Fodor's

COLORADO

WELCOME TO COLORADO

A playground for nature lovers and outdoor enthusiasts, Colorado has majestic landscapes, raging rivers, and winding trails perfect for activities from biking to rafting. The heart of the Rocky Mountains has scores of snow-capped summits towering higher than 14,000 feet and trails from easy to challenging for exploring them—as well as roads offering spectacular drives. Skiers flock to the slopes here for the champagne powder and thrilling downhill runs. Need a break from the outdoors? Urban adventures await in cool cities like Denver, Boulder, and Aspen.

TOP REASONS TO GO

★ **Mountains:** The stunning views from the state's many commanding peaks can't be beat.

★ **Outdoor Activities:** Hiking, biking, horseback riding, and fishing are all excellent.

★ **Local Flavors:** Grass-fed meats, microbrews, green chilies, and stream-raised trout.

★ **Hip Cities:** Cosmopolitan Denver, trendy Boulder, and glamorous Aspen entice.

★ **Skiing:** Fluffy powder, top-notch runs, and posh resorts draw skiers of all levels.

★ **National Parks:** Rocky Mountain, Mesa Verde, and Black Canyon of the Gunnison.

12
TOP EXPERIENCES

Colorado offers terrific experiences that should be on every traveler's list. Here are Fodor's top picks for a memorable trip.

1 Skiing

The perfect powder of the Rocky Mountains and variety of alpine terrain attract skiers of all levels. Après ski, relax at a bar or restaurant in one of the state's posh resorts. (Ch. 4, 5, 6, 9, 10)

2 Mesa Verde National Park

Wandering through some of the nearly 600 ancient Puebloan dwellings carved into high sandstone cliffs at this park is truly awe-inspiring. *(Ch. 11)*

3 Microbrews

Coloradoans craft some superb microbrews. Pop into local establishments for tours and tastings, or take away a growler for an outdoor picnic. *(Ch. 1, 7)*

4 Dude Ranches

Staying at a dude ranch is a true Western experience. Guests can ride horses through gorgeous terrain and then dine family-style on grass-fed meat. *(Ch. 10)*

5 Wildlife Spotting

Colorado's national parks offer excellent opportunities to spot all kinds of wildlife, from the small (marmots, pika) to the large (bears, moose, elk). *(Ch. 1, 8)*

6 Old West Mining Towns

Relive the boom times of the West in the state's colorful mining communities. Many historic buildings have been converted into museums and hotels. *(Ch. 10)*

7 Aspen Glamour

One of the U.S.'s fabled resort towns, Aspen defines glitz, glamour, and glorious skiing. Top-notch restaurants and high-end shops provide diversions year-round. *(Ch. 6)*

8 Rocky Mountain National Park

This premier national park teems with lush forests, alpine lakes, snowcapped peaks, and more than 350 miles of hiking trails. With any luck, you'll spot bighorn sheep, elk, and mule deer here. *(Ch. 8)*

9 Outdoor Activities

Whether it's fishing, hiking, biking, horseback riding, or rafting, the fresh-air activities here are sure to satisfy all tastes. *(Ch. 1)*

10 Scenic Drives and Train Trips

Eye-opening vistas of dramatic canyons, verdant forests, or undulating landscapes await on grand journeys around the state. (Ch. 1)

11 Pikes Peak

The inspiration for the song "America the Beautiful," Pikes Peak beguiles with its breathtaking views. Take the world's highest cog train all the way to the summit. (Ch. 12)

12 Cities

Vibrant, trendy cities like Denver, Boulder, and Aspen lure visitors from the mountains with their top-notch dining, shopping, and nightlife scenes. (Ch. 2, 6, 7)

CONTENTS

CONTENTS

MAPS

ABOUT THIS GUIDE

Fodor's Recommendations

Everything in this guide is worth doing—we don't cover what isn't—but exceptional sights, hotels, and restaurants are recognized with additional accolades. Fodor'sChoice★ indicates our top recommendations; and **Best Bets** calls attention to notable hotels and restaurants in various categories. Care to nominate a new place? Visit Fodors.com/contact-us.

Trip Costs

We list prices wherever possible to help you budget well. Hotel and restaurant price categories from $ to $$$$ are noted alongside each recommendation. For hotels, we include the lowest cost of a standard double room in high season. For restaurants, we cite the average price of a main course at dinner or, if dinner isn't served, at lunch. For attractions, we always list adult admission fees; discounts are usually available for children, students, and senior citizens.

Hotels

Our local writers vet every hotel to recommend the best overnights in each price category, from budget to expensive. Unless otherwise specified, you can expect private bath, phone, and TV in your room. For expanded hotel reviews, facilities, and deals, visit Fodors.com.

Top Picks	Hotels &
★ Fodor'sChoice	Restaurants
	⌂ Hotel
Listings	↳ Number of
⌨ Address	rooms
⌨ Branch address	⦿ Meal plans
☎ Telephone	✕ Restaurant
🖷 Fax	⌨ Reservations
⊕ Website	⌂ Dress code
✉ E-mail	▤ No credit cards
⌨ Admission fee	$ Price
⊘ Open/closed times	
	Other
Ⓜ Subway	⇨ See also
✛ Directions or	☞ Take note
Map coordinates	🏌 Golf facilities

Restaurants

Unless we state otherwise, restaurants are open for lunch and dinner daily. We mention dress code only when there's a specific requirement and reservations only when they're essential or not accepted. To make restaurant reservations, visit Fodors.com.

Credit Cards

The hotels and restaurants in this guide typically accept credit cards. If not, we'll say so.

EUGENE FODOR

Hungarian-born Eugene Fodor (1905–91) began his travel career as an interpreter on a French cruise ship. The experience inspired him to write *On the Continent* (1936), the first guidebook to receive annual updates and discuss a country's way of life as well as its sights. Fodor later joined the U.S. Army and worked for the OSS in World War II. After the war, he kept up his intelligence work while expanding his guidebook series. During the Cold War, many guides were written by fellow agents who understood the value of insider information. Today's guides continue Fodor's legacy by providing travelers with timely coverage, insider tips, and cultural context.

EXPERIENCE
COLORADO

WHAT'S WHERE

The following numbers refer to chapters.

2 Denver. Colorado's capital and largest city, Denver is unmatched in its combination of urban pleasures and easy access to outdoor recreation.

3 The Rockies near Denver. Scenic highway I–70 ascends into the foothills through historic towns like Golden, Idaho Springs, and Georgetown.

4 Summit County. The ski resorts of Keystone, Breckenridge, Copper Mountain, and Arapahoe Basin cluster near I–70 as it rises in the Rockies. Lake Dillon and its port towns attract summer visitors.

5 Vail Valley. Vail, the world's largest single-mountain ski resort, sits in a narrow corridor bounded by steep peaks. Also in the valley: upscale ski area Beaver Creek and sleepy Minturn.

6 Aspen and the Roaring Fork Valley. Glitzy Aspen is a serious skiing draw. Farther west, Victorian charmer Glenwood Springs centers on a massive hot springs pool.

7 Boulder and North Central Colorado. College town Boulder balances high-tech with bohemia. Estes Park abuts Rocky Mountain National Park's eastern entrance, while Grand Lake is its quieter western gateway.

8 Rocky Mountain National Park. The wilderness and alpine tundra here welcome wildlife and outdoor enthusiasts year-round.

9 Northwest Colorado and Steamboat Springs. Where the Rockies transition into an arid desert, Grand Junction is the region's hub. Nearby are the Colorado and Dinosaur National Monuments, and Steamboat Springs.

10 Southwest Colorado. Evergreen-clad peaks and red desert beckon outdoor enthusiasts to mountain-biking birthplace Crested Butte, Black Canyon of the Gunnison, idyllic Telluride, and historic Durango.

11 Mesa Verde National Park. Designated a park in 1906, this protected series of canyons provides a peek into the lives of the Ancestral Puebloan people who made their homes among the cliffs.

12 South Central Colorado. Next to Pikes Peak, Colorado Springs' mineral waters still flow. Cañon City is a rafting hub; Buena Vista and Salida are two artists' colonies. To the south, explore Great Sand Dunes National Park and Preserve.

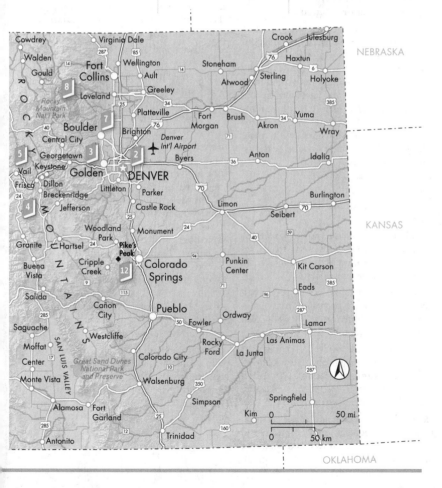

COLORADO PLANNER

When to Go

The Colorado you experience will depend on the season you visit. Summer is a busy time. Hotels in tourist destinations book up early, especially in July and August, and hikers crowd the backcountry. Ski resorts buzz from December to early April, especially around Christmas and Presidents' Day. Many big resorts are popular summer destinations.

If you don't mind capricious weather, rates drop and crowds are nonexistent in spring and fall. Spring's pleasures are somewhat limited, since snow usually blocks the high country—and mountain-pass roads—well into June. But spring is a good time for fishing, rafting, birding, and wildlife-viewing. In fall, aspens splash the mountainsides with gold, wildlife comes down to lower elevations, and the angling is excellent.

Festivals and Events

Summer in Colorado is full of food and culture celebrations. Here are some highlights:

Bravo! Vail Valley Music Festival This festival brings national orchestras to venues around the Valley. ⊠ *Vail* ☎ *877/812–5700* ⊕ *www.bravovail.org.*

Country Jam. The likes of Keith Urban and Tim McGraw party in Grand Junction. ⊠ *Grand Junction* ☎ *800/780–0526* ⊕ *www.countryjam.com.*

Crested Butte Music Festival. A variety of genres are played among the wildflowers at this summer festival. ⊠ *Crested Butte* ☎ *970/349–0619* ⊕ *www.crestedbuttemusicfestival.com.*

Strings in the Mountains Music Festival. Chamber music, jazz, rock, blues, world beat, and country shows take place in Steamboat Springs during this festival.

⊠ *Steamboat Springs* ☎ *970/879–5056* ⊕ *www.stringsmusicfestival.com.*

Telluride Bluegrass Festival. The top acts in bluegrass take music to new levels in a stunning setting. ⊠ *Telluride* ☎ *800/624–2422* ⊕ *www.bluegrass.com.*

Telluride Film Festival. You'll find movie premieres, workshops, and the chance to rub elbows with celebs at this film fest. ⊠ *Telluride* ☎ *510/665–9494* ⊕ *www.telluridefilmfestival.org.*

Vail International Dance Festival. For two weeks every summer, all types of dance are presented in this series at the beautiful Vilar Center in Beaver Creek or the Gerald R. Ford Amphitheater in Vail. ⊠ *Vail* ☎ *888/920–2787* ⊕ *www.vaildance.org.*

How's the Weather?

Summer in the Rocky Mountains begins in late June or early July. Days are warm, with highs often in the 80s; nighttime temperatures fall to the 40s and 50s. Afternoon thunderstorms are common over the higher peaks. Fall begins in September; winter creeps in during November, and deep snows arrive by December. Temperatures usually hover near freezing by day, thanks to the warm mountain sun, and drop overnight, occasionally as low as −60°F. Winter tapers off in March, though snow lingers into April on valley bottoms and into July on mountain passes.

At lower elevations (Denver, the eastern plains, and the southwest), summertime highs above 100°F are not uncommon, and winters are cold, with highs in the 20s and 30s. The entire state sees snowy winters, even on the plains.

1

What to Bring?

Colorado is famous for its "Rocky Mountain formal" dress code, which means cowboy attire is accepted everywhere, even in the fanciest restaurants, so bring your jeans and leave your formal wear at home. It's wise to be prepared for rapidly changing weather, however, as well as cooler nights (even when daytime temperatures hit summer highs).

If your plans include outdoor activities such as golf, skiing, or mountain biking, most major towns and cities have rental equipment available.

High-Altitude Tips

The three things to consider with high-altitude travel are altitude sickness, dehydration, and sunburn.

■ If you are coming from sea level and plan to visit the mountains, it's worth taking a day or two in Denver or another lower-elevation area to acclimate. Either way, take it easier than usual.

■ Drink plenty of water and avoid alcohol.

■ Always wear sunscreen and protective clothing. Sunglasses and a hat also are must-haves at higher elevation.

Getting Here and Around

⇨ *For more detailed information, see Travel Smart Colorado.*

Modern and busy, **Denver International Airport** (DEN ☎ *800/247–2336* ⊕ *www. flydenver.com*) moves travelers in and out efficiently. There's also **Colorado Springs Airport** (COS ☎ *719/550–1900* ⊕ *www. flycos.com*) and a number of smaller airports near resorts—Steamboat Springs, Aspen, and Telluride.

In Denver some of the hotels provide free shuttles, and the free Mall shuttle and light rail make it easy to get around the metro area. You can travel to some major ski areas by prearranged shuttle van. **Amtrak** (☎ *303/825–2583* ⊕ *www. amtrak.com*) has stops in Denver, Winter Park, Glenwood Springs, Grand Junction, Trinidad, and La Junta.

Any other travel requires a car. Always check on road conditions, as the weather can be unpredictable. **Colorado Road Condition Hotline** (☎ *303/639–1111 near Denver, statewide 511* ⊕ *www.cotrip.org*).

Dining

Dining in Colorado has evolved, and there are now more options than ever. However, the dress code remains casual. Reservations are recommended in most areas, and are essential in the high country, especially during the winter ski season, and in places where golf, mountain biking, and water sports are popular during the summer.

Lodging

Plan well ahead for lodging in resort towns, particularly during ski season and midsummer, when festivals dominate. Condos can be a value during high season, especially if you have a group or family, because you can save money on dining or share expenses. While ski-area lodges can offer the closest access, they also will be the most expensive.

To rent vacation homes, condos, and chalets throughout the state, visit Vacation Rental By Owner (⊕ *www.vrbo.com*). If you're looking for a short-term rental, try Airbnb (⊕ *www.airbnb.com*)

QUINTESSENTIAL COLORADO

The Great Outdoors

Colorado gets more than 300 sunny days per year, and that's a big part of why the natives get restless when forced to spend too much time inside. On any given day you'll find folks figuring out ways to get out there, from biking to work along the intricate veins of multiuse paths to hiking with the dog around expanses of open space, to soccer and jogging at the well-planned parks scattered around cities. In fact, Coloradans talk about the outdoors the way some people elsewhere talk about meals. They want to know where you just skied, hiked, biked, or rafted, and the next outdoor challenges on your list.

Hot Springs

In the late 1800s people came to Colorado not for gold or skiing, but for the restorative powers of the mineral-rich hot springs that had been discovered all over the state. Doc Holliday was one such patient. Suffering from consumption, he spent his final days breathing the sulfurous fumes in Glenwood Springs. To this day there are nearly two-dozen commercial hot-springs resorts, most with lodging or other activities attached, and many more pools have been identified where people can go for the private backcountry experience. Some hot springs have been left in their natural state, while others are channeled into Olympic-size swimming pools and hot tubs. Either way, they have become destinations for all who long to take advantage of their therapeutic benefits.

Colorado is famous as one big playground, from snowcapped ski resorts and biking and hiking trails to white-water rivers and hot springs. So do as the locals do and experience some of the allure of Colorado.

Summits Without the Sweat

As fanatic as the famous "Fourteeners" (peaks over 14,000 feet) bunch can be, not everyone is as enthusiastic about spending entire days to get the good views. Luckily, there are other ways to get high enough to see something spectacular. In summer a ride on the gondola in Telluride between the town and Mountain Village is free and provides magnificent views. Road trips through the Rockies will give you great views. You can drive to the tops of Mount Evans and Pikes Peak or take the Pikes Peak Cog Railway to the summit, or take a road trip to Aspen and drive the route over Independence Pass. Another terrific drive is Shrine Pass—Exit 180 off I–70 toward Vail Pass—especially in fall, which allows you to see the Mount of the Holy Cross and the Tenmile, Gore, and Sawatch ranges.

Land of the Lost

Colorado definitely has a thing for dinosaurs—no surprise, considering that the state sits on prime dino real estate, with plenty of sandstone and shale perfect for preservation. Dinosaur Ridge, close to Morrison, features a trail where you can see, touch, and photograph Jurassic-period bones and Cretaceous footprints. Both the Denver Museum of Nature & Science and the University of Colorado Museum of Natural History have collections of fossil specimens. Other attractions, such as the Denver Botanic Gardens and Red Rocks Amphitheatre, offer regular dino-theme events. There's even a town called Dinosaur, which sits near Dinosaur National Monument in the northwest part of the state. Parfet Prehistoric Preserve east of Golden and Picketwire Canyonlands south of La Junta have hiking trails with extensive sets of dinosaur tracks.

OUTDOOR ADVENTURES

HORSEBACK RIDING

Horseback riding in the Rocky Mountains can mean a quick trot on a paved trail through craggy red rocks or a weeklong stay at a working dude ranch, where guests rise at dawn and herd cattle from one mountain range to another. Horse-pack trips are great ways to visit the backcountry, because horses can travel distances and carry supplies that would be impossible for hikers.

What to Wear

Clothing requirements are minimal. A sturdy pair of pants, a wide-brim sun hat, and outerwear to protect against rain are about the only necessities. Ask your outfitter for a list of things you'll need. June through August is the peak period for horse-pack trips.

Choosing a Dude Ranch

Dude ranches fall roughly into two categories: working ranches and guest ranches. Working ranches, where you participate in such activities as roundups and cattle movements, sometimes require experienced horsemanship. Guest ranches offer a wide range of activities in addition to horseback riding, including fishing, four-wheeling, spa services, and cooking classes. At a typical dude ranch you stay in log cabins and are served family-style meals in a lodge or ranch house; some ranches now have upscale restaurants on-site, too. For winter, many ranches have snow-oriented amenities.

When choosing a ranch, consider whether the place is family-oriented or adults only, and check on the length-of-stay requirements and what gear, if any, you are expected to bring. Working ranches plan around the needs of the business, and thus often require full-week stays for a fixed price, while regular guest ranches operate more like hotels.

Contacts Colorado Dude Ranch Association. ⊕ *www.coloradoranch.com.*

Best Horseback Rides

Academy Riding Stables, Colorado Springs. Ideal for visitors who have only a short time in the area but long to do a half-day trail ride, Academy brings red-rock country up close at the Garden of the Gods, with pony rides for kids and hay wagon or stagecoach rides for groups.

C Lazy U Guest Ranch, Granby. One of the finest ranches in the state, C Lazy U offers a relaxing upscale experience, from daily horseback rides with a horse chosen for the duration of the visit to supervised kids' activities and chef-prepared meals, deluxe accommodations, a spring-fed pool, fly-fishing, and an on-site spa.

Colorado Cattle Company & Guest Ranch, New Raymer (near Fort Collins). The real deal, the adults-only Colorado Cattle Company is two hours from Denver International Airport and seconds from turning you on to a true Western experience, with cattle drives through the fall, branding, fencing, and roping on a 7,000-acre ranch with 450 head of cattle.

Devil's Thumb Ranch, Tabernash (near Winter Park). Their commitment to the environment, use of renewable resources, and focus on the finest quality, from the organic ingredients in the restaurant to the luxurious bed linens in the rustic yet upscale cabins, makes Suzanne and Bob Fanch's spread a deluxe getaway. There's a spa on the premises, along with superior horseback-riding, cross-country skiing, and ice-skating programs.

SKIING AND SNOWBOARDING

The champagne powder of the Rocky Mountains can be a revelation for new-comers. Forget treacherous sheets of rock-hard ice, single-note hills where the bottom can be seen from the top, and mountains that offer only one kind of terrain from every angle. In the Rockies the snow builds up quickly, leaving a solid base that hangs tough all season, only to be layered upon by thick, fluffy powder that holds an edge, ready to be groomed into rippling corduroy or left in giddy stashes along the sides and through the trees. Volkswagen-size moguls and half-pipe–studded terrain parks are the norm, not the special attractions.

Many resorts have a wide variety of ter-rain at all levels, from beginner (green circle) to expert (double black diamond). Turn yourself over to the rental shops, which provide expert help in planning your day and outfitting you with the right equipment. Renting is also a great chance for experienced skiers and snowboarders to sample the latest technology.

Lift Tickets

Shop around for lift tickets before you leave home. Look for package deals, multiple-day passes, and online discounts. The traditional ski season usually runs from mid-December until early April, with Christmas, New Year's, and the month of March being the busiest times at the resorts.

What to Wear

Skiing the Rockies means preparing for all kinds of weather, sometimes in the same day, because the high altitudes can start a day off sunny and bright but kick in a blizzard by afternoon. Layers help, as well as plenty of polypropylene to wick away sweat in the sun, and a water-resis-tant outer layer to keep off the powdery wetness that's sure to accumulate—espe-cially if you're a beginner snowboarder certain to spend time on the ground. Must-haves: plenty of sunscreen, because the sun is closer than you think, and a helmet, because so are the trees.

Contacts Colorado Ski Country USA. ☎ *303/ 825–7669* ⊕ *www.coloradoski.com.*

Best Slopes

Aspen. Part "Lifestyles of the Rich and Famous" and part sleepy ski town, pic-turesque Aspen offers four mountains of widely varied terrain within easy access and some of the best dining in the state.

Breckenridge. Five terrain parks and four pipes, each designed to target a skill level and promote advancement, give snow-boarders the edge at this hip resort, which manages to make skiers feel just as wel-come on its big, exposed bowls.

Keystone. Near Breckenridge and Copper Mountain, Keystone has a high percent-age of beginner and intermediate offerings and is small enough to navigate easily.

Vail. Those looking for the big-resort experience head to Vail, where modern comforts and multiple bowls mean a diz-zying variety of runs and every possible convenience, all laid out in a series of con-temporary European-style villages.

Winter Park. Winter Park has retained the laid-back vibe of a locals' mountain, and is still one of the better values on the Front Range. Mary Jane offers a mogul a min-ute, while the gentler Winter Park side gives cruisers a run for their money.

HIKING

Hiking is easily the least expensive and most accessible recreational pursuit. Sure, you could spend a few hundred dollars on high-tech hiking boots, a so-called personal hydration system, and a collapsible walking staff made of space-age materials, but there's no need for such expenditure. All that's really essential are sturdy athletic shoes, water, and the desire to see the landscape under your own power.

Hiking in the Rockies is a three-season sport that extends as far into fall as you're willing to tromp through snow, though in the arid desert regions it's possible to hike year-round without snowshoes. One of the greatest aspects of this region is the wide range of hiking terrain, from high-alpine scrambles that require stamina to flowered meadows that invite a relaxed pace to confining slot canyons where flash floods are a real danger.

Safety

There are few real hazards to hiking, but a little preparedness goes a long way. Know your limits, and make sure the terrain you are about to embark on does not exceed your abilities. It's a good idea to check the elevation change on a trail before you set out—a 1-mile trail might sound easy, until you realize how steep it is—and be careful not to get caught on exposed trails at elevation during afternoon thunderstorms in summer. Bring layers of clothing to accommodate changing weather, and always carry enough drinking water. Make sure someone knows where you're going and when to expect your return.

Contacts Colorado Mountain Club.
⊕ *www.cmc.org*.

Best Hikes

Bear Lake Road, Rocky Mountain National Park. A network of trails threads past alpine lakes, waterfalls, aspens, and pines. Stroll 1 mile to Sprague Lake on a wheelchair-accessible path, or take a four-hour hike past two waterfalls to Mills Lake, with its views of mighty Longs Peak.

Black Canyon of the Gunnison National Park. These are serious trails for serious hikers. There are six routes down into the canyon, which can be hot and slippery, and supersteep. But the payoff is stunning: a rare look into the canyon's heart and the fast-moving Gunnison River.

Chautauqua Park, Boulder. Meet the locals (and their dogs) as you head up into the mountains to look back down at the city or to get up close and personal with the Flatirons. There's even a grassy slope perfect for a picnic.

Colorado National Monument, Grand Junction. Breathe in the smell of sagebrush and juniper as you wander amid red-rock cliffs, canyons, and monoliths.

The Colorado Trail. The beauty of this epic hike, which starts just north of Durango and goes 500 miles all the way to Denver, is that you can do it all or just pieces of it.

Green Mountain Trail, Lakewood. Part of Jefferson County Open Space, the easy, mostly exposed trail affords panoramic views of downtown Denver, Table Mesa, Pikes Peak, and the Continental Divide from the top. You must share the trail with bikers and dogs, as well as other critters.

Maroon Bells, Aspen. Bring your camera and take your shot at the twin, mineral-streaked peaks that are one of the most-photographed spots in the state.

BICYCLING

The Rockies are a favorite destination for bikers. Wide-open roads with great gains and losses in elevation test (and form) the stamina for road cyclists, while riders who prefer pedaling fat tires have plenty of mountain and desert trails to test their skills. Many cyclists travel between towns (or backcountry huts or campsites) in summer. Unmatched views often make it difficult to keep your eyes on the road.

Bike Paths

Most streets in the larger cities have bike lanes and separated bike paths, and Denver, Boulder, Fort Collins, Durango, Crested Butte, and Colorado Springs are especially bike-friendly. Cities and biking organizations often offer free maps.

Bike Rentals

Thanks to the popularity of the sport here, it's usually easy to find a place that rents bicycles, both entry-level and high-end. Bike shops are also a good bet for information on local rides and group tours.

Safety

On the road, watch for trucks and stay as close as possible to the side of the road, in single file. On the trail, ride within your limits and keep your eyes peeled for hikers and horses (both of which have the right of way), as well as dogs. Always wear a helmet and carry plenty of water.

Contacts Bicycle Colorado. ☎ 303/417–1544 ⊕ www.bicyclecolo.org.

Best Rides

Breckenridge. Groups of mixed-skill level bikers make for Summit County, where beginners stick to the paved paths, the buffs take on Vail Pass, and single-track types test their technical muscles in the backcountry.

Cherry Creek Bike Path, LoDo, and Cherry Creek. The ultimate urban trek, the paved trail along the burbling creek is part of 850 miles of linked Denver greenway.

Crested Butte. Pearl Pass is the storied birthplace of mountain biking (check out the museum devoted to it in town). If your legs are not quite ready for that 40-mile, 12,700-foot challenge, there are plenty of paths more suitable to mere mortals.

Durango. Bikes seem to be more popular than cars in Durango, another fabled biking center. You can bike around town or into the mountains with equal ease.

Grand Junction/Fruita. With epic rides such as The Edge Loop and Kokopelli's Trail, these areas beckon single-track fanatics with their wavy-gravy loop-de-loops and screaming downhill payoffs. Beware: the heat can be intense.

Keystone. Serious downhillers head to Keystone's Drop Zone, the resort's expert section packed with rock gardens and high-speed jumps. Don't like the grunt-filled climb? Hop on a chairlift and smile away the sweet downhill.

Matthews/Winters Park, Morrison. With expansive views of the Red Rocks Park, the moderate to challenging combination of double-track and single-track mountain biking is crowded at sunrise and sunset.

Rangely. From the Raven Rims, you can see the town from nearly every point along this fun mountain-bike ride that starts in the corrals at Chase Draw.

Winter Park. Home to the fabled Fat Tire Classic bike ride, Winter Park features tree-lined single-track trails that vary from gentle, meandering jaunts to screaming roller-coaster rides.

RAFTING

Rafting brings on emotions as varied as the calm induced by flat waters surrounded with stunning scenery and wildlife and the thrill and excitement of charging a raging torrent of foam. Beginners and novices should use guides, but experienced rafters may rent watercraft.

Choosing a Guide

Seasoned outfitters know their routes and their waters as well as you know the road between home and work. Many guides offer multiday trips in which they do everything, including searing your steak and rolling out your sleeping bag. Waters are ranked from Class I (the easiest) to Class VI (think Niagara Falls).

Select an outfitter based on recommendations from the local chamber, experience, and word of mouth. Ask your guide about the rating on your route before you book. Remember, ratings can vary greatly throughout the season due to runoff and weather events.

"Raft" can mean any number of things: an inflated raft in which passengers do the paddling; an inflated raft or wooden dory in which a licensed professional does the work; a motorized raft on which some oar work might be required. Be sure you know what kind of raft you'll be riding— or paddling—before booking.

What to Wear

Wear a swimsuit or shorts and sandals and bring along sunscreen and sunglasses. Outfitters are required to supply a life jacket for each passenger that must be worn. Most have moved to requiring helmets, as well. Early summer, when the water is highest, is the ideal time to raft, although many outfitters stretch the season, particularly on calmer routes.

Contacts Colorado River Outfitters Association. ☎ 720/260–4135 ⊕ www.croa.org.

Best River Runs

Animas River, Durango. Even at high water, the Lower Animas stays at Class III, which makes for a great way to see the Durango area. Meanwhile, the Upper Animas runs between Class III and Class IV, with a few spots at Class V, and gives little time to appreciate the mountain scenery and canyon views that race by.

Arkansas River, Buena Vista, and Salida. The Arkansas rages as a Class V or murmurs as a Class II, depending on the section and the season. It's *the* white-water rafting destination in the state.

Blue River, Silverthorne. The Class I–III stretches of the Blue that run between Silverthorne and Columbine Landing are ideal for first-time paddlers. Be sure to check the flows; the season is short.

Clear Creek River, Idaho Springs. One of the state's most popular rafting spots, this snowmelt-fed river offers everything from Class I to V. Only 30 miles outside of Denver, it's perfect for day trips. Peak season is from mid-May to August.

Colorado River in Glenwood Canyon, Glenwood Springs. Choose a wild ride through the Shoshone Rapids (up to Class IV) or a mellow float down the Lower Colorado.

Eagle River, Vail. Three sections offer fun for beginners to expert paddlers. The water levels vary, as this alpine river is not dam-controlled and rises and falls according to snowmelt.

Gunnison River, north of Black Canyon of the Gunnison National Monument. Packhorses carry your equipment into this wild area that leads into Gunnison Gorge, where Class I–III waters take you past granite walls while bald eagles fly overhead.

FISHING

Trout do not live in ugly places.

And so it is in Colorado, where you'll discover unbridled beauty, towering pines, rippling mountain streams, and bottomless pools. It's here that blue-ribbon trout streams remain much as they were when Native American tribes, French fur trappers, and a few thousand miners, muleskinners, and sodbusters first placed a muddy footprint along their banks.

Make the Most of Your Time

To make the best use of that limited vacation, consider hiring a guide. You could spend days locating a great fishing spot, learning the water currents and fish behavior, and determining what flies, lures, or bait the fish are following. A good guide will cut through the options, get you into fish, and turn your excursion into an adventure complete with a full creel.

If you're not inclined to fork over the $250-plus that most quality guides charge per day for two anglers and a boat, your best bet is a stop at a reputable fly shop. They'll shorten your learning curve, tell you where the fish are, what they're biting on, and whether you should be "skittering" your dry fly on top of the water or "dead-drifting" a nymph.

What to Bring

If you're comfortable with your fishing gear, bring it along, though most guides loan or rent equipment. Bring a rod and reel, waders, vest, hat, sunglasses, net, tackle, hemostats, and sunscreen.

Know the Rules

Fishing licenses, available at tackle shops and a variety of stores, are required in Colorado for anyone over the age of 16. Famed fisherman Lee Wolff wrote that "catching fish is a sport. Eating fish is not a sport." Most anglers practice "catch and release" to maintain productive fisheries and to protect native species. A few streams are considered "private," in that they are stocked by a local club; other rivers are fly-fishing or catch-and-release only.

When to Go

The season is always a concern when fishing. But as many fishing guides will attest, the best time to come and wet a line is whenever you can make it.

Contacts **Colorado Parks and Wildlife.** ☎ 303/297–1192 ⊕ *www.wildlife.state. co.us.*

Best Fishing

Arkansas River, Buena Vista, and Cotopaxi. Fly-fish for brown or rainbow trout through Browns or Bighorn Sheep Canyon, or combine white-water rafting with fishing by floating on a raft through the Royal Gorge.

Gunnison River, Almont. In a tiny hamlet near Crested Butte and, more importantly, near the headwaters of the Gunnison, they *live* fly-fishing.

Lake Dillon, Dillon. Pick your spot along 26 miles of shoreline and cast away for brown and rainbow trout and kokanee salmon. The marina has rental boats and a fully stocked store.

Lake Granby, Grand Lake. Can't wait for summer? Try ice fishing on Lake Granby, on the western side of the Rockies.

Roaring Fork River, Aspen. Uninterrupted by dams from its headwaters to its junction with the Colorado, the Roaring Fork is one of the last free-flowing rivers in the state, plus it has a healthy population of 12- to 18-inch trout.

FLAVORS OF COLORADO

Despite a short growing season in much of the state, Colorado enjoys a strong culinary reputation for its commitment to organic, sustainable farming practices, farmers' markets, and chef-fueled focus on buying and dining locally. Locally produced microbrews and wine, a robust agricultural foundation, and a continual roster of food-theme festivals make it easy for the traveler to snag a taste of Colorado while passing through. The region also is known for its many steak houses that keep the state's reputation as cattle country thriving.

Festivals of Local Bounty

Nearly every region of Colorado has some kind of fruit or vegetable that grows so well it makes a name for itself—which inevitably leads to a festival. The alternating swathes of high altitude and low valley are credited with providing a head start or a late blast of sun that in turn pumps that produce with extra flavor.

Peach Festival, Palisade. The small town of Palisade, which also is blessed with a climate ideal for growing wine grapes, is noted for several types of fruits, including their famous peaches, which are celebrated in August.

Wild Mushroom Festival, Crested Butte. The climate above 9,000 feet in Crested Butte is just right for fungi, which leads to a celebration of the result every August.

Stream-Raised and Grass-Fed

Colorado is famous for its trout, beef, bison, and lamb, so much so that vegetarian restaurants have been slower in proliferating than in other parts of the country. The state also offers visitors the chance to pluck the trout right from its many rivers and lakes—rainbow, cutthroat, brook, brown, and, of course, lake—although so many get shipped out that it's as likely to be frozen as not at restaurants, so be sure to ask. Meanwhile, whether or not the beef and bison seen grazing across the West are natural (meaning no hormones, steroids, or antibiotics), every town, large or small, boasts a steak house. And it's the grasses in their mountain diet that have been credited with the superior flavor and texture of the Colorado lamb.

Buckhorn Exchange, Denver. More than 500 pairs of eyes stare down at you during the meal, but it's what's on your plate that will keep your attention: dry-aged, prime-grade Colorado steaks served with hearty sides. Since 1893 this has been one of the state's game-meat specialists, as well.

The Fort Restaurant, Morrison. Bison is a particular specialty at this replica of Bent's Fort, a former Colorado fur-trade mecca, but the steaks, trout, elk, and other meats are delicious, as well.

Game Creek Club, Vail. With the word "game" in the name, it's not hard to imagine that the tony eatery does a good job with meats. The Bavarian-style lodge is open to the public for dinner.

Green Chile

Not the pepper itself but a gravy-like stew is what Coloradans refer to when they talk about *chile verde,* the heady mixture that migrated with families who made their way from Mexico up through New Mexico and Texas and over from California to settle the high country. Its recipes vary as much across the state as minestrone does across Italy and pot-au-feu across France, but you can usually count on a pork-based concoction with jalapeños, sometimes tomatoes, and maybe tomatillos, the heat ranging from mellow to sinus-clearing. Green chile can smother just about anything—from enchiladas to huevos—but a plain bowlful with a warmed tortilla is all the purist requires, and it's the best hangover cure ever.

Dos Hombres, Grand Junction. The regular green chile at this cheerful spot is tomato-based, with a variety of chilies and pork for a thick, colorful mixture. They also offer milder, vegetarian, and New Mexican–style versions.

Fiesta Jalisco, Avon, Breckenridge, Colorado Springs, Steamboat. Light on chilies but packed with pork, the green here is medium-spicy and perfect on a burrito. The margaritas are special, too.

Jack 'n' Grill, Denver. This family-run joint pulls its chilies from New Mexico and makes its green chile stew into a fire-breathing brew made of cooked-down, chopped green chilies that they roast themselves, so hot it separates the serious from the simply curious.

Artisan Markets

Recently, an influx of creative chefs to Colorado have taken advantage of the state's abundance of local farms and working ranches. Many have opened restaurants attached to artisan food markets. With chefs butchering their own meats, growing produce on their own farms, and creating signature culinary offerings with local farmers, these markets offer a delicious and unique option for appreciative diners.

Mercantile Dining & Provision. Housed inside the Union Station train station in Denver's lower downtown (LoDo), Mercantile Dining & Provision exudes charm and provides a comfortable ambience. There's a large meat and cheese counter that sells handmade charcuterie and high-end cheeses. Add in chef Alex Seidel's ever-changing menu with ingredients from his own gardens, local meats delivered from Colorado ranches, and fresh seafood from the coast, and you have all the ingredients for a memorable meal.

Blackbelly Market, Boulder. Helmed by chef Hosea Rosenberg, this restaurant is part butcher shop, part food truck, part restaurant, and part bar. The display counters showcase fresh cuts of meat from the in-house butcher. The menu in the dining room features a mélange of flavors. Ask for a seat at the chef's table where you can watch Rosenberg and his team create culinary delights.

Local Wines

Microbrews may rule, but Colorado's wine country continues to get kudos for producing reasonably priced, award-winning vino. The wines run the gamut, from lightweight whites to heavy-duty reds, and Colorado varietals as well as wines made from California grapes that don't grow well in the short season (such as red Zinfandel). Cabernet Sauvignon, Merlot, and Chardonnay are the most popular, but the Viognier and Riesling offerings have gotten good press, too. Another of Colorado's best-kept secrets is its winery tours through Palisade and Grand Junction.

Balistreri Vineyards, Denver. This family-owned winery offers free tastings of their popular Chardonnay, Viognier, Merlot, Cabernet, or more than a dozen other wines. The tasting room also serves small plates for lunch on weekdays.

Two Rivers Winery & Chateau, Grand Junction. With its setting evocative of rural France, this inn set among the vines is the ideal spot for a sip of Burgundian-style Chardonnay after a tour of the Colorado national monuments.

MICROBREWS IN COLORADO

Colorado is crazy for microbrews. Since the first microbrewery opened in Boulder in 1979, the state has wholeheartedly embraced the craft beer movement. As of this writing, there are more than 235 establishments making fresh beer throughout the state. With a governor who once was a brewer (John Hickenlooper), a family that helped define American brewing (the Coors), and a youthful demographic, craft beer is booming like never before in Colorado.

While most towns have their own brewpub or brewery, many of the best ones are located in three cities in the Front Range of the Rocky Mountains: Denver, Fort Collins, and Boulder. Many breweries have attached restaurants or food trucks that offer everything from pub grub to upscale cuisine. Much like wineries, they offer tasting flights so that visitors can sample the full range of their beers. Most microbreweries also have tasting rooms open to the public, where bottled beer and growlers (half-gallon glass jugs filled with fresh beer) can be purchased for takeout.

The Great American Beer Festival, the country's largest and most prestigious beer festival, attracts more than 1,300 breweries from across the country each fall in downtown Denver. For a list of the microbrews in the state, visit the Colorado Brewers Guild (⊕ *coloradobeer.org*).

Where to Go

Aspen Brewing Company, Aspen. One of the most beautiful places in the state, Aspen is home to a local brewery turning out some fine beers. Independence Pass Ale pays homage to the 12,000-foot-high pass and "back road" into town that is closed all winter due to snow. The taproom is open daily noon–midnight.

Avery Brewing Company, Boulder. The beers at Avery Brewing Company range from big bold IPAs to subtly smooth porters. Their state-of-the-art, technologically advanced brewery, which opened in 2015, has a suspended catwalk that allows you to take your own self-guided tour while sipping a cold one.

Boulder Beer Company, Boulder. Learn about Colorado's first craft brewery on the free tours and tastings at Boulder Beer Company. You can grab a bite to eat afterward at the brewhouse's pub; in summer, you can enjoy the grub and suds on the patio.

Crooked Stave Artisan Beer Project, Denver. When owner Chad Yakobson opened his brewery in the Denver neighborhood of LoDo he had one plan: to create superior sour and experimental beers. His barrel-aged beers are proof of his success.

Elevation Beer Co, Poncha Springs. In Chaffee County, surrounded by 14,000-foot peaks and next to the Arkansas River headwaters, Elevation makes some of the state's best barrel-aged and specialty beers. The tasting room is open daily noon–8.

New Belgium Brewing Company, Fort Collins. This gorgeous brewery is often referred to as the "cathedral of beer." It is employee-owned, fully wind-powered, and one of the largest breweries in the country. Famous for its Fat Tire Amber Ale, New Belgium Brewing Company always has an array of flavorful beers in their taproom. Tours are available Tuesday through Sunday 11:30–4:30.

COLORADO WITH KIDS

Colorado is an outdoor adventure playground that offers memorable experiences for both adults and kids on its many mountains, waterways, parks, lakes, and bustling urban areas. In the winter, families can whoosh down the state's many ski slopes, while in summer they can hike through its numerous trails and then gather around a campfire at night.

There are a few things to remember when traveling with kids in Colorado. Throughout much of the state, you will be at a high altitude, which will affect every member of the family. Make sure children drink plenty of water, are protected from the sun, and have plenty of down time.

Stock up on sunscreen, water, and extra food if you plan to undertake a family hike. Keep an eye on all members of your group when enjoying the outdoors and watch that no one strays too close to rivers or mountain overlooks.

Where to Go

Cheyenne Mountain Zoo, Colorado Springs. This superlative zoo is loaded with interactive exhibits that allow kids to really learn about the animals they are seeing. Animal lovers can feed giraffes by hand and more daring tykes can soar in a gondola that flies over the zoo.

Children's Museum of Denver, Denver. One of the best children's museums in the country, the Children's Museum of Denver has an impressive range of hands-on exhibits. There's a fire station with a fire truck and pole, and an assembly line where kids can design and build various items.

Dinosaur Journey, Colorado National Monument. What kids aren't intrigued by dinosaurs? This museum provides interactive experiences for curious young ones: they can look for fossils in a mock quarry, examine dino prints, and be wowed by animatronic dinosaurs.

Georgetown Loop Railroad, Georgetown. This 3-mile narrow gauge loop ascends over 640 feet of mountainous terrain between the mining towns of Georgetown and Silver Plume. It feels as if you're being transported back to an earlier era as the steam engine slowly chugs up the tracks.

Glenwood Caverns Adventure Park, Glenwood Springs. This once sleepy resort town, renowned for its hot springs, has transformed itself into one of the state's best family vacation spots. The Glenwood Caverns Adventure Park has a thrilling alpine coaster, a fun zip-line ride, and a rollercoaster that overhangs a cliff. Add in several caves, two rivers, and miles of hiking trails and your family is guaranteed to stay busy.

Great Sand Dunes National Park, San Luis Valley. While the largest sand dunes in the United States may seem entirely out of place amid the state's soaring mountains, they provide unique adventures for families. Kids enjoy amazing hikes, nighttime stargazing, tours to spot the bison in the southwest part of the park, and, if they're particularly adventurous, climbing the massive dunes.

COLORADO WILDLIFE

(A) Bighorn Sheep: Clambering along rocky ledges, muscular bighorn sheep fascinate with their ability to travel so easily where the rest of us can't. In winter the docile herd animals descend to lower elevations. Rams have heavy, curled horns, while ewes' horns are short and slightly bent. From afar it's easy to spot both sexes' white rumps, which stand out brightly against their furry brown coats.

(B) Bison: The shaggy, grouchy American bison may not be the western frontier's most charismatic ungulate, but it's certainly the most iconic. A bison can reach 6 feet at the shoulder, and males can weigh a ton (females typically weigh about 1,000 pounds). Bulls and cows alike sport short, curved horns, which they'll use to gore predators (or tourists who invade their space).

(C) Black Bear: So common in Colorado that residents in some areas must chase them out of garbage cans and backyards, the black bear is in a constant battle for space and food. "Black" refers to the species, not the color, so don't be confused if you see gold, tan, or rust; it's the same family. In any case, the way not to see one is to hike loudly, especially in Rocky Mountain National Park and other heavily forested areas from mid-March to November. Hang a bear bag while camping and pack out your trash.

(D) Coyote: This foraging omnivore's indiscriminate diet includes carrion, small mammals, insects, and grasses. They're about 30 pounds or more, distinguishing them from much larger wolves. The graytan canines thrive throughout the western United States. They travel alone or in small packs and, with rare exceptions, pose little threat to humans.

(E) Elk: A bull's antlers can weigh 40 pounds and, in summer, shed a soft fur known as antler velvet. Elk congregate where forest meets meadows, summering

at high elevations before migrating lower in winter. In September and October, bulls attract a "harem" of mating partners by bugling, a loud and surreal whistling.

(F) Marmot: A few species of marmots like to live high up among granite rock piles of talus slopes and along riverbanks, so if you see them, it's likely to be along high-country trails. The rocky strongholds help protect these furry ground squirrels from such natural predators as eagles and hawks.

(G) Moose: Feeding on fir, willows, and aspens, the moose is the largest member of the deer family: the largest bulls stand 7 feet tall at the shoulders and weigh up to 1,600 pounds. Distinctive characteristics include its antlers, which lie flat like palmate satellite dishes. Keep your distance if you come upon a moose; they are notoriously territorial and protective of their offspring.

(H) Mountain Lion: Although the mountain lion is an occasional predator, chances are you won't see him at most of the parks. They're tawny colored, can be 8 feet long, and weigh up to 200 pounds. They're capable of taking down a mule deer or elk.

Mule Deer: Often seen grazing in meadows and forests are mule deer, with their black-tipped tails and pronounced antlers. Their name comes from the shape of their ears, which resemble mules' ears. Their unusual gait—all four feet can hit the ground at once—gives them an advantage over predators, as they move faster over scrubby terrain and can change directions instantly. Watch for them at peak feeding times at dawn and dusk, especially when you're driving along remote mountain roads.

GREAT ITINERARIES

FIRST-TIMER'S ITINERARIES: DENVER, BOULDER, AND ROCKY MOUNTAIN NATIONAL PARK, 7 DAYS

Denver, Days 1–3

Denver is filled with folks who stopped to visit and never left. After a few days in the Mile High City and surrounding metro area it's easy to see why: Colorado's capital has much to recommend it, including a thriving cultural scene, restaurants representing every ethnicity, plenty of sunshine, outdoor options galore, and snowcapped peaks for visual variety.

After you've settled into your hotel, head downtown, or if you're already staying there—always a good option to explore the city—make your way to Lower Downtown, or **LoDo**. The historic district is home to many of the city's famous brewpubs, art galleries, and **Coors Field**, as well as popular restaurants and some of the area's oldest architecture.

Hop on the free MallRide, the shuttle bus run by RTD, to head up the 16th Street Mall, a pedestrian-friendly, shopping-oriented strip that runs through the center of downtown. From there you can walk to **Larimer Square** for more shopping and restaurants. You can also visit the **Denver Art Museum, Union Station, the History Colorado Center, the Colorado State Capitol, the Molly Brown House,** and the **U.S. Mint.**

Logistics: Light rail is an excellent way to navigate the city. Vending machines at each station for the RTD Light Rail service show destinations and calculate your fare ($2.25–$4 depending on the number of zones crossed). Children under age five ride free when accompanied by a fare-paying adult. RTD buses also provide an excellent way to get around; schedules are posted inside shelters and are available at Civic Center Station at the south end of the 16th Street Mall and Market Street Station toward the north end. Fares are $2.25 one-way.

Day 4: Boulder

Boulder takes its fair share of ribbing for being a Birkenstock-wearing, tofu-eating, latter-day hippie kind of town, but the truth is that it is healthy, wealthy, and exceedingly popular. Stroll along the **Pearl Street Mall** and sample the excellent restaurants and shops, catching one of the dozens of street performers; or head just outside the city to tour **Celestial Seasonings,** the tea manufacturer; or to **Chautauqua Park** to hike in the shadow of the dramatic Flatiron Mountains. In winter, Eldora Mountain Resort is a 21-mile jaunt up a steep, switchback-laden road with no lift lines as payoff. The University of Colorado campus here means there is a high hip quotient in much of the nightlife.

Logistics: You can take an RTD bus to Boulder from Denver, but it's just as easy to drive up U.S. 36 (one hour by car). If you're going to go beyond the Pearl Street Mall in Boulder, it's nice to have a car once you're there. Parking, though, can be quite tight.

Days 5–7: Rocky Mountain National Park

Rocky Mountain National Park (RMNP) is a year-round marvel, a park for every season: hiking in the summer, spotting elk in the fall, snowshoeing in winter, and snapping photos of wildflowers in spring. There are several hikes that shouldn't be missed in the park. For

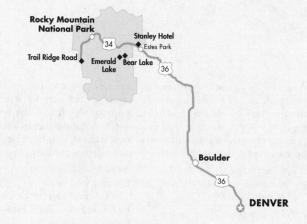

Rocky Mountain
National Park

Trail Ridge Road

Emerald
Lake

Bear Lake

Stanley Hotel
Estes Park

Boulder

DENVER

lovely scenery, opt for the one that goes from **Bear Lake to Emerald Lake.** There are some steep sections along the way, but the spectacular mountain views more than make up for it. Also not to be missed is a drive along **Trail Ridge Road,** the world's highest continuous paved highway. You'll enjoy awesome views of waterfalls, lakes, mountain vistas, glaciers, and emerald meadows. Give yourself four hours to complete the drive, and check the weather conditions before you start.

There are five campgrounds in the park, but those looking for more comfort should opt for **Estes Park.** This picturesque town is the gateway to RMNP and a worthwhile destination itself, a small town swelling to a large one with the tourists who flock to its Western-theme shops and art galleries. The **Stanley Hotel,** the inspiration for Stephen King's novel *The Shining,* provides great lodging in a historic setting.

Logistics: Estes Park is a hop-skip from Denver and Boulder, about 65 miles northwest of Denver via I–25 and then CO–66 and U.S. 36. To get to RMNP, simply take U.S. 34 or U.S. 36 into the park (a 15-minute drive).

SKIING THE ROCKIES, 5 DAYS

With its champagne-powder runs and wide variety of alpine terrain, Colorado is a winter paradise. In less than a week, you can ski some of the most iconic resorts in the state.

Days 1–2: Aspen
World-class dining, upscale shopping, and possible celebrity sighting await in Aspen, along with some of the best skiing in North America. Aspen's four ski areas—**Aspen Highlands, Aspen Mountain, Buttermilk,** and **Snowmass**—all have amazing runs through fluffy champagne powder. After an afternoon of whooshing down the slopes, visit some of the fabled restaurants and nightlife options in downtown Aspen, or relax at a hotel spa.

Days 3–4: Vail Valley
Roughly 2 hours (102 miles) from Aspen via I–70 W and CO–82 E

The Bavarian-themed village at the base of **Vail Mountain** offers as much as the resorts in the Alps. The back side of the mountain, with its thrilling series of bowls, delivers enough glades and bumps to challenge even the most dedicated skier. But beginners and moderate skiers need not worry; the front side of

Vail Mountain has plenty of cruisers to satisfy skiers of all levels. The free shuttle in town runs every 15 minutes and links the three base villages. At night, you can wander along the quaint cobbled streets and pop into the European-style cafés.

Day 5: Breckenridge

Roughly 50 minutes (38 miles) from Vail via CO–9 N and I–70 W

Breckenridge is a great place to unwind after spending four days at its bigger and better-known cousins. The town has the sort of laid-back ski-country vibe that Colorado is known for. With a downtown filled with Victorian houses left over from its mining heyday, the area is filled with affordable restaurants, comfy bars, and interesting shops. The mountain itself is one of the larger ski areas in America with five separate peaks offering a variety of terrain from beginner to expert.

EXPLORING THE COLORADO SOUTHWEST, 10 DAYS

The southwest corner of Colorado is a study in contrasts. From the soaring peaks of the Sangre de Cristo Mountains to the serene beauty of the San Luis Valley, it is a region that offers a multitude of experiences. It is less crowded than the more popular areas of the state, with more wide-open spaces. As you head across the numerous mountain passes, the gradual changes in fauna and terrain are awe-inspiring.

Days 1–2: Denver

Spend a few days acclimating to the altitude change in Denver, visiting the city's top-notch museums and exploring the LoDo area. In preparation for your

journey, pop into the massive **REI** flagship store in the Central Platte Valley neighborhood. It's full of any gear you might need, including sturdy hats, lightweight rain jackets, comfortable boots, packs, and other necessities.

Days 3–4: Colorado Springs and Nearby

The Colorado Springs area is dominated by 14,115-foot **Pikes Peak**—the inspiration for the song "America the Beautiful"—and getting to its summit, whether by cog railway, foot, or car, is a memorable experience. But there are other worthy options along this popular corridor, such as strolling through the red rocks of the **Garden of the Gods,** peeking at the tunnel in **Cave of the Winds,** checking out the animals at the **Cheyenne Mountain Zoo,** taking advantage of the healing vibes in the artists' community at **Manitou Springs,** or exploring the old gold-mining town of **Cripple Creek.**

Logistics: Colorado Springs is 70 miles south of Denver on I–25. You'll enjoy mountain views on most of the drive; Pikes Peak is visible on clear days. Take U.S. 24 west from I–25 to reach Manitou Springs; follow CO–67 south from U.S. 24 west to visit Cripple Creek.

Days 5: Salida

Surrounded by the Collegiate Peaks, **Salida** is a good jumping-off point for the many outdoor activities available in this mountainous region. Salida is also a haven for artists who specialize in Western-oriented themes and grassroots sensibilities.

Logistics: Take CO–115 south from Colorado Springs to Canyon City; continue west on U.S. 50 toward Salida. As you head into Salida the Sangre de Cristo Mountains offer stunning views.

Day 6: Black Canyon of the Gunnison National Park

From Salida head west on U.S. 50 toward Montrose, and then continue north on CO–347 to **Black Canyon of the Gunnison National Park**. The trip takes about two-and-a-half hours. This national park offers sheer cliffs rising more than 2,000 feet above the river and stunning views that rival the Grand Canyon. Stay overnight in nearby **Montrose**, about 15 miles west of the park.

Days 7–8: Telluride and Nearby

Telluride, though famous for its film and bluegrass festivals, presents a less glitzy face than other ski resorts like Aspen and Vail, but is still well worth the visit. The **San Juan Skyway**, a 236-mile loop that connects Durango, Telluride, Ouray, and Silverton, is a gloriously scenic drive that winds you through mountains, alpine forests, and wildflower meadows.

Logistics: To get to Telluride from Montrose head south on U.S. 550 to Ridgeway, continue west on CO–62 toward Placerville, and then head south on CO–145 to Telluride. The entire journey is roughly 66 miles and takes about 90 minutes.

Day 9: Mesa Verde National Park

Mesa Verde National Park safeguards the 1,400-year-old cliff dwellings of the Ancestral Puebloans. Take a ranger-led tour to the primary cliff-dwelling sites like the **Balcony House, Cliff Palace,** and **Spruce Tree House.** Make time for the **Chapin Mesa Archaeological Museum,** where you can learn the history of the Ancestral Puebloan culture. Afterward, drive to Durango to spend the night.

Logistics: Mesa Verde is a 1½-hour drive from Telluride, heading south on CO–145. From Mesa Verde head east on U.S. 160 toward Durango, an approximately one-hour drive.

Day 10: Durango

Durango is an Old West mining town that has retained much of its Victorian charm. Mountain bikers make it a mission to try their mettle on the tough trails surrounding the town; in winter, the **Purgatory at Durango Mountain Resort** routinely has deep powder and short lift lines.

Logistics: To get back to Denver head east from Durango on U.S. 160 until you get to Walsenburg (approximately four-hours); then head north on I–25 to Denver. Telluride and Durango have airports with limited service from major carriers.

MOUNTAIN FINDER

To help you decide which of Colorado's ski slopes are best for you, we've rated each major mountain according to several categories. To give some sense of cost, we have included the price of a peak-season one-day adult lift ticket at the time of this writing, as well as a category that covers affordable lodging options. Don't think this chart is only for winter visitors though—we've also rated the mountain areas on their summer offerings, too. *You should also consult the regional chapters.*

	LIFT TICKET COST	VARIETY OF TERRAIN	SNOWBOARDER FRIENDLY	OTHER SNOW SPORTS	FAMILY FRIENDLY	DINING VARIETY	NIGHTLIFE	AFFORDABLE LODGING	OFF-SLOPE ACTIVITIES	SUMMER ACTIVITIES	CONVENIENCE FACTOR
Arapahoe Basin	$85	◑	●	○	◑	●	●	●	○	○	●
Aspen	$129	●	◑	●	◑	●	●	●	●	●	◑
Beaver Creek	$159	◑	●	◑	●	◑	●	◑	●	●	◑
Breckenridge	$130	◑	●	●	●	◑	◑	◑	●	●	◑
Copper Mountain	$138	●	●	●	●	◑	◑	●	◑	◑	◑
Crested Butte	$108	◑	●	◑	●	◑	◑	●	●	●	○
Purgatory at Durango Mountain Resort	$81	◑	◑	●	◑	●	●	●	○	○	○
Eldora	$89	◑	●	◑	◑	●	●	●	○	○	◑
Keystone	$99	●	◑	◑	●	◑	◑	●	◑	◑	●
Loveland	$57	◑	●	○	●	◑	●	●	○	○	●
Monarch	$69	◑	◑	○	●	●	●	●	○	○	◑
Ski Cooper	$50	○	◑	○	●	●	●	●	○	○	◑
Snowmass	$129	◑	◑	◑	●	◑	◑	●	◑	◑	◑
Steamboat	$119	◑	●	●	●	◑	◑	◑	●	◑	◑
Telluride	$114	◑	◑	◑	◑	●	◑	◑	◑	●	○
Vail	$129	●	◑	●	●	●	●	◑	●	●	◑
Winter Park	$129	●	●	◑	●	◑	◑	●	●	◑	◑
Wolf Creek	$65	◑	◑	○	●	●	●	●	○	○	○

KEY: ○ few or none   ◐ moderate   ◑ substantial   ● noteworthy

DENVER

Updated by
Kyle Wagner

You can tell from its skyline alone that Denver is a major metropolis, with a Major League Baseball stadium at one end of downtown and the State Capitol building at the other. But look to the west to see where Denver distinguishes itself in the majestic Rocky Mountains, snow-peaked and breathtakingly huge, looming in the distance. This combination of urban sprawl and proximity to nature is what gives the city character and sets it apart as a destination.

Many Denverites are unabashed nature lovers who can also enjoy the outdoors within the city limits by walking along the park-lined river paths downtown. (Perhaps as a result of their active lifestyle, Denverites are among the "thinnest" city residents in the United States, and the city is named annually as one of the healthiest in the nation.) For Denverites, preserving the environment and the city's rich mining and ranching heritage are of equally vital importance to the quality of life.

LoDo, a business-and-shopping area, buzzes with jazz clubs, restaurants, and art galleries housed in carefully restored century-old buildings. The culturally diverse populace avidly supports the Denver Art Museum, the Denver Museum of Nature & Science, the Museo de las Americas, and the new History Colorado Center (formerly the Colorado History Museum). The Denver Performing Arts Complex is the nation's second-largest theatrical venue, bested in capacity only by New York's Lincoln Center. An excellent public transportation system, including a popular, growing light-rail system and 850 miles of bike paths, makes getting around easy.

ORIENTATION AND PLANNING

GETTING ORIENTED

Denver's downtown is laid out at a 45-degree angle to the rest of the metro area. Interstate 25 bisects Denver north to south, and I–70 runs east to west. University Boulevard is a major north–south road and Speer Boulevard is a busy diagonal street. Most Denverites are tied to their vehicles, but the light-rail works well if you're going to certain areas.

If you're staying downtown, you can visit LoDo, Capitol Hill, and Larimer Square by walking or using light-rail or the free Mall shuttle. The Central Platte Valley can be accessed by taking the Mall shuttle all the way north to the end and then walking across the pedestrian-only Millennium Bridge. You will need a car to get to Cherry Creek or City Park, however, but once there, those sections also are easy to explore on foot.

2

TOP REASONS TO GO

Denver Art Museum: Visitors are treated to Asian, pre-Columbian, and Spanish Colonial works along with a world-famous collection of Native American pieces.

Denver Botanic Gardens: Creatively arranged displays of more than 15,000 plant species from around the world draw garden enthusiasts year-round.

Larimer Square: Specialty stores, superior people-watching, and some of the city's top restaurants and nightlife bring tourists and locals alike to the city's oldest area.

LoDo: Lower downtown's appeal lies in its proximity to Coors Field, the newly renovated Union Station and the convenient and free 16th Street Mall shuttle. Shops and galleries are busy during the day, and it's also a hot spot at night.

Red Rocks Park and Amphitheatre: Even if you aren't attending a concert, the awe-inspiring red rocks of this formation-turned-venue are worth a look, and there are hiking trails nearby.

Downtown. With its pedestrian-friendly numbered streets, free Mall shuttle, and plethora of restaurants, galleries, and museums within easy walking distance, downtown is a logical starting point for exploring.

Central Platte Valley. Just west of downtown, the Central Platte Valley is a destination for daytime activities along the Platte River and evening pursuits such as dining, music, and dancing.

City Park and Nearby. East of downtown, the 330-acre oasis that is City Park also serves as a jumping-off point for the Denver Zoo and the Denver Museum of Nature & Science.

PLANNING

WHEN TO GO

Denver defies easy weather predictions. Although its blizzards are infamous, snowstorms are often followed by beautiful spring weather just a day or two later. Ski resorts are packed from roughly October to April, and Denver itself often bears the traffic. Summers are festival-happy, with a rock-concert slate and films on the big screen at nearby Red Rocks Park and Amphitheatre. Local bands and nationally known acts perform at venues around the city such as City Park and Civic Center Park. Perhaps the best times to visit, though, are spring and fall, when the heat isn't so intense, the snow isn't so plentiful, and crowds are relatively thin. Ski resorts are still as scenic, but less expensive.

PLANNING YOUR TIME

An easy way to organize the first day of a visit to Denver is to start at one end of the pedestrian-friendly downtown, which is laid out at a 45-degree angle to the rest of the metro area, and work your way to the other using the free 16th Street Mall shuttle. The Central Platte Valley neighborhood (a short walk across Millennium Bridge) and LoDo sit at one end, with Larimer Square on the way toward Capitol Hill at the other. Along the way, a few blocks' walk from the Mall can take you to attractions such as the Denver Art Museum, the History Colorado Center, and the U.S. Mint.

A car or bus ride is necessary to visit City Park or Cherry Creek, but once there, these areas also are easily navigated on foot and can offer a second day's worth of attractions, including the Denver Zoo, Denver Botanic Gardens, and the Denver Museum of Nature & Science at City Park, and the plethora of shopping and restaurants of Cherry Creek North.

GETTING HERE AND AROUND

AIR TRAVEL

Denver International Airport (DEN) is 15 miles northeast of downtown, but it usually takes about a half hour to 45 minutes to travel between them, depending on the time of day. It's served by most major domestic carriers and many international ones. Arrive at the airport with plenty of time before your flight, preferably two hours; the airport's check-in and security-check lines are particularly long.

TRANSFERS Between the airport and downtown, Super Shuttle makes door-to-door trips. The region's public bus service, Regional Transportation District (RTD), runs SkyRide to and from the airport; the trip takes 50 minutes, and the fare is $18–$26 each way. There's a transportation center in the airport just outside baggage claim. A taxi ride to downtown costs $60–$70.

Airport Contact Denver International Airport (*DEN*). ⊠ *8500 Peña Blvd.* ☎ *800/247–2336* ⊕ *www.flydenver.com.*

Airport Transfers Regional Transportation District/SkyRide. ⊠ *Denver* ☎ *303/299–6000 for route and schedule information* ⊕ *www.rtd-denver.com.* **Super Shuttle.** ☎ *303/370–1300* ⊕ *www.supershuttle.com.*

BUS TRAVEL

In downtown Denver, free shuttle-bus service operates about every 10 minutes from 5 am weekdays (5:30 am Saturday; 6:30 am Sunday and holidays) until 1:35 am, running the length of the 16th Street Mall (which bisects downtown) and stopping at one-block intervals. In addition, the Free MetroRide offers weekday rush-hour service between Union Station and Civic Center Station, making limited stops along 18th and 19th streets. If you plan to spend much time outside downtown, a car is advised, although Denver has one of the best city bus systems in the country.

The region's public bus service, RTD, is comprehensive, with routes throughout the metropolitan area. The service also links Denver to outlying towns such as Boulder, Longmont, and Nederland. You can buy bus tokens at grocery stores or pay with exact change on the bus. Fares vary according to time and zone. Within the city limits, buses cost $2.25.

Bus Contacts RTD. ☎ *303/299–6000, 800/366–7433* ⊕ *www.rtd-denver.com.*

CAR TRAVEL

Rental-car companies include Advantage, Alamo, Avis, Budget, Dollar, Enterprise, Hertz, Thrifty, and National. All have airport and downtown representatives.

Reaching Denver by car is fairly easy, except during rush hour. Interstate highways 70 and 25 intersect near downtown; an entrance to I–70 is just outside the airport.

■ TIP→ **When you're looking for an address within Denver, make sure you know whether it's a street or avenue.** Speer Boulevard runs alongside Cherry Creek from northwest to southeast through downtown; numbered streets run parallel to Speer and most are one-way. Colfax Avenue (U.S. 287) runs east–west through downtown; numbered avenues run parallel to Colfax. Broadway runs north–south. Other main thoroughfares include Colorado Boulevard (north–south) and Alameda Avenue (east–west). Try to avoid driving in the area during rush hour, when traffic gets heavy. Interstates 25 and 225 are particularly slow during those times; although the Transportation Expansion Project (T-REX) added extra lanes, a light-rail system along the highways, bicycle lanes, and other improvements, expansion in the metro area outpaced the project.

PARKING Finding an open meter has become increasingly difficult in downtown Denver, especially during peak times such as Rockies games and weekend nights. Additionally, most meters have two-hour limits until 10 pm, and at 25¢ for 10 minutes in some downtown areas, parking in Denver is currently more expensive than in New York City or Chicago (although the city has made it easier to pay by switching most meters to accept debit/credit cards as well as change). However, there's no shortage of pay lots for $5 to $25 per day.

CAR SERVICES Hailed solely via smartphone app, car services in the metro area give taxis a ride for their money, particularly because the ride can be considerably cheaper and arrive faster. The downside, though, is that at peak times, Uber and Lyft prices soar to "surge pricing." Expect to pay about $1.13–$2.14 base and 17¢–20¢ a minute and $1.41–$1.57 per mile at non-peak times and up to four times as much during surge pricing.

Car Service Companies Lyft. ⊕ *www.lyft.com.* **Uber.** ⊕ *www.uber.com.*

TAXI TRAVEL

Taxis can be costly and difficult to simply flag down as in some major metropolitan areas; instead, you usually must call ahead to arrange for one. Cabs are $2–$2.60 minimum and $2–$2.60 per mile, depending on the company. However, at peak times—during major events, and at 2 am when the bars close—taxis are very hard to come by.

Taxi Companies Freedom Cab. ☎ *303/444–4444.* **Metro Taxi.** ☎ *303/333–3333.* **Yellow Cab.** ☎ *303/777–7777.*

TRAIN TRAVEL

Historic Union Station in the heart of downtown has undergone extensive redevelopment and features an open-air train hall behind the refurbished historic building, where passengers once again can hop aboard the California Zephyr as it stops in Denver on its runs between Chicago and San Francisco.

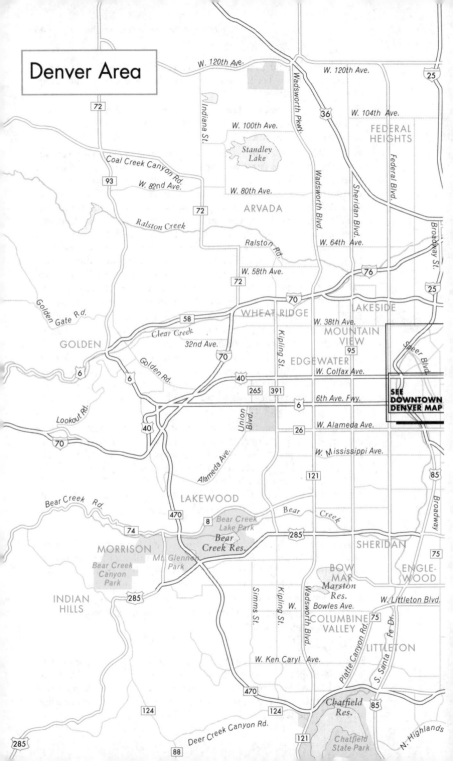

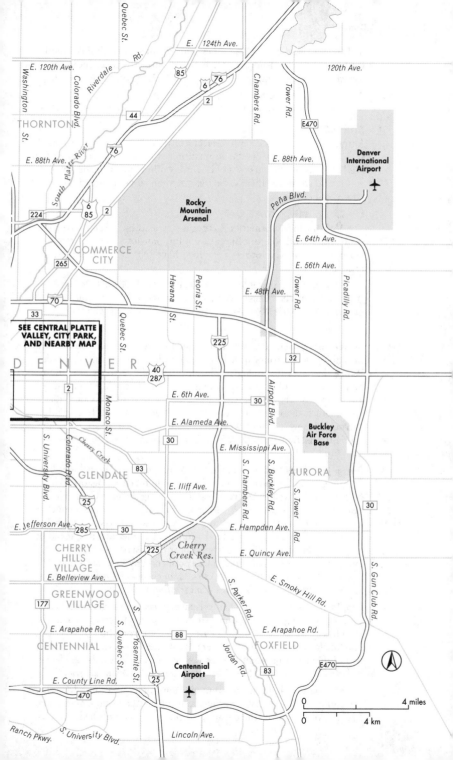

RTD's Light Rail service's six lines and 47 miles of track links southwest, southern, and northeast Denver to downtown, including new service from Union Station. The peak fare is $2.25 within the city limits.

Contacts Amtrak. ✉ *Union Station, 1701 Wynkoop St.* ☎ *800/872–7245* ⊕ *www.amtrak.com.* **RTD Light Rail.** ☎ *303/299–6000* ⊕ *www.rtd-denver.com.*

SAFETY

Although Denver is a generally peaceful city, the crime rate has increased slightly in recent years as the population has boomed. There are a few shadier areas on the outskirts of downtown, but violent crimes are few and far between. As always, paying attention to your surroundings is your best defense.

VISITOR INFORMATION

The Visitors and Information Center is operated by VISIT Denver, the Convention and Visitors Bureau. It's located downtown at the corner of 16th and California. They also have self-guided walking-tour brochures.

Visitor Information Lower Downtown District, Inc. ☎ *303/628–5428* ⊕ *www.lodo.org.* **VISIT Denver, The Convention and Visitors Bureau.** ✉ *1555 California St., LoDo* ☎ *303/892–1505, 800/233–6837* ⊕ *www.denver.org.*

TOURS

FAMILY **Denver History Tours.** Personalized, guided tours of historic Denver are available, as are tours to select surrounding areas along the Front Range, in buses (for groups only) and on walking tours for a minimum of two people; prices and times vary according to the tour. Guides are knowledgeable locals eager to tailor the tour to individual tastes and interests, and work to accommodate varying fitness levels within a group. Trains, the Old West, and "haunted" Denver are particular specialties. ✉ *Denver* ☎ *720/234–7929* ⊕ *www.denverhistorytours.com* 💲 *From $20.*

Denver Microbrew Tour. This guided walking tour in LoDo includes beer sampling at several microbreweries and a comprehensive history of local beer making as well as Denver's history; a swing through Coors Field is also included. The fee covers the samples along the way and a voucher for a full pint, as well. A new tour through the hip arts district RiNo (River North) recently was added and includes cider tastings, too (but not Coors Field). The guides are all beer enthusiasts who thoroughly enjoy sharing beer trivia, and can recommend anything beer-related in Denver. ✉ *Denver* ☎ *303/578–9548* ⊕ *www.denvermicrobrewtour.com* 💲 *From $29* ⏱ *Tours Fri.–Sun. Call for times.*

Gray Line. This company offers the usual expansive and exhaustive coach tours of anything and everything, from shopping in Cherry Creek to visiting Rocky Mountain National Park. Tours last from three to 10 hours, and lunch is sometimes included at a local eatery. Guides run the gamut from informed-to-a-point yet enthusiastic to expert locals. ✉ *Denver* ☎ *800/472–9546, 303/289–2841* ⊕ *www.grayline.com* 💲 *From $35.*

My 420 Tours. A handful of cannabis tour companies are addressing the confusion for tourists over where to buy and consume marijuana. My 420 offers one of the cheapest, if not the most polished, options.

After meeting in the lobby of a cannabis-friendly hotel that also can be booked for an overnight stay (a vaporizer is delivered to the room for personal use), a group of up to 35 is then escorted in a luxury bus—complete with laser lighting and accompanying music—to a variety of marijuana-related activities. Expect to visit at least two marijuana shops, which offer discounts to the group, as well as a "grow," a facility engaged in actively cultivating marijuana crops, and a local eatery. Depending on the timing, the tour can incorporate local cultural activities, as well. My 420 also offers cannabis cooking classes and will customize a private tour. ⊠ *Denver* ☎ *855/694–2086* ⊕ *www.my420tours. com* ⊠ *From $129.*

EXPLORING DENVER

For many out-of-state travelers Denver is a gateway city, a transitional stop before heading into the nearby Rocky Mountains. Often, visitors will simply fly into Denver International Airport, rent a car, ask for directions to I–70, and head west into the mountains. But it's worth scheduling an extra few days, or even a few hours, to delve into the city itself. The city is an easy place to maneuver, with prominent hotels such as the Brown Palace, excellent shopping at Cherry Creek and Larimer Square, a full range of professional sports teams, and plenty of (expensive) parking.

DOWNTOWN

Denver's downtown is an intriguing mix of well-preserved monuments from the state's frontier past and modern high-tech marvels. You can often catch the reflection of an elegant Victorian building in the mirrored glass of a skyscraper. Hundreds of millions of dollars were poured into the city in the 1990s in such projects as Coors Field, the downtown home of Denver's baseball Rockies; the relocation of Elitch Gardens, the first amusement park in the country to move into a downtown urban area; and an expansion of the light-rail system to run from downtown into the southern suburbs (and more recently, west toward Golden). Lower downtown, or LoDo, is a Victorian warehouse district revitalized by the ballpark, loft condominiums, and numerous brewpubs, nightclubs, and restaurants.

TIMING

Downtown is compact and can be toured on foot in an hour or less, but a car is recommended for exploring outside of downtown proper. The Denver Art Museum merits at least two to three hours, and the Colorado History Museum, renamed the History Colorado Center in spring 2012 after moving to a new three-story building a few blocks from the previous location, can be covered in an hour or two. Save some time for browsing and people-watching along the 16th Street Mall and Larimer Square. LoDo is a 25-plus square-block area that takes a few hours to meander through.

LODO

TOP ATTRACTIONS

Fodor's Choice
★

Larimer Square. This square, on the oldest street in the city, was immortalized by Jack Kerouac in his seminal book *On the Road.* It was saved from the wrecker's ball by a determined preservationist in the 1960s, when the city went demolition-crazy in its eagerness to present a more youthful image. Much has changed since Kerouac's wanderings: Larimer Square's rough edges have been cleaned up in favor of upscale retail and chic restaurants. The Square has also become a serious late-night party district thanks to spillover from the expanded LoDo neighborhood and Rockies fans flowing out from the baseball stadium. Shops line the arched redbrick courtyards of **Writer Square,** one of Denver's most charming shopping districts. ⊠ *Larimer and 15th Sts., LoDo* ☎ *303/534–2367* ⊕ *www.larimersquare.com.*

LoDo. Officially, the Lower Downtown Historic District, the 25-plus square-block area that was the site of the original 1858 settlement of Denver City, is nicknamed LoDo. It's home to art galleries, chic shops, nightclubs, and restaurants ranging from Denver's most upscale to its most down-home. This part of town was once the city's thriving retail center, then it fell into disuse and slid into slums. Since the early 1990s LoDo has been transformed into the city's cultural center, thanks to its resident artists, retailers, and loft dwellers who have taken over the old warehouses and redbricks. ⊠ *From Larimer St. to South Platte River, between 14th and 22nd Sts., LoDo* ⊕ *www.lodo.org.*

OFF THE
BEATEN
PATH

Forney Museum of Transportation. Inside a converted warehouse are an 1898 Renault coupe, Amelia Earhart's immaculately maintained "Goldbug," and a Big Boy steam locomotive, among other historic vehicles. Other exhibits in this eccentric museum consist of antique bicycles, cable cars, and even experimental car-planes. This trivia-laden showcase is outside of the downtown loop: Go north on Brighton Boulevard; the museum is adjacent to the Denver Coliseum on the south side of I–70. ⊠ *4303 Brighton Blvd., Globeville* ☎ *303/297–1113* ⊕ *www.forneymuseum.org* ⊜ *$9.75* ☉ *Mon.–Sat. 10–4, Sun. noon–4.*

16th Street Mall. Outdoor cafés and tempting shops line this pedestrian-only 15-block, 1¼-mile thoroughfare, shaded by red-oak and locust trees. The mall's businesses run the entire socioeconomic range. There are popular meeting spots for business types at places like the Irish pub Katie Mullen's in the Sheraton Hotel; a front-row view of the many street performers and goings-on from the sidewalk patio at the Paramount Cafe, around the corner from the Paramount Theatre; and plenty of fast-food chains. Although some Denverites swear by the higher-end Cherry Creek Shopping District, the 16th Street Mall covers every retail area and is a more affordable, diverse experience. You can find Denver's best people-watching here. Catch one of the free shuttle buses at any corner that run the length of downtown. Pay attention when you're wandering across the street, as the walking area and bus lanes are the same color and are hard to distinguish. ⊠ *From Broadway to Wewatta St., LoDo* ⊕ *16thstreetmalldenver.com.*

WORTH NOTING

Brown Palace. The grande dame of Denver hotels was built in 1892, and is still considered the city's most prestigious address. Famous guests have included President Dwight D. Eisenhower, Winston Churchill, and Beyoncé. Even if you aren't staying here, the Brown Palace lobby is a great place to sit on comfortable old couches, drink tea, and listen to piano standards (or harp, during afternoon tea). Reputedly this was the first atrium hotel in the United States; its ornate lobby and nine stories are crowned by a Tiffany stained-glass window. ⊠ *321 17th St., LoDo* ☎ *303/297–3111* ⊕ *www.brownpalace.com.*

Daniels & Fisher Tower. This 330-foot-high, 20-floor structure emulates the Campanile of St. Mark's Square in Venice, and it was the tallest building west of the Mississippi when it was built in 1909. William Cooke Daniels originally commissioned the tower to stand adjacent to his five-story department store. Today it's an office building with a cabaret in the basement as well as the city's most convenient clock tower. It's particularly striking—the clock is 16 feet high—when viewed in concert with the fountains in the adjacent Skyline Park. ⊠ *1601 Arapahoe St., at 16th St., LoDo.*

FAMILY **Denver Firefighters Museum.** Denver's first firehouse was built in 1909 and now serves as a museum where original items of the trade are on view, including uniforms, nets, fire carts and trucks, bells, and switchboards. Artifacts and photos document the progression of firefighting machinery from horses and carriages in the early 1900s to the flashy red-and-white trucks of today. ⊠ *1326 Tremont Pl., LoDo* ☎ *303/892–1436* ⊕ *www. denverfirefightersmuseum.org* 🎟 *$6* ☉ *Mon.–Sat. 10–4.*

CIVIC CENTER

TOP ATTRACTIONS

Clyfford Still Museum. Though he showed very little of his work and sold even less during his lifetime, artist Clyfford Still has nonetheless been credited as a significant contributor to the abstract expressionist movement, if not one of the most instrumental in its development. The vast majority of his extensive body of work had been sealed from the public since his death in 1980, but in 2004 his second wife chose Denver as the final resting place for a carefully curated portion—a little more than a hundred works of the more than 2,400 pieces, including paintings, drawings, and sculpture. In late 2011, the austere and easily navigable museum opened in a building designed by architect Brad Cloepfil. The nine galleries reveal Still's progression in chronological displays, and true to Still's wishes, it offers no restaurant. Periodically, the museum refreshes the works on display to present a new side of the artist's vision. ⊠ *1250 Bannock St., Golden Triangle* ☎ *720/354–4880* ⊕ *www.clyffordstillmuseum.org* 🎟 *$10* ☉ *Tues.–Thurs. and weekends 10–5, Fri. 10–8.*

FAMILY
Fodor's Choice
★
Denver Art Museum. Unique displays of Asian, pre-Columbian, Spanish Colonial, and Native American art are the hallmarks of this model of museum design. Among the museum's regular holdings are John DeAndrea's sexy, soothing, life-size polyvinyl painting *Linda* (1983); Claude Monet's dreamy flowerscape *Le Bassin des Nympheas* (1904);

and Charles Deas's red-cowboy-on-horseback *Long Jakes, The Rocky Mountain Man* (1844). The works are thoughtfully lighted, though dazzling mountain views through hallway windows sometimes steal your attention. Imaginative hands-on exhibits, game- and puzzle-filled Family Backpacks, and video corners will appeal to children; the Adventures in Art Center has hands-on art classes and exploration for children and adults. The museum doubled in size in 2007 with the opening of the Frederic C. Hamilton building, a 146,000-square-foot addition designed by architect Daniel Libeskind that has prompted debate: some say the glass and titanium design has ruined the view, while others think the building is a work of art in its own right. To the east of the museum is an outdoor plaza—you'll know it by the huge orange metal sculpture—that leads to the Denver Public Library next door. ⊠ *100 W. 14th Ave. Pkwy., Civic Center* ☎ *720/865–5000* ⊕ *www.denverartmuseum. org* ⊠ *$13* ☉ *Tues.–Thurs. and weekends 10–5; Fri. 10–8.*

QUICK
BITES

Palettes. The Denver Art Museum's restaurant, which serves lunch Tuesday through Sunday and dinner only on Fridays, is the product of local culinary artist chef Kevin Taylor. He fills the menu with colorful dishes like his signature soft-egg ravioli with black truffle butter and shiitake tamales. The prix-fixe menu is popular with local theatergoers. There's also a coffee shop and wine bar, **Mad Beans and Wine Cafe,** on the second floor of the museum, as well as **Mad Greens Inspired Eats,** a sandwich and salad spot on Martin Plaza across from the museum's main entrance, with outdoor tables on the plaza between the museum and the Denver Public Library. ⊠ *100 W. 14th Ave. Pkwy.* ☎ *303/534–1455* ⊕ *www.denverartmuseum.org/tags/palettes* ☉ *Closed Mon.*

FAMILY **Denver Public Library's Central Library.** A life-size horse on a 20-foot-tall chair and other sculptures decorate the expansive lawn of this sprawling complex with round towers and tall, oblong windows. Built in the mid-'50s, the Central Library underwent a massive, Michael Graves–designed renovation in 1995. The map and manuscript rooms, Gates Western History Reading Room (with amazing views of the mountains), and Schlessman Hall (with its three-story atrium) merit a visit. The library houses a world-renowned collection of books, photographs, and newspapers that chronicle the American West, as well as original paintings by Remington, Russell, Audubon, and Bierstadt. The children's library is notable for its captivating design and its unique, child-friendly multimedia computer catalog. ⊠ *10 W. 14th Ave. Pkwy., Civic Center* ☎ *720/865–1111* ⊕ *www.denverlibrary.org* ☉ *Mon. and Tues. 10–8, Wed.–Fri. 10–6, Sat. 9–5, Sun. 1–5.*

FAMILY **History Colorado Center.** The three-story, interactive History Colorado Center opened in April 2012, replacing the flagship museum of the Colorado Historical Society that sat two blocks away. Right from the lobby "time machines" that showcase oddball events from around the state (the "Tomato Wars" and the Leadville Ice Palace, for instance), the museum puts visitors on notice that this won't be the typical placard-reading experience. In addition to revamped versions of the

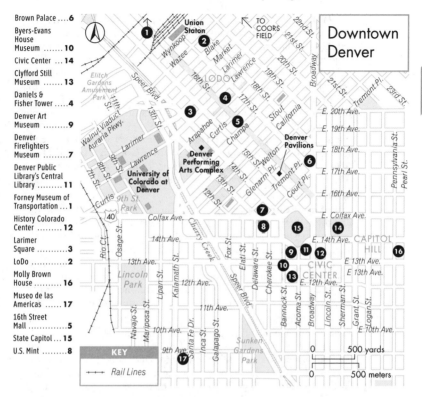

previous collections depicting state history from 1800 to the present, new exhibitions combine technology, artifacts, and multimedia presentations. Milk a life-size replica of a cow, drive a Model T Ford on the plains, or try a virtual ski jump, and then see what you would have looked like in a classroom in the late 1800s. ⊠ *1200 Broadway, Civic Center* ☎ *303/447–8679* ⊕ *www.historycoloradocenter. org* ⊡ *$12* ⊘ *Daily 10–5.*

**OFF THE
BEATEN
PATH**

Museo de las Americas. The region's first museum dedicated to the achievements of Latinos in the Americas has a permanent collection as well as rotating exhibits that cover everything from Latin Americans in the state legislature to Latin American female artists in the 20th century. Among the permanent pieces are the oil painting *Virgin of Solitude* (circa 1730) and a Mayan polychrome jar (circa 650–950), as well as contemporary works, and the exhibit "La Cocina" displays one full-size 18th-century kitchen as well as numerous smaller partial dioramas of a variety of Latino cooking cultures from around the world. The museum is in the second phase of renovation that is to be completed in 2018; until then, the pre-Columbian gallery is closed. In addition to the regular hours, the museum is open (with free admission) the first Friday evening of each month from 5 to 9. ⊠ *861 Santa Fe Dr., Lincoln Park* ☎ *303/571–4401* ⊕ *www.museo.org* ⊡ *$5* ⊘ *Tues.–Sat. noon–5.*

U.S. Mint. Tour this facility to catch a glimpse of the coin-making process, as presses spit out thousands of coins a minute. There are also exhibits on the history of money and a restored version of Denver's original mint prior to numerous expansions. More than 14 billion coins are minted yearly, and the nation's second-largest hoard of gold is stashed away here. To schedule a tour and prepare for your visit (there are strict security guidelines), visit the Mint's website. Reservations are required for all tours, which are guided, free, and available most weekdays from 8 to 3:30. The gift shop, which sells authentic coins and currency, is in the Tremont Center, across Colfax Avenue from the Mint. ⊠ *320 W. Colfax Ave., Civic Center* ☎ *303/405–4761* ⊕ *www.usmint.gov/mint_tours* ⊠ *Free* ☉ *Tours by reservation Mon.– Thurs. 8–3:30. Gift shop Mon.–Thurs. 8–5.*

WORTH NOTING

Byers-Evans House Museum. Sprawling and detailed, red and black, this elaborate Victorian went up in 1883 as the home of *Rocky Mountain News* publisher William Byers. Restored to its pre–World War I condition, the historic landmark has occasional exhibitions and regular tours. Its main appeal is the glimpse it provides into Denver's past, specifically 1912 through 1924. The furnishings are those the Evans family acquired during the 80-some years they lived here. ⊠ *1310 Bannock St., Civic Center* ☎ *303/620–4933* ⊕ *www.historycolorado.org* ⊠ *$6* ☉ *Mon.–Sat. 10–4.*

Civic Center. A peaceful respite awaits in this three-block park in the cultural heart of downtown, site of the state capitol. A 1919 Greek amphitheater is in the middle of one of the city's largest flower gardens, and in summer, it's the site of free bike-in movies at dusk. Festivals such as Cinco de Mayo, Taste of Colorado, and the People's Fair keep things lively here in spring and summer, and on Tuesdays and Thursdays, food trucks offer lunchtime alternatives. The park was born in 1906, when Mayor Robert Speer asked New York architect Charles Robinson to expand on his vision of a "Paris on the Platte." Two of the park's statues, *Bronco Buster* and *On the War Trail*, depicting a cowboy and an Indian on horseback, were commissioned in the 1920s. ⊠ *Bannock St. to Broadway south of Colfax Ave. and north of 14th Ave., Civic Center* ⊕ *www.civiccenterconservancy.org.*

CAPITOL HILL

TOP ATTRACTIONS

Molly Brown House. This Victorian celebrates the life and times of the scandalous, "unsinkable" Molly Brown. The heroine of the *Titanic* courageously saved several lives and continued to provide assistance to survivors back on terra firma. Costumed guides and period furnishings in the museum, including flamboyant gilt-edge wallpaper, lace curtains, tile fireplaces, and tapestries, evoke bygone days. The museum collects and displays artifacts that belonged to Brown, as well as period items dating to 1894–1912, when the Browns lived in the house. Tours run every half hour; you won't need much more than that to see the whole place. A bit of trivia: Margaret Tobin Brown was known as Maggie, not Molly—allegedly a Hollywood invention that Brown did not like—during her lifetime. ⊠ *1340 Pennsylvania St.,*

Capitol Hill ☎ *303/832–4092* ⊕ *www.mollybrown.org* 🖼 *$8* ☉ *Sept.–May, Tues.–Sat. 10–3:30, Sun. noon–3:30; June–Aug., Mon.–Sat. 10–3:30, Sun. noon–3:30.*

State Capitol. Built in 1886, the capitol was constructed mostly of materials indigenous to Colorado, including marble, granite, and rose onyx. Especially inspiring is the gold-leaf dome, a reminder of the state's mining heritage, and once again open for tours after a $17 million, eight-year renovation that re-gilded portions with more than 65 ounces of gold and restored the cast-iron exterior. The dome is open for tours by appointment on the hour and 30 people at a time can go to the top (using a 99-step staircase from the third floor) to take in the 360-degree view of the Rockies. Historical tours and a legislative tour are available. Outside, a marker on the 13th step indicates where the elevation is exactly 1 mile high (above sea level). The legislature is generally in session from January through May, and visitors are welcome to sit in third-floor viewing galleries above the House and Senate chambers. ✉ *200 E. Colfax Ave., Capitol Hill* ☎ *303/866–2604 dome tours* ⊕ *www.colorado.gov* 🖼 *Free* ☉ *Weekdays 7:30–5. Tours weekdays 10–3.*

CENTRAL PLATTE VALLEY

Less than a mile west of downtown is the booming Central Platte Valley. Once the cluttered heart of Denver's railroad system, it's now overflowing with attractions. The imposing glass facade of the NFL Broncos' Sports Authority Field at Mile High, the stately Pepsi Center sports arena, the Downtown Aquarium, and the flagship REI outdoors store are four of the biggest attractions. New restaurants, a couple of coffeehouses, and a few small, locally owned shops, including a wine boutique, make it appealing to wander around. The sights in this area are so popular that the light-rail line was extended to connect the attractions with downtown.

The South Platte River valley concrete path, which extends several miles from downtown to the east and west, snakes along the water through out-of-the-way parks and trails. The 15th Street Bridge is particularly cyclist- and pedestrian-friendly, connecting LoDo with growing northwest Denver in a seamless way. The most relaxed, and easiest, way to see the area is on one of the half-hour or hour-long tours on the **Platte Valley Trolley** (☎ *303/458–6255* ⊕ *www.denvertrolley.org*), which can be accessed by parking at the Children's Museum and catching the streetcar east of the lot by the river.

TIMING

You can easily spend a full day in this area, especially if you have kids or would like to explore the Greenway. Older kids tend to blaze through the Children's Museum in a morning or afternoon, but the under-six set can spend all day here. The Aquarium can make a good four- to six-hour stop. If you want to do both the Elitch Gardens water park and main park, plan on spending a full day there.

TOP ATTRACTIONS

FAMILY

Fodor'sChoice

★

Children's Museum of Denver. This is one of the finest museums of its kind in North America, with constantly changing hands-on exhibits that engage children up to about age eight in discovery. Fire Station No. 1 is a real fire hall with a pole and kitchen. Children can build a car on an assembly line and send it careening down a test ramp at the Assembly Plant. Or, little ones can enter Bubbles Playscape, where science and soap collide in kid-made bubbles up to 6 feet long. One of the biggest attractions is the Center for the Young Child, a 3,700-square-foot playscape aimed at newborns and toddlers and their caregivers. ■TIP→ The museum is in the midst of a major expansion, and some exhibits are closed or moving to make room for new ones; updates are posted on the website through the project completion in late 2015. ⊠ *2121 Children's Museum Dr., off Exit 211 of I–25, Jefferson Park* ☎ *303/433–7444* ⊕ *www.mychildsmuseum.org* ⊠ *$9* ⊗ *Weekdays 9–4 (Wed. open until 7:30), weekends 10–5.*

FAMILY

Downtown Aquarium. On the north side of the South Platte across from Elitch Gardens, this is the only million-gallon aquarium between Chicago and the West Coast. It has four sections that show aquatic life in all its forms, from the seas to the river's headwaters in the Colorado mountains. The 250-seat Aquarium Restaurant surrounds a 50,000-gallon tank filled with sharks and fish. Other highlights include an expanded stingray touch pool, a gold-panning area, animatronic creatures, and an interactive shipwreck. The aquarium also has a lounge with a weeknight happy hour, and the truly adventurous can learn how to scuba dive or snorkel in the tanks. ⊠ *700 Water St., off Exit 211 of I–25, Jefferson Park* ☎ *303/561–4450* ⊕ *www.aquariumrestaurants.com* ⊠ *$18.99* ⊗ *Sun.–Thurs. 10–9, Fri. and Sat. 10–9:30.*

FAMILY

Elitch Gardens. This elaborate and thrilling park was a Denver family tradition long before its 1995 relocation from northwest Denver to its current home on the outskirts of downtown. The park's highlights include hair-raising roller coasters and thrill rides; for younger kids and squeamish parents there are also plenty of gentler attractions such as bumper cars and tea cups. Twister II, an update of the classic, wooden Mister Twister, is from the original Elitch Gardens, as is a 100-foot-high Ferris wheel that provides sensational views of downtown. A 10-acre water-adventure park is included in the standard entry fee. You can spend a whole day at either the water park or the main park. ■TIP→ Locker and stroller rentals are available; discounted tickets are available online. ⊠ *I–25 and Speer Blvd., Auraria* ☎ *303/595–4386* ⊕ *www.elitchgardens.com* ⊠ *$45.99 unlimited-ride pass* ⊗ *June–mid-Aug., daily; Apr., May, and late Aug.–Oct., Fri.–Sun.; hrs vary.*

WORTH NOTING

FAMILY

Platte River Greenway. Just behind the REI flagship store, this serene park is at the center of the South Platte River valley path. Its rocks and rapids are especially attractive in summer for kayakers, bicyclists, and hikers. Sidewalks extend down the South Platte to the east toward the suburbs and west toward Sports Authority Field at Mile High. A pathway in yet another direction leads to LoDo. From the park it's about a 20-minute walk to the 16th Street Mall and Coors Field, which makes it a healthy way to sightsee when the weather is good. ⊠ *1615 Platte St., Jefferson Park* ⊕ *www.thegreenwayfoundation.org.*

CITY PARK AND NEARBY

Acquired by the city in 1881, City Park, Denver's largest public space (330 acres), contains rose gardens, lakes, a golf course, tennis courts, and a huge playground. A shuttle runs between two of the city's most popular attractions: the Denver Zoo and the Denver Museum of Nature & Science, both on the site. City Park is east of downtown Denver, and runs from East 17th Avenue to East 26th Avenue, between York Street and Colorado Boulevard.

TIMING

If you have children or are an animal lover, you could easily spend half a day in City Park. Plan to arrive early on weekends, as parking can be difficult to obtain (it's free at the attractions, but goes fast), and in warm-weather months pack a picnic, as the park itself is a delightful daytime rest area, with plenty of room to stretch.

TOP ATTRACTIONS

Denver Botanic Gardens. More than 15,000 plant species from Australia, South Africa, the Himalayas, and especially the western United States compose the horticultural displays in the thoughtfully laid-out theme gardens here. They are at their peak in July and August, when garden enthusiasts could spend half a day here; the tropical conservatory alone is worth an hour's visit in the off-season. Spring brings a brilliant display of wildflowers to the world-renowned rock alpine garden, primarily in late May and early June. The OmniGlobe simulates the climate and atmospheric changes on Earth; other environmental attractions include a "green roof" atop the café and a children's garden that covers part of the parking structure. Tea ceremonies take place some summer weekends in the tranquil Japanese garden, and artists such as rock musician Chris Isaak, singer–songwriter Jewel, and blues legend B.B. King have performed as part of the summer concert series. ⊠ *1007 York St., Cheesman Park* ☎ *720/865–3500, 720/865–3585 info desk* ⊕ *www.botanicgardens.org* 🗐 *$12.50* ⊙ *May–Sept., daily 9–9; Oct.–Apr., daily 9–5.*

FAMILY

Fodor's Choice
★

Denver Museum of Nature & Science. Founded in 1900, the museum has amassed more than 775,000 objects, making it the largest natural history museum in the western United States. It houses a rich combination of traditional collections—dinosaur remains, animal dioramas, a mineralogy display, an Egyptology wing—and intriguing hands-on exhibits. In Expedition Health you can test your health and fitness on a variety of contraptions and receive a personalized health profile. The Prehistoric Journey exhibit covers the seven stages of Earth's development. The massive complex also includes an IMAX movie theater and a planetarium, where the Space Odyssey exhibit simulates a trip to Mars. An impressive eating-and-relaxation area has a full-window panoramic view of the Rocky Mountains. ⊠ *2001 Colorado Blvd., City Park* ☎ *303/370–6000, 800/925–2250* ⊕ *www.dmns.org*

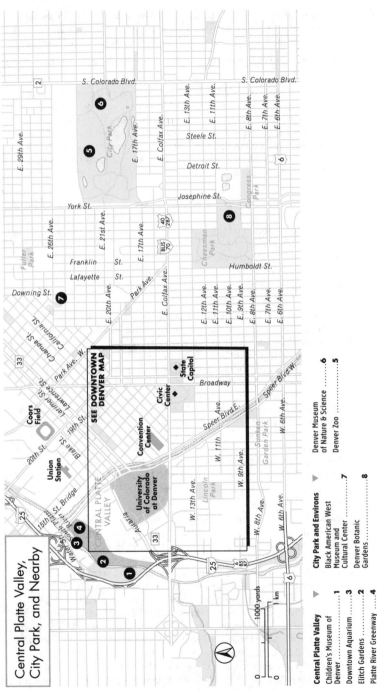

Central Platte Valley, City Park, and Nearby

Central Platte Valley ▶

Children's Museum of
Denver **1**
Downtown Aquarium **3**
Elitch Gardens **2**
Platte River Greenway **4**

City Park and Environs ▶

Black American West
Museum and
Cultural Center **7**
Denver Botanic
Gardens **8**

Denver Museum
of Nature & Science **6**
Denver Zoo **5**

0 ─── 1000 yards
0 ─── 1 km

✉ Museum $14.95, IMAX $9.95, planetarium $19.95; $21.95–26.95 for combined pass (any two or all three) ⊙ Daily 9–5, IMAX and planetarium showtimes vary.

QUICK BITES

Pete's Kitchen. This old-fashioned, 24/7, greasy-spoon diner specializes in Greek food, huge pancakes, and spicy huevos rancheros. It's a short drive from the Denver Museum of Nature & Science, and it's often packed, particularly on Sunday mornings. ✉ *1962 E. Colfax Ave., Cheesman Park* ☎ *303/321–3139* ⊕ *www.petesrestaurants.com.*

FAMILY **Denver Zoo.** A bright peacock greets you at the door to the state's most popular cultural attraction, whose best-known exhibit showcases man-eating Komodo dragons in a lush re-creation of a cavernous riverbank. The newest exhibit is the much-anticipated, $50-million, 10-acre Toyota Elephant Passage, which houses elephants, gibbons, clouded leopards, and tapirs, along with other animals from the Asian continent. The Conservation Carousel ($2) rotates in the center of the 80-acre zoo, with handcrafted endangered species as mounts. A 7-acre Primate Panorama houses 31 species of primates in state-of-the-art environments that simulate the animals' natural habitats. Other highlights include a nursery for baby animals; seal shows; the world's only painting rhinoceros, Mshindi; the electric Safari Shuttle, which snakes through the property as you are treated to a lesson on the zoo's inhabitants; and the usual lions, tigers, bears, giraffes, and monkeys. The exhibits are spaced far apart along sprawling concrete paths, so build in plenty of time to visit. ✉ *2300 Steele St., City Park* ☎ *720/337–1400* ⊕ *www. denverzoo.org* ✉ *Nov.–Feb. $13, Mar.–Oct. $17* ⊙ *Nov.–Feb., daily 10–4; Mar.–Oct., daily 9–5.*

WORTH NOTING

Black American West Museum and Cultural Center. The revealing documents and artifacts here depict the vast contributions that African Americans made to opening up the West. Nearly a third of the cowboys and many pioneer teachers and doctors were African Americans. One floor is devoted to black cowboys; another to military troops, including the Buffalo Soldiers. Changing exhibits focus on topics such as the history of black churches in the West. ✉ *3091 California St., Five Points* ☎ *720/242–7428* ⊕ *www.blackamericanwestmuseum.org* ✉ *$10* ⊙ *Fri. and Sat. 10–2.*

SPORTS AND THE OUTDOORS

Denver is a city that can consistently and enthusiastically support three professional sports teams. Unfortunately, it has more than that—the Colorado Rockies, Colorado Avalanche, Denver Broncos, Denver Nuggets, and Colorado Rapids (soccer). Until recently, the Nuggets and Rapids had been the odd teams out, as the Rockies, Avalanche, and Broncos have all reached or won championships in their respective sports. But here and there the Nuggets have come close to catching up, and fans patiently await their year.

What's great about Denverites is that most aren't just spectators. After a game, they go out and do stuff—hiking, bicycling, kayaking, and, yes, playing team sports themselves. The city and its proximity to outdoor pursuits encourage a fit lifestyle.

BASEBALL

Coors Field. The Colorado Rockies, Denver's National League baseball team, play April through October in Coors Field. Because it's set in high altitude and thin air, the park is among the best in the major leagues for home-run hitters—and likewise, one of the worst for pitchers. ⊠ *2001 Blake St., LoDo* ☎ *303/292–0200, 800/388–7625* ⊕ *www.coloradorockies.com.*

BASKETBALL

Pepsi Center. From November to April, the Denver Nuggets play at the Pepsi Center. The 19,000-seat arena is also the primary indoor venue for large musical acts such as U2 and Justin Timberlake. Tours of the facilities are available several days a week. ⊠ *1000 Chopper Circle, Auraria* ☎ *303/405–8555* ⊕ *www.pepsicenter.com.*

BICYCLING AND JOGGING

Bicycle Doctor/Edgeworks. This facility just south of downtown repairs road and mountain bikes and rents them for $20 to $70 a day. ⊠ *860 Broadway, Golden Triangle* ☎ *303/831–7228, 877/245–3362* ⊕ *www.bicycledr.com.*

Cherry Creek Bike Path. A well-kept path runs from Cherry Creek Shopping Center to Larimer Square downtown alongside the peaceful creek of its name. ⊠ *Cherry Creek, LoDo.*

Deer Creek Canyon. Running through forested foothills southwest of Denver near the intersection of C–470 and Wadsworth Boulevard, the Deer Creek Canyon trail system is popular with mountain bikers. ⊠ *C–470 and Wadsworth Blvd., Littleton* ⊕ *www.co.jefferson.co.us/openspace.*

Denver Parks Department. With more than 400 miles of off-road paths in and around the city to choose from, cyclists can move easily between urban, mountain, and rural settings. Denver Parks Department has suggestions for bicycling and jogging paths throughout the metropolitan area's 250 parks, including the popular Cherry Creek and Chatfield Reservoir State Recreation areas. ⊠ *Denver* ☎ *720/913–0696* ⊕ *www.denvergov.org/parks.*

High Line Canal. Sixty-six miles of mostly dirt paths through the metropolitan area run along the scenic canal at almost completely level grade. ⊠ *Auraria, Cherry Creek, LoDo* ⊕ *www.denverwater.org/recreation/highlinecanal.*

Matthews/Winters Park. West of the city, paved paths wind through Matthews/Winters Park near both Golden and Morrison. It's dotted with plaintive pioneer graves amid the sun-bleached grasses, thistle, and columbine. ⊠ *South of I–70 on CO 26, Golden* ⊕ *jeffco.us/open-space/parks/matthews-winters-park/.*

South Platte River. Twelve miles of paved paths run along the river as it heads into downtown. ✉ *Central Platte Valley, LoDo* ⊕ *www. greenwayfoundation.org.*

FOOTBALL

Sports Authority Field at Mile High. The team that introduced America to quarterback John Elway—the National Football League's Denver Broncos—plays September through December at Sports Authority Field at Mile High. Every game has sold out for more than 30 years, so tickets are not easy to come by, but not impossible. ✉ *1701 Bryant St., Exit 210B off I–25, Sun Valley* ☎ *720/258–3000* ⊕ *www.denverbroncos.com.*

GOLF

NON-CITY OWNED COURSES

With their sprawling layouts and impressively appointed greens, these four public clubs merit a special look over their city-operated counterparts simply because of their more rural settings. On any Denver-area course, though, out-of-town golfers should keep in mind that the high altitude affects golf balls as it does baseballs—which is why the Rockies have so many more home runs when they bat at home. It's generally agreed that your golf ball will go about 10%–15% farther in the thin air here than it would at sea level.

Arrowhead Golf Club. Designed by Robert Trent Jones Jr., this private course with rolling terrain is set impressively among red sandstone spires. It's 45 minutes from downtown in Roxborough State Park, which means that any members of your group who don't want to golf can hike nearby. The slow-paced play is made up for by allowing more time to spend looking at the spectacular scenery. ✉ *10850 W. Sundown Trail, Littleton* ☎ *303/973–9614* ⊕ *www.arrowheadcolorado. com* 🖃 *$110 weekdays, $160 weekends* 🏌 *18 holes, 6636 yards, par 72.*

Buffalo Run. A Keith Foster–designed private course and the site for the 2004 Denver Open, the bargain-priced Buffalo Run counts wide-open views of the plains surrounding its lake-studded course among its charms, which also include streams running through it and the Bison Grill Restaurant. Some of the greens play fast, and the exposed terrain can mean sloppy conditions after a run of wet weather, so call ahead for an update. ✉ *15700 E. 112th Ave., Commerce City* ☎ *303/289–1500* ⊕ *www.buffalorungolfcourse.com* 🖃 *$27 weekends, $44 weekends* 🏌 *18 holes, 7411 yards, par 72.*

Fodor's Choice ★ **Ridge at Castle Pines North.** Tom Weiskopf designed this 18-hole course with great mountain views and dramatic elevation changes. It's ranked among the nation's top 100 public courses. It's in Castle Rock, about 45 minutes south of Denver on I–25. One of the course's distinguishing features is its commitment to pace of play; a series of programs have been implemented to help golfers stick to a schedule without cramping golfing styles. ✉ *1414 Castle Pines Pkwy., Castle Rock* ☎ *303/688–4301* ⊕ *www.playtheridge.com* 🖃 *$115 weekdays, $145 weekends* 🏌 *18 holes, 7013 yards, par 71* ⚑ *Reservations essential.*

Riverdale Golf Courses. It's two golf courses in one: Riverdale has the Dunes, a Scottish-style links course designed by Pete and Perry Dye that sits on the South Platte River and offers railroad ties, plenty of bunkers, and water; while the Knolls has a more gnarly, park-inspired layout. Both courses are shaded by plenty of trees, and you can't beat the price for this public facility maintained as pristinely as a private one. While you're here, be sure to peruse the on-site Colorado Golf Hall of Fame showcases. ✉ *13300 Riverdale Rd., Brighton* ☎ *303/659–4700* ⊕ *www. riverdalegolf.com* ✉ *Knolls $26 weekdays, $29 weekends for 18 holes; Dunes $39 weekdays, $48 weekends* ⚑ *Knolls: 18 holes, 6771 yards, par 71; Dunes: 18 holes, 7064 yards, par 72.*

CITY-OWNED PUBLIC COURSES

Eight courses—City Park, Harvard Gulch, Evergreen, Kennedy, Overland Park, Wellshire, and Willis Case, along with Aqua Golf, a water driving range—are operated by the City of Denver and are open to the public. Green fees for all range from $25 to $37. For advance reservations golfers must use the City of Denver Golf Reservation System (on the Web or by phone) up to seven days in advance. For same-day tee times you can call the starters at an individual course. Reservations can be made up to 14 days in advance with a Denver Golf Loyalty card, free by visiting any Denver golf course location.

City Park. Since 1920, City Park's tree-lined public course at the north end of the park has been a popular go-to for an urban golf experience. The fairways are narrow but easily navigated, with welcome city skyline and mountain views from many of its mostly short, flat holes, primarily at the east end of the course. The Denver Zoo and Denver Museum of Nature & Science are almost within putting distance, so those in the group who don't want to golf have options. ✉ *2500 York St., City Park* ☎ *303/295–2096* ⊕ *www.cityofdenvergolf.com* ✉ *$27 weekdays; $37 weekends* ⚑ *18 holes, 6740 yards, par 72.*

Evergreen Golf Course. Situated 30 minutes from Denver and at an altitude of 7,220 feet, this public course offers golfers even more bang for their buck in terms of yardage—but they may feel the extra exertion of walking along this rolling, public 18-hole executive course, as well. With its setting along Bear Creek in the midst of a pine-heavy forest, the course is a favorite byway for elk. ✉ *29614 Upper Bear Creek Rd.* ☎ *303/674–6351* ⊕ *www.cityofdenvergolf.com* ✉ *$25 weekdays, $36 weekends* ⚑ *18 holes, 4877 yards, par 69.*

Kennedy Golf Course. The sprawling, rolling hills of this course feature magnificent mountain views and plenty of putting practice on the greens. Technically located in suburban Aurora southeast of Denver, the 27-hole regulation course has quite a bit of variety, with the short, tight Creek nine; longer, wider West nine; and a combination of both in the Babe Lind nine—any two of which can be combined to make up your 18 holes. Miniature golf is on-site, as well. ✉ *10500 E. Hampden Ave., Aurora* ☎ *720/865–0720* ⊕ *www.cityofdenvergolf.com* ✉ *$27 weekdays; $37 weekends* ⚑ *West Course: 9 holes, 3455 yards, par 36; Creek Course: 9 holes, 3304 yards, par 35; Babe Lind Course: 9 holes, 3580 yards, par 36.*

Overland Park. Touted as the oldest continuously operating golf course west of the Mississippi—it was once the Denver Country Club—Overland Park has appealing city and mountain views as well as narrow but open fairways; small, easily read and well-bunkered greens; and fast play. The course is peppered with trees but sports only one water hazard, and the flat terrain makes for a fairly effortless walk. ✉ *1801 S. Huron St., Overland* ☎ *303/698–4975* ⊕ *www.cityofdenvergolf.com* ⊠ *$27 weekdays; $37 weekends* ⅃ *18 holes, 6676 yards, par 72.*

Wellshire Golf Course. Designed in 1926 by Donald Ross and famously played by Ben Hogan, Wellshire Golf Course is known for its classic layout; small, slightly elevated greens; and intermittent mountain views. The foliage-heavy course is mostly flat and contains a handful of water hazards; fairways are narrow and sometimes run parallel to each other. The Wellshire has retained some of its old-time country club charm in the clubhouse and restaurant. ✉ *3333 S. Colorado Blvd., South Denver* ☎ *303/692–5636* ⊕ *www.cityofdenvergolf.com* ⊠ *$27 weekdays; $37 weekends* ⅃ *18 holes, 6541 yards, par 72.*

Willis Case. Out of Denver's city-owned golf courses, arguably the best mountain views can be found at Willis Case, whose old-growth-covered, beautifully landscaped, gently rolling terrain can be found right off I–70. The first tee feels as if you are aiming straight for the Rockies, and the sloping fairways, guarded greens, and strategically placed bunkers make for moderately challenging play. ✉ *4999 Vrain St., North Denver* ☎ *720/865–0700* ⊕ *www.cityofdenvergolf.com* ⊠ *$27 weekdays; $37 weekends* ⅃ *18 holes, 6306 yards, par 72.*

HIKING

Green Mountain. Part of Jefferson County Open Space and a piece of William Frederick Hayden Park (City of Lakewood), Green Mountain is the first named foothill as you head west from Denver toward the mountains. The easy, mostly exposed trails here afford panoramic views of downtown Denver, Table Mesa, Pikes Peak, and the Continental Divide from the top (895 feet in elevation gain). There are multiple trails from several trailheads, including a 6½-mile loop and a 3-mile loop. You must share the experience with bikers and dogs (as well as other critters). ✉ *Lakewood* ✛ *I–70 west to CO 470 to W. Alameda Pkwy., turn left to trailhead entrance* ⊕ *www.lakewood.org/HaydenPark* ☾ *Open daily 5 am–10 pm.*

Mount Falcon Park. Looking down on Denver and across at Red Rocks, this park is amazingly tranquil, laced with meadows and streams, and shaded by conifers. The trails are well marked. ✉ *Aurora* ✛ *Off Rte. 8, Morrison exit, or U.S. 285, Parmalee exit* ⊕ *www.jeffco.us/open-space/parks/mount-falcon-park.*

Fodor's Choice ★ **Red Rocks Park and Amphitheatre.** Fifteen miles southwest of Denver, Red Rocks Park and Amphitheatre is a breathtaking wonderland of vaulting oxblood-and-cinnamon-color sandstone spires. The outdoor music stage is in a natural 9,000-seat amphitheater (with perfect acoustics, as only nature could have designed). Visit even when there's no show. The 5-mile scenic drive offers a glorious glimpse of the 868 acres of sandstone, and there are picnic and parking areas along the way for photos and a rest. If you're feeling particularly spunky, follow the locals' lead and run the steps for a real workout. The Trading Post loop hiking trail, at 6,280 feet, is 1½ miles long and quite narrow with drop-offs and steep grades. ⊠ *17598 W. Alameda Pkwy., Morrison ✢ I–70 west to Exit 259, turn left to park entrance* ⊕ *www.redrocksonline. com* ☽ *Open daily (non-show days) one hr before sunrise to one hr after sunset.*

Roxborough State Park. An easy, wheelchair-accessible 2-mile loop trail in the park goes through rugged rock formations; there are also myriad harder hikes that offer striking vistas and a unique look at metropolitan Denver and the plains. ⊠ *Littleton ✢ I–25 south to Santa Fe exit, take Santa Fe Blvd. south to Titan Rd., turn right and follow signs* ⊕ *www. parks.state.co.us/parks/roxborough* ☒ *$7 for a day pass.*

HOCKEY

Colorado Avalanche. This wildly popular Denver-based National Hockey League team won the Stanley Cup in 1996 and beat the New Jersey Devils for an encore in 2001. It continues to be beloved by locals and plays October to April in a packed 19,000-seat Pepsi Center arena. ⊠ *1000 Chopper Pl., Auraria* ☎ *303/428–7645* ⊕ *www. coloradoavalanche.com.*

STOCK SHOWS

FAMILY **National Western Stock Show.** Thousands of cowpokes retrieve their string ties and worn boots and indulge in two weeks of hootin', hollerin', and celebratin' the beef industry during the National Western Stock Show each January.

Whether you're a professional rancher or bull rider, or just plan to show up for the people-watching, the Stock Show is a rich, colorful glimpse of Western culture. The pros arrive to make industry connections, show off their livestock, and perhaps land a few sales. The entertainment involves nightly rodeo events, presentations of prized cattle (some going for thousands of dollars), and "Mutton Bustin'." The latter is one of those rowdy rodeo concepts that usually has no place in a genteel metropolis like Denver: kids, ages 5–7, don huge hockey-goalie helmets and hold for dear life onto the backs of bucking baby sheep. At the trade show you can buy hats and boots as well as yards of beef jerky and quirky gift items.

The yearly event is held at the Denver Coliseum. Just be sure to call first and ask for directions; although parking is plentiful it can move around based on volume and livestock needs, and the Coliseum, usually home of straightforward sporting and entertainment events, becomes a labyrinth of lots and shuttles during the Stock Show. Daily admission prices depend on the day's events. ⊠ *Denver Coliseum, 4600 Humboldt St., Elyria ✢ East of I–25 on I–70* ☎ *303/295–6124, 866/464–2626 for tickets* ⊕ *www.nationalwestern.com* ☒ *$10–$19.*

WHERE TO EAT

As befits a multiethnic crossroads, Denver lays out a dizzying range of eateries. Head for LoDo, the Highland District, the up-and-coming RiNo Art District, or south of the city for the more inventive kitchens. Try Federal Street for cheap ethnic eats—especially Mexican and Vietnamese—and expect authentic takes on classic Italian, French, and Asian cuisines. Throughout Denver, menus at trendy restaurants focus on locally sourced, organic, and healthier options; Denver's top chefs continue to gain the attention of national food magazines and win culinary competitions.

WHAT IT COSTS

	$	$$	$$$	$$$$
Restaurants	under $13	$13–$18	$19–$25	over $25

Restaurant prices are the average cost of a main course at dinner or, if dinner is not served, at lunch.

Use the coordinates (✣ B2) at the end of each listing to locate a site on the corresponding map.

DOWNTOWN

LODO

$$$ FRENCH 🍴 **Coohills.** Classic French cooking is merged with modern techniques and regionally sourced ingredients at this chic, sprawling space that's filled with natural light. Situated at the edge of LoDo and run by the Coohills, a veteran restaurateur couple—he's the chef, she runs the front of the house—the eatery is known for its free weekly outdoor concerts featuring local bands in the summer and year-round chef's counter, a large communal table alongside the open kitchen that's set up for tasting menus of five to ten courses with optional wine pairings. Fans of authentic French fare can't go wrong with the pâté, Burgundy-style snails in Pernod butter, or the foie gras torchon; check the blackboard for each day's more contemporary takes, and check in with the sommelier for suggestions from the smart and ever-rotating wine list. [$] *Average main: $24* ✉ *1400 Wewatta St., LoDo* ☎ *303/623–5700* 🌐 *www.coohills.com* 🕒 *Closed Sun. No lunch* ✍ *Reservations essential* ✣ *C2.*

$$$$ STEAKHOUSE 🍴 **Denver ChopHouse & Brewery.** This was one of the first brewpubs to pop up near the Coors Field ballpark, and it has withstood the test of time. Housed in the old Union Pacific Railroad warehouse, the restaurant, similar to the ones in Washington, D.C., and Boulder, is clubby, with dark-wood paneling and exposed brick. The food is basic American, and there's plenty of it: steaks, seafood, pizzas, and chicken served with hot corn bread and honey butter, and "bottomless" salads tossed at the table. [$] *Average main: $27* ✉ *1735 19th St., LoDo* ☎ *303/296–0800* 🌐 *www.denverchophouse.com* ✍ *Reservations essential* ✣ *B4.*

$ MODERN MEXICAN 🍴 **Illegal Pete's.** With a half-dozen metro-area locations around Denver and Boulder (the original) and one in Fort Collins, this hip, homegrown chain of burrito joints gives larger operations like Chipotle a run for their money by using hormone-free meats and locally sourced ingredients and by offering five-hour daily happy hours and live music. The burritos are enormous—they even do a tasty fish version—and breakfast (chorizo, yes) is a nice option. Bonus: the kitchen is open until midnight during the week and until 2:30 am on weekends. $ *Average main: $7* ✉ *1530 16th St., LoDo* ☎ *303/623–2169* ⊕ *www.illegalpetes.com* ▭ *No credit cards* ⩔ *Reservations not accepted* ✛ *A5.*

$$$

SEAFOOD

✕ **Jax Fish House & Oyster Bar.** A popular oyster bar serves as the foyer to the ever-busy Jax, whose brick-lined back dining room packs in the crowds, especially when there's a ball game at Coors Field three blocks away. A dozen different types of oysters are freshly shucked each day, and they can be paired with one of the house-made, fruit-infused vodkas or chili-fired shooters. Main courses make use of fresh catches flown in from both coasts such as ahi tuna, scallops, snapper, and shrimp, and although there are a couple of meat dishes, only the truly fish-phobic should not go there. The sides are fun, too: buckwheat waffles, fries tossed with maple sugar, and radish kimchi. $ *Average main: $25* ✉ *1539 17th St., LoDo* ☎ *303/292–5767* ⊕ *www.jaxdenver.com* ☉ *No lunch* ⩔ *Reservations essential* ✛ *A5.*

$$

MODERN
AMERICAN

✕ **The Kitchen Next Door Union Station.** With more reasonably priced offerings and a more casual setting than the other Kitchens in Boulder and Glendale, Next Door's comfortable pub style fits in well at Union Station and provides a much-needed selection of healthy salads—the organic kale and apple salad is crunchy and satisfying and part of its proceeds is donated to community school gardens—burgers and sandwiches. It's also a great happy-hour stop (daily 3–6 pm), with snacks for $3–$5 and drink prices to match. $ *Average main: $14* ✉ *1701 Wynkoop St., Suite 100, LoDo* ☎ *720/460–3730* ⊕ *www.thekitchen. com/next-door-union-station* ⩔ *Reservations not accepted* ✛ *A4.*

$$

ITALIAN
FAMILY

✕ **Mangiamo Pronto!** Snag a booth at this small, casual café three blocks from Coors Field. The name is Italian for "let's eat now!" A larger version of the tiny original in Santa Fe, New Mexico, Mangiamo serves three well-executed, Italian-inspired meals every day but Sunday. Menu items include frittatas and homemade oatmeal for breakfast; Caprese salads, thin-crusted pizzas, and thickly packed panini for lunch; and those same pizzas and panini along with a variety of bruschetta, pastas, and other Mediterranean specialties at dinner—try the melt-in-your-mouth veal saltimbocca. Afterward, good luck choosing just one of the many gelato flavors for dessert. Don't miss the inexpensive Italian wines by the bottle. $ *Average main: $16* ✉ *1601 17th St., LoDo* ☎ *303/297–1229* ⊕ *www.denveritalianrestaurants.net* ▭ *No credit cards* ☉ *Closed Sunday* ⩔ *Reservations essential* ✛ *A5.*

$$$$

MODERN
AMERICAN

Fodor'sChoice
★

✕ **Mercantile Dining & Provisions.** Brought to you by the same team that created Fruition, Mercantile features the same ingredients from their farm and creamery as well as the emphasis on fresh and local; this is the very essence of seasonal dining. The pretty space, with its powder-blue upholstery and milky-white walls, calms and invites lingering, ideal for a menu that includes starters doubling as small plates—the bone marrow brûlée has become legendary, and the "provisions" platter pulls from the farm's cheeses and pickles that are also available at the on-site market—although it's hard to stop there when a roasted Colorado lamb shoulder and a crispy half chicken are options. Sit at the counter for a quicker meal or to snack, and try one of the creative cocktails from a snappy list that also includes pricey but uncommon wines. Breakfast and lunch, using the same tip-top-fresh produce, are also available daily. $ *Average main: $26* ✉ *1701 Wynkoop St., Suite 155, LoDo* ☎ *720/460–3733* ⊕ *www.mercantiledenver.com* ⌫ *Reservations essential* ✚ *A4.*

$$$$
STEAKHOUSE

✕ **Morton's The Steakhouse.** The Denver outpost of this nationally revered steak house is as swanky and overwhelming as the rest, with dark woods, white linens, and the signature steak knives at each place setting. Diners are greeted by expert staff wielding the cuts of the day and their accompaniments, and once choices are made the experience is almost always seamless. The steaks themselves are superb—prime, well aged, and unadorned. All sides cost extra, but they're big enough to feed two or three. The extensive wine list is pricey, and the delicious desserts are enormous. $ *Average main: $45* ✉ *1710 Wynkoop St., LoDo* ☎ *303/825–3353* ⊕ *www.mortons.com/denver* ◷ *No lunch* ⌫ *Reservations essential* ✚ *A4.*

$$$$
MODERN
AMERICAN

✕ **The Squeaky Bean.** The original location was a tiny storefront in the Highland, but it was obvious early on that the popular Bean, with herbs and produce from its own gardens and a deceptively simple yet inventive menu, was going to grow. Now situated in the historic Saddlery Building in LoDo, the spacious dining room balances contemporary furnishings with a vintage setting and serves a seasonal menu that also changes monthly and is heavy on bold, bright flavors: mint and cumin on lamb with pappardelle, or yellow curry and rhubarb atop halibut. It's worthwhile to at least check out the impressive cheese cart for dessert. Service is brisk and attentive and the wine list is remarkably well priced and includes many by-the-glass options. $ *Average main: $28* ✉ *1500 Wynkoop St., Suite 101, LoDo* ☎ *303/623–2665* ⊕ *www.thesqueakybean.net* ◷ *Closed Mon. No dinner Sun.* ⌫ *Reservations essential* ▬ *No credit cards* ✚ *A5.*

$$$$
SEAFOOD
Fodor'sChoice
★

✕ **Stoic & Genuine.** Known for their eateries Rioja and Euclid Hall, Jennifer Jasinski and Beth Gruitch bring fresh seafood and oysters to Union Station in an oddly configured but ultimately comfortable space that features two somewhat cramped raw-bar areas and a row of regular seating, as well as a spacious patio that offers excellent people-watching. The oyster roster is expansive and impeccably fresh and comes with a choice of granitas—savory semifrozen ices with flavors such as citrus-chili and tarragon-cucumber. Hot and cold seafood highlights include lobster roll and tuna tartare, and there are a couple of land-based dishes for those who prefer turf over surf. But it's the little details that stand out: Cornbread arrives hot in a cast-iron cornstick pan, and Swedish fish are scattered atop the check for a whimsical and welcome touch. $ *Average main: $26* ✉ *1701 Wynkoop St., LoDo* ☎ *303/640–3474* ⊕ *www.stoicandgenuine.com* ⌫ *Reservations essential* ✚ *A4.*

$$$$
MODERN
AMERICAN

✕ **Vesta Dipping Grill.** Both the remodeled building and the interior space designed to house this modern grill, named after Vesta, the Roman hearth goddess, have won national architectural awards, and it's easy to see why: the sensual swirls of fabric and copper throughout the room make diners feel as though they're inside a giant work of art, and the clever, secluded banquettes are among the most sought-after seats in town. The menu is clever, too, and the competent grill masters in the kitchen put out expertly cooked meats, fish, and vegetables, all of which can be paired with some of the more than two-dozen dipping sauces that get their inspiration from chutneys, salsas, mother sauces, and barbecue. The wine list is as cool as the clientele. $ *Average main: $28* ⊠ *1822 Blake St., LoDo* ☎ *303/296–1970* ⊕ *www.vestagrill.com* ⊗ *No lunch* ⚑ *Reservations essential* ✥ *B5.*

LARIMER SQUARE

$$$$ ✕ **Capital Grille.** In a town that loves its steaks, the Rhode Island–based
STEAKHOUSE chain was taking a chance moving in and pretending to offer anything different from the other high-end big-boy steak houses. That said, Capital Grille—housed in a dark, noisy, broodingly decorated room typical of the genre—has much to recommend it, including a drop-dead Delmonico, textbook French onion soup, and terrific skin-on mashed potatoes. If you were ever to try steak tartare, this would be the place to do it, and the lobster is one of the best in town. The wine list is long, important, and expensive, but the service is remarkably fresh-faced and eager to please. $ *Average main: $42* ⊠ *1450 Larimer St., Larimer Square* ☎ *303/539–2500* ⊕ *www.thecapitalgrille.com/pages/locations/?id=8018* ⊗ *No lunch weekends* ⚑ *Reservations essential* ✥ *A6.*

$$ ✕ **Euclid Hall Bar & Kitchen.** The most casual eatery from Jennifer Jasinski
AMERICAN and Beth Gruitch (Rioja, Stoic & Genuine), Euclid Hall is a tavern in an 1883 building that once housed the beloved old bar Soapy Smith's. The irreverent menu pulls comfort foods from around the world: poutine, schnitzels, po'boys and the like, all homemade and done with the usual Jasinski attention to detail. The beers are arranged with unnecessarily complicated mathematical references to algebra and trigonometry, but the well-rounded selection itself makes perfect sense. ∎ TIP➔ **They accept reservations for parties of seven or more.** $ *Average main: $14* ⊠ *1317 14th St., Larimer Square* ☎ *303/595–4255* ⊕ *www.euclidhall.com* ⊗ *No lunch weekends* ⚑ *Reservations not accepted* ✥ *A6.*

$$ ✕ **Osteria Marco.** The Bonannos, whose restaurants number a dozen
ITALIAN now and are all among the best in town, continue to have success with
FAMILY this reasonably priced, casual eatery. High-backed wooden booths, dish towels as napkins, and exposed-brick walls provide a hip, urban setting below street level for wood-fired pizzas topped with Frank Bonanno's homemade or imported cheeses and house-cured meats. Or try one of the sampler trays from the *formaggi* and *salumi* (fresh cheese and meats) bar, the Italian version of an artisan deli that greets you at the entrance. Salads are large enough to eat as entrées. The mostly locally sourced meat dishes shine—especially Sunday night's roast suckling pig special. $ *Average main: $18* ⊠ *1453 Larimer St., Larimer Square* ☎ *303/534–5855* ⊕ *www.osteriamarco.com* ⚑ *Reservations essential* ✥ *A6.*

$$$ ✕ **Rioja.** Chef Jennifer Jasinski's intense attention to detail is evident in
MEDITERRANEAN her tribute to Mediterranean food with contemporary flair. The 2013
Fodor'sChoice James Beard winner for Best Chef Southwest, she partners in this ven-
★ ture with two other women: Beth Gruitch runs the front of the house

2

while sous chef Dana Rodriguez helps in the back, and together this trio makes intriguing and compelling combinations like seared sea scallops with black truffle vinaigrette and Colorado lamb with preserved lemon yogurt. The restaurant is hip and artsy, with exposed brick and blown-glass lighting, arched doorways, and textured draperies. The wine list presents Riojas galore, and is well priced for Larimer Square. The tiny bar is a nice stop for dessert. $ *Average main: $25* ✉ *1431 Larimer St., Larimer Square* ☎ *303/820–2282* ⊕ *www.riojadenver.com* ☯ *No lunch Mon. and Tues.* ⚮ *Reservations essential* ✛ *A6.*

$$$$
ASIAN FUSION

✕ **TAG.** At first glance, the menu at TAG seems to be all over the place, but after a few bites of chef/owner Troy Guard's eclectic, self-described "continental social food," it all starts to make sense. The dishes are inspired by his Hawaiian upbringing but also draw heavily from Asian and Latin American influences, and the result is a lot of bold flavors that work surprisingly well together. Try the signature taco sushi with charred ahi and guacamole, or the miso pork belly. Between lunch and dinner (2–6 pm), the kitchen offers a delightful $5 menu of drinks and snacks, including an appealing ginger beer–based mule. $ *Average main: $29* ✉ *1441 Larimer St., Larimer Square* ☎ *303/996–9985* ⊕ *www.tag-restaurant.com* ☯ *No lunch weekends* ⚮ *Reservations essential* ✛ *A6.*

$$$
MEXICAN

✕ **Tamayo.** Chef–owner Richard Sandoval brought his popular concept of modern, upscale Mexican cuisine from New York to Denver, and it's just as welcome here. The food is classic Mexican with a twist, such as seafood tacos, *huitlacoche* (edible fungus) dumpling soup, elaborate moles, and empanadas for dessert. The tequila flights are a favorite at the large, inviting bar, which is highlighted by a mural made of semiprecious stones by artist and restaurant namesake Rufino Tamayo. Screens made from blond wood and Spanish art fill the interior, and in season the outdoor patio supplies a rare view of the mountains. $ *Average main: $25* ✉ *1400 Larimer St., Larimer Square* ☎ *720/946–1433* ⊕ *www.richardsandoval.com/tamayo* ⚮ *Reservations essential* ✛ *A6.*

RINO AND FIVE POINTS

$$
MODERN
AMERICAN

✕ **Acorn.** The cavernous space in the former foundry now called The Source sports graffiti-style art, exposed brick and ductwork as its main decor elements, but the lack of warmth is more than made up for in the Acorn's hipness quotient, which comes through in the extensive roster of cleverly assembled sharing plates—things like crispy fried pickles with green goddess aioli and Wagyu beef tartare with truffle cheese—that are large enough to serve as meals themselves. The tables are close, so don't plan to share anything too private, but the chef's line is also a great place to sit and be close to the action, watching the kitchen do its thing while you eat, the wood-fired grill and pizza oven mere feet away. $ *Average main: $17* ✉ *3350 Brighton Blvd., RiNo* ☎ *720/542–3721* ⊕ *www.denveracorn.com* ☯ *No lunch Sun.* ⚮ *Reservations essential* ✛ *D1.*

$$
INDIAN

✕ **Biju's Little Curry Shop.** Colorado cyclists already knew the culinary genius of Biju Thomas from his *Feed Zone* cookbooks with Boulderite Allen Lim of Skratch Labs—the two are famous for having fed and watered elite athletes at the Tour de France, as well as local races—and so the second Thomas opened his colorful curry shop, folks came

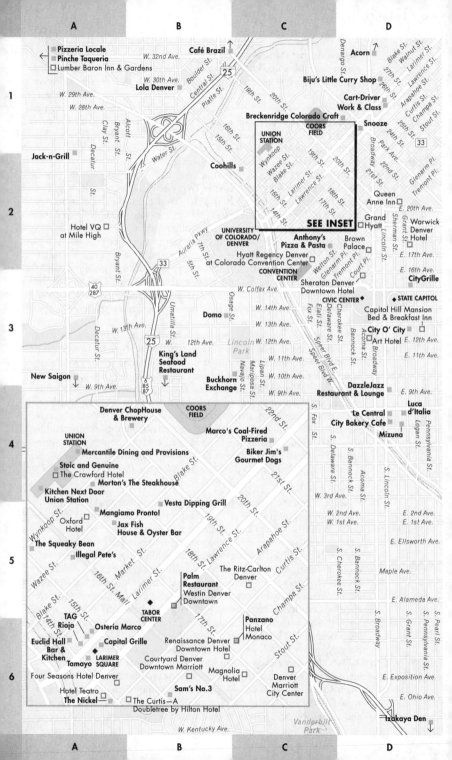

Map labels:

- Pizzeria Locale
- Pinche Taqueria
- Lumber Baron Inn & Gardens
- Café Brazil
- W. 32nd Ave.
- W. 30th Ave.
- Lola Denver
- W. 29th Ave.
- W. 28th Ave.
- Boulder St.
- Central St.
- Platte St.
- Acorn
- Biju's Little Curry Shop
- Cart-Driver
- Work & Class
- Breckenridge Colorado Craft
- Snooze
- COORS FIELD
- UNION STATION
- Jack-n-Grill
- Coohills
- Wynkoop St.
- Wazee St.
- Blake St.
- Larimer St.
- Lawrence St.
- Hotel VQ at Mile High
- Queen Anne Inn
- Grand Hyatt
- Warwick Denver Hotel
- SEE INSET
- UNIVERSITY OF COLORADO/DENVER
- Anthony's Pizza & Pasta
- Brown Palace
- CityGrille
- Hyatt Regency Denver at Colorado Convention Center
- CONVENTION CENTER
- Sheraton Denver Downtown Hotel
- CIVIC CENTER
- STATE CAPITOL
- Capitol Hill Mansion Bed & Breakfast Inn
- Domo
- W. Colfax Ave.
- W. 14th Ave.
- W. 13th Ave.
- City O' City
- Art Hotel
- Lincoln Park
- W. 12th Ave.
- King's Land Seafood Restaurant
- W. 11th Ave.
- New Saigon
- W. 9th Ave.
- Buckhorn Exchange
- W. 10th Ave.
- DazzleJazz Restaurant & Lounge
- Luca d'Italia
- Le Central
- City Bakery Cafe
- Mizuna

Inset map labels:

- Denver ChopHouse & Brewery
- COORS FIELD
- Marco's Coal-Fired Pizzeria
- UNION STATION
- Mercantile Dining and Provisions
- Biker Jim's Gourmet Dogs
- Stoic and Genuine
- The Crawford Hotel
- Morton's The Steakhouse
- Kitchen Next Door Union Station
- Vesta Dipping Grill
- Mangiamo Pronto!
- Oxford Hotel
- Jax Fish House & Oyster Bar
- The Squeaky Bean
- Illegal Pete's
- The Ritz-Carlton Denver
- Palm Restaurant
- Westin Denver Downtown
- TAG
- Rioja
- Osteria Marco
- TABOR CENTER
- Panzano Hotel Monaco
- Euclid Hall Bar & Kitchen
- Capital Grille
- Renaissance Denver Downtown Hotel
- Tamayo
- LARIMER SQUARE
- Courtyard Denver Downtown Marriott
- Magnolia Hotel
- Denver Marriott City Center
- Four Seasons Hotel Denver
- Hotel Teatro
- The Nickel
- Sam's No.3
- The Curtis—A Doubletree by Hilton Hotel
- Vanderbilt Park
- W. Kentucky Ave.
- Izakaya Den

Street names:

- Denargo St.
- Blake St.
- Walnut St.
- Larimer St.
- Lawrence St.
- 27th St.
- 26th St.
- 25th St.
- 24th St.
- Arapahoe St.
- Curtis St.
- Champa St.
- Stout St.
- Park Ave.
- Broadway
- 22nd St.
- 21st St.
- Glenarm Pl.
- Tremont Pl.
- Sherman St.
- E. 20th Ave.
- E. 17th Ave.
- E. 16th Ave.
- Lincoln St.
- Welton St.
- Glenarm Pl.
- Tremont Pl.
- Court Pl.
- E. 12th Ave.
- E. 11th Ave.
- E. 9th Ave.
- Pennsylvania St.
- Logan St.
- Grant St.
- Clarkson St.
- Washington St.
- Pearl St.
- S. Broadway
- S. Grant St.
- S. Pennsylvania St.
- S. Pearl St.
- S. Lincoln St.
- S. Cherokee St.
- S. Bannock St.
- S. Acoma St.
- S. Delaware St.
- S. Fox St.
- Cherokee St.
- Bannock St.
- Acoma St.
- Delaware St.
- Fox St.
- Elati St.
- Speer Blvd.
- Osage St.
- Umatilla St.
- Mariposa St.
- Navajo St.
- Lipan St.
- Auraria Pkwy.
- 7th St.
- 5th St.
- Clay St.
- Bryant St.
- Alcott St.
- Decatur St.
- Water St.
- 14th St.
- 15th St.
- 19th St.
- 20th St.
- 18th St.
- 17th St.
- 16th St. Mall
- Market St.
- Larimer St.
- Wynkoop St.
- Wazee St.
- Blake St.
- Arapahoe St.
- Champa St.
- Stout St.
- Curtis St.
- E. 2nd Ave.
- E. 1st Ave.
- E. Ellsworth Ave.
- Maple Ave.
- E. Alameda Ave.
- E. Exposition Ave.
- E. Ohio Ave.
- W. 3rd Ave.
- W. 2nd Ave.
- W. 1st Ave.

Highway markers: 25, 33, 40, 287, 6, 85, 87

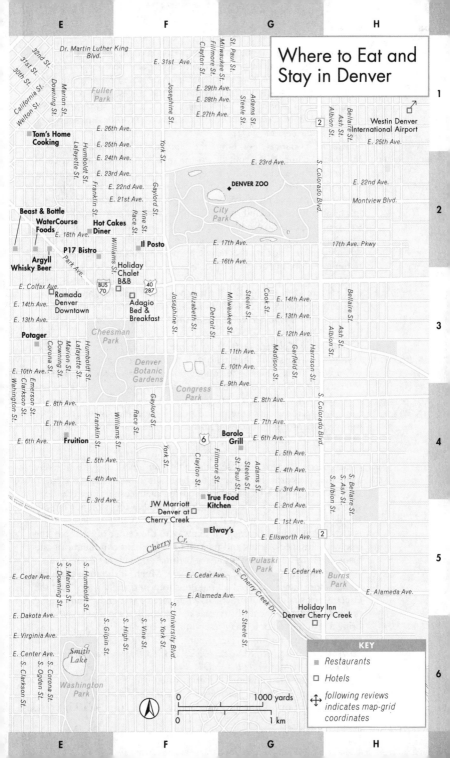

Where to Eat and Stay in Denver

KEY

- ■ *Restaurants*
- □ *Hotels*
- ↔ *following reviews indicates map-grid coordinates*

Tom's Home Cooking

Beast & Bottle

WaterCourse Foods

Hot Cakes Diner

Il Posto

P17 Bistro

Argyll Whisky Beer

Holiday Chalet B&B

Ramada Denver Downtown

Adagio Bed & Breakfast

Potager

Fruition

Barolo Grill

True Food Kitchen

JW Marriott Denver at Cherry Creek

Elway's

Holiday Inn Denver Cherry Creek

Westin Denver International Airport

DENVER ZOO

0   1000 yards
0   1 km

from all over to get at the South Indian foods of his youth. The menu comprises but a few dishes; start with a protein (or not; you can go vegetarian) and build from there with jasmine rice or biryani, and then add as you wish—sauces and vegetables and spices, until you have a masterpiece in a bowl. [$] *Average main: $14* ✉ *1441 26th St., RiNo* ☎ *303/292–3500* 🌐 *www.littlecurryshop.com* 🕓 *Closed Sun.* ✍ *Reservations not accepted* ✥ *D1.*

$ HOT DOG 🍴 **Biker Jim's Gourmet Dogs.** Quite the character, Biker Jim was hawking his gourmet hot dogs—split down the middle, with Coca-Cola-caramelized onions and a squirt of cream cheese as a topping option—for years on the 16th Street Mall until someone finally convinced him to open his own raucous place. Now he's got two (the second location is in Highlands Ranch) and they're both always packed with folks eager to try an elk jalapeño cheddar dog or a wild boar dog or a duck-cilantro dog. Sure, Biker Jim will do a plain all-beef version, but why go there when there are a dozen other delectable possibilities? On the side there's nothing healthy, but deep-fried pickles and fried mac-and-cheese beckon anyway. Chipotle-fired brownies with ice cream sandwiched inside make for an ideal ending. **TIP→ It's open until 3 am Friday and Saturday.** [$] *Average main: $7* ✉ *2148 Larimer St., Five Points* ☎ *720/746–9355* 🌐 *www.bikerjimsdogs.com* ✍ *Reservations not accepted* 💳 *No credit cards* ✥ *C4.*

$$ AMERICAN 🍴 **Breckenridge Colorado Craft.** Years before Coors Field moved in, Breckenridge Brewery set up shop with its top-notch brews and some snacks to go with. It has stayed the course, renaming this location and now offering about three-dozen made-in-Colorado microbrews, as well as a solid roster of big, juicy burgers (which can be made with bison, too), hefty sandwiches (the pulled pork is nice and spicy) and other pub grub befitting a spacious, noisy, TV-filled sports bar. [$] *Average main: $16* ✉ *2220 Blake St., Five Points* ☎ *303/297–3644* 🌐 *www.breckbrewcocraft.com* ✍ *Reservations not accepted* ✥ *D1.*

$$ PIZZA 🍴 **Cart-Driver.** Two repurposed shipping containers are the unlikely industrial backdrop for some of the best pizza and oysters in Denver. The owners of Cart-Driver have modeled their casual, unpretentious spot after truck stops in Italy—the Autogrills that focus on putting out simple, easily worked menus that focus on high quality—and the result is crusts that hold their crisp all the way to the center of each pie (the one with littleneck clams and pancetta is a brilliant combination) and briny-fresh oysters, satiny mousses of tuna and chicken liver, and an odd but intriguing roster of canned beers. Much of the food from the rather short menu is served on baking sheets and in jelly jars, and the effect is not smarmy but practical, while service is friendly and chaotic in the face of an almost-always packed place. Be prepared to wait, or bring a group of eight to snag reservations—or come very late, because they serve until midnight every night. [$] *Average main: $13* ✉ *2500 Larimer St., Suite 100, RiNo* ☎ *303/292–3553* 🌐 *www.cart-driver.com* ✍ *Reservations not accepted* ✥ *D1.*

$$ PIZZA FAMILY 🍴 **Marco's Coal-Fired Pizzeria.** Pizzerias often claim to serve authentic Neapolitan pizza, but in this casual, brick-lined, case, it's true: Marco's pies come out of the coal-fired ovens with a crispy-crackly crust,

generously topped with fresh mozzarella and fresh basil, and just the right amount of homemade sauce made from San Marzano tomatoes. If New York–style is more your thing, they have that, too (try the Bronx, with meatballs). A freshly made cannoli is the only way to finish. Weekend brunch pairs egg-topped pizzas with bottomless mimosas—don't knock it until you've tried it. $ *Average main: $15* ✉ *2129 Larimer St., Five Points* ☎ *303/296–7000* ⊕ *www.marcoscoalfiredpizza.com* ⩓ *Reservations essential* ✢ *C4*.

$ ✕ **Snooze.** The line for this Ballpark neighborhood joint starts just before
AMERICAN the 6:30 am weekday opening and sometimes an hour before it opens on weekends, because the lavish breakfasts are well worth the wait. The hollandaise-smothered creations alone—for instance, the Bella!, with Taleggio cheese and prosciutto on toasted ciabatta—inspire extra workouts, and the pineapple upside-down pancakes, with vanilla crème anglaise and cinnamon butter, require a plan to not eat the rest of the day. Get a cup of coffee and get to know your line neighbor, or try your luck at one of the six other metro-area locations, including Union Station. $ *Average main: $12* ✉ *2262 Larimer St., Five Points* ☎ *303/297–0700* ⊕ *www.snoozeeatery.com* ⩓ *Reservations not accepted* ✢ *D1*.

$ ✕ **Tom's Home Cookin'.** Get there early, because Tom's usually runs out
SOUTHERN of the abundant portions of finger-licking-good Southern-style comfort foods and soul food made from scratch. Tom Unterwagner and Steve Jankousky—partners in life and business—offer "meat and twos" (as in, one meat item and two side dishes) as a deal each day, and it's a tough choice; you can call ahead to find out what will be on the white board, anything from crispy fried chicken to roast turkey to meatloaf to country-fried steak; it's all good. Fried catfish is often on there, as well as fried okra, mashed potatoes, and the best mac-and-cheese in town as sides, and be sure to have the sweet tea, the real deal from their Atlanta, Georgia, roots. Also, loosen your belt for fresh peach cobbler or Coca-Cola cake when they have them. ■TIP➔ **Cash only.** $ *Average main: $10* ✉ *800 E. 26th Ave., Five Points* ☎ *303/388–8035* ⊙ *Closed weekends. No breakfast or dinner* ⩓ *Reservations not accepted* ▭ *No credit cards* ✢ *E1*.

$ ✕ **Work & Class.** A former chef for several Jennifer Jasinski restaurants,
LATIN AMERICAN including Rioja, Dana Rodriguez now has a place of her own that's a well-conceived realization of her Latina heritage. Well executed in a shipping container in the trendy burgeoning RiNo Arts District, guests sit at a communal table or at one of the two bars, where you can watch the line cooks shred pork for the tender *cochinita pibil* (a savory slow-roasted Yucatán favorite) or cut off haunches of citrus-zesty short ribs—meat comes priced by weight, from a quarter to a full pound. In keeping with the name, the rest of the menu is indeed "regular folks' food," but turned up a notch: think shrimp and grits or cheesy tomato mac spiked with chipotles. Happy hour is a big deal from 4 to 6 pm daily, with $3–$5 snacks and $3 beers. ■TIP➔ **No reservations or groups over seven, but if you do have to wait, the drinks are only $4.** $ *Average main: $12* ✉ *2500 Larimer St., Suite 101, RiNo* ☎ *303/292–0700* ⊕ *www. workandclassdenver.com* ⊙ *Closed Mon. No lunch* ⩓ *Reservations not accepted* ▭ *No credit cards* ✢ *D1*.

CAPITOL HILL

$$
BRITISH

✕ **Argyll Whisky Beer.** A gastropub that didn't make it the first time around in Cherry Creek, Argyll is definitely better in its second incarnation uptown, with the ideal roomy lounge space that sprawls beyond an inviting bar. The menu, created by beloved local chef John Broening, features tender-inside, crisp-outside fish and steak-fry-style chips so good some people plan their week around them. The menu is expectedly British and a tad on the heavier side—bangers and mash, Scotch eggs, green curry—but there are salads and surprises, such as "spot of tea," a broth with ramen noodles and gooey egg. The lamb burger is a marvel of moistness and flavor, complemented by a yogurt-cucumber relish. Not surprisingly, the beer roster is brilliant and nicely priced; same goes for the whiskeys. Brunch is not to be taken lightly; the corned beef hash is the dish to have. $ *Average main: $15* ✉ *1035 E. 17th Ave., Capitol Hill* ☎ *303/847–0850* ⊕ *www.argylldenver.com* ⌕ *Reservations essential* ✛ *E2.*

$$$
MODERN
AMERICAN

✕ **Beast + Bottle.** A cozy space that's just right for couples and small get-togethers, this Uptown eatery is aptly named for its constantly rotating roster of small plates and handful of entrées that focus on a fish, a couple of meat options, and always one or two vegetarian dishes. The kitchen proclaims a focus on "using the whole animal," with an attempt to introduce diners to new cuts or unusual preparations—they make all the broths and sauces from scraps and bones and offer organ meats in delectable ways—and their extensive list of small plates makes for a fun evening of sharing and grazing (the country lamb ribs with cinnamon salt, for instance). The provenance of each ingredient is shared on a large board behind diners, and the wine program endeavors to match the daring food with little-known varietals; all the wines are available by the glass, three-quarter bottle, or liter pour. The sidewalk patio and intimate bar are great dining options, as well. $ *Average main: $25* ✉ *719 E. 17th Ave., Capitol Hill* ☎ *303/623–3223* ⊕ *www.beastandbottle.com* ☾ *Closed Mon. No lunch Tues.–Fri.* ⌕ *Reservations essential* ✛ *E2.*

$
AMERICAN

✕ **CityGrille.** Politicians and construction workers rub shoulders while chowing down on the well-crafted sandwiches, soups, and salads at this casual eatery across the street from the State Capitol. CityGrille has earned national attention for both the burger, a half-pounder of ground sirloin, and the chile, a gringo stew of pork, jalapeños, and tomatoes that's spicy and addictive. The three-martini lunch lives on in this power-packed spot, and you can get a meal here until 11 pm (midnight on weekends). $ *Average main: $12* ✉ *321 E. Colfax Ave., Capitol Hill* ☎ *303/861–0726* ⊕ *www.citygrille.com* ✛ *D3.*

$
VEGETARIAN

✕ **City O' City.** Brought to Denver by the same folks who run the vegetarian-friendly WaterCourse, City O' City is a welcoming, casual, three-meals-daily bakery and café that offers gluten-free, vegan, and all manner of other dietary options in a bright, breezy atmosphere. Add cheese and eggs if you like, go macrobiotic, or imbibe from the wine and beer list—there are no judgements here. Happy hour starts at 2 pm daily and involves $2–$5 snacks. The opulent-looking items in the pastry case are entirely vegan. $ *Average main: $12* ✉ *206 E. 13th Ave., Capitol Hill* ☎ *303/831–6443* ⊕ *www.cityocitydenver.com* ⌕ *Reservations not accepted* ✛ *D3.*

$ DINER FAMILY 🍴 **Hot Cakes Diner.** This jumping Capitol Hill spot is a breakfast and lunch hangout. Weekend brunch draws crowds of bicyclists and newspaper readers in search of the croissant French toast, "health nut" pancakes, and colossal omelets. Even bigger are the scrumptious one-dish skillets; a popular one tops grilled pork chops with home fries, chili, cheddar, and eggs. They're open weekdays at 6 am and weekends at 7 am; closed each day at 2 pm. [$] *Average main: $9 ✉ 1400 E. 18th Ave., Capitol Hill ☎ 303/832–4351 🌐 www.eathotcakes.com ⏲ No dinner ✍ Reservations not accepted ✥ E2.*

$$$ MODERN ITALIAN 🍴 **Il Posto.** The menu, written on a chalkboard on the wall, changes daily in the austere but inviting Il Posto (The Place), where chef/owner Andrea Frizzi cooks intricately layered Italian dishes based on what's fresh. Two risotto dishes are offered daily, along with a handful of pastas, a few fish dishes, and one or two meat-based meals. Get anything with foie gras, nasturtiums, or fennel—all of which can be easily paired with the eatery's focused and well-priced Italian-only wine list. The bench-style booth seating along the wall is the most comfortable, but hipsters prefer the communal table in the middle. In temperate weather, try for a sidewalk seat for people-watching over 17th Avenue. [$] *Average main: $24 ✉ 2011 E. 17th Ave., Capitol Hill ☎ 303/394–0100 🌐 www.ilpostodenver.com ⏲ No lunch weekends ✍ Reservations essential ✥ F2.*

$$$ MODERN AMERICAN 🍴 **Potager.** The menu changes monthly at this industrial-designed restaurant, whose name, French for "kitchen garden," refers to the herb-rimmed back patio. Exposed ducts and a high ceiling make for a trendy dining room, and the floor-to-ceiling front windows allow the hip to be seen and the twinkling lights outside and in to be reflected for a warm glow. The menu always includes a selection of salads along with fish dishes and a thin-crust pizza from the wood-fired oven. The wine list is all over the map but it's well priced and changes monthly to go with the menu; the servers are among the most savvy in town. [$] *Average main: $25 ✉ 1109 Ogden St., Capitol Hill ☎ 303/832–5788 🌐 www.potagerrestaurant.com ⏲ Closed Sun. and Mon. No lunch ✍ Reservations not accepted ✥ E3.*

$$$ ASIAN FUSION 🍴 **P17 Bistro.** A complete overhaul of the menu transformed the former Parallel Seventeen into a bistro that serves Asian-inspired dishes with an emphasis on seasonal and locally sourced ingredients, and includes a lengthy roster of small plates. The atmosphere remains casually chic, and at night, the cozy patio with its twinkly lights beckons with a happy hour devoted to fun cocktails. The popular weekend brunch also features small plates—try the beignets with housemade apple butter—as does lunch, where the duck confit tacos are a must. [$] *Average main: $20 ✉ 1600 E. 17th Ave., Capitol Hill ☎ 303/399–0988 🌐 www.p17denver.com 💳 No credit cards ✍ Reservations essential ✥ E2.*

$$ VEGETARIAN 🍴 **WaterCourse Foods.** In a town known for its beef, WaterCourse stands out as a devoted vegan eatery in spacious digs uptown, after having made the decision in 2014 to drop all eggs, dairy, and other animal products completely from its kitchen. This casual, low-key place serves herbivores three meals a day, most of which are based on fruits, vegetables, whole grains, and meat-like soy substitutes. There are also

macrobiotic dishes available. The Reuben, with sauerkraut, portobellos, and Swiss on grilled rye, is amazing, as are the seitan-based faux Buffalo wings and the cauliflower-based "chicken and waffles." They also offer a small but nice selection of organic wines as well as slow-pressed organic juices. $ *Average main: $16* ⊠ *837 E. 17th Ave., Capitol Hill* ☎ *303/832–7313* ⊕ *www.watercoursefoods.com* ✢ *E2.*

CENTRAL DOWNTOWN

$ ✕ **Anthony's Pizza & Pasta.** This two-story dive, with a standing counter
PIZZA as well as a sit-down dining area upstairs crammed with ramshackle chairs and tables in various stages of disrepair, is the closest Denver gets to a New York slice. Fold each triangle in half, tilt it to let it drip, and inhale. Sweet- and spicy-sauced spaghetti with a side of meatballs offers an alternative for those who don't want pizza. $ *Average main: $8* ⊠ *1550 California St., Downtown* ☎ *303/573–6236* ⊕ *www.anthonyspizzaandpasta.com* ☽ *Closed Sun.* ✍ *Reservations not accepted* ✢ *C2.*

$$$$ ✕ **The Nickel.** An ambitious contemporary American menu makes a meal
MODERN an adventure at The Nickel, the restaurant that took over the space
AMERICAN once occupied by the now-closed Prima and replaced Restaurant Kevin Taylor as the premiere eatery in the Hotel Teatro. The room has been remodeled to take terrific advantage of the natural light that floods the space, making it feel much more impressive and special, and the sumptuous leather wingback chairs make it hard to leave once you have settled in. That allows you to take your time with a menu that changes monthly and pulls from Asian and Mediterranean influences. A wood-fired grill adds another element (it's what makes the rack of lamb and half chicken winners) to the menu, as do the rooftop bees for in-house honey, house-cured charcuterie, and homemade pickles. There's a lot going on here, but that's a good thing. $ *Average main: $27* ⊠ *1100 14th St., Downtown* ☎ *720/889–2128* ⊕ *www.thenickeldenver.com* ✍ *Reservations essential* ✢ *A6.*

$$$$ ✕ **Palm Restaurant.** This Denver outpost of the longtime New York steak
STEAKHOUSE house serves meat, seafood, pork chops, and other American dishes à la carte. The walls are bedecked with caricatures of local celebrities, and there's a chance you might see one in person—the restaurant is a favorite of local politicians, executives, and athletes, and with good reason: The steaks and the portions are both superlative. $ *Average main: $42* ⊠ *1672 Lawrence St., Downtown* ☎ *303/825–7256* ⊕ *www.thepalm. com/Denver* ☽ *No lunch weekends* ✍ *Reservations essential* ✢ *B5.*

$$$$ ✕ **Panzano.** This dining room in Hotel Monaco is filled with fresh flow-
ITALIAN ers and windows that let in natural light, making the space cheerful and
Fodor'sChoice bright. Three meals a day are served, but it's lunch and dinner that focus
★ on true Italian cuisine. Everything on the menu is multilayered, such as grilled flatbread topped with cheese, prosciutto, truffle oil, and balsamic vinegar; or risotto made with an ever-changing and ever-pleasing variety of cheeses and fresh produce. The breads are baked in-house. The superior service and accommodating staff make for a pleasant dining experience. The large, roomy bar is available for dining, too. $ *Average main: $26* ⊠ *909 17th St., Downtown* ☎ *303/296–3525* ⊕ *www. panzano-denver.com* ✍ *Reservations essential* ✢ *C6.*

$ DINER FAMILY 🍴 **Sam's No. 3.** Greek immigrant Sam Armatas opened his first eatery in Denver in 1927, and his three sons use the same recipes their father did in their updated version of his all-American diner, from the famous red and green chilis to the Coney Island–style hot dogs and creamy rice pudding. The retro diner resembles a fancy Denny's, and the bar is crowded with theatergoers and hipsters after dark. Good luck choosing: the menu is 12 pages long, with Greek and Mexican favorites as well as diner classics. The chunky mashed potatoes rule, and breakfast, which is served all day, comes fast. [$] *Average main: $10* ✉ *1500 Curtis St., Downtown* ☎ *303/534–1927* 🌐 *samsno3.com* ✍ *Reservations not accepted* ✣ *B6.*

CITY PARK AND NEARBY

$$$$ ITALIAN 🍴 **Barolo Grill.** This restaurant looks like a chichi Italian farmhouse, with dried flowers in brass urns, hand-painted porcelain, and straw baskets everywhere. The food isn't pretentious in the least, however. It's more like Santa Monica meets San Stefano—bold yet classic, healthful yet flavorful. Duckling stewed in red wine; fresh pastas, including veal-stuffed agnolotti; and risotto with mixed wild mushrooms, are all well made and fairly priced. The reasonably priced five-course tasting menu is a smart way to sample more of the kitchen's talents; adding the wine pairings ups the cost, but it improves the value. [$] *Average main: $30* ✉ *3030 E. 6th Ave., Central Denver* ☎ *303/393–1040* 🌐 *www.barologrilldenver.com* 🕒 *Closed Sun. and Mon. No lunch* ✍ *Reservations essential* ✣ *G4.*

$$$$ STEAKHOUSE 🍴 **Buckhorn Exchange.** Rumor has it that Buffalo Bill was to the Buckhorn what Norm Peterson was to *Cheers*. But if hunting makes you queasy, don't enter this Denver landmark and taxidermy shrine, where more than 500 pairs of eyes stare down at you from the walls. The handsome men's-club look—with pressed-tin ceilings, burgundy walls, red-checker tablecloths, rodeo photos, shotguns, and those trophies—probably hasn't changed much since the Buckhorn first opened in 1893. The dry-aged, prime-grade Colorado steaks are huge, juicy, and magnificent, as is the game. Try the smoked buffalo sausage or navy-bean soup to start. [$] *Average main: $35* ✉ *1000 Osage St., Central Denver* ☎ *303/534–9505* 🌐 *www.buckhorn.com* 🕒 *No lunch weekends* ✍ *Reservations essential* ✣ *C3.*

$ AMERICAN FAMILY 🍴 **City Bakery Cafe.** Everything is made from scratch at this charming little bakery and café, including the stocks for the French onion soup and other daily restoratives offered alongside the stacked-high sandwiches. Freshly baked for more than a hundred local restaurants, the dozens of varieties of breads are also available to take home or eat at a booth in the light-filled space. On Fridays, owner and baker Michael Bortz references his native Pennsylvania and his heritage as a third-generation chocolatier from the Philadelphia area—by offering cheesesteaks and shoofly pie, and if you're there when he makes his buttery, golden-shelled crab cakes, order extra to take home. Bortz is also the one responsible for the delectable tiramisu, éclairs, real-butter croissants, and other pastries in the front case, and he makes a mean *marjolaine*, the classic French dessert of layers of hazelnuts and pastry cream. $ *Average main: $8* ✉ *726 Lincoln St., Central Denver* ☎ *303/292–3989* ⊕ *www.citybakerydenver.com* ⊙ *Closed Sun. No dinner* ⟁ *Reservations not accepted* ✛ *D4.*

$$
AMERICAN

✕ **DazzleJazz Restaurant & Lounge.** If it's martinis and jazz you're after, come to this art deco space that allows for a groovy bar scene on one side and groovy dining on the other. The menu is as retro as the atmosphere, with an emphasis on comfort foods with a twist (check out the updated macaroni and cheese or the baked casserole dips) and small plates, and live music most nights makes this a laid-back spot. The cocktail roster, printed inside old jazz albums, is one of the most intricate around, and the Sunday jazz brunch swings. $ *Average main: $17* ✉ *930 Lincoln St., Central Denver* ☎ *303/839–5100* ⊕ *www.dazzlejazz. com* ⊙ *No lunch Mon.–Thurs.* ✛ *D3.*

$$$
JAPANESE

✕ **Domo.** Domo's owners pride themselves on fresh flavors and the painstaking preparation of Japanese country foods, as well as one of the largest sake selections in town. Everything is prepared to order, and it's worth the wait: this is where you can find some of Denver's best seafood, curry dishes, and vegetarian fare. The house specialty is *wanko sushi*—three to five courses of sushi accompanied by rice, soup, and six of Domo's tantalizing side dishes. The restaurant also houses a cultural-education center, a museum, and a Japanese garden. $ *Average main: $20* ✉ *1365 Osage St., Central Denver* ☎ *303/595–3666* ⊕ *www.domorestaurant.com* ⟁ *Reservations not accepted* ✛ *B3.*

$$$$
MODERN
AMERICAN
Fodor's Choice
★

✕ **Fruition.** Well-crafted, elegant comfort food made from seasonal ingredients is served in compelling combinations, like roasted pork with fennel, sausage-stuffed squash blossoms, and Colorado lamb loin served with ricotta tortellini. The bonus is that the cheese is made from sheep's milk at chef/owner Alex Seidel's own farm. A nightly offering of two courses of delightful dishes includes many vegetarian options, but many diners choose to make a meal from the amazing appetizer roster. The two small but nicely spaced dining rooms are gently lighted for a warm-toned atmosphere that fades into the background, allowing the evening to focus on the food and the expertly chosen and fairly priced wine list. $ *Average main: $28* ✉ *1313 E. 6th Ave., Central Denver* ☎ *303/831–1962* ⊕ *www.fruitionrestaurant.com* ⊙ *No lunch* ⟁ *Reservations essential* ✛ *E4.*

$$
FRENCH

✕ **Le Central.** A real find, this homey bistro serves excellent mussel dishes and provincial French specialties, including beef bourguignon (braised in red wine and garnished with mushrooms and onions), salmon *en croûte* (wrapped in pastry and baked), and steak au poivre. You can depend on Le Central for fabulous food, great service, and a surprisingly low tab. Weekend brunch is a big favorite. $ *Average main: $18* ✉ *112 E. 8th Ave., Central Denver* ☎ *303/863–8094* ⊕ *www.lecentral. com* ⟁ *Reservations essential* ✛ *D4.*

$$$$
ITALIAN

✕ **Luca d'Italia.** The restaurant's steel-gray, orange-and-red contemporary decor belies the fact that it's one of the most authentic Italian restaurants in the city. Chef-owner Frank Bonanno summons the memory of his Italian grandmother to re-create small-town Italy through wild boar with pappardelle, goat-stuffed *caramelle* (pasta shaped like candy wrappers), and house-cured capocollo and homemade cheeses. His tiramisu and chocolate sorbet have to be tasted to be believed. Service, overseen by Jacqueline Bonanno, is as impeccable as it is at Bonanno's many other restaurants (Mizuna, Osteria Marco, Salt & Grinder, and Bones, to name a few), and the wine list is agreeably priced and heavy on interesting Italians. [$] *Average main: $29* ✉ *711 Grant St., Central Denver* ☎ *303/832–6600* 🌐 *www.lucadenver.com* ⏲ *Closed Sun. and Mon. No lunch* ✍ *Reservations essential* ✣ *D4.*

2

$$$$ MODERN AMERICAN Fodor's Choice ★

🍴 **Mizuna.** Chef-owner Frank Bonanno knows how to transform butter and cream into comforting masterpieces at this cozy eatery with warm colors and intimate seating. His menu is reminiscent of California's French Laundry—witness the foie gras torchon and butter-poached lobster—but his Italian heritage has given him the ability to work wonders with housemade pastas and gnocchi, and he often offers a ragout or other long-stewed sauce. Be sure to try the creative desserts (such as brown butter pot de crème, an update on the classic French custard), and expect to be served by the most professional staff, trained by Jacqueline Bonanno, in town. [$] *Average main: $38* ✉ *225 E. 7th Ave., Central Denver* ☎ *303/832–4778* 🌐 *www.mizunadenver.com* ⏲ *Closed Sun. and Mon. No lunch* ✍ *Reservations essential* ✣ *D4.*

GREATER DENVER

HIGHLAND

$$ BRAZILIAN

🍴 **Café Brazil.** This always-packed spot is worth the trip to Highland for such fare as shrimp and scallops sautéed with fresh herbs, coconut milk, and hot chilies; *feijoada completa,* the Brazilian national dish of black-bean stew and smoked meats, accompanied with fried bananas; or grilled chicken breast in a sauce of palm oil, red chili, shallots, and coconut milk. There's a party style in this festive café with its vivid paintings and colorful traditional masks, and it's frequented by locals in the know. [$] *Average main: $18* ✉ *4408 Lowell Blvd., Highland* ☎ *303/480–1877* 🌐 *www.cafebrazildenver.com* ⏲ *Closed Sun. and Mon. No lunch* ✍ *Reservations essential* ✣ *B1.*

$$$ MEXICAN Fodor's Choice ★

🍴 **Lola Denver.** This casual eatery with valet parking brings in a young, hip clientele and provides a spectacular view of the city skyline from most of the sunny dining room, bar, and patio. Tableside guacamole, more than 90 tequilas, superior margaritas, and a clever, glass-lined bar area are just a few of the reasons the lovely Lola remains a locals' hangout. The food is modern Mexican, with fresh seafood in such dishes as *escabeche* (marinated, poached fish), *ceviche* (lime-cooked fish), and salads, in addition to smoked rib eye and *pollo frito* (fried chicken). A Mexican-style brunch is served Saturday and Sunday. [$] *Average main: $24* ✉ *1575 Boulder St., Highland* ☎ *720/570–8686* 🌐 *www.loladenver.com* ⏲ *No lunch* ✍ *Reservations essential* ✣ *B1.*

$ MODERN MEXICAN

🍴 **Pinche Taqueria.** The name has stirred up quite a bit of controversy since the owners first used it for their food truck—it refers to a kitchen helper in Spain, but something more sinister in Mexico—so look for a sign that says "Tacos Tequila Whiskey" instead. It turns out that's exactly what this taqueria specializes in, anyway, particularly the first thing, tacos street-style. Get to know your fellow diners at the communal tables or the long bar, or sit on the patio that opens from the dining area through the garage door. $ *Average main: $8* ⊠ *3300 W. 32nd Ave., Highland* ☎ *720/502–4608* ⊕ *www.tacostequilawhiskey. com* ⊘ *No lunch Mon.* ⌖ *Reservations not accepted* ✛ *A1.*

$
PIZZA
FAMILY

✕ **Pizzeria Locale.** The team at this casual pizzeria (already known for Boulder's Frasca) set out to make inexpensive pizza the way it was done in Italy 150 years ago: in under two minutes in a blistering-hot oven, with a light, thin, bubbly crust, and sparingly topped with fresh ingredients. The unexpected ingredients are the ones that impress—charred broccolini, crème fraîche with corn, ricotta with Calabrian chilies. A miniature cup of butterscotch pudding is the perfect amount of dessert. $ *Average main: $8* ⊠ *3484 W. 32nd Ave., Highland* ☎ *303/302–2451* ⊕ *www.pizzerialocale.com* ⌖ *Reservations not accepted* ✛ *A1.*

NORTH DENVER

$
MEXICAN
FAMILY

✕ **Jack–n–Grill.** The friendly family that runs this small, pepper-decorated place moved to Denver from New Mexico, and they brought their love of chilies with them. The green chili is fire-breathing spicy, and the red is a smoky, complex brew. The best item, though, is the plate of chicken or beef *vaquero* tacos, slathered with a sticky-sweet barbecue sauce and served on buttery tortillas. Get it with a bowl of freshly roasted corn off the cob. Lunch is always packed, so arrive early, and don't be afraid to tackle a gigantic breakfast burrito, either. There's a mean margarita and there are *cervesas*, too. $ *Average main: $11* ⊠ *2524 Federal Blvd., North Denver* ☎ *303/964–9544* ⊕ *www.jackngrill.com* ⌖ *Reservations not accepted* ✛ *A1.*

CHERRY CREEK

$$$$
STEAKHOUSE

✕ **Elway's.** You won't see the big guy very often here—or at the company's downtown Ritz-Carlton–Denver, Denver International Airport, or Vail locations, either—but that doesn't keep sports fans from packing it in, hopeful. And when the toothy-grinned former Broncos QB (and current executive vice president of football operations) John Elway doesn't show, diners console themselves with some of the best steak-house fare in town, particularly the porterhouse (big enough for half a football team) and the huge side of chunky-creamy Yukon gold mashed potatoes. While you eat, ease back into the intimately set-up, camel-color suede booths and watch waterfalls cascade over granite slabs, choose from the pricey but appealing wine list, and save room for make-your-own s'mores. $ *Average main: $45* ⊠ *2500 E. 1st Ave., Cherry Creek* ☎ *303/399–5353* ⊕ *www.elways.com* ⌖ *Reservations essential* ✛ *F5.*

$$
CONTEMPORARY

✕ **True Food Kitchen.** Holistic health guru Dr. Andrew Weil has opened restaurants in select locations in Arizona and California, and this venture in Cherry Creek, where his intensive focus is on anti-inflammatory preparations and antioxidant ingredients prepared with an international flair, has met with great success. Don't expect all-vegetarian, however; the menu offers plenty of meat, particularly lean bison and turkey, as well as fish, but there are also tempeh and other meat substitutes. Trendy cocktails—cucumber margarita or blueberry acai mojito, anyone?—and natural sodas add to the appeal for the younger crowds that flock to the communal tables for small plates and thin-crust pizzas. The kids' menu is impressively healthy and appealing with its turkey sloppy joes and almond butter–and-banana sandwiches. $ *Average main: $18* ✉ *2800 E. 2nd Ave., Cherry Creek* ☎ *720/509–7661* ⊕ *www.truefoodkitchen.com* ▭ *No credit cards* ⌨ *Reservations essential* ✛ *F4.*

SOUTH DENVER

$$ ✕ **Izakaya Den.** A larger and slightly more reasonably priced offer-
JAPANESE ing from the brothers who own Sushi Den next door, Izakaya Den is supposed to be like a Japanese *izakaya*, an informal and inexpensive drinking place where snacks are served. Instead, it's more like a typical upscale American take on a tapas bar, with pricier small plates and an extensive sake roster. That said, the high quality of fish imported from the owners' market in Japan is unparalleled in Denver, and several dishes—the hamachi, the crispy tuna, and the Wagyu carpaccio—are stellar. They offer a popular sushi-making class, and happy hour is a much cheaper way to try some of the better dishes, but you have to sit at one of the bars. $ *Average main: $18* ✉ *1487 S. Pearl St., South Denver* ☎ *303/777–0691* ⊕ *www.izakayaden.net* ☉ *Closed Sun. and Mon. No lunch Tues.–Fri.* ⌨ *Reservations essential* ✛ *D6.*

WEST DENVER

$ ✕ **King's Land Seafood Restaurant.** Like a Chinese eatery in New York or
CHINESE San Francisco, King's Land does dim sum to perfection, serving it daily during the week for lunch and during their crazy, jam-packed week-ends. Choose from dozens of dumplings, buns, and steamed dishes that are wheeled to you on carts, or go with the regular menu, also available at night, which includes delectable duck and seafood special-ties. The dining room is huge and always noisy, and the staff doesn't speak much English, so just close your eyes and point. Reservations are accepted for parties of six or more. $ *Average main: $12* ✉ *2200 W. Alameda Ave., West Denver* ☎ *303/975–2399* ✛ *B3.*

$$ ✕ **New Saigon.** Denver's best Vietnamese restaurant is always crowded
VIETNAMESE with folks trying to get at their crispy egg rolls, shrimp-filled spring rolls, and cheap but hefty noodle bowls. With nearly 200 dishes on the menu—priced and portioned for sharing—this vast, avocado-color eatery has everything Vietnamese covered, including 30-some vegetar-ian dishes and 10 with succulent frogs' legs. Service can be spotty, and not much English is spoken, but the staff goes overboard trying to help and never steers anyone wrong. It's best to go at off times to ensure a seat. Reservations are accepted for parties of six or more. $ *Aver-age main: $16* ✉ *630 S. Federal Blvd., West Denver* ☎ *303/936–4954* ⊕ *www.newsaigon.com* ☉ *Closed Mon.* ✛ *A3.*

WHERE TO STAY

Denver's lodging choices include the stately Brown Palace, bed-and-breakfasts, and business hotels. Unless you're planning a quick escape to the mountains, consider staying in or around downtown, where most of the city's attractions are within walking distance. Many of the hotels cater to business travelers, with accordingly lower rates on weekends—many establishments slash their rates in half on Friday and Saturday. The three hotels in the vicinity of Cherry Creek are about a 10- to 15-minute drive from downtown. *Hotel reviews have been shortened. For full information, visit Fodors.com.*

WHAT IT COSTS				
	$	**$$**	**$$$**	**$$$$**
For two people	under $121	$121–$170	$171–$230	over $230

Hotel prices are the lowest cost of a standard double room in high season, excluding service charges and 14.85% tax.

Use the coordinates (✣ B2) at the end of each listing to locate a site on the corresponding map.

DOWNTOWN

LODO

$$$$ HOTEL Fodor's Choice ★ **Brown Palace.** This grande dame of Colorado lodging has hosted public figures from President Eisenhower to the Beatles since it first opened its doors in 1892, and the details are exquisite: a dramatic nine-story lobby is topped with a glorious stained-glass ceiling, and the Victorian rooms have sophisticated wainscoting and art deco fixtures. **Pros:** sleeping here feels like being part of history; exceptional service; spacious and comfortable rooms. **Cons:** restaurants feel dated; parking costs extra. [$] *Rooms from: $240* ✉ *321 17th St., LoDo* ☎ *303/297–3111, 800/321–2599* 🌐 *www.brownpalace.com* 🛏 *205 rooms, 36 suites* 🍴 *No meals* ✣ *D2.*

$$$$ HOTEL Fodor's Choice ★ **The Crawford Hotel.** The lobby—which guests can view from each floor—is the newly renovated Union Station, a retro delight of desks with chain-pull lamps, long wooden benches, and constant bustle; the nostalgic sense of being on a train journey is carried elegantly into the 112 rooms, each of which offers a unique layout and design. **Pros:** centralized location; never have to leave Union Station; large choice of excellent restaurants. **Cons:** pricey; lobby chaos at peak times can be jarring. [$] *Rooms from: $289* ✉ *1701 Wynkoop St., LoDo* ☎ *720/460–3700, 855/362–5098* 🌐 *www.thecrawfordhotel.com* 🛏 *107 rooms, 5 suites* 🍴 *No meals* ✣ *A4.*

$$ B&B/INN **Lumber Baron Inn & Gardens.** The Keller family has made a plush, stylish, and romantic bed-and-breakfast out of a dilapidated Highland apartment building originally constructed for a lumber baron and his family in the 1890s. **Pros:** romantic, appealing mix of historic and modern; intimate spaces. **Cons:** not downtown. [$] *Rooms from: $149* ✉ *2555 W*

37th Ave., LoDo ☎ 303/477–8205, 888/214–2790 🌐 www.lumberbaron.com 💳 No credit cards 🛏 1 room, 3 suites 🍴 Breakfast ✣ A1.

$$$$ HOTEL Fodor's Choice ★ **Oxford Hotel.** During the Victorian era this hotel was an elegant fixture on the Denver landscape, and civilized touches like complimentary shoe shines, afternoon sherry, and morning coffee remain. **Pros:** prime LoDo location; gorgeous historic setting; great restaurants on-site and nearby. **Cons:** noisy ballpark crowds in season turn LoDo area into a big party. [$] *Rooms from: $290 ✉ 1600 17th St., LoDo ☎ 303/628–5400, 800/228–5838 🌐 www.theoxfordhotel.com 🛏 79 rooms, 9 suites 🍴 No meals ✣ A5.*

CAPITOL HILL AND CIVIC CENTER

$$$ B&B/INN **Adagio Bed & Breakfast.** One of the new "Bud + Breakfast" B&B experiences cropping up around the state, this is a good place to stay if you love music and marijuana, as the Adagio and its sister B&B in Silverthorne are committed to making sure guests can enjoy cannabis during a visit by providing the necessary paraphernalia and a place to use it. **Pros:** pretty, cozy rooms; within driving distance of major attractions; breakfast available when you want it. **Cons:** not within walking distance of downtown or Cherry Creek; limited amenities due to size. [$] *Rooms from: $179 ✉ 1430 Race St., Capitol Hill ☎ 303/370–6911, 800/533–4640 🌐 www.budandbfast.com 🛏 4 rooms, 2 suites 🍴 Breakfast ✣ F3.*

$$$$ HOTEL Fodor's Choice ★ **The ART Hotel.** Each floor of rooms in this nine-story building is dedicated to a different artist, with original art in every room by the artist, as well—you can't miss the entry-level greeting *Wall Drawing #397* by Sol Lewitt or the video art in the elevators—it's quickly apparent that this is going to be a different lodging experience. **Pros:** compelling art collection; comfortable, stylish rooms; stellar service. **Cons:** one of the most expensive hotels in Denver; restaurant still working out the kinks. [$] *Rooms from: $359 ✉ 1201 Broadway, Civic Center ☎ 303/572–8000 🌐 www.thearthotel.com 🛏 131 rooms, 14 suites 🍴 No meals ✣ D3.*

$$ B&B/INN **Capitol Hill Mansion Bed & Breakfast Inn.** The dramatic turret and intense rust color of this Richardson Romanesque Victorian mansion built in 1891 is enough to draw you into the eight elegantly appointed rooms done in varying themes, such as Rocky Mountain, Victorian, and Colonial. **Pros:** welcoming hosts; inviting rooms. **Cons:** walls are thin; place feels remote compared to rest of downtown. [$] *Rooms from: $154 ✉ 1207 Pennsylvania St., Capitol Hill ☎ 303/839–5221, 800/839–9329 🌐 www.capitolhillmansion.com 🛏 5 rooms, 3 suites 🍴 Breakfast ✣ D3.*

$ B&B/INN FAMILY **Holiday Chalet B&B.** Stained-glass windows and homey accents throughout make this 1896 Victorian brownstone in Capitol Hill, the neighborhood immediately east of downtown, exceptionally appealing. **Pros:** welcoming staff; delightful teas; enchanting style. **Cons:** parking can be a challenge; creaky house with thin walls; noisy neighborhood. [$] *Rooms from: $105 ✉ 1820 E. Colfax Ave., Capitol Hill ☎ 303/437–8245 🌐 www.theholidaychalet.com 🛏 5 rooms, 5 suites 🍴 Breakfast ✣ F3.*

$ HOTEL **Ramada Denver Downtown.** This Ramada is within walking distance of the capitol, as well as nine blocks east of downtown and the 16th Street

Mall. **Pros:** very reasonable rates; easy to get downtown. **Cons:** not the safest part of Colfax Avenue late at night; can be noisy. $ *Rooms from: $107* ⊠ *1150 E. Colfax Ave., Capitol Hill* ☎ *303/831–7700, 800/272–6232* ⊕ *www.ramada.com* ⤴ *135 rooms, 8 suites* �|○| *No meals* ✥ *E3.*

CENTRAL DOWNTOWN

$$$
HOTEL

🔲 **Courtyard Denver Downtown Marriott.** This stunning building (it used to be Joslins Department Store) sits right on the 16th Street Mall, which means everything downtown is a few blocks or a free Mall shuttle away. **Pros:** great location and views; deluxe rooms have sofabeds. **Cons:** pricey for the style; rooms nothing fancy. $ *Rooms from: $199* ⊠ *934 16th St., Central Downtown* ☎ *303/571–1114, 888/249–1810* ⊕ *www. marriott.com* ⤴ *166 rooms, 11 suites* �|○| *No meals* ✥ *B6.*

$$
HOTEL
FAMILY

🔲 **The Curtis — A Doubletree by Hilton Hotel.** Each floor here has a pop-culture theme, from classic cars to TV to science fiction, and the rooms are spacious and groovy, with speakers for your MP3 player and comfy, mod furnishings. **Pros:** across the street from Denver Performing Arts Complex; pet- and kid-friendly; reasonably priced for location. **Cons:** can be noisy; high-traffic area; some of the rooms feel small. $ *Rooms from: $150* ⊠ *1405 Curtis St., Central Downtown* ☎ *303/571–0300, 800/525–6651* ⊕ *www.thecurtis.com* ▭ *No credit cards* ⤴ *331 rooms, 5 suites* �|○| *No meals* ✥ *A6.*

$$$
HOTEL

🔲 **Denver Marriott City Center.** Definitely geared toward the business traveler, the Denver Marriott is a three-block walk from the Denver Convention Complex and has 25,000 square feet of meeting space of its own. **Pros:** nice gym and pool; close to the convention center. **Cons:** not much maneuvering space in the rooms; bland chain-hotel feel. $ *Rooms from: $179* ⊠ *1701 California St., Central Downtown* ☎ *303/297–1300, 800/228–9290* ⊕ *www.denvermarriott.com* ⤴ *601 rooms, 14 suites* �|○| *No meals* ✥ *C6.*

$$$$
HOTEL
Fodor'sChoice
★

🔲 **Four Seasons Hotel Denver.** Rooms at this famously service-oriented hotel manage the rare feat of being simply decorated—with cream-colored walls, white linens, wine upholstery, and brown-leather accents—while still maintaining a sense of luxury. **Pros:** noteworthy service; central location; comfortable rooms. **Cons:** pricey. $ *Rooms from: $325* ⊠ *1111 14th St., Central Downtown* ☎ *303/389–3000* ⊕ *www. fourseasons.com* ⤴ *218 rooms, 21 suites* ⏐○⏐ *No meals* ✥ *A6.*

$$$$
HOTEL
FAMILY

🔲 **Grand Hyatt.** Close to Larimer Square, the theaters, the 16th Street Mall, and the Colorado Convention Center and with unpretentious, comfortable rooms—downtown hotels don't get much better than this. **Pros:** great views from upper floors; top-notch gym; lavish concierge lounge services. **Cons:** has chain-hotel vibe; cavernous space can be overwhelming. $ *Rooms from: $279* ⊠ *1750 Welton St., Central Downtown* ☎ *303/295–1234, 800/233–1234* ⊕ *www.grandhyattdenver.com* ⤴ *491 rooms, 25 suites* ⏐○⏐ *No meals* ✥ *D2.*

$$$$
HOTEL

🔲 **Hotel Monaco.** Celebrities and business travelers check into this hip property, which occupies the historic 1917 Railway Exchange Building and the 1937 art moderne Title Building, for the modern perks and art deco–meets–classic French style. **Pros:** one of the pet-friendliest hotels in town; welcoming complimentary wine hour; central location. **Cons:** may be too pet-friendly; hotel has decidedly business rather than romantic feel. [$] *Rooms from: $254* ✉ *1717 Champa St., Central Downtown* ☎ *303/296–1717, 800/990–1303* 🌐 *www.monaco-denver.com* ⇆ *157 rooms, 32 suites* 🍽 *No meals* ✣ *C6.*

$$$$ **HOTEL** 🏨 **Hotel Teatro.** Black-and-white photographs, costumes, and scenery from plays that were staged in the Denver Performing Arts Complex across the street decorate the grand public areas of this hotel. **Pros:** great location for theater and other downtown pursuits; excellent restaurants; lovely rooms and hotel spaces. **Cons:** noisy and chaotic area; costly parking; some rooms are tiny. [$] *Rooms from: $259* ✉ *1100 14th St., Central Downtown* ☎ *303/228–1100, 888/727–1200* 🌐 *www.hotelteatro.com* ⇆ *102 rooms, 7 suites* 🍽 *No meals* ✣ *A6.*

$$ **HOTEL** 🏨 **Hyatt Regency Denver at Colorado Convention Center.** A much-needed and extensive 2014 remodel updated rooms to include expanded workstations, LCD-screen TVs, and a fresh palette (slate, beige, pine); the hotel caters to business-focused guests. **Pros:** spacious rooms with large workstations; large health club with lap pool; central location. **Cons:** noisy convention atmosphere. [$] *Rooms from: $144* ✉ *650 15th St., Central Downtown* ☎ *303/436–1234* 🌐 *www.denverregency.hyatt.com* ⇆ *1,040 rooms, 60 suites* 🍽 *No meals* ✣ *C2.*

$$$$ **HOTEL** 🏨 **Magnolia Hotel.** The Denver outpost of this Texas-based chain has remarkably spacious, elegant rooms with sophisticated furnishings—some with fireplaces—and warm colors, all built within the confines of the 1906 former American Bank Building. **Pros:** pretty, comfortable rooms; nice complimentary breakfast buffet; good restaurants. **Cons:** although classy, can feel like a generic chain hotel. [$] *Rooms from: $279* ✉ *818 17th St., Central Downtown* ☎ *303/607–9000, 888/915–1110* 🌐 *www.magnoliahoteldenver.com* ⇆ *240 rooms, 57 suites* 🍽 *Breakfast* ✣ *C6.*

$$ **B&B/INN** 🏨 **Queen Anne Inn.** Just north of downtown in the regentrified Clements historic district (some of the neighboring blocks have yet to be reclaimed), this inn made up of adjacent Victorians is a delightful, romantic getaway. **Pros:** lovely rooms; welcoming hosts; hearty fare. **Cons:** not right downtown; neighborhood can be noisy. [$] *Rooms from: $155* ✉ *2147 Tremont Pl., Central Downtown* ☎ *303/296–6666, 800/432–4667* 🌐 *www.queenannebnb.com* ⇆ *9 rooms, 4 suites* 🍽 *Breakfast* ✣ *D2.*

$$$ **HOTEL** 🏨 **Renaissance Denver Downtown Hotel.** The Renaissance's gorgeous hotel lobby is part of the original 1925 Colorado National Bank building, whose 16 vivacious Western-themed murals have been painstakingly restored; rooms are remarkably stylish, with sparkly glitter accents on pillows and blues and browns complementing the plush white linens. **Pros:** central location; attentive service; excellent restaurant and lounge. **Cons:** some rooms get outside noise. [$] *Rooms from: $199* ✉ *918 17th St., Central Downtown* ☎ *303/867–8100* 🌐 *www.rendendowntown.com* ⇆ *221 rooms, 9 suites* 🍽 *No meals* ✣ *B6.*

$$$$ **HOTEL** 🏨 **The Ritz-Carlton, Denver.** This beautiful property features warm woods, elaborate glass fixtures, and luxurious details, and the pampering service is typical of the chain. **Pros:** gracious service; room-service fare delicious and prompt; inviting public spaces. **Cons:** this part of town can be noisy; feels away from the action. [$] *Rooms from: $319*

✉ *1881 Curtis St., Downtown* ☎ *303/312–3800* 🌐 *www.ritzcarlton.com* 🛏 *155 rooms, 47 suites* 🍴 *No meals* ✣ *C5.*

$$$ HOTEL 🏨 **Sheraton Denver Downtown Hotel.** Guest rooms at the ever-bustling Sheraton are roomy and streamlined, with unfussy furniture and nice workstations that appeal primarily to the business traveler. **Pros:** great location; many amenities; friendly and accommodating staff. **Cons:** front area where cars come in is chaos central; feels like nothing but conventions. [$] *Rooms from: $179* ✉ *1550 Court Pl., Downtown* ☎ *303/893–3333, 866/716–8134* 🌐 *www.sheratondenverhotel.com* 🛏 *1,149 rooms, 82 suites* 🍴 *No meals* ✣ *D3.*

$$$ HOTEL FAMILY 🏨 **Warwick Denver Hotel.** This stylish midsize business- and family-friendly hotel is ideally located on the edge of downtown, and the spacious rooms have been updated with comfortable beds and the latest in high-tech perks to complement the brass and mahogany furnishings and roomy marble bathrooms. **Pros:** reasonable rates; motivated and friendly staff; oversize rooms, rare downtown swimming pool. **Cons:** more than walking distance from the business district; lower rates sometimes attract large, noisy groups. [$] *Rooms from: $175* ✉ *1776 Grant St., Central Downtown* ☎ *303/861–2000, 800/525–2888* 🌐 *www.warwickdenver.com* 🛏 *103 rooms, 58 suites* 🍴 *No meals* ✣ *D2.*

$$$$ HOTEL 🏨 **Westin Denver Downtown.** This sleek, luxurious high-rise opens right onto the 16th Street Mall and all the downtown action. **Pros:** convenient location on Mall; contemporary rooms; nice pool with great city view. **Cons:** the Palm is pricey; breakfast options are also expensive. [$] *Rooms from: $289* ✉ *1672 Lawrence St., Central Downtown* ☎ *303/572–9100, 800/937–8461* 🌐 *www.westin.com* 🛏 *418 rooms, 12 suites* 🍴 *No meals* ✣ *B5.*

GREATER DENVER

CHERRY CREEK

$$ HOTEL 🏨 **Holiday Inn Denver-Cherry Creek.** The Cherry Creek shopping district is 4 miles away, and the major museums and the zoo are a five-minute drive from this bustling hotel, which provides coveted mountain views from many of its rooms. **Pros:** good for business travelers; location bridges gap for folks who want both museums and downtown; free shuttle weekdays. **Cons:** not walking distance to any attractions; far from downtown; can be noisy. [$] *Rooms from: $139* ✉ *455 S. Colorado Blvd., Cherry Creek* ☎ *303/388–5561, 800/388–6129* 🌐 *www.cherrycreekhoteldenver.com* 🛏 *256 rooms, 13 suites* 🍴 *No meals* ✣ *G6.*

$$$$ HOTEL 🏨 **JW Marriott Denver at Cherry Creek.** The hip atmosphere and location smack in the middle of Cherry Creek's shopping district has made this upscale outpost of the Marriott family popular with tourists and locals alike. **Pros:** friendly staff; great location for shopping; bus to downtown a block away. **Cons:** feels very much like a chain; feels far from downtown; pricey. [$] *Rooms from: $259* ✉ *150 Clayton La., Cherry Creek* ☎ *303/316–2700* 🌐 *www.marriott.com* 🛏 *191 rooms, 5 suites* 🍴 *No meals* ✣ *F5.*

DENVER INTERNATIONAL AIRPORT

$$$$ HOTEL **Westin Denver International Airport.** This on-site airport hotel offers impressively soundproofed accommodations, local art throughout the rooms and the hotel itself, and some of the best views of the mountains and the plains in the state. **Pros:** only hotel right at the airport; stunning views; soundproofing so outstanding you won't realize you're next to an international airport. **Cons:** feels rather isolated; until TSA rules change, only the Westin's restaurants are accessible. [$] *Rooms from: $240* ✉ *8300 Peña Blvd., East of Downtown* ☎ *303/317–1800* 🌐 *www.starwoodhotels.com* 🛏 *484 rooms, 35 suites* 🍴 *No meals* ✣ *H1.*

NIGHTLIFE AND PERFORMING ARTS

Friday's *Denver Post* (🌐 *www.denverpost.com*) publishes a calendar of the week's events, as does the slightly alternative *Westword* (🌐 *www.westword.com*), which is free and published on Thursday. Downtown and LoDo are where most Denverites go at night. Downtown has more mainstream entertainment, whereas LoDo is home to fun, funky rock clubs and small theaters. Remember that Denver's altitude can intensify your reaction to alcohol.

TicketMaster. Selling tickets to almost all concerts, sporting events, and plays that take place in the Denver area, the ubiquitous TicketMaster is Denver's prime agency. ✉ *Denver* ☎ *800/745–3000* 🌐 *www.ticketmaster.com.*

PERFORMING ARTS

PERFORMANCE VENUES

Denver Performing Arts Complex. This huge complex, composed of an impressively high-tech group of theaters, hosts more shows—from classical orchestras to Jay Leno to *Wicked*—than any other performing arts center in the world. Spread over a four-block area, the theaters are connected by a soaring glass archway to a futuristic symphony hall. The complex anchors are the round Temple Hoyne Buell Theatre, built in 1991, and the ornate Ellie Caulkins Opera House, which occupies the former Auditorium Theatre built in 1908. The other five theaters include the small Garner Galleria Theatre and the midsize Space Theatre. The symphony, ballet, and opera have their seasons here. The complex has been run by the Denver Center for the Performing Arts since 1972, and 90-minute guided tours that take you behind the scenes are available by reservation Monday and Saturday for $8 per person; customized tours can also be arranged. ✉ *Box office, 1101 13th St., Central Downtown* ☎ *303/893–4100, 800/641–1222* 🌐 *www.denvercenter.org.*

Paramount Theatre. Designed by renowned local architect Temple H. Buell in the art deco style in 1930, the lovingly maintained Paramount in downtown Denver is both an elegant place to see shows and a rowdy, beer-serving party location for rock fans to enjoy large-scale concerts. ✉ *1631 Glenarm Pl., Central Downtown* ☎ *303/623–0106* 🌐 *www.paramountdenver.com.*

Fodor'sChoice   **Red Rocks Amphitheatre.** The exquisite 9,000-seat Red Rocks Amphi-
★   theatre, amid majestic geological formations in nearby Morrison, is
renowned for its natural acoustics, which have awed the likes of Leop-
old Stokowski and the Beatles. Although Red Rocks is one of the best
places in the country to hear live music, be sure to leave extra time
when visiting—parking is sparse, crowds are thick, paths are long and
extremely uphill, and seating is usually general admission. ⊠ *18300 W.
Alameda Pkwy., Morrison* ✛ *Off U.S. 285 or I–70* ☎ *720/865–2494*
⊕ *www.redrocksonline.com.*

SYMPHONY, OPERA, AND DANCE

Colorado's premier orchestra, opera company, and ballet company are
all in residence at the Denver Performing Arts Complex.

Colorado Ballet. From September through March, the Colorado Ballet specializes in the classics, with performances primarily at the Ellie
Caulkins Opera House. ⊠ *1278 Lincoln St., Downtown* ☎ *303/837–
8888* ⊕ *www.coloradoballet.org.*

Colorado Symphony Orchestra. From September to June, the orchestra
performs in the Boettcher Concert Hall, as well as playing ensemble
concerts at venues around the city and a popular summer Symphony on
the Rocks series at Red Rocks Park and Amphitheatre near Morrison.
⊠ *Boettcher Concert Hall, 13th and Curtis Sts., LoDo* ☎ *303/623–
7876, 877/292–7979* ⊕ *www.coloradosymphony.org.*

Opera Colorado. World-renowned for its superior acoustics and a Figaro
seat-back tilting system that allows attendees to follow the text of the
opera, the magnificent Ellie Caulkins Opera House has red-velvet seating and a lyre shape, ideal for full-bodied sound travel. The cherry-
wood-accented theater, in the renovated Newton Auditorium, is where
Opera Colorado presents its spring season, often with internationally renowned artists. ⊠ *1101 13th St., Downtown* ☎ *303/778–1500,
303/468–2030 tickets* ⊕ *www.operacolorado.org.*

THEATER

Bug Theatre Company. Based in Denver's trendy Highland neighborhood,
this small nonprofit theater produces cutting-edge, original works.
⊠ *3654 Navajo St., Highland* ☎ *303/477–5977* ⊕ *www.bugtheatre.org.*

Curious Theatre Company. Inspiring, innovative, and even edgy theater is
held in the same venue in which Curious's founders first met more than
15 years ago—a 19th-century church in Denver's artsy Golden Triangle.
Each season begins in September. ⊠ *1080 Acoma St., Golden Triangle*
☎ *303/623–0524* ⊕ *www.curioustheatre.org.*

Denver Center Theatre Company. Presenting high-caliber repertory theater,
including new works by promising playwrights, this company takes
over the stage at the Bonfils Theatre Complex, part of the Denver Performing Arts Complex. ⊠ *14th and Curtis Sts., LoDo* ☎ *303/893–4100,
800/641–1222* ⊕ *www.denvercenter.org.*

NIGHTLIFE

LODO

BARS AND BREWPUBS

Denver ChopHouse & Brewery. This high-end microbrewery is on the site of the old Union Pacific Railroad headhouse—with the train paraphernalia to prove it. It's a bit expensive for a brewpub, but if you hang out after Broncos games you might encounter local sports celebrities celebrating or commiserating, and certainly you will find fellow fans. ✉ *1735 19th St., LoDo* ☏ *303/296–0800* ⊕ *www.denverchophouse.com.*

Mynt Mojito Lounge. Near the 16th Street Mall, Mynt Mojito Lounge has established a chichi reputation with its namesake mojitos, Miami-style pastel colors, Cuban food, and fruity martinis—try the refreshing cha-cha, with fresh raspberries. ✉ *1424 Market St., LoDo* ☏ *303/825–6968* ⊕ *www.myntmojitolounge.com.*

Wynkoop Brewing Company. One of the city's best-known bars has anchored LoDo since it was a pre–Coors Field warehouse district. The Wynkoop Brewing Company is now more famous for its founder—Colorado governor and former Denver mayor John Hickenlooper—than for its brews, food, or ambience, but it remains a relaxing, slightly upscale, two-story joint filled with halfway-decent bar food, the usual pool tables, and games and beers of all types. ✉ *1634 18th St., LoDo* ☏ *303/297–2700* ⊕ *www.wynkoop.com.*

COMEDY CLUBS

Comedy Works. Denver comics have honed their skills at Comedy Works for more than 30 years, and nationally known performers make it a tour stop. A second location, The Landmark in Greenwood Village, has an upscale lounge and restaurant attached. ✉ *1226 15th St., LoDo* ☏ *303/595–3637* ⊕ *www.comedyworks.com.*

JAZZ CLUBS

El Chapultepec. This fluorescent-lighted, bargain-basement Mexican dive with a checkerboard floor and pool tables in the back feels cramped. Still, the limos parked outside hint at its enduring popularity: "the Pec" is where Ol' Blue Eyes used to pop in, and where visiting musicians, including the Marsalis brothers and former president Bill Clinton, still jam after hours. Cash only. ✉ *1962 Market St., LoDo* ☏ *303/295–9126* ⊕ *www.thepeclodo.com.*

Herb's Bar. Hidden in the back of a parking lot, the hipster favorite Herb's Bar, known locally by its previous name, Herb's Hideout, is a gloriously nostalgic bar with dim lighting, comfortable booths, and inexpensive cocktails. ✉ *2057 Larimer St., LoDo* ☏ *303/299–9555* ⊕ *www.herbsbar.com.*

CAPITOL HILL AND CITY PARK

DANCE CLUBS

The Church. Multiple rooms on three floors in a decommissioned church host DJ-spun Goth, indie, and industrial dance music on Sunday nights as well as progressive trance, hip-hop, and global on Friday and bachata, reggeton, salsa, cumbia, and Latin house music on Saturday. ✉ *1160 Lincoln St., Capitol Hill* ☏ *303/832–8628* ⊕ *www.coclubs.com/the-church* ☾ *Closed Mon.–Thurs.*

Legalized Marijuana in Colorado

HOW TO PURCHASE

On January 1, 2014, Colorado became the first state to allow legal recreational marijuana sales for any purpose to anyone over 21. Purchasing marijuana in Colorado at a licensed recreational shop is as simple as walking into the store, showing your ID, and buying it in the desired form. Dispensaries are medical-only, however, and require a doctor-issued medical card for entry, while some buildings are designated as offering medical and recreational.

The amount a person is legally allowed to purchase is dependent on residency; Colorado residents with a valid ID may buy up to one ounce of marijuana per day, while those with an out-of-state ID may purchase a quarter ounce of marijuana. No personal information is collected, and your ID is used only for proof of age and residency.

Recreational marijuana stores are located in cities and towns around the state, but the vast majority of the licenses are held in Denver. Some cities, such as Colorado Springs, have banned recreational stores. In addition, many cities limit store hours (in Denver, for instance, they can't be open past 7 pm). Call ahead to find out if a shop takes credit or debit cards, as many are still cash-only. *The Denver Post's The Cannabist* and the weekly *Westword* publish online guides that list shops, as well as reviews and information on the latest marijuana products.

WHERE TO CONSUME

Where to smoke marijuana is considerably more restricted. Marijuana products cannot be consumed on-site at a retail outlet, nor can it be smoked in public spaces, including ski areas or national parks (both of which are on federal lands, where getting caught can result in jail time or hefty fines, as marijuana possession is still illegal under federal law). Under Colorado's Clean Indoor Air Act, pot smoking is banned anywhere that cigarette smoking is also banned. A handful of private cannabis clubs have opened with membership fees, and some hotels advertise as "cannabis-friendly," meaning they allow consumption in designated smoking areas on-property. References to "420"—a once-obscure, insider allusion to all things marijuana-related—are meant as an indication of an establishment's openness to assisting clientele in procurement or consumption.

You can drive legally while possessing marijuana in a vehicle the same way you can with alcohol: It needs to be sealed. Driving stoned is against the law, and legal limits have been established for the amount of THC a driver can have in his or her system. Taking marijuana on a plane is illegal, as is transporting it to another state, even to a state where it's also legal.

Several tour groups offer marijuana-based services that include airport transfers, tours of marijuana-growing operations, transport to recreational shops, and enough time in party-style buses to smoke, consume edible marijuana products and visit local eateries, explore museums and other cultural events, and then get dropped off for a stay at a "cannabis-friendly" hotel.

Funky Buddha Lounge. This nighttime spot distinguishes itself with two outdoor rooftop bars for dancing and mingling, and DJs four nights a week. On Sunday during the season, the flat-screen TVs broadcast the football games. ⊠ *776 Lincoln St., Capitol Hill* ☎ *303/832–8628* ⊕ *www.funkybuddha.co* ⊙ *Closed Mon. and Tues.*

GAY BARS

Charlie's Denver. Charlie's has country-western atmosphere, music, and dancing, and a drag show at least one night a week. ⊠ *900 E. Colfax Ave., Capitol Hill* ☎ *303/839–8890* ⊕ *www.charliesdenver.com.*

Hamburger Mary's Bar & Grille. Drag queens rule the scene here on weekends, with events such as "Mary-oke" and the town's premier drag revue, all of which take place on the stage side of this restaurant/club. The front windows open to the 17th Avenue sidewalk for people-watching (both ways), and the restaurant crowd, gay and straight, seems to agree that this bar offers one of the town's best burgers, with tater tots as a side option. The huge patio out back is always a party. ⊠ *700 E. 17th Ave., Capitol Hill* ☎ *303/832–1333* ⊕ *www.hamburgermarys.com/denver.*

ROCK CLUBS

Bluebird Theater. Of Denver's numerous old-school music hangouts, the most popular is the regally restored Bluebird Theater, which showcases local and national acts, emphasizing rock, hip-hop, Americana, and ambient genres. ⊠ *3317 E. Colfax Ave., City Park* ☎ *303/377–1666, 888/929–7849 tickets* ⊕ *www.bluebirdtheater.net.*

Fillmore Auditorium. Denver's classic San Francisco concert hall spin-off looks dumpy on the outside, but it's elegant and impressive inside. Before catching a big-name act such as Rise Against, Lady Antebellum, or Marilyn Manson, scan the walls for color photographs of past club performers. ⊠ *1510 Clarkson St., Capitol Hill* ☎ *303/837–0360* ⊕ *www.fillmoreauditorium.org.*

Hi-Dive. This energetic, hip club located in the Baker neighborhood just south of Capitol Hill, books a diverse and eclectic range of talented indie rockers. The crowd is young, likes Red Bull, and tends to revel in the discovery of obscure underground music. ⊠ *7 S. Broadway, Capitol Hill* ☎ *303/733–0230* ⊕ *www.hi-dive.com.*

Lion's Lair. The Lion's Lair is a dive where punk-rock bands and occasional name acts—the Black Keys played here a couple of times years ago, as did British rocker Graham Parker— squeeze onto a tiny stage just above a huge, square, central bar. ⊠ *2022 E. Colfax Ave., Cheesman Park* ☎ *303/320–9200* ⊕ *www.lionslairlounge.squarespace.com.*

Ogden Theatre. This classic old theater showcases alternative-rock and hip-hop acts such as Band of Horses, The Jesus and Mary Chain, and Jurassic 5. ⊠ *935 E. Colfax Ave., Capitol Hill* ☎ *888/929–7849, 303/832–1874* ⊕ *www.ogdentheatre.net.*

CENTRAL DOWNTOWN

BARS AND BREWPUBS

Rock Bottom Restaurant & Brewery. This is a perennial favorite, thanks to its rotating special brews and reasonably priced pub grub. ⊠ *1001 16th St., Central Denver* ☎ *303/534–7616* ⊕ *www.rockbottom.com.*

COMEDY CLUBS

Bovine Metropolis Theater. Eight times a week, a rotating cast of characters offers improv at Bovine Metropolis Theater, which also stages satirical productions and teaches classes in the genre. ⊠ *1527 Champa St., Central Downtown* ☎ *303/758–4722* ⊕ *www.bovinemetropolis. com* ⊗ *Closed Sun.*

DANCE CLUBS

La Rumba. DJ-spun, Latin-based dance weekends, with bachata, cumbia, and reggaeton, as well as live salsa Saturday nights and salsa classes several times a week, is what's on deck at La Rumba. ⊠ *99 W. 9th Ave., Golden Triangle* ☎ *303/572–8006* ⊕ *www.larumba-denver.com* ⊗ *Closed Sun.–Wed.*

JAZZ CLUBS

DazzleJazz Restaurant & Lounge. This is a cozy, casual spot for nightly live jazz in the Golden Triangle. *Downbeat* magazine has named it one of the 100 best jazz clubs in the world; it offers acoustically treated walls in the dining room and the lounge, where the audience can get up close and personal with the musicians. ⊠ *930 Lincoln St., Golden Triangle* ☎ *303/839–5100* ⊕ *www.dazzlejazz.com.*

ROCK CLUBS

Mercury Café. Tripling as a health-food restaurant with sublime tofu fettuccine, fringe theater, and rock club in a downtown neighborhood, the Mercury Café specializes in acoustic sets, progressive, and newer wave music. Weekly swing and salsa dance lessons upstairs and poetry readings in a side room add to the appeal. No credit cards; there is an ATM on-site. The eatery also prides itself on its self-reliance on solar and wind energy and neighborhood tree and urban garden programs. ⊠ *2199 California St., Five Points* ☎ *303/294–9258* ⊕ *www. mercurycafe.com* ⊗ *Closed Mon.*

SOUTH DENVER

BARS AND BREWPUBS

Skylark Lounge. A vintage-style poolroom is just one reason to stop by the beloved Skylark Lounge, which counts live music, pinball machines, comfortable seating, and friendly staffers among its many charms. ⊠ *140 S. Broadway, South Denver* ☎ *303/722–7844* ⊕ *www. skylarklounge.com* ⊗ *Closed Sun.–Wed.*

GREATER DENVER

BARS AND BREWPUBS

PS Lounge. Considered by some Denverites as the best bar in town, the laid-back, casual, slightly divey PS Lounge has a well-stocked jukebox and an owner, known to all simply as Pete, who hands out a free shot to anyone who behaves and seems to be having a good time. Cash only. ⊠ *3416 E. Colfax Ave., Congress Park* ☎ *303/320–1200.*

COUNTRY MUSIC CLUBS

Grizzly Rose. Classic-rock bands are big here, as are country acts big and small. The Grizzly Rose has miles of dance floor, hosts regional and national bands, gives two-step dancing lessons, and sells plenty of Western wear, from cowboy boots to spurs. Sunday nights are for all ages until 11 pm. ⊠ *5450 N. Valley Hwy., I–25 at Exit 215, Globeville* ☎ *303/295–1330* ⊕ *www.grizzlyrose.com* ⊗ *Closed Mon.*

Stampede Mesquite Grill & Dance Emporium. This suburban country club and bar is a cavernous boot-scooting spot, with dance lessons and a restaurant. ⊠ *2430 S. Havana St., Aurora* ☎ *303/696–7686* ⊕ *www. stampedeclub.net* ⊗ *Closed Sun.–Tues.*

ROCK CLUBS

Gothic Theatre. Sitting south of downtown, this theater came of age in the early '90s, with a steady stream of soon-to-be-famous alternative-rock acts such as Nirvana and the Red Hot Chili Peppers. It still showcases the old and new, from Leon Russell to Glass Animals and T.J. Miller, but also operates as a community venue for theater, music, and charity events. ⊠ *3263 S. Broadway, Englewood* ☎ *303/789–9206* ⊕ *www.gothictheatre.com.*

Herman's Hideaway. In a south Denver neighborhood, down-home Herman's Hideaway showcases mostly local rock, with a smattering of reggae and blues thrown in. ⊠ *1578 S. Broadway, Overland* ☎ *303/777–5840* ⊕ *www.hermanshideaway.com.*

SHOPPING

Denver may be the best place in the country for shopping for recreational gear. Sporting-goods stores hold legendary ski sales around Labor Day. The city's selection of books and Western fashion is also noteworthy.

DOWNTOWN

LODO

CRAFTS AND ART GALLERIES

LoDo has the trendiest galleries, many in splendidly and stylishly restored Victorian warehouses.

David Cook Fine Art. Historic Native American art and regional paintings, particularly Santa Fe modernists, are David Cook's speciality. ⊠ *1637 Wazee St., LoDo* ☎ *303/623–8181* ⊕ *www.davidcookfineart. com* ⊗ *Tues.–Sat. 10–6.*

Mudhead Gallery. This gallery in the Titanium Lofts building sells museum-quality Southwestern and Native American art, with an especially fine selection of Santa Clara and San Ildefonso pottery and Hopi kachinas. ⊠ *1720 Wazee St., LoDo* ☎ *303/293–0007* ⊕ *www. mudheadgallery.net* ⊗ *Tues.–Sat. 10–6.*

MALLS AND SHOPPING DISTRICTS

Denver Pavilions. This three-story, open-air retail and entertainment complex in downtown Denver houses national chain stores like Barnes & Noble, Forever 21, Ann Taylor Loft, and Gap. There are also restaurants, including Denver's Hard Rock Cafe, and a 15-screen movie theater, the UA Denver Pavilions. Don't expect distinctive local flavor, but it's a practical complement to Larimer Square a few blocks away. ⊠ *16th St. Mall between Tremont and Welton Sts., LoDo* ☎ *303/260–6000* ⊕ *www.denverpavilions.com.*

Writer Square. Writer Square is a small but charming and pedestrian-friendly gathering place with shops and restaurants popular with downtown business types on their lunch breaks. The quirky galleries make for amusing window-shopping. ⊠ *1512 Larimer St., LoDo.*

WESTERN PARAPHERNALIA

Cry Baby Ranch. This Larimer Square store's move to a larger space means more room for its rambunctious assortment of 1940s and '50s cowboy kitsch, as well as modern attire for cowpokes of both sexes. ⊠ *1419 Larimer St., LoDo* ☎ *303/623–3979, 888/279–2229* ⊕ *www.crybabyranch.com* ⊗ *Weekdays 10–7, Sat. 10–6, Sun. noon–5.*

CIVIC CENTER

SPORTING GOODS

Sports Authority. At this huge, multistory shrine to Colorado's love of the outdoors, entire floors are given over to a single sport. There are other branches throughout Denver. ⊠ *1000 Broadway, Civic Center* ☎ *303/863–2260* ⊕ *www.sportsauthority.com* ⊗ *Mon.–Sat. 9–9:30, Sun. 9–8.*

CAPITOL HILL

BOOKSTORES

Fodor's Choice
★

Tattered Cover Book Store. A must for all bibliophiles, the Tattered Cover may be the best bookstore in the United States, not only for the near-endless selection (more than 400,000 books on two floors at the Colfax Avenue location and 300,000 in LoDo, along with much smaller versions of the stores at Union Station and Denver International Airport) and helpful, knowledgeable staff, but also for the incomparably refined atmosphere. Treat yourself to the overstuffed armchairs, reading nooks, and afternoon readings and lectures, and stop by the café for an espresso drink and bakery treat at the Capitol Hill site in the renovated historic Lowenstein Theater. ⊠ *2526 E. Colfax Ave., Capitol Hill* ☎ *303/322–7727* ⊕ *www.tatteredcover.com* ⊗ *Mon.–Sat. 9–9, Sun. 10–6.*

SPAS

The Woodhouse Day Spa. Situated in an 1886 house, Woodhouse Spa has more than a dozen rooms devoted to pampering, which happens from the moment guests receive a glass of wine or cocktail at the front door to the post-treatment relaxation in a cozy parlor-style area. The setting has the genteel feel of a favorite great aunt's home, with antiques and period reproductions. The four-handed massage is a worthy indulgence, with two therapists simultaneously performing a hypnotically soothing full-body rub-down, and the unique Minkyti facial combines resurfacing with anti-aging products. ⊠ *941 E. 17th Ave., Capitol Hill* ☎ *303/813–8488* ⊕ *www.denver.woodhousespas.com* ⊗ *Mon.–Wed. 9–7, Thurs.–Sun. 9–8* ☞ *$100 50-min massage, $240 spa package. Services: Aromatherapy, body wraps, facials, massage, nail services.*

GOLDEN TRIANGLE

CRAFTS AND ART GALLERIES

Native American Trading Company. The collection of crafts, jewelry, and regional paintings here is outstanding. ⊠ *213 W. 13th Ave., Golden Triangle* ☎ *303/534–0771* ⊕ *www.nativeamericantradingco.com* ⊗ *Wed.–Fri. 10–5, Sat. 11–4.*

CENTRAL PLATTE VALLEY

CRAFTS AND ART GALLERIES

John Fielder's Colorado. Few photographers capture the state's magnificent landscape the way John Fielder does, and his work is displayed along with a rotating roster of noted world photographers. ⊠ *833 Santa Fe Dr., Lincoln Park* ☎ *303/744–7979* ⊕ *www.johnfielder.com* ⊗ *Tues.–Sat. 9–5.*

SPORTING GOODS

REI. Denver's REI flagship store, one of four such shops in the country, is yet another testament to the city's adventurous spirit. The store's 94,000 square feet are packed with all stripes of outdoors gear and some special extras: a climbing wall, a mountain-bike track, a white-water chute, and a "cold room" for gauging the protection provided by coats and sleeping bags. There's also a Starbucks inside. Behind the store is the Platte River Greenway, a park path and water area that's accessible to dogs, kids, and kayakers. ⊠ *1416 Platte St., Jefferson Park* ☎ *303/756–3100* ⊕ *www.rei.com* ⊗ *Mon.–Sat. 9–9, Sun. 10–7.*

GREATER DENVER

ANTIQUES

Brass Armadillo Antique Mall. More than 600 dealers are crammed into a treasure-hunter's paradise, where prices and quality vary. Plan to spend the day if you're serious about searching. ⊠ *11301 W. I–70 Frontage Rd., Wheat Ridge* ☎ *303/403–1677, 877/403–1677* ⊕ *www. brassarmadillo.com* ⊗ *Daily 9–9.*

CRAFTS AND ART GALLERIES

Old Santa Fe Pottery. The 20 rooms are crammed with Mexican masks, pottery, and rustic Mexican furniture—and there's even a chip dip and salsa room. ⊠ *2485 S. Santa Fe Dr., Overland* ☎ *303/871–9434* ⊕ *www.oldsantafevillage.com* ⊗ *Mon.–Sat. 10–6, Sun. 10–5.*

Pismo Fine Art Glass. Cherry Creek has its share of chic galleries, including Pismo Fine Art Glass, which showcases exquisite handblown-glass art. ⊠ *2770 E. 2nd Ave., Cherry Creek* ☎ *303/333–2879* ⊗ *Mon.–Sat. 10–6, Sun. 11–5.*

MALLS AND SHOPPING DISTRICTS

Cherry Creek. In a pleasant, predominantly residential neighborhood 2 miles from downtown, the Cherry Creek shopping district has retail blocks and an enclosed mall. ⊠ *Cherry Creek.*

Cherry Creek Shopping Center. At Milwaukee Street, the granite-and-glass behemoth Cherry Creek Shopping Center holds some of the nation's top retailers. Its more than 160 stores include Banana Republic, Burberry, H&M, Tiffany & Co., Louis Vuitton, Neiman Marcus, and Macy's. ⊠ *3000 E. 1st Ave., Cherry Creek* ☎ *303/388–3900, 866/798–0889* ⊕ *www.shopcherrycreek.com* ⊗ *Mon.–Sat. 10–9, Sun. 11–6.*

Cherry Creek North. Just north of the Cherry Creek Shopping Mall is Cherry Creek North, an open-air development of tree-lined streets and shady plazas with art galleries, specialty shops, and fashionable restaurants. ⊠ *Between 1st and 3rd Aves. from University Blvd. to Steele St., Cherry Creek* ☎ *303/394–2904* ⊕ *www.cherrycreeknorth.com.*

Park Meadows. The upscale Park Meadows is a mall designed to resemble a ski resort, with a 120-foot-high log-beam ceiling anchored by two massive stone fireplaces. The center includes more than 100 specialty shops. On snowy days, "ambassadors" scrape your windshield while free hot chocolate is served inside. ⊠ *I–25, 5 miles south of Denver at County Line Rd., Littleton* ⊕ *www.parkmeadows.com.*

SPAS

Indulgences Day Spa. This popular Highland spa is well known for its down-to-earth setting (the space is nice but not overly fancy), and the staff is focused on guest comfort levels rather than upselling products. The essential oil wrap—particularly welcome in Colorado's dry climate—and the warm-stone massage that begins with an all-over body brushing are two of the more popular offerings, as is time in the complimentary steam room. Indulgences also has become a go-to spa for couples looking for a laid-back massage together. ⊠ *4100 Federal Blvd., Highland* ☎ *303/561–0566* ⊕ *www.indulgencesdayspa.com* ☞ *$70 60-min massage, $130 spa package. Steam room. Services: Facials, waxing, massage, body wraps, spray tanning.*

3

THE ROCKIES
NEAR DENVER

Updated by
Kyle Wagner

If you ever wondered why folks living along the Front Range—as the area west of Denver and east of the Continental Divide is known—continually brag about their lifestyles, you need only look at the western horizon where the peaks of snowcapped Rocky Mountains rise just a 35-minute drive from downtown. For those drawn to the Front Range, a morning workout might mean an hour-long single-track mountain-bike ride at Winter Park, a half-hour kayak session in Golden's Clear Creek, or a 40-minute hike in Mount Falcon Park.

The allure of this area, which rises from the red-rock foothills cloaked in lodgepole pine and white-barked aspens to the steep mountainsides draped with the occasional summer snowfields, has brought increasing recreational pressures as mountain bikers, equestrians, hikers, dog lovers, hunters, and conservationists all vie for real estate that is increasingly gobbled up by McMansion sprawl. On the Front Range the days of the elitist "Native" bumper stickers are long since gone; almost everyone here is from somewhere else. Finding an outdoor paddling, climbing, or skiing partner is about as difficult as saying hello to the next person you meet on the trail.

ORIENTATION AND PLANNING

GETTING ORIENTED

The Front Range mountains, the easternmost mountains in Colorado, stretch more than 180 miles from the Wyoming border to Cañon City. The Continental Divide flows along much of the northern portion of this spine, which includes several "Fourteeners," 14,000-foot or higher peaks. A boon for high-country lovers, the Rockies near Denver are easily accessed from the metro area via I–70, Colorado's major east–west interstate, or U.S. 285, the major route heading southwest into the mountains toward Fairplay in the now infamous South Park, one of the largest high-altitude valleys in the country. (Trey Parker, co-creator of the animated sitcom *South Park,* went to Evergreen High School.) Interstate 70 stitches together Denver, Golden, Idaho Springs, and Georgetown before crossing the Continental Divide through the Eisenhower Tunnel, right next to Loveland Ski Resort.

Foothills Near Denver. Less than 40 minutes from the city's heart, there are fast, cooling escapes in the mountain towns of Golden, Morrison, and Evergreen. Try your luck at the gaming towns of Central City and Black Hawk, or explore the former mining town of Idaho Springs.

TOP REASONS TO GO

Explore the Rockies: This section of mountains butts up against the Denver metro area, so it's easy to explore interesting towns and enjoy the mountain lifestyle.

Hit the slopes at Winter Park Resort: There's a blocked-off area for beginners, an outstanding children's program, and chutes and in-bounds off piste–style terrain for experts.

Ride the Georgetown Loop Railroad: Peering out the window at the raw, steep mountainside and the rickety trestle bridge on the vintage train ride from Georgetown to Silverplume provides an eye-opening lesson in 1800s transportation.

Tour the MillerCoors Brewery: An entertaining (and free) tour ends in a sudsy stop at the end for an informal tasting. You'll see the steeping, roasting, and milling of the barley, then tour the Brew House where the "malt mash" is cooked in massive copper kettles.

Explore Mount Evans: The highest paved road in the United States leads to the summit of 14,264-foot-high Mount Evans, and you can drive or bike nearly to the top or hike as much or as little of it as you like, passing mountain goats, bighorn sheep, and other animals along the way.

Continental Divide Area. Colorado's gold- and silver-mining heritage is the highlight of Georgetown, within an hour's drive of Denver along I–70. Highway 40 climbs northwest from I–70, west of Idaho Springs, making a switchback ascent up Berthoud Pass before dropping into the resort town of Winter Park.

PLANNING

WHEN TO GO

Summers are hot in the city, but when you go higher up in the Front Range the days may be warm but the nights are cool. It's a time of year when many hikers and bikers head for the higher peaks. Heavy traffic on I–70 during weekends and holidays has become a sad fact of life for those wanting to explore the Front Range and Colorado's High Country. Slowdowns peak on Friday and Sunday afternoon when stop-and-go jams are the norm, particularly around Idaho Springs and Georgetown. Winter weekend and holiday traffic fares little better, with regular slowdowns in the morning rush to the Summit County ski resorts and afternoon returns.

Many locals claim that the best times to visit Colorado are the spring "mud season" and autumn, when the tourists are gone and the trails are empty. In spring the Front Range mountains are carpeted with fresh new growth, while late September brings the shimmering gold of turning aspens. The interstate is well maintained. It's rare, but atop the mountain passes and at the Eisenhower Tunnel it's possible to see a bit of snow during the summer.

GETTING HERE AND AROUND

AIR TRAVEL

Denver International Airport is east of Denver, about a 35-minute taxi ride from the city center and a two-hour drive from the Continental Divide when the roads are clear and traffic is normal.

Airport Contact Denver International Airport (DEN). ☎ 800/247-2336 ⊕ www.flydenver.com.

Airport Transfers Home James. ☎ 800/359-7503 *shuttle service from Denver International Airport to Winter Park and Grand County* ⊕ www.ridehj.com.

CAR TRAVEL

The most convenient place to rent a car is at Denver International Airport. You can save money if you rent from the other offices of major car companies, but you'll have to take a shuttle or taxi to the city locations.

Although it is often severely overcrowded on weekends and holidays, I-70 is still the quickest and most direct route from Denver to the High Rockies. It slices through the state, separating it into northern and southern halves. Idaho Springs is along I-70. Winter Park is north of I-70, on U.S. 40 and over Berthoud Pass, which has gorgeous views but also has several hairpin turns. U.S. 285 is the southwest route to Buena Vista, Salida, and the High Rockies. Any mountain road or highway can be treacherous when a winter storm blows in. Drive defensively, especially downhill to Denver and Dillon where runaway truck ramps see a fair bit of use.

Gasoline is readily available along I-70 and U.S. 285, but not so in more-remote areas like Mount Evans and Guanella Pass. Blinding snowstorms can appear out of nowhere on the high passes at any time of the year. In the fall, winter, and early spring, it's a good idea to bring chains and a shovel along. Road reports and signage on the highways will indicate whether chains or four-wheel-drive vehicles are required. Keep your eyes peeled for wildlife, especially along the stretch of I-70 from Idaho Springs to the Eisenhower Tunnel. Bighorn sheep, elk, and deer frequently graze along the north side of the highway.

PARKS AND RECREATION AREAS

Arapaho & Roosevelt National Forests. Much of the northern Front Range region is within the Arapaho & Roosevelt National Forests. The **Indian Peaks Wilderness Area** is northwest of Denver and encompasses a rugged area of permanent snowfields, alpine lakes, and peaks reaching 13,000 feet and higher. It's a popular wilderness area for Denver and Front Range residents because it's easily reachable for overnight trips. Some of the trailheads on the eastern side are about one hour from Boulder and almost two hours from Denver. Because 90% of the people enter from the east side of the forests, visitors entering from the west side will find more solitude. ⊠ *Fort Collins* ☎ *303/541-2500* ⊕ *www.fs.usda.gov/arp.*

Clear Creek. For Class II to IV rafting and kayaking, try Clear Creek Rafting Company, which offers rafting on Clear Creek near Idaho Springs and on the Arkansas River during the early spring snowmelt season and throughout the summer. ⊠ *350 Whitewater Rd., Idaho Springs* ☎ *800/353-9901* ⊕ *www.clearcreekrafting.com.*

Golden Gate Canyon State Park. Just west of Golden, Golden Gate Canyon State Park has great hiking and wildlife-viewing, and offers some of the best car camping in the metro area. ⊠ *Golden* ☎ *303/582–3707* ⊕ *www.parks.state.co.us.*

Jefferson County Open Space Parks. Most recreational lands in the foothills west of Denver are protected by Jefferson County Open Space Parks. These relatively small county parks are heavily used and have excellent hiking, mountain-biking, and horse-riding trails. ☎ *303/271–5925* ⊕ *www.co.jefferson.co.us/openspace/index.htm.*

Meyer Ranch Park. A homestead in the early 1870s, Meyer Ranch is now one of the most popular hiking areas in Jefferson County Open Space, as well as a sledding mecca in the winter and a leaf-peeping spot in fall. The park offers more than 4 miles of trails winding through meadows of wildflowers and small, hilly stands of lodgepole pine and aspens; biking and horseback riding also are allowed. ■ TIP→ **There is a scenic picnic area along Owl's Perch Trail.** The park is open from one hour before sunrise to one hour after sunset. Address is for parking lot. ⊠ *10508 S. Turkey Creek Rd.* ✛ *30 mins west of Denver off Hwy. 285* ☎ *303/271–5925 Jeffco administrative office* ⊕ *www.jeffco.us.*

RESTAURANTS

Front Range dining draws primarily from the Denver metro area; you'll find standard chains, mom-and-pop restaurants, upscale dining, and good ethnic food choices like Mexican and Thai with the occasional Middle Eastern restaurant thrown in.

HOTELS

In summertime, out-of-state and regional visitors flock to Georgetown and Idaho Springs to explore the rustic ambience, tour a mine, and hike or mountain bike on trails that thread the mountainsides; or to Golden to tour the MillerCoors Brewery. You won't find megaresorts or grand old lodges; but there are bed-and-breakfasts, condominiums, a few nice hotels in Golden, and some chain properties. Winter Park Resort has a mix of hotels and motels, plus a few upscale ranches. In Black Hawk and Central City, where gambling is allowed, there are several big hotels with casinos on the main floor, plus a few smaller casinos tucked into historical storefronts. *Hotel reviews have been shortened. For full information, visit Fodors.com.*

WHAT IT COSTS			
$	$$	$$$	$$$$
Restaurants	under $13	$13–$18	$19–$25	over $25
Hotels	under $121	$121–$170	$171–$230	over $230

Restaurant prices are the average cost of a main course at dinner or, if dinner is not served, at lunch, excluding 7.1%–8.9% tax. Hotel prices are the lowest cost of a standard double room in high season, excluding service charges and 8.9% tax.

VISITOR INFORMATION

Contact Clear Creek County Tourism Bureau. ⊠ *Idaho Springs* ☎ *303/567–4660, 866/674–9237* ⊕ *www.clearcreekcounty.org.*

FOOTHILLS NEAR DENVER

If you want to head into the High Country for a few hours, take the MillerCoors tour in Golden, then head up to the Buffalo Bill Museum. If you want to climb even higher, take a walk around the lake in the center of Evergreen and visit some of the local shops in the tiny downtown area.

GOLDEN

15 miles west of Denver via I–70 or U.S. 6 (W. 6th Ave.).

Golden was once the territorial capital of Colorado. City residents have smarted ever since losing that distinction to Denver by "dubious" vote in 1867, but in 1994 then-Governor Roy Romer restored "ceremonial" territorial-capital status to Golden. Today it is one of Colorado's fastest-growing cities, boosted by the high-tech industry as well as MillerCoors Brewery and Colorado School of Mines. Locals love to kayak along Clear Creek as it runs through Golden; there's even a racecourse and a white-water park on the water.

GETTING HERE AND AROUND

Golden is a 30-minute drive from downtown Denver via U.S. 6. Downtown Golden is compact and easily walkable. You may want to drive to the Colorado School of Mines area of town; it's about a mile away from the downtown area, and you'll want a car to reach the Buffalo Bill Museum, which is several miles away. The parking area for the MillerCoors tours is within walking distance of downtown.

TIMING

You can explore downtown and tour the MillerCoors Brewery in three hours or so.

ESSENTIALS

Visitor Information Greater Golden Chamber of Commerce. ⊠ *1010 Washington Ave.* ☎ *303/279–3113* ⊕ *www.goldencochamber.org.*

EXPLORING

TOP ATTRACTIONS

Bradford Washsburn American Mountaineering Museum. Even if you never intend to go climbing, you may enjoy learning about lofty adventures showcased at the American Mountaineering Museum here. Visual exhibits display photos and items from experiences climbing some of the world's highest mountains. Artifacts from famous climbs are alongside exhibits about the 10th Mountain Division—men who fought in Italy in World War II, some of whom founded several of Colorado's ski resorts. ⊠ *710 10th St.* ☎ *303/996–2755* ⊕ *www.mountaineeringmuseum.org* ᧒ *$5* ☉ *Mon., Wed., and Thurs. 9–6, Tues. 9–7, Fri. 9–4, Sat. noon–5.*

FAMILY **Buffalo Bill Museum and Grave.** The drive up **Lookout Mountain** to the Buffalo Bill Museum and Grave provides a sensational panoramic view of Denver that alone is worth the price of admission. It was this view that encouraged Bill Cody—Pony Express rider, cavalry scout, and tireless promoter of the West—to request Lookout Mountain as his burial site. Adjacent to the grave is a small museum with art and artifacts

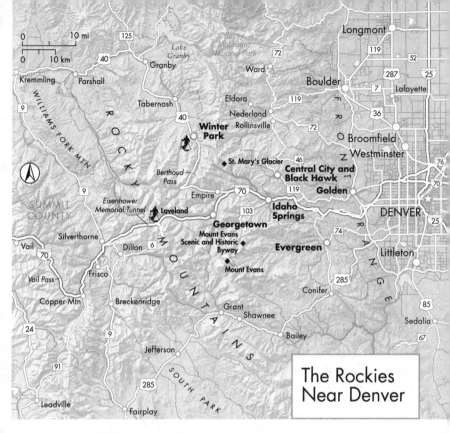

The Rockies
Near Denver

detailing Cody's life and times, as well as a souvenir shop. The grave is 100 yards past the gift shop on a paved walkway. ⊠ 987½ Lookout Mountain Rd. ✛ Rte. 5 off I–70 Exit 256, or 19th Ave. out of Golden ☎ 303/526–0744 ⊕ www.buffalobill.org ⊠ $5 ⊘ Museum May–Oct., daily 9–5; Nov.–Apr., Tues.–Sun. 9–5; grave daily dawn–dusk.

Clear Creek History Park. This park interprets the Golden area circa 1843–1900 via restored structures and reproductions, including a tepee, prospector's camp, one-room schoolhouse, and cabins. It is also populated with live chickens and bees. On select days, guides in period clothing lead 45-minute tours, but you can stroll the park and peek into the buildings anytime. ⊠ 11th and Arapahoe Sts. ☎ 303/278–3557 ⊕ www.goldenhistory.org ⊘ Daily dawn–dusk; call for tour times.

Golden History Museums. Three properties—the Astor House, the Golden History Center, and Clear Creek History Park—have combined under the name of Golden History Museums, and are all available for a $5 combination ticket (you can wander the History Park for free, however, or one museum for $3). The Astor House Museum is a restored Western hotel and boardinghouse which dates to the late Victorian period; exhibits explore the material culture and local life of the era. ⊠ Astor House, 822 12th St. ☎ 303/278–3557 ⊕ www.goldenhistory.org ⊠ $5 ⊘ Tues.–Sat. 10–4:30, Sun. noon–4:30.

Fodor's Choice   **MillerCoors Brewery.** Thousands of beer lovers make the pilgrimage to the
★   venerable MillerCoors Brewery each year. Founded in 1873 by Adolph
Coors, a 21-year-old German stowaway, today it's the largest single-site
brewery in the world and part of MillerCoors. The free self-paced tour
explains the malting, brewing, and packaging processes. Informal tastings are held at the end of the tour, and you can buy souvenirs in the gift
shop. A free shuttle runs from the parking lot to the brewery. ⊠ *13th
and Ford Sts.* ☎ *303/277–2337, 866/812–2337* ⊕ *www.millercoors.
com* ☉ *June–mid-Aug., Mon.–Sat. 10–4, Sun. noon–4; mid-Aug.–May,
Thurs.–Sat. and Mon. 10–4, Sun. noon–4* ☞ *Children under 18 must
be accompanied by an adult.*

12th Street. A National Historic District, Golden's 12th Street has a row
of handsome 1860s brick buildings. ⊠ *Golden.*

WORTH NOTING

FAMILY   **Colorado Railroad Museum.** Just outside Golden is the Colorado Railroad
Museum, a must-visit for any choo-choo lover. More than 100 vintage locomotives and cars are displayed outside the museum. Inside the
replica-1880 masonry depot are historical photos and memorabilia of
Puffing Billy (the nickname for steam trains), along with an astounding
model train set that steams through a miniature-scale version of Golden.
In the Roundhouse you can witness a train's restoration in progress,
and in winter, the popular tale of *The Polar Express* is theatrically
performed. ⊠ *17155 W. 44th Ave.* ☎ *303/279–4591, 800/365–6263*
⊕ *www.coloradorailroadmuseum.org* ☜ *$10* ☉ *Daily 9–5.*

FAMILY   **Heritage Square.** A colorful re-creation of an 1880s frontier town, Heritage Square has a music hall, a rip slide (an inflatable water slide), an
alpine slide, and some specialty shops. A vaudeville-style review ends
each evening's entertainment. ⊠ *18301 W. Colfax Ave.* ⊹ *Off I-70 at
the Golden exit; then 1 mile north on Colfax/U.S. 40* ☎ *303/277–0040*
⊕ *www.heritagesquare.info* ☜ *Entrance to park is free; admission varies
per ride* ☉ *Shops daily 11–5. Rides Apr., May, Sept., and Oct., select
weekends; June–Aug., daily. Hrs vary.*

SPORTS AND THE OUTDOORS
GOLF

Fodor's Choice   **Fossil Trace Golf Club.** Created by James Engh, this spectacular 18-hole
★   course is set into an old quarry. You play along fairways that have been
set into deep gouges in the earth created when the quarry was mined,
and you hit past pillars of sandstone to reach some of the greens. Along
the way, players can stop to look at fossils of triceratops' footprints
in an aeons-old rock wall, and relics of old clay-mining equipment.
⊠ *3050 Illinois St.* ☎ *303/277–8750* ⊕ *www.fossiltrace.com* ☜ *$78
weekdays, $88 weekends* ⚑ *18 holes, 6831 yards, par 72.*

HIKING

Mount Falcon Park. This park is a great way to explore the true foothills
of the Front Range, and the comparatively low elevation makes it a
good warm-up for higher ventures. Early in the morning mule deer can
be seen grazing on the adjacent slopes. Take the **Turkey Trot Trail** from
the east parking lot in the Morrison Town Park marked with a "hikers
only" sign. The trail winds 1¾ miles up the east face of Mount Falcon

through brushy slopes before curving behind the mountain up a forested draw to top out at around 7,000 feet. The trail loops back around and connects to the Castle Trail for a 1¼-mile easy return to the parking lot. Allow about 90 minutes. ⚠ **Stay on the path to avoid critters, including rattlesnakes, that lie in the grass.** ✉ *Jefferson County Open Space, start at east parking lot* 🌐 *www.jeffco.us/parks.*

WHERE TO EAT AND STAY

$$ PIZZA FAMILY Fodor's Choice ★ 🍴 **Woody's Wood Fired Pizza.** Woody's has a full menu, with pastas, chicken, calzones, and burgers, but it's more fun to choose the $11.97 all-you-can-eat pizza, soup, and salad bar. The choices on the pizza bar range from classic to It's Greek to Me and Margherita, and the salad is always fresh. Woody's is so popular that the pies are always just out of the oven. Don't be surprised if you have to join the throng of families and college students waiting outside for a table on a busy night. [$] *Average main: $15* ✉ *1305 Washington Ave.* ☎ *303/277–0443* 🌐 *www.woodysgolden.com* ✍ *Reservations not accepted.*

$$$ HOTEL 🏨 **Golden Hotel.** Right in the heart of Golden, this hotel is a comfortable place to stay midway between downtown Denver and the mountains. **Pros:** downtown and riverside setting; spacious rooms. **Cons:** this hotel caters to businesspeople, so you may see many suits; understaffed. [$] *Rooms from: $178* ✉ *800 11th St.* ☎ *800/233–7214, 303/279–0100* 🌐 *www.TheGoldenHotel.com* 🛏 *59 rooms, 3 suites* 🍽 *No meals.*

EVERGREEN

20 miles southwest of Golden via U.S. 6 east, Hwy. 470, I–70 west, and Hwy. 74 (Evergreen Pkwy.); 28 miles west of Denver.

Once a quiet mountain town, today Evergreen is a tony community filled with upscale, extravagantly designed homes. The downtown core remains rustic in feel, however, and on warm-weather weekends it's filled with tourists and Denverites escaping the city heat. Visitors browse the eclectic mix of shops and mingle with locals walking their dogs on the path, which circles Lake Evergreen.

GETTING HERE AND AROUND

It's a 45-minute drive from downtown Denver. Once you're in the heart of town, it's easy to find parking and explore on foot.

WHEN TO GO

Evergreen Jazz Fest. The annual, multiday Evergreen Jazz Fest in July features musicians from around the country, such as New Orleans' beloved New Black Eagle Jazz Band. Ticket prices vary; concerts are offered in five venues around town. ✉ *Evergreen* 🌐 *www.evergreenjazz.org* 🎟 *From $50.*

EXPLORING

Hiwan Homestead Museum. Built between 1890 and 1930, this restored log cabin shows a popular and relaxed mountain summertime lifestyle. The museum, which includes three other buildings, has an exceptional collection of Southwestern Indian artifacts. ✉ *4208 S. Timbervale Dr.* ☎ *720/497–7650* 🎟 *Free* 🕒 *June–Aug., Tues.–Sun. 11–5; Sept.–May, Tues.–Sun. noon–5.*

WHERE TO EAT AND STAY

$ VEGETARIAN 🍴 **Dandelions Café & Bakery.** Nearly everything at Dandelions is made from scratch, from the ginger-infused limeade and lemon-tarragon salad dressing to the honey oat bread and superb gluten-free brownies. Pizza is their specialty, and the pies come individually sized and loaded with toppings. The small dining area is inviting and open to the kitchen, where the owners cook as they chat with the customers. [$] *Average main: $9* ✉ *32156 Castle Ct.* ☎ *303/674–5000* 🌐 *www.dandelionsevergreen.com* 💳 *No credit cards* 🕒 *Closed Sun. No dinner* ✍ *Reservations not accepted.*

$$ VIETNAMESE 🍴 **Saigon Landing.** Gracious service and exceptional Vietnamese food have made Saigon Landing an Evergreen favorite. The dining room, decorated with imported knick-knacks, serves as a relaxing and romantic backdrop for live piano music on the weekends. This is the place to try exotic dishes such as frog's legs, grilled quail, and stuffed squid; more traditional offerings like lemongrass beef and sesame chicken are exemplary as well. [$] *Average main: $16* ✉ *28080 Douglas Park Rd.* ☎ *303/674–5421* 🌐 *www.saigonlanding.com* 💳 *No credit cards* ✍ *Reservations essential.*

$ AMERICAN FAMILY 🍴 **The Wildflower Cafe.** This tiny but friendly café serves breakfasts so scrumptious that there's a line out the door most days. It's well worth the wait, especially for the jalapeño-studded huevos rancheros Benedict. Thursday sushi nights (the only time the place is open for dinner) are such a hit that Denverites sometimes make the drive. The burgers are above average, and kids are particularly well catered to with Mickey Mouse pancakes and yogurt with granola for less than $4. [$] *Average main: $8* ✉ *28035 Hwy. 74* ☎ *303/674–3323* 🌐 *www.wildflowerevergreen.com* 🕒 *No dinner Fri.–Wed.* ✍ *Reservations not accepted.*

$$ B&B/INN Fodor's Choice ★ 🏨 **Highland Haven Creekside Inn.** Within walking distance of downtown Evergreen, this inn has a combination of standard and luxury rooms, suites, and cottages set alongside Bear Creek, where guests can go trout fishing. **Pros:** mountain town locale but only 35 minutes from downtown Denver or Georgetown; very quiet; romantic. **Cons:** bathrooms tend to be small; you'll have to stroll into Evergreen or drive for dinner. [$] *Rooms from: $170* ✉ *4395 Independence Trail* ☎ *303/674–3577, 800/459–2406* 🌐 *www.highlandhaven.com* 🛏 *6 rooms, 5 suites, 7 cottages* 🍽 *Breakfast.*

SHOPPING

ART GALLERIES

Evergreen Gallery. This gallery has an excellent collection of contemporary decorative and useful ceramics, art glass, photographs, and other fine craft work. ✉ *28195 Hwy. 74* ☎ *303/674–4871, 877/389–3375* 🌐 *www.theevergreengallery.com.*

SPAS

TallGrass Aveda Spa and Salon. Tucked at the end of a windy road, the warmly rustic TallGrass is remote enough that you may see deer or elk outside as you wait for your treatment. Scrubs are a top pick to slough off skin dried by the Colorado climate, and the Arnica-based Recovery Massage targets stress and muscle fatigue. Note that prices are higher for services on weekends, but the spa also offers discounts at the last minute. A healthy spa lunch can be added to the experience. ✉ *997 Upper Bear Creek Rd.* ☎ *303/670–4444* ⊕ *www.tallgrassspa. com* ☞ *$100 50-min massage, $360 half-day escape. Hair salon, steam room. Services: Aromatherapy, body wraps, facials, massage, nail services.*

CENTRAL CITY AND BLACK HAWK

18 miles west of Golden via U.S. 6 and Hwy. 119; 38 miles west of Denver.

Changes to the gambling laws created a "gold rush" to Black Hawk and Central City, allowing the casinos to stay open 24/7 and offer craps and roulette; the betting limit was also raised to $100. The two former mining towns edge up against each other with more than 20 casinos, several of which are topped by big hotels. Central City offers a fleeting sense of what the original mining town looked like.

GETTING HERE AND AROUND

Both towns are about a 45-minute drive from Denver. If you want to start in Black Hawk, take the narrow and winding Highway 119. If you'd rather start in Central City, head up I–70 and take the wide Central City Parkway. Bus transportation is also available from Denver and Golden through most of the casinos and the Opera House.

TIMING

You can cover Central City and Black Hawk's main attractions in a few hours on foot, although they're hard to find amid the crowds of gamblers.

EXPLORING

There are more than 20 casinos in Black Hawk and Central City. Many of the casinos in Central City are in buildings dating from the 1860s—from jails to mansions—and their plush interiors have been lavishly decorated to re-create the Old West era, a period when this town was known as the "Richest Square Mile on Earth." Black Hawk looks like builders stuck a load of glitzy hotels and casinos right in the middle of once-quiet mountainous terrain. Virtually every casino has a restaurant with the usual all-you-can-eat buffet. The biggest casinos are in newer buildings in Black Hawk. Hotel deals are common.

Gilpin History Museum. At the Gilpin History Museum, photos and reproductions, as well as vintage pieces from different periods of Gilpin County history, paint a richly detailed portrait of life in a typical rowdy mining community. ✉ *228 E. 1st High St., Central City* ☎ *303/582–5283* ⊕ *www.gilpinhistory.org* 🎟 *$6* ☉ *Late May–early Sept., Tues.–Sun. 10–4; rest of year by appointment only.*

WHERE TO EAT AND STAY

$$$$
STEAKHOUSE
✕**White Buffalo Grille.** Inside Black Hawk's Lodge Casino, this upscale spot serves steaks, seafood such as honey-bourbon-glazed salmon, a top-notch bison burger, and Colorado rack of lamb. Garlic-herb mashed potatoes, creamed corn, and rice pilaf can be ordered as sides. The views from the all-glass enclosure on a bridge above Richmond Street are divine. 🟊 *Average main: $28* ✉ *Lodge Casino, 240 Main St., Black Hawk* ☎ *303/582–6375* ⊕ *www.thelodgecasino.com* ☉ *No lunch.*

$ B&B/INN **Chase Creek B&B.** At this small historic house on the banks of namesake Chase Creek, the Yankee and Sleepy Hollow rooms are done up in a Victorian style with lace curtains and pastel walls, while the attic Polar Star room has mission-style furniture. **Pros:** two rooms have private hot tubs; in a quiet area. **Cons:** almost all the nearby restaurants are in big casinos; a drive to Central City; only three rooms, so book far in advance. [$] *Rooms from: $95* ✉ *250 Chase St., Black Hawk* ☎ *303/582–3550* 🌐 *www.chasecreekinn.com* 🛏 *3 rooms* 🍴 *Breakfast.*

PERFORMING ARTS

OPERA

Central City Opera House. Opera has been staged at the Central City Opera House, the nation's fifth-oldest opera house, almost every year since opening night in 1878. Lillian Gish has acted, Beverly Sills has sung, and many other greats have performed here. Performances are held in summer only. ✉ *124 Eureka St., Central City* ☎ *303/292–6700, 800/851–8175 Denver box office* 🌐 *www.centralcityopera.org* 🕒 *Late June–early Aug.*

SHOPPING

SPAS

Ameristar Casino Resort Spa Black Hawk. Opened in 2009, the upscale hotel Ameristar upped the ante for size and amenities, and nowhere is the opulence more apparent than in the modern but restful Ara Spa, which offers aromatherapy and hot stone massages, a variety of tub soaks, and a detox wrap. Before or after treatment, guests can take advantage of the steam room, sauna, and whirlpool; if you aren't indulging in a treatment, a $50 day-use fee Monday-Friday garners use of the water amenities, including the steam room and whirlpool (but not on weekends). The well-equipped fitness center and rooftop pool are added incentives to spend the day; use is free by leaving your photo ID. ✉ *111 Richman St., Black Hawk* ☎ *720/946–4000, 866/667–3386* 🌐 *www.ameristar.com/Black_Hawk.aspx* ☞ *$100 50-min massage, $300 3-hr, 3-treatment spa package. Hair salon, sauna, steam room. Services: Aromatherapy, body wraps, facials, hydrotherapy, massage.*

IDAHO SPRINGS

11 miles south of Central City via Central City Pkwy. and I–70; 33 miles west of Denver via I–70.

Colorado prospectors struck their first major vein of gold here on January 7, 1859. That year local mines dispatched half of all the gold used by the U.S. Mint—ore worth a whopping $2 million. Today the quaint town recalls its mining days, especially along portions of Colorado Boulevard, where pastel Victorians will transport you back to a century giddy with all that glitters.

GETTING HERE AND AROUND

After taking one of the I–70 Idaho Springs exits, it's hard to get lost, because the central part of this small town is bordered by the highway on one side and landlocked by a steep mountainside just a few blocks away. Head to the center of town, park, and walk around.

EXPLORING

TOP ATTRACTIONS

FAMILY **Argo Gold Mine & Mill.** During gold-rush days the Argo Gold Mine & Mill processed more than $100 million worth of the precious metal. To transport the ore from mines in Central City, workers dug through solid rock to construct a tunnel to Central City, 4½ miles away. When completed in 1910 the Argo Tunnel was the longest in the world. During a tour of the mine and mill, guides explain how this monumental engineering feat was accomplished. Admission includes the small museum and a gold-panning lesson. ⊠ *2350 Riverside Dr.* ☎ *303/567–2421* ⊕ *www.historicargotours.com* ⌨ *$16* ⊘ *Daily 9–5, weather permitting.*

Fodor'sChoice **Mount Evans Scenic and Historic Byway.** The incomparable Mount Evans ★ Scenic and Historic Byway—the highest paved road in the United States—leads to the summit of 14,264-foot-high Mount Evans. This is one of only two Fourteeners in the United States that you can drive up (the other is her southern sister, Pikes Peak). More than 7,000 feet are climbed in 28 miles, and the road tops out at 14,134 feet, 130 feet shy of the summit, which is a ¼-mile stroll from the parking lot. The toll road winds past placid lakes and through stands of towering Douglas firs and bristlecone pines. This is one of the best places in the state to catch a glimpse of shaggy white mountain goats and regal bighorn sheep. Small herds of the nimble creatures stroll from car to car looking for handouts. Feeding them is prohibited, however. Keep your eyes peeled for other animals, including deer, elk, and feather-footed ptarmigans. ⊠ *U.S. Forest Service fee station, State Rd. 3* ✛ *From Idaho Springs, State Rd. 103 leads south 14 miles to the entrance to Hwy. 5, which is the beginning of the scenic byway* ☎ *303/567–3000* ⊕ *www.mountevans.com* ⌨ *$10* ⊘ *The road is open only when road conditions are safe. Generally, the last 5 miles to summit, Memorial Day–Labor Day.*

Phoenix Gold Mine. At the Phoenix Gold Mine a seasoned miner leads tours underground, where you can wield 19th-century excavating tools or pan for gold. Whatever riches you find are yours to keep. ▪TIP➜ This is cash only. ⊠ *Off Trail Creek Rd.* ☎ *303/567–0422* ⊕ *www.phoenixgoldmine.com* ⌨ *$15; $10 for tour only* ⊘ *May–Oct., daily 10–5; Nov.–Apr., daily 10–4, weather permitting.*

Fodor'sChoice **St. Mary's Glacier.** This is a great place to enjoy a mountain hike and ★ the outdoors for a few hours. From the exit, it's a beautiful 10-mile drive up a forested hanging valley to the glacier trailhead. The glacier, technically a large snowfield compacted in a mountain saddle at the timberline, is thought to be the southernmost glacier in the United States. During drought years it all but vanishes; a wet winter creates a wonderful Ice Age playground throughout the following summer. Most visitors are content to make the steep ¾-mile hike on a rock-strewn path up to the base of the glacier to admire the snowfield and sparkling sapphire lake. The intrepid hiker, with the right type of gear, can climb up the rocky right-hand side of the snowfield to a plateau less than a mile above for sweeping views of the Continental Divide. Because of its proximity to Denver, St. Mary's Glacier is a popular weekend getaway for summer hikers, snowboarders, and skiers. There are two pay parking lots with about 140 spaces between them; the cost is $5 per vehicle per day, with restrooms and trash facilities available at both. Don't look for a St. Mary's Glacier sign on I–70; it reads "St. Mary's Alice" to refer to the nearby ghost towns. ✉ *Idaho Springs* ✣ *I–70 Exit 238, west of Idaho Springs.*

WORTH NOTING

Charlie Taylor Water Wheel. Near Indian Hot Springs Resort is a 600-foot waterfall, Bridal Veil Falls. The imposing Charlie Taylor Water Wheel—the largest in the state—was constructed in the 1890s by a miner who attributed his strong constitution to the fact that he never shaved, took baths, or kissed women. ✉ *Idaho Springs* ✣ *South of Idaho Springs on I–70.*

FAMILY **Indian Hot Springs Resort.** Idaho Springs presently prospers from the hot springs at Indian Hot Springs Resort. Around the springs, known to the Ute natives as the "healing waters of the Great Spirit," are geothermal caves that were used by tribes as a neutral meeting site. The hot springs, a translucent dome–covered mineral-water swimming pool, mud baths, and geothermal caves are the primary draws for the resort. You don't need to be an overnight guest to soak in the mineral-rich waters; day rates start at $20 for the geothermal cave baths (depending on type of bath and day of week), $22.50 for outdoor Jacuzzi baths, and $16 for the pool. The plain but comfortable spa offers massages and facials. ✉ *302 Soda Creek Rd.* ☎ *303/989–6666* 🌐 *www.indianhotsprings.com* 🎫 *Varies by bath and pool; prices higher on weekends* ⏲ *Daily 7:30 am–10:30 pm.*

Oh-My-Gawd Road. Although most travelers heading to Central City take the new highway from I–70, adventurous souls can take the Oh-My-Gawd Road. Built in the 1870s to transfer ore, this challenging drive climbs nearly 2,000 feet above Idaho Springs to Central City. After traveling along a series of hairpin curves you arrive at the summit, where you are treated to sweeping views of Mount Evans. The dusty road is often busy with mining traffic, so keep your windows up and your eyes open. ✉ *Hwy. 279* ✣ *From Idaho Springs (Exit 240), drive west through town on Colorado Blvd. Turn right on 23rd Ave., left on Virginia St., and right at Virginia Canyon Rd. (279).*

WHERE TO EAT

$ PIZZA FAMILY 🍴 **Beau Jo's Pizza.** This always-hopping pizzeria is the area's original après-ski destination. Be prepared for a wait on winter weekends, because Denverites often stop in Idaho Springs for dinner until the traffic thins down. Topping choices for the famous olive oil–and-honey pizza crust range from traditional to exotic—andouille sausage, Hatch green chile, tofu—and they've added a decent version of a gluten-free crust, as well. [$] *Average main: $12* ✉ *1517 Miner St.* ☎ *303/567–4376* 🌐 *www.beaujos.com* ✍ *Reservations not accepted.*

$$ AMERICAN 🍴 **Tommyknocker Brewery & Pub.** Harking back to gold-rush days, this casual bar and restaurant is usually filled with skiers in winter and travelers or Denverites year-round who want to meet High Country friends halfway. The suds have a distinctly local flavor and sporty names like Alpine Glacier Pilsner and Pick Axe IPA. In addition to fare such as

buffalo burritos and "monster" wings, the brewery has plenty of vegetarian options. $ *Average main: $14* ✉ *1401 Miner St.* ☎ *303/567–2688* ⊕ *www.tommyknocker.com* ⚹ *Reservations not accepted.*

SHOPPING

ART GALLERIES

Sawtooth Gallery. In a historic downtown building, Sawtooth Gallery displays works from more than a dozen Colorado artists, most from Clear Creek County. The pieces on display run the gamut in quality as well as medium, but are often inspired by the surrounding area. ✉ *1634 Miner St.* ☎ *303/569–2143* ⊕ *www.sawtoothgallery.com.*

GIFTS AND SOUVENIRS

The Wild Grape. This store is filled with an eclectic collection of gift items and souvenirs and an outstanding collection of greeting cards. ✉ *1435 Miner St.* ☎ *303/567–4670.*

CONTINENTAL DIVIDE AREA

As I–70 climbs higher into the Rockies, the population and air begin to thin. Georgetown is a former mining town; Winter Park is a mountain resort town with a more recent history. Nearby Loveland is smaller, but one of the locals' favorite ski areas because of its proximity to Denver.

WINTER PARK

36 miles west of Idaho Springs; 67 miles west of Denver via I–70 and U.S. 40.

Winter Park Resort is easily navigable from the small village at the base anchored by Zephyr Mountain Lodge and the Fraser Crossing and Founders Pointe condominiums. The Village Cabriolet—an open gondola—takes day skiers from a big parking lot to one end of the village, and they must walk past most of the shops, restaurants, and bars before reaching the lifts at the base of the resort.

GETTING HERE AND AROUND

In winter you can catch a ride on shuttle buses that move between the resort and the town of Winter Park, a few miles away. But in summer you'll need a car to vacation here. Amtrak stops at nearby Fraser and Granby.

WHEN TO GO

From late November to mid-April good snow attracts winter sports lovers. Winter Park is equally popular in summer with hikers, bicyclists, and golfers, but has few tourist attractions besides its natural beauty. Mountain bikers flock here because of the diversity of the trails and the growing emphasis on downhill mountain biking.

ESSENTIALS

Visitor Information Winter Park/Fraser Valley Chamber of Commerce. ✉ 78841 U.S. 40 ☎ 970/726–4221, 800/903–7275 ⊕ www.playwinterpark.com. **Winter Park Resort.** ✉ 100 Winter Park Dr. ☎ 800/977–7669, 970/726–1564 ⊕ www.winterparkresort.com.

DOWNHILL SKIING AND SNOWBOARDING

Winter Park. This ski park is really two interconnected areas: Winter Park and Mary Jane, both open to skiers and snowboarders. Between the two peaks there are four distinct skiable sections: Winter Park; the "Jane"; Vasquez Ridge, which is primarily intermediate cruising; and Vasquez Cirque, which has seriously steep in-bounds off-piste terrain. Pick a meeting place for lunch in case you and your friends get separated.

The skiing on the Winter Park and Vasquez Ridge trails is generally family-friendly, and there are segregated areas for beginners. Winter Park's runs promise lots of learning terrain for beginners and easy cruising for intermediates. On busy weekends Vasquez Ridge is a good place for escaping crowds, partly because this area is a bit more difficult to find, but the run-outs can be long.

Mary Jane is famous for its bumps and chutes, delivering 1,766 vertical feet of unrelenting moguls on a variety of trails, although there are a couple of groomed intermediate runs. Experts gravitate toward the far end of the Jane to runs like Trestle and Derailer, or to Hole-in-the-Wall, Awe, and other chutes. Expert skiers and riders seeking inbound off piste–style terrain hike over to the Vasquez Cirque.

The resort's Eagle Wind terrain has advanced steeps and deeps tucked among the trees. Panoramic Express, the highest six-person lift in North America, provides access to above-the-tree-line skiing at Parsenn Bowl, Perry's Peak, and Forever Eva, as well as terrain and gladed sections. The pitch in many areas of Parsenn's is moderate, making the bowl a terrific place for intermediate skiers to try powder and crud-snow skiing.

The resort's Rail Yard, with its superpipe and terrain parks, is specially designed for freestylers. A progressive park system allows skiers and snowboarders to start small and work their way up to the bigger and more difficult features. There is also a limited-access park, the Dark Territory, which is for experts only and requires an additional fee. **Facilities:** 143 trails; 3,081 acres; 3,060-foot vertical drop; 26 lifts. ⊠ *100 Winter Park Dr.* ☎ *800/729–5813, 970/726–5587* ⊕ *www.winterparkresort. com* ⊠ *Lift ticket $129.*

LESSONS AND PROGRAMS

National Sports Center for the Disabled. Winter Park is home to the National Sports Center for the Disabled, one of the country's largest and best programs for skiers with disabilities. ☎ *970/726–1540* ⊕ *www.nscd.org.*

Winter Park Ski and Ride School. For adult skiers and snowboarders, the Winter Park Ski and Ride School has half-day lessons starting at $129. Daylong children's programs, which include lunch, start at $189. ⊠ *Balcony House* ☎ *800/729–7907* ⊕ *www.winterparkresort.com.*

RENTALS

Winter Park Resort Rentals. This rental agency rents skiing and snowboarding gear from its Village location and west Portal location and includes free overnight storage. Rental equipment is also available from shops downtown. ⊠ *Zephyr Mountain Lodge, 201 Zephyr Way* ☎ *970/726–1664 Village location, 970/726–1662 west Portal location.*

NORDIC SKIING
BACKCOUNTRY SKIING
Berthoud Pass. South of Winter Park, Berthoud Pass is a hard place to define. At the top of the pass there is a former downhill skiing area—its lifts have been removed—that is popular with some backcountry skiers. There's no regular avalanche control on these former runs. Skiers and snowboarders venturing in must have their own rescue equipment, including beacons, shovels, and probes. Backcountry skiing on the slopes of the former ski area or anywhere else on Berthoud Pass is only for very experienced, well-conditioned, and properly prepared skiers and riders. You must check current avalanche conditions before starting out, although that's no guarantee. In addition to skiing the slopes of the former ski areas, many people pull into parking areas elsewhere alongside the highway over Berthoud Pass and go crosscountry or backcountry skiing. At many spots along the highway you'll see signs warning of avalanche blasting at any time with long-range weaponry. (This blasting is done to help prevent avalanches from covering the highway.) ⊠ *U.S. 40* ⊕ *berthoudpass.com.*

TRACK SKIING
Devil's Thumb Ranch. About 8 miles northwest of Winter Park, Devil's Thumb Ranch grooms about 62 miles of cross-country trails. Some skiing is along fairly level tree-lined trails; some is with more ups and downs and wide-open views. The ranch has rentals, lessons, and backcountry tours. ⊠ *3530 County Rd. 83, Tabernash* ☎ *970/726–5632, 970/726–5632* ⊕ *www.devilsthumbranch.com* 🎫 *Trail fee $20.*

Snow Mountain Ranch. Twelve miles northwest of Winter Park, Snow Mountain Ranch has a 62-mile track system that includes almost 3 miles of trails lighted for night skiing. The ranch is a YMCA facility (with discounts for members) and has added bonuses such as a sauna and an indoor pool. Lessons, rentals, and on-site lodging are available. ■TIP➔ **No trail fee for overnight guests.** ⊠ *1101 Hwy. 53, Granby* ☎ *970/887–2152, 888/613–9622* ⊕ *www.snowmountainranch.org* 🎫 *Trail fee $20.*

OTHER SPORTS AND THE OUTDOORS
GOLF
Golf Granby Ranch. Formerly known as Headwaters, Golf Granby Ranch is an 18-hole course nestled against the Rocky Mountains. The original course by Micheal Asmundson was redesigned by the Nicklaus Design firm to turn it into a more walkable course; two "family holes" were added to offer a golf experience for novices. The back nine is fraught with interesting challenges and fast greens. ⊠ *1000 Village Rd., Granby* ☎ *970/887–2709, 888/850–4615* ⊕ *www.granbyranch.com* 🎫 *$75 weekdays, $90 weekends* ⅀ *18 holes, 7210 yards, par 72.*

Pole Creek Golf Club. Designed by Denis Griffiths, Pole Creek has three 9-hole, par-36 courses and fantastic views of the mountains. You can play any combination of 18 holes, but try to get on the Ridge 9, which has particularly challenging holes with slippery greens and one of the best views in the state. The on-site eatery Bistro 28 ($$) serves three well-executed meals daily. ⊠ *5827 Hwy. 51* ☎ *970/887–9195* ⊕ *www.*

polecreekgolf.com 🎟 *$93 weekdays, $99 weekends* ⛳ *Meadow/Ranch: 18 holes, 3074 yards, par 36; Ranch/Ridge: 18 holes, 3143 yards, par 36; Ridge/Meadow: 18 holes, 3377 yards, par 36.*

HIKING

Byers Peak. At 12,804 feet, Byers Peak is one of the tallest mountains overlooking Fraser, and the highest point in the Byers Peak Wilderness Area. The trail climbs the northern ridge of Byers through lodgepole pine and Engelmann spruce forests before entering the spaciousness of the alpine tundra at around 11,200 feet. Climbers are rewarded with views of the Indian Peaks Wilderness, the Gore Range, and Middle Park. The trail is only 1½ miles, but it climbs 2,400 feet. If you aren't used to it, high altitude can catch you off guard. Take plenty of water with you and slather on the sunscreen. In summer an early morning start is best. Afternoon thunderstorms are frequent, and you should never be above the tree line during a storm with lightning. Plan on three hours for the round-trip hike. ✉ *Sulphur Ranger District, Arapaho & Roosevelt National Forests* ☎ *970/887–4100.*

HORSEBACK RIDING

Cabin Creek Stables at Devil's Thumb Ranch. For leisurely horseback-riding tours of the Fraser Valley, your best bet is Cabin Creek Stables at Devil's Thumb Ranch. ✉ *3530 Hwy. 83, Tabernash* ☎ *800/933–4339* 🌐 *www.devilsthumbranch.com* 🎟 *From $55.*

MOUNTAIN BIKING

Vasquez Creek. Winter Park is one of the leading mountain-biking destinations in the Rockies, with some 30 miles of trails crisscrossing the main part of the resort and 600 more miles off the beaten path. Vasquez Creek is an easy but fun 4½-mile trail that runs along a forest of blue spruce, fir, and aspen. The trail sticks to dirt roads with easy grades; the elevation gain is barely 600 feet. For more serious bikers the side trails have challenging climbs and rewarding vistas. ✉ *Trailhead: parking garage next to the visitor center at the junction of U.S. 40 and Vasquez Rd.*

SNOWMOBILING

Grand Adventures. This company offers snowmobile rentals and guided tours. Rates range from $85 per hour to $205 for a full-day tour. ✉ *81699 U.S. 40 S* ☎ *970/726–9247, 800/726–9247* 🌐 *www.grandadventures.com.*

SNOW TUBING

FAMILY **Fraser Snow Tubing Hill.** You can slide down this hill on an oversize inner tube and then hop on a magic carpet for a ride up to the top to do it all over again. When you get cold, head into the warming hut nearby. The hill is lighted at night, and the rate is $18 per hour. ✉ *Hwy. 72 and Fraser Valley Pkwy.* ☎ *970/726–5954* 🌐 *frasertubinghill.com* 🎟 *$18.*

WHERE TO EAT

$ AMERICAN 🍴 **Carvers.** Long a local and Denverite favorite for breakfast, this casual joint—in a new and larger location—makes Belgian waffles that are as delicious as the variety of Benedicts and scrambles with fresh orange or grapefruit juice. Lunch is also served. [$] *Average main: $8* ✉ *Kings Crossing Center, 78336 U.S. 40* ☎ *970/726–8202* 🌐 *www.carvers-wp.com* 🕒 *No dinner* ✍ *Reservations not accepted.*

$$$ AMERICAN 🍴 **Deno's Mountain Bistro.** A sizable selection of beers from around the world helps make this casual establishment the liveliest spot in town. But what sets it apart is a wine list that's comprehensive and fairly priced—a rarity in low-key Winter Park. The cellar full of fine vintages is a labor of love for Deno and his son, the powerhouse duo behind the restaurant. The menu ranges from seared yellowfin tuna to certified Angus center-cut filet, all expertly prepared and served by friendly staffers who know their stuff. [$] *Average main: $20* ✉ *78911 U.S. 40* ☎ *970/726–5332* 🌐 *www.denoswp.com* ✍ *Reservations essential.*

$$$$ AMERICAN Fodor's Choice ★ 🍴 **The Dining Room at The Lodge at Sunspot.** Reached via chairlift during the day and gondola at night, this massive log-and-stone structure set at 10,700 feet above sea level is a real stunner. Douglas-fir beams, Southwestern rugs on the walls, and a huge stone fireplace in the bar add to the rustic charm. The real draw is the view of the surrounding mountains, including the peaks marching along the Continental Divide. A prix-fixe menu includes game and fish paired with side dishes such as wild rice and potatoes roasted in olive oil and herbs. Elk Tournedos—elk tenderloin with a sun-dried cherry demi-glace and red roasted potatoes—is one example of a signature dish. Wines can be chosen to complement your meal. [$] *Average main: $38* ✉ *Top of Zephyr Express Lift* ☎ *970/726–1446* 🌐 *www.winterparkresort.com* 🕒 *Hrs vary with the season* ✍ *Reservations essential.*

$$ PIZZA FAMILY 🍴 **Hernando's Pizza and Pasta Pub.** Bring along a dollar bill that you're willing to leave on the wall. It will join thousands of others that have been drawn on, written on, and tacked up in rows around and above the bar. Nothing fancy here, just good pasta and pizzas that keep locals and regular resort visitors coming back. If you're in a creative mood, build your own pie, with a combination of the ordinary toppings, from pepperoni to sausage, then add more unusual extras like almonds or jalapeños. **TIP→ They don't take reservations, but you can call ahead for priority seating.** [$] *Average main: $14* ✉ *78199 U.S. 40* ☎ *970/726–5409* 🌐 *www.hernandospizzapub.com* ✍ *Reservations not accepted.*

$$ SOUTHERN FAMILY 🍴 **Smokin' Moe's Ribhouse & Saloon.** You can fill up here on delicious spicy smoky ribs, smoked BBQ chicken, or Southern-fried catfish served in huge portions, plus a choice of sides including creamy coleslaw, mashers and gravy, or smoky beans. Diners are served at long tables covered with checkered tablecloths, and there's a salad bar for a lighter option. While you eat, there's likely to be live music, and sometimes it's a full-on hoedown. Check out "Moe," a lifelike mannequin slouched down on a bar stool hiding behind sunglasses. [$] *Average main: $15* ✉ *63 Cooper Creek Way* ☎ *970/726–4600* 🌐 *www.smokinmoes.com* ✍ *Reservations not accepted.*

WHERE TO STAY

$$$$ RESORT FAMILY Fodor's Choice ★ 🏨 **Devil's Thumb Ranch.** Many visitors come to this 6,000-acre ranch outside Winter Park for unrivaled cross-country skiing, with 60 miles of groomed trails, but they wind up staying for the resort's comfort and privacy. **Pros:** terrific cross-country skiing and horseback riding; top-notch restaurant. **Cons:** in winter getting there can be rough; one of the pricier properties in the state; must drive to eat in any other restaurant or cook your own meals. [$] *Rooms from: $265* ✉ *3530 Hwy.*

83, Tabernash ☎ 800/933–4339 ⊕ www.devilsthumbranch.com ➵ 83 rooms, 4 suites, 15 cabins †◎† No meals.

$$$
RENTAL

☷ **Iron Horse Resort.** On the banks of the Fraser River, this condo-style hotel is ski-in ski-out, but it's removed from the resort's base village. **Pros:** truly ski-in ski-out; set in a quiet location. **Cons:** isolated area, so you must drive to the base village or to town for all the restaurants and shops; must create your own nightlife. $ *Rooms from: $230* ✉ *101 Iron Horse Way* ☎ *970/726–8851, 800/621–8190* ⊕ *www.ironhorse-resort.com* ➵ *38 suites* †◎† *No meals.*

$$
B&B/INN

☷ **Vasquez Creek Inn.** The owners of Devil's Thumb Ranch bought the little Gasthaus Eichler alongside Vasquez Creek and remodeled in a similar vein, softening the rooms with puffy pillows atop the remarkably comfortable beds and recasting in creams, golds and rusts. **Pros:** comfortable rooms; great restaurant; walking distance to town. **Cons:** you're right in the middle of town, and on busy weekends the streets in front of the hotel can be busy. $ *Rooms from: $150* ✉ *78786 U.S. 40* ☎ *970/722–1188* ⊕ *www.vasquezcreekinn.com* ➵ *15 rooms* †◎† *Breakfast.*

$$
HOTEL
FAMILY

☷ **Vintage Hotel.** Right next to the Village Cabriolet lift, the Vintage is the best value if you want to be close to the resort base. **Pros:** from door to base village in five minutes on the cabriolet; pet-friendly property. **Cons:** its popularity means it might get a bit noisy at times; you'll need to drive or take a shuttle to the town of Winter Park. $ *Rooms from: $135* ✉ *100 Winter Park Dr.* ☎ *970/726–8801, 800/472–7017* ⊕ *www. vintagehotel.com* ➵ *110 rooms, 8 suites* †◎† *No meals.*

$$$
B&B/INN

☷ **Wild Horse Inn.** Tucked into the woods on the way to Devil's Thumb Ranch, this mountain retreat is a bit off the beaten path, but your reward is complete relaxation. **Pros:** quiet at night; after an exhausting day of skiing you can book an hour with the on-site massage therapist. **Cons:** it's a 10- to 15-minute drive to get into Winter Park; must create your own nightlife; the largest, loveliest room is on the first floor near the entrance area. $ *Rooms from: $200* ✉ *1536 County Rd. 83* ☎ *970/726–0456* ⊕ *www.wildhorseinn.com* ➵ *7 rooms, 3 cabins* †◎† *Breakfast.*

$$$
RENTAL

☷ **Zephyr Mountain Lodge, Frasier Crossing, Founders Pointe, and Parrys Peak Lofts.** These are all condo complexes—some with individual hotel rooms, too—that are in the village at the base a short walk from the base lifts. **Pros:** nice places to stay in the wintertime, because they are all close to the lifts; fireplaces in most units; walk out the door and there are a few restaurants and bars. **Cons:** no air-conditioning and only limited air circulation in the units; will need a car or shuttle to head into the town of

Winter Park; owned units vary in decor. $ *Rooms from: $186* ⊠ *Zephyr Mountain Lodge, 201 Zephyr Way* ☎ *800/979–0332, 970/726–8400* ⊕ *www.zephyrmountainlodge.com* ⤳ *220 rooms* ⦿ *No meals.*

NIGHTLIFE

Cheeky Monk. One of the hot spots in the base village is the colorful Cheeky Monk, which bills itself as a Belgian beer café. ⊠ *Winter Park Village, 130 Parry Peak Way, base of lifts* ☎ *970/726–6871* ⊕ *www. thecheekymonk.com.*

Crooked Creek Saloon. For a bit of local color, head down to Fraser and the Crooked Creek Saloon. The motto here is "Eat till it hurts, drink till it feels better." Locals show up for the cheap beer during happy hour. ⊠ *401 Zerex St.* ☎ *970/726–9250* ⊕ *www.crookedcreeksalooncolorado.com.*

Ullrs Tavern. This tavern provides the closest thing to real nightlife in the area. Ullrs Tavern's small, somewhat ramshackle space attracts a younger crowd, with live music on the weekends, a DJ other nights, and a handful of pool tables. ⊠ *78415 U.S. 40* ☎ *970/726–3026.*

Winter Park Pub. The under-30 crowd tends to hang out at the lively Winter Park Pub, grooving to local bands. ⊠ *78260 U.S. 40* ☎ *970/726–4929.*

SHOPPING

SHOPPING DISTRICTS

FAMILY **Cooper Creek Square.** This square is filled with inexpensive souvenir shops and fine jewelers, upscale eateries and local cafés, plus live entertainment all summer in the courtyard. ⊠ *47 Cooper Creek Way* ☎ *970/726–8891* ⊕ *coopercreeksquare.com.*

GEORGETOWN

32 miles southwest of Winter Park via U.S. 40 and I–70; 50 miles west of Denver via I–70.

Georgetown rode the crest of the silver boom during the second half of the 19th century. Most of the impeccably maintained brick buildings that make up the town's historic district date from that period. Georgetown hasn't been tarted up, so it provides a true sense of what living was like in those rough-and-tumble times. It's a popular tourist stop in the summertime. Be sure to keep an eye out for the state's largest herd of rare bighorn sheep that often grazes alongside I–70 in this region.

GETTING HERE AND AROUND

Just west of where I–70 and U.S. 40 intersect, the downtown historic area is just a few blocks long and a few blocks wide, so park and start walking.

TIMING

Georgetown is close enough to attract day-trippers from Denver, but much of the summer the town is filled with vacationers who have come here to ride the Georgetown Loop Railroad. Weekdays are quieter than weekends.

ESSENTIALS

Visitor Information Georgetown. ⊠ *Georgetown City Hall, 404 6th St.* ☎ *303/569–2555, 888/569–1130* ⊕ *georgetown-colorado.org.* **Loveland Snow Report.** ☎ *800/736–3754* ⊕ *www.skiloveland.com.*

CLOSE UP

Eisenhower Memorial Tunnel

As you travel west along I-70 you'll reach one of the world's engineering marvels, the 8,941-foot-long Eisenhower Memorial Tunnel. Most people who drive through take its presence for granted, but until the first lanes were opened in 1973 the only route west through the mountains was the perilous Loveland Pass, a heart-pounding roller-coaster ride. In truly inclement weather the eastern and western slopes were completely cut off from each other. Authorities first proposed the tunnel in 1937. Geologists warned about unstable rock, and through more than three decades of construction, their direst predictions came true as rock walls crumbled, steel girders buckled, and gas pockets caused mysterious explosions. When the project was finally completed, more than 500,000 cubic yards of solid granite had been removed from Mount Trelease. The original cost estimate was $1 million. By the time the second bore was completed in 1979 the tunnel's cost had skyrocketed to $340 million. Today there can be a long wait during busy weekends because so many travelers use I-70.

EXPLORING

FAMILY
Fodor's Choice
★

Georgetown Loop Railroad. This 1920s narrow-gauge train connects Georgetown with the equally historic community of Silver Plume. The 6-mile round-trip excursion takes about 70 minutes, and winds through vast stands of pine and fir before crossing the 95-foot-high Devil's Gate Bridge, where the track actually loops back over itself as it gains elevation. You can add on a tour of the **Lebanon Silver Mill and Mine,** which is a separate stop between the two towns, as well as meals in the dining car. In fall and around the holidays, special trains run, including popular rides with Santa. ⊠ *100 Loop Dr.* ☎ *888/456–6777* ⊕ *www.georgetownlooprr.com* ⊠ *$25.95 for train; $34.95 with mine tour* ☉ *May–Oct., daily 10:25–2:55; Nov.–Jan. 4, dates and times vary.*

Guanella Pass Scenic Byway. South of Georgetown, the Guanella Pass Scenic Byway treats you to marvelous views of the Mount Evans Wilderness Area. Along the way—while negotiating some tight curves, especially as you head down to Grant—you'll get close views of Mount Evans as well as Grays and Torrey's peaks—two Fourteeners. It takes about 40 minutes to cross the 22-mile dirt and asphalt road. ⊠ *Hwy. 381.*

Hotel de Paris. The elaborate Hotel de Paris, built almost single-handedly by Frenchman Louis Dupuy in 1878, was one of the Old West's preeminent hostelries. Now a museum, the hotel depicts how luxuriously the rich were accommodated: Tiffany fixtures, lace curtains, and hand-carved furniture re-create an era of opulence. ⊠ *409 6th St.* ☎ *303/569–2311* ⊕ *www.hoteldeparismuseum.org* ⊠ *$7* ☉ *Jan.–Sept., Mon.–Sat. 10–5, Sun. noon–5; Oct.–Dec., Sat. 10–5, Sun. noon–5.*

DOWNHILL SKIING AND SNOWBOARDING

Loveland Ski Area. Because of its proximity to Denver (an hour's drive), lack of resort facilities and hotels, and few high-speed lifts, Loveland Ski Area is often overlooked by out-of-staters, but that's just the way locals like it. Loveland has some of the highest runs in Colorado spread across a respectable 1,800 acres serviced by 10 lifts. It's split between Loveland Valley, a good place for beginners, and Loveland Basin, a good bet for everyone else. Loveland Basin has excellent glade and open-bowl skiing and snowboarding, especially on the 2,210-foot vertical drop. Best of all, it opens early and usually stays open later than any other ski area except Arapahoe Basin. **Facilities:** 93 trails; 1,800 acres; 2,210-foot vertical drop; 10 lifts. ✉ *Georgetown* ✣ *I–70 Exit 216, 12 miles west of Georgetown* ☎ *303/571–5580, 800/736–3754* 🌐 *www.skiloveland.com* 🎟 *Lift ticket $57* 🕓 *Mid-Oct.–May, weekdays 9–4, weekends 8:30–4.*

HIKING THE CONTINENTAL DIVIDE

The Continental Divide, that iconic geographic division that sends raindrops to either the Atlantic or Pacific Ocean, makes a worthy pilgrimage for day hikers and backpackers alike in summer. The easiest way to reach the divide is to drive up U.S. Highway 6 over Loveland Pass at the Eisenhower Tunnel on I–70 and park on top of the divide. Hiking trails lead both east and west along the divide. Bring cash or a check for the $5 parking fee, and car pool if you can—parking is limited and tight during nice weather.

LESSONS AND PROGRAMS

Loveland Ski School. This ski school offers 2½-hour group "Newcomer Packages" beginning at 10 am and 1 pm for $112 including all rental gear and an all-day lift ticket. Advanced half-day lessons (a maximum of four people per group) are $92 or $102 with rental gear. ✉ *Georgetown* ☎ *303/571–5580 ext. 170* 🌐 *www.skiloveland.com.*

RENTALS

Loveland Rental Shop. Loveland Rentals has two on-mountain locations, at the basin next to the Sport Shop and in the valley next to the restaurant. You can purchase sport packages for $31, and performance packages for $45. Snowboard packages are $45; helmets run $10. ✉ *Georgetown* ☎ *303/571–5580 ext. 113 Basin Rental Shop, 303/571–5580 ext. 155 Valley Rental Shop* 🌐 *www.skiloveland.com.*

WHERE TO EAT AND STAY

$$ EUROPEAN 🍴 **Euro Grill.** Hearty portions of reasonably priced Eastern European dishes are served in this sparsely decorated but roomy eatery with alpine views. Menu options include goulash, sauerbraten, and potato pancakes, as well as superb chicken, veal, and pork schnitzels. The apple schnitzel is also worth saving room for at the end. The selection of Czech beers is ideal for the menu, and the patio is a welcome warm-weather option. [$] *Average main: $16* ✉ *1025 Rose St.* ☎ *303/569–2126* 🌐 *www.eurogrillrestaurant.com* 💳 *No credit cards.*

$$ HOTEL FAMILY **Georgetown Mountain Inn.** Next door to the Old Georgetown Railroad, this basic inn has rooms decorated with Western-style wood furniture and Southwestern blankets. **Pros:** right by the station for the Georgetown Loop railroad; Colorado rooms enhanced with pine-paneled walls and hand-hewn log headboards and bedside tables are particularly nice. **Cons:** several blocks away from the historic downtown; some guests have complained about noise. [$] *Rooms from: $145* ✉ *1100 Rose St.* ☎ *303/569–3201, 800/884–3201* 🌐 *www.georgetownmountaininn.com* 🛏 *32 rooms, 1 suite* 🍴 *No meals.*

$$ B&B/INN **Hotel Chateau Chamonix.** With its log exterior and green roof, this hotel doesn't look exceptional for the region outside, but inside it's a lovely property put together with care by local owners. **Pros:** some rooms overlook a stream and have a two-person hot tub on a porch; extras like espresso-cappuccino machines in the rooms. **Cons:** on one of the town's busy main streets; not within easy walking distance of the historic downtown area. [$] *Rooms from: $155* ✉ *1414 Argentine St.* ☎ *303/569–1109, 888/569–1109* 🌐 *www.HotelChateauChamonix.com* 🛏 *10 rooms* 🍴 *Breakfast.*

SHOPPING

ART GALLERIES

Grizzly Creek Gallery. This gallery has wonderfully scenic large-scale photographs of the Rockies and wildlife. ✉ *512 6th St.* ☎ *303/569–0433* 🌐 *www.grizzlycreekgallery.com.*

4

SUMMIT COUNTY

Updated by
Aimee Heckel

Summit County, a mere hour's drive from the Denver Metro Area on a straight shot up I–70, is Denver's playground. The wide-open mountain park ringed by 13,000- to 14,000-foot peaks greets westbound travelers minutes after they pop out the west portal of the Eisenhower Tunnel. The sharp-toothed Gore Range rises to the northwest and the Tenmile Range gathers up behind Breckenridge. Resting in the center of this bowl are the sapphire waters of Dillon Reservoir, an artificial lake fed by Blue River.

In winter, Summit County is packed with tourists and Front Range day-trippers skiing the steeps at Breckenridge, Keystone, Arapahoe Basin, and Copper Mountain. The high density of first-rate ski resorts generally keeps lift lines low, particularly on weekdays. In summer, the steady westbound traffic is mostly SUVs stacked high with kayaks and mountain bikes.

Summit County, as its name implies, is relatively high. The town of Breckenridge sits at 9,603 feet (Aspen by comparison is at 7,908 feet), and the resort's highest ski lift tops out just shy of 13,000 feet. Visitors from sea level should take their time getting acclimated. Even Denverites find themselves breathless in the thin air. Drink lots of water and rest your first few days. There will be plenty of time to play.

ORIENTATION AND PLANNING

GETTING ORIENTED

The great east–west Colorado corridor I–70 cleaves through the heart of Summit County, punching west from Denver past Idaho Springs and Georgetown. The traffic here can be heavy and fast; everyone is in a hurry to make it through the Eisenhower Tunnel, the traditional gateway to Summit County. Those with an extra half hour and a yearning for hairpin turns, shaggy mountain goats, and 100-mile views opt for U.S. 6 over Loveland Pass and the Continental Divide. As it drops into the Summit County Basin on the west side of the divide, U.S. 6 passes Arapahoe Basin and Keystone Ski Resort before merging with I–70. Both roads skirt Dillon Reservoir with its shoreline communities of Dillon and Frisco. The highway quickly disappears back into a narrow mountain valley and climbs to Copper Mountain and then up and over Vail Pass.

Keystone and Arapahoe Basin. Tucked up a western valley off the Continental Divide, Keystone and Arapahoe Basin tend to attract more of a local—and hardier—ski crowd; and hikers in summer. Keystone is an intimate resort town but "A-Basin" is little more than a ski area.

TOP REASONS TO GO

Festival fun: Breckenridge hosts numerous festivals, including the aptly named Spring Fever Festival in April, and the weeklong Ullr Festival in January.

Mining heritage: It was gold that built Colorado in the 1800s, and this legacy is alive and well in the rejuvenated mining town of Leadville.

Mountain waters: Nothing beats a day of lake kayaking or fishing among the many wooded islets on Lake Dillon, the reservoir that is the heart of Summit County.

Skiing choices: You won't find more choices to ski and ride within snowball-throw's distance of one another than in Summit County, many a mere hour's drive from the Denver Metro Area.

Trail biking: Sure, there are plenty of single-track rides, but the real draw is the glorious paved bike trail that runs from Dillon up and over the mountains to Vail.

4

Lake Dillon and Breckenridge. Dillon and Frisco are twin towns hugging the shores of Dillon Reservoir, a sparkling human-made lake. Skiers will bypass both for Breckenridge, the largest ski area in Summit County. "Breck" has a blend of authentic Colorado character with a flashy dose of upscale lodges and high-end condos.

Copper Mountain and Leadville. Farther west on I–70, Copper Mountain makes up for a lack of mountain charm with its near-perfect ski mountain. The high-altitude mountain town of Leadville will leave you breathless, both from the thin air and from the gorgeous views of Colorado's highest peak, 14,440-foot Mount Elbert.

PLANNING

WHEN TO GO

Summit County is a haven for winter enthusiasts: the resorts of Arapahoe Basin and Breckenridge—and nearby Loveland in Clear Creek County—are so high that the ski season often dawns here weeks before it does in the rest of the state, with Arapahoe Basin and Loveland competing to see who has the longest season, which can begin as early as October and end as late as July. The altitude also means that it can snow on any day of the year, so be prepared. Traffic, particularly on the I–70 approaches to the Eisenhower Tunnel and the Georgetown-to–Idaho Springs stretch, moves at a snail's pace around weekend rush hours—noon to 10 pm on Friday and all day Sunday.

GETTING HERE AND AROUND

AIR TRAVEL

Denver International Airport (DEN) is the gateway to the attractions and ski resorts in Summit County. The airport is an hour's drive from the Continental Divide along I–70.

TRANSFERS To and from Summit County (Breckenridge, Copper Mountain, Dillon, Frisco, and Keystone), use Colorado Mountain Express and 453 Taxi, which have regular service to and from the Denver airport.

Airport Contact **Denver International Airport (DEN).** ✉ *8500 Pena Blvd., Denver* ☎ *800/247–2336* ⊕ *www.flydenver.com.*

Airport Transfer **Colorado Mountain Express.** ☎ *970/926–9800, 800/525–6363* ⊕ *www.coloradomountainexpress.com.* **453-Taxi.** ☎ *970/453–8294.*

BUS OR SHUTTLE TRAVEL

All the resorts run free or inexpensive shuttles between the ski villages and the slopes. Summit Stage provides free public transportation to town and ski areas, in and between ski areas in Summit County.

Shuttle Contact **Summit Stage.** ☎ *970/668–0999* ⊕ *www.summitstage.com.*

CAR TRAVEL

The hardest part about driving in the High Rockies is keeping your eyes on the road. A glacier-carved canyon off to your left, a soaring mountain ridge to your right, and there, standing on the shoulder, a bull elk. Some of the most scenic routes aren't necessarily the most direct. The Eisenhower Tunnel sweeps thousands of cars daily beneath the mantle of the Continental Divide, whereas only several hundred drivers choose the slower, but more spectacular, Loveland Pass. Some of the most beautiful byways, like the Mount Evans Scenic and Historic Drive, are one-way roads.

Although it is severely overcrowded, I–70 is still the quickest and most direct route from Denver to Summit County. The interstate slices through the state, separating it into northern and southern halves. Breckenridge is south of I–70 on Highway 9; Leadville and Ski Cooper are south of I–70 along U.S. 24 and Highway 91.

The most convenient place for visitors to rent a car is at the Denver International Airport. Gasoline is readily available along I–70 and its arteries, but when venturing into more remote areas be sure that you have enough fuel to get there and back. Blinding snowstorms can appear out of nowhere on the high passes at any time of the year. Chains aren't normally required for passenger vehicles on highways, but it's a good idea to carry them. A shovel isn't a bad idea, either. The highway shuts down during severe snowstorms and blizzards. Keep your eyes peeled for mule deer and for bighorn sheep, especially along the stretch of I–70 from Idaho Springs to the Eisenhower Tunnel.

PARKS AND RECREATION AREAS

Summit County is perched in a 9,000-foot-high park (a wide valley surrounded by peaks) with Lake Dillon at its recreational heart.

Arapaho National Forest. The wild Gore Range northwest of Lake Dillon is protected within the Eagles Nest Wilderness Area, administered by the Arapaho National Forest. As in all wilderness areas in Colorado, motorized or mechanized vehicles (forestry-speak for mountain bikes) are prohibited. You can tackle the backcountry peaks on your own two feet or on horseback. ☎ *970/295-6600* ⊕ *www.fs.fed.us.*

The Blue River, which bisects the county south to north and is the lifeblood of Lake Dillon, has gold-medal fishing beginning below Lake Dillon to the Green Mountain Reservoir.

RESTAURANTS

Whereas the restaurants in the celeb resorts of Aspen and Vail mimic the sophistication and style of New York and Los Angeles, Summit County eateries specialize in pub food and Mexican cuisine for calorie-hungry hikers, skiers, and boaters, with the exception of a few more urbane spots in Breckenridge. You won't find much sushi here, but you will find fish tacos, shepherd's pies, and burgers with every imaginable topping. Hearty, reasonably priced comfort food is served at a number of cozy brewpubs along with handcrafted local suds like Dam Straight Lager, Avalanche Ale, and Backcountry Brewery.

HOTELS

Summit County is a great place for history buffs looking for redone Victorian mining mansions–cum–bed-and-breakfasts and budget hunters who want affordable rooms close to the slopes. The county probably has the highest density of condominium units in the state. The competition tends to keep prices lower than in other resort towns. Note that staff at hotels in the region are sometimes young and inexperienced, which may result in less-than-desirable service at some otherwise excellent properties. Also note that many accommodations do not have air-conditioning—beware that rooms with southern exposure warm up quickly. Summer nights, however, are often cool enough in the mountains that opening the windows will do the trick. *Hotel reviews have been shortened. For full information, visit Fodors.com.*

WHAT IT COSTS				
	$	**$$**	**$$$**	**$$$$**
Restaurants	under $13	$13–$18	$19–$25	over $25
Hotels	under $121	$121–$170	$171–$230	over $230

Restaurant prices are the average cost of a main course at dinner or, if dinner is not served, at lunch, excluding 7.75%–12.7% tax. Hotel prices are the lowest cost of a standard double room in high season, excluding service charges and 8.8%–12.1% tax.

KEYSTONE AND ARAPAHOE BASIN

Just 90 miles west of Denver over Loveland Pass or through the Eisenhower Tunnel, Keystone and Arapahoe Basin are among the closest ski resorts to the Front Range. Given their location hugging the Continental Divide's western flank—both are surrounded by high-altitude peaks topping 12,000 feet—they are also among the highest resorts in the state. You can reach both by taking I–70 across the divide to Dillon and then following U.S. 6 south and east up the narrow valley.

KEYSTONE

8 miles southeast of Dillon via U.S. 6; 69 miles west of Denver.

Fodor's Choice ★ One of the region's most laid-back destinations, Keystone is understandably popular with families and, as the state's largest night skiing operation (with lifts running until 8 pm), has long been a local favorite. Its trails are spread across three adjoining peaks: Dercum Mountain, North Peak, and the Outback. Through the years, as the resort added more runs, it morphed from a beginner's paradise on Keystone Mountain to an early-season training stop for the national ski teams that practice on the tougher and bumpier terrain on North Peak. Keystone also has full-day guided snowcat tours. Today it's a resort for all types of skiers and riders, whether they prefer gentle slopes, cruising, or high-adrenaline challenges on the Outback's steep bowls.

The planners were sensitive to the environment, favoring colors and materials that blend inconspicuously with the natural surroundings. Lodging, shops, and restaurants are in Lakeside Village, the older part of the resort, and in River Run, a newer area at the base of the gondola that has become the heart of Keystone. Everything here is operated by Keystone, which makes planning a vacation one-stop shopping.

GETTING HERE AND AROUND
The easiest way to travel to and around Summit County is to rent a car at Denver International Airport. Catching one of the numerous shuttles up to the ski areas and then taking advantage of the free transportation by Summit Stage (taxi service is also available) is a more economical route, but requires patience and a good timetable. You'll want a car to reach both resorts, but once there both Keystone and A-Basin are easily navigated on foot.

WHEN TO GO
From late October to late April winter sports rule. But Keystone is quickly becoming a magnet in summer, with a small lake for water sports, mountain biking and hiking trails, two highly respected golf courses, and outdoor concerts and special events.

ESSENTIALS
Transportation Contacts 453-Taxi. ☎ *970/453–8294.*

Visitor Information Keystone Resort. ☎ *970/496–2316, 877/625–1556* ⊕ *www.keystoneresort.com.* **Keystone Snow Report.** ☎ *970/496–4111 Press 1* ⊕ *www.keystoneresort.com/ski-and-snowboard/snow-report.aspx.*

DOWNHILL SKIING AND SNOWBOARDING

FAMILY
Fodor's Choice ★ **Keystone.** What you see from the base of the mountain is only a fraction of the terrain you can enjoy when you ski or snowboard at Keystone. There's plenty more to Keystone Mountain, and much of it is geared to novice and intermediate skiers. The Schoolmarm Trail has 3½ miles of runs where you can practice turns. Dercum Mountain is easily reached from the base via high-speed chairs or the River Run gondola. You can ski or ride down the back side of Dercum Mountain to reach North Peak, a mix of groomed cruising trails and ungroomed bump runs. Keystone recently added a family ski trail, along with green/

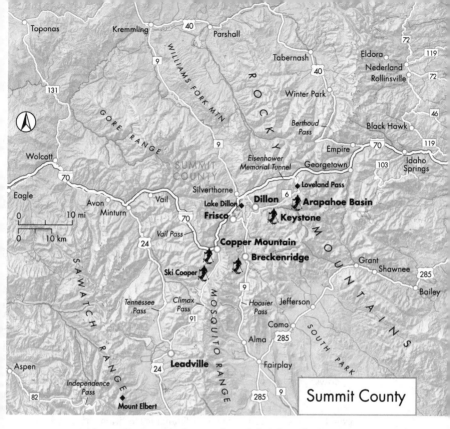

Summit County

blue trails through the woods with kid-friendly features, like tunnels and bridges. Keystone has a variety of instructional programs, from half-day group lessons to specialty clinics, including mogul classes and women's seminars.

If you prefer to bypass North Peak, the River Run gondola is a short walk from the Outpost gondola, which takes you to the Outpost Lodge (home to the Alpenglow Stube, which at 11,444 feet above sea level is advertised as the "highest gourmet restaurant in the country"). From here it's an easy downhill run to the third mountain, appropriately named the Outback because of its wilderness setting. Some glades have trees thinned just enough for skiers and riders who are learning to explore gladed terrain; other sections are reserved for advanced skiers. Weather permitting, the resort also has snowcat tours that whisk you up to powder skiing on some of the state's steepest terrain.

One of the most popular nonskiing or -boarding sports at Keystone is tubing. Both Adventure Point at the summit of Dercum Mountain and the Keystone Nordic Center have tube rentals and runs. Adventure Point's hills are lift-serviced, whereas the Nordic Center is more of a traditional sledding hill designed for younger kids. Personal sleds and tubes are not allowed.

Rental packages (skis, boots, and poles, or snowboards and boots) start at around $34 per day for a basic package but increase quickly for high-performance gear. Cheaper ski and snowboard stores are in Breckenridge, Dillon, and Frisco. **Facilities:** 131 trails; 3,148 acres; 3,128-foot vertical drop; 20 lifts. ⊠ *U.S. 6* ☎ *800/239–1639* ⊕ *www.keystoneresort.com* ⊠ *Lift ticket from $99* ☉ *Early Nov.–early Apr.; call for hrs.*

> **BIGHORN SHEEP**
>
> Keep your eyes peeled on the northern slopes of I–70 as you drive up to Summit County from Denver (your right side). Herds of bighorn sheep congregate around Georgetown, often right off the highway.

NORDIC SKIING

Keystone Nordic Center. This center has 9 miles of groomed trails and access to 35 miles of trails available for skiing and snowshoeing. Lessons and rentals of cross-country skis and snowshoes are available. ⊠ *155 River Course Dr.* ☎ *970/496–4275* ⊕ *www.keystoneresort.com/activities/nordic-center.aspx.*

OTHER SPORTS AND THE OUTDOORS

GOLF

Keystone Golf. With 36 challenging holes, Keystone lures golfers as soon as the snow melts. **Keystone Ranch,** designed by Robert Trent Jones Jr., has a links-style front nine; the back nine has a traditional mountain-valley layout. Holes play past lodgepole pines, meander around sage meadows, and include some carries across water. **The River Course** is a par-71 stunner designed by Michael Hurdzan and Dana Fry. The front nine runs around the Snake River, whereas the back nine threads through a stand of lodgepole pines. Dramatic elevation changes, bunkers, and water hazards combine to test golfers of all abilities. Add magnificent views of the Continental Divide and Lake Dillon, and it's easy to see why this course is so popular. ⊠ *1239 Keystone Ranch Rd.* ☎ *800/464–3494* ⊕ *www.keystonegolf.com* ⊠ *Keystone Ranch, $125; The River Course, $150* ⅄ *Keystone Ranch: 18 holes, 7090 yards, par 72; The River Course: 18 holes, 6886 yards, par 71.*

ICE-SKATING

FAMILY **Ice-Skating Rink.** In winter, 5-acre Keystone Lake freezes to become the country's largest outdoor ice-skating rink. You can rent skates, sleds, or even hockey sticks for an impromptu game. Lessons in figure skating and hockey are available. Weather permitting, skating runs from late November to early March. Another smaller ice rink is also available in River Run. ⊠ *Lakeside Village* ☎ *800/354–4386* ⊕ *www.keystoneresort.com* ⊠ *From $6.*

WHERE TO EAT

$$$$ ✕ **Alpenglow Stube.** The competition has heated up in recent years, but
AMERICAN Alpenglow Stube remains among the finest mountaintop restaurants in
Fodor'sChoice Colorado. The exposed wood beams, a stone fireplace, and floral uphol-
★ stery make it elegant and cozy. At night the gondola ride to get here alone is worth the cost of the meal. Dinner is à la carte or a seven-course extravaganza, starting perhaps with the signature ragoût of blue crab,

and followed by delights such as pepper-dusted wild boar tenderloin. In winter, lunch is two or four courses and equally delectable, with excellent pasta specials. Sunday brunch features seafood and dessert bars. Remove your ski boots and put on the plush slippers reserved for diners. [$] *Average main: $110* ✉ *North Peak, 21996 U.S. 6* ☎ *970/496–4386* 🌐 *www.keystoneresort.com* 🕓 *Closed late Apr.–early June and mid-Sept.–late Nov.* ✍ *Reservations essential.*

$ AMERICAN 🍴 **Inxpot.** A blend of books, coffee, martinis, and some of the best breakfast and lunch sandwiches you can get your hands on make this cozy shop a local favorite. Collages covering ceiling tiles and worn couches give this spot its character, and the après-ski rehashing and games of chess bring in the community. Order the Frenchman for a croissant loaded with turkey breast, spinach, and melted brie, and slathered with craisin pecan mayo. If you're thirsty, try one of several local brews or a steamy, hot buttered rum on chilly days. [$] *Average main: $10* ✉ *195 River Run Rd., River Run Village* ☎ *970/262–3707* 🌐 *www.inxpot.com.*

$$$$ AMERICAN 🍴 **Keystone Ranch.** This 1930s homestead was once part of a working cattle ranch, and cowboy memorabilia is strewn throughout, nicely blending with stylish throw rugs and Western crafts. The gorgeous and massive stone fireplace is a cozy backdrop for dessert, or sipping an aperitif or after-dinner coffee. The seasonal five-course menu emphasizes local ingredients, including farm-raised game and fresh fish. You're in luck if the menu includes elk with wild mushrooms in juniper sauce with quince relish. [$] *Average main: $78* ✉ *Keystone Ranch Golf Course, 1239 Keystone Ranch Rd.* ☎ *970/496–4386* 🌐 *www.keystoneresort.com* 🕓 *No lunch Oct.–May. Closed Sun. and Mon.* ✍ *Reservations essential.*

$$ AMERICAN 🍴 **Kickapoo Tavern.** This rustic bar and grill in Jackpine Lodge has local microbrews on tap and big portions of home-style dishes such as Cajun pasta, hearty two-mile-high meatloaf, and burritos said to be "as big as a barn." The central location, pleasant outdoor patio, and TVs tuned to sporting events keep the place hopping both après ski and après night ski. [$] *Average main: $18* ✉ *129 River Run Rd., River Run Village* ☎ *970/468–0922* 🌐 *www.kickapootavern.com.*

$$$$ MODERN AMERICAN 🍴 **Ski Tip Lodge Restaurant.** In this ski lodge dating from the 1880s, almost everything on the menu melts in your mouth. The four-course, prix-fixe dinner is a favorite in the area for Colorado-spun American cuisine. Main courses have included whiskey sage–glazed muscovy duck, peppered bacon-wrapped buffalo tenderloin, and thyme-seared wild Alaskan halibut. The delicious homemade bread and soup make for a memorable beginning. Adjourn to the cozy lounge for the decadent desserts and specialty coffees. Swing by for après ski in winter and cocktails on the patio in summer. It's closed briefly during the fall and spring shoulder seasons. [$] *Average main: $75* ✉ *764 Montezuma Rd., 1 mile off U.S. 6* ☎ *970/496–4386, 800/354–4386* 🌐 *www.keystoneresort.com* 🕓 *No lunch* ✍ *Reservations essential.*

WHERE TO STAY

$$$ RESORT 🏨 **Keystone Lodge & Spa.** The cinder-block structure gives no hint of the gracious, pampered living just inside the door. **Pros:** one of the larger properties in the resort; spa; dog-friendly. **Cons:** rooms are small; hot tubs get crowded. [$] *Rooms from: $215* ✉ *22010 U.S. 6* ☎ *877/753–9786, 970/496–4500* 🌐 *www.keystoneresort.com* 🛏 *152 rooms* 🍴 *No meals.*

$$ B&B/INN 🏨 **Ski Tip Lodge.** Opened as a stop along the stagecoach route back in the 1880s, this property was turned into the state's first ski lodge in the 1940s by skiing pioneers Max and Edna Dercum. **Pros:** good location for the price; on-site restaurant; romantic. **Cons:** small rooms; not near the lifts; some rooms share bathrooms. [$] *Rooms from: $149* ✉ *764 Montezuma Rd., Dillon* ☎ *970/496–4500, 877/753–9786* 🌐 *www.keystoneresort.com* 🛏 *10 rooms* 🍴 *Breakfast.*

KEYSTONE LODGING ALTERNATIVES

Keystone Resort. This company operates many of the lodgings at the resort, which range from hotel-style rooms at the Keystone Lodge and the Inn at Keystone, to a wide range of condominiums. Many of the accommodations are centered around Lakeside Village and River Run, among other neighborhoods. Free shuttles ferry visitors to other parts of the resort. ✉ *100 Dercum Square* ☎ *877/753–9786* 🌐 *www.keystoneresort.com* ☞ *With any two-night stay or longer booked through Keystone, kids 12 and younger ski for free.*

NIGHTLIFE

Goat Soup and Whiskey. Across from Mountain View Plaza, the Goat Soup and Whiskey has two bars filled with twenty- and thirtysomethings drinking whiskey and beer. There's live music during ski season. ✉ *22954 U.S. 6* ☎ *970/513–9344* 🌐 *www.soupandwhiskey.com.*

Snake River Saloon. Live music with rock and roll leanings makes the Snake River Saloon a good spot to stop for a beer. The fun-loving crowd spans all ages. In case you want dinner before dancing, the restaurant is a local favorite for American fare like surf & turf and Colorado T-bone steak. ✉ *23074 U.S. 6* ☎ *970/468–2788* 🌐 *www.snakeriversaloon.com.*

SHOPPING

SPAS

Spa at Keystone Lodge. Beyond a deceiving cinder block stairwell, this spa is blessedly warm and naturally lighted. It includes 11 treatment rooms where guests can layer on signature treatments as part of a Journey series, like 100 minutes of massage and facial (Bliss) or five hours of true pampering that includes a scrub, manicure, and pedicure (Head in the Clouds). Guests sip complimentary champagne or Tazo tea before their treatments in the relaxation room. Arrive 30 minutes ahead of time to properly unwind or jumpstart your relaxation with a quick steam or sauna. Use of outdoor heated pool, indoor and outdoor Jacuzzis, dry sauna, steam room, and fitness facilities are complimentary. ✉ *Keystone Lodge & Spa, 22101 U.S. 6* ☎ *970/496–4118* 🌐 *www.keystoneresort.com.*

ARAPAHOE BASIN

6 miles northeast of Keystone via U.S. 6.

Arapahoe Basin was the first ski area to be built in Summit County. It has changed—but not too much—since its construction in the 1940s, and most of A-Basin's dedicated skiers like it that way. It's America's highest ski area, with a base elevation of 10,780 feet and a summit of 13,050 feet. Many of the runs start above the timberline, ensuring breathtaking views (and the need for some extra breaths). Aficionados love the seemingly endless intermediate and expert terrain and the wide-open bowls that stay open into June (sometimes July). "Beachin' at the Basin" has long been one of the area's most popular summer activities.

GETTING HERE AND AROUND

Given the remoteness of Arapahoe Basin, a car is the best way to go.

WHEN TO GO

Skiing is the highlight here. That said, winter in this high-country spot can begin in early October and last into June. In the summer, go hiking, mountain biking or sign up for Yoga on the Mountain and the Summit Challenge Trail Run and BBQ.

ESSENTIALS

Visitor Information Arapahoe Basin Ski Area. ☎ *970/468–0718, 888/272–7246* ⊕ *www.arapahoebasin.com.* **Arapahoe Basin Snow Report.** ☎ *970/468–0718* ⊕ *www.arapahoebasin.com.*

DOWNHILL SKIING AND SNOWBOARDING

Arapahoe Basin. What makes Arapahoe Basin delightful is also what makes it dreadful in bad weather: its elevation. Much of Arapahoe's skiing is above the tree line, and when a storm moves in, you can't tell up from down.

If that sounds unpleasant, consider the other side of the coin: on sunny spring days Arapahoe is a wonderful place, because the tundra surrounded by craggy peaks is reminiscent of the Alps. Intermediate-level skiers can have a great time here on the easier trails. But A-Basin is best known for its expert challenges: the East Wall, a steep face with great powder-skiing possibilities; Pallavicini, a wide tree-lined run; and the West Wall, from which skiers of varying degrees of bravado like to launch themselves. After a long battle with the U.S. Forest Service, A-Basin won permission to install a snowmaking machine for certain trails. Daily ski-rental packages (skis, boots, and poles) start at $29, and snowboard packages at $37. Ski stores in Breckenridge, Dillon, and Frisco are even cheaper. **Facilities:** 109 trails; 960 acres; 2,270-foot vertical drop; 8 lifts. ✉ *28194 U.S. 6, Keystone* ☎ *970/468–0718, 888/272–7246* ⊕ *www.arapahoebasin.com* 🎫 *Lift ticket from $85* ☉ *Late Oct.–mid-June or early July.*

LESSONS AND PROGRAMS

Arapahoe Basin Central Reservations. Contact Arapahoe Basin Central Reservations for information on regular classes and ski clinics. ☎ *970/468–0718* ⊕ *www.arapahoebasin.com.*

LAKE DILLON AND BRECKENRIDGE

Lake Dillon, a 3,233-acre artificial reservoir with four narrow arms and almost 27 miles of shoreline, sits at the heart of Summit County. The lake is guarded on the northwest by the steep Gore Range and on the southwest by the Tenmile Range (a part of the Mosquito Range), and to the east by the Continental Divide. Along the northern shore sit Dillon and her sister town Silverthorne, while Frisco hugs a southwest arm of the lake. Breckenridge is roughly 5 miles south of Lake Dillon, backed up against the Tenmile Range.

DILLON

73 miles west of Denver via I–70.

Dillon can't seem to sit still. Founded in 1883 as a stagecoach stop and trading post for men working in the mines, Dillon has had to pack up and move three times since. It was first relocated to be closer to the Utah and Northern Railroad, and then to take advantage of the nearby rivers. Finally, in 1955, bigwigs in Denver drew up plans to dam the Blue River so they could quench the capital's growing thirst. The reservoir would submerge Dillon under more than 150 feet of water. Once again the town was dismantled and moved, this time to pine-blanketed hills mirrored in sapphire water. Residents agreed that no building in the new location would be taller than 30 feet, so as not to obstruct the view of the reservoir, which is appropriately called Lake Dillon.

GETTING HERE AND AROUND

Private car is the best way to explore Dillon, although in summer a network of bicycle trails around the reservoir makes pedaling an attractive option.

WHEN TO GO

Dillon is a hub for all seasons. In winter, during ski season, Dillon is the place to get gas, groceries, and directions before heading to Keystone, A-Basin, Breck, or Copper. Beginning with the snowmelt in May, Dillon unfolds as a center for hiking, biking, and water sports. Dillon also is home to Summit County's largest farmers' market every Friday in warmer weather.

ESSENTIALS

Visitor Information Summit Chamber of Commerce. ☎ *970/668–2051* ⊕ *www.summitchamber.org.*

EXPLORING

Fodor's Choice ★ **Lake Dillon.** Resting in the heart of Summit County at 9,017 feet is the Front Range's answer to a day at the beach—beautiful Lake Dillon and her two ports, Dillon, just off I–70 on the south, and Frisco, off I–70 and Highway 9 on the west. The lake is actually backed up by a 231-foot earth-filled dam that fills the valley where Dillon once sat. During the frequent Western droughts, when water levels can drop dramatically, collectors wander along the exposed shores hunting for artifacts from this Rocky Mountain Atlantis.

It was these droughts that inspired the Denver Water Board to construct the reservoir and divert the water through the Harold D. Roberts Tunnel, beneath the Continental Divide. Below the mile-long dam the Blue River babbles past the outlet shopping haven and turns into miles of gold-medal fly-fishing waters on its journey north.

The lake has been an aquatic boon to both the Front Range and the exploding Summit County population. There are more than 27 miles of gravel beaches, marshes, peninsulas, and wooded islets for picnickers to enjoy, many accessible from a 7½-mile paved trail along the northern shores, or from the informal dirt paths elsewhere. Gaze out at the deep blue waters from Sapphire Point Lookout (a short ½-mile hike on the south side of the lake) any nice day, and you'll see a flotilla of motorboats, sailboats, canoes, kayaks, and sailboarders dancing in the waves. Dillon Reservoir is the highest deep-water marina in North America and attracts sailors from all over the world to participate in regattas. In winter the frozen waters are enjoyed by ice anglers and cross-country skiers.

Because the lake is considered a drinking-water source, swimming is not permitted, and the lake is patrolled vigorously by Summit County sheriffs. Just because you don't see a patrol boat doesn't mean they can't see you; their surveillance is done with binoculars. ⊠ *Dillon.*

SPORTS AND THE OUTDOORS

BICYCLING

Fodor's Choice ★ Summit County attracts cyclists with its 55 miles of paved bike paths and extensive network of backcountry trails. There are dozens of trailheads from which you can travel through gentle rolling terrain, up the sides of mountains, and along ridges for spectacular views. Starting in Dillon, you could bike around the reservoir to Frisco. From there you could ride the Blue River Pathway, largely along the river, to Breckenridge. Or you could ride through beautiful Tenmile Canyon all the way to Copper Mountain. If you're really fit, you could even continue your ride over Vail Pass and down into Vail Village.

Summit County Chamber of Commerce Information Center. This information center has detailed information about bike trails in the area. Ask for a free Summit County Bike Trail Guide that outlines, with great detail, your options. Listings include distance, difficulty, and elevation changes. ⊠ *246 Rainbow Dr., Frisco* ☎ *970/668–2051* ⊕ *www. summitchamber.org.*

BOATING

Dillon Marina. At Dillon Marina you can rent a sailboat, pontoon boat, or runabout to play on the water, or get certified by the American Sailing Association through the sailing school. Reserve ahead in high season. It claims to be the world's highest deep-water marina, and also offers lakeside dining at 2 miles above sea level. ⊠ *Take I–70 Exit 205 to U.S. 6, and follow signs to the marina, Lake Dillon* ☎ *970/468–5100* ⊕ *www.dillonmarina.com.*

FAMILY **Frisco Bay Marina.** This marina is less crowded than Dillon and has quick access to the numerous pine-cloaked islands along the western shores. Here you can rent pontoon boats, fishing boats, canoes, and kayaks.

Take I–70 Exit 203 to Highway 9 to Main Street, and follow signs to the marina. ✉ *902 E. Main St., Frisco* ☎ *970/668–4334* 🌐 *www.townoffrisco.com/play/frisco-bay-marina/general-info*.

FISHING

Cutthroat Anglers. A favorite with locals, Cutthroat Anglers has a pro shop chock-full of gear for avid fly-fishermen. Their wade trips are good for beginners; full-day float-trip adventures are a favorite for those with a bit more experience. The wade trip is available in half-day and full-day versions. ✉ *400 Blue River Pkwy., Silverthorne* ☎ *970/262–2878* 🌐 *www.fishcolorado.com*.

GOLF

Raven Golf Club at Three Peaks. *Colorado Avid Golfer* magazine named this 18-hole beauty the best mountain course and the best golf experience in Colorado, both for its technically challenging layout and for its rich, natural beauty, including stands of pine and aspen trees and visiting elk and deer herds. Each hole on the par-72 course has dramatic views of the Gore Mountain range. ✉ *2929 N. Golden Eagle Rd., Silverthorne* ☎ *970/262–3636* 🌐 *www.ravenatthreepeaks.com* 🎫 *$169* ⛳ *18 holes, 7413 yards, par 72*.

WHERE TO EAT

$$ AMERICAN 🍴 **Dillon Dam Brewery.** At this popular brewery, one of the largest brewpubs in the nation, you can belly up to the horseshoe-shape bar and sample ales and lagers while you munch on burgers, sandwiches, or pub grub. The menu is steps above average bar food. Start with the Asiago ale dip, made with the brewery's own extra pale ale. Other tasty options include the honey sriracha salmon entrée and the bison meat loaf. Carnivores and vegetarians alike have plenty to choose from, and there are also many gluten-free items. [$] *Average main: $18* ✉ *100 Little Dam St.* ☎ *970/262–7777* 🌐 *www.dambrewery.com*.

$$ SOUTHWESTERN FAMILY 🍴 **Red Mountain Grill.** The colorful decor of this American Southwest joint is something you'll remember. High-backed chairs ring the tables, stone buttresses arch toward vaulted ceilings, and mobiles of round- and star-shaped metal lights dangle above. The menu is packed with surprises, like Fat Tire Ale–battered fish tacos or a green-chili cheeseburger made with local beef. If you go during a football game, be prepared to wait on drinks and tables, or you can escape to the patio, a perfect place for taking advantage of happy hour during the summer. [$] *Average main: $15* ✉ *703 E. Anemone Trail* ☎ *970/468–1010* 🌐 *www.redmountaingrill.com*.

SHOPPING

Outlets at Silverthorne. A sprawling complex with more than 50 discount factory outlets, the shops here are color-coded for your shopping convenience. The Blue Village has Calvin Klein, J.Crew, Polo Ralph Lauren, and other upscale clothing shops. If you need outdoor gear, the Red Village is home to Eddie Bauer and Columbia Sportswear. For kids' clothing, head to the Gymboree Outlet in the Green Village. ✉ *246-V Rainbow Dr., I–70 Exit 205* ☎ *970/468–9440* 🌐 *www.outletsatsilverthorne.com*.

CLOSE UP

Colorado Golf

It isn't easy to define "golf" in Colorado, because the topography varies so dramatically, from the rolling plains near the Kansas state line to the flat-top buttes and mesas at the western end of the state. In the Rockies, the state's central spine, the courses climb up and down mountainsides; in the foothills the fairways roll over more gentle terrain and over canyons; and down in the cities many layouts march back and forth in confined spaces.

ROCKY MOUNTAIN COURSES

Mountain golf has unique challenges, but vacationers flock to the high-country golf courses because of their dramatic scenery. "Aim for that peak" is an oft-repeated phrase. It doesn't matter whether you are playing the Jack Nicklaus–designed 27-hole municipal course in Breckenridge, the Club at Crested Butte, or the golf course at the Snowmass Club, there's bound to be a hole where that description fits.

Resort courses, often available only to guests, are spread around mountain towns from Snowmass and Steamboat to Vail and Telluride. For example, if you stay at certain properties in Vail and Beaver Creek, you get access to the Tom Fazio course (woven through sagebrush-covered hills) and the Greg Norman course (spread around a broad valley with shots across ravines) at the posh, private Red Sky Golf Club in Edwards, 15 minutes west of Beaver Creek. Even if you're not staying in a hotel that has preferred tee times at specific resort courses, a good concierge (or your own Web search) will obtain tee times at many entertaining courses, such as the Raven at

Three Peaks in Summit County and Rollingstone Ranch Golf Club in Steamboat.

When playing high-altitude golf, you do have to deal with mountain lies and illusions. The thrill of a clean hit and watching the ball fly 300 yards downhill may be deflected by the agony of seeing a putt topple off the back edge of a green because you "knew" that the green tilted left, although it actually sloped right. Lowland golfers who come to the mountains to play golf quickly learn they may have to change club lengths and lofts, because balls fly 10%–15% farther in the thinner air and land on never-level terrain. Greens are especially difficult to read, because the ball will try to roll from the highest mountain peak to the nearest valley—unless the course architect foxes players by building up the green's lower end to counterbalance that pull. Ask the pro in the golf shop for tips before setting out.

CITY COURSES

If you aren't heading up to the mountains, there are plenty of public and semiprivate courses in and around the bigger cities. Some city-owned courses in Denver proper tend to be unimaginative layouts in confined spaces, but there's a variety of challenging and award-winning courses in the surrounding burbs, especially in Lakewood, Littleton, and Parker. On the western slopes, a big standout is the Golf Club at Redlands Mesa in Grand Junction. This Jim Engh public course is woven among mesas and sand-color flat-top buttes.

4

FRISCO

9 miles north of Breckenridge via Hwy. 9.

Keep going past the hodgepodge of strip malls near the interstate and you'll find that low-key Frisco has a downtown district trimmed with restored B&Bs. The town is removed from the ski lifts, but is a low-cost lodging alternative to pricier resorts in the surrounding communities.

GETTING HERE AND AROUND

Private car is the best way to arrive in Frisco, but the town is compact enough for walking or biking.

EXPLORING

FAMILY **Historic Park & Museum.** This sprawling museum re-creates Frisco's boom days. Stroll through 11 buildings dating from the 1880s, including a fully outfitted one-room schoolhouse, a trapper's cabin with snowshoes and pelts, the town's original log chapel, and a jail with an exhibit on mining. ✉ *120 Main St.* ☎ *970/668–3428* 🌐 *www.townoffrisco.com* 🎟 *Free* 🕒 *May–Sept., Tues.–Sat. 9–5, Sun 9–3; Oct.–Apr., Tues.–Sat. 10–4, Sun. 10–2.*

SPORTS AND THE OUTDOORS

FISHING

Blue River Anglers. This company runs fly-fishing tours on the Blue, Colorado, South Platte, Eagle, Arkansas, and Williams Fork rivers, as well as various lakes and streams in the area. If you're lucky, you may catch 10- to 20-inch rainbow and brown trout. ✉ *281 Main St.* ☎ *888/453–9171, 970/668–2583* 🌐 *www.blueriveranglers.com.*

WHERE TO EAT

$ AMERICAN 🍴 **Butterhorn Bakery & Café.** There's usually a wait at this popular breakfast and lunch spot, where meals are cheap, portions are large, and the Vail Mountain Coffee is perfect. Try Eggs Butterhorn, a croissant sandwich with poached eggs, avocado, Canadian bacon, and red-pepper sauce. For those with a sweet tooth, opt for Eggy Bread: French toast made with cinnamon fruit bread. Snag a seat on the patio on weekends when the restaurant can get packed and loud. You can get cakes and baked goods here, too. [$] *Average main: $10* ✉ *408 Main St.* ☎ *970/668–3997* 🌐 *www.butterhornbakery.com* 🕒 *No dinner.*

$$$$ MODERN AMERICAN 🍴 **Food Hedz World Café.** "Hidden gem" describes this strip mall café perfectly because it's unlikely you'd stumble across this creative outpost on your own. But local foodies and tourists who do their research know where to go for lunch in the summer. Starting around Thanksgiving, you can get dinner here, too. Grab one of the family-style tables and dig in to meals like a sauté of shrimp, scallops, and cod or a wood-grilled chicken salad with curried mayonnaise and toasted pumpkin seeds. The menu occasionally changes, but the chef, who works in an open kitchen so that he can converse with customers, may occasionally sneak you something made to order. [$] *Average main: $35* ✉ *842 Summit Blvd.* ☎ *970/668–2000* 🌐 *www.foodhedzcafe.com* 🕒 *Closed Sun. and Mon.*

$$$ AMERICAN SEAFOOD 🍴 **Silverheels Bar and Grill.** At this longtime favorite you can join locals who gather around the bar for margaritas and treat appetizers like entrées throughout the day. For lunch you can try lighter fare like the

haddock tacos or Joel's Bowl—stir-fried chicken and vegetables over sushi rice. Kick dinner off with a tasty appetizer like snow-crab empanadas or Thai scallops, and for the main course head right for the classic trout plates: trout stuffed with corn-bread stuffing, trout almondine, or lemon pepper trout. If fish dishes aren't your thing, there's always a great stash of beef and pork plates. Ⓢ *Average main: $25* ✉ *601 Main St.* ☎ *970/668–0345* ⊕ *www.silverheelsrestaurant.com.*

WHERE TO STAY

$$ 🏨 **Frisco Lodge.** This 1885 stagecoach stop has morphed into a Euro-
B&B/INN   pean-style boutique hotel complete with a chalet facade and a garden courtyard. **Pros:** great location on Main Street; outdoor hot tub and fireplace; courtyard garden. **Cons:** street noise audible; thin walls. Ⓢ *Rooms from: $150* ✉ *321 Main St.* ☎ *800/279–6000* ⊕ *www.friscolodge.com* ⬧ *18 rooms, 14 with bath* ⦿ *Breakfast.*

$$ 🏨 **Hotel Frisco.** This Main Street hostelry is a great home base for skiers
B&B/INN   wanting to hit Breckenridge, Copper, Keystone, and Arapahoe Basin. **Pros:** centrally located. **Cons:** small bathrooms; no elevator. Ⓢ *Rooms from: $134* ✉ *308 Main St.* ☎ *970/668–5009, 800/262–1002* ⊕ *www. hotelfrisco.com* ⬧ *20 rooms, 2 suites* ⦿ *No meals.*

NIGHTLIFE

Backcountry Brewery. Boisterous Backcountry Brewery is home to Great American Beer Festival gold medal–winner Telemark IPA and other homemade brews on rotation. ✉ *720 Main St.* ☎ *970/668–2337* ⊕ *www.backcountrybrewery.com.*

Moose Jaw. The Moose Jaw is a locals' hangout. Pool tables beckon, and a plethora of old-time photographs, trophies, and newspaper articles makes the barn-wood walls all but invisible. ✉ *208 Main St.* ☎ *970/668–3931.*

BRECKENRIDGE

22 miles southwest of Keystone via U.S. 6, I–70, and Hwy. 9.

Breckenridge was founded in 1859, when gold was discovered in the surrounding hills. For the next several decades the town's fortunes rose and fell as its lodes of gold and silver were discovered and exhausted. Throughout the latter half of the 19th century and the early 20th century, Breckenridge was famous as a mining camp that "turned out more gold with less work than any camp in Colorado," according to the *Denver Post.* Dredging gold out of the rivers continued until World War II. Visitors today can still see evidence of gold-dredging operations in the surrounding streams.

At 9,603 feet above sea level and surrounded by higher peaks, Breckenridge is the oldest continuously occupied town on the western slope. Much of the town's architectural legacy from the mining era remains, so you'll find stores occupying authentic Victorian storefronts, and restaurants and bed-and-breakfasts in Victorian homes. Surrounding the town's historic core, condos and hotels are packed into the woods and along the roads threading the mountainsides toward the base of Peak 8.

GETTING HERE AND AROUND

Most people arrive by car or a shuttle from Denver International Airport. Getting around is easiest by car, but can also be done by local shuttles and taxis.

WHEN TO GO

The ski season runs from November to April, but festivals and warm-weather activities attract visitors year-round.

FESTIVALS Festivals run rampant here, and it's rare to show up when locals aren't celebrating. Among the best festivals are the annual U.S. Snowboard Grand Prix (⊕ *www.ussnowboarding.com*) and the International Snow Sculpture championships in winter, and Genuine Jazz (⊕ *www. genuinejazz.com*) in June. Summer events include the Toast of Breckenridge food and wine festival and the National Repertory Orchestra (⊕ *www.nromusic.com*) performances at the Riverwalk Center near the center of town.

ESSENTIALS

Transportation Contact Breckenridge Free Ride. ⊠ *Breckenridge* ☎ *970/547–3140* ⊕ *www.breckfreeride.com.*

Visitor Information Breckenridge Tourism Office. ⊠ *111 Ski Hill Rd.* ☎ *888/251–2417* ⊕ *www.gobreck.com.* **Breckenridge Snow Report.** ⊠ *Breckenridge* ☎ *970/496–4111* ⊕ *www.breckenridge.com.*

TOURS

FAMILY **Breckenridge Heritage Alliance.** The Breckenridge Heritage Alliance leads lively tours of downtown Breckenridge, Colorado's largest National Historic District. The schedule varies seasonally. ⊠ *203 S. Main St.* ☎ *970/453-9767* ⊕ *www.breckheritage.com* ⊠ *From $5.*

EXPLORING

FAMILY **Country Boy Mine.** Ever since gold was discovered here in 1887, the Country Boy Mine has been one of the region's top producers, along with lead and zinc, which were vital for U.S. efforts in World War II. During tours of the facility you can belly up to the stove in the restored blacksmith shop or pet the donkeys that roam the area. The mine has a 55-foot ore chute you can slide down in summer, and gold panning all year round. ⊠ *0542 French Gulch Rd.* ☎ *970/453–4405* ⊕ *www. countryboymine.com* ⊠ *Mine tours $25.95 for adults* ☉ *Days and hrs vary seasonally; call ahead in winter.*

FAMILY **Edwin Carter Discovery Center.** Dating from 1875, the Edwin Carter Discovery Center is dedicated to the "log cabin naturalist" who helped to create Denver's Museum of Nature and Science. Look for realistic stuffed animals, including a large buffalo and a burro carrying a miner's pack. The interactive exhibits also include a hands-on taxidermy workbench. ⊠ *111 N. Ridge St.* ☎ *970/453–9767* ⊕ *breckheritage.com/ edwin-carter-discovery-center* ⊠ *Free, or $5 donation.*

Historic District. Downtown Breckenridge's Historic District is one of Colorado's largest, with about 250 buildings on the National Register of Historic Places. The district is roughly a compact 12 square blocks, bounded by Main, High, and Washington streets and Wellington Road. There are some 171 buildings with points of historical interest, from simple log cabins to Victorians with lacy gingerbread trim. ⊠ *Breckenridge* ⊕ *www.townofbreckenridge.com.*

DOWNHILL SKIING AND SNOWBOARDING

Fodor's Choice ★ **Breckenridge.** With plenty of facilities for snowboarders, Breckenridge is popular with young people. There are several terrain parks and an area where you can learn to free-ride. The resort's slopes are spread across five interconnected moun-

tains in the Tenmile Range, named Peaks 6, 7, 8, 9, and 10. Peak 6 includes 543 acres, 3 bowls (2 at an intermediate level), and 10 trails to the ski area. The highest chairlift in North America—a high-speed quad lift on Peak 8—tops out at an air-gulping 12,840 feet. Peak 7 and Peak 8 have above-the-timberline bowls and chutes. The lower reaches of Peak 7 have some of the country's prettiest intermediate-level terrain accessible by a lift. Peak 8 and Peak 9 have trails for all skill levels. Peak 10 has long trails with roller-coaster runs.

In line with the town's proud heritage, some runs are named for old mines, including Bonanza, Cashier, Gold King, and Wellington. During one week each January the town declares itself an "independent kingdom" during the wild revel called Ullr Fest, which honors the Norse god of snow.

Rental packages (skis, boots, and poles; snowboards and boots) start around $45 per day. Prices vary, but not dramatically. **Facilities:** 187 trails; 2,908 acres; 3,398-foot vertical drop; 34 lifts. ⊠ *1599 Ski Hill Rd.* ☎ *970/453–5000* ⊕ *www.breckenridge.com* 🎫 *Lift Ticket $130* ☉ *Nov.–Apr., daily 8:30–4.*

LESSONS AND PROGRAMS

Breckenridge Ski & Ride School. Contact the Breckenridge Ski & Ride School for information about lessons and specialty clinics. ⊠ *Breckenridge* ☎ *888/576–2754* ⊕ *www.breckenridge.com.*

NORDIC SKIING

BACKCOUNTRY SKIING

They don't call this place Summit County for nothing—mountain passes above 10,000 feet allow relatively easy access to high-country terrain and some of the area's best snow. But remember: avalanche-related deaths are all too common in Summit County. Don't judge an area solely on appearances or the fact that other skiers or snowmobilers have been there before, as even slopes that look gentle may slide. Never head into the backcountry without checking weather conditions, letting someone know where you're going, and wearing appropriate clothing. Always carry survival gear and travel with a buddy.

Dillon Ranger District Office of the White River National Forest. For information on snow conditions and avalanche dangers, contact the Dillon Ranger District Office of the White River National Forest. ⊠ *Breckenridge* ☎ *970/468–5400* ⊕ *www.dillonrangerdistrict.com.*

Summit County Huts Association. One popular touring route for backcountry skiing is the trip to Boreas Pass, just south of Breckenridge. The 6½-mile-long trail follows the route of a former railroad, with good views of distant peaks along the way. The Summit County Huts Association has four backcountry cabins where skiers can spend the night (two are open for summer hikers). ⊠ *524 Wellington Rd.* ☎ *970/453–8583* ⊕ *www.summithuts.org.*

10th Mountain Division Hut Association. If you're traveling far afield in Breckenridge during your backcountry skiing adventures, there are cabins available through the 10th Mountain Division Hut Association. ⊠ *Breckenridge* ☎ *970/925–5775* ⊕ *www.huts.org.*

TRACK SKIING

Breckenridge Nordic Center. This center has 22 miles of groomed tracks for classic and skate skiing, as well as ungroomed trails in the Golden Horseshoe. There are also 11 miles of marked snowshoe trails. Swing into the lodge, Oh, Be Joyful, to warm up. ⊠ *1200 Ski Hill Rd.* ☎ *970/453–6855* ⊕ *www.breckenridgenordic.com.*

OTHER SPORTS AND THE OUTDOORS

FISHING

Mountain Angler. This company organizes fishing trips, including float trips on the Colorado River, half-day trips on streams near Breckenridge, and all-day trips on rivers farther away. ⊠ *311 S. Main St.* ☎ *970/453–4665, 800/453–4669* ⊕ *www.mountainangler.com.*

GOLF

Breckenridge Golf Club. This is the world's only municipally owned course designed by Jack Nicklaus. You may play any combination of the three 9-hole sets: the Bear, the Beaver (with beaver ponds lining many of the fairways), or the Elk. The course resembles a nature reserve as it flows through mountainous terrain and fields full of wildflowers. ⊠ *200 Clubhouse Dr.* ☎ *970/453–9104* ⊕ *www.breckenridgegolfclub.com* ⊠ *$134* ⚐ *27 holes, 7276 yards, par 72.*

KAYAKING

FAMILY **Breckenridge Kayak Park.** With splash rocks, eddy pools, and S-curves, the 1,800-foot Breckenridge Kayak Park is a playground for kayakers. This public park on the Blue River behind the Breckenridge Recreation Center is free and generally open from May through August. ⊠ *880 Airport Rd.* ☎ *970/453–1734* ⊕ *www.townofbreckenridge.com.*

RAFTING

Breckenridge Whitewater Rafting. This outfitter runs white-water rafting and fishing trips on stretches of the Colorado, Arkansas, Eagle, and Blue rivers in Summit County, and Clear Creek on the Front Range. They also offer zipline, rock climbing, fly fishing, hiking, and horseback tours. ⊠ *411 S. Main St.* ☎ *800/370–0581, 970/236–9402* ⊕ *www. breckenridgewhitewater.com.*

Performance Tours Whitewater Rafting. This outfitter leads expeditions on the Blue and Colorado rivers for newcomers looking for some action and experienced rafters ready for extremes. The company is based in Buena Vista, but will pick up groups in Breckenridge and has a sales office in town. ⊠ *101 Ski Hill Rd.* ☎ *800/328–7238* ⊕ *www.performancetours.com.*

SNOWMOBILING

Good Times Adventures. This company runs snowmobile and dog-sledding trips on more than 40 miles of groomed trails, through open meadows and along the Continental Divide to 11,585-foot-high Georgia Pass. ✉ *6061 Tiger Rd.* ☎ *970/547–1386* 🌐 *www.goodtimesadventures.com.*

WHERE TO EAT

$ AMERICAN 🍴 **Blue Moose.** Locals flock here for the hearty breakfasts of eggs, oatmeal, pancakes, and much more, so you can expect a wait unless you get there early. Neither the food nor the decor is fancy, and the service—while friendly—can be slow. But a meal here will hit the spot. Be sure to bring cash or checks; they don't accept credit cards. Blue Moose will also consider trades for food. [$] *Average main: $10* ✉ *540 S. Main St.* ☎ *970/453–4859* 💳 *No credit cards* 🕒 *No dinner* ✍ *Reservations not accepted.*

$$$ AMERICAN 🍴 **Park & Main.** Taking pride in good sandwiches goes a long way, as the hip eatery/wine bar Park & Main proves. The curried turkey club is made of slow-roasted curried turkey, apple, walnut and dried cranberry salad, Swiss cheese, and smoked bacon. Even the chicken shawarma has fans driving in from other counties. There are dinner and dessert specials every night, like a Nutella-pressed panino, and all-day beverages for those who like mimosas for happy hour. [$] *Average main: $20* ✉ *500 S. Main St.* ☎ *970/453–9493* 🌐 *www.parkandmainfood.com.*

WHERE TO STAY

$$$$ RENTAL 🏨 **Grand Lodge on Peak 7.** Luxury comes in the form of other people's timeshares at this ultracozy, high-end lodge at the base of the Independence Superchair in Breckenridge Ski Resort. **Pros:** proximity to Peak 6; family-friendly amenities; full-service spa. **Cons:** limited rooms available during peak weekends; limited parking; no bathrooms by ski lockers. [$] *Rooms from: $350* ✉ *1979 Ski Hill Rd.* ☎ *866/423–9372, 970/453–3330* 🌐 *www.grandlodgeonpeak7.com* 🛏 *180 rooms* 🍽 *No meals.*

$$$$ HOTEL Fodor's Choice ★ 🏨 **Lodge at Breckenridge.** This lodge more than compensates for its location on a mountainside beyond the downtown area with breathtaking views of the Tenmile Range from nearly every angle. **Pros:** great mountain views; complimentary Continental breakfast and shuttle to town or resort; recently renovated. **Cons:** no room service. [$] *Rooms from: $259* ✉ *112 Overlook Dr.* ☎ *970/453–9300, 800/736–1607* 🌐 *www.thelodgeatbreckenridge.com* 🛏 *45 rooms, 2 houses* 🍽 *Breakfast.*

$$ B&B/INN 🏨 **Mountain Stream Lodge.** This timber-frame bed-and-breakfast includes five mountain-style bedrooms with fireplaces and private decks or patios overlooking a willow-lined river and mountains. **Pros:** all rooms are within earshot of the river; gas fireplaces; friendly owners. **Cons:** rooms fill fast; reservations are essential. [$] *Rooms from: $169* ✉ *303B N. Main St.* ☎ *970/453–2975, 800/795–2975* 🌐 *www.mountainstreamlodge.com* 🛏 *4 rooms* 🍽 *Breakfast.*

$$$$ RENTAL 🏨 **Mountain Thunder Lodge.** Rising above the trees, this lodge constructed from rough-hewn timber brings to mind old-fashioned ski lodges. **Pros:** family-size suites; close to ski lifts; free Wi-Fi. **Cons:** short walk to main street. [$] *Rooms from: $250* ✉ *500 Mountain Thunder Dr.* ☎ *888/400–9590* 🌐 *www.breckresorts.com* 🛏 *88 rooms* 🍽 *No meals.*

$$$$ RENTAL **Village at Breckenridge.** The word "village" puts it mildly, as this sprawling resort is spread over 14 acres of mountainous terrain alongside a beautiful river and right across from historic Main Street. **Pros:** great concierge; ski-in ski-out. **Cons:** some rooms have better style than others; decor depends on individual owners. [$] *Rooms from: $240* ✉ *535 S. Park Ave.* ☎ *970/453–5192, 888/400–9590* 🌐 *www.breckresorts.com* 🛏 *200 rooms* 🍴 *No meals.*

LODGING ALTERNATIVES

Summit Mountain Rentals. This rental agency has more than 145 condos and private homes for rent around Frisco and Breckenridge. ✉ *111 Ski Hill Rd.* ☎ *970/453–7370, 800/383–7382* 🌐 www.summitrentals.com 🛏 *More than 145 properties.*

NIGHTLIFE

BARS AND LOUNGES

Breckenridge Brewery & Pub. This establishment serves various microbrews, from Avalanche Ale to Oatmeal Stout, and has an extensive and kid-friendly pub menu. It's a great après-ski spot. ✉ *600 S. Main St.* ☎ *970/453–1550* 🌐 *www.breckbrewpub.com.*

Cecilia's. On the lower level of La Cima Mall, Cecilia's is a martini and cigar lounge with mouthwatering libations. Smokers head to the cigar patio. Stick around for the DJs and dance party later. ✉ *520 S. Main St.* ☎ *970/453–2243* 🌐 *www.cecilias.tv.*

COPPER MOUNTAIN AND LEADVILLE

Skiers head to Copper Mountain because the runs make sense—you can start easy and progress to harder slopes without having to crisscross the mountain. It also offers the largest expanse of skiing in Summit County. Although nearby Leadville has a small ski resort (Ski Cooper) and plenty of snowmobiling trails, this rustic mining town is more popular as a summer base for hiking forays to nearby Mount Elbert, the highest peak in Colorado.

COPPER MOUNTAIN

7 miles south of Frisco via I–70.

Once little more than a series of strip malls, Copper Mountain is now a thriving resort with a bustling base. The resort's heart is a pedestrian-only village anchored by Burning Stones Plaza, which is prime people-watching turf. High-speed ski lifts march up the mountain on one side of the plaza, and the other three sides are flanked by condominiums with retail shops and restaurants on the ground floors. Lodgings extend west toward West Village and east to Center and East villages, where a six-pack high-speed lift ferries skiers.

GETTING HERE AND AROUND

The easiest way to reach Copper Mountain is by car. The resort is foot-friendly, and there is also a free resort shuttle service around town.

WHEN TO GO

Skiing is from November to mid-April. In summer the resort tends to be quieter, as most visitors gravitate to the Lake Dillon area for hiking and biking.

ESSENTIALS

Visitor Information Copper Mountain Resort. ⊠ *Copper Mountain* ☏ *970/968–2882, 800/458–8386* ⊕ *www.coppercolorado.com.*
Copper Mountain Snow Report. ⊠ *Copper Mountain* ☏ *970/968–2100.*

DOWNHILL SKIING AND SNOWBOARDING

Copper Mountain. This mountain is popular with locals because the resort's 2,465 acres are spread across several peaks where the terrain is naturally separated into areas for beginners, intermediates, and expert skiers and snowboarders, making it easy to pick your slope. As you move from east to west, trails decrease in difficulty. East Village is home to the expert terrain, Center Village hosts intermediate terrain, and West Village is where you'll find almost all of the beginner terrain. The Union Creek area contains gentle, tree-lined trails for novices. The slopes above the Village at Copper and Copper Station are an invigorating blend of intermediate and advanced trails. Several steep mogul runs are clustered on the eastern side of the area, and have their own lift. At the top of the resort and in the vast Copper Bowl there's challenging high-alpine terrain. Freeriders gravitate to the Woodward Central and the Bouncer Park. Weather permitting, on Friday and weekends, expert skiers can grab a free first-come, first-served snowcat ride up Tucker Mountain for an ungroomed, wilderness-style ski experience.

Rental packages (skis, boots, and poles) start at $29 per day for the junior package and go as high as $59 per day for high-performance equipment. Snowboard rental packages (snowboard and boots) start at $42 for adults. Helmet rentals begin at $10. Purchase your rental equipment one day in advance over the phone or by booking online and you'll save 20%. **Facilities:** more than 140 trails; 2,465 acres; 2,601-foot vertical drop; 23 lifts. ⊠ *209 Ten Mile Circle* ☏ *970/968–2882, 800/458–8386* ⊕ *www.coppercolorado.com* 🎿 *Lift Ticket $138 in peak season; $70 in early season* ☉ *Nov.–mid-Apr., weekdays 9–4; weekends and holidays 8:30–4.*

LESSONS AND PROGRAMS

FAMILY **Ski and Ride School.** Copper Mountain's Ski and Ride School has classes for skiers and snowboarders, private lessons, men- and women-only groups, and special competitive lessons (to help you make a quantum leap in skills). Copper's Youth Seasonal Programs, divided into groups based on age and skill level, are designed to both teach and entertain. There's also Kids' Night Out, popular among parents who want an evening without the children. ⊠ *Copper Mountain* ☏ *970/968–2318.*

OTHER SPORTS AND THE OUTDOORS

ATHLETIC CENTER

FAMILY **Woodward at Copper.** Hone your best tricks at this massive snowboard, skateboard, and BMX training facility and indoor playground nicknamed "The Barn." Strap on a snowboard or skis specially fitted with wheels to take on the Jumps and Pump track before landing in one of the foam pits. You can also practice tricks on five Olympic trampolines or jump even higher on the Supertramp, one of the first in the world offered at a public gym. There is also space for skateboarders and BMX and mountain-bike riders of all levels. Camps throughout the summer teach children as young as eight how to own the slopes. ✉ *0505 Ten Mile Circle* ☎ *888/350–1544* 🌐 *www.woodwardatcopper.com.*

BICYCLING

Gravitee Snowboard Shop. Hundreds of miles of bike paths weave around Copper Mountain Resort, leading up and down mountainsides and through high-country communities. In summer, find all kinds of organized rides. Gravitee has all the gear you need for cycling in the area. ✉ *Tucker Mountain Lodge, 0164 Copper Rd.* ☎ *970/968–0171* 🌐 *www.gravitee.com.*

GOLF

Copper Creek Golf Club. Right at the Copper Mountain Resort is a course designed by Pete and Perry Dye. The highest-elevation 18-hole golf course in North America, it flows up and down some of the ski trails at the base of the mountain and between condos and town homes in the resort's East Village. ✉ *104 Wheeler Pl.* ☎ *866/286–1663* 🌐 *www.coppercolorado.com* 🎟 *$74* ⛳ *18 holes, 6057 yards, par 69.*

WHERE TO EAT AND STAY

$$ AMERICAN 🍴 **Endo's Adrenaline Café.** Just a few ski-boot steps from the American Eagle Lift, Endo's Adrenaline Café is one of the more hopping sports bar/restaurants. Enjoy rock music as you climb atop a high bar stool and catch a game on one of the TVs, or pick a table for a more intimate lunch or dinner at this high-energy establishment. Try the fish tacos or a mountainous plate of Endo's Mondo Nachos—a heaping portion of chips covered in melted cheddar, jalapeños, and guacamole. [$] *Average main: $14* ✉ *209 Ten Mile Circle* ☎ *970/968–3070* 🌐 *www.coppercolorado.com.*

$ RENTAL FAMILY 🏨 **Copper Mountain Resort.** Copper Mountain Resort manages the majority of lodging in the area, ranging from standard hotel rooms to spacious condos and town homes. **Pros:** centrally located; wide range of accommodations. **Cons:** village can be noisy; quality of rooms varies greatly. [$] *Rooms from: $99* ✉ *0509 Copper Rd.* ☎ *970/968–2318, 888/219–2441* 🌐 *www.coppercolorado.com.*

NIGHTLIFE

Endo's Adrenaline Café. At the base of the American Eagle lift, Endo's Adrenaline Café is the place to be for après-ski cocktails. ✉ *209 Ten Mile Circle* ☎ *970/968–3070* 🌐 *www.coppercolorado.com.*

JJ's Rocky Mountain Tavern. The East Village is home to JJ's Rocky Mountain Tavern, the best place for a beer after a long day on the bumps. Musician Moe Dixon, a favorite with the locals, has people dancing on the tables when he covers everyone from John Denver to Jimmy Buffett some nights during ski season. ✉ *102 Wheeler Circle* ☎ *970/968–3062* 🌐 *www.coppercolorado.com.*

LEADVILLE

24 miles south of Copper Mountain via Hwy. 91.

Sitting in the mountains at 10,152 feet, Leadville is America's highest incorporated city. The 70 square blocks of Victorian architecture and adjacent mining district hint at its past as a rich silver-mining boom-town. In the history of Colorado mining, perhaps no town looms larger. Two of the state's most fascinating figures lived here: mining magnate Horace Tabor and his second wife, Elizabeth Doe McCourt (nicknamed Baby Doe), the central figures in John LaTouche's Pulitzer prize–winning opera *The Ballad of Baby Doe.*

Tabor amassed a fortune of $9 million, much of which he spent building monuments to himself and his mistress "Baby Doe." His power peaked when his money helped him secure a U.S. Senate seat in 1883. He married Baby Doe after divorcing his first wife, the faithful Augusta. The Tabors incurred the scorn of high society by throwing their money around in what was considered a vulgar fashion. After the price of silver plummeted, Tabor died a pauper in 1899 and Baby Doe became a recluse, rarely emerging from her tiny, unheated cabin beside the mine entrance. She froze to death in 1935.

GETTING HERE AND AROUND

A car is the only reasonable mode of transportation into Leadville. Once in town, the main street, lined with shops and restaurants, and the cozy surrounding neighborhoods make for pleasant walks in summer.

WHEN TO GO

FESTIVALS **Leadville Boom Days.** Eccentricity is still a Leadville trait, as witnessed by the 21-mile International Pack Burro Race over Mosquito Pass and a local parade. The annual event is part of Leadville Boom Days, held the first weekend of August. The event is immortalized with thousands of T-shirts and bumper stickers that read, "Get Your Ass Over the Pass." ⊠ *Leadville* ⊕ *www.leadvilleboomdays.com.*

ESSENTIALS

Visitor Information Leadville Lake County Chamber of Commerce.
⊠ *809 Harrison St.* ☎ *719/486–3900* ⊕ *www.leadvilleusa.com.*

EXPLORING

TOP ATTRACTIONS

Historic Tabor Opera House and Museum. The three-story Tabor Opera House opened in 1879, when it was proclaimed the "largest and best west of the Mississippi." It hosted luminaries such as Harry Houdini, John Philip Sousa, and Oscar Wilde. Shows on the current schedule are mostly music and dance, like the Zikr Dance Ensemble and The Denver Concert Band, but there's also a community talent show to give local stars a spotlight on the famous stage. ⊠ *308 Harrison Ave.* ☎ *719/486–8409* ⊕ *www.taboroperahouse.net* ⊠ *Call for ticket prices.*

FAMILY **Leadville, Colorado & Southern Railroad Company.** Still chugging along is the Leadville, Colorado & Southern Railroad Company, which can take you on a breathtaking 2½-hour trip to the Continental Divide. The train leaves from Leadville's century-old depot and travels beside the Arkansas River to its headwaters at Freemont Pass. The return trip takes you down to French Gulch for views of Mount Elbert, Colorado's highest peak. ⊠ *326 E. 7th St.* ☎ *719/486–3936, 866/386–3936* ⊕ *www. leadville-train.com* ✉ *$37* ☉ *Late May–early Oct., daily; call for hrs.*

Mount Elbert. The massive, snowcapped peak watching over Leadville is Mount Elbert. At 14,433 feet it's the highest mountain in Colorado and the tallest peak in the entire Rocky Mountain Range, second in height in the contiguous 48 states only to California's 14,495-foot Mount Whitney. ⊠ *Leadville.*

FAMILY   **National Mining Hall of Fame and Museum.** This museum covers virtually every aspect of mining, from the discovery of precious ore to fashioning it into coins and other items. Dioramas in the beautiful brick building explain extraction processes. ⊠ *120 W. 9th St.* ☎ *719/486–1229* ⊕ *www.mininghalloffame.org* ✉ *$7* ☉ *June–mid-Nov. daily 9–5; mid-Nov.–May, Tues.–Sun. 9–5.*

WORTH NOTING

Healy House and Dexter Cabin. On a tree-lined street in downtown Leadville you'll find the Healy House and Dexter Cabin, an 1878 Greek Revival house and an 1879 log cabin—two of Leadville's earliest residences. The lavishly decorated rooms of the clapboard house provide a sense of how the town's upper crust, such as the Tabors, lived and played. ⊠ *912 Harrison Ave.* ☎ *719/486–0487* ⊕ *www.historycolorado. org/museums/history-healy-house-dexter-cabin* ✉ *$6* ☉ *Mid-May–early Oct., daily 10–4:30.*

Heritage Museum. This museum paints a vivid portrait of life in Leadville at the turn of the last century, with dioramas depicting life in the mines. There's also furniture, clothing, and toys from the Victorian era. ⊠ *102 E. 9th St.* ☎ *719/486–1878* ⊕ *www.leadvilleheritagemuseum.com* ✉ *$6* ☉ *Memorial Day–last weekend in Sept., daily 10–5.*

DOWNHILL SKIING AND SNOWBOARDING

FAMILY   **Ski Cooper.** Nine miles west of Leadville, Ski Cooper is one of those undiscovered boutique ski areas in the Rockies. It has 400 acres skiable via lift and another 2,400 acres of backcountry powder accessible by snowcat. The 26 groomed runs are perfect for beginning or intermediate skiers. Rental packages (skis, boots, and poles) start at $28 per day, among the cheapest in the state. Snowboarding packages start at $20. **Facilities:** 39 trails; 400 acres; 1,200-foot vertical drop; 4 lifts. ⊠ *U.S. 24* ☎ *719/486–3684, 800/707–6114* ⊕ *www.skicooper.com* ✉ *Lift ticket $50* ☉ *Late Nov.–early Apr., daily 9–4.*

LESSONS AND PROGRAMS

Chicago Ridge Snowcat Tours. These tours are for expert backcountry skiers who want the off-piste adventure of scripting their signature across acres of untracked powder. You'll get your fill of a hot lunch, beacons, powder skis or boards, and après-ski refreshments. The terrain has tree glades and open bowls. You must be over 18 (or be accompanied by an adult) and fit; the runs are up to 10,000 feet long, and some vertical drops top 2,000 feet. Wide powder skis are available for rent for those who really want to float. ⊠ *Leadville* ☎ *719/486–2277* ⊕ *skicooper. com/snowcat-tours* ✉ *From $299.*

Ski Cooper Ski School. This ski school covers the gamut for skiers and snowboarders. A "First-Timer" two-hour group lesson with magic carpet lift ticket and rental gear is $79. You can also book private lessons, race and telemark clinics, and lessons for your children, which can be extended as part of the all-day child-care programs. Lessons for skiers with disabilities are available by appointment.

Ski Cooper has a number of options for children, including their popular Panda Patrol for children ages 5 to 12. A full-day package (from 10 am to 3 pm) includes a group ski lesson, equipment rental, lunch, and full-mountain lift ticket for $99. The Panda Cubs program caters to four-year-olds and provides a two-hour lesson, lift ticket, rental package, lunch, and afternoon daycare for $84. ⊠ *232 County Rd. 29* ☎ *719/486–2277* ⊕ *www.skicooper.com.*

OTHER SPORTS AND THE OUTDOORS

CANOEING AND KAYAKING

Twin Lakes Canoe & Kayak Adventures. There's no better way to see the high country than by exploring its alpine lakes. Twin Lakes Canoe & Kayak Adventures offers guided tours of Twin and Turquoise lakes to beginners, and equipment rentals to more experienced paddlers and stand-up paddleboarders. ⊠ *6451 Hwy. 82, about 20 miles south of Leadville* ☎ *719/251–9961* ⊕ *www.twinlakescanoeandkayak.com.*

GOLF

Mt. Massive Golf Course. Play North America's highest 9-hole green at 9,680 feet—and watch your distance increase in the thin mountain air. Just west of Leadville in the Arkansas River valley, this public golf course was opened in the 1930s to the delight of the mining community. True green fairways replaced sagebrush flats after a $50,000 grant in the 1970s heralded an automated irrigation system. ⊠ *259 County Rd. 5* ☎ *719/486–2176* ⊕ *www.mtmassivegolf.com* 🎫 *$24* ⛳ *9 holes, 3150 yards, par 36.*

HORSEBACK RIDING

Halfmoon Packing & Outfitting. If you're feeling that it's time to hit the trail, Halfmoon Packing & Outfitting has a stable of horses ready for you. Also ask about wagon rides, stagecoach rides, and two-day to one-week trips. ⊠ *1100 County Rd. 18* ☎ *719/486–4570* ⊕ *www.halfmoonpacking.com.*

SNOWMOBILING

Leadville Ski Country. There's more than one way to explore the terrain of Summit County, and Leadville Ski Country has everything you need to see it by snowshoe, ski, snowboard, and snowmobile. Zoom around the 20-mile loop circling Turquoise Lake on a snowmobile for a 2- or 3-hour rental. At $20 for ski rentals and $28 for snowboard rentals, you'll be hard-pressed to find better deals. ⊠ *116 E. 9th St.* ☎ *719/486–3836, 800/500–5323* ⊕ *www.leadvilleskicountry.com.*

WHERE TO EAT AND STAY

$ ╳ **Cookies With Altitude.** If the aroma of frosting-topped cookies or hunks
BAKERY of fudge doesn't get you in the door, paninis made with locally grown produce when in season—a rare find in smaller mountain towns—should do the trick. Try the veggie delight: roasted veggies, feta, and

hummus. End by sinking your teeth into one of the several cookies in the display case, like the brownie-meets-cookie indulgence of The Dark Side, The Great Pumpkin's maple glaze, or seasonal Berry Delightful Oatmeal—a cookie stuffed with raisins, blueberries, cherries, and more. $ *Average main: $10* ⊠ *717½ Harrison Ave.* ☎ *719/486–1026.*

$ ✕ **The Grill.** Run by the Martinez family since 1965, this locals favorite
MEXICAN draws a standing-room-only crowd. The service is sometimes slow,
FAMILY but that leaves time for another of the marvelous margaritas. New Mexican cuisine is the specialty here, including dishes with hand-roasted green chilis. In summer you can retreat to the patio and dine with views of the two highest Colorado mountains. $ *Average main: $12* ⊠ *715 Elm St.* ☎ *719/486–9930* ⊕ *www.grillbarcafe.com* ☯ *No lunch. Closed Tues.*

$$ 🏨 **Delaware Hotel.** This artfully restored 1886 hotel is one of the best
HOTEL examples of high Victorian architecture in the area, so it's no surprise that it's listed on the National Register of Historic Places. **Pros:** loaded with gold-rush character; great mountain views; very friendly staff. **Cons:** lobby is one large store; the altitude in Leadville can be tough if you're arriving from sea level. $ *Rooms from: $129* ⊠ *700 Harrison Ave.* ☎ *719/486–1418, 800/748–2004* ⊕ *www.delawarehotel.com* ↝ *36 rooms, 4 suites* ◉| *Breakfast.*

$ 🏨 **Twin Lakes Inn.** You'll be hard-pressed to find better views than at this
B&B/INN 1879 inn on the shores of Colorado's largest glacial lake and at the base of Mount Elbert, Colorado's tallest peak. **Pros:** lovely location; excellent restaurant; rooms with mountain views. **Cons:** no air-conditioning; small rooms; shared bathrooms. $ *Rooms from: $79* ⊠ *6435 E. State Hwy. 82* ☎ *719/486–7965* ⊕ *www.thetwinlakesinn.com* ↝ *11 rooms* ◉| *Breakfast.*

SHOPPING

Melanzana. If you're in the market for cold-weather gear, forget the big-name brands and opt instead for the hand-stitched, high-end Polartec gear from this local outdoor clothing company. The Leadville-based employees design, cut, sew, and sell their creations in their main street storefront. Young employees are bent over sewing machines behind the register while you shop for a plush, fuzzy hoodie, or water- and windproof vest. It's a source of local pride to be caught wearing Melanzana. The –20°F winters may require you to stock up the next time you're in town anyway. ⊠ *716 Harrison Ave.* ☎ *719/486–3245* ⊕ *www.melanzana.com.*

VAIL VALLEY

Updated by
Aimee Heckel

If Aspen is Colorado's Hollywood East, then her rival Vail is Wall Street West. So popular is this ski resort with the monied East Coast crowd that locals sometimes refer to particularly crowded weeks as "212" weeks, in reference to the area code of so many visitors. The attraction for vacationers from all over is the thin, aspen-cloaked Vail Valley, a narrow corridor slit by I–70 and bounded by the rugged Gore Range to the north and east and the tabled Sawatch escarpments to the south. Through it all runs the sparkling Eagle River.

The resorts begin just west of Vail Pass, a saddle well below tree line, and stretch 20 miles through the communities of Vail, Eagle-Vail, Minturn, Avon, Beaver Creek, Arrowhead, and Edwards. The vibe in these places varies dramatically, from Beaver Creek, a gated community of second (and sometimes third) megahomes, to Edwards, a rapidly growing and increasingly affluent worker town, to Vail, filled with styles of lodging, dining, and shopping appealing to many tastes.

In winter this region is famous for the glittering resorts of Vail and Beaver Creek. Between these two areas skiers and snowboarders have just over 7,000 acres at their disposal, including the unforgettable Back Bowls far beyond the noise of I–70 traffic. In summer these resorts are great bases from which you can explore the high country on foot, horseback, raft, or bike.

ORIENTATION AND PLANNING

GETTING ORIENTED

Finding your way around the Vail Valley is relatively easy; the valley runs east and west, and everything you need is less than a mile off the I–70 corridor (and the constant drone of traffic), which parallels the Eagle River. The Gore Range to the north and east is one of the most rugged wilderness areas in Colorado—the peaks are jagged and broken, and any hiking here immediately involves a steep and sustained climb. To the south, the tabled heights of the Sawatch Mountain Range are gentler, and give Vail her superb skiing, particularly in the famed Back Bowls. Beaver Creek feels more isolated, being set off the highway behind a series of gates that control access to the posh communities within.

Vail. European-style cafés and beautifully cobbled streets lined with boutiques are more than just window dressing—Vail is no longer just known for its serious skiing. The nearby town of Minturn is a much more modest burg.

TOP REASONS TO GO

High-altitude golf: The thin air at this elevation lets your Titleist fly much farther—enjoy those hero swings at more than a dozen venues.

Romantic meals: A number of intimate restaurants are hidden away among the peaks, reachable by ski, on horseback, and even by horse-drawn sleigh.

Rugged scenery: The Gore Range presents some of the most sharp-spined backcountry in the state,

with ice-cold tarns, sheer cliffs, and shaggy white mountain goats.

The slopes: Vail is as real and challenging a ski mountain as you'll find anywhere in the western United States, with the steeps and back bowls to prove it.

Summer festivals: Check out some of Vail's many cultural activities—summer is full of music, culinary, and dance festivals.

Beaver Creek. As the entrance gates will remind you, Beaver Creek is the most exclusive skiing community in Colorado. This is resort-to-resort skiing set among gorgeous glades of aspens; it never seems to get crowded. The smaller and more prosaic town of Edwards, which has a growing batch of shops and restaurants, lies just 4 miles west.

PLANNING

WHEN TO GO

Winter is by far the most crowded time in Vail Valley, with early spring seeing the highest number of visitors hoping to catch that blissful blend of thick powder and china-blue skies. Naturally, prices are highest then as well, though you can sometimes get pre- and postseason deals. Although summer is quickly gaining in popularity, the real deals can be had in the shoulder seasons—late autumn and late spring when the ski slopes are closed. Restaurants will often have two-for-one entrées with a bottle of wine, and hotels run deeply cut rates. Traffic through the I–70 corridor moves at a good clip unless snows have stacked up truckers putting on chains on either side of Vail Pass. The pass itself is low, and stays below tree line, affording it some protection from drifting and blowing snow.

GETTING HERE AND AROUND
AIR TRAVEL

Denver International Airport (DEN), the gateway to the High Rockies, is 119 miles east of Vail. It's a 90-minute drive from Vail, but ski traffic can double the time (expect it to take much longer if a blizzard hits). The Vail Valley is served by Eagle County Airport (EGE), 34 miles west of Vail. Air Canada, American, Delta, and United have nonstop flights to Eagle County from several gateways (Air Canada and Delta only during ski season).

If possible, try snagging a direct flight straight into the Eagle County Airport from your hometown. But if your trip involves a connection through Denver or another hub, it is often faster to rent a car and make the scenic 90-minute drive through the mountains or catch one of the many shuttle services. Although winter mountain weather can be fickle and delay flights, the two high passes on I–70 between Denver–Loveland and Summit County–Vail are rarely closed, though traffic might slow to a creep.

Airport Contacts Denver International Airport (DEN). ⊠ *8500 Peña Blvd., Denver* ☎ *800/247-2336* ⊕ *www.flydenver.com.* **Eagle County Airport (EGE).** ⊠ *219 Eldon Wilson Rd., Gypsum* ☎ *970/328-2680* ⊕ *www.eaglecounty.us/airport.*

Airport Transfers Colorado Mountain Express. ⊠ *Edwards* ☎ *970/754-7433, 800/525-6363* ⊕ *www.coloradomountainexpress.com.* **453-Taxi.** ⊠ *Breckenridge* ☎ *970/453-8294* ⊕ *www.453-taxi.com.*

BUS AND SHUTTLE TRAVEL

All the resorts run free or inexpensive shuttles between the ski villages and the slopes. Locals and visitors alike hop the free Town of Vail buses up and down from East Vail to West Vail (a distance of nearly 6 miles, with Lionshead at the center). For trips to Beaver Creek, catch the ECO Transit bus from the Vail Transportation Center in Vail Village, beside the Vail Information Center. Town of Avon buses depart throughout the day from Elk Lot (located near the main gates of Beaver Creek) and Covered Bridge Bus Stop in Beaver Creek.

Contacts Avon/Beaver Creek Transit. ⊠ *Avon* ☎ *970/748-4120* ⊕ *www.avon. org.* **Colorado Mountain Express.** ⊠ *Edwards* ☎ *800/525-6363, 970/754-7433* ⊕ *www.coloradomountainexpress.com.* **ECO Transit.** ⊠ *Gypsum* ☎ *970/328-3520* ⊕ *www.eaglecounty.us/Transit.* **Town of Vail.** ⊠ *75 S. Frontage Rd. W, Vail* ☎ *970/477-3456, 866/650-9020* ⊕ *www.vailgov.com/transportation-services.*

CAR TRAVEL

The most convenient place for visitors to rent a car is at Denver International Airport. Most major agencies have offices in Eagle County Airport as well.

Although it is often severely overcrowded, I–70 is still the quickest and most direct route from Denver to Vail. For the first 45 minutes it climbs gradually through the dry Front Range mountains before ducking into the Eisenhower Tunnel. The last 45 minutes are through the high Summit County Basin and up and over the mellow grade of Vail Pass.

PARKS AND RECREATION AREAS

The Vail Valley has two wilderness areas in close proximity—the truly untrammeled Eagle's Nest Wilderness Area to the northeast in the Gore Range, and the more popular Holy Cross Wilderness to the southwest.

The Eagle River, whose headwaters are on the north side of Tennessee Pass, is an excellent fishing stream, mostly for brook and brown trout in the 6- to 12-inch range. Public access is easiest upriver of Red Cliff on Forest Service land. There's some superb rafting in Gore Canyon on the Colorado River west of Vail, particularly in spring when the river is boiling with snow runoff.

FAMILY **White River National Forest.** The land between the wilderness areas of Eagle's Nest and Holy Cross, including most of the ski resorts' slopes, is part of the White River National Forest. ⊠ *Administrative Office, Glenwood Springs* ☎ *970/945–2521* ⊕ *www.fs.usda.gov/whiteriver.*

RESTAURANTS

Unlike the nearby Summit County ski resorts, which pride themselves on standard "mining fare" like surf and turf, Vail has a distinctly European dining style. This is the town in which to sample creamed pheasant soup or bite into a good cut of venison. For the most romantic options, look into a slope-side restaurant like Beano's, where the fixed-course menus and unique transportation (horses in summer and sleighs in winter) make the experience more than just a meal. The farther down-valley you move, the more the prices drop.

HOTELS

Vail and Beaver Creek are purpose-built resorts, so you won't find any quaint historic Victorians converted into bed-and-breakfasts here as you will in Breckenridge and Aspen. Instead, Vail lodgings come in three flavors—European chalets that blend with the Bavarian architecture, posh chain resorts up side canyons, and loads of small but serviceable condominiums perfect for families. Down-valley in Edwards and Minturn you'll find that accommodation prices drop, but so does the accessibility to the slopes. *Hotel reviews have been shorted. For full information, visit Fodors.com.*

WHAT IT COSTS				
	$	$$	$$$	$$$$
Restaurants	under $13	$13–$18	$19–$25	over $25
Hotels	under $121	$121–$170	$171–$230	over $230

Restaurant prices are the average cost of a main course at dinner or, if dinner is not served, at lunch, excluding 4.4%–8.4% tax. Hotel prices are the lowest cost of a standard double room in high season, excluding service charges and 5.4%–9.8% tax.

VAIL

100 miles west of Denver via I–70.

Fodor's Choice ★ Consistently ranked as one of North America's leading ski destinations, Vail has a reputation few can match. The four-letter word means Valhalla for skiers of all skill levels. Vail has plenty of open areas where novices can learn the ropes. It can also be an ego-building mountain for intermediate and advanced skiers who hit the slopes only a week or two a season. Some areas, like Blue Sky Basin, can make you feel like a pro.

Although Vail is a long, thin town spread for several miles along the Eagle River and comprising East Vail, Vail Village, Lionshead in the center, and West Vail, the hub of activity in winter and summer revolves around Vail Village, and the recently redone Lionshead, which has

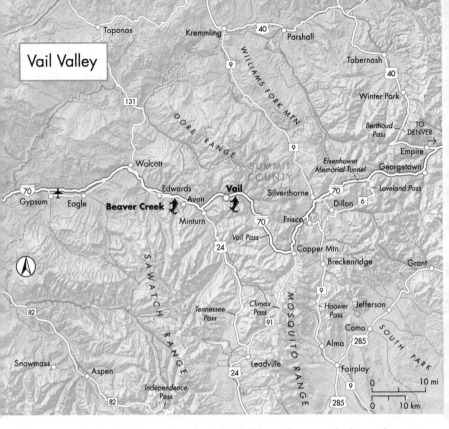

shops, restaurants, a heated gondola, and even a glockenspiel tower. Vail Village is also a hub of retail and dining with direct lift access to the mountain.

In terms of size, Vail overwhelms nearly every other ski area in North America. There are 5,289 acres popular with skiers and riders of all skill levels. Areas are clearly linked by a well-placed network of lifts and trails. The Front Side is draped with long trails; the infamous Back Bowls beckon powder skiers. A few hours of adventure skiing in Blue Sky Basin is a must for intermediate to advanced skiers and riders.

When the snows melt and two-for-one dinners are advertised in restaurant windows, you can be sure of two things—Vail is in the heart of the mud season, and the tranquillity won't last long. With the blooming of summer columbines come the culture crowds for music and culinary festivals and self-enrichment in the form of writing workshops and health-food seminars. While the valley teems with visitors, hikers and mountain bikers stream up the steep slopes on foot and via the Eagle Bahn Gondola to head into the network of trails that web the seemingly endless backcountry.

GETTING HERE AND AROUND

The best way to get to the Vail Valley is with a rental car. Once in the valley, a free shuttle makes it easy to get around town, and inexpensive bus service runs between Vail and Beaver Creek.

WHEN TO GO

Vail has grown into a year-round resort, skiing being the main attraction from December through March, and outdoor pursuits like hiking, biking, and fishing the rest of the year. While May and June have pleasant temperatures, many of the hiking and biking trails are still buried beneath snowdrifts. For those interested in seeing wildflowers, mid-July is the time to hit the peaks. The colorful aspen trees generally turn bright gold sometime in September.

FESTIVALS Vail hosts a wide variety of festivals, starting with the GoPro Mountain Games (⊕ *www.mountaingames.com*), showcasing such sports as kayaking, rafting, and mountain biking. Then there are Taste of Vail (⊕ *www.tasteofvail.com*), Gourmet on Gore, Spring Back to Vail, Snow Daze, Bravo!, and the Vail International Dance Festival, to name just a few. There are also free outdoor concerts by up-and-coming musicians, as well as concerts both on and off the mountain by some of the biggest names in the business.

Fodor's Choice **Bravo! Vail Valley Music Festival** Stretching from late June/early July
★ through early August, the annual Bravo! Vail Valley Music Festival is a month-and-a-half-long celebration of classical music. Among the performers in residence for a few days or more than a week are the New York Philharmonic, Dallas Symphony Orchestra, and Philadelphia Orchestra. Chamber-music concerts, many performed by the ensemble-in-residence, are popular events. While main orchestral events are held at Vail's Gerald R. Ford Amphitheater, you can find chamber music events and free concerts at various venues throughout the Vail Valley. ⊠ *Vail* ☎ *877/812–5700* ⊕ *www.bravovail.org.*

Vail International Dance Festival. Held in late July and early August, the annual Vail International Dance Festival hosts an unparalleled collection of ballet and modern dance groups from around the globe. The performers vary from year to year, but frequently include guest artists from the New York City Ballet, American Ballet Theatre, Pacific New Ballet, and other world-class companies. In recent years stars from reality TV hits like *Dancing With the Stars* and *So You Think You Can Dance* have appeared. Most performances are at the Gerald R. Ford Amphitheater, an outdoor venue where some people sit in the seats, but many more recline on blankets on the surrounding lawn. ⊠ *Gerald R. Ford Amphitheater, 530 S. Frontage Rd. E* ☎ *970/777–2015* ⊕ *www.vaildance.org* ⊠ *Varies.*

ESSENTIALS

Visitor Information Vail Resorts, Inc. ⊠ *Vail* ☎ *800/404–3535* ⊕ *www.vail.com.* **Vail Snow Report.** ⊠ *Vail* ☎ *970/754–4888* ⊕ *www.snow.com.*

TOURS

Nova Guides. Vail's Nova Guides runs Jeep and all-terrain-vehicle tours, as well as rafting, fishing, snowmobiling, and hiking expeditions. For something different, try a snow coach tour in a heated, four-track vehicle. Nova Guides can also arrange accommodation in a cabin or the large Camp Hale Lodge. ⊠ *7088 U.S. Hwy. 24* ☏ *719/486–2656* ⊕ *www.novaguides.com* ✉ *From $50.*

Timberline Tours. One of the oldest outfitters in the state, Timberline offers guided Jeep and rafting excursions in Vail Valley, with water activities like stand-up paddleboarding, rafting, and kayaking for every experience and adrenaline level. ⊠ *23698 U.S. Hwy. 24, Minturn* ☏ *800/831–1414, 970/476–1414* ⊕ *www.timberlinetours. com* ✉ *From $89.*

EXPLORING

Betty Ford Alpine Gardens. At 8,250 feet above sea level, the Betty Ford Alpine Gardens are the highest public botanical gardens in North America. This oasis of columbines, alpine plants, colorful perennials, and wild roses offers stunning views of the Rocky Mountains from meandering pathways that pass beside streams and waterfalls. The gardens are free to the public and open year-round; peak flower season is June through August. Guided tours are available. ⊠ *Ford Park, 530 S. Frontage Rd.* ☏ *970/476–0103* ⊕ *www.bettyfordalpinegardens.org* ✉ *Free* ⊙ *Daily dawn–dusk.*

Colorado Ski & Snowboard Museum and Hall of Fame. The Colorado Ski & Snowboard Museum and Hall of Fame traces the development of the sport throughout the world, with an emphasis on Colorado's contributions. On display are century-old skis and tows, early ski fashions, and an entire room devoted to the 10th Mountain Division, an army division that trained nearby. Snowboard enthusiasts will get a kick out of two original "snurfers"—prehistoric boards from 1966 and 1967, along with some vintage Burton boards. ⊠ *231 S. Frontage Rd. E* ☏ *970/476–1876* ⊕ *www.skimuseum.net* ✉ *$3 suggested donation* ⊙ *Late June–Sept., Tues.–Sun. 10–6; mid-Nov.–Apr., daily 10–6.*

DOWNHILL SKIING AND SNOWBOARDING

Fodor's Choice
★

Vail. Year after year, Vail logs more than a million "skier days" (the ski industry's measure of ticket sales), perpetuating its ranking as one of the top two or three most popular resorts in North America. From the top of China Bowl to the base of the Eagle Bahn Gondola at Lionshead, the resort is more than 7 miles across. The vast acreage is roughly divided into three sections: the Front Side, the Back Bowls, and Blue Sky Basin. Snowboarders will find plenty of steeps on the Front Side, and technical challenges at the Golden Peak or Bwana terrain parks, but they should avoid the Back Bowls, where long catwalks can get slow in the afternoon sun.

In 2013, Vail introduced Gondola One, one of the fastest 10-passenger gondolas in the world, clocking in at 1,200 feet per minute. The heated gondola with Wi-Fi and cushioned seats replaced the Vista Bahn. From Mid-Vail, the Mountain Express Lift (No. 4) has also been upgraded from a high-speed quad to a high-speed six-passenger chairlift.

Vail is perhaps best known for its legendary **Back Bowls,** more than 3,000 acres of wide-open spaces that are sensational on sunny days. Standing in any one of them, it's difficult to get a visual perspective, as skiers on the far side resemble Lilliputians. These bowls stretch from the original Sun Up and Sun Down to Game Creek on one side and Teacup, China, Siberia, and Outer Mongolia bowls on the far side. The terrain ranges from wide, groomed swatches for intermediate skiers to seemingly endless bump fields to glades so tight that only an expert boarder can slither between the trees. When there's fresh powder, these bowls beckon skiers intermediate and above. But after the fresh snow has been tracked up by skiers and pummeled by wind and sun, it may be wise for less-than-expert skiers to stay in the groomed sections of the bowls.

The **Front Side** of Vail Mountain delivers a markedly different experience. Here there's lots of wide-trail skiing, heavily skewed toward groomed intermediate runs, especially off the Northwood Express, Mountaintop Express, and Avanti Express lifts, as well as the slopes reachable via the Eagle Bahn Gondola. Pockets of advanced and expert terrain are tucked in and around the blue-marked slopes. The upper parts of Riva and the top of Look Ma are just a few of the places you'll find skilled skiers. The best show in town is on Highline (you can see it while riding Chair 10), where the experts groove through the moguls and those with a bit less experience careen around the bumps. The other two extremely difficult double-black-diamond trails off this slow lift are the best cruisers on the mountain for skilled skiers.

It takes time (as long as 45 minutes) to reach **Blue Sky Basin,** made up of three more bowls, but it's worth the effort. Tucked away in a secluded corner of Vail, this 645-acre area has been left in a wilder state, and the majority of the terrain is never groomed. Intermediate skiers will find a few open trails with spectacular views of rugged mountain peaks. For advanced and expert skiers, the real fun is playing in glades and terrain with names such as Heavy Metal, Lovers Leap, the Divide, and Champagne Glade. **Facilities:** 195 trails; 5,289 acres; 3,450-foot vertical drop; 31 lifts. ⊠ *Vail* ☎ *970/476–5601* ⊕ *www.vail.com* ✍ *Lift ticket $129* ⊗ *Late Nov.–mid-Apr., daily 8:30–4.*

LESSONS AND PROGRAMS

FAMILY **Vail Ski & Snowboard School.** This respected operation runs classes, workshops, and clinics for skiers of all levels. The more than 1,000 instructors teach in 22 languages. Beginners can take three-day courses that include equipment rental and lift passes. Workshops for women, teen sessions, and telemark courses are among the programs targeting specific groups. ⊠ *Vail* ☎ *970/754–8245* ⊕ *www.vail.com* ✍ *From $150* ⊗ *Closed in summer.*

RENTALS

Vail Sports. Within steps of the lifts and with 10 locations along the mountainside in Vail Village and Lionshead, this shop rents a wide range of ski gear, including high-end equipment. Prices for skis range from $47 to $67 a day. Book online for discounts. ⊠ *151 Vail La.* ☎ *970/477–5740* ⊕ *www.vailsports.com.*

NORDIC SKIING

BACKCOUNTRY SKIING

Paragon Guides. It's a good idea to hire a guide if you're unfamiliar with the area's backcountry trails. Paragon's capable guides can lead you along 100 different trails on foot or by bike, snowshoes, skis, and more. ⊠ *210 Edwards Village Blvd., Edwards* ☎ *970/926–5299* ⊕ *www.paragonguides.com.*

Fodor's Choice
★ **10th Mountain Division Hut and Trail System.** This famed network is one of Colorado's outdoor gems. Its 34 huts are in the mountains near Camp Hale, where the decorated namesake World War II division trained. Skiers and snowshoers in winter (snowmobiles are not permitted to approach the huts) and hikers and mountain bikers in summer tackle sections of the more than 350 miles of trails linking new and rustic cabins on day trips or weeklong expeditions. Apart from the joy of a self-reliant adventure among rugged mountains, travelers enjoy the camaraderie of communal living (there are very few private rooms in the huts), and evenings spent swapping stories by the glow of a wood-burning stove or the twinkle of summer stars. Hut reservations should be made at least a month in advance. ⊠ *Vail* ☎ ⊕ *www.huts.org.*

> **KNOW YOUR SNOW**
>
> Vail is known for its "powder": slopes puffed with light, fluffy flakes that make you feel that you are gliding on silk. Ungroomed runs, however, can quickly turn to "crud" as they get "tracked out" (scarred with deep tracks). That's when it's time to hunt up the "corduroy"—freshly groomed runs.

OTHER SPORTS AND THE OUTDOORS

FAMILY **Adventure Ridge.** In summer, Adventure Ridge, at Eagle's Nest high above Lionshead, is the hub of Vail Mountain activities. It's cool and high, and it has the views, especially from the zip-line and ropes course. It also has tons of activities like Friday Afternoon Club live bands, beer, sunset watching, the Dino Dig (a large sandbox with buried plastic dinosaur bones for kids), horseshoe pits, Frisbee golf, a climbing wall, tubing, and free guided nature hikes through the Gore Range Natural Science School's Discovery Center. Winter activities include tubing, snowmobiling, zip-lining, or ski-bike and (free) snowshoe tours. ⊠ *Atop Front Side of Vail Mountain, Eagle's Nest* ☎ *970/476–9090* ⊕ *www.vail.com.*

BICYCLING

A popular summer destination for both road bikers and mountain bikers, Vail has a variety of paved bike paths (including one that leads up to Vail Pass), plus dozens of miles of dirt mountain-bike trails. You can take bikes on lifts heading uphill, then head downhill on an array of routes.

Vail Bike Tech. Known as Vail Ski Tech in the winter, this shop rents and repairs bikes the rest of the year. Best of all, they are only steps from the Eagle Bahn Gondola, a summer gateway to the ski-slope trails. They also offer shuttle service to Vail Pass for downhill mountain biking. ⊠ *555 E. Lionshead Circle* ☎ *800/525–5995* ⊕ *www.vailbiketech.com.*

GOLF

Golfers who love to play mountain courses know that some of the best are in Vail Valley. These courses meander through the valleys dividing the area's soaring peaks. The region is home to more than a dozen courses, and there are another half dozen within easy driving distance. It's all just a matter of where you're staying and how much you want to spend. Some courses are only open to members and to guests at certain lodges.

Sonnenalp Golf Course. This Robert Cupp–Jay Morrish design threads through an upscale neighborhood 13 miles west of Vail. There are some serious elevation changes. Guests at the Sonnenalp Resort get preferred tee times. ⊠ *1265 Berry Creek Dr., Edwards* ☎ *970/477–5372* ⊕ *www. sonnenalp.com* ⊟ *$170, $140 for hotel guests* ⏃ *18 holes, 7100 yards, par 71* ⏃ *Reservations essential.*

Vail Golf Club. The area's municipal course rolls along between homes and condominiums in East Vail. ⊠ *1778 Vail Valley Dr.* ☎ *970/479– 2260* ⊕ *www.vailgolfclub.net* ⊟ *$109* ⏃ *18 holes, 7024 yards, par 71* ⏃ *Reservations essential.*

HIKING

Fodor's Choice
★

Booth Lake. This is one of Vail's most popular hikes, so get on the trail early or pick a weekday during the summer high season. It's a sustained 6-mile one-way climb from 8,400 feet to Booth Lake at 11,500 feet, right above the tree line. Fit hikers can do this in about seven hours. En route, you can cool off at the 60-foot Booth Creek Falls; at only 2 miles in, this is also a great spot to turn around if you're feeling winded (this should take about two to three hours round-trip, and is a great option for an easier hike). The reward for pushing on is a nice view of Booth Lake cradled among the alpine tundra. ⊠ *Trailhead: Take Exit 180 from I–70 to end of Booth Falls Rd.*

FAMILY **Eagle's Loop.** This trail starts from atop the Eagle Bahn Gondola at 10,350 feet, but it's a mellow, 1-mile stroll along the mountaintop ridge with panoramic views of the Mount of the Holy Cross. Allow about half an hour. A one-day lift ticket for the 14-minute gondola ride is $30 for adults. Adventurous types may prefer to skip the gondola (and the $30 fee) and hike the intermediate, often steep, 4½-mile trail through aspen trees and wildflowers to the beginning of the Eagle Loop trail. ⊠ *Trailhead: Top of Eagle Bahn Gondola.*

OUTFITTERS AND EXPEDITIONS

Paragon Guides. In summer, this backcountry adventure company offers rock climbing, mountain biking, and day and overnight llama treks in and around Vail Valley. In winter the company runs daylong ski trips through the backcountry, and three- to six-day trips along the 10th Mountain Division Hut System. ⊠ *210 Edwards Village Blvd., Edwards* ☎ *970/926–5299* ⊕ *www.paragonguides.com.*

NATURE CENTERS

FAMILY **Vail Nature Center.** This nature center occupies an old homestead just across from the Betty Ford Alpine Gardens. In summer, you can sign up for half-day and full-day backcountry hikes, wildflower walks, morning birding expeditions, and evening beaver-pond tours. Kids can sign up for art and fly-fishing classes, and families can join the "S'mores and More" family campfire program. ✉ *Adjacent to Ford Park, 601 Vail Valley Dr.* ☎ *970/479–2291* 🌐 *www.walkingmountains.org/locations/vail-nature-center* 🕒 *Mid-June–late Sept., daily 9–5.*

SNOWMOBILING

FAMILY **Adventure Ridge.** This outfitter at the top of Lionshead leads snowmobile excursions for kids, as well as snowshoeing, ski biking, zip-lining, and tubing for adventure-seekers of all ages. ✉ *Atop Front Side of Vail Mountain* ☎ *970/476–9090.*

Nova Guides. This is a good source for snowmobile rentals and guided "snowcoach" tours on a 13-passenger snowcat. ✉ *7088 U.S. Hwy. 24* ☎ *719/486–2656* 🌐 *www.novaguides.com.*

Vail Valley Tours. This snowmobiling outfit offers complimentary pickup in Vail, Avon, and Beaver Creek for two-hour, half-day, and custom guided tours into the White River National Forest. ✉ *2111 N. Frontage Rd. W* ☎ *970/476–7749* 🌐 *www.vailvalleytours.com* 🎟 *From $99.*

WHERE TO EAT

$$$$ MODERN AMERICAN FAMILY Fodor's Choice ★

🍴 **Atwater on Gore Creek.** The huge, seasonal menu includes highlights like a high-end Colorado Kobe steak served with asparagus spears and bleu cheese fritters, a crispy pork shank with a sherry-apricot glaze, and a variety of delicious sandwiches, pizzas, and lighter, tapas-style plates. Meals are rounded out with expert wine and beer pairings that make this somewhat out-of-the-way restaurant well worth the free shuttle from the village. [$] *Average main: $35* ✉ *Vail Cascade Resort, 1300 Westhaven Dr., Cascade Village* ☎ *970/479–7014* 🌐 *www.vailcascade.com/atwater.*

$$ AMERICAN

🍴 **Bart & Yeti's.** Grilled portobello-mushroom sandwiches, spicy Southwestern green chile, and Mike Flynn's beef stew are among the choices at this laid-back, rustic restaurant. If you want a full meal, try the most popular entrée, barbecued baby back ribs. The deck is a gathering spot in warm weather. The place is in Lionshead, just north of the Eagle Bahn Gondola. [$] *Average main: $13* ✉ *553 E. Lionshead Circle, Lionshead* ☎ *970/476–2754* 🌐 *www.bartnyetis.com.*

$$$$ AMERICAN Fodor's Choice ★

🍴 **Flame.** For a high-end restaurant in the high-end Four Seasons Vail hotel, this modern mountain steak house provides an appropriately high-end dining experience with surprisingly informal, family-friendly service. Small bites like the spicy tuna tacos or elk corn dogs served with house-made ketchup and aioli are perfect for sharing, which is highly encouraged, but the emphasis is on big here. Big windows and a big patio with mountain views; a new bar with a big (165-inch) TV; and big bites. Order any piece of meat—there are 17 cuts, including the exclusive, Colorado-raised, pure Wagyu beef—and you'll appreciate why the chef dry-ages his meat a second 28 days after buying it. The flavor and tenderness is unmatched. Be sure to leave room for some decadent sides, perhaps crispy brussels sprouts kimchi or Maine lobster mashed potatoes. [$] *Average main: $55* ✉ *Four Seasons Vail, 1 Vail Rd.* ☎ *970/477–8650* 🌐 *www.flamerestaurantvail.com.*

$$$$ FRENCH **Fodor's Choice** ★ ✕ **Game Creek Restaurant.** Getting to this restaurant is certainly half the fun, as you must catch a gondola up the mountain, then hop on a snowcat to get across Game Creek Bowl during the winter. During the summer you can travel by shuttle or walk. The Bavarian-style lodge is members-only for lunch, but open to the public for dinner all year and for an outstanding Sunday brunch in summer. Be prepared to linger over a multicourse meal as you enjoy spectacular views of the slopes and the mountains beyond. The menu is prix fixe—you might start with goat cheese burrata followed by duck with fava beans, red lentil dal, and piquillo peppers. [$] *Average main: $100* ✉ *278 Hanson Ranch Rd.* ☎ *970/754–4275* 🌐 *www.gamecreekvail.com* 🕒 *Closed Sun. and Mon. No lunch* ✍ *Reservations essential.*

$$$ MODERN AMERICAN ✕ **Larkspur Events and Dining.** An open kitchen bustling with activity is the backdrop at Larkspur, popular with a parka-clad crowd at lunch and well-dressed diners in the evening. Owner and chef Thomas Salamunovich has a talent for blending cuisines, so the menu is filled with creative entrées such as crispy chickpea cake or mushroom pizza with leeks and truffle-lemon vinaigrette for lunch and veal scaloppine with twice-baked potatoes, creamed spinach, and a lemon beurre fondue for dinner. Leave room for decadent desserts such as flourless chocolate cake and lemon-infused doughnuts with almond–poppy seed anglaise. Larkspur offers a grab-and-go market (8–5 daily in winter) with coffees, sandwiches, soups, burgers, and other hot goodies. [$] *Average main: $23* ✉ *Golden Peak Lodge, 458 Vail Valley Dr., Vail Village* ☎ *970/754–8050* 🌐 *www.larkspurvail.com* 🕒 *Closed summer. No dinner Sun.–Thurs. in winter* ✍ *Reservations essential.*

$$$$ MODERN FRENCH ✕ **La Tour.** In the heart of Vail Village, this contemporary French restaurant has been a local favorite for years and shouldn't be missed. Chef and owner Paul Ferzacca demonstrates his modern take on French cuisine with dishes like succulent bacon-wrapped pork with roasted cauliflower and a black-fig mostarda and chicken paillard with a beurre blanc sauce, crème fraîche potato puree, asparagus, cherry tomatoes, and capers. For dessert, try the chef-original peanut butter mousse with peanut brittle and grape sorbet. The service is top-notch, and the behemoth wine list is dominated by French and California labels. When the restaurant is busy in the summer, grab a seat on the patio for a quieter, breezier meal. [$] *Average main: $40* ✉ *122 E. Meadow Dr., Vail Village* ☎ *970/476–4403* 🌐 *www.latour-vail.com.*

$$$$ TAPAS ✕ **Leonora.** The swanky decor, complete with circular, crushed-velvet booths, a ceiling-high clear column of 1,000 wine bottles in the center of the restaurant, and cozy mood lighting from oversized shades filled with round, dim bulbs inspires the lively clientele to swap their ski gear for fancier nightlife gear for happy hour and dinner here. The loungey vibe is a big draw, but it's the food that keeps people coming back. Enjoy seafood, steak, or stew, or assemble a table of light tapas. The portions are smaller than at some other upscale ski resorts, but the flavors are big. [$] *Average main: $30* ✉ *16 Vail Rd., Lionshead* ☎ *970/477–8050* 🌐 *www.thesebastianvail.com/dining/leonora* 🕒 *Closed Mon. and Tues. in summer.*

5

$$$$ ✕**Mountain Standard.** This casual lunch and dinner stop prepares its
AMERICAN   meat and fish with a deft hand and the age-old way—over an open
wood fire. The menu changes often, but usually includes popular dishes
such as the spring pea bruschetta, a fall-off-the-bone pork chop with
charred okra succotash and cornbread crumble, and a whole Rocky
Mountain trout with grilled pole bean salad and smoked almond milk.
For dessert, splurge on a s'mores pie. From the dining room, you can
watch chefs prepare your food in the open kitchen, but summer has the
better view, with foodies and families alike congregating on the patio
overlooking Gore Creek. $ *Average main: $29* ⊠ *193 Gore Creek Dr.*
☎ *970/476–0123* ⊕ *www.mtnstandard.com* ▭ *No credit cards.*

$$$$ ✕**The 10th.** Find respite from the usual mountain fare at this high-end,
AMERICAN   high-up restaurant at the base of Look Ma run. There are spectacular
views of the Gore Range, a cozy bar and lounge with fireplace, and a
south-facing outdoor deck with heated tables. Warm your bones with
dishes like the heritage chicken-and-pheasant potpie with heirloom veggies and vermouth cream, and buffalo-and-elk bolognese on baked ziti
pasta. And there's no reason to tromp around in your ski boots—the
restaurant offers complimentary slippers, and bathrooms have hair dry-
ers, mouthwash, and hairspray to help with mid-ski grooming issues.
This place gets packed, so make reservations or plan on coming before
or after the rush. $ *Average main: $38* ⊠ *At the base of Look Ma
run, Mid-Vail* ☎ *970/754–1010* ⊕ *www.the10thvail.com* ☽ *No lunch
Mon.–Thurs. in summer, no dinner summer; no dinner Sun. and Mon.
in winter* ⌲ *Reservations essential.*

$$$$ ✕**Terra Bistro.** With spacious glass windows and track lighting, this
MODERN   sleek, sophisticated space in the Vail Mountain Lodge & Spa looks
AMERICAN   as if it belongs in a big city. Only the fireplace reminds you that this is
Vail. The menu focuses on contemporary American cuisine that throws
in a few Asian, Mediterranean, and Southwestern influences. Salmon
tartare with cucumber, ginger, jalapeño, and lime, and grilled Rocky
Mountain trout with sautéed kale are headliners; organic produce and
free-range meat and poultry are used whenever possible. $ *Average
main: $36* ⊠ *Vail Mountain Lodge, 352 E. Meadow Dr., Vail Village*
☎ *970/476–6836* ⊕ *www.terrabistrovail.com.*

$ ✕**Yellowbelly.** Fried-chicken joints usually require several napkins to
AMERICAN   mop up the grease and a long workout the next day to make up for
FAMILY   the indulgence—not so at Yellowbelly. Order the fried white or fried
Fodor'sChoice   dark plate—this gluten-free recipe is as tasty as it gets without weight-
★   ing you down too much for an afternoon on the slopes. Emphasizing
locally sourced (and never frozen) ingredients, this in-and-out lunch
spot serves great sides, and you get two with your main dish. Consider
brussels slaw, citrus quinoa, macaroni pie, or the sea-salted "smashed
potatoes." At the Boylan soda fountain, enjoy cane-sugar root beer and
black-cherry sodas. The location in West Vail Mall is inconvenient if
you don't have a car, but it's worth finding a way to get here. $ *Average
main: $10* ⊠ *2161 N. Frontage Rd., No. 14* ☎ *970/343–4340* ⊕ *www.
yellowbellychicken.com* ▭ *No credit cards.*

WHERE TO STAY

$$$$
RESORT
Arrabelle at Vail Square. Surrounded by shops, restaurants, and galleries, and just steps away from an ice-skating rink and the Eagle Bahn Gondola (which runs right to the top of Vail Mountain), the Arrabelle is a star in Lionshead Village. **Pros:** ski valet; pet-friendly; great location; fabulous on-site spa. **Cons:** the valet parking entrance is hard to find. $ *Rooms from: $515* ⊠ *675 Lionshead Pl.* ☎ *970/754–7777, 866/662–7625* ⊕ *www.arrabelle.rockresorts.com* ⬅ *60 rooms, 22 condominiums* ⊚ *No meals.*

$$$$
RESORT
FAMILY
Fodor'sChoice
★
Four Seasons Resort Vail. One of the newest luxury properties in Vail, the swanky Four Seasons has quickly overtaken the competition in the village, despite having fewer rooms than the other high-end chains. **Pros:** large guest rooms with luxurious bathrooms; family-friendly, with a kids' club and teen center. **Cons:** a slight walk from slopes. $ *Rooms from: $1,000* ⊠ *1 Vail Rd.* ☎ *970/477–8600, 800/819–5053* ⊕ *www.fourseasons.com/vail* ⬅ *121 rooms, 24 suites* ⊚ *No meals.*

$$$$
RENTAL
Galatyn Lodge. This luxury lodge in a quiet part of Vail Village maintains a low profile, which is just the approach its hard-core skiing regulars prefer. **Pros:** outdoor heated pool; high percentage of return guests; apartment style. **Cons:** no children's programs; no restaurant or bar. $ *Rooms from: $375* ⊠ *365 Vail Valley Dr., Vail Village* ☎ *970/479–2418, 800 /943–7322* ⊕ *www.thegalatynlodge.com* ⬅ *5 condos* ⊚ *No meals.*

$$$$
B&B/INN
Gasthof Gramshammer. Pepi Gramshammer, a former Austrian Olympic ski racer who runs some of the country's best intensive ski programs, operates this guesthouse. **Pros:** European flavor; village location. **Cons:** no room service. $ *Rooms from: $306* ⊠ *231 E. Gore Creek Dr., Vail Village* ☎ *970/476–5626, 800/610–7374* ⊕ *www.pepis.com* ⬅ *31 rooms, 6 suites, 1 penthouse* ⊚ *Breakfast.*

$$$$
HOTEL
Lodge at Vail. One of the first hotels to open in Vail, in 1962, the sprawling lodge—modeled after the Lodge at Sun Valley—is popular with skiers and families because of its fabulous location only 150 feet from the village's main lift, the Gondola One. Ski valets ready your skis every morning and collect your gear for drying in the evening. **Pros:** located near main ski lift; popular steak house, Elway's, on-site. **Cons:** pricey; quality of rooms varies. $ *Rooms from: $419* ⊠ *174 E. Gore Creek Dr., Vail Village* ☎ *970/754–7800, 877/528–7625* ⊕ *www.lodgeatvail.rockresorts. com* ⬅ *80 rooms, 84 condos, 3 chalets* ⊚ *No meals.*

$$$$
HOTEL
FAMILY
Fodor'sChoice
★
The Sebastian. Manhattan chic meets Colorado ski lodge at this boutique hotel where you will find the work of Mexican abstract artist Manuel Felguérez throughout, and the lively Frost Bar with its craft cocktails and street-fare–style bites. **Pros:** great location; attention to detail and top-notch service; family-friendly, with pop-up tents in room, a camp, and playroom. **Cons:** many rooms overlook the freeway. $ *Rooms from: $605* ⊠ *16 Vail Rd.* ☎ *970/477–8000, 800/354–6908* ⊕ *www.thesebastianvail. com* ▭ *No credit cards* ⬅ *84 rooms, 16 suites* ⊚ *No meals.*

$$$$
HOTEL
Fodor'sChoice
★
Sitzmark Lodge. This cozy family-run lodge offers balconies that look out onto Vail Mountain or Gore Creek and a lively and diverse feel, thanks to the international guests who return year after year. **Pros:** friendly; easy access to ski lifts; international ambience. **Cons:** no spa. $ *Rooms from: $300* ⊠ *183 Gore Creek Dr., Vail Village*

5

☎ *970/476–5001, 888/476–5001* 🌐 *www.sitzmarklodge.com* 🛏 *34 rooms* 🍴 *Breakfast.*

$$$$ HOTEL 🏨 **Sonnenalp Resort.** It's the sense of family tradition and European elegance that makes the Sonnenalp Resort the most romantic of all hotels in the faux-Tyrolean village of Vail. **Pros:** classic alpine ambience; excellent buffet breakfasts; spa and beautiful indoor-outdoor pool. **Cons:** removed from lifts; wooden beams can make ceilings feel low. [$] *Rooms from: $650* ✉ *20 Vail Rd., Vail Village* ☎ *970/476–5656, 800/654–8312* 🌐 *www.sonnenalp.com* 🛏 *15 rooms, 112 suites* 🍴 *Breakfast.*

$$$$ RESORT FAMILY 🏨 **Vail Cascade Resort & Spa.** Down-to-earth yet luxurious, this family-oriented hotel offers excellent amenities and is one of Vail's only true ski-in ski-out places to stay. **Pros:** right on the slope; large spa and health club; stunning views of creek. **Cons:** staff can be hard to find; concrete exterior; expensive parking. [$] *Rooms from: $300* ✉ *1300 Westhaven Dr., Cascade Village* ☎ *970/476–7111, 800/420–2424* 🌐 *www.vailcascade.com* 🛏 *292 rooms, 27 suites, 80 condominiums* 🍴 *No meals.*

$$$$ HOTEL 🏨 **Vail Mountain Lodge.** This upscale boutique hotel on Gore Creek is perfectly located for outdoor enthusiasts, but its private fireplaces, soaking tubs, and feather beds, as well as the comprehensive spa, fitness center, and Vitality center may tempt guests to spend the entire stay indoors. **Pros:** spacious rooms; great fitness club; incredibly comfortable beds. **Cons:** no hotel-specific parking but valet available. [$] *Rooms from: $499* ✉ *352 E. Meadow Dr.* ☎ *970/476–0700, 888/794–0410* 🌐 *www.vailmountainlodge.com* 🛏 *20 rooms, 7 condos* 🍴 *Breakfast.*

LODGING ALTERNATIVES

Vail/Beaver Creek Reservations. This is your one-stop source for buying lift tickets, arranging ski and snowboard lessons, getting updates on events and activities, and booking lodging at many of the hotels and condominium properties in the Vail Valley. ✉ *Vail* ☎ *800/525–2257* 🌐 *www.beavercreek.com.*

Vail Valley Partnership. This central reservations service reps properties in Vail, Avon, and Beaver Creek. ✉ *Vail* ☎ *970/477–4002* 🌐 *www.visitvailvalley.com.*

NIGHTLIFE

Bol. An upscale bar and restaurant with a bowling alley, Bol specializes in burgers and pizza but also serves more substantial steaks and seafood grills. ✉ *141 E. Meadow Dr., Vail Village* ☎ *970/476–5300* 🌐 *www.bolvail.com.*

Frost Bar. DJs spin Fridays and Saturdays to the young, überhip, and occasionally famous patrons that pack in for après and stay until closing. The bar features hand-blown glass accents and a glass floor and boasts the largest collection of scotch and tequila in Vail. Drink craft cocktails and munch on elevated street food, such as lobster mac and cheese and steak tacos. In summer, the special mojito menu features drinks made from several varieties of mint fresh from the garden. ✉ *16 Vail Rd., Vail Village* ☎ *970/477–8000* 🌐 *www.thesebastianvail.com.*

Garfinkel's. Near the gondola in Lionshead, Garfinkel's has plenty of video monitors for watching games. It's open until 2 am on weekends. ⌧ *536 E. Lionshead Circle* ☎ *970/476–3789* ⊕ *www.garfsvail.com.*

Matsuhisa. Head to this high-end sushi spot for the best bar counter in town: a long, sleek wooden bar sitting in front of floor-to-ceiling windows that offer stunning views of the mountain and the village. The expertly crafted menu here draws a savvy crowd (try the yellowtail jalapeño sashimi), while the cold and warm sake selection and craft cocktails, exclusive to this restaurant, keep the place hopping until late. ⌧ *141 E. Meadow Dr.* ☎ *970/476–6628* ⊕ *www.matsuhisavail.com.*

Red Lion. This popular spot is a tradition in Vail. It's standing-room-only in the afternoon, and a bit mellower in the evening. Most nights there's guitar or piano music, and there's bingo in the winter. ⌧ *304 Bridge St.* ☎ *970/476–7676* ⊕ *www.theredlion.com.*

Sarah's Lounge. Located in Christiania at Vail, this lively spot showcases Helmut Fricker, a Vail institution who plays accordion while yodeling up a storm on Friday evenings in ski season. ⌧ *356 E. Hanson Ranch Rd.* ☎ *970/476–5641.*

10th Mountain Whiskey Tasting Room. Warm your belly with a flight of mountain magic at this industrial-cool but cozy tasting room in the heart of the village. Samples of locally distilled potato vodka, corn moonshine, bourbon, whiskey, and cordial are served up with a history of the 10th Mountain Division. ⌧ *286 Bridge St.* ☎ *970/470–4215* ⊕ *www.10thwhiskey.com.*

SHOPPING

ART GALLERIES

Claggett/Rey Gallery. This is the place to purchase paintings and sculptures by some of the finest Western and Native American artists living in North America. ⌧ *100 E. Meadow Dr., Bldg. 10* ☎ *970/476–9350* ⊕ *www.claggettrey.com.*

BOUTIQUES

Axel's. Across from the Children's Fountain, this is a great pick for high-end European fashions including Italian suede pants, riding boots, silver and gold handmade belt buckles, and shearling coats. ⌧ *201 Gore Creek Dr.* ☎ *970/497–4888* ⊕ *www.axelsltd.com.*

Gorsuch. Gorsuch specializes in high-end apparel for the mountain lifestyle, spanning luxurious sweaters to ski gear. Also find a branch in the Four Seasons. ⌧ *263 E. Gore Creek Dr.* ☎ *970/476–2294* ⊕ *www.gorsuch.com* ⌧ *61 Avondale La., Avon* ☎ *970/949–8091.*

Luca Bruno. Children keep pace with their stylish parents at this boutique that carries James Perse and Nanette Lepore for the grown-ups, and Hartford sweaters and button-ups for the little ones. ⌧ *141 E. Meadow Dr., Vail Village* ☎ *970/479–0050.*

Pepi Sports. Look to this chic boutique for ski clothing, equipment, and accessories from designers such as Bogner, Skea, Descente, and Spyder. Also find jewelry, clothes, shoes, and home furnishings here. ⌧ *231 Bridge St.* ☎ *970/476–5206* ⊕ *www.pepisports.com.*

Perch. Tory Burch, Elizabeth and James, Theory, and Diane von Furstenberg fill the racks in this perfectly upscale boutique. The inviting space carries all of the latest trends and trendsetters, eschewing steadfast mountain style for cocktail dresses. Read: there are no Nordic sweaters. ⊠ *122 E. Meadow Dr., Vail Village* ☎ *970/688–5947* ⊕ *www.perchvail.com.*

SPAS

Aria Athletic Club & Spa. This 78,000-square-foot facility in the Vail Cascade Resort & Spa is one of the best places in Vail to relax and rejuvenate. Enjoy pampering treatments inspired by the natural beauty of the surrounding area, like a massage with heated river stones and oils infused with balsam fir, juniper, and pine to relieve tension; exuberating mineral scrubs and wraps to build immunity; and healing hand and foot rubs to pamper after days in mittens and boots. Fourteen treatment rooms plus mani-pedi stations and childcare and kids' programs ensure a relaxing visit. On the invigoration front, take advantage of facilities that include racquetball, basketball, indoor tennis courts, an indoor running track, and a full gym with a full schedule of classes, from Pilates to FitWall to yoga and Spinning. ⊠ *1300 Westhaven Dr.* ☎ *970/479–5942, 888/824–5772* ⊕ *www.vailcascade.com.*

RockResorts Spa at The Arrabelle. Step into this 10,000-square-foot oasis that mimics the peaceful, mountainous surroundings: cream-colored walls, reclaimed-wood and natural-stone accents, and blues that match bluebird days, bringing the outside in. Arrive early to take advantage of the peaceful setting and the whirlpool, sauna, and eucalyptus steam room, as well as the separate his and hers relaxation rooms with chaise lounges. Most treatments use organic ingredients and local flora, such as lavender and mountain juniper. The Fruit and Spice Body Peel and Wrap is the ultimate indulgence, with a hydrating pumpkin peel, cinnamon-sugar scrub, and scalp massage. ⊠ *675 Lionshead Pl.* ☎ *970/754–7754* ⊕ *www.arrabelle.rockresorts.com.*

Sonnenalp Spa. This lovely spa in Sonnenalp Resort is a European-style facility where you can relax on one of the lounge chairs around a crackling fireplace as you sip tea or spa water. Aspen trees stand over the heated outdoor tranquility pool, which has its own waterfall. Quench parched skin with a moisturizing HydraFacial, which diminishes wrinkles and shrinks pores (it's similar to microdermabrasion, but without the redness). You can also reduce altitude headaches with a hit from the oxygen bar. Beyond the massages and body wraps, you can stimulate other senses with sound, vibration, and light therapies. Any treatment longer than an hour will cost a pretty penny, but the serene, inviting atmosphere is worth it for a splurge. Book ahead for manicures and pedicures—they fill up year-round. Nonguests can use the facilities for $35 a day. ⊠ *20 Vail Rd.* ☎ *970/479–5404* ⊕ *www.sonnenalpspa.com.*

The Spa at Four Seasons Vail. This 14,000-square-foot, award-winning, full-service spa is the height of decadence. Unwind next to the relaxation lounge's oversized fireplace in the winter or in the relaxation garden during warmer times of year. The grotto-inspired hot tub and cold plunge rotation wake up the body, and a dedicated slumber room lulls you to sleep. A dry cedar sauna and a eucalyptus steam room ends or begins the journey. Aside from the 13 treatment rooms, there are two couples' suites with dual massage tables, a giant soaking tub for pre- and post-treatment relaxation, and a private patio for a meal under the stars. ⊠ *1 Vail Rd.* ☎ *970/477–8600* ⊕ *www.fourseasons.com/vail.*

BEAVER CREEK

12 miles west of Vail; 110 miles west of Denver via I–70.

As with the majority of the area's resorts, the heart of Beaver Creek is a mountainside village. What sets Beaver Creek apart is that it's a series of cascading plazas connected by escalators. In this ultraposh enclave even boot-wearing skiers and snowboard-hauling riders take the escalators from the hotels and shuttle stops on the lower levels. Opened in 1980 as a smaller version of Vail, Beaver Creek has somewhat overshadowed its older sibling in glamour. In fact, its nearest rival in the luxury market is Utah's Deer Valley.

Locals know that Beaver Creek is the best place to ski on weekends, when Vail is too crowded, or anytime there's fresh powder. Beaver Creek is just far enough from Denver that it doesn't get the flood of day-trippers who flock to Vail and the other Front Range resorts. The slopes of Beaver Creek Mountain are connected to those of even ritzier Bachelor Gulch. These are close to Arrowhead, creating a village-to-village ski experience like those found in Europe.

Savvy travelers have learned that Beaver Creek is even lovelier in summer, when diners can enjoy a meal on a spacious patio, mountain bikers can hitch a ride uphill on the chairlift, and golfers can play on the beautiful Beaver Creek Course or on one of the dozen others in the Vail Valley. On special evenings you can attend concerts, get tickets to the theater, or head to a performance at the Vilar Performing Arts Center. In Beaver Creek you have easy access to all the activities in Vail Valley.

GETTING HERE AND AROUND
Driving is the most convenient way to get around Beaver Creek, but there are private shuttles and public buses. Expect to pay for parking.

WHEN TO GO
Beaver Creek's seasons are the same as Vail's; winter is great for snow sports and summer also attracts outdoor enthusiasts.

ESSENTIALS
Transportation Contacts Avon/Beaver Creek Transit. ⊠ *Avon* ☎ *970/748–4120* ⊕ *www.avon.org.* **Colorado Mountain Express.** ⊠ *Edwards* ☎ *800/525–6363, 970/754–7433* ⊕ *www.coloradomountainexpress.com.*

DOWNHILL SKIING AND SNOWBOARDING

Fodor's Choice ★ **Beaver Creek.** Beaver Creek is a piece of nirvana, partly because of its system of trails and partly because of its enviable location two hours from Denver. Although only a third the size of Vail, Beaver Creek is seldom crowded. The skiable terrain extends from the runs down Beaver Creek to the slopes around Bachelor Gulch to the network of trails at

Arrowhead. You can easily ski from one village to another. The omnipresent and helpful ambassadors are always willing to point you in the right direction, and carry your skis to the liftside.

Beaver Creek has a little of everything, from smoother slopes for beginners to difficult trails used for international competitions. Grouse Mountain, in particular, is famed for its thigh-burning bump runs. Beginners have an entire peak, at the summit of Beaver Creek Mountain, where they can learn to ski or practice on novice trails. And newcomers can return to the village on one of the lifts if they are too tired to take the long trail all the way to the bottom. Intermediate-level skiers have several long cruising trails on the lower half of Beaver Creek Mountain and in Larkspur Bowl. Both locations also have black-diamond trails, so groups of skiers and snowboarders of varying abilities can ride uphill together. The Birds of Prey runs, like Peregrine and Golden Eagle, are aptly named, because the steepness of the trails can be a surprise for skiers who mistakenly think they are skilled enough to take on this challenging terrain. The days of snowboarders getting snubbed in Beaver Creek are long gone, and shredders can tackle a series of terrain parks with increasing difficulty from Park 101 to the Zoom Room and on to the Moonshine half-pipe.

The slopes of neighboring **Bachelor Gulch** are a mix of beginner and intermediate trails. Here you can often find fresh powder hours after it's gone elsewhere. Many of the open slopes weave past multimillion-dollar homes; cost of real estate is even higher than in Beaver Creek. The Ritz-Carlton Bachelor Gulch, which sits at the base of the Bachelor Gulch Express Lift, is one of the region's most beautiful hotels. A stop here is a must for any architecture buff. Many skiers plan to arrive in time for a hearty lunch at Buffalos or an après-ski cocktail in the Buffalo Bar or the Bachelors Lounge. There are shuttles handy to take you back to Beaver Creek.

The third village in the area, **Arrowhead,** has the best and usually the least crowded intermediate terrain. Locals take advantage of sunny days by sitting on the spacious deck at the Broken Arrow restaurant. It's not much more than a shack, but the burgers can't be beat. The European concept of skiing from village to village was introduced here in 1996, when Vail Associates decided to connect Arrowhead, Beaver Creek, and Bachelor Gulch via lifts and ski trails. **Facilities:** 150 trails; 1,832 acres; 3,340-foot vertical drop; 24 lifts. ⊠ *Beaver Creek* ☎ *800/404–3535* ⊕ *www.beavercreek.com* ✉ *Lift ticket $159* ☼ *Late Nov.–mid-Apr., daily 9–4.*

LESSONS AND PROGRAMS

Beaver Creek Ski & Snowboard School. At Beaver Creek's excellent ski and snowboard school there are about 600 instructors; lessons are available in more than 20 languages. Special clinics run throughout the year, like workshops for women, teen sessions, and telemark courses. The school boasts numerous beginner through advanced ski and snowboard lessons for all ages, with a focus on small class sizes. ⊠ *Beaver Creek* ☎ *970/754–8245* ⊕ *www.beavercreek.com.*

CLOSE UP

Skiing and Snowboarding Tips

Although downhill skiing has long been the classic winter activity, snowboarding—once the bastion of teenage "riders" in baggy pants—is fast catching up as a mainstream sport. Telemarking and cross-country skiing still have loyal followings, though these skiers tend to prefer the wide-open backcountry to the more populated resorts.

Although it snows somewhere in the Colorado high country every month—and resorts can open their lifts as early as October and close as late as the Fourth of July—the traditional ski season usually runs from late November until early April. Christmas through New Year's Day and the month of March (when spring-breakers arrive) tend to be the busiest periods for most ski areas. The slower months of January and February often yield good package deals, as do the early and late ends of the season.

EQUIPMENT RENTAL

Rental equipment is available at all ski areas and at ski shops around resorts or in nearby towns. It's often more expensive to rent at the resort where you'll be skiing, but then it's easier to go back to the shop if something doesn't fit. Experienced skiers can "demo" (try out) premium equipment to get a feel for new technology before upgrading.

LESSONS

In the United States, the Professional Ski Instructors of America (PSIA) has devised a progressive teaching system that is used at most ski schools. This allows skiers to take lessons at different ski areas. Classes range in length from hour-long skill clinics to half- or full-day workshops.

Deals can be had for first-time and beginner skiers and snowboarders who attend morning clinics and then try out their new skills on beginner and intermediate slopes for the remainder of the day.

Most ski schools follow the PSIA teaching approach for children, and many also incorporate SKIwee, another standardized teaching technique. Classes for children are arranged by ability and age group; often the ski instructor chaperones a meal during the teaching session. Children's ski instruction has come a long way in the last 10 years; instructors specially trained in teaching children and equipment designed for little bodies mean that most children can now begin to ski successfully as young as three or four. Helmets are often de rigueur.

LIFT TICKETS

With some lift ticket prices increasing every year, the best advice is to shop around. Single-day, adult, holiday-weekend passes cost the most, but better bargains can be had through off-site purchase locations (check newspaper Sunday sections and local supermarkets, such as King Soopers and Safeway), online discounts, multiple-day passes, and season passes. You can always call a particular resort's central reservations line to ask where discount lift tickets can be purchased. With a little legwork you should never have to pay full price.

TRAIL RATING

Ski areas mark and rate trails and slopes—Easy (green circle), Intermediate (blue square), Advanced (black diamond), and Expert (double black diamond).

5

RENTALS

Beaver Creek Sports. Adult ski rentals range from $68 to $83 a day, depending on the package. Find six Beaver Creek Sports locations in Vail Valley. ⊠ *1 Beaver Creek Pl., Avon* ☎ *970/754–5430* ⊕ *www. beavercreeksports.com.*

NORDIC SKIING

TRACK SKIING

Beaver Creek Nordic Sports Center. Lessons, equipment rentals, and guided tours are available here. ⊠ *Strawberry Park Condo Bldg., at the bottom of Chair 12* ☎ *970/745–5313* ⊕ *www.beavercreek.com/ski-and-snowboard-school/nordic-center* ⊘ *Closed mid-Apr.–mid-Dec.*

McCoy Park. The prettiest place for cross-country skiing is this park with more than 19 miles of trails groomed for traditional cross-country skiing, skate skiing, and snowshoeing, all laid out around a mountain peak. To get here, take the Strawberry Park chairlift—a plus because it gets you far enough from the village that you're in a pristine environment. The groomed tracks have a fair amount of ups and downs (or perhaps because the elevation begins at 9,840 feet, it just seems that way). ⊠ *Beaver Creek* ☎ *970/754–5313* ⊕ *www.beavercreek.com* ⊘ *Closed mid-Apr.–mid-Dec.*

OTHER SPORTS AND THE OUTDOORS

GOLF

Eagle Ranch Golf Club. This 6,600-foot-high course was landscaped in the lush wetlands of the Brush Creek Valley. Caddies like to joke that the perfect club might actually be a fly rod. Arnold Palmer, who designed the 18-hole course, said, "The fairways are very playable and the roughs are not extremely rough." ⊠ *0050 Lime Park Dr., Eagle* ☎ *970/328–2882, 866/328–3232* ⊕ *www.eagleranchgolf.com* ☑ *$99* ⅃ *18 holes, 7500 yards, par 72* ⚓ *Reservations essential.*

Red Sky Ranch & Golf Club. At this tony private course a few miles west of Beaver Creek members alternate with guests on two courses designed by Tom Fazio and Greg Norman. The Tom Fazio Course's front nine are laid out on sagebrush-covered hills, but the back nine flows up and down a mountainside covered with groves of junipers and aspens. The Greg Norman Course sprawls through a broad valley. Some shots require carries across jagged ravines. Norman's signature bunkers abound, guarding slippery greens. In order to play at Red Sky Golf Club you must be staying in the Lodge at Vail, the Pines Lodge in Beaver Creek, the Ritz-Carlton Bachelor Gulch, other hotels owned by Vail Resorts, or other partner properties. Nonmembers must book caddies a day in advance. ⊠ *376 Red Sky Rd., Wolcott* ☎ *970/754–8377* ⊕ *www.redskygolfclub.com* ☑ *$250* ⅃ *Greg Norman: 18 holes, 7580 yards, par 72; Tom Fazio: 18 holes, 7113 yards, par 72* ⚓ *Reservations essential.*

HIKING

Holy Cross Wilderness Area. This wilderness region southwest of Beaver Creek offers plenty of outdoor adventures. One great hike is the 4½-mile Missouri Lakes trail. It's easy to access and provides a fun loop and moderate hike through the wilderness. See high alpine lakes and great views at the mouth of a mini canyon. Take the switchbacks to Fancy Pass and Cross Creek trails for a bird's-eye view of the area. ✉ *Holy Cross Ranger District, White River National Forest* ☎ *970/827–5715* 🌐 *www.fs.usda.gov/whiteriver.*

HORSEBACK RIDING

Beaver Creek Stables. Here you can book outings ranging from one-hour rides to all-day excursions. Many trips include a tasty picnic lunch. In the evening, ride your horse to Beano's Cabin for dinner. Horseback-riding lessons are also available. ✉ *93 Elk Track Rd., Avon* ☎ *970/845–7770* 🌐 *www.beavercreekstables.com.*

5

WHERE TO EAT

$$$$ MODERN AMERICAN Fodor's Choice ★

🍴 **Beano's Cabin.** One of the memorable experiences during a trip to Beaver Creek is traveling in a sleigh to this former hunting lodge. In summer you can get here on horseback or by wagon. During the journey, your driver will undoubtedly fill you in on some local history. The pine-log cabin, warmed by a crackling fire, is an unbeatable location for a romantic meal. On the prix-fixe menu, choose from entrées such as potato dumplings with bing cherries and chanterelles, or a wood-grilled Rocky Mountain elk chop with sweet corn–rabbit belly hash. The menu changes seasonally. [$] *Average main: $100* ✉ *Larkspur Bowl* ☎ *970/754–3463* 🌐 *www.beanoscabinbeavercreek.com* ⏲ *Closed mid-Apr. and Oct. to mid-Nov., depending on snowfall* ✍ *Reservations essential* ☞ *Lunch for members only in winter.*

$$$ SEAFOOD

🍴 **Dive Fish House.** Dive is all about seafood, flown in daily from Hawaii and both coasts. This oyster and crudo bar also offers the likes of Carolina grits and charred tomato sauce, and calamari and squid ink pasta with lemon beurre blanc cioppino. Check out Wednesday's "hump day" oysters and champagne special, all night long. [$] *Average main: $22* ✉ *56 Edwards Village Blvd., No. 230, Edwards* ☎ *970/926–3433* 🌐 *www.divefishhouse.com* ⏲ *Closed Sun. and Mon. No lunch.*

$$$ AMERICAN

🍴 **The Gashouse.** This longtime hangout set inside a 1930s-era log cabin has walls covered with hunting trophies. (If stuffed animal heads aren't your thing, think twice about eating here.) Locals swear by the buffalo, prime rib, and elk, and also the fresh seafood. Stop in for a brew and some buffalo wings and watch how some of the Vail Valley residents kick back. [$] *Average main: $24* ✉ *34185 U.S. 6, Edwards* ☎ *970/926–3613* 🌐 *www.gashouse-restaurant.com.*

$$$$ AMERICAN Fodor's Choice ★

🍴 **Grouse Mountain Grill.** The stately appearance of this Pines Lodge restaurant belies its friendly, welcoming attitude. The fresh, farm-raised, cage-free food philosophy makes for quality ingredients, and the chef here truly knows how to make the food sing. The pretzel-crusted pork chops have been a favorite for years, but also check out the Ritz-crusted walleye with duck-fat fries and an herb tartar sauce, or the baby beets with house-made ricotta beignets. There's live music most nights, with local musician Tony Gulizia a popular regular. If you get chilly on the patio, the waitstaff brings out blankets. Complimentary valet is offered. $ *Average main: $40* ✉ *141 Scott Hill Rd.* ☎ *970/949–0600* ⊕ *www. grousemountaingrill.com* ☉ *No lunch in summer.*

$$$ ✕ **Maya.** In 2013, celeb chef Richard Sandoval transformed his Cima
MODERN restaurant at the Westin Riverfront into Maya, switching his plates from
MEXICAN contemporary Latin to modern Mexican. Oversized windows brighten
Fodor's Choice the already warm space filled with hand-blown glass light fixtures,
★ wood, and Mexican-tile accents, and a bar lined with house-infused tequilas. Guacamole is smashed together tableside, and the skillet pork carnitas and roasted chicken mole dishes are simple reminders that delicious, authentic Mexican isn't confined to hole-in-the-wall outposts. Don't miss the serrano-pepper-infused tequila margaritas. For something different, try a drink with smoky mezcal. $ *Average main: $25* ✉ *Westin Riverfront Resort & Spa, 126 Riverfront La., Avon* ☎ *970/790–5500* ⊕ *www.richardsandoval.com/mayabc.*

$$$ ✕ **The Metropolitan.** For a quick, but nevertheless indulgent, bite, the Met
TAPAS is a fine choice après ski or as a midshopping nosh break. The wine and tapas bar looks like an oenophile's cafeteria, complete with a wine fountain that dispenses three pour sizes of 16 different wines. Make a meal of a few small plates, like the tasty shrimp and grits with bacon or sweet and salty brussels sprouts. The butter-poached Maine lobster tacos, with ancho chili cream and pico de gallo, and the signature jerk shrimp tacos are not to be missed. Note the colorful cocktails, including honeydew-melon-cucumber sangria and the Spicy Beaver, a blend of tequila, cilantro, lime, jalapeño, and agave nectar. The restaurant also contains a high-end espresso bar that uses Colorado-based Dazbog Coffee beans. $ *Average main: $25* ✉ *210 Offerson Rd., Suite 201C* ☎ *970/748–3123* ⊕ *www.themetbc.com.*

$$$$ ✕ **Mirabelle.** In a restored farmhouse at the entrance to Beaver Creek,
EUROPEAN Mirabelle is one of the area's loveliest restaurants. Owner and chef Daniel Joly serves superb Belgian–French cuisine. His preparations are a perfect blend of colors, flavors, and textures. The menu changes regularly, but if it's available, try warm foie gras with caramelized peaches, and roasted elk fillet with rhubarb jam. Depending on your point of view, the elaborate desserts are either heavenly or sinful. The wine list is roughly two-thirds European—to match the menu—and a third domestic. $ *Average main: $50* ✉ *55 Village Rd., Avon* ☎ *970/949–7728* ⊕ *www.mirabelle1.com* ☉ *Closed mid-Apr.–late-May and mid-Oct.– mid-Nov., and Sun. No lunch.*

$$$$ ✕ **Spago.** At the Ritz-Carlton, Wolfgang Puck's restaurant is housed in
MODERN an expansive dining room whose vegetable-dyed wood paneling and
AMERICAN enlarged black-and-white photographs achieve a sleekly modern look without contradicting the resort's rustic mountain sensibility. Puck's seasonal menu often favors Asian accents and regional ingredients. In late autumn the menu's butternut squash soup is deliciously intensified with cranberry chutney, spiced cream, and pumpkin-seed brittle. The Colorado lamb chops spiced with Hunan eggplant and cilantro-mint vinaigrette is not to be missed and for dessert the *kaiserschmarren*, a

souffléd crème fraîche pancake with strawberry sauce, is otherwordly. Service is impeccable, if a touch formal; those who prefer a low-key (or less bank-breaking) meal might consider dining in the bar area. $ *Average main: $45 ⊠ Ritz-Carlton Bachelor Gulch, 0130 Daybreak Ridge, Avon ☎ 970/343–1555 ⊕ www.wolfgangpuck.com ⊙ No lunch spring–fall; closed Mon. and Tues. in summer ⌂ Reservations essential.*

$$$$
MODERN
AMERICAN
✕ **Splendido at the Chateau.** With elegant marble columns and custom-made Italian linens, this posh eatery is the height of opulence. Owner and chef David Walford is a master of contemporary American cuisine, and he borrows freely from many traditions. He is equally adept at turning out rack of lamb with charmoula-spiced carrot purée as he is grilling an elk loin with sunflower seed risotto. Retire for a nightcap to the classically elegant piano bar, where Peter Vavra entertains. $ *Average main: $35 ⊠ 17 Chateau La., Beaver Creek Village ☎ 970/845–8808 ⊕ www.splendidobeavercreek.com ⊙ Closed mid-Apr.–June, mid-Oct.–mid-Nov, and Mon. and Tues. in summer. No lunch.*

$$$
WINE BAR
✕ **Vin48.** Good vino is not hard to find at Vin48, a casual, upscale wine bar in Avon. Enjoying the benefits of Vin48's Enomatic preservation system, you can explore 40 wines by the glass or half glass (with help from an on-staff sommelier) as you go. Choose from a selection of small plates, such as crispy veal sweetbreads, fried chicken drumettes, and grilled summer-vegetable ravioli. Or sink your teeth into heartier fare, like the pecan wood–smoked flat-iron steak with braised heirloom cherry tomatoes and scamorza-cheese croutons. A wall of glass doors folds open in the summer for fresh air, and young and old wine enthusiasts can savor their pours on the outdoor patio. The daily happy hour is fantastic. $ *Average main: $25 ⊠ 48 E. Beaver Creek Blvd., Avon ☎ 970/748–9463 ⊕ www.vin48.com ⊙ No lunch.*

$$$$
MODERN ITALIAN
✕ **Zino Ristorante.** Sister restaurant to Vail's famed Sweet Basil, Zino has earned a loyal fan base for its house-made pastas and wood-fired pizzas. The ravioli are filled with Maine lobster, ricotta, and fennel, and there's a delicious fettuccine topped with slow-cooked wild boar Bolognese and house-made pancetta. Also consider the seared diver scallops with an heirloom-cauliflower ragu. The two-story restaurant has a large bar, ideal for lighter bites or a cocktail. In summer, dine alfresco on the riverside patio or keep busy with a game of bocce on the regulation-size court. $ *Average main: $32 ⊠ 27 Main St., Edwards ☎ 970/926–0777 ⊕ www.zinoristorante.com ⊙ No lunch.*

WHERE TO STAY

$$$$
HOTEL
🛏 **Beaver Creek Lodge.** A large central atrium that doubles as an art gallery grabs all the attention at this modern hotel a few hundred yards from the lifts. **Pros:** room layouts great for families; good value; friendly service. **Cons:** a short walk to the lifts; fee for parking and resort fee; no spa. $ *Rooms from: $429 ⊠ 26 Avondale La., Beaver Creek Village ☎ 970/845–9800 ⊕ www.beavercreeklodge.net ⌨ 70 suites* ❰❰❰ *Breakfast ⌁ All-suite hotel.*

$$$$
HOTEL
🛏 **Charter at Beaver Creek.** With its elegantly angled blue-slate roof, this sprawling property is one of the area's largest accommodations. **Pros:** on-site spa; ski-in ski-out. **Cons:** small rooms; mediocre breakfasts

(not included); pools can be noisy with children. $ *Rooms from: $490* ⊠ *120 Offerson Rd., Beaver Creek Village* ☎ *970/949–6660, 800/525–6660* ⊕ *www.thecharter.com* ⟿ *156 individual condos* ⦿ *No meals.*

$$$$ 🛏 **Lodge & Spa at Cordillera.** An aura of isolated luxury prevails at this
HOTEL   ridge-top lodge with a style that calls to mind the finest alpine hotels, and is popular with return guests. **Pros:** spa; fireplaces in rooms. **Cons:** must take shuttle or drive to lifts or town; $40 daily resort fee. $ *Rooms from: $269* ⊠ *2205 Cordillera Way, Edwards* ☎ *970/926–2200, 800/877–3529* ⊕ *www.cordilleralodge.com* ⟿ *56 rooms* ⦿ *No meals.*

$$$$ 🛏 **The Osprey at Beaver Creek, A Rock Resort.** You can't get any closer
HOTEL   to a ski run in the United States than the Osprey, unless you sleep on
Fodor'sChoice the lift. **Pros:** best ski location at Beaver Creek; rooms are fresh and
★   light; romantic. **Cons:** often sold out well in advance. $ *Rooms from: $419* ⊠ *10 Elk Track La.* ☎ *970/429–5042, 866/621–7625* ⊕ *www. ospreyatbeavercreek.rockresorts.com* ⟿ *45 rooms* ⦿ *Breakfast.*

$$$$ 🛏 **Park Hyatt Beaver Creek Resort & Spa.** With magnificent antler chande-
RESORT   liers, and towering windows opening out onto the mountain, the lobby
Fodor'sChoice of this slope-side hotel manages to be both cozy and grand. **Pros:** beau-
★   tiful on-site spa; cozy Colorado mountain vibe; ski-in ski-out. **Cons:** fee for parking; small rooms; a big-resort feel. $ *Rooms from: $499* ⊠ *136 E. Thomas Pl., Beaver Creek Village* ☎ *970/949–1234* ⊕ *www. beavercreek.hyatt.com* ⟿ *190 rooms, 23 suites* ⦿ *No meals.*

$$$$ 🛏 **Pines Lodge.** This Swiss-style ski-in ski-out lodge is a winner for ski-
HOTEL   ers, combining upscale accommodations with an unpretentious atti-
        tude. **Pros:** traditional European chalet decor; slope-side; on-site ski shop and ski concierge. **Cons:** a short walk to the village; valet parking only. $ *Rooms from: $600* ⊠ *141 Scott Hill Rd., Beaver Creek Village* ☎ *970/429–5043, 855/279–3430* ⊕ *www.pineslodge.rockresorts.com* ⟿ *60 rooms, 4 condos, 5 townhouses* ⦿ *No meals.*

$$$$ 🛏 **Ritz-Carlton, Bachelor Gulch in Beaver Creek.** The stone-and-timber
RESORT   resort crowns Beaver Creek Mountain above the bustle of Vail Valley
FAMILY   like one of King Ludwig's Bavarian castles. **Pros:** the most luxurious
Fodor'sChoice property on the mountain; excellent guest service; ski-in ski-out. **Cons:**
★   high altitude (9,000 feet); removed from the Village. $ *Rooms from: $399* ⊠ *0130 Daybreak Ridge, Bachelor Gulch Village* ☎ *970/748– 6200, 800/241–3333* ⊕ *www.ritzcarlton.com* ⟿ *180 rooms, 40 suites* ⦿ *No meals.*

$$$$ 🛏 **The Westin Riverfront Resort & Spa at Beaver Creek Mountain.** What this
RESORT   rambling, contemporary resort lacks in ski-village charm (it's located in the nearby town of Avon, a free shuttle trip from the village), it makes up for with big, airy rooms, the stunningly serene 27,000-square-foot Spa Anjali and Athletic Club, and an outdoor heated lap pool— all completely renovated in 2015. **Pros:** rooms are sleek and upscale; good value; first-rate facilities, from the spa to the restaurant. **Cons:** located outside the ski village; steep resort and parking fees; staff may try to pitch you on timeshares. $ *Rooms from: $319* ⊠ *126 Riverfront La., Avon* ☎ *970/790–6000* ⊕ *www.westinriverfrontbeavercreek.com* ⟿ *230 rooms* ⦿ *No meals.*

NIGHTLIFE AND PERFORMING ARTS

PERFORMING ARTS

Vilar Performing Arts Center. With gold-color wood paneling and an etched-glass mural re-creating with bold strokes the mountains outside, this dazzling performance venue is itself a work of art. Seating more than 500, the horseshoe-shaped auditorium has great views from just about every seat. Throughout the year there's a stellar lineup of events, including concerts by orchestras and pop stars, great theater, and aerial dancers. In the surrounding plazas you'll find many art galleries. Just walking around Beaver Creek is a feast for the eyes, because sculptures are set almost everywhere you look. ✉ *68 Avondale La.* ☎ *970/845–8497, 888/920–2787* ⊕ *www.vilarpac.org.*

NIGHTLIFE

Coyote Café. This boisterous spot is a kick-back-and-relax sort of place right on the pedestrian mall, where locals hang out at the bar and enjoy the patio. The kitchen doles out Mexican food, sandwiches, and burgers. ✉ *210 The Plaza, Avon* ☎ *970/949–5001* ⊕ *www.coyotecafe.net.*

Dusty Boot Steakhouse & Saloon. For the best après-ski scene among both visitors and locals, head to this rollicking saloon complete with Wild West decor, including cowboy hats and buffalo skulls over the pine-wood bar. When the ski slopes close, the bar is usually three-deep. The happy-hour menu includes an appetizer and a draft beer. The dinner menu features hand-cut steaks and local barbecue. Tables fill fast and reservations aren't accepted. ✉ *St. James Place, Beaver Creek Village* ☎ *970/748–1146* ⊕ *www.dustyboot.com.*

8100 Mountain Bar & Grill. This is a great option for an upscale drink with heart—here, the wines are organic and the brews local. The faux candlelight, modern chandeliers, and lounge-y vibe lure an upper-crust crowd who knock back favorites like Colorado Wildflower: a mix of local honey, vodka, mint, and fresh-squeezed orange juice. The appetizers are just as delish—consider the shucked oysters with a Colorado hot sauce. ✉ *Park Hyatt Beaver Creek Resort, 50 W. Thomas Pl., Beaver Creek Village* ☎ *970/827–6600* ⊕ *www.8100barandgrill.com.*

Osprey Lounge. Delicious tapas at this upscale après-ski hangout perfectly complement the well-poured cocktails. The menu always changes, but often includes popular dishes like wild-mushroom quesadillas and braised veal cheeks. The golden-hued back-lit bar and stacked, cylindrical cords of wood behind it create a mountain-chic ambience at this intimate, slope-side space beside the Strawberry Park Express Lift. The lounge was recently renovated to offer more seats. ✉ *10 Elk Track La., Beaver Creek Village* ☎ *970/754–7400* ⊕ *www. ospreyatbeavercreek.rockresorts.com.*

5

SHOPPING

ANTIQUES

Shaggy Ram. Although the Shaggy Ram sounds as if it would stock mostly Western items, this colorful shop is filled with French and English antiques. Items range from fringed lamps to crystal decanters to elegant old desks. ✉ *210 Edwards Village Blvd., Edwards Village Center, Edwards* ☎ *970/926–7377* ⊙ *Closed end of ski season–late June.*

ART GALLERIES

Walt Horton Fine Art. Well known for his expressive, playful bronze sculptures, Walt Horton features several of his own pieces and works by other local oil painters and sculptors in his gallery. ✉ *156 Plaza, Beaver Creek Village* ☎ *970/949–1660* ⊕ *www.walthortonfineart.com.*

CLOTHING

SmartWool. The first North American SmartWool–brand store is stocked with your every Merino wool need: light- and mid-weight base layers, ultralight underwear, and the coziest socks on the slopes. ✉ *15 W. Thomas Pl., Avon* ☎ *970/331–0835* ⊕ *www.smartwool.com.*

SPAS

It's easy to find a full-body massage in Beaver Creek, as many hotels have full-service spas included.

Allegria Spa. In the Park Hyatt Beaver Creek, the 30,000-square-foot Allegria Spa—inspired by Roman bathhouses—has a self-guided healing water tour called Aqua Sanitas. Dip in and out of five water rituals, alternating from hot to cold, including a 105-degree mineral pool, cooling showers, and steam rooms with soothing fiber-optic displays. There are a few tables for room-service meals (they're even happy to serve you cocktails and bar drinks). The spa offers a full range of services, including a wonderful "barefoot" massage. The signature "ginger peach cure" treatment comprises a scrub, full-body massage, wrap, and Swiss shower (with 12 jetted nozzles). ✉ *136 E. Thomas Pl.* ☎ *970/748–7500* ⊕ *www.allegriaspa.com.*

Bachelor Gulch Spa at The Ritz-Carlton. Despite being one of the larger spas in the area (with 19 treatment rooms), the spa at Bachelor Gulch cultivates an intimate vibe. Stone-lined grottos ease the day's stress before your treatment even starts. Take a signature soak in the copper tub—alone or with a significant other—or indulge in the Hot Toddy, a body scrub to soften rough patches and soothe achy muscles. Guys can pamper themselves with the Mountain Man spa package, which remedies post-slope woes by working out knots with massage, wind-burned skin with a facial, and beat-up limbs with hand-and-foot grooming. The fitness center classes include yoga, Pilates, Barre, Zumba, morning meditation, and seasonal offerings like guided hikes and outdoor yoga (with an option to finish with an alfresco massage) once the weather warms up. ✉ *0130 Daybreak Ridge, Avon* ☎ *970/748–6200* ⊕ *www.ritzcarlton.com.*

ASPEN AND THE ROARING FORK VALLEY

Updated by
Whitney Bryen

The Roaring Fork Valley—and Aspen, its crown jewel—is the quintessential Colorado Rocky Mountain High. A row of the state's famed Fourteeners (peaks over 14,000 feet) guards this valley. There are only two ways in or out: over the precipitous Independence Pass in summer or up the four-lane highway through the booming Roaring Fork Valley, which stretches 40 miles from Glenwood Springs to Aspen.

Outside Aspen, Colorado natives regard the city and its mix of longtime locals, newly arrived ski bums, hard-core mountaineers, laser-sculpted millionaires, and tanned celebs with a mixture of bemusement and envy. The "real Aspenites," who came for the snow and stayed for summers, have been squeezed out by seven-digit housing prices. Most have migrated down-valley to the bedroom communities of Basalt and Carbondale.

The quest for wealth in the valley dates back to the mid-1800s, when the original inhabitants, the Ute people, were supplanted by gold prospectors and silver miners, who came to reap the region's mineral bounty. The demonetization of silver in 1893 brought the quiet years, as the population dwindled and ranching became a way of life. Nearly half a century later the tides turned again as downhill skiing gave new life to Aspen. Today the Roaring Fork Valley weaves together its past and present into a blend of small-town charm and luxurious amenities, all surrounded by the majestic beauty of central Colorado's 2-million-acre White River National Forest.

ORIENTATION AND PLANNING

GETTING ORIENTED

Wedged in a valley between the Elk Mountain palisades to the southwest and the high-altitude massifs of the Sawatch Range in the east, the Roaring Fork Valley is a Rocky Mountain Shangri-la. The charm and beauty of this isolation makes reaching Aspen a scenic journey, but also one that can be frustrating.

The only land-based way in or out of Aspen is Highway 82—heading either across the Roaring Fork Valley or (in summer) over Independence Pass across the eastern side of the mountains (the pass begins at the junction of U.S. 24 and Highway 82). Aspen's explosive growth hasn't come without some headaches. Despite expanded lanes, Highway 82 quickly clogs with skiers and day commuters.

Aspen. Head here for a dose of the high life in an almost too-pretty town. The aspen-draped Maroon Bells peaks are one of the state's iconic images.

The Roaring Fork Valley. Snowmass is a year-round family resort destination rather than a true town. The historic towns of Glenwood Springs, Carbondale, Redstone, and Basalt offer a pleasant—and less expensive—alternative experience, and have great fly-fishing and rafting in summer.

TOP REASONS TO GO

Fine fare: Restaurants in Aspen, Basalt, Carbondale, and Glenwood Springs are used to being praised for climbing gastronomic heights, and the dishes that many offer, from locally raised Wagyu beef to Russian caviar, are as upscale as the clientele.

Historic hotels: Thanks to moneyed preservationists, the Victorian Hotel Jerome in Aspen and the Medici-inspired Hotel Colorado in Glenwood Springs still stand.

Hot springs: The 93°F mineral-water pool at Glenwood Springs has been a therapeutic retreat since the Ute Indians called it "healing waters."

The mountains: You'll find postcard Colorado in the 14,000-foot Maroon Bells, especially when these steep-faced peaks are reflected in Maroon Lake.

The scene: You'll see it all in Aspen—Hollywood celebs in cowboy boots, high-heeled Brazilians, tanned European ski instructors, and fascinating and friendly locals.

PLANNING

6

WHEN TO GO

Aspen and the Roaring Fork Valley are a year-round destination. If it's skiing you're after, February and March historically have the best snow (deepest base and most terrain open) plus the warmest winter weather. Aspen summers are legendary for their food, art, and music festivals. Although more than 6,000 locals call Aspen home, the area population swells to more than 14,000 during ski season and to more than 21,000 in summer. June and early July are best for rafting (snowmelt makes for high-octane rapids); most high-country biking and hiking trails are cleared of snowdrift by mid-June, when brilliant wildflowers emerge and remain in bloom through early August. Mid-September brings hotel-room deals, cooler days, photogenic snow dustings on the Maroon Bells, and flame-orange aspen groves.

PLANNING YOUR TIME

The drive from Glenwood Springs at the northwest tip of the Roaring Fork Valley to Aspen is less than an hour, making it easy for visitors to set up a base camp anywhere along "the valley" with convenient access to nearby activities. For those seeking local flavor, Carbondale and Basalt offer cozy accommodations that are centrally located between the larger towns of Glenwood Springs and Aspen. Snowmass and Aspen are closest to the mountains for winter skiing but Sunlight Mountain Resort near Glenwood Springs offers a less crowded, budget-friendly winter wonderland.

GETTING HERE AND AROUND

AIR TRAVEL

Aspen/Pitkin County Airport (ASE) is 3 miles from downtown Aspen and 7 miles from Snowmass Village. Airline schedules vary seasonally, but you can count on several daily nonstop departures to Denver on United Airlines. American Airlines and United also typically offer nonstop flights to Dallas, Houston, Chicago, Miami, and Los Angeles during ski season.

TRANSFERS   If you aren't renting a car, your best bet for traveling to and from Aspen and Snowmass Village is Roaring Fork Transportation Authority, which provides bus service from Aspen/Pitkin County Airport to the Rubey Park bus station near the base of the ski mountain. Colorado Mountain Express, a shared-van shuttle service, connects Aspen with Denver International Airport and Eagle County Airport (winter). High Mountain Taxi, based in Aspen, can provide local rides and charter service outside the Roaring Fork Valley. ⊠ 233 E. Airport Rd., Aspen ☎ 970/920–5384 ⊕ www.aspenairport.com. **Denver International Airport (DEN).** ⊠ 8500 Peña Blvd., Denver ☎ 800/247–2336 ⊕ www.flydenver.com. **Eagle County Airport (EGE).** ⊠ 219 Eldon Wilson Rd., Gypsum ☎ 970/328–2680 ⊕ www.eaglecounty.us/airport.

Airport Contacts Aspen/Pitkin County Airport (ASE).

Airport Transfers Colorado Mountain Express. ☎ 970/926–9800, 800/525–6363 ⊕ www.ridecme.com. **High Mountain Taxi.** ☎ 970/925–8294 ⊕ www.hmtaxi.com.

CAR TRAVEL

In summer the 160-mile, three-hour drive from Denver to Aspen is a delightful journey up the I–70 corridor and across the Continental Divide through the Eisenhower Tunnel (or by way of the slower, but more spectacular, Loveland Pass), down along the eastern ramparts of the Collegiate Peaks along State Highway 91 and U.S. Highway 24, with a final push on twisty State Highway 82 up and over 12,095-foot Independence Pass.

The scenery, particularly south of Leadville on U.S. 24, is among the best in Colorado, with views to the west of 14,433-foot Mount Elbert, the highest mountain in the state. Independence Pass is closed in winter (the timing depends on snowfall, typically late October–late May), but motorists should always drive cautiously. Blinding snowstorms—even in July—can erase visibility and make the pass treacherously icy. Be especially careful on the western side, where the road narrows and vertigo-inducing drop-offs plunge thousands of feet from hairpin curves. Both Route 82 and I–70, like all Colorado roads, should be driven with caution, especially at night when elk, bighorn sheep, and mule deer cross without warning.

Generally speaking, driving to Aspen from Denver in winter is more trouble than it's worth, unless you plan to stop along the way. The drive west on I–70 and east on Route 82 takes more than three hours at best, depending on weather conditions and, increasingly, ski traffic. On the other hand, the 3-mile drive from the Aspen/Pitkin County Airport (ASE) is a breeze along the flat valley floor. The 70-mile drive from the Eagle County Airport (EGE)—which doesn't cross any mountain passes—is another option. Whenever you visit, the traffic and parking may try your patience.

SHUTTLE TRAVEL

The Roaring Fork Transportation Authority provides bus service up and down the valley; many resorts have free private shuttles.

Shuttle Contact Roaring Fork Transportation Authority. ✉ *430 E. Durant Ave., Aspen* ☎ *970/925–8484* ⊕ *www.rfta.com.*

PARKS AND RECREATION AREAS

The Roaring Fork Valley is surrounded by recreational land, wilderness areas, and national forests. To the southeast, in the Collegiate Peaks Wilderness area, more 14,000-foot summits beckon hikers than anywhere else in the Lower 48.

The often overlooked Hunter-Fryingpan Wilderness Area is one of Colorado's hidden secrets—a thin-air spine of unnamed peaks and excellent trout rivers in the Williams Mountains just east of Aspen. On the other side of the Continental Divide, the Hunter-Fryingpan becomes the Mount Massive Wilderness Area, named for Colorado's second-highest peak, which stands 14,421 feet tall. Most of these wilderness areas are encompassed within the much larger—and more fragmented—White River National Forest.

RESTAURANTS

Sushi? Coconut curry? Bison and lobster? Colorado's culinary repertoire is at its broadest in Aspen. With all the Hummers and designer handbags come an equal number of menus with high-end ingredients and showy preparations. Plates can be pricey, particularly in Aspen, but many eateries have at least a few moderately priced entrées (usually pastas) and bar menus as a nod to the budget-conscious. For those who want a break from Aspen, there are excellent dining options down-valley in Basalt and Carbondale as well.

HOTELS

There's no shortage of lodging in Aspen and the Roaring Fork, but you'll pay the highest rates in the state. Downriver alternatives like Carbondale and Glenwood Springs are attractive for budget hunters—but you'll face heavy traffic when commuting to Aspen. Before booking down-valley, however, look for special deals in town that might include lift tickets and parking. If you're staying for more than a weekend or are traveling with a large group, condominiums offer the added bonus of a kitchen. *Hotel reviews have been shortened. For full information, visit Fodors.com.*

WHAT IT COSTS				
	$	$$	$$$	$$$$
Restaurants	under $13	$13–$18	$19–$25	over $25
Hotels	under $121	$121–$170	$171–$230	over $230

Restaurant prices are the average cost of a main course at dinner or, if dinner is not served, at lunch, excluding 8.2%–8.6% tax. Hotel prices are the lowest cost of a standard double room in high season, excluding service charges and 8.6%–10.7% tax.

ASPEN

200 miles west of Denver via I–70 and Hwy. 82.

Fodor's Choice ★ One of the world's fabled resorts, Aspen practically defines glitz, glamour, and glorious skiing. To the uninitiated, Aspen and Vail might be synonymous. Between the galleries, museums, music festivals, and other glittering social events, there's so much going on in Aspen that even in winter many people come simply to "do the scene," and never make it to the slopes. High-end boutiques have been known to serve free cocktails après ski.

At the same time, Aspen is a place where some people live average lives, sending their children to school and working at jobs that may or may not have to do with skiing. It is, arguably, America's original ski-bum destination, a fact that continues to give the town's character an underlying layer of humor and texture. You can come to Aspen and have a reasonably straightforward, enjoyable ski vacation, because once you've stripped away the preciousness, Aspen is simply a great place to ski.

GETTING HERE AND AROUND

The rich arrive by private planes, but almost everyone else arrives in Aspen by car or shuttle bus. Parking is a pricey pain, and traffic, especially on weekends, clogs the streets. The Roaring Fork Transportation Authority has bus service connecting the resort with the rest of the valley. The easiest way to get around Aspen is on foot or by bike. For longer trips hop aboard the free Aspen Skiing Company shuttles, which connect Aspen, Aspen Highlands, Buttermilk, and Snowmass base areas.

WHEN TO GO

The summer season in the Roaring Fork Valley runs from mid-June to Labor Day, and winter season starts at Thanksgiving until the ski lifts close in mid-April.

Fodor's Choice ★ **Aspen Music Festival and School.** Focusing on everything from chamber music to jazz, the Aspen Music Festival and School begins in June and runs through mid-August. Musicians like Joshua Bell and Sarah Chang make pilgrimages here to perform at more than 300 events held at the 2,050-seat Benedict Music Tent, the Victorian Wheeler Opera House, and the Harris Concert Hall. Tickets are readily available online. A quarter of the performances are free, and one of the great pleasures of the festival is showing up on the free-seating lawn outside the Benedict Music Tent with some friends, a blanket, and a bottle of something good. ⊠ *225 Music School Rd.* ☎ *970/925–9042* ⊕ *www.aspenmusicfestival.com.*

ESSENTIALS

Visitor Information Aspen Chamber Resort Association. ⊠ *425 Rio Grande Pl.* ☎ *970/925–1940, 800/670–0792* ⊕ *aspenchamber.org.* **Aspen/Snowmass Snow Report.** ☎ *970/925–1221, 800/525–6200* ⊕ *www.aspensnowmass.com.*

TOURS

Aspen Carriage and Sleigh. A romantic (albeit pricey) way to get acquainted with the backcountry is by taking a private sleigh ride with Aspen Carriage and Sleigh. They also have carriage tours around downtown and the historic West End. ⊠ *Aspen* ☎ *970/925–3394* ⊕ *www.aspencarriage.com* ⊠ *From $275 for up to 4 people.*

Independence Pass

From Memorial Day to Labor Day, the most beautiful route to Aspen is over Independence Pass. From the Vail–Leadville–Buena Vista corridor on the east side of the Sawatch Mountains, Highway 82 climbs up and over 12,095-foot Independence Pass and switchbacks down to Aspen, along the way passing above tree line and making some spectacular white-knuckle hairpin turns (drive slowly to appreciate the scenery, and also because you might have to yield to oncoming traffic in narrow, one-lane sections).

The pass divides the Mount Massive Wilderness to the north from the Collegiate Peaks to the south. The trip's not for the fainthearted, given the long exposed drops and the possibility for snow at any time of the year. Elk and mule deer herds can sometimes be seen at dawn and dusk, grazing in the willow thickets beside Lake Creek as it cascades down the eastern flank of the pass. As soon as the autumn snow flies, however, the pass closes and Aspen becomes a cul-de-sac town accessible only via Glenwood Springs.

EXPLORING

TOP ATTRACTIONS

Aspen Art Museum. Opened in 2014, the $72 million Aspen Art Museum turned heads with its giant, crate-like design and firmly established the museum as a must-visit for contemporary art (and architecture) lovers. Designed by Shigeru Ban, the 33,000-square-foot facility is a three-story glass cube encased in a woven, wood-veneer exterior screen that allows glimpses of the museum's exhibitions to passersby. Inside, a glass elevator and ceilings with an open-plane design create a bright space and the rooftop sculpture garden offers prime views of Aspen Mountain. The Aspen Art Museum is a non-collecting museum so the majority of the works exhibited here are new pieces from top national and international artists, often commisioned by the museum. An endowment keeps admission free. ⊠ *637 E. Hyman Ave.* ☎ *970/925–8050* ⊕ *www. aspenartmuseum.org* ⊡ *Free* ☾ *Tues.–Sun. 10–8.*

QUICK BITES

Ink! Coffee Follow the locals to Ink! Coffee, where you can sample hot and cold coffee, tea, and other drinks, including the signature Blended Black and White—iced espresso mixed with black and white chocolate and milk. The café also serves sandwiches, salads, snacks, and pastries. In summer the patio is a nice place to relax. ⊠ *520 E. Durant Ave.* ☎ *970/544–0588* ⊕ *www.inkcoffee.com.*

FAMILY
Fodor'sChoice
★

Maroon Bells. The majestic Maroon Bells are twin peaks more than 14,000 feet high. The colorful mountains, thanks to mineral streaking, are so vivid you'd swear they were blanketed with primrose and Indian paintbrush. It's one of the most photographed spots in the state. Before 8 am and after 5 pm in the summer, cars can drive all the way up to Maroon Lake (and vehicles with children in car seats are permitted at any time). Otherwise, cars are allowed only partway, but the Roaring

6

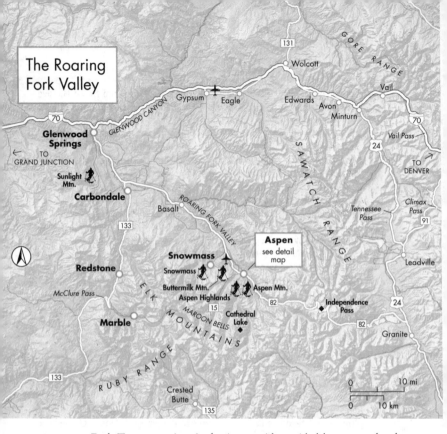

The Roaring Fork Valley

Fork Transportation Authority provides guided bus tours that leave regularly in summer months from Aspen Highlands. The Perfect Summer Package pass, available for $30, includes one trip to the Maroon Bells and three days of gondola and chairlift rides in Aspen and Snowmass, where concerts, nature walks, amazing hiking, and other activities await you. ⊠ *White River National Forest, Maroon Creek Rd., 10 miles southwest of Aspen.*

WORTH NOTING

Wheeler/Stallard House Museum. You can get a taste of Victorian high life at the Queen Anne–style Wheeler/Stallard House Museum, which displays memorabilia collected by the Aspen Historical Society and features revolving historical exhibits. Your admission fee here also covers entrance to the Holden/Marolt Ranching and Mining Museum, a hands-on exploration of Aspen's past housed in an old ore-processing building on the western edge of town (open summer only). ⊠ *620 W. Bleeker St.* ☎ *970/925–3721* ⊕ *www.aspenhistory.org* ⊠ *$6* ⊙ *Sept.– early June, Tues.–Sat. 1–5; mid-June–July, Tues.–Sat. 10:30–4:30.*

DOWNHILL SKIING AND SNOWBOARDING

Aspen is really four ski areas rolled into one resort. Aspen Highlands, Aspen Mountain (Ajax, to locals), Buttermilk, and Snowmass can all be skied with the same ticket. Three are clustered close to downtown Aspen, but Snowmass is down the valley in Snowmass Village. A free shuttle system connects the four.

> ### WHEN DO THE WILDFLOWERS PEAK?
>
> The Maroon Bells–Snowmass Wilderness Area southwest of Aspen is famed for dramatic cliffs and alpine meadows. The bloom will start first in the valleys and eventually climb above the 11,500-foot tree line. Most Colorado wildflowers reach their peak from just before the summer solstice until mid-July.

Fodor's Choice ★ **Aspen Highlands.** Locals' favorite Aspen Highlands is essentially one long ridge with trails dropping off either side. Aspen Highlands has thrilling descents at Golden Horn, Olympic Bowl, and Highland Bowl, a hike-in experience unlike any in Colorado. The steep and often bumpy cluster of trails around Steeplechase and Highland Bowl makes this mountain one of the best places to be on a good-powder day. Aspen Highlands has a wide-open bowl called Thunder Bowl that's popular with intermediate skiers, as well as plenty of lower-mountain blue runs. The best overall downhill run is Highland Bowl. Besides the comparatively short lift lines and some heart-pounding runs, a highlight of Aspen Highlands is your first trip to the 12,392-foot summit. The view, which includes the Maroon Bells and Pyramid Peak, is the most dramatic in the area, and one of the best in the country. **Facilities:** 122 trails; 1,040 acres; 3,635-foot vertical drop; 5 lifts. ⊠ *Maroon Creek Rd.* ☎ *970/925–1220, 800/525–6200* ⊕ *www.aspensnowmass.com* 🎫 *Lift ticket $129* ☉ *Mid-Dec.–mid-Apr., daily 9–4.*

Aspen Mountain. Open since 1947, Aspen Mountain is a dream destination for mogul and steep skiers. Bell Mountain provides some of the best bump skiing anywhere, followed by Walsh's (also a favorite for snowboarders), Hyrup's, and Kristi's. Those wanting long cruisers head to the ridges or valleys: Ruthie's Run and International are the classics. There are no novice-level runs here: this is a resort where nearly half the trails are rated advanced or expert, and a black-diamond trail here might rank as a double black diamond elsewhere. The narrow ski area is laid out on a series of steep, unforgiving ridges with little room for error. Most skiers spend much of the morning on intermediate trails off the upper-mountain quad. Then they head for lunch on the deck of Bonnie's, the mid-mountain restaurant that on sunny days is one of the great people-watching scenes in the skiing world. After a big storm there's snowcat skiing on the back side of the mountain. Many trails funnel into Spar Gulch, so it can be quite crowded late in the day. For an alternate route, head down the west side of the mountain below the Ruthie's chair and take the road back to the main base area. **Facilities:** 76 trails; 675 acres; 3,267-foot vertical drop; 8 lifts. ⊠ *E. Durant Ave.* ☎ *970/925–1220, 800/525–6200* ⊕ *www.aspensnowmass.com* 🎫 *Lift ticket $129* ☉ *Late Nov.–mid-Apr., daily 9–4.*

6

Fodor's Choice
★

Buttermilk. If you're looking for an escape from the hustle and bustle of Aspen, spend a day at Buttermilk—a family-friendly place where it's virtually impossible to get into trouble. Buttermilk is terrific for novices, intermediates, and freestylers, thanks to the superpipe and Buttermilk Park (which has over 100 features). It's a low-key, lighthearted sort of place, and an antidote to the kind of hotdogging you might encounter at Aspen Mountain. Red's Rover on West Buttermilk is a mellow long run for beginners, while Racer's Edge appeals to speed demons. Among the featured attractions is a hangout for children named Fort Frog. The Tiehack section to the east, with sweeping views of Maroon Creek valley, has several advanced runs (though nothing truly expert). It also has superb powder, and the deep snow sticks around longer because many serious skiers overlook this mountain. Buttermilk's allure hasn't been lost on pros, however: it's the longtime host of the Winter X Games. **Facilities:** 44 trails; 470 acres; 2,030-foot vertical drop; 8 lifts. ⊠ *W. Buttermilk Rd.* ☎ *970/925–1220, 800/525–6200* ⊕ *www.aspensnowmass. com* ⛷ *Lift ticket $129* ☉ *Mid-Dec.–early Apr., daily 9–4.*

LESSONS AND PROGRAMS

Aspen Mountain Powder Tours. This company provides access to 1,100 acres on the back side of Aspen Mountain via a 12-person snow cat. Most of the backcountry terrain can be handled by confident intermediates, with about 10,000 vertical feet constituting a typical day's skiing. Reservations are required and should be made as early as possible beginning November 1. Full-day trips include a hearty lunch, snacks, drinks, two guides, and all the skiing you want. ⊠ *Aspen* ☎ *970/920–0720, 800/525–6200* ⛷ *From $449.*

Aspen Skiing Company. Aspen Skiing Company gives lessons at all four mountains. Full-day adult group lessons start at $153, and a private full-day lesson for up to five other people will cost you $730. Beginner's Magic is a package for first-time adult skiers and snowboarders that includes a full-day lesson, lift ticket, and gear rental for $219. Aspen Skiing Company also offers women-only clinics, children's lessons, and freestyle camps just for teens; check availability in advance. ⊠ *Aspen* ☎ *970/925–1220, 800/525–6200* ⛷ *From $153.*

RENTALS

Numerous ski shops in Aspen rent equipment. Rental packages (skis, boots, and poles) start at around $50 per day and rise to $75 or more for the latest and greatest equipment. Snowboard packages (boots and boards) run about $60 per day. Reserve your gear online before you arrive in town to save 10%–20%. For convenience, consider ski-rental delivery to your hotel or condo.

Aspen Sports. This sporting-goods store has a huge inventory of winter gear to choose from. There are five locations in Aspen and five in Snowmass. ⊠ *408 E. Cooper Ave.* ☎ *970/925–6331* ⊕ *www. aspensports.com.*

Black Tie Ski Rentals. Reserve your ski or snowboard package online or over the phone, and Black Tie Ski Rentals will deliver your gear directly to your condominium or hotel room. ⊠ *Aspen* ☎ *800/925–8544, 970/925–8544* ⊕ *www.blacktieskirentals.com.*

Four Mountain Sports. Owned by Aspen Skiing Company, Four Mountain Sports has an impressive fleet of ski and snowboard rental equipment and an equally impressive fleet of stores; there are nine locations, including one at the base of all four mountains. ✉ *520 E. Durant Ave.* ☎ *970/920–2337* ⊕ *www.aspensnowmass.com.*

NORDIC SKIING

BACKCOUNTRY SKIING

Alfred A. Braun Hut System. The Alfred A. Braun Hut System is one of Aspen's major backcountry networks. The system's seven huts are located near the tree line in the Elk Mountains. Take the usual precautions, because the trails cover terrain that's prone to avalanche. Huts sleep 7 to 14 people. They're open in winter only, and reservations for non-members can be made beginning June 1 through the 10th Mountain Division Hut Association. ☎ *970/925–5775* ⊕ *www.huts.org* ✉ *$25 per person per night, 4-person minimum.*

Aspen Alpine Guides. If you're unfamiliar with the hut system in Aspen or are inexperienced in backcountry travel, you should hire a guide. One highly reputable company is Aspen Alpine Guides. ☎ *970/925–6618* ⊕ *www.aspenalpine.com.*

10th Mountain Division Hut Association. Named in honor of the U.S. Army's 10th Mountain Division, whose troops trained in the central Colorado mountains, the 10th Mountain Division Hut Association is a nonprofit organization that maintains nearly three-dozen huts in the backcountry, including a handful of huts that are located just a few miles from Aspen like McNamara and Margy's Hut, built by the former secretary of defense Robert McNamara in memory of his wife. You must be in good shape and have some backcountry skiing experience to reach the huts in the winter months. There is a fair amount of skiing along tree-lined trails and a good bit of high-alpine ups and downs. Accommodations in the huts vary, but you can count on mattresses and pillows, wood-burning stoves, and utensils for cooking. Huts sleep 6 to 20 people (more if you're willing to cuddle). ✉ *1280 Ute Ave., Suite 21* ☎ *970/925–5775* ⊕ *www.huts.org* ✉ *$33 and up per person per night.*

TRACK SKIING

Ashcroft Ski Touring Center. About 12 miles from Aspen, the Ashcroft Ski Touring Center is sequestered in the high-alpine Castle Creek Valley. The 21 miles of groomed trails are surrounded by the high peaks of the Maroon Bells–Snowmass Wilderness; a novice section passes by the old ghost town of Ashcroft. Rental gear and guided tours are available. ✉ *11399 Castle Creek Rd.* ☎ *970/925–1971* ⊕ *www. pinecreekcookhouse.com/ashcroft.*

6

Aspen Cross-Country Center. Lessons and rentals for track skiing are offered at the Aspen Cross-Country Center. Diagonal, skating, and racing setups are available. ⊠ *39551 Hwy. 82* ☎ *970/925–2145 Nov.–Mar., 970/925–2849 Apr.–Oct.*

Aspen/Snowmass Nordic Council. Subsidized by local taxes, the Aspen/Snowmass Nordic Council charges no fee for more than 60 miles of maintained trails in the Roaring Fork Valley, making it the largest free groomed Nordic-trail system in North America. For a longer ski, try the Owl Creek Trail, connecting the Aspen Cross-Country Center trails with the Snowmass Club trail system. More than 10 miles long, the trail leads through some lovely scenery. ☎ *970/429–2039* ⊕ *www. aspennordic.com.*

OTHER SPORTS AND THE OUTDOORS

FAMILY **Aspen Center for Environmental Studies** (*ACES*). This nonprofit environmental science education center runs workshops ranging from what animals you might find on local trails to how to survive in the wilderness. ACES naturalist guides offer snowshoe walks in winter or private guides on Aspen Mountain, at Snowmass, and in the historic ghost town of Ashcroft. Summer brings guided hikes in Aspen, Snowmass, and the Maroon Bells, as well as oodles of educational classes for kids, teens, and adults. Its Aspen location is a 25-acre nature preserve on Hallam Lake, but ACES also operates a working farm at Rock Bottom Ranch down-valley between Basalt and Carbondale. ⊠ *100 Puppy Smith St.* ☎ *970/925–5756* ⊕ *www.aspennature.org.*

FISHING

Aspen Trout Guides. This company, which is in the Hamilton Sports shop, runs guided fly-fishing tours of local waterways in Aspen. ⊠ *520 E. Durant Ave.* ☎ *970/379–7963* ⊕ *aspentroutguides.com.*

Roaring Fork River. Fast, deep, and uninterrupted by dams from its headwaters to its junction with the Colorado, the Roaring Fork River is one of the last free-flowing rivers in the state. The healthy populations of rainbow and brown trout—of the hefty 12- to 18-inch variety—make the Roaring Fork a favorite with anglers. From the headwaters at Independence Pass to within 3 miles of Aspen most of the river access is on public lands, and is best fished in summer and early fall. Downstream from Aspen the river crosses through a checkerboard pattern of private and public land; it's fishable year-round. ⊕ *www.wildlife.state.co.us/fishing.*

HIKING

Cathedral Lake. You'll get a taste of several ecozones as you tackle Cathedral Lake, a 5½-mile round-trip trail. The popular day hike starts gently in aspen and pine groves, but you're likely to break out in a sweat during the long, steep climb into a high valley above tree line. Another series of steep, short switchbacks ascend a headwall, followed by a scree field. From there it's a short walk to a shallow alpine lake cupped by a wall of granite cliffs. When the high-country snows melt off in mid-July, the meadows and willow thickets surrounding the lake are colored with blooming wildflowers. ⊠ *Castle Creek Rd.* ☎ *970/925–3445.*

Fodor'sChoice **Maroon Bells–Snowmass Wilderness Area.** Aspen excels at high-altitude
★ scenery (seven of the state's 54 Fourteeners are in the Elk Mountains
range), and nowhere is the iconic image of the Colorado Rockies more
breathtaking than in the Maroon Bells–Snowmass Wilderness Area. In
summer, shuttle buses take visitors up Maroon Creek Road to the base
of the Maroon Bells from 8 am until 5 pm. Private cars are allowed at
all other times (there is a $10 recreational fee). More ambitious sight-
seers can select from a number of hiking trails. Friendly forest rangers
staff the Aspen Ranger District office on the west side of town, where
you can get recommendations for your ability level. ⊠ *Aspen Ranger
District, 199 Prospector Rd.* ☎ *970/925–3445.*

HORSEBACK RIDING

Maroon Bells Guide & Outfitters. For day or overnight horseback tours
into the spectacular Maroon Bells, try Maroon Bells Guide & Outfitters, which offers sleigh rides in the winter. ⊠ *3133 Maroon Creek Rd.*
☎ *970/920–4677* ⊕ *www.maroonbellsaspen.com.*

ICE-SKATING

Aspen Recreation Center. Home to an indoor ice rink big enough for
National Hockey League games, the Aspen Recreation Center (or ARC
to locals) also has a fitness center, climbing wall, Olympic-size swimming pool, and water play area with a lazy river and waterslide. ⊠ *0861
Maroon Creek Rd.* ☎ *970/544–4100* ⊕ *www.aspenrecreation.com.*

Silver Circle/CP Burger Ice Rink. For outdoor ice-skating, try this good-
size rink across the street from the Rubey Park bus station downtown.
Skate rentals are available. In the summer the rink transforms into
a mini-golf course. ⊠ *433 E. Durant Ave.* ☎ *970/925–3056* ⊕ *www.
cpburger.com/sk8.*

KAYAKING

Aspen Kayak & SUP Academy. Long-time Aspen paddler Charlie MacArthur
runs the Aspen Kayak & SUP Academy, where you can learn to roll and
drop in on a wave in a kayak. You can also sample stand-up paddling.
⊠ *315 Oak Ln.* ☎ *970/925–4433* ⊕ *www.aspenkayakacademy.com.*

MOUNTAIN BIKING

Aspen Sports. This store has a wide selection of rental bikes, as well as
trail-a-bikes and trailers for kids. ⊠ *408 E. Cooper Ave.* ☎ *970/925–
6331* ⊕ *www.aspensports.com.*

Blazing Adventures. This company leads biking, as well as hiking, Jeep, and
rafting tours through Aspen and the surrounding valleys. ⊠ *555 E. Durant
Ave.* ☎ *970/923–4544, 800/282–7238* ⊕ *www.blazingadventures.com.*

Hub of Aspen. Hub of Aspen has high-performance mountain and road
bikes. ⊠ *315 E. Hyman Ave.* ☎ *970/925–7970* ⊕ *www.hubofaspen.com.*

PARAGLIDING

Aspen Paragliding. This company provides everything you need for a
safe and memorable tandem flight above Aspen and the surrounding
valley. There is no experience necessary—even children as young as
five can fly with an experienced pilot. ⊠ *426 S. Spring St.* ☎ *970/925–
6975, 970/379–6975* ⊕ *www.aspenparagliding.com* ⊡ *$250 per tan-
dem flight.*

RAFTING

Blazing Adventures. For the truly adventurous, Blazing Adventures runs mild to wild rafting excursions on the Roaring Fork, Colorado, and Arkansas rivers. This outfitter also offers hiking, biking, and Jeep tours. ✉ *555 E. Durant Ave.* ☎ *970/923–4544, 800/282–7238* ⊕ *www. blazingadventures.com.*

WHERE TO EAT

Use the coordinates (✛ B2) at the end of each listing to locate a site on the corresponding map.

$$$$
AMERICAN
✕ **Ajax Tavern.** So close to the gondola you can keep your boots on, this upbeat restaurant is mountainside in The Little Nell. Most of the tavern has big glass windows, and there's also a spacious patio with slope-side views. Wide-plank floors and brick walls with dark wood paneling define this spot, which is popular both for its location and hearty surf-n-turf dishes (they also have a stellar raw bar). The menu changes seasonally, and focuses on Colorado ingredients. Two great items you can count on year-round are Parmesan truffle fries and the Ajax double cheeeburger made with locally raised, grass-fed beef. Ⓢ *Average main: $27* ✉ *675 E. Durant St.* ☎ *970/920–4600* ⊕ *www. thelittlenell.com* ✛ *C5.*

$$
AMERICAN
✕ **Aspen Over Easy.** In this funky diner, visitors and locals can be heard planning outdoor adventures or raving about the nearby resorts while devouring delicious breakfast dishes served all day. Mix and match unexpected eggs Benedict, like the blue crab and Baja chipotle lime, or build your own omelet. Wash down your breakfast with an organic juice from the bar—try the owner's favorite Aspen Body, which blends carrots, celery, cucumber, kale, beets, and apple in a satisfying morning jolt. Salads, sandwiches, and burgers are also offered on the lunch and dinner menu. Ⓢ *Average main: $13* ✉ *304 E. Hopkins Ave.* ☎ *970/429–8693* ⊕ *www.aspenovereasy.com* ✛ *B4.*

$$$$
MODERN
AMERICAN
✕ **Cache Cache.** Trained in classic French fundamentals, chef Chris Lanter brings a Continental influence to sophisticated, yet filling entrées, such as veal osso buco and calves' liver with cherry wood–smoked bacon. With a focus on locally raised meats, the chic bistro's Colorado rack of lamb and 7X Ranch Colorado NY strip are perennial favorites. In the warm-weather months, vegetable accompaniments reflect whatever is freshest from area farms. Pastas and rotisserie items are sensational, and desserts are worth leaving room for. For those on a budget, belly up to the raucous bar for $20 entrées. Ⓢ *Average main: $38* ✉ *205 S. Mill St.* ☎ *970/925–3835* ⊕ *www.cachecache.com* ☾ *Closed Mon. and Tues. No lunch* ✛ *B4.*

$$$$
ECLECTIC
✕ **Chef's Club by Food and Wine.** Every year, a handful of different visionary "Best New Chefs" from *Food & Wine* magazine collaborate on the fine-dining menu at this sophisticated restaurant inside the St. Regis Aspen Resort. From Asian to Italian, the various dishes and cuisines blend together beautifully under the guardianship of executive chef Todd Slossberg. The chefs change annually and the menu changes often—all the more reason to return regularly. You can expect

an attentive waitstaff, expansive wine list, and clever cocktails. $ $ *Average main: $35* ⊠ *St. Regis Aspen, 315 E. Dean St.* ☎ *970/429–9581* ⊕ *www.chefsclub.com/aspen* ⊙ *No lunch* ✛ *C4.*

$ ✕ **CP Burger.** Casual CP Burger offers gourmet beef, chicken, tuna, and
BURGER   falafel burgers for takeout or eating in. Also on the menu are hot dogs,
FAMILY   grilled cheese, and kale salad, a locals' favorite. In the summer, take
your burger, fries (regular, sweet potato, or Parmesan truffle), and shake
(spiked for adults, if you like) outside to eat under white umbrellas and
watch the kids on the mini-golf course. In the winter, the course transforms into an ice rink, and you can warm up inside CP Burger with a hot
chocolate. $ *Average main: $9* ⊠ *433 E. Durant Ave.* ☎ *970/925–3056*
⊕ *www.cpburger.com* ✛ *C5.*

$$$$ ✕ **Element 47.** The seasonal menu at this swanky restaurant high-
MODERN   lights locally sourced produce, meat, and game raised on Colorado
AMERICAN   ranches. Aspen's elite book dinner tables here not only for the beauti-
Fodor'sChoice   fully presented entrées—that might include locally raised Wagyu beef
★   or Columbia River king salmon—but also the exquisite service and the
20,000-bottle wine cellar. For a lighter meal, head to the bar, which
features Colorado beers and spirits. $ *Average main: $35* ⊠ *675 E.
Durant Ave.* ☎ *970/920–6330* ⊕ *www.element47aspen.com* ⌂ *Reservations essential* ✛ *C5.*

$$ ✕ **Hickory House Ribs.** Tie on your bib and dig in. No one will mind
SOUTHERN   if your hands and face are covered in the secret sauce that tops the
slow-cooked meats and chicken at this log cabin–style joint with a
grizzly bear over the door. These hickory-smoked baby back ribs
have won more than 40 national competitions. Feeling brave? Bring
a buddy and try "The Feast," one-and-a-half racks of baby back
ribs, barbecue chicken, smoked pork and beef, along with cole slaw,
corn, garlic bread, potatoes, and baked beans ($54). And after a late
night on the town, nothing beats a hearty breakfast of ribs and eggs.
$ *Average main: $17* ⊠ *730 W. Main St.* ☎ *970/925–2313* ⊕ *www.
hickoryhouseribs.com* ✛ *C2.*

$$$$ ✕ **L'Hostaria.** This subterranean hot spot is sophisticated yet rustic, with
ITALIAN   an open-beam farmhouse ceiling, sleek blonde-wood chairs, contempo-
rary art, and a floor-to-ceiling glass wine "cellar" in the main room. The
menu relies on simple, subtle flavors in specialties such as grilled beef
tenderloin with a Mediterranean sauce, and traditional pasta dishes like
house-made fettuccine Bolognese, spinach pappardelle, and spaghetti
topped with Maine lobster. $ *Average main: $30* ⊠ *620 E. Hyman Ave.*
☎ *970/925–9022* ⊕ *www.hostaria.com* ✛ *B5.*

$$ ✕ **Main Street Bakery & Café.** Perfectly brewed coffee and hot breakfast
CAFÉ   buns and pastries are served daily at this café, along with a full break-
fast menu that includes homemade granola and plenty of egg dishes.
Lunch brings soups, salads, sandwiches, and comfort-food favorites
like chicken pot pie. On sunny days, sit on the umbrella-covered back
patio. $ *Average main: $14* ⊠ *201 E. Main St.* ☎ *970/925–6446* ⊙ *No
dinner* ✛ *B4.*

$$$$ ✕ **Matsuhisa.** Although you shouldn't expect to see celebrity chef Nobu
JAPANESE   Matsuhisa in the kitchen of his hopping restaurant in an 1887 Victorian on Main Street, his recipes and techniques are unmistakable.

6

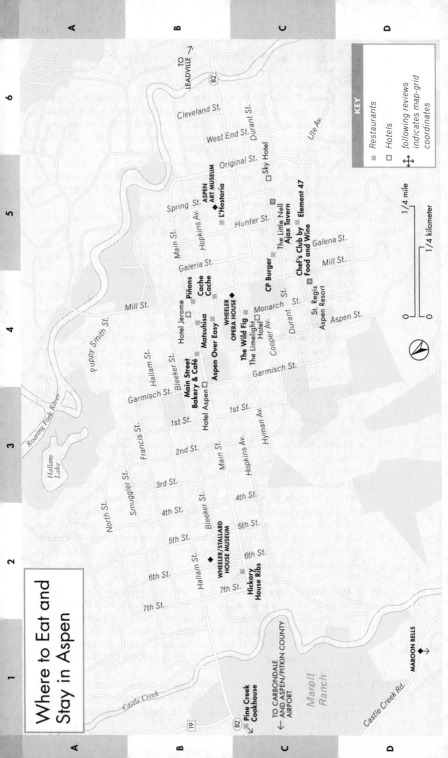

Where to Eat and Stay in Aspen

TO LEADVILLE →

82

Cleveland St.

West End St.

Durant St.

Ute Av.

Original St.

Sky Hotel

Spring St.

ASPEN ART MUSEUM

L'Hostaria

Hopkins Av.

Hunter St.

The Little Nell

Ajax Tavern

Element 47

Chef's Club by Food and Wine

Galena St.

Mill St.

Main St.

Galeria St.

Piñons

Cache Cache

Mill St.

Hotel Jerome

WHEELER OPERA HOUSE

CP Burger

Monarch St.

St. Regis Aspen Resort

Matsuhisa

Cooper Av.

Aspen St.

Aspen Over Easy

The Wild Fig

The Limelight Hotel

Durant St.

Hallam St.

Main Street Bakery & Café

Garmisch St.

Garmisch St.

Hotel Aspen

1st St.

1st St.

Hyman Av.

Francis St.

2nd St.

Main St.

Hopkins Av.

North St.

Smuggler St.

3rd St.

4th St.

4th St.

Bleeker St.

5th St.

5th St.

Hallam St.

WHEELER/STALLARD HOUSE MUSEUM

6th St.

6th St.

Hickory House Ribs

7th St.

7th St.

Roaring Fork River

Hallam Lake

Puppy Smith St.

Bleeker St.

Maroon Bells

MAROON BELLS

Castle Creek

82

19

Pine Creek Cookhouse

TO CARBONDALE AND ASPEN/PITKIN COUNTY AIRPORT

Marolt Ranch

Castle Creek Rd.

KEY

■ Restaurants

□ Hotels

✛ following reviews indicates map-grid coordinates

0   1/4 mile

0   1/4 kilometer

Nobu's shrimp skewers with wasabi pepper sauce are scrumptious, his king crab tempura is delicious, his new-style sashimi marvelous, and his prices astronomical. Check out the additional seating upstairs (or outdoors in warm weather) for cocktails and a limited but still superb menu. [$] *Average main: $32* ✉ *303 E. Main St.* ☎ *970/544–6628* 🌐 *www.matsuhisaaspen.com* ⏲ *No lunch* ✍ *Reservations essential* ✥ *B4.*

$$$$ MODERN AMERICAN

🍴 **Pine Creek Cookhouse.** In the winter, the only way to get to this homey log cabin with breathtaking views of the Elk Mountains is via snowshoe, cross-country ski, or horse-drawn sleigh. In the summer, you can drive to the front door, but you should consider hiking here to compensate for the filling American alpine fare you'll enjoy at lunch or dinner: wild game, such as bison and elk, plus smoked trout and river salmon. In the cold-weather months, don't miss the authentic Nepalese Sherpa stew. Wintertime dinners are prix fixe starting at $95, which includes four courses and gear for skiing or snowshoeing. [$] *Average main: $35* ✉ *12500 Castle Creek Rd.* ☎ *970/925–1044* 🌐 *www.pinecreekcookhouse.com* ✍ *Reservations essential* ✥ *C1.*

$$$$ MODERN AMERICAN

🍴 **Piñons.** The open, modern dining room at Piñons has a bit of Old West flair, with leather-wrapped railings and a faux-tin ceiling. The contemporary American menu scores high on creativity. Try the spicy sashimi tuna tacos as an appetizer, and the pan-seared buffalo tenderloin with huckleberry sauce as an entrée. The service and wine list are impeccable. The interior tends to fill up fast, but you can always eat at the lively bar, with its bargain-friendly, two-course $35 prix-fixe menu. In the summer, the cozy patio provides fabulous views of Aspen Mountain. [$] *Average main: $40* ✉ *105 S. Mill St.* ☎ *970/920–2021* 🌐 *www.pinons.net* ⏲ *No lunch* ✥ *B4.*

$$$$ MEDITERRANEAN Fodor's Choice ★

🍴 **The Wild Fig.** For Mediterranean and Middle Eastern tastes, head to The Wild Fig, a friendly brasserie with an unbeatable location right off the pedestrian mall. The restaurant is small but cozy, with a cheerful yellow ceiling and white-tiled walls trimmed in dark wood. In addition to favorites like house-made saffron fettuccine with clams, The Wild Fig also has one of Aspen's more unusual plates: "fish in a bag," in which the fish of the night is cooked and served in a brown paper bag. For dessert, try the beignets with crème anglaise. [$] *Average main: $30* ✉ *315 E. Hyman Ave.* ☎ *970/925–5160* 🌐 *www.thewildfig.com* ⏲ *No lunch Sept.–Jun.* ✥ *C4.*

WHERE TO STAY

Use the coordinates (✥ B2) at the end of each listing to locate a site on the corresponding map.

$$$ HOTEL

🏨 **Hotel Aspen.** Just a few minutes from the mall and the mountain, this hotel on the town's main drag is a great find. **Pros:** great location; free parking; private hot tubs with mountain views in some rooms. **Cons:** faces busy Main Street; no restaurant. [$] *Rooms from: $199* ✉ *110 W. Main St.* ☎ *970/925–3441, 877/442–3991* 🌐 *www.hotelaspen.com* 🛏 *34 rooms, 1 apartment, 11 suites* 🍽 *Breakfast* ✥ *B4.*

$$$$
HOTEL
FAMILY
Fodor'sChoice
★

Hotel Jerome. Fresh from a multimillion-dollar makeover, the luxurious Hotel Jerome, first opened in 1889, has swapped its Victorian style for an upbeat, private club–like decor that retains the stately hotel's historic integrity but gives it a sumptuous new sheen. **Pros:** historic property with modern amenities; central location; top-notch service; game room for kids. **Cons:** small spa and fitness center; very expensive, with rates that don't include resort fee. $ *Rooms from: $750* ⊠ *330 E. Main St.* ☎ *970/920–1000, 800/367–7625* ⊕ *hoteljerome.aubergeresorts.com* ☜ *78 rooms, 15 suites* ❍| *No meals* ✛ *B4.*

$$$$
HOTEL
Fodor'sChoice
★

The Limelight Hotel. This classic is the place to stay for families who want to enjoy a taste of luxury without tip-heavy service (guest services such as bellhops are available upon request). **Pros:** family- and pet-friendly; downtown location; complimentary snowshoes and cruiser bikes. **Cons:** busy; often fully booked in high season. $ *Rooms from: $450* ⊠ *355 S. Monarch St.* ☎ *970/925–3025, 855/925–3025* ⊕ *www.limelighthotel.com* ☜ *120 rooms, 5 suites, 1 penthouse* ❍| *Breakfast* ✛ *C4.*

$$$$
HOTEL
Fodor'sChoice
★

The Little Nell. Right at the base of the gondola, this hotel is the only true ski-in ski-out property in town. **Pros:** best location in town; great people-watching; luxurious. **Cons:** extremely expensive; difficult to get a room in high season. $ *Rooms from: $1,050* ⊠ *675 E. Durant Ave.* ☎ *970/920–4600, 855/920–4600* ⊕ *www.thelittlenell.com* ☜ *78 rooms, 14 suites* ❍| *No meals* ✛ *C5.*

$$$$
HOTEL

Sky Hotel. Aspen's trendiest hotel, part of the playful Kimpton boutique-hotel group, attracts a young crowd with its sleek style and excellent location across the street from the slopes. **Pros:** dramatic style; great location for skiers; some rooms have balconies. **Cons:** valet parking only; some guest-room doors open to exterior. $ *Rooms from: $299* ⊠ *709 E. Durant Ave.* ☎ *970/925–6760, 800/882–2582* ⊕ *www.theskyhotel.com* ☜ *84 rooms, 6 suites* ❍| *No meals* ✛ *C5.*

$$$$
HOTEL
Fodor'sChoice
★

St. Regis Aspen Resort. A longtime fixture in Aspen, the St. Regis Aspen resembles a stately yet contemporary mountain chalet. **Pros:** one of Aspen's most luxurious properties; close to the slopes; ultraposh spa. **Cons:** very expensive; only valet parking. $ *Rooms from: $1,149* ⊠ *315 E. Dean St.* ☎ *970/920–3300, 888/627–7198* ⊕ *www.stregisaspen.com* ☜ *154 rooms, 25 suites* ❍| *No meals* ✛ *C4.*

NIGHTLIFE AND PERFORMING ARTS

PERFORMING ARTS

Jazz Aspen Snowmass. In June and September, Jazz Aspen Snowmass hosts popular music festivals that feature world-class pop, rock, jazz, and country bands and musicians. JAS partners with the Town of Snowmass Village to bring free concerts to Fanny Hill on Thursday nights in summer. ⊠ *Aspen* ☎ *970/920–4996* ⊕ *www.jazzaspensnowmass.org.*

Wheeler Opera House. This intimate, historic performance hall hosts big-name classical, jazz, pop, and opera performers. Comedy shows and local musical theater also take place here. ⊠ *320 E. Hyman Ave.* ☎ *970/920–5770* ⊕ *www.wheeleroperahouse.com.*

NIGHTLIFE

BARS AND LOUNGES

Downtown's East Hyman Avenue is an ideal place for barhopping, with a cluster of nightspots sharing the same street address and additional options for drinking and dancing on the Hyman Avenue Mall.

Eric's Bar. Whiskey—and lots of it—is the claim to fame of Eric's Bar, a hip little watering hole that attracts a rowdy crowd. There's a varied lineup of at least a dozen microbrews and other beers on tap. ⊠ *315 E. Hyman Ave.* ☎ *970/920–6707.*

J-Bar. You can't say you've seen Aspen until you've set foot in the historic Hotel Jerome's lively J-Bar. The Aspen Crud, a bourbon milkshake, was invented here during Prohibition. ⊠ *Hotel Jerome, 330 E. Main St.* ☎ *970/920–1000* ⊕ *www.hoteljerome.com.*

Justice Snow's. Named for a 19th-century Aspen justice of the peace, Justice Snow's is known for its creative, handcrafted cocktails. Pull up a chair at the sophisticated, Victorian-era bar to sample an absinthe fountain, share a frothy punchbowl, or sip house-infused spirits in vintage glassware. ⊠ *328 E. Hyman Ave.* ☎ *970/429–8192* ⊕ *www.justicesnows.com.*

MUSIC AND DANCE CLUBS

Belly Up Aspen. This live-concert venue has hosted musical acts ranging from Kenny Rogers and country western musicians to 80s rock bands and The Offspring. The nightclub accommodates 450 for intimate shows. ⊠ *450 S. Galena St.* ☎ *970/544–9800* ⊕ *www.bellyupaspen.com.*

SHOPPING

ART GALLERIES

Baldwin Gallery. This modern galley is the place to see and be seen at receptions for nationally known artists. ⊠ *209 S. Galena St.* ☎ *970/920–9797* ⊕ *www.baldwingallery.com.*

Galerie Maximillian. This gallery is the place to find 19th- and 20th-century prints, sculpture, and paintings—including original Picassos and Chagalls. ⊠ *602 E. Cooper Ave.* ☎ *970/925–6100* ⊕ *www.galeriemax.com.*

BOOKS

Explore Booksellers. Located in a historic Victorian house, Explore Booksellers stocks more than 20,000 books in its multiple, cozy rooms. This independent bookstore is especially strong in politics, travel, and literature. The upstairs, vegetarian-friendly Pyramid Bistro is a perfect place for a light meal or snack. ⊠ *221 E. Main St.* ☎ *970/925–5336 bookstore, 970/925–5338 bistro* ⊕ *www.explorebooksellers.com.*

BOUTIQUES

Boogie's. Spacious and colorful Boogie's sells shoes, accessories, and a wide variety of jeans, casual shirts, and cowboy boots. ⊠ *534 E. Cooper Ave.* ☎ *970/925–6111.*

Pitkin County Dry Goods. Founded in 1969, Pitkin County Dry Goods may be one of Aspen's oldest clothing stores, but it carries contemporary, casual apparel for men and women, as well as fun and funky belts, scarves, and jewelry. ⊠ *520 E. Cooper Ave.* ☎ *970/925–1681* ⊕ *www.pitkincountydrygoods.com.*

MARKETS

Aspen Saturday Market. Show up in downtown Aspen any Saturday from mid-June to mid-October and you can enjoy the Aspen Saturday Market, a sort of farmers' market–meets–arts fair. White tents cluster along the corner of Galena and Hopkins and then extend to the intersection of Hyman and Galena. Everything here is Colorado made, from pottery and paintings to peppers and peaches. Enjoy live music and ready-made foods to eat on the spot. ⊠ *Aspen.*

Brand Building. For chic boutiques, check out the Brand Building, home to Gucci and Christian Dior, as well as the modern Baldwin Gallery. ⊠ *Hopkins Ave. between Mill and Galena Sts., Hopkins Ave. between Mill and Galena Sts.*

SPAS

Remède Spa at St. Regis Aspen Resort. Be sure to arrive early at Remède Spa to enjoy the extensive amenities here: a co-ed confluence waterfall pool (bring a bathing suit), plus a soothing steam cave with eucalyptus, hot soaking tub, and cool plunge pool. The customized massage includes aromatherapy, warm paraffin foot wrap, and scalp massage on a heated table for no extra charge. Afterward, snuggle under a chenille throw on a chaise in a dimly lit room, where you can breathe pure oxygen through a cannula while sipping champagne. ⊠ *315 E. Dean St.* ☎ *970/429–9650* ⊕ *www.stregisaspen.com/features/services-amenities/remede-spa* ☞ *$165 60-min massage. Hot tubs, nail salon, sauna, steam. Gym with: Cardiovascular machines, free weights, weight-training equipment. Services: Aromatherapy, body wraps, body scrubs, facials, massage, waxing.*

SpaAspen at Aspen Club & Spa. With 34 treatment rooms and a huge, mazelike women's locker room, SpaAspen at the Aspen Club & Spa is the largest full-service spa in the Aspen area. Fitness enthusiasts often book therapeutic massages here to soothe sore muscles after a day of skiing or hiking. Spa clients who spend more than $85 on treatments have full access to the Aspen Club's comprehensive fitness center, as well as a full schedule of group fitness classes. The Aspen Club & Spa is located on the outskirts of town, but a complimentary shuttle pickup is a phone call away. ⊠ *1450 Crystal Lake Rd.* ☎ *970/925–8900* ⊕ *www.aspenclub.com* ☞ *$135 50-min massage. Hair salon, hot tub, nail salon, sauna, steam. Gym with: Cardiovascular machines, free weights, weight-training equipment. Services: Aromatherapy, body wraps, body scrubs, facials, manicures, massage, pedicures, waxing. Classes: Aquaerobics, Pilates, ski conditioning, yoga, Zumba.*

SPORTING GOODS

Ute Mountaineer. This sporting-goods store sells and rents a variety of backcountry gear, and also carries outdoor clothing and guidebooks. ⊠ *201 S. Galena St.* ☎ *970/925–2849* ⊕ *www.utemountaineer.com.*

THE ROARING FORK VALLEY

Moving down-valley from Aspen along the Roaring Fork River, down past the family resort of Snowmass, is a journey to a much less ritzy Colorado. The landscape changes, too, going from lush aspen groves to the drier Western Slope steppe.

SNOWMASS

10 miles northwest of Aspen via Hwy. 82.

One of four ski mountains owned by Aspen Skiing Company and one of the best intermediate hills in the country, Snowmass has more ski-in ski-out lodgings and a slower pace than Aspen. Snowmass was built in 1967 as Aspen's answer to Vail—a ski-specific resort—and although it has never quite matched Vail's panache or popularity, it has gained stature with age, finding its identity as a resort destination rather than the village it once called itself. In general, Snowmass is better for families with young children, leaving the town of Aspen to a more up-at-the-crack-of-noon crowd.

The town at the mountain's base, Snowmass Village, has a handful of boutiques and upscale restaurants, but it's less self-absorbed and more family-oriented and outdoorsy than Aspen.

GETTING HERE AND AROUND

Heading east along Highway 82 toward Aspen, you'll spot the turn-offs (Brush Creek and Owl Creek roads) to the Snowmass ski area. Snowmass is best navigated with your own car or the free Aspen Skiing Company shuttle bus, which runs roughly every 15 minutes. All parking in Snowmass is free during the summer, but there's usually a fee in the winter season.

WHEN TO GO

Snowmass Village is a year-round resort, though the peak times are June through September for hiking and November through April for skiing.

EXPLORING

Snowmass Ice Age Discovery Center. In 2010, a bulldozer operator stumbled upon some strange-looking bones near Snowmass Village. They were later identified as belonging to several ancient, large mammals, such as the American mastodon, Columbian mammoth, giant bison, ground sloth, and camel. This soon became known as the best high-elevation Ice Age site anywhere. Displays at the Snowmass Ice Age Discovery Center detail the work that scientists from the Denver Museum of Nature & Science have done to unearth, catalog, and preserve the bones. There are some nifty hands-on activities for kids, too, including coloring sheets, skeleton puzzles, a green-screen photo station, and a cozy book nook. ⊠ *54 Snowmass Village Mall, Snowmass Village* ☎ *970/922–2277* ⊕ *www.snowmassiceage.com* ☒ *Free* ☺ *June–Sept., daily 10–5.*

FAMILY **Treehouse Kids' Adventure Center.** Interactive age-appropriate play areas and a full menu of activities for older children and teens make the Treehouse Kids' Adventure Center in the Snowmass Base Village a good headquarters for family fun. Summer camp activities include mountain biking, fishing, skateboarding, mountain boarding, and paintball. When winter comes, it serves as an upbeat base camp for ski lessons. ☒ *120 Carriage Way, Snowmass Village* ☎ *970/923–8733* ⊕ *www.aspensnowmass.com/ski-and-snowboard-schools/treehouse-kids-adventure-center.*

DOWNHILL SKIING AND SNOWBOARDING

Fodor's Choice ★

Snowmass. This sprawling ski area is the biggest of the four Aspen-area mountains. Aspen Highlands, Aspen Mountain, Buttermilk, and Snowmass can all be skied with the same ticket. A free shuttle system connects all four. Snowmass includes shops and restaurants, the Elk Camp Gondola, and Elk Camp Meadows Activity Center. There are six major chairlifts: Elk Camp, High Alpine–Alpine Springs, Big Burn, Sam's Knob, Two Creeks, and Campground. Except for the last two, all these sectors funnel into the pedestrian mall at the base. Snowmass is probably best known for Big Burn, itself a great sprawl of wide-open, intermediate skiing. Experts head to such areas as Hanging Valley Wall and the Cirque for the best turns. For powder stashes among the trees, head to the glades on Burnt Mountain (to the east of Longshot), Hanging Valley, Sneaky's, and Powerline.

At Snowmass nearly 50% of the 3,332 skiable acres are designated for intermediate-level skiers. The route variations down Big Burn are essentially inexhaustible, and there are many other places on the mountain for intermediates to find entertainment. The novice and beginning-intermediate terrain on the lower part of the mountain makes Snowmass a terrific place for younger children.

Don't overlook the fact that Snowmass is four times the size of Aspen Mountain, and has triple the black- and double-black-diamond terrain of its famed sister, including several fearsomely precipitous gullies at Hanging Valley. Although only 30% of the terrain is rated expert, this huge mountain has enough difficult runs, including the consistently challenging Powderhorn and the more relaxed Sneaky's Run, to satisfy skilled skiers.

This mountain has one of the most comprehensive snowboarding programs in the country, with the heart of the action in the Headwall Cirque. The terrain map points out the numerous snowboard-friendly trails and terrain parks while steering riders away from flat spots. You'll want to visit Snowmass Park's halfpipe in the Coney Glade area. **Facilities:** 94 trails; 3,332 acres; 4,406-foot vertical drop; 15 lifts. ☒ *West of Aspen via Brush Creek Rd. or Owl Creek Rd., Snowmass Village* ☎ *970/925–1220, 800/525–6200* ⊕ *www.aspensnowmass.com* ☒ *Lift ticket $129* ☉ *Late Nov.–mid-Apr., daily 9–4.*

LESSONS AND PROGRAMS

Aspen Skiing Company. This company runs a top-notch Ski & Snowboard School at Snowmass and Aspen's other mountains. ☒ *Lower Snowmass Village Mall, Snowmass Village* ☎ *970/925–1220, 800/525–6200.*

RENTALS

Numerous ski shops in Snowmass rent equipment. Rental packages (skis, boots, and poles) start at around $50 per day and rise to $75 or more for the latest and greatest equipment. Snowboard packages (boots and boards) run about $60 per day. Reserve your package online before you arrive in town to save 10%–20%. For convenience, consider ski-rental delivery to your hotel or condo.

Aspen Sports. This sporting-goods store is one of the best-known ski out-fitters in Snowmass. ⊠ *50 Carriage Way, Snowmass Village* ☎ *970/923-6111* ⊕ *www.aspensports.com.*

Four Mountain Sports. Owned by the Aspen Skiing Company, Four Mountain Sports has an impressive list of premium skis and snowboards in its rental fleet. ⊠ *Snowmass Village Mall, Snowmass Village* ☎ *970/920-2337* ⊕ *www.aspensnowmass.com.*

Incline Ski & Board Shop. Locally owned and operated, Incline Ski & Board Shop is steps from the shuttle-bus stop. ⊠ *1 Snowmass Village Mall, Snowmass Village* ☎ *800/314-3355* ⊕ *www.inclineski.com.*

NORDIC SKIING
TRACK SKIING

Aspen/Snowmass Nordic Council. This council maintains more than 60 miles of trails in the Roaring Fork Valley. Probably the most varied, in terms of scenery and terrain, is the 5-mile Snowmass Club trail network. For a longer ski, try the Owl Creek Trail, connecting the Snowmass Club trail system and the Aspen Cross-Country Center trails. More than 10 miles long, the trail provides both a good workout and a heavy dose of woodsy beauty, with many ups and downs across meadows and aspen-gladed hillsides. Best of all, you can take the bus back to Snowmass Village when you're finished. ⊠ *Snowmass Village* ☎ *970/429-2039* ⊕ *www.aspennordic.com.*

OTHER SPORTS AND THE OUTDOORS
BALLOONING

Unicorn Balloon Company. Take to the skies on an early-morning balloon ride for panoramic views of Aspen, Snowmass, and the surrounding rugged landscapes. ☎ *970/925-5752* ⊕ *www.unicornballoon.com.*

DOGSLEDDING

Krabloonik. Ride behind a sled-dog team through snowy wilderness, across open meadows, and around exciting banked turns. Krabloonik's trips, beginning at 10 am and 12:15 pm and costing about $300, include lunch at the Krabloonik restaurant, which offers gourmet mountain fare with wild-game specialties. Twilight rides (at 4 pm with dinner following) are also available for a slightly higher fee. ⊠ *4250 Divide Rd., Snowmass Village* ☎ *970/923-3953* ⊕ *krabloonik.com/dog-sledding.*

MOUNTAIN BIKING

Aspen Skiing Company. Pick up a summer trail map of area mountain biking trails from the Aspen Skiing Company. The company can also sell you a lift ticket so you won't have to ride uphill. ⊠ *97 Lower Mall, Snowmass Village Mall, Snowmass Village* ☎ *970/925-1220* ⊕ *www.aspensnowmass.com.*

WHERE TO EAT

$$$$ MODERN AMERICAN 🍴 **Eight K.** Inside the Viceroy Snowmass hotel, Eight K restaurant—named for its 8,000-foot elevation—commands stunning views of the surrounding mountains. In the spacious dining room, diners chow down on gourmet mountain fare with Southern influences. Chef Will Nolan's Cajun roots come out in such menu items as barbecued shrimp and grits, duck and andouille gumbo, Wagyu beef burger, and cast-iron–seared bass. The menu varies seasonally and focuses on fresh, locally sourced ingredients whenever possible. Check out the restaurant's impressive wine wall, cozy lounges in front of a roaring fireplace, and the 87-foot glass bar lit up in blue neon. [$] *Average main: $38* ✉ *Viceroy Snowmass, 130 Wood Rd., Snowmass Village* ☎ *970/923–8000* 🌐 *www.viceroyhotelsandresorts.com/en/snowmass/dining_and_nightlife/eightk* 💳 *No credit cards* 🕒 *No lunch.*

$$$$ AMERICAN 🍴 **Krabloonik.** Eskimo for "bushy eyebrows," Krabloonik is located in a rustic yet elegant log cabin tucked into the mountain, which means you'll be treated to wonderful views on your drive there. Dine sumptuously on some of the best game in Colorado, like caribou, elk, and wild boar, as well as house-smoked trout and wild-mushroom soup. The wine list is extensive. [$] *Average main: $48* ✉ *4250 Divide Rd., Snowmass Village* ☎ *970/923–3953* 🌐 *krabloonik.com* 🕒 *Closed Sun.–Thurs. in winter. No lunch in winter.*

$ AMERICAN 🍴 **New Belgium Ranger Station.** It's best to arrive at the New Belgium Ranger Station as soon as it opens for lunch on sunny winter days, since this tiny, slope-side restaurant fills up fast with hungry skiers. Patrons squeeze in for the soft Bavarian-style pretzels with choose-your-own dipping sauces, such as Fat Tire fondue cheese sauce or hazelnut cocoa spread. Seating is also cozy during late-afternoon après ski and into dinner. There are several beers on tap from New Belgium Brewing, based in Fort Collins. [$] *Average main: $10* ✉ *100 Elbert Rd., Snowmass Village* ☎ *970/236–6277* 🌐 *www.rangerstation.org* 💳 *No credit cards.*

WHERE TO STAY

$$$$ HOTEL 🏨 **Holiday Inn Express Snowmass.** Retro-chic decor, a laid-back staff, and reasonable room rates make the Wildwood Snowmass a favorite among young, cost-conscious skiers. **Pros:** affordable price; lively bar; pool. **Cons:** tiny rooms with motel-like exterior entry; can be noisy. [$] *Rooms from: $259* ✉ *40 Elbert La., Snowmass Village* ☎ *970/923–8400* 🌐 *www.wildwoodsnowmass.com* 🛏 *145 rooms, 6 suites.*

$$ HOTEL 🏨 **Snowmass Inn.** One of Snowmass's original digs, the Snowmass Inn commands a prime location in the middle of the Snowmass Village Mall, a short walk from the slopes. **Pros:** good location for skiers; great price for Snowmass. **Cons:** minimal customer service; shared pool with next-door lodge. [$] *Rooms from: $140* ✉ *67 Daly La., Snowmass Village* ☎ *800/843–1579* 🛏 *39 rooms* 🍽 *No meals.*

$$$$ HOTEL 🏨 **Stonebridge Inn.** Slightly removed from the hustle and bustle of the Village Mall, this hotel has a lobby and bar that are streamlined and elegant, with mood lighting, art that reflects the region's ski history, and rustic lodge furniture. **Pros:** quiet location; good on-site restaurant. **Cons:** not ski-in ski-out. [$] *Rooms from: $285* ✉ *300 Carriage Way, Snowmass Village* ☎ *970/923–2420, 866/939–2471* 🌐 *www.stonebridgeinn.com* 🛏 *88 rooms, 5 suites* 🍽 *No meals.*

$$$$ HOTEL Fodor's Choice ★ **Viceroy Snowmass.** Perched like a palace overlooking the Roaring Fork Valley, the Viceroy Snowmass is the undisputed king of the village. **Pros:** ski-in ski-out; stellar spa; ski valet. **Cons:** a short walk or gondola ride to the main village; small gym. [$] *Rooms from: $600* ✉ *130 Wood Rd., Snowmass Village* ☎ *888/622–4567, 970/923–8000* 🌐 *www.viceroyhotelsandresorts.com/snowmass* 🛏 *163 rooms* 🍴 *No meals.*

$$$$ HOTEL **The Westin Snowmass Resort.** The modern, airy Westin Snowmass Resort has the best location in Snowmass, right on top of Fanny Hill. **Pros:** ski-in ski-out; on-site gourmet restaurant; big, year-round outdoor pool area. **Cons:** no-frills, small spa. [$] *Rooms from: $659* ✉ *100 Elbert La., Snowmass Village* ☎ *970/923–8200* 🌐 *www.westinsnowmass.com* 🛏 *236 rooms, 18 suites* 🍴 *No meals.*

NIGHTLIFE

The Bar at Wildwood. Colorado's famed New Belgium beers reign supreme at this colorful, funky bar and restaurant inside the Wildwood Snowmass hotel. Retro modular seating in the lounge invites mingling. ✉ *40 Elbert La., Snowmass Village* ☎ *970/923–8451* 🌐 *www.wildwoodsnowmass.com/snowmass-restaurants.*

Venga Venga Cantina & Tequila Bar. A huge patio with warming fire pits makes this casual bar and restaurant a prime après-ski location at the edge of the Snowmass Village Mall and the ski hill. Look for happy-hour specials and dozens of tequilas and mezcals to sample into the night. ✉ *105 Daly La., Snowmass Village* ☎ *970/923–7777* 🌐 *www.richardsandoval.com/vengavenga.*

Zane's Tavern. Free-spirited locals gather at this classic mountain-town bar with billiards, foosball, shuffleboard, a jukebox, and $2.50 happy-hour drafts. ✉ *10 Snowmass Village Sq., Snowmass Village* ☎ *970/923–3515* 🌐 *www.zanestavern.com.*

SHOPPING

ART GALLERIES

Anderson Ranch Arts Center. Pottery, jewelry, and art supplies are sold at ArtWorks, the museum-style gift shop at Anderson Ranch Arts Center. The center also hosts visiting artists, summer workshops, and lectures. ✉ *5263 Owl Creek Rd., Snowmass Village* ☎ *970/923–3181* 🌐 *www.andersonranch.org.*

SPAS

The Spa at Viceroy Snowmass. Combo treatments at The Spa at Viceroy Snowmass are dubbed "rituals," based on Nordic, Asian, and Ute Indian cultures. Massage or facial "journeys" are offered as well. No matter what your service is called at this (faux) candlelit spa, you'll begin the experience in a dramatic relaxation room. Here, an attendant pours warm water over your feet and dries them with a fluffy towel. After your treatment, you can soak in a mosaic-tiled hot tub with a waterfall in the locker room. ✉ *130 Wood Rd., Snowmass Village* ☎ *970/923–8000* 🌐 *www.viceroyhotelsandresorts.com/en/snowmass/spa_and_wellness* ☞ *$135 60-min massage. Hair salon, hot tub, nail salon. Gym with: Cardiovascular machines, free weights, weight-training equipment. Services: Aromatherapy, body wraps, body scrubs, facials, manicures, massage, pedicures, Vichy shower, waxing.*

CARBONDALE

30 miles northwest of Aspen on Hwy. 82.

The artsy, outdoorsy town of Carbondale sits under looming Mount Sopris (12,965 feet). Its Main Street is lined with century-old brick buildings that house clothing boutiques, art galleries, and excellent restaurants. Locals gather there on the first Friday of every month for an outdoor block party that features music, street performers, artists' receptions, wine tastings, kids' activities, and more.

The paved Rio Grande recreation trail runs through town; bicycles are the preferred method of commuting for many area employees. Otherwise you'll find Carbondale's fit residents hiking and mountain biking below Mount Sopris's twin summits, fly-fishing the Crystal River, kayaking, rafting, and tubing the Roaring Fork River, and Nordic skiing at Spring Gulch above town.

SPORTS AND THE OUTDOORS

BICYCLING

Ajax Bike and Sport. There's a large selection of mountain and road bikes for sale and rent at Ajax Bike and Sport. The shop also sells accessories and apparel. ✉ *571 Hwy. 133* ☎ *970/963–0128* 🌐 *www.ajaxbikeandsport.com.*

FISHING

Alpine Angling. This company has the gear you need to get fishing, including rods, wheels, waders, and flies. The smart staff here can recommend best places for visitors to catch (and release) local trout, and offers lessons and guided trips. ✉ *995 Cowen Dr., Suite 102* ☎ *800/781–8120* 🌐 *www.roaringforkanglers.com.*

GOLF

River Valley Ranch Golf Club. Jay Moorish designed this course on the banks of the Crystal River. There is lots of water, a constant breeze, and superb—if not downright distracting—views of Mount Sopris. ✉ *303 River Valley Ranch Dr.* ☎ *970/963–3625* 🌐 *www.rvrgolf.com* 🎫 *$89 weekdays, $94 weekends for 18 holes; $50 for 9 holes* ⛳ *18 holes, 6027 yards, par 72.*

WHERE TO EAT AND STAY

$$ MODERN AMERICAN Fodor's Choice ★

🍴 **Town.** Sporting an open kitchen, exposed brick walls, and red leather banquettes, this chic bistro offers inventive, cleverly presented meals. The eclectic dinner menu includes starters such as "jars"—small Mason jars filled with yummy spreads like chicken-liver pâté and served with grilled bread or toast. Roasted vegetable sides, and the beloved gnocchi salad with asparagus and mushrooms delight vegetarians, while carnivores revel in such options as rabbit tacos, and cherry barbecue–glazed pork shoulder. A front counter serves baked goods and coffee in the morning, and eat-in salads, sandwiches, and small plates in the afternoon. [$] *Average main: $17* ✉ *348 Main St.* ☎ *970/963–6328* 🌐 *www.towncarbondale.com* 💳 *No credit cards.*

$$ AMERICAN

🍴 **Village Smithy.** Locals flock to "the Smithy" for beloved breakfast items served daily from 7 am 'til 2 pm, such as applewood bacon and eggs, chorizo scramble, and seasonal pancakes with turkey-maple sausages. Vegetarians are taken care of here as well with tasty tofu scramble, fresh spinach and wild mushroom omelets, and deep-fried French toast. Wooden tables are packed into every nook and cranny of this brick building that was once a blacksmith shop, but a covered porch provides more space. $ *Average main: $14* ⊠ *26 S. Third St.* ☎ *970/963–9990* ⊕ *www.villagesmithy.com* ▭ *No credit cards.*

$
B&B/INN
⬚ **Ambiance Inn.** This comfortable, two-story, three-bedroom B&B features spacious guest rooms, all with private bathrooms. **Pros:** friendly innkeepers; central location; full breakfast; private baths. **Cons:** children welcomed "selectively"; not your typical historic B&B. $ *Rooms from: $95* ⊠ *66 N. 2nd St.* ☎ *970/963–3597, 800/350–1515* ⊕ *www.ambianceinn.com* ▭ *No credit cards* ⊅ *2 rooms, 1 suite* ⧆ *Breakfast.*

REDSTONE AND MARBLE

17 miles south of Carbondale via Hwy. 133.

About an hour's drive from Aspen, Redstone is ringed by the impressive sandstone cliffs from which the town draws its name. The entire town is a National Historic District, developed in 1902 for coal miners and their families; since the 1930s, it's been known as an artists' colony. Summer brings streams of visitors strolling the main drag, Redstone Boulevard, lined with shops and galleries; in winter, horse-drawn carriages or sleighs carry people along the snow-covered road.

GETTING HERE AND AROUND

The best way to reach Redstone and Marble is by car, both because the scenery demands plenty of stops and (more important) there isn't any public transportation available anyway.

WHEN TO GO

Redstone and Marble are popular destinations June through August for hiking in the nearby Elk Mountains and fly-fishing. From September to October there is usually a brief autumn, which peaks with the blazing turning of the aspen trees. In the winter months, the area offers backcountry skiing and ice climbing.

EXPLORING

Marble. A few miles up Highway 133 from Redstone lies Marble, a sleepy town that attracts seekers of rural solitude who make it their summer residence and winter retreat. The tiny hamlet was incorporated in 1899 to serve workers of the Colorado Yule Marble Quarry, whose extraordinary stone graces the Lincoln Memorial and the Tomb of the Unknowns in Washington, D.C. Walk the Marble Mill Park Trail to see remnants of the old marble-processing mill. Other historic sites include a two-story schoolhouse now used by the Marble Historical Society Museum, and the Marble Community Church. Marble is also the gateway to one of Colorado's most-photographed places: the **Crystal Mill**. Set on a craggy cliff overlooking the river, the 1893 mill harkens back to the area's mining past; it's also the perfect place to enjoy a picnic lunch in the solitude of the Colorado Rockies. A four-wheel-drive vehicle is needed to get you here in good weather (your feet will have to do on rainy days when the road isn't passable). ⊠ *Marble* ⊕ *www.mcrchamber.org.*

6

Redstone Castle. Redstone's history dates to the late 19th century when J.C. Osgood, director of the Colorado Fuel and Iron Company, built Cleveholm Manor, now known as Redstone Castle. Here he entertained other titans of his day, including John D. Rockefeller, J.P. Morgan, and Teddy Roosevelt. Among the home's embellishments are gold-leaf ceilings, ruby-red velvet walls, silk brocade upholstery, marble and mahogany fireplaces, and Tiffany chandeliers. Call ahead or check the castle's website to verify tour availability. ⊠ *58 Redstone Blvd., Redstone* ☎ *970/963–9656* ⊕ *www.redstonecastle.us* 🎫 *$15* ☉ *Tours: Memorial Day–Oct., daily 1:30; winter, weekends at 1:30, with additional tours in Dec.*

WHERE TO EAT AND STAY

$$
AMERICAN

✕ **Crystal Club Cafe.** Slow-cooked baby back ribs smothered in home-made BBQ sauce are what the Crystal Club Cafe is known for. But this pastel-colored, riverside restaurant with a wraparound porch also serves comfort-food staples like beef tenderloin with a raspberry chipotle sauce and Colorado lamb chops with rosemary mint sauce. Plenty of picnic tables on a grassy lawn beckon in the warm-weather months. $ *Average main: $17* ⊠ *467 Redstone Blvd., Redstone* ☎ *970/963–9515* ⊕ *www. crystalclubcafe.com* ⊟ *No credit cards.*

$$
B&B/INN

▦ **Crystal Dreams Bed & Breakfast and Spa.** Built in 1994 in the Redstone National Historic District, this three-story Victorian has all the charm along with the benefits of modern construction. **Pros:** beautiful views; romantic place for couples; impressive breakfast. **Cons:** no credit cards accepted; no children under 12; two-night minimum. $ *Rooms from: $165* ⊠ *0475 Redstone Blvd., Redstone* ☎ *970/963–8240* ⊕ *www. crystaldreamsgetaway.com* ⊟ *No credit cards* ⇆ *3 rooms* ⦿| *Breakfast.*

SHOPPING

Redstone Art Gallery. The gallery at the Redstone Art Gallery displays watercolor and oil paintings, photography, pottery, woodwork, and jewelry, mostly by Colorado artists. There's also a fanciful gift shop, pretty backyard sculpture garden, workshops, classes, and artists' receptions here. ⊠ *173 Redstone Blvd., Redstone* ☎ *970/963–3790* ⊕ *www. redstoneart.com.*

GLENWOOD SPRINGS

40 miles northwest of Aspen via Hwy. 82; 160 miles west of Denver via I–70.

Once upon a time, Glenwood Springs, the famed spa town that forms the western apex of a triangle with Vail and Aspen, was every bit as tony as those chic resorts are today, attracting a faithful legion of the pampered and privileged who came to enjoy the healing waters of the world's largest outdoor natural hot-springs pool, said to cure everything from acne to rheumatism.

GETTING HERE AND AROUND

The easiest way to arrive is by car on I–70, the main east–west highway in Colorado. Public transport is more limited than in Aspen, so you'll need a vehicle to explore much beyond the main street.

WHEN TO GO

Glenwood Springs comes into its own in the early summer, when rafters, anglers, and spa goers arrive to sample the gifts of the Colorado River and its underground mineral springs.

ESSENTIALS

Visitor Information Glenwood Springs Chamber Resort Association.
⊠ *802 Grand Ave.* ☎ *970/945–6589* ⊕ *glenwoodchamber.com.*

EXPLORING

Glenwood Canyon. Along I–70 east of Glenwood Springs is the 16-mile-long Glenwood Canyon. Nature began the work as the Colorado River carved deep granite, limestone, and quartzite gullies—buff-tint walls brilliantly streaked with lavender, rose, and ivory. This process took a half-billion years. Then man stepped in, seeking a more direct route west. In 1992 the work on I–70 through the canyon was completed, at a cost of almost $500 million. Much of the expense was attributable to the effort to preserve the natural landscape. When contractors blasted cliff faces, for example, they stained the exposed rock to simulate nature's weathering. Bike the striking canyon on a paved, riverside recreation path or venture up the steep hiking trail to the hauntingly beautiful **Hanging Lake,** with its emerald-green pool under a gushing waterfall. The trail is extremely popular in the summer months; arrive early to find a place to park at the trailhead. ⊠ *Glenwood Springs.*

FAMILY **Glenwood Caverns Adventure Park.** Glenwood is home to the Historic Fairy Caves, whose subterranean caverns, grottoes, and labyrinths are truly a marvel of nature (the area was touted the "Eighth Wonder of the World" when it opened to the public in the 1890s). Now part of Glenwood Caverns Adventure Park, the still-amazing caves are easily accessible year-round via the Iron Mountain Tramway, a 10-minute gondola ride with a bird's-eye view of downtown, the Colorado River, and surrounding mountains. Choose from two different 50-minute walking tours of the caves. Or opt for the crawl-on-your-belly "Wild Tour" spelunking adventure. For a second helping of adrenaline, try the gravity-powered alpine coaster that drops 3,400 feet; sail out over 1,300 feet above Glenwood Canyon on a giant swing; or ride a twisty roller coaster that overhangs a cliff. ⊠ *51000 Two Rivers Plaza Rd.* ☎ *800/530–1635, 970/945–4228* ⊕ *www.glenwoodcaverns.com* 🎫 *$49.*

FAMILY **Glenwood Hot Springs.** Even before the heyday of the adjacent Hotel Colorado, Western notables such as gunslinger Doc Holliday came to take the curative waters of the world's largest outdoor natural mineral-springs pool. The smaller pool at Glenwood Hot Springs is 100 feet long and maintained at 104°F. The larger is four times that size, and contains more than a million gallons of constantly filtered water that is completely refilled every six hours and maintained at a soothing 90–93°F. Other facilities include a children's wading pool, two waterslides, a stellar full-service spa, and a fitness center. ⊠ *401 N. River St.* ☎ *970/947–2955, 800/537–7946* ⊕ *www.hotspringspool.com* 🎫 *$15.75* ☉ *Memorial Day–Labor Day, daily 7:30–10; after Labor Day–Memorial Day, daily 9–10.*

Hot Springs Vapor Caves. Part of the Yampah Spa & Salon, the Hot Springs Vapor Caves are a series of three natural underground, geothermal steam baths. Mineral-filled water from a natural hot spring runs about 125°F under the floors of the only known natural vapor caves in North America, creating steam temperatures of 110–112°F within the rock chambers, where there are marble benches for you to sit on while you inhale the steam. Each chamber is successively hotter than the last, but you can take a break in an adjacent cooling room or the upstairs solarium when you need it. A variety of spa treatments is also available, including massages, body wraps, and private mineral baths. ⊠ *Yampah Spa & Salon, 709 E. 6th St.* ☎ *970/945–0667* ⊕ *www.yampahspa.com* ⊠ *$15 for caves, additional cost for treatments* ☉ *Daily 9–9.*

DOWNHILL SKIING AND SNOWBOARDING

Sunlight Mountain Resort. Twenty-five minutes south of Glenwood Springs, Sunlight Mountain Resort is affordable Colorado skiing at its best. Overshadowed by world-class neighbors, the resort sees far less traffic than typical Colorado slopes. Fresh powder, typically skied off at Aspen within an hour, can last as long as two days here on classic downhill runs like Sun King and Beaujolais; you'll rarely, if ever, stand in lines at the three lifts. The resort has 67 trails, including a series of double-black steeps on the East Ridge. The varied terrain, sensational views, and lack of pretension make this a local favorite. The lift tickets cost a fraction of what they do at nearby Aspen and every slope meets at the bottom base lodge. A terrain park for freestyling skiers and boarders features rails, boxes, and jumps. For winter-sports enthusiasts who don't want to ride a chairlift, there's a 20-mile network of cross-country ski and snowshoe trails just off the slopes. Parking at the resort is free.

Half-day ski and snowboard lessons (including gear rental and lift ticket) for adults cost $95; full-day lessons are $145. The Children's Center offers lessons for children ages three to six. The resort also has ski-stay-swim packages at a number of Glenwood Springs hotels. The deal includes one night's lodging, a full-day lift ticket for adults, free skiing for kids 12 and under, and a full day at the Glenwood Hot Springs Pool. **Facilities:** 67 trails; 680 acres; 2,010-foot vertical drop; 3 lifts. ⊠ *10901 County Rd. 117* ☎ *970/945–7491, 800/445–7931* ⊕ *www.sunlightmtn.com* ⊠ *Lift ticket $60* ☉ *Early Dec.–early Apr., daily 9–4.*

RENTALS

Sunlight Mountain Resort. The shop at the base of Sunlight Mountain has complete ski-rental packages starting at $25 a day. ⊠ *10901 County Rd. 117* ☎ *970/945–7491, 800/445–7931* ⊕ *www.sunlightmtn.com.*

Sunlight Ski and Bike Shop. The resort's retail outlet, Sunlight Ski and Bike Shop, is in downtown Glenwood Springs. Prices for ski rentals here are typically a little cheaper than at the mountain. ⊠ *309 9th St.* ☎ *970/945–9425* ⊕ *www.sunlightmtn.com/rental-shop.*

OTHER SPORTS AND THE OUTDOORS
BICYCLING
Glenwood Canyon Bike Path. A concrete trail sandwiched between the Colorado River and the highway traffic, Glenwood Canyon Bike Path runs about 16 miles from Dotsero southwest to Glenwood Springs through the spectacular depths of Glenwood Canyon. The path generally runs below, and out of sight of the interstate, and the roar of the river drowns out the sound of traffic. Because of the mild climate on Colorado's Western Slope, it's closed in the winter months during heavy snow years and occasionally in the spring when water levels are high in the Colorado River. The Ute trail—a single-track dirt trail—branches off of the concrete path offering a detour at Dotsero for mountain bikers and hikers. A choice ride is the 18-mile round-trip from Glenwood Springs east up to the trailhead at Hanging Lake, where you can leave your bike and hike a steep mile (climbing 1,000 feet) to the beautiful emerald lake. Horseshoe Bend, about 2 miles from the Vapor Caves, is a perfect picnic spot, since the highway ducks out of sight into a series of tunnels. ⊠ *Trailhead: enter path from either the Yampah Spa Hot Springs Vapor Caves in Glenwood Springs or farther east on I–70 at Grizzly Creek rest area.*

OUTFITTERS AND RENTALS **Canyon Bikes.** Canyon Bikes will shuttle you 14 miles up Glenwood Canyon. You can then enjoy the downhill bike ride on a paved recreation path back to the shop at Hotel Colorado. Shuttle rides are $18 per person or $39 including bike rental. ⊠ *319 6th St.* ☎ *970/945–8904, 877/945–6605* ⊕ *www.canyonbikes.com.*

Sunlight Ski and Bike Shop. Downtown's Sunlight Ski and Bike Shop rents mountain and comfort bikes, as well as tandem bikes and tag-a-longs for young riders. ⊠ *309 9th St.* ☎ *970/945–9425* ⊕ *www.sunlightmtn.com/rental-shop.*

FISHING
Roaring Fork Anglers. This shop leads wade and float trips throughout the area, and sells a variety of fly-fishing gear. ⊠ *2205 Grand Ave.* ☎ *970/945–0180* ⊕ *www.roaringforkanglers.com.*

RAFTING
Colorado River. When the ski season is over and Colorado's "white gold" starts to melt, many ski instructors swap their sticks for paddles and hit the mighty Colorado River for the spring and summer rafting seasons. Stomach-churning holes, chutes, and waves beckon adrenaline junkies, while calmer souls can revel in the shade of Glenwood Canyon's towering walls. ⊠ *Glenwood Springs.*

OUTFITTERS

FAMILY **Blue Sky Adventures.** At this outfitter, you can book a "Pedals & Paddles" package that includes a half-day raft trip with Blue Sky Adventures, followed by a bike rental from next-door sister company, Canyon Bikes. ⊠ *319 6th St.* ☎ *970/945–6605, 877/945–6605* ⊕ *www.blueskyadventure.com.*

Rock Gardens Rafting. In addition to half- and full-day trips on the Colorado River, Rock Gardens Rafting rents inflatable kayaks and stand-up paddleboards. ⊠ *1308 County Rd. 129* ☎ *800/970–6737* ⊕ *www.rockgardens.com.*

Whitewater Rafting, LLC. This company offers tours that include the "Double Shoshone" tour, where you run the area's most hair-raising white-water rapids—twice. ✉ *2000 Devereux Rd.* ☎ *970/945–8477, 800/993–7238* 🌐 *www.coloradowhitewaterrafting.com.*

WHERE TO EAT

$ BURGER 🍴 **Grind.** The owners of this burger joint actually grind their own beef, lamb, chicken, pork, and buffalo for the most exquisite gourmet patties this side of the Mississippi. The focus is on locally raised, grass-fed meats, and unusual toppings. Try, for example, the Cordon Bleu, a chicken burger with Swiss cheese, sautéed apples and pears, ham, and mustard. Even the vegetarian options—homemade falafel with tzatziki sauce or black bean with chipotle mayonnaise and pumpkin-seed salsa—are excellent. Milk shakes and classic arcade games please kids, while parents can enjoy a variety of Colorado microbrews. [$] *Average main: $8* ✉ *720 Grand Ave., 2nd fl.* ☎ *970/230–9258* 🌐 *www.grindglenwood.com* 💳 *No credit cards.*

$$ INDIAN 🍴 **Nepal Restaurant.** Finding good Asian fare in Glenwood Springs is no easy feat, but this little eatery, tucked into a strip mall beside the highway on the west side of town, has tasty Nepalese, Tibetan, and Indian food. Dishes are so authentic that you might think for a second that you're in the high Himalayas. Try fish *kawab* (marinated overnight and then baked in a tandoor) with a side of garlicky *naan* (chewy flat bread) if you're skeptical. [$] *Average main: $13* ✉ *6824 Hwy. 82* ☎ *970/945–8803* 🌐 *www.nepalrestaurant.us.com.*

$$ MODERN AMERICAN 🍴 **The Pullman.** With its exposed redbrick walls, pendant lighting, loftlike high ceilings, and zinc-topped bar, The Pullman exudes a sophisticated, urban vibe. It's across the street from the Amtrak train station (thus, the name) in Glenwood's historic downtown area. This laid-back restaurant welcomes all types of casual diners with a contemporary American menu that specializes in pork. Depending on the season, the menu might include truffled seasonal pork rinds, roasted pork shoulder, or garlic-bacon mashed potatoes. The salads and pasta dishes are excellent as well. [$] *Average main: $17* ✉ *330 7th St.* ☎ *970/230–9234* 🌐 *www.thepullmangws.com* 💳 *No credit cards.*

$ AMERICAN 🍴 **Slope & Hatch.** Pick your poison or mix and match tacos and hot dogs at this small but popular spot just off the main drag and near the Roaring Fork River. Tacos range from traditional fried fish with fresh pico de gallo to unexpected thai veggie stir-fry topped with edamame and coconut curry. Local dogs are equally enticing, like the Glenwood Completo with avocado and ancho remoulade and the Carolina dog with pulled pork, chipotle BBQ, and slaw. Rotating Colorado beers offer the perfect pairing. [$] *Average main: $9* ✉ *208 7th St.* ☎ *970/230–9652* 🌐 *slopeandhatchgws.com* 💳 *No credit cards.*

$$ BARBECUE 🍴 **Smoke.** Homemade bold and tangy, thick and sweet, and smoky and spicy sauces on every table add extra flavor to the perfectly cooked traditional barbecue dishes, prepared in an open kitchen. Popular picks at this modern space include Louisana shrimp and grits or a pulled pork and smoked chicken combo plate. House-made mustard sauce pairs perfectly with the jalapeño beef sausage. Southern sides

Rafting the Roaring Fork Valley

The key to understanding white-water rafting is the rating system. Rivers are rated from Class I, with small waves where you really don't need to paddle to avoid anything, to Class VI, where a mistake can be fatal. To confuse matters, rivers often get more difficult when the water level is high (measured in cubic feet of water per second). May and June are peak rafting seasons for those who want the adrenaline rush of fighting spring runoff. By mid-August many rivers are little more than lazy float trips.

The Roaring Fork, a free-flowing river (no dams), has several different sections that generally range from Class II to Class IV. Because it runs away from major highways through the heart of ranch country, you're liable to see more wildlife than on the Colorado; in June your guides may point out a nest full of croaking bald eaglets while riding the Cemetery Rapids, a half-mile churning stretch of white water.

The portion of the mighty Colorado that runs through the steep, spectacular walls of Glenwood Canyon alongside I–70 includes the rough-and-tumble Shoshone section, considered Class IV during the peak runoff season, with aptly named rapids like Maneater and Baptism. The lower Colorado has some exciting stretches, too, including Maintenance Shack, a Class III rapid that can flip a large raft when the water is running high. By July and August you can hit the same rapid sideways or backward and barely get wet. The lower stretches of the Colorado pass by several hidden, and not-so-hidden shallow hot springs. If you'd like to warm up in them, ask your guides.

and unique cocktails complement the hearty entrées. $ *Average main: $14 ⊠ 713 Grand Ave.* ✢ *Under the bridge* ☎ *970/230–9795* ⊕ *www. smokemodernbbq.com.*

WHERE TO STAY

$$$$ **Glenwood Hot Springs Lodge.** Perfectly located, just steps from the
HOTEL Glenwood Hot Springs Pool (which is used to heat the property), the
FAMILY attractive rooms in this lodge are decorated in blues and earth tones that reflect the colors of the mountains and water. **Pros:** right next to the hot springs. **Cons:** no restaurant or bar; breakfast is at next-door pool. $ *Rooms from: $249 ⊠ 415 E. 6th St.* ☎ *970/945–6571, 800/537–7946* ⊕ *www.hotspringspool.com* ⌷ *104 rooms, 3 suites* ⦿ *Breakfast.*

$$ **Hotel Colorado.** When you catch sight of the graceful sandstone colon-
HOTEL nades and Italianate campaniles of this exquisite building, you won't be surprised that it's listed in the National Register of Historic Places. **Pros:** one of the most historic properties in the valley; across the street from the hot springs. **Cons:** most rooms don't have air-conditioning; some rooms are small. $ *Rooms from: $159 ⊠ 526 Pine St.* ☎ *970/945–6511, 800/544–3998* ⊕ *www.hotelcolorado.com* ⌷ *100 rooms, 30 suites* ⦿ *No meals.*

$$$
HOTEL

⚅ **Hotel Denver.** Right across from Glenwood Springs' train station, this historic hotel has some rooms that look out on a three-story New Orleans–style atrium, which is accented by colorful canopies. **Pros:** downtown; romantic; on-site brewpub. **Cons:** no dedicated concierge; no room service. Ⓢ *Rooms from: $229* ✉ *402 7th St.* ☎ *970/945–6565, 800/826–8820* ⊕ *www.thehoteldenver.com* ⤢ *69 rooms* ⦿ *No meals.*

SHOPPING

SPAS

Spa of the Rockies at Glenwood Hot Springs. The full-service Spa of the Rockies, housed in a 19th-century sandstone bathhouse at Glenwood Hot Springs, pays tribute to the healing pools just outside its doors with a focus on mineral-based treatments. You can add a private aromatherapy herbal soak or mineral bath to any service. The small, co-ed relaxation room has windows that directly face the popular Glenwood Hot Springs pool. ✉ *415 E. 6th St.* ☎ *877/947–3331* ⊕ *www. spaoftherockies.com* ⤲ *$115 60-min massage. Nail salon, private baths, steam room. Services: Aromatherapy, body wraps, body scrubs, facials, manicures, massage, pedicures, Vichy shower, waxing.*

BOULDER AND NORTH CENTRAL COLORADO

With Estes Park and Grand County

Updated by
Avery Stonich

With spectacular scenery and an equally appealing climate, north central Colorado contains a string of sophisticated yet laid-back cities and endless opportunities for outdoor adventure along Colorado's Front Range. Restaurants serving cuisines from around the world, celebrated universities, eclectic shopping, high-tech industries, ranching, Colorado's best-known breweries, bustling nightlife, and concerts are mere minutes from the wilderness, with hiking, rock climbing, bicycling, skiing, and kayaking.

North central Colorado encompasses three counties—Boulder, Grand, and Larimer—each with its own unique appeal. Despite their differences, these areas share a few common traits: natural beauty, rich history, and an eclectic cultural scene.

This part of Colorado also encompasses the northern Front Range, the easternmost edge of the Rocky Mountains—where the Rockies meet the Great Plains. The Front Range is Colorado's most populous area. It's just west of what's known as the I–25 Corridor, a strip that includes the cities of Fort Collins, Denver, Colorado Springs, and Pueblo, which line up almost perfectly along the north–south interstate. The Front Range is known for its blend of historic cities and towns, verdant landscapes, and wealth of outdoor recreation opportunities.

ORIENTATION AND PLANNING

GETTING ORIENTED

Outside of Denver, Boulder and Fort Collins are the second and third most prominent cities in the region. Between these two energetic university towns you'll find the sprawling cities of Loveland and Longmont and a few former coal-mining towns with homey, small-town character (like Marshall, Louisville, Lafayette, and Erie). To the west are the proud, independent mountain hamlets of Lyons, Nederland, Ward, and Jamestown. Beyond the high peaks are broad valleys dotted with unpretentious ranching communities like Granby and Kremmling, and right in the middle of it all is the area's crown jewel, Rocky Mountain National Park, with its two gateways, Grand Lake and Estes Park.

Boulder. Even though every conceivable trend in food, alternative health care, education, and personal style has come through town, Boulder still feels wild. It's also very much a college town—home to the scenic University of Colorado at Boulder campus.

TOP REASONS TO GO

The arts: Theater buffs have enjoyed the Colorado Shakespeare Festival every summer since 1958, and music lovers engage their ears and intellect at the Colorado Music Festival's stunning performances.

Boulder Dushanbe Teahouse: This traditional Central Asian teahouse was carved and painted by master artisans and gifted to Boulder by its sister city of Dushanbe, Tajikistan.

Chautauqua Park: You can still attend a lecture, silent film, or classical concert here much like visitors did 100 years ago. Enjoy a picnic on the green or eat in the hall before the event.

Hiking near Boulder and in the Indian Peaks Wilderness: On weekends year-round you'll find the trails packed. The views are spectacular, especially when the wildflowers bloom in midsummer.

The local breweries: This is basically the Napa Valley of beer. You could fill a whole vacation with the myriad ales, stouts, and lagers on offer. In late June the state's small brewers congregate in Fort Collins for the Colorado Brewers' Festival.

Side Trips from Boulder. Nederland, Niwot, and Lyons are easy to explore from Boulder—all can be reached in less than an hour. Each is known for its natural beauty, historic character, and funky atmosphere.

Estes Park. The eastern gateway to Rocky Mountain National Park, resort town Estes Park is nestled against Roosevelt National Forest on its other three sides.

Grand County. West of Rocky Mountain National Park, guest ranches and golf courses dot the landscape. In Grand Lake, waterskiing, sailing, canoeing, ice fishing, and snowmobiling dominate the scene.

Fort Collins. Famous for Colorado State University, as well as its open spaces and beer, Fort Collins has a rich history and vibrant cultural scene.

PLANNING

WHEN TO GO

Visiting the Front Range is pleasurable in any season. Winter in the urban corridor is generally mild, but can be cold and snowy in the mountainous regions. Snowfall along the Front Range is highest in spring, particularly March, making for excellent skiing but unpredictable driving and potentially lengthy delays. Spring is unpredictable—75°F one day and a blizzard the next—and June can be hot or cool (or both). July typically ushers in high summer, which can last through September, although most 90°F-plus days occur in July and early August and at lower elevations. In the higher mountains, summer temperatures are generally 15–20°F cooler than in the urban corridor. Afternoon spring and summer thunderstorms can last 10 minutes or a few hours. Fall brings crisp sunny days and cool nights, some cold enough for frost in the mountains.

Art and music festivals start up in May and continue through September. With them comes an increase in visitor traffic. Spring and summer are typically the best times to fish or watch for wildlife.

PLANNING YOUR TIME

You could pass a weekend or a year in this area and still leave stones unturned. At a minimum, spend a long weekend in Boulder, exploring the trails, eating and drinking to your heart's content, and people-watching along the Pearl Street Mall. If you have a bit more time, drive to Estes Park for a few days, stopping in Lyons along the way to see where the river jumped its banks in 2013. Stop for a beer to help revitalize this resilient town.

In Estes Park, stay for a few days to check out Rocky Mountain National Park and take in the stunning mountain views. If you still have time, drive over Trail Ridge Road and see how Grand Lake compares. Tack on a week-long stay at a dude ranch near Granby, and you might never want to leave.

GETTING HERE AND AROUND

AIR TRAVEL

Denver International Airport, known to locals as DIA (although its airport code is DEN), 23 miles northeast of downtown Denver, is the primary commercial passenger airport serving north central Colorado. Boulder, Fort Collins, and Granby have municipal airports but no commercial service.

TRANSFERS The Denver Airport's Ground Transportation Information Center assists visitors with car rentals, door-to-door shuttles, public transportation, wheelchair services, charter buses, and limousine services. Boulder is approximately 45 miles (45 minutes to 1 hour) from Denver International Airport; Granby approximately 110 miles (a little more than 2 hours); Fort Collins approximately 70 miles (just over an hour); and Estes Park approximately 75 miles (about 1½ hours).

Estes Park Shuttle (reservations essential) serves Estes Park and Rocky Mountain National Park from Denver, Denver International Airport, and Boulder. Super Shuttle and Green Ride serve Fort Collins and Boulder. Home James serves Granby, Grand Lake, and the guest ranches of Grand County.

Airport Contacts Denver International Airport (DEN). ⊠ *8500 Peña Blvd., Denver* ☎ *800/247–2336, 303/342–2000* ⊕ *www.flydenver.com.* **Fort Collins–Loveland Municipal Airport (FNL).** ⊠ *4900 Earhart Rd., Loveland* ☎ *970/962–2850* ⊕ *www.fortloveair.com.*

Airport Shuttles Estes Park Shuttle. ⊠ *Estes Park* ☎ *970/586–5151* ⊕ *www.estesparkshuttle.com.* **Green Ride Colorado Shuttle.** ☎ *970/226–5533 Fort Collins, 303/997–0238 Boulder* ⊕ *www.greenrideco.com.* **Ground Transportation Information Center.** ☎ *303/342–4059* ⊕ *www.flydenver.com/parking_transit/transportation_den.* **Home James.** ☎ *970/726–5060, 800/359–7503* ⊕ *www.homejamestransportation.com.* **Super Shuttle.** ☎ *970/482–0505, 800/258–3826* ⊕ *www.supershuttle.com.*

BUS TRAVEL

The expansive network of the Regional Transportation District (RTD) includes service from Denver and Denver International Airport to and within Boulder, Lyons, Niwot, Nederland, and the Eldora Mountain Resort. The Hop bus (part of the RTD network) is a circulator that makes for easy carless travel within Boulder between the university, the Hill, the Twenty-Ninth Street shopping area, and downtown. Transfort serves Fort Collins's main thoroughfares.

Bus Contacts Regional Transportation District (RTD). ☎ *303/299–6000, 800/366–7433* ⊕ *www.rtd-denver.com.* **Transfort.** ☎ *970/221–6620* ⊕ *www.ridetransfort.com.*

CAR TRAVEL

Interstate 25, the most direct route from Denver to Fort Collins, is the north–south artery that connects the cities in the urban corridor along the Front Range. From Denver, U.S. 36 runs through Boulder, Lyons, and Estes Park to Rocky Mountain National Park. The direct route from Denver to Grand County is I–70 west to U.S. 40 (Empire exit) and to U.S. 34. If you're driving directly to Fort Collins or Estes Park and Rocky Mountain National Park from Denver International Airport, take the E–470 tollway to I–25. U.S. 36 between Boulder and Estes Park is heavily traveled, while Highways 119, 72, and 7 have much less traffic.

Gasoline and service are available in all larger towns and cities in the region. Bicyclists are common except on arteries; state law gives them the same rights and holds them to the same obligations as those using any other vehicle. Expect a fair amount of road construction along the northern Front Range; arterial routes, state highways, and city streets are being rebuilt to accommodate increasing traffic in the urban corridor. Although the state plows roads regularly, a winter snowstorm can slow traffic and create wet, slushy, or icy conditions. Note that you can't always count on having cell-phone service in sparsely populated or mountainous areas.

Car Travel Contacts AAA Colorado. ☎ *303/753–8800* ⊕ *www.colorado. aaa.com.* **Colorado Department of Transportation Road Information.** ☎ *303/639–1111* ⊕ *www.codot.gov.* **Colorado State Patrol.** ☎ *303/239–4501, *277 from cell phone to report an aggressive driver* ⊕ *www.colorado.gov/csp.* **Rocky Mountain National Park Road Information.** ☎ *970/586–1333.*

TRAIN TRAVEL

Amtrak provides passenger rail service to and within north central Colorado. The Chicago–San Francisco *California Zephyr* stops in downtown Denver, Winter Park/Fraser, and Granby, once each day in both directions.

Train Contact Amtrak. ☎ *800/872–7245 reservations, 303/534–2812 train status only* ⊕ *www.amtrak.com.*

PARKS AND RECREATION AREAS

Rocky Mountain National Park is known for its scenery, hiking, wildlife-watching, camping, and snowshoeing. ⇨ *See Chapter 8, Rocky Mountain National Park.*

North central Colorado has six state parks: Eldorado Canyon, Barr Lake, and St. Vrain, all close to Boulder; and Boyd Lake, State Forest, and Lory, all close to Fort Collins. In Boulder and Fort Collins you can literally walk out your door, up the street, and into the mountains or foothills on a hiking trail. There are also plenty of riparian trails and open-space paths within the city limits that can take you for miles; they usually have plenty of access points.

Arapaho and Roosevelt National Forests and Pawnee National Grassland. The Arapaho and Roosevelt National Forests and Pawnee National Grassland, an enormous area that encompasses 1.5 million acres, has fishing, sailing, canoeing, and waterskiing, as well as hiking, mountain biking, birding, and camping. Contained within the Arapaho National Forest is the **Arapaho National Recreation Area (ANRA)**, a 35,000-acre expanse adjacent to Rocky Mountain National Park that contains Lake Granby, Shadow Mountain Lake, Monarch Lake, and Willow Creek and Meadow Creek reservoirs. Toss in neighboring Grand Lake and you have what's known as Colorado's Great Lakes. ⊠ *USDA Forest Service Sulphur Ranger District, 9 Ten Mile Dr., Granby* ☎ *970/887–4100* ⊕ *www.fs.usda.gov/main/arp/home.*

Indian Peaks Wilderness. Spanning the Continental Divide between Grand Lake and Nederland just south of Rocky Mountain National Park, Indian Peaks Wilderness is a 76,711-acre expanse that lies within the Arapaho and Roosevelt national forests and is a favorite destination for hiking and backcountry camping. Permits are required for camping from June 1 to Sept. 15, with popular spots selling out in advance. ⊠ *Boulder Ranger District, 2140 Yarmouth Ave., Boulder* ☎ *303/541–2500* ⊕ *www.fs.usda.gov/recarea/arp/recarea/?recid=80803.*

RESTAURANTS

Thanks to the influx of people from around the world, you have plenty of options here. Restaurants in north central Colorado run the gamut from simple diners with tasty, homey basics to elegant establishments with extensive wine lists. The hot trend is organic and sustainable ingredients, with many restaurants offering dishes made from local ingredients. Some restaurants take reservations, but many, particularly those in the middle price range, seat on a first-come, first-served basis.

HOTELS

The area's ever-popular guest ranches and spas are places to escape and be pampered after having fun outdoors. In the high-country resorts of Estes Park and Grand Lake and nearby towns, high elevations keep the climate cool, which means that there are few accommodations with air-conditioning—but you really don't need it. The region is also full of chain motels and hotels, often on the outskirts of cities. *Hotel reviews have been shortened. For full information, visit Fodors.com.*

WHAT IT COSTS				
	$	$$	$$$	$$$$
Restaurants	under $13	$13–$18	$19–$25	over $25
Hotels	under $121	$121–$170	$171–$230	over $230

Restaurant prices are the average cost of a main course at dinner or, if dinner is not served, at lunch, excluding 5.75%–8.46% tax. Hotel prices are the lowest cost of a standard double room in high season, excluding service charges and 5.75%–12.40% tax.

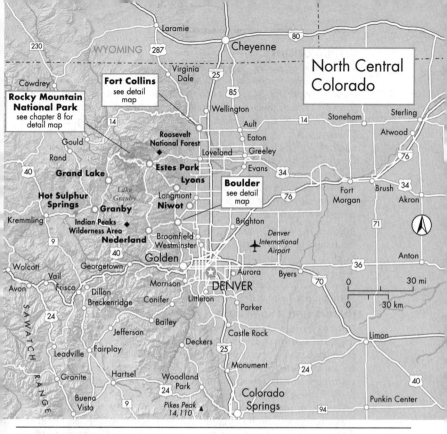

BOULDER

No place in Colorado better epitomizes the state's outdoor mania than Boulder, where sunny weather keeps locals busy through all seasons. The bicycle count rivals the car tally in this uncommonly beautiful and beautifully uncommon city. Boulder has more than 150 miles of trails for hiking, walking, jogging, and bicycling.

One of Boulder's most endearing features is its setting. In 1960 Boulder citizens voted to start buying land surrounding the city to protect it from urban sprawl and preserve its historic and ecological resources. Residents started taxing themselves in 1967 in order to buy a greenbelt, and the city now owns more than 45,000 acres of open space—120,000 acres if you lump in lands owned by Boulder County Parks & Open Space. This means that there's three times as much protected land surrounding the city as developed land. Even in winter, residents bicycle to work and jog on the open-space paths. It's practically a matter of civic pride to spend a lunch hour playing Frisbee, going on a bike ride with coworkers, hiking with the family dog, and even rock climbing on the Flatirons.

GETTING ORIENTED

One of the best places to take a first look at this beautiful town is from the scenic overlook on Davidson Mesa (pull out at the scenic overlook on westbound U.S. 36, at the crest of the hill about 8 miles outside of town). In the distance are the craggy (and often snowcapped) peaks in Roosevelt National Forest, Indian Peaks Wilderness, and Rocky Mountain National Park. Closer by, to the southwest, are Bear Peak and the Devil's Thumb on its left slope, near the entrance to Eldorado Canyon. Just north of there are Green Mountain and the trademark red-sandstone Flatirons, which you can see from many vantage points in town. These massive rock upthrusts, named for their flat faces, are popular among rock climbers and hikers. To the east are flat plains, dotted with parks and reservoirs.

In town, the red-tile roofs of the University of Colorado dominate the landscape on University Hill ("the Hill"), just south of downtown. Boulder Creek courses along the south side of downtown, with a multi-use path alongside it. At the northeastern end of town is Boulder Reservoir, a 700-acre park used for swimming, rowing, kayaking, sailing, stand-up paddleboarding, windsurfing, and waterskiing.

GETTING HERE AND AROUND

Although a 10-minute walk separates downtown from the Hill, each area has a distinct flavor. Downtown—particularly the Pearl Street pedestrian mall—bustles with families, street performers, upscale boutiques, and eateries, while the Hill pulsates with trendy shops, packed coffeehouses, bars and rock clubs, and restaurants geared more to students. Parking and driving in these sections of Boulder can be frustrating and time-consuming. Leave your car at the hotel and try the Hop, a bus that circulates in both directions through downtown, Twenty-Ninth Street, the Hill, and the university for about the cost of an hour of parking. Buses run in both directions every 9–15 minutes.

Boulder B-cycle. For a quick trip, borrow a bike from B-cycle, Boulder's bike-sharing service, which has nearly 40 stations all over town. Pick up from one station and return to any other. The rate structure encourages trips of 30 minutes or less. ⊠ *Boulder* ☎ *303/532–4412* ⊕ *www.boulder.bcycle.com.*

WHEN TO GO

Like the rest of the Front Range, Boulder has beautiful weather year-round. The city definitely feels livelier when school is in session, especially on big football weekends, and summer weekends often bring big crowds of tourists (including day-trippers from Denver).

FAMILY **Boulder Creek Festival.** Held each Memorial Day weekend, the Boulder Creek Festival converts a stretch along Boulder Creek into a giant party, complete with carnival rides, live music, 500-plus vendors, food and beer pavilions, and the signature event: a rubber duck race on Boulder Creek. Children have fun with dance, theater, and hands-on activities at the Kids' Place. The fest runs between Arapahoe Avenue and Canyon Boulevard between 9th and 14th streets. ⊠ *Boulder* ⊕ *www.bceproductions.com/boulder-creek-festival.*

ESSENTIALS

Transportation Contacts Boulder Custom Rides. ✉ *Boulder* ☎ *303/442–4477* ⊕ *www.bouldercustomrides.com.* **303-Limovan.** ☎ *303/5466–826* ⊕ *303limovan.com.* **Yellow Cab.** ✉ *Boulder* ☎ *303/777-7777* ⊕ *www.boulderyellowcab.com.*

Visitor Information Boulder Convention & Visitors Bureau. ✉ *2440 Pearl St.* ☎ *303/442-2911* ⊕ *www.bouldercoloradousa.com.*

TOURS

Banjo Billy's Bus Tours. Banjo Billy's Bus Tours offer 90-minute tours of downtown Boulder, Chautauqua Park, the Hill, part of the University of Colorado, and other notable sites, aboard a bus that has been retrofitted to look like a shack. The tour's lighthearted, quirky commentary focuses on ghosts, history, and crime stories. Your seat may be a saddle, couch, or bench upholsterd with funky, mismatched fabrics. ✉ *Boulder* ☎ *720/938-8885* ⊕ *www.banjobilly.com* ⊠ *From $22.*

Historic Boulder. Historic Boulder provides free brochures for seven self-guided walking tours, including the University of Colorado at Boulder, the Hill, Chautauqua Park, the Mapleton Historic District, and the Downtown Boulder Historic District. Call or stop by the office at 1123 Spruce Street, or pick up a general walking-tour map of Boulder in the kiosk just east of 13th Street on the Pearl Street Mall. ✉ *1123 Spruce St.* ☎ *303/444-5192* ⊕ *www.historicboulder.org.*

EXPLORING

TOP ATTRACTIONS

Boulder Museum of Contemporary Art. View local and worldwide contemporary art exhibits and performance art at this innovative museum with frequently changing exhibitions. Admission is free during the farmers' market, which takes place in front of the museum from May to November on Saturday 8–2; and May to October on Wednesday 4–8. All other times, the museum charges $1. ✉ *1750 13th St.* ☎ *303/443–2122* ⊕ *www.bmoca.org* ⊠ *$1* ☉ *Tues.–Sun. 11–5* ⌁ *Closed 2 wks every 3 months during exhibition changes.*

Fodor'sChoice
★
Chautauqua Park. For the prettiest views of town, follow Baseline Road west from Broadway to Chautauqua Park, nestled at the base of the Flatirons. Bring a picnic and relax on the expansive lawn, or use the park as a launching point to miles of hiking trails. Chautauqua is also home to an historic dining hall (now a tasty restaurant) and auditorium, which hosts the Colorado Music Festival. For a bird's-eye view of Boulder, keep going west on Baseline (which turns into Flagstaff Road) 1 mile to Panorama Point, and then 3½ miles to Realization Point. ✉ *Grant St. and Baseline Rd.* ⊕ *www.bouldercolorado.gov/parks-rec/chautauqua-park.*

Downtown Boulder Historic District. The late-19th- and early-20th-century commercial structures of the Downtown Boulder Historic District once housed mercantile stores and saloons. The period architecture—including Queen Anne, Italianate, and Romanesque styles in stone or brick—has been preserved, but stores inside cater to modern tastes, with fair-trade coffees and Tibetan prayer flags. ⊠ *Boulder* ⊹ *Bounded by the south side of Spruce St. between 10th and 16th Sts., Pearl St. between 9th and 16th Sts., and the north side of Walnut St. between Broadway and 9th St.*

Eldorado Canyon State Park. With steep canyon walls, a rushing creek, verdant pine forests, 30 streamside picnic tables, and 12 miles of trails, this park attracts thrill-seekers and nature lovers alike. Rock climbers scale the sandstone walls, kayakers charge the rapids of South Boulder Creek, and anglers cast lines for brown and rainbow trout. The **Streamside Trail** parallels South Boulder Creek for ½ mile (wheelchair accessible for 300 feet). The 1-mile (one-way) **Fowler Trail** is wheelchair accessible, with interpretive signs and great views for climbers. For Continental Divide views, take the 3½-mile (round-trip) **Rattlesnake Gulch Trail**, which climbs 800 feet. Snowshoeing is popular here in winter. Mountain bikers crank on Rattlesnake Gulch Trail and the Walker Ranch Loop (accessed from the Crescent Meadows trailhead off Gross Dam Road). Hikers and horses can climb the 3½-mile (one-way) **Eldorado Canyon Trail** to Crescent Meadows. ⊠ *9 Kneale Rd.* ⊹ *Drive south on Broadway (Hwy. 93) 3 miles to Eldorado Canyon Dr. (Rte. 170); paved road ends at the village of Eldorado Springs. Drive through town to park entrance* ☎ *303/494–3943* ⊕ *www.parks.state.co.us/ Parks/eldoradocanyon* ☞ *$8 per vehicle* ☉ *Daily dawn–dusk.*

The Hill. Across Broadway from the University of Colorado campus is the Hill, a favorite student hangout. The neighborhood is home to restaurants, music venues, bars, coffeehouses, and boutiques. ⊠ *Broadway and 13th St. between University Ave. and College Ave.*

Fodor'sChoice ★ **Pearl Street.** Between 8th and 20th streets in the downtown area, Pearl Street is the city's hub, an eclectic collection of boutiques, consignment shops, bookstores, art galleries, cafés, bars, and restaurants. From 11th and 15th streets is a pedestrian mall, replete with street performers and people-watching. ⊠ *Boulder* ⊕ *www.boulderdowntown.com.*

University of Colorado at Boulder. The campus of the University of Colorado at Boulder began in 1875 with the construction of Old Main, which borders the Norlin Quadrangle, now on the National Register of Historic Places, a broad lawn where students sun themselves or play a quick round of Frisbee between classes. The university's red sandstone buildings with tile roofs, built in the "Rural Italian" architectural style that Charles Z. Klauder created in the early 1920s, complement the campus's green lawns and small ponds. You can take a walking tour of the campus year-round. ⊠ *University Memorial Center* ☎ *303/492–1411 CU main number, 303/492–6301 Admissions Office* ⊕ *www.colorado.edu/admissions/undergraduate/visit/ dailytours* ☉ *Campus tours weekdays at 9:30 and 1:30; most Sat. at 10:30* ☞ *Reservations essential.*

CU Heritage Center. The mission of this museum is to document the history of the University of Colorado and alumni accomplishments. It has seven galleries dedicated to such topics as Glenn Miller, who was a swing music pioneer and has a campus ballroom named after him; notable alumni; space exploration, including a moon rock sample and wreckage of the Space Shutte Challenger, which had alum Ellison Onizuka on board; and athletics. ⊠ *Old Main Bldg., Third Floor, 459 UCB* ☏ *303/492–6329* ⊕ *www.cuheritage.org* ⊙ *Mon.–Sat. 10–4.*

University of Colorado Museum of Natural History. This museum houses more than 4 million objects, from dozens of countries. Think fossils, archaeological finds, dinosaur relics, plants, and invertebrates. There are permanent and changing exhibits, and a discovery corner for kids. ⊠ *Henderson Bldg., 15th and Broadway* ☏ *303/492–6892* ⊕ *cumuseum.colorado.edu* ⊠ *$3 (suggested donation)* ⊙ *Weekdays 9–5, Sat. 9–4, Sun. 10–4.*

WORTH NOTING

Boulder Beer Company. The scent of hops fills the air during free 45-minute tours and tastings at the Boulder Beer Company, Colorado's first craft brewery. Arrive early to make sure you get a spot as space is limited. The brewhouse's pub is open weekdays 11 am to 10 pm, and Saturday from noon to 10 pm. Chill out on the pleasant patio during the summer and listen to live music on Thursday and Saturday from 5 to 9 pm. ⊠ *2880 Wilderness Pl.* ☏ *303/444–8448* ⊕ *www.boulderbeer.com* ⊠ *Free* ⊙ *Tours weekdays at 2, Sat. at 2 and 4.*

Fiske Planetarium. This dome puts on planetarium shows and star talks, as well as laser shows choreographed to music like Pink Floyd, Bob Marley, and Queen. Showtimes vary somewhat, but generally laser shows take place on Thursday, Friday, and Saturday night; and star shows are sprinkled throughout the week, including some family matinees. There are also live talks on Thursday evening. The Sommers–Bausch Observatory is open for free public viewing every Friday, weather permitting, when CU classes are in session. ⊠ *2414 Regent Dr.* ☏ *303/492–5002* ⊕ *fiske.colorado.edu* ⊠ *$10.*

Mapleton Historic District. Three blocks north of Pearl Street and west of Broadway this neighborhood of turn-of-the-20th-century homes is shaded by old maple and cottonwood trees. ⊠ *Boulder* ⊹ *Bounded roughly by Broadway, the alley between Pearl and Spruce Sts., 4th St., and the alley between Dewey St. and Concord Ave.*

FAMILY **National Center for Atmospheric Research.** Talking about the weather is *not* boring at the National Center for Atmospheric Research, where the hands-on exhibits and tours fire up kids' and adults' enthusiasm for what happens in the sky. If you can't make the guided tour, self-guided, audio, and tablet tours are available during regular hours. The distinctive buildings, designed by architect I.M. Pei, stand majestically on a mesa at the base of the mountains, where you can see mule deer and other wildlife. After browsing the visitor center, follow the interpretive NCAR Weather Trail to learn about local weather, climate, plants, and wildlife. The nearly ½-mile loop is wheelchair accessible. ⊠ *1850 Table Mesa Dr.* ⊹ *From southbound Broadway, turn right onto Table Mesa Dr.* ☏ *303/497–1174* ⊕ *ncar.ucar.edu* ⊙ *Weekdays 8–5, weekends and holidays 9–4. Tours Mon., Wed., and Fri. at noon.*

SPORTS AND THE OUTDOORS

BICYCLING

IN BOULDER

Fodor's Choice ★ **Boulder Creek Path.** This multi-use path winds through town for about 5½ miles, from Boulder Canyon in the west to the Stazio Ballfields (near the intersection of Arapahoe and 55th) in the east, connecting to more than 100 miles of city and greenbelt trails and paths. You can access paths from nearly every cross street in town, but don't always count on parking nearby. Find maps and other resources on the website. ⊠ *Trailheads: From downtown, the best access points are behind the public library parking lot on south side of Canyon Blvd. between 9th St. and Broadway or in Central Park on 13th St., between Canyon Blvd. and Arapahoe Rd.* ⊕ *www.bouldercolorado.gov/goboulder.*

Marshall Mesa/Community Ditch/Doudy Draw/Greenbelt Plateau Trails. This moderate 8-mile mountain-bike loop takes you up through pine stands and over a plateau where you can look down on Boulder, with the Flatirons and the Rockies in full view. Start from the Marshall Mesa Trailhead. Head right toward Highway 93, cross through the underpass, and continue along Community Ditch. Turn left on the Doudy Draw Trail, then left up Flatirons Vista to circle back via the Greenbelt Plateau and cross back over 93. Grab a trail map before heading out since you can add on other trails to make an even longer ride. ⊠ *Trailhead: Just east of intersection of Hwy. 93 and Marshall Rd. Parking available.* ⊕ *www. bouldercolorado.gov/osmp/basic-trail-information.*

IN THE MOUNTAINS

Betasso Preserve. For a fun mountain-bike ride that's not too difficult, head to Betasso Preserve, about 6 miles outside Boulder to the west. The Canyon Loop Trail is 3¼ miles, with the option to add the 2½-mile Benjamin Loop. ⊠ *Boulder* ✛ *Trailhead: From the western edge of Boulder, drive west on Canyon Blvd./Hwy. 119 for about 4 miles, then turn right at Sugarloaf Rd. After about a mile, turn right onto Betasso Rd. Look for the turnout on the left.* ⊕ *www.bouldercounty.org/os/parks/pages/ betassopreserve.aspx* ⊗ *Closed to bikes on Wed. and Sat.*

Switzerland Trail. A scenic spin that's not too technical, the Switzerland Trail is a 14-mile ride one-way that follows the route of an old narrow-gauge railroad, taking you past the historic mining town of Sunset. ⊠ *Boulder* ✛ *Trailhead: From Broadway, drive west 5 miles on Canyon Blvd./Hwy. 119 and turn right onto Sugarloaf Rd./Hwy. 72. After 5 miles, turn right onto Sugarloaf Mountain Rd. The parking area is 1 mile farther.*

Walker Ranch. For a strenuous mountain-bike ride, head 10 miles west out of town to Walker Ranch. The 7¾-mile loop has several big climbs and two extended descents. ⊠ *Trailhead: Off Flagstaff Rd., about 10 miles west of Baseline Rd.*

OUTFITTERS

Full Cycle. The conveniently located Full Cycle sells a full selection of bicycles and gear, and also offers mountain-bike rentals (helmets and locks included) for same-day, 24-hour, and week-long periods. ⊠ *1795 Pearl St.* ☎ *303/440–1002* ⊕ *www.fullcyclebikes.com.*

University Bicycles. Stop here to rent town, mountain, road, and kids' bikes for one day to one week. Rental fee includes helmet, lock, flat-repair kit, and map. ⊠ *839 Pearl St.* ☎ *303/444–4196* ⊕ *www.ubikes.com.*

BIRD-WATCHING

Eldorado Canyon State Park. Red-tailed hawks, prairie falcons, and golden eagles soar along the steep cliffs of Eldorado Canyon State Park. Owls, chickadees, nuthatches, and woodpeckers are at home in the pine forests along South Boulder Creek in the park. Wild turkeys have been sighted in Crescent Meadows. ⊠ *9 Kneale Rd., Eldorado Springs* ✢ *Drive south on Broadway (Hwy. 93) 3 miles to Eldorado Canyon Dr. (Rte. 170); paved road ends at the village of Eldorado Springs. Drive through town to park entrance* ☎ *303/494–3943* ⊕ *www.parks.state.co.us/ Parks/eldoradocanyon* ⤳ *$8 per vehicle.*

Walden Ponds Wildlife Habitat. Bring your binoculars (and bug repellant) to stroll the grounds of these former gravel pits, which now attract songbirds, waterfowl, raptors, and other wildlife. Explore via nearly 3 miles of trails, including boardwalks through wetland habitat with interpretive signs. Dawn and dusk are best for species-spotting, especially in April and May when many birds migrate through the Front Range on their way to summer homes. ⊠ *Jay Rd. and N. 75th St.* ✢ *Drive north on 28th St. (U.S. 36) and turn right at Valmont Rd. Drive east 4 miles and turn left at 75th St. Sign marking ponds is about ½ mile farther* ⊕ *www.bouldercounty.org/os/parks* ◷ *Daily dawn–dusk.*

FISHING

Eldorado Canyon State Park offers excellent fly-fishing. Fish generally measure between 8 and 14 inches long, although anglers bring in a few specimens up to 24 inches long each year. See ⊕ *www.wildlife.state. co.us/fishing* for more information.

OUTFITTERS

Rocky Mountain Anglers. Buy some flies here or sign up for a guided tour. The guides have access to private ranches and know where to find secluded fishing holes on public lands, including Rocky Mountain National Park. Fees include transportation and all your gear—plus lunch on full-day trips. You'll need a fishing license, available at the store. ⊠ *1904 Arapahoe Ave.* ☎ *303/447–2400* ⊕ *www.rockymtanglers. com* ⤳ *From $195 for a half-day trip.*

GOLF

FAMILY **Indian Peaks Golf Course.** Designed by Colorado native Hale Irwin, this public championship golf course is a local favorite, partially owing to its views of the high peaks of the Continental Divide, which aren't visible from Boulder. Wildlife like great blue herons, birds of prey, and foxes also love this place, due to its numerous trees, six lakes, and two winding creeks. The well-maintained course has excellent greens and plays well for low and high handicappers. It's also a great spot to learn, with six sets of tees. ⊠ *2300 Indian Peaks Trail, Lafayette* ✢ *Baseline Rd. to Indian Peaks Trail, 10 miles east of Boulder* ☎ *303/666–4706* ⊕ *www.indianpeaksgolf.com* ⤳ *$44 weekdays, $51 weekends* ⚑ *18 holes, 5486 yards, par 72.*

HIKING

City of Boulder's Open Space and Mountain Parks. The City of Boulder manages 145 miles of trails, with 35 trailheads and 66 access points in and around Boulder, offering a vast array of opportunties to commune with nature. Most trails are open to dogs, provided they are leashed or under voice and sight control and registered with the city's Voice and Sight Tag Program. Most trailheads are free; a few require a $5 parking permit for non-resident vehicles. You can purchase a daily pass either at self-serve kiosks at trailheads or at the Open Space and Mountain Parks administration office on Cherryvale Road. ⊠ *66 S. Cherryvale Rd.* ☏ *303/441–3440* ⊕ *www.osmp.org* ⊙ *Weekdays 8–5.*

IN BOULDER

Fodor'sChoice
★
Boulder Creek Path. For a relaxing amble with pleasant scenery, take the Boulder Creek Path, which winds from west of Boulder through downtown and past the university to the eastern part of the city. Access the multi-use trail from almost any cross street. Within the eastern city limits, the path winds past wetlands, gaggles of Canada geese, and prairie-dog colonies. People-watching is also great, with everyone from cyclists in full spandex, to runners, and parents pushing their babies in jogging strollers. Walk west along the path from Broadway to Boulder Canyon for views of kayakers negotiating the rapids and inner-tubers cooling off in the summer heat. Downtown delivers great mountain views. ⊠ *Boulder* ⊕ *www.bouldercolorado. gov/goboulder.*

Even a short walk up the grassy slope between **Chautauqua Park** and the base of the mountains brings out hikers and their dogs to take in some sun. On sunny summer mornings the dining hall at Chautauqua Park fills with hungry people ready for a hearty breakfast. Afternoon walkers relax on the park's gently sloping lawn with a picnic and gaze up at the foothills stretching along the Front Range. To reach the parking lot, take Baseline Road west from Broadway. The park is on the left just past the intersection with 9th Street.

Fodor'sChoice
★
Chautauqua Trailhead. Miles of trails snake up into the hills from the Chautauqua Trailhead. For a nice intro, hike up through the meadow on the Chautauqua Trail, turn left onto the Bluebell/Baird Trail, and then left again to return to the parking lot via the Mesa Trail, roughly a 1½-mile loop. The trail is a long slope at the beginning, but once you're in the trees you won't gain much more elevation. There are many other hiking options here as well. Study the map at the trailhead or stop in at the visitor center (next to the main parking lot), which is open daily 9–4 from November to April, and on weekends at other times of year. ⊠ *Trailhead at main parking lot, Grant St. and Baseline Rd.* ⊕ *www. bouldercolorado.gov/osmp/chautauqua-trailhead.*

Royal Arch Trail. The roughly 3¼-mile round-trip hike to Royal Arch Trail provides an up-close look at Boulder's own rock arch. It is definitely worth the steep hike (1,400 feet of elevation gain) for views of the foothills and cities of the Front Range. The trail spurs off the Chautauqua Trail loop and follows the base of the Flatirons before a steep climb. Go under the arch to the precipice for the best views.

If you turn around, the arch frames a couple of Flatirons for a good photo. ⊠ *Trailhead at main parking lot, 900 Baseline Rd.* ⊕ *www. bouldercolorado.gov/osmp.*

IN THE MOUNTAINS

Flagstaff Mountain. There are many hiking options here—you can start from the base of Flagstaff Road and climb to the top of the mountain on foot, or drive 3½ miles up to the summit road and access trails from the Sunrise Amphitheater. Park at Gregory Canyon to access the Flagstaff Trail from town. From the amphitheater, the **Boy Scout Trail** is an easy ¾-mile jaunt to May's Point, with views of high-alpine peaks. ⊠ *Boulder* ✣ *Trailhead: Drive west on Baseline Rd. to sharp curve to right that is Flagstaff Rd. (turn left for the Gregory Canyon trailhead). Or drive 3½ miles to the Summit Rd. The Boy Scout Trail starts from the parking area about ½ mile in* ⊕ *www.bouldercolorado.gov/osmp/ flagstaff-trailhead* ▣ *$5 parking fee for non-resident vehicles.*

Green Mountain. Beginning at the Gregory Canyon trailhead, you can string together a vareity of trails to climb this 8,144-foot peak, which rewards ambitious hikers with beautiful vistas of the Front Range and the Indian Peaks. Make a 5-mile loop with more than 2,000 feet of elevation gain by heading up the Gregory Canyon and Ranger trails, then return- ing via the E.M. Greenman and Saddle Rock trails. Allow three to four hours. Or drive 4½ miles up Flagstaff Road to the West Ridge Trail to shave the journey hike to less than 3 miles. ⊠ *Flagstaff Road and Baseline Rd.* ✣ *Trailhead (Gregory Canyon Trail): Drive west on Baseline Rd. to Flagstaff Rd., and turn left immediately after curve. Parking area is at end of short road where trail starts* ⊕ *www.bouldercolorado.gov/osmp/ gregory-canyon-trailhead* ▣ *$5 parking fee for non-resident vehicles.*

Sanitas Valley Loop. Known locally as Mount Sanitas, the Sanitas Valley Loop is a challenging 3-mile hike with stunning views of snowcapped peaks to the west and Boulder to the east. From the trailhead, head left to climb the western ridge, which starts with steep steps and maintains a steady incline up 1,300 feet to the 6,863-foot summit. Descend the East Ridge Trail, a series of rugged switchbacks that drop down to Sani- tas Valley, then take the Sanitas Valley Trail, or veer left onto Dakota Ridge Trail, which parallels the valley back to the parking lot. Be sure not to take the sharp left at the Dakota Ridge intersection, which leads straight downhill to town. Allow two hours. ⊠ *Trailhead: Mapleton Ave., 1 mile west of Broadway on the left* ⊕ *https://bouldercolorado. gov/osmp/mount-sanitas-trailhead.*

Settlers Park/Red Rocks. Carry a picnic and enjoy the mountain and city views from this mountain park, which includes a series of intercon- nected trails that skirt around a scenic rock outcropping. Head up from Settlers Park at the west end of Pearl and find your way to a lovely bench overlook east of the rocks, about ¼ mile. If you have time, continue down the other side to Sunshine Canyon and come back the same way or pick a different route. ⊠ *Trailhead: Settlers Park, where Pearl and Canyon meet at the western edge of town* ⊕ *www.bouldercolorado.gov/ osmp/basic-trail-information.*

INNER-TUBING

In July and August, when daytime temperatures can reach the 90s, Boulderites take to tubing in **Boulder Creek**—especially near Eben G. Fine Park, at the mouth of Boulder Canyon near the junction of Arapahoe Avenue and Canyon Boulevard on the western end of town.

Conoco. Need a tube to float the creek? The Conoco gas station, which is about a block away from Boulder Creek, sells inner tubes ($15 plus tax). The station is open from 7 am until 9 pm Monday through Saturday, and 8 am to 8 pm Sunday. ⊠ *1201 Arapahoe Ave., at Broadway* ☎ *303/442–6293.*

KAYAKING AND CANOEING

Serious kayakers run the slaloms in Clear Creek, Lefthand Canyon, and the South Platte, but Boulder Creek—from within Boulder Canyon midway into the city—is one of the locals' favorites. Water in the creek can create Class II–III rapids when summer conditions are right.

Boulder Reservoir. If calm waters are what you want, you can rent a canoe, kayak, or stand-up paddleboard at the Boulder Reservoir, a 700-acre recreation area with photo-worthy Flatirons views. ⊠ *5565 N. 51st St. ✛ 6 miles northeast of downtown. Drive northeast on Hwy. 119 and turn left at Jay Rd. Turn right immediately onto 51st St. and follow it to a sign that marks entrance station* ☎ *303/441–3461* ⊕ *www. bouldercolorado.gov/parks-rec/boulder-reservoir* ⊠ *$6.25 entrance fee, not including boat rentals* ☉ *Closed Labor Day–Memorial Day.*

OUTFITTER

Boulder Outdoor Center. This outfit offers a full range of guided outdoor adventures, including rafting trips, canoeing and kayaking instruction, hiking, stand-up paddleboarding, snowmobiling, snowcat skiing, and more—plus gear rentals, too. ⊠ *2525 Arapahoe Ave., Suite E4–228* ☎ *303/444–8420* ⊕ *www.boc123.com.*

RACES

Fodor's Choice ★ **BolderBOULDER.** Memorial Day brings the annual 10-km (6.2-mile) BolderBOULDER, when more than 50,000 runners, including top international competitors, run in the country's third-largest foot race. Nearly 100,000 spectators line the route and fill CU's Folsom Stadium to cheer on participants. Along the racecourse are rock bands, jazz musicians, African drumming groups, Elvis impersonators, belly dancers, and classical quartets to spur on runners. The race ends in Folsom Stadium with a ceremony that includes a flyover by U.S. Air Force fighter jets and skydivers who parachute onto the stadium field. ⊠ *Boulder* ☎ *303/444–7223* ⊕ *www.bolderboulder.com* ⊠ *From $45.*

SNOWSHOEING

Brainard Lake Recreation Area. In Roosevelt National Forest, Brainard Lake Recreation Area has well-marked trails and gorgeous views of the snow-covered Indian Peaks and Continental Divide. ⊠ *Brainard Lake Rd., 4 miles west of Hwy. 72 on Brainard Lake Rd. (Rte. 102) at Ward, Ward ✛ Drive west on Hwy. 119 to Nederland and turn north at Hwy. 72* ☎ *303/541–2500* ⊕ *www.fs.usda.gov/goto/arp/brainard.*

WHERE TO EAT

Use the coordinates (✣ B2) at the end of each listing to locate a site on the corresponding map.

$$$ LATIN AMERICAN 🍴 **Aji.** Enjoy a South American cocktail like a *caipirinha, mojito*, or pisco sour before dinner in this busy restaurant, which has one of Boulder's most popular happy hours. Large windows let in plenty of light, seating is spacious in the festive dining room, and the service is great. Try *ceviche* (shrimp or fish marinated in lime juice) or *empanadas* (savory pastries) to start. For dinner, dig into Brazilian seafood stew, veggie enchiladas, or *carne asada*, all artfully prepared and plated. A slice of *tres leches* cake and a cup of French-press coffee round out a meal here. [$] *Average main: $21* ✉ *1601 Pearl St.* ☎ *303/442–3464* 🌐 *www.ajirestaurant.com* ✣ *G5.*

$$$ AMERICAN Fodor's Choice ★ 🍴 **Blackbelly.** Those seeking a sophisticated yet casual culinary experience away from the hustle of downtown will delight in Blackbelly, a restaurant that serves farm-to-table freshness to a packed house every night. Chef Hosea Rosenberg, who won season five of Bravo TV's *Top Chef*, crafts a frequently updated menu using ingredients from the restaurant's farm as well as other local sources. Pork takes center stage, including house-made sausages and *salumi*, and a signature dish of prawns and pork belly served with cheddar grits. Vegetarian mouths can opt for the seasonal pasta, which might feature local mushrooms, fiddleheads, or spinach. Blackbelly's market, attached to the restaurant, serves grab-and-go breakfast and lunch. [$] *Average main: $20* ✉ *1606 Conestoga St. No. 3* ☎ *303/247–1000* 🌐 *www.blackbelly.com* ✍ *Reservations essential* ✣ *H3.*

$$$$ BISTRO 🍴 **Black Cat Farm to Table Bistro.** This intimate eatery delivers an authentic farm-to-table experience, with a menu that changes daily, drawing from whatever the restaurant is harvesting from its four farms. The menu might include heirloom beet salad with candied pecans and goat cheese mousse, Colorado beef with warm farro salad, or house-raised Tunis lamb with lentils and smoked apricots. Diners relax in leather couches at wall-side tables, with excellent views of the kitchen and its cookbook-lined shelves. If you indulge in the tasting menu ($68)—which includes six courses chosen by the chef—then also splurge for the wine pairings ($48). [$] *Average main: $32* ✉ *1964 13th St.* ☎ *303/444–5500* 🌐 *www.blackcatboulder.com* ⏲ *No lunch* ✍ *Reservations essential* ✣ *G6.*

$$ INTERNATIONAL Fodor's Choice ★ 🍴 **Boulder Dushanbe Teahouse.** Feast your eyes on the intricately carved walls, pillars, and ceiling at this unique teahouse, which was a gift from Boulder's sister city Dushanbe, Tajikistan, and opened in 1998. Tajik artisans decorated the building in a traditional style, with ceramic Islamic art and a riot of colorful wood. The menu presents a culinary cross section of the world, with dishes such as North African harissa chicken, spicy Indonesian peanut noodles, and Tajik shish kabob. Relax during high tea at 3 pm (reservations required) to sip one of nearly 100 varieties of tea accompanied by a selection of sandwiches and sweets. Outside, rose bushes surround a charming patio, where some tables overlook an offshoot of Boulder Creek. [$] *Average main: $17* ✉ *1770 13th St.* ☎ *303/442–4993* 🌐 *www.boulderteahouse.com* ✣ *G6.*

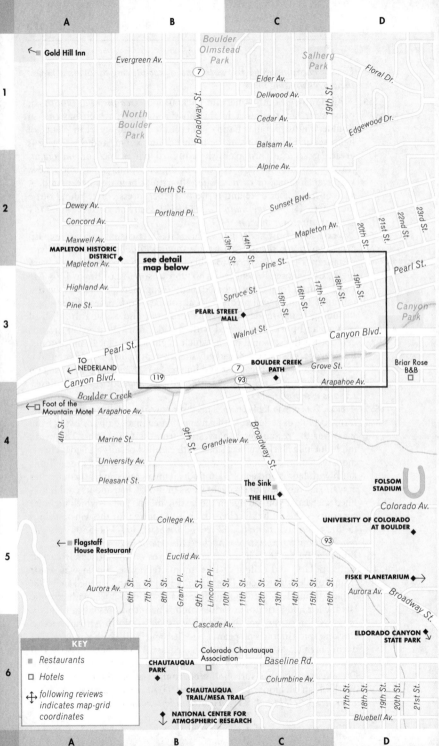

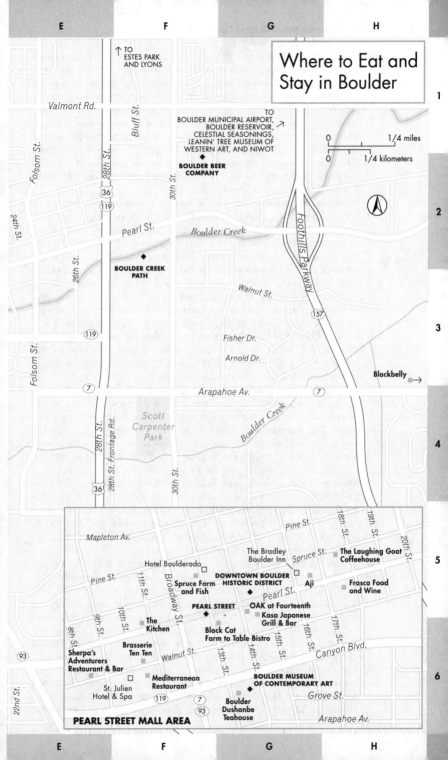

Where to Eat and Stay in Boulder

E   F   G   H

1

↑ TO
ESTES PARK
AND LYONS

Valmont Rd.

Bluff St.

TO
BOULDER MUNICIPAL AIRPORT,
BOULDER RESERVOIR,
CELESTIAL SEASONINGS,
LEANIN' TREE MUSEUM OF
WESTERN ART, AND NIWOT →

♦ BOULDER BEER
COMPANY

0   1/4 miles
0   1/4 kilometers

2

Folsom St.

24th St.

28th St.

30th St.

36
119

Pearl St.

Boulder Creek

Foothills Parkway

26th St.

♦ BOULDER CREEK
PATH

Walnut St.

157

3

119

Fisher Dr.

Arnold Dr.

Folsom St.

7

Arapahoe Av.

7

Blackbelly →

4

28th St.

28th St. Frontage Rd.

30th St.

Scott
Carpenter
Park

Boulder Creek

36

PEARL STREET MALL AREA

5

Mapleton Av.

Pine St.

18th St.

19th St.

Hotel Boulderado

The Bradley
Boulder Inn

Spruce St.

The Laughing Goat
Coffeehouse

20th St.

Pine St.

11th St.

Broadway St.

Spruce Farm
and Fish

♦ DOWNTOWN BOULDER
HISTORIC DISTRICT

Aji

Frasca Food
and Wine

Pearl St.

PEARL STREET
♦

OAK at Fourteenth

Kasa Japanese
Grill & Bar

16th St.

17th St.

9th St.

10th St.

The
Kitchen

Black Cat
Farm to Table Bistro

13th St.

14th St.

15th St.

Canyon Blvd.

6

8th St.

Sherpa's
Adventurers
Restaurant & Bar

Brasserie
Ten Ten

St. Julien
Hotel & Spa

Walnut St.

Mediterranean
Restaurant

119   7
93

♦ BOULDER MUSEUM
OF CONTEMPORARY ART

Grove St.

93rd St.

Boulder
Dushanbe
Teahouse

Arapahoe Av.

E   F   G   H

$$$ FRENCH Fodor's Choice ★ 🍴 **Brasserie Ten Ten.** A festive atmosphere and excellent food attract locals to this vibrant bistro, which serves French-style cuisine. Start with oysters, jambon, and Gruyère crepes, a charcuterie and cheese plate, or the simple salad—a long-standing favorite with butter lettuce, fried capers, pine nuts, and miso vinagrette. Don't miss the *brique poulet*, a mouthwatering chicken served with delectable French fries and *beurre blanc*. This restaurant can get crowded, but you can water down the wait at the marble bar, choosing from nearly 30 beers, 10 specialty cocktails, 6 varieties of single-malt scotch, and an extensive selection of wines by the glass. [$] *Average main: $20* ✉ *1011 Walnut St.* ☎ *303/998–1010* 🌐 *www.brasserietenten.com* ⊕ *F6.*

$$$$ AMERICAN 🍴 **Flagstaff House Restaurant.** This is Boulder's most opulent restaurant, with valet parking, formal service, five-star food, and stunning views. Executive chef Mark Monette has fresh fish flown in daily, grows some of his own herbs, and is noted for his exquisite combinations of ingredients and fanciful presentations. The menu changes daily—you might get duck three ways with couscous and mustard greens; Colorado lamb rack, loin, and shank with truffle-infused polenta; or ruby-red trout and diver-caught scallops with English pea purée. Stop in for a less formal bite on the cocktail deck in the summer. The wine list is remarkably comprehensive. Casual attire is not acceptable. [$] *Average main: $52* ✉ *1138 Flagstaff Rd.* ⊕ *Drive west on Baseline Rd. and turn right onto Flagstaff Rd. Follow it up the hill for about ¾ mile, then look for the restaurant on your right.* ☎ *303/442–4640* 🌐 *www.flagstaffhouse.com* ⏲ *No lunch* ✍ *Reservations essential* ⊕ *A5.*

$$$$ ITALIAN Fodor's Choice ★ 🍴 **Frasca Food and Wine.** This restaurant, one of Boulder's best, serves meticulously prepared food in the style of the Friuli-Venezia region of northeastern Italy, with expert wine pairings, drawing from a vast cellar. The bustling dining room has a backlit wine wall, while the waitstaff provides attentive but not intrusive service. Start with *salumi*, a platter of cured meats. From there, a four-course prix-fixe menu is de rigueur—you might feast on an antipasto like fresh fish crudo, a house-made pasta with pork belly or seasonal vegetables, or a main of lamb with eggplant or tilefish with porcini mushrooms. Ask the sommelier to suggest the perfect wine for each course. The four-course tasting menu is $78 per person. [$] *Average main: $78* ✉ *1738 Pearl St.* ☎ *303/442–6966* 🌐 *www.frascafoodandwine.com* ⏲ *Closed Sun. No lunch* ✍ *Reservations essential* ⊕ *H5.*

$$$$ AMERICAN 🍴 **Gold Hill Inn.** About 10 miles from downtown Boulder on the dirt road going through the historic town of Gold Hill, this humble cabin hardly looks like a bastion of haute cuisine, but its six-course, $36 prix-fixe dinner is something to rave about. Entrées change daily but stick to a mountain gourmet theme, and may include roast duck with raspberry sauce or leg of lamb marinated in buttermilk, juniper berries, and cloves. Portions are generous—try to save room for dessert. Or opt for a lighter meal with your choice of three courses for $28. The inn also hosts "murder mystery" nights, featuring professional actors, in the adjacent Bluebird Lodge. [$] *Average main: $36* ✉ *401 Main St., Gold Hill* ⊕ *Take Mapleton Ave. west from Broadway up Sunshine Canyon Dr. to Gold Hill, then Main St.* ☎ *303/443–6461*

CLOSE UP

Quick Bites in Boulder

Not every meal requires a lengthy restaurant visit. Boulder has plenty of healthy, inexpensive, and prepared-to-order food, as well.

Abo's Pizza. A Boulder institution that's been serving exquisite pizza for nearly 40 years, Abo's Pizza cooks up thin and crispy pies that won't disappoint. ✉ *2761 Iris Ave.* ☎ *303/443–1921* 🌐 *www.abospizza.com.*

Breadworks Bakery and Cafe. For a delicious homemade meal, head to Breadworks Bakery and Cafe, a north Boulder eatery with quick counter service and plenty of seating. Breakfast options include tasty pastries, brioche, steel-cut oatmeal, or scrambled eggs. For lunch, choose from hot paninis, soups, casseroles, pizza, or salads. ✉ *2644 Broadway* ☎ *303/444–5667* 🌐 *www.breadworks.net* 🕒 *No dinner* ✍ *Reservations not accepted.*

Falafel King. Bite into excellent pita pockets of hot and crispy falafel, spicy gyros, or marinated grilled chicken breast, or combine it all in a bowl. Add on tabouli, hummus, or dolmas (stuffed grape leaves) to round out lunch. ✉ *1314 Pearl St.* ☎ *303/449-9321* 🌐 *www.falafelkingboulder.com* ✍ *Reservations not accepted.*

Illegal Pete's. Feast on hefty burritos and other Mexican fare made to order with fresh ingredients and a choice of five salsas. There's also a location on The Hill at 1124 13th Street. ✉ *1447 Pearl St.* ☎ *303/440–3955* 🌐 *www.illegalpetes.com.*

Salvaggio's Deli. If you're hankering for a delicious Philly cheese steak, sub, or other classic sandwich, Salvaggio's Deli is a local favorite, with three locations—26th and Pearl, Pearl Street Mall at 14th Street, and the Hill at Broadway and University. Hours vary by location. ✉ *2609 Pearl St.* ☎ *303/938–1981* 🌐 *www.salvaggiosdeli.net.*

🌐 *www.goldhillinn.com* 🕒 *No lunch. Closed Tues. and Jan.–Apr.; closed Mon. Sept.–Mar.; closed weekdays Nov. and Dec.* ✍ *Reservations essential* ✥ *A1.*

$$ JAPANESE 🍴 **Kasa Japanese Grill & Bar.** Head to this spot for traditional Japanese specialties as well as fusion-style sushi and sashimi, with fresh fish flown in from around the world. The interior is an elegant space designed by architect Edward Suzuki, with black-granite tables, wooden flooring, imported Japanese tiles, and inverted white umbrellas hanging from (or rather, composing) the ceiling (*kasa* means "umbrella" in Japanese). For a splurge, call ahead and ask for the *omakase*—a four-course chef's choice menu (starting at $80). [$] *Average main: $17* ✉ *1468 Pearl St.* ☎ *303/938–8888* 🌐 *www.kasasushiboulder.com* 🕒 *Closed Mon.* ✥ *G5.*

$$$ AMERICAN Fodor's Choice ★ 🍴 **The Kitchen.** This bistro offers elegant, relaxed meals with great service, emphasizing local food in a community atmosphere. The menu changes regularly, but you can always count on tasty combinations—perhaps a pork chop with polenta and Colorado cherries, or grilled aspargus with lemon zest and capers. The Kitchen's version of happy hour is Community Hour (weekdays from 3 to 5). Monday is Community

Night, with the option to reserve a spot at the community table for a four-course family-style dinner. $ *Average main: $24* ✉ *1039 Pearl St.* ☎ *303/544–5973* ⊕ *www.thekitchen.com* ✛ *F6.*

$ ✕ **The Laughing Goat Coffeehouse.** This bohemian-style café two blocks
CAFÉ west of the pedestrian mall serves bagels, muffins, pastries, and oatmeal for breakfast, and panini sandwiches and soups for lunch. The lattes, made with cow, goat, soy, hemp, or almond milk, are excellent. This is where Boulder's creative community and young tech start-up entrepreneurs rub shoulders, sometimes literally, thanks to the charmingly tight seating. You can hear live entertainment nightly, with poetry by locals on Monday. Beer and wine happy-hour deals are from 4 to 8 pm. $ *Average main: $5* ✉ *1709 Pearl St.* ⊕ *www.thelaughinggoat.com* ✛ *H5.*

$$ ✕ **Mediterranean Restaurant.** After work, when most of Boulder seems to
MEDITERRANEAN show up for happy hour at "the Med," this place becomes a real scene. If the crowd gets to be too much, try a table on the patio. The decor is Portofino meets Santa Fe, with abstract art, terra-cotta floors, and brightly colored tile. The open kitchen turns out diverse Mediterranean flavors of Italy, Spain, France, Greece, Morocco, and Lebanon, with a giant list of tapas, like hummus, bacon-wrapped dates, lamb skewers, and crisp calamari. Mains include dishes like paella, tomato-braised pork-ricotta meatballs, and *piccata di pollo*—all complemented by an extensive, well-priced wine list. $ *Average main: $18* ✉ *1002 Walnut St.* ☎ *303/444–5335* ⊕ *www.themedboulder.com* ✛ *F6.*

$$$$ ✕ **OAK at fourteenth.** Foodies, first dates, and business diners alike flock to
AMERICAN this bustling restaurant on Pearl Street Mall for its seasonal cuisine that centers around an oak-fired oven, locally sourced meats and vegetables, and house-made pastas. The menu includes a wide selection of small and large plates, with staples like shaved apple and kale salad, shrimp and grits, and tomato-braised meatballs, as well as rotating dishes such as oak-braised beef short ribs and oak-grilled duck breast. Sit at the chef's counter for a view of the kitchen. $ *Average main: $27* ✉ *1400 Pearl Street* ☎ *303/444–3622* ⊕ *www.oakatfourteenth.com* ✛ *G5.*

$$ ✕ **Sherpa's Adventurers Restaurant & Bar.** A favorite of Boulder's many
NEPALESE health-conscious athletes and world travelers, this restaurant is owned and run by Sherpas, and offers a voluminous menu with Himalayan favorites, like curry and tandoori chicken. It oozes mountain culture, with a cozy lounge that is both a bar and travel library, and a chef who has summited Everest 10 times. Owner Pemba Sherpa also offers guiding services in Nepal. The restaurant's service is some of the friendliest in town, but the pacing—much like a trek up Everest—can be woefully slow. As soon as you sit down, order the *saag* dip ($6), a creamy garlic, cumin, ginger, and spinach dish served with warm naan bread. Don't be afraid to try the yak, it's delicious. $ *Average main: $13* ✉ *825 Walnut St.* ☎ *303/440–7151* ⊕ *www.sherpasrestaurant.com* ▭ *No credit cards* ✛ *E6.*

$ ✕ **The Sink.** For decades, students have flocked to this spot on the Hill,
AMERICAN where Robert Redford worked as a janitor in the 1950s for a stint while studying at CU. Tables are dispersed in a labyrinth of rooms, where colorful caricatures and murals decorate the walls. The menu includes a broad selection of pub food. Try the famous Sinkburger, which is smothered in barbecue sauce, or the POTUS pizza, named after President

Obama, who ate here during a surprise visit in 2012. $ *Average main: $12* ✉ *1165 13th St.* ☎ *303/444–7465* ⊕ *www.thesink.com* ✛ *C4.*

$$$ ✕ **Spruce Farm & Fish.** Coffered ceilings, stained-glass windows, and
SEAFOOD mosaic tile floors create a classic setting for this fish-focused restaurant, which is located in the Hotel Boulderado. Settle in for happy hour at the spruce-wood bar to savor farm-fresh oysters accompanied by hand-crafted cocktails, or stay for dinner in the stylish dining room, which includes comfortable booths, tables, and a fully enclosed porch. The menu evolves seasonally, with an emphasis on seafood and local foods, which transform into dishes like Maine lobster pasta with artichokes and capers, or filet mignon with gnocchi and mushrooms. Sweet tooths will delight in the postdinner offerings, such as flourless chocolate cake and blueberry apple buckle. $ *Average main: $24* ✉ *2115 13th St.* ☎ *303/442–4880* ⊕ *www.spruceboulderado.com* ✛ *F5.*

WHERE TO STAY

Use the coordinates (✛ B2) at the end of each listing to locate a site on the corresponding map.

$$$$ 🏨 **The Bradley Boulder Inn.** Elegant and contemporary, this downtown
B&B/INN inn has a spacious great room with warm tones and an inviting stone fireplace, and local artwork is on display throughout. **Pros:** quiet inn one block from Pearl Street shopping and dining; daily wine-and-cheese hour; privileges at nearby gym. **Cons:** books early; no children under 14. $ *Rooms from: $270* ✉ *2040 16th St.* ☎ *303/545–5200,* ⊕ *www. thebradleyboulder.com* ☾ *Closed the first 2 wks of Jan.* ⌖ *12 rooms* ⍩ *Breakfast* ✛ *G5.*

$$ 🏨 **Briar Rose B&B.** This lovely bed-and-breakfast in a historic house pro-
B&B/INN vides an intimate, homey experience under the mindful and compassion-ate care of its innkeeper Gary Hardin, a Zen monk. **Pros:** the only B&B in central Boulder; close to downtown shopping and dining; delicious (and healthy) breakfast. **Cons:** on a busy and noisy street; small inn that books early. $ *Rooms from: $154* ✉ *2151 Arapahoe Ave.* ☎ *303/442–3007* ⊕ *www.briarrosebb.com* ⌖ *10 rooms* ⍩ *Breakfast* ✛ *D3.*

$$$ 🏨 **Colorado Chautauqua Association.** Surrounded by nature, this cluster of
RENTAL historic cottages plus two lodge buildings is at the base of the Flatirons
Fodor'sChoice in Chautauqua Park, one of the loveliest parts around Boulder. **Pros:**
★ unique lodging; arts, dining, and recreation on property; well-kept cab-ins; amazing views of town and mountains. **Cons:** no maid service; park is crowded. $ *Rooms from: $185* ✉ *900 Baseline Rd.* ☎ *303/952–1611* ⊕ *www.chautauqua.com* ⌖ *15 rooms, 58 cottages, 8-bedroom Mission House* ⍩ *No meals* ✛ *B6.*

$ 🏨 **Foot of the Mountain Motel.** This cute, no-frills mom-and-pop place is
HOTEL the best value around, especially given its location adjacent to the Boul-der Creek Path near the mouth of Boulder Canyon. **Pros:** excellent value for the area; quiet neighborhood; close to recreation. **Cons:** no-frills accommodations; no on-site restaurant; no air conditioning. $ *Rooms from: $99* ✉ *200 W. Arapahoe Ave.* ☎ *303/442–5688, 866/773–5489* ⊕ *www.footofthemountainmotel.com* ⌖ *18 rooms, 2 suites* ⍩ *Break-fast* ✛ *A4.*

$$$$ HOTEL Fodor's Choice ★ 🏨 **Hotel Boulderado.** This 1909 beauty beckons with a soaring stained-glass ceiling and large helpings of Victorian charm in its gracious lobby. **Pros:** well-maintained historic building; downtown location; excellent restaurants. **Cons:** on busy and noisy streets; large, busy hotel. [$] *Rooms from: $269* ✉ *2115 13th St.* ☎ *303/442–4344, 800/433–4344* 🌐 *www.boulderado.com* 🛏 *139 rooms, 21 suites* 🍴 *No meals* ✥ *F5.*

$$$$ HOTEL Fodor's Choice ★ 🏨 **St Julien Hotel & Spa.** Unwind in the luxury of this classy yet casual hotel and its stellar spa. **Pros:** convenient downtown location; close to outdoor activities and mountains; dreamy spa. **Cons:** large hotel; quite busy; some rooms are small. [$] *Rooms from: $349* ✉ *900 Walnut St.* ☎ *720/406–9696, 877/303–0900* 🌐 *www.stjulien.com* 🛏 *189 rooms, 12 suites* 🍴 *No meals* ✥ *F6.*

NIGHTLIFE AND PERFORMING ARTS

PERFORMING ARTS

ARTS FESTIVALS

Colorado Music Festival. From July to early August, the Colorado Music Festival brings classical music, chamber music, and a mashup series to the historic Chautauqua Auditorium. Since 1976, this long-running festival has hosted a variety of musical talent, representing many genres. Evening meals are available in the dining hall, or you can picnic on the lawn to take in mountain views before the show. ✉ *Chautauqua Park, 900 Baseline Rd.* ☎ *303/664–0599* 🌐 *www.comusic.org* 🎟 *From $5.*

Fodor's Choice ★ **Colorado Shakespeare Festival.** This annual festival runs from early June to mid-August and presents the Bard's comedies and tragedies in two venues on the University of Colorado campus—the stunning Mary Rippon Outdoor Theater, and the indoor University Theater. ✉ *University of Colorado Campus* ☎ *303/492–8008 box office, 303/492-1527 administrative offices* 🌐 *www.coloradoshakes.org* 🎟 *From $20* 🕐 *Closed mid-Aug.–May.*

THEATER, MUSIC, AND DANCE

Boulder Philharmonic Orchestra. Boulder's professional orchestra presents its own concert season, frequently including some of the biggest names in classical music. The "Boulder Phil" also collaborates with the Boulder Ballet Ensemble to present the *Nutcracker* each holiday season. ✉ *University of Colorado, Macky Auditorium, 17th St. and University Ave.* ☎ *303/449–1343* 🌐 *www.boulderphil.org* 🎟 *From $13* 🕐 *Closed May–Aug.*

Boulder's Dinner Theatre. Dine here and then see a popular musical, with actors who double as your waitstaff. The theater stages four productions a year, plus a few cabaret and children's shows. ✉ *5501 Arapahoe Ave.* ☎ *303/449–6000* 🌐 *www.bdtstage.com* 🎟 *From $38, including dinner.*

Fodor's Choice ★ **Boulder Theater.** The historic 1930s art deco–style Boulder Theater is a gem of a venue. It hosts musical performances in a wide variety of genres, from jazz to bluegrass to disco to rock. The theater also presents special events like film festivals. ✉ *2032 14th St.* ☎ *303/786–7030* 🌐 *www.bouldertheater.com.*

Chautauqua Auditorium. Concerts take place throughout the summer at this historic auditorium. Performers have included Josh Ritter, Branford Marsalis, Lucinda Williams, Indigo Girls, and Toots and the Maytals, among others. ⊠ *900 Baseline Rd.* ☎ *303/442–3282* ⊕ *www. chautauqua.com.*

College of Music. The University of Colorado's superb College of Music presents concerts year-round, including chamber music by the internationally renowned Takács String Quartet during the academic year. ⊠ *302 UCB* ☎ *303/492–8008* ⊕ *www.cupresents.org.*

Dairy Center for the Arts. Located in an old dairy building, this center is a hub for the arts community, housing gallery shows and providing a venue for films as well as locally produced plays, music, and dance performances. ⊠ *2590 Walnut St.* ✛ *Enter from 26th St.* ☎ *303/440–7826* ⊕ *www.thedairy.org.*

Department of Theater and Dance. The University of Colorado–Boulder's theater and dance department stages excellent student productions during the academic year. ⊠ *University of Colorado Theater Building* ☎ *303/492–7355 administrative offices, 303/492-8008 box office* ⊕ *www.colorado.edu/theatredance.*

NIGHTLIFE

BARS AND LOUNGES

Fodor's Choice ★ **The Bitter Bar.** With an intimate, couch-lined space modeled after old-time speakeasies (complete wih a secret back entrance), this could very well be Boulder's greatest bar. The staff is passionate about handcrafted cocktails, and they're not shy with advice—including the perfect ice shape to suit your booze. Eat before you go since food is limited to a few snacks, and a taco truck in the parking lot on weekends. ⊠ *835 Walnut St.* ☎ *303/442–3050* ⊕ *www.thebitterbar.com.*

Centro Latin Kitchen & Refreshment Palace. Try happy hour with a Latin twist at this happening spot, which has one of Boulder's most vibrant patios—not to mention perhaps the best margarita in town. The long, wavy bar wraps around two sides, with large garage doors that open to the outside. ⊠ *950 Pearl St.* ☎ *303/442–7771* ⊕ *www. centrolatinkitchen.com.*

Corner Bar. Business lunches and after-work gatherings take place at the Corner Bar in the Hotel Boulderado, a contemporary American pub with both indoor and outdoor seating. The happy hour, from 3 to 6, brings $3 beers and $6 martinis along with 40% off wines and appetizers. ⊠ *2115 13th St.* ☎ *303/442–4560* ⊕ *www.cornerbarboulderado.com.*

Pearl Street Pub & Cellar. This laid-back pub has bucked the gentrification trend of downtown. Sidle up to the long wooden bar upstairs, or head to the basement for a game of pool, foosball, or darts. ⊠ *1108 Pearl St.* ☎ *303/939–9900.*

Rio Grande Mexican Restaurant. This festive place has gained a reputation for its strong margaritas—so potent that there's a three-per-person limit. If you need some grub to soak up the booze, dig into Mexican fare in the cavernous dining room or on the rooftop patio. ⊠ *1101 Walnut St.* ☎ *303/444–3690* ⊕ *www.riograndemexican.com.*

West End Tavern. Beer and bourbon are the name of the game at this upscale pub, which also serves tasty barbecue and burgers. Try to nab a spot on the rooftop deck. ⊠ *926 Pearl St.* ☎ *303/444–3535* ⊕ *www. thewestendtavern.com.*

BREWPUBS AND BREWERIES

FATE Brewing Company. Boulder's first brew-bistro opened in 2013 and became an instant favorite, with 30 beers on tap and an artisan approach to food, specializing in fresh smoked meats from the Yoder Smoker out back. Pints are $3.50 during happy hour (weekdays from 3 to 5:30). For cask tappings, stop by Wednesday at 3. Or come for a leisurely Sunday brunch (ask for a table on the back patio) and stay for the brewery tour at 4. ⊠ *1600 38th St.* ☎ *303/449–3283* ⊕ *www. fatebrewingcompany.com.*

Mountain Sun Pub & Brewery. This casual brewery crafts nearly 100 beers throughout the year, and always has 20 on tap. A favorite is the FYIPA, a dry-hopped American IPA with a citrusy flavor. Tours are available upon request. Stay for a cheeseburger and hand-cut fries, or live music on Sunday night starting at 10. ⊠ *1535 Pearl St.* ☎ *303/546–0886* ⊕ *www.mountainsunpub.com.*

Sanitas Brewing Co. This brewery crafts delicious beers with distinctive personality. Twelve taps flow with three regular brews, as well as a rotating cast of seasonal and short-run offerings. Cheap eats are available from the McDevitt Taco Supply truck that parks alongside the spacious patio. ⊠ *3550 Frontier Ave., Unit A* ✛ *SE corner of the building* ☎ *303/442–4130* ⊕ *www.sanitasbrewing.com.*

Walnut Brewery. Large windows offer a peek into brewing operations while you sample beer and a full menu at Boulder's original brewpub, which opened in 1990. Walnut Brewery always has a selection of its own creations on draught. Try the Buffalo Gold ale or the malty St. James Irish Red Ale. A new seasonal is tapped each month on the second Thursday, with a free pint of it for anyone who shows up between 6 and 6:30. The excellent beer goes well with the upscale pub fare, which includes fish tacos, smoked salmon fish-and-chips, and buffalo fajitas. ⊠ *1123 Walnut St.* ☎ *303/447–1345* ⊕ *www. walnutbrewery.com.*

West Flanders Brewing Company. Hand-crafting is the focus at this downtown brewery, which makes its own beer, bread, sauerkraut, pickles, and more. The pub-style gourmet fare is also crafted with care. Locals pack the house on Monday night for live bluegrass jams starting at 8. ⊠ *1125 Pearl St.* ☎ *303/447–2739* ⊕ *www.wfbrews.com.*

MUSIC AND DANCE CLUBS

Fox Theatre. The Fox—a former movie palace—is now the premier live music venue in Boulder. It holds just over 600 people and hosts a wide variety of musical talent, including fledgling groups that go on to become world-famous, as well as acts that are already legends. ⊠ *1135 13th St.* ☎ *303/447–0095* ⊕ *www.foxtheatre.com.*

SHOPPING

ANTIQUES

The Amazing Garage Sale. You never know what you might discover here as you browse the glorious antique and midcentury furniture, home decor, jewelry, and other treasures. Inventory moves fast, so get it while you can. ✉ *4919 N. Broadway* ☎ *303/447–0417* ⊕ *www. theamazinggaragesale.com* ☾ *Mon.–Sat. 10–6, Sun. 11–5.*

BOOKSTORES

Boulder has one of the largest concentrations of used-book sellers in the United States. Most shops are on Pearl Street between 8th and 20th streets.

Fodor'sChoice
★
Boulder Bookstore. Boulder's largest independent bookstore stocks thousands of new and used books, including a great selection of photography, history, and art books about Colorado. The bookstore hosts hundreds of community events each year. ✉ *1107 Pearl St.* ☎ *303/447–2074* ⊕ *www.boulderbookstore.net* ☾ *Mon.–Sat. 10–10, Sun. 10–8.*

Trident Booksellers and Cafe. Channel your inner intellectual here while browsing the eclectic collection of new and used books, which focuses on art, religion, poetry, culture, and literature. At the attached tea and coffee shop, you can read while you sip. ✉ *940 Pearl St.* ☎ *303/443–3133* ⊕ *www.tridentcafe.com.*

CHILDREN'S ITEMS

FAMILY **Grandrabbit's Toy Shoppe.** A Boulder institution since 1977, Grandrabbit's is every kid's dream come true, with shelves stocked from floor to ceiling. The independently owned speciality toy store has grown to three Colorado locations and is known as the place to go to find toys that contribute to learning and development. It's not uncommon to find adults wandering the aisles, sans children, their eyes soft with nostalgia. ✉ *The Village, 2525 Arapahoe Ave.* ☎ *303/443–0780* ⊕ *www.grtoys.com.*

FAMILY **Into the Wind.** This shop carries traditional and out-of-the-ordinary kites, plus an imaginative selection of unique toys. ✉ *1408 Pearl St.* ☎ *303/449–5356* ⊕ *www.intothewind.com.*

CLOTHING BOUTIQUES

Alpaca Connection. This shop sells gorgeous alpaca garments—including sweaters, hats, socks, and gloves—as well as cotton and linen dresses, mostly from Peru. ✉ *1326 Pearl St.* ☎ *303/447–2047* ⊕ *www. thealpacaconnection.com* ☾ *Daily 11–6.*

Fresh Produce. This Boulder-based company makes brightly colored and whimsically designed clothing for women and children. ✉ *1218 Pearl St.* ☎ *303/442–7507* ⊕ *freshproduceclothes.com* ☾ *Mon.–Sat. 10–7, Sun. 11–5.*

Jacque Michelle. Shop here for fashionably casual and unique women's clothing and accessories, as well as clever, appealing gifts. ✉ *2670 Broadway* ☎ *303/786–7628* ⊕ *www.jacquemichelle.com.*

7

CRAFTS AND ART GALLERIES

Art Source International. This long-running business is Colorado's largest antique print and map dealer. If you're looking for rare maps or historic photos of Colorado, this is the place to go. Framing is also available. ⊠ *1237 Pearl St.* ☏ *303/444–4080* ⊕ *www.rare-maps.com.*

Boulder Arts & Crafts Gallery. Owned and operated by 28 artists, the gallery features works by more than 100 Colorado artists. It's a popular place to find unique gifts and decorative items, such as photographs, pottery, hand-painted silk scarves, leather handbags, furniture, and glass objets d'art. ⊠ *1421 Pearl St.* ☏ *303/443–3683* ⊕ *www. boulderartsandcrafts.com.*

SmithKlein Gallery. At this fine art gallery on the Pearl Street Mall, you can browse an eclectic mix of contemporary and traditional art, including glass and bronze sculpture, jewelry, and paintings. ⊠ *1116 Pearl St.* ☏ *303/444–7200* ⊕ *www.smithklein.com.*

FARMERS' MARKET

Fodor's Choice ★ **Boulder County Farmers Market.** This bustling farmers' market brings a hive of activity to 13th Street between Arapahoe Avenue and Canyon Boulevard on Wednesday and Saturday, spring through fall. Bring some cash and purchase produce, baked goods, flowers, wines, cheeses, meats, and more straight from the local producers (cherries and peaches are prime in late summer). If drooling over all of these goodies makes you hungry, visit the cluster of food vendors for an immediate meal. The market is open from 4 to 8 pm Wednesday from early May to early October, and Saturday from 8 am until 2 pm early April to mid-November. ⊠ *13th St. between Canyon Blvd. and Arapahoe Ave.* ☏ *303/910–2236* ⊕ *bcfm.org.*

GIFT STORES

Bliss. This locally owned and operated gift shop is a treasure trove of trendy collectibles and unique home accents from around the globe. ⊠ *1643 Pearl St.* ☏ *303/443–0355* ⊕ *www.blissboulder.com.*

Two Hands Paperie. Elegant European stationery, handmade paper, and handcrafted, leather-bound journals are among the finds here. The store cultivates a sense of community through art classes, craft parties, and community-making events. ⊠ *803 Pearl St.* ☏ *303/444–0124* ⊕ *www. twohandspaperie.com.*

Where the Buffalo Roam. Come here for quirky T-shirts, CU and Colorado souvenirs, and a variety of trinkets. ⊠ *1320 Pearl St.* ☏ *303/938–1424.*

HOME AND GARDEN

Fodor's Choice ★ **Peppercorn.** A Boulder mainstay, this shop offers a dizzying selection of crockery, cookware, table linen, and kitchen utensils, as well as upscale food items and cookbooks. Kids love the balloon artist who often lingers outside the front door (although he's not affiliated with the store). ⊠ *1235 Pearl St.* ☏ *303/449–5847, 800/447–6905* ⊕ *www. peppercorn.com.*

SHOPPING NEIGHBORHOODS

Flatiron Crossing. If it's a traditional indoor mall that you seek, head to Flatiron Crossing, one of the metro area's most popular shopping centers. It's about 10 miles southeast of Boulder on U.S. Highway 36. Shoppers can hit stores such as Nordstrom, Coach, Williams-Sonoma, J. Crew, and more; browse at a few locally owned jewelers and galleries; and take a break in the food court or in one of the full-service restaurants. ⊠ *One W. Flatiron Crossing Dr., Broomfield* 🕾 *720/887–7467* ⊕ *www.flatironcrossing.com* 🕙 *Mon.–Sat. 10–9, Sun. 11–6.*

FAMILY **Pearl Street Mall.** This is the heart of Boulder, a four-block pedestrian mall with upscale boutiques, art galleries, bookstores, shoe shops, and stores with home and garden furnishings. Outside merchant doors, a slew of street performers, musicians, magicians, caricaturists, and a balloon-artist keeps strollers amused. ⊠ *Pearl St. between 11th and 15th Sts.*

Twenty-Ninth Street. Stroll along Twenty-Ninth Street, a pleasant outdoor mall with lovely views, and pick up a pair of shoes, some outdoor gear, a yoga outfit, or a new smartphone. The outdoor mall has plenty of nationally known clothiers, a movie theater, coffee shops, and eateries. ⊠ *29th St. between Arapahoe Ave. and Pearl St.* 🕾 *303/444–0722* ⊕ *www.twentyninthstreet.com* 🕙 *Mon.–Sat. 10–9, Sun. 11–6 (individual store hrs vary).*

University Hill. Known as "the Hill," University Hill is a great place for hip clothes, new and used CDs, and CU apparel. ⊠ *13th St. between College Ave. and Pennsylvania St.*

SPORTING GOODS

Fodors Choice **McGuckin Hardware.** A Boulder institution, McGuckin Hardware stocks
★ home appliances and gadgets, hardware, and a mind-boggling array of outdoor merchandise. The seemingly omniscient salespeople know where everything is. ⊠ *Village Shopping Center, 2525 Arapahoe Ave., Unit D1* 🕾 *303/443–1822* ⊕ *www.mcguckin.com.*

REI. The Boulder branch of REI sells a broad range of outdoor equipment, and rents snowshoes, bear canisters, and trekking poles. The store also has full-service professional bike and ski/snowboard shops, offering maintenance and repair. ⊠ *1789 28th St.* 🕾 *303/583–9970* ⊕ *www. rei.com/stores/44.*

SIDE TRIPS FROM BOULDER

Boulder has a few neighboring towns that are interesting destinations in their own right, well worth a drive and a short stop if not a longer layover. Mountainous Nederland, rural Niwot, and stunning Lyons all have quirky, distinctive (albeit small) downtown areas and gorgeous surroundings filled with mountains, forests, and streams.

NEDERLAND

16 miles west of Boulder via Hwy. 119.

A former mining and mill town at the top of Boulder Canyon and on the scenic Peak to Peak Highway, "Ned" embodies that small, mountain-town spirit in look and attitude: laid-back, independent, renegade, and friendly.

GETTING HERE AND AROUND

Nederland is an easy drive from Boulder. Take Highway 119 (Canyon Boulevard) west.

FESTIVALS

Frozen Dead Guy Days. Inspired by a guy who wanted to be kept on ice after his death (his body is in a Tuff Shed near Nederland), this quirky festival brings out the oddball spirit of this town. The three-day event in March includes live music, a hearse parade, coffin races, icy turkey bowling, a salmon toss, and a charity polar plunge into (usually frozen) Chipeta Park Pond. ⊠ *Chipeta Park and Town Square* ☎ *303/506–1048* ⊕ *frozendeadguydays.org.*

NedFest. In late August, this festival brings a weekend of bluegrass, rock and roll, and jazz music to the west shore of Barker Reservoir. A few thousand people come to relax in the sun, dance, drink beer, and browse the vendor stands. ⊠ *Jeff Guercio Memorial Baseball Field, 132 East St.* ☎ *720/539–5370* ⊕ *www.nedfest.org* 🎟 *$38–$50 for 1 day, $83–$90 for 2 days, $128–$420 for 3 days.*

ESSENTIALS

Visitor Information Nederland Area Chamber of Commerce and Visitor Center. ⊠ *4 W. 1st St.* ☎ *303/258–3936.*

EXPLORING

FAMILY **Carousel of Happiness.** No visit to Nederland is complete without a dollar spin on the Carousel of Happiness, a restored 1910 carousel featuring 56 hand-carved, hand-painted animals running around to the tune of a 1913 Wurlitzer band organ. The complex also includes a gift shop and a puppet theater. ⊠ *20 Lakeview Dr.* ☎ *303/258–3457* ⊕ *www.carouselofhappiness.org* 🎟 *$1.*

Peak to Peak Scenic and Historic Byway. The Peak to Peak Scenic and Historic Byway (Highways 119, 72, and 7), a 55-mile stretch that winds from Central City through Nederland to Estes Park, is not the quickest route to the eastern gateway to Rocky Mountain National Park, but it's certainly the most scenic. You'll pass through the old mining towns of Ward and Allenspark and enjoy spectacular mountain vistas. Mount Meeker and Longs Peak rise magnificently behind every bend in the road. The descent into Estes Park provides grand vistas of snow-covered mountains and green valleys.

An afternoon drive along this route is especially memorable in fall, when the sky is deeper blue and stands of aspens contrast with the evergreen pine forests. ⊠ *Nederland* ✚ *From Central City, drive north on Hwy. 119. From Nederland, drive north on Hwy. 72. Turn left at intersection with Hwy. 7 and continue to Estes Park* ⊕ *www.codot.gov/travel/scenic-byways.*

SPORTS AND THE OUTDOORS

HIKING

DeLonde Trail/Blue Bird Loop. At the Caribou Ranch Open Space, the DeLonde Trail/Blue Bird Loop is an easy 4½-mile walk through forests and wildflower-filled meadows. An elk herd resides on the open space, so listen for the bulls bugling in fall. The 1¼-mile DeLonde Trail starts to the left of the trailhead information kiosk and connects to the Blue Bird Loop just before the former DeLonde homestead site. You can take a break at the picnic table overlooking the pond near the ranch house before continuing on the loop to the former Blue Bird Mine complex. Allow two hours to complete the hike. Note that there are no dogs allowed. ⊠ *Nederland* ✢ *Trailhead: From Nederland, drive north on Hwy. 72 to County Rd. 126, turn left, and go 1 mile* ☎ *303/678–6200* ⊕ *www.bouldercounty.org/os/parks.*

Indian Peaks Wilderness. Offering some of the most popular hiking in the area, Indian Peaks Wilderness is a place where you'll always have company in summer. The area encompasses more than 50 lakes, 133 miles of trails, and six mountain passes crossing the Continental Divide. Wildflowers are prolific, and peak in late July and early August. Cinquefoil, harebell, stonecrop, flax, wild geranium, yarrow, larkspur, lupine, and columbine (the state flower) all mix in a mosaic of colors on the slopes and in the meadows. Parking at trailheads outside the wilderness area is limited, so plan to start out early in the day. "No Parking" signs are posted, and, if the designated parking lot is full, the etiquette is to park your car on the outbound side of the road at a spot where there's still room for vehicles to pass. There's no central access point to the area; contact the U.S. Forest Service or check the Arapaho Roosevelt National Forest website for trail information and driving directions. Permits are not required for day visitors but are for camping. All dogs must be on leash.

The easy 2¾-mile (round-trip) hike to **Lost Lake** is just outside the wilderness boundary and has enough altitude to give you views of the high peaks under the brilliant blue sky. It's a good option for those visiting from the flatlands, as you'll gain a mere 800 feet on this two-hour walk. To get to the trailhead from Nederland, drive south on Highway 119 to County Road 130. About 1 mile after the pavement ends, look for a road on the left that goes sharply downhill (marked Hessie Trail). Do not venture down this lower road without a high-clearance vehicle. For most cars, it's best to park above along the county road and hike ½ mile to the trailhead.

The well-traveled trail to **Diamond Lake** starts out as the Arapaho Pass Trail at the Fourth of July trailhead. It's steep as you climb through the pines, but the elevation gain between the trailhead and the lake is only 800 feet. The trail delivers terrific views of Jasper Peak and the Arapaho Peaks. In late July, when the snowfields are gone, the wildflowers cover the slopes and meadows with bursts of color. At the junction with the Diamond Lake trailhead to the left, the trail passes a waterfall and crosses a stream (with a bridge) before it descends to Diamond Lake. Relax at the lake and enjoy the views before returning. Allow three hours to hike the 5-mile round-trip. To get to the trailhead from Nederland, drive south on Highway 119 to County Road 130. About 5 miles after the pavement ends, look for signs for the Fourth of July trailhead. ✉ *Boulder Ranger District Office, Arapaho National Forest, 2140 Yarmouth Ave.* ☎ *303/541–2500* 🌐 *www.fs.usda.gov/recarea/arp/recarea/?recid=80803.*

SKIING AND SNOWBOARDING

Eldora Mountain Resort. Boulder's backyard ski resort, Eldora Mountain Resort offers ski and snowboard terrain to suit every ability, as well as two terrain parks, and a Nordic Center with 25 miles (40 km) of groomed trails. Eldora's summit is 10,800 feet, and it's often windy, so dress warmly. Head for the the base lodge for ski rentals, cafeteria-style meals, and ski school. The resort offers a full range of lessons for children and adults. There's no lodging on-site, so set up home base in Nederland or Boulder. **Facilities:** 53 trails; 680 acres; 1,600-foot vertical drop; 11 lifts. ✉ *2861 Eldora Ski Rd.* ✣ *5 miles west of Nederland off Hwy. 119 and Eldora Rd.* ☎ *303/440–8700* 🌐 *www.eldora.com* 🎟 *Lift ticket $89* 🕒 *Mid-Nov.–mid-Apr., daily 9–4.*

WHERE TO EAT AND STAY

$ INDIAN 🍴 **Kathmandu Restaurant.** This bustling Nepali and Indian restaurant serves a full range of traditional fare at reasonable prices. Kathmandu has received accolades for its vegetarian food, but everything is good here. The menu spans the gamut from starters like momos and samosas, to *saag panir* (creamed spinach), *aloo gobi* (cauliflower and potatoes), and tandoori chicken, lamb, and curries. If you're really hungry, stop in for the daily lunch buffet from 11 to 3. [$] *Average main: $12* ✉ *110 N. Jefferson St.* ☎ *303/258–1169* 🌐 *www.nepalidining.com.*

$$ CAFÉ 🍴 **Sundance Cafe and Lodge.** Locals love this place for its low-key atmosphere and great, diner-style breakfasts, lunches, and dinners. The blue-checked tablecloths and wood-paneled bar and walls create a homey feel. Dinner features steak, chicken, pasta dishes, and crab legs. Lunch (served all day) is more casual, with burgers and sandwiches. Try the Robbie Burger, which is topped with bacon and Brie. From both the deck and the inside, you enjoy great views of the Indian Peaks to the west, Boulder to the east, and Roosevelt National Forest on all sides. [$] *Average main: $15* ✉ *23492 Hwy. 119* ✣ *1 mile south of Nederland* ☎ *303/258–0804* 🌐 *www.sundancelodgecolorado.com* ✍ *Reservations not accepted.*

$$ BARBECUE 🍴 **Wild Mountain Smokehouse & Brewery.** This brewpub has it all: handcrafted beer, delicious barbecue, and a truly spectacular deck. It's a festive atmosphere, whether you're sitting outside or in the lodge-style dining room, where there's a fireplace, cathedral ceilings, and cheery red and green walls. Stop in for some seriously smoky meats or a salad topped with maple-glazed salmon. Choose from six barbecue sauces and 11 sides, and pair it all with a pint of home brew. [$] *Average main: $14* ✉ *70 E. 1st St.* ☎ *303/258–9453* 🌐 *www.wildmountainsb.com.*

$$ B&B/INN 🏨 **Magnuson Hotel Lodge at Nederland.** This is an excellent choice for those who want to be smack dab in the middle of Nederland, 10 minutes from Eldora Ski Resort. **Pros:** property has mountain style; quiet; good value for location. **Cons:** Nederland can feel remote unless you're spending a lot of time hiking and skiing; on a heavily traveled road. [$] *Rooms from: $131* ✉ *55 Lakeview Dr., Nederland* ☎ *303/258–9463, 800/279–9463* 🌐 *www.magnusonhotels.com/1st-Inn-Nederland* 🛏 *14 rooms, 9 suites* 🍽 *Breakfast.*

NIWOT

10 miles northeast of downtown Boulder via Hwy. 119.

Niwot is the Arapaho Indian word for "left hand," and this is where Chief Niwot (born circa 1820) and his tribe lived along the banks of Left Hand Creek until the early 1860s. European settlers arrived in the latter half of the 1800s to take up farming, after gold mining in the mountains became less lucrative. The town's importance grew after the arrival of the railroad in the 1870s. These days its most famous business is Crocs footwear, which was started in Niwot in 2004. Antiques aficionados have made Niwot a prime destination in Boulder County. The compact historic district, replete with brick buildings decorated with flower boxes, runs along 2nd Avenue between the cross streets Franklin and Murray.

EXPLORING

EN ROUTE

Celestial Seasonings. Spicy aromas greet you in the parking lot of Celestial Seasonings, North America's largest herbal-tea producer (sealing 10 million tea bags daily). The factory offers free 45-minute tours, which include a jolting trip into the famous "Mint Room," waking your senses and clearing your sinuses. Before the tour, check out original paintings of tea-box art and sample more than 80 varieties of tea. You can also grab a bite to eat at the on-site café. ✉ *4600 Sleepytime Dr., Boulder* ✢ *8 miles northeast of downtown Boulder. Take Hwy. 119 to Jay Rd., turn right. After about 1 mile, turn left onto Spine Rd. After about ½ mile, turn left onto Sleepytime Dr.* ☎ *303/530–5300* 🌐 *www.celestialseasonings.com* ⏲ *Tours on the hr Mon.–Sat. 10–4, Sun. 11–3.*

EN ROUTE

Leanin' Tree Museum of Western Art. This is one of the country's largest privately owned collections of Western art, with more than 250 paintings of Western landscapes, wildlife, and pioneer life, and 100 bronze sculptures. See work by renowned artists such as Bill Hughes, Allan Houser, and Frank McCarthy. The museum sells a wide variety of its own greeting cards as well as gifts in its unique shop. ✉ *6055 Longbow Dr., Boulder* ✢ *About 8 miles northeast of Boulder. From Hwy. 119, take 63rd St. south, then Longbow Dr. west* ☎ *303/530–1442* 🌐 *www.leanintreemuseum.com* 🎟 *Free* ⏲ *Weekdays 8–6, Sat. 9–5, Sun. 10–5.*

WHERE TO EAT AND STAY

$$$$ MEDITERRANEAN

🍴 **Colterra.** Southern French and Northern Italian cuisine are the specialty of this farm-to-table restaurant, whose highlight is a large sandstone-patio dining area fringed with vegetable garden beds and shaded by leafy trees. You can select from a frequently changing menu that might include Colorado Wagyu beef, ragout of local Boulder lamb, or oven-roasted chicken breast with polenta. Although not listed on the menu, risotto is a daily offering, featuring seasonal ingredients. Can't decide on dessert? Go for the dark chocolate symphony, which includes five chocolate delights. [$] *Average main: $26* ✉ *210 Franklin St.* ☎ *303/652–0777* 🌐 *www.colterra.com.*

$$$ ✕**Treppeda's Italian Restaurant.** This casual but elegant Italian café has
ITALIAN   outdoor seating, a cozy terra-cotta-painted dining room, and a long
wooden bar along one wall. At lunch, order at the counter and enjoy
tasty grilled paninis made from authentic ingredients and fresh focaccia.
Dinner is more formal, with traditional dishes like steamed mussels in
white wine, *spaghetti alla carbonara*, veal marsala, and sea bass with
olives, capers, and garlic, as well as pizza and daily specials. The wine
list hails largely from Italy, with more than 170 selections. Desserts
include tiramisu, crème brûlée, and gelato. $ *Average main: $25 ⊠ 300
2nd Ave.* ☎ *303/652–1606* ⊕ *www.treppedas.com* ⊘ *Closed Sun. No
lunch Sat.* ⌂ *Reservations essential.*

$$ ▦**Niwot Inn and Spa.** This small inn has a cozy, Southwestern lodge feel,
B&B/INN   right down to the hardwood floors and woven wool rugs in the com-
mon areas. **Pros:** great Continental breakfast buffet; close to excellent
restaurants. **Cons:** can hear the train passing; drive to Boulder can be
congested during rush hour; no elevator. $ *Rooms from: $159 ⊠ 342
2nd Ave.* ☎ *303/652–8452* ⊕ *niwotinn.com* ⇄ *13 rooms, 1 suite, 1
2-bedroom apartment* ⋈| *Breakfast.*

LYONS

17 miles north of Boulder via U.S. 36.

Lyons is a peaceful, down-to-earth community of 2,000 residents that's
tucked inside the red-sandstone foothills at the confluence of the North
St. Vrain and South St. Vrain creeks. Founded in 1881, it's crammed
with historic buildings—there are 15 structures listed in the National
Register of Historic Places—and the whole downtown area feels like
a turn-of-the-20th-century frontier outpost. The cafés, restaurants, art
galleries, and antiques stores attract lots of visitors, who also come for
the recreation opportunities and top-notch music festivals.

GETTING HERE AND AROUND
To drive to Lyons from Boulder, travel north on U.S. 36.

FESTIVALS
Planet Bluegrass. At the end of July, Planet Bluegrass presents Rocky-
Grass—an internationally renowned bluegrass festival that features a
combination of well-known and legendary artists as well as up-and-
comers. The venue—an idyllic outdoor setting under red-rock cliffs on
the banks of the St. Vrain River—is also host to FolksFest in August.
In addition, the indoor Wildflower Pavilion stages weekly concerts in
the spring and fall. (Planet Bluegrass is also the organizer of Telluride
Bluegrass Festival, held each June in southwest Colorado, a seven-hour
drive from Lyons.) ⊠ *500 W. Main St.* ☎ *303/823–0848, 800/624–2422*
⊕ *www.bluegrass.com.*

ESSENTIALS
Visitor Information Lyons Area Chamber of Commerce.
⊠ *350 Broadway* ⊹ *In the visitor center at Sandstone Park.* ☎ *303/823–6622*
⊕ *www.lyons-colorado.com.*

EXPLORING

Lyons Classic Pinball. You wouldn't expect such a pinball extravaganza in tiny Lyons, but there it is, behind the Oskar Blues brewpub, with nearly 40 classic pinball games. The change machines (and fellow gamers) make it a simple and fun stop. ✉ *339-A Main St.* ☎ *303/823–6100* 🌐 *www.lyonspinball.com* 🕓 *Thurs. 5–10, Fri. and Sat. 3–11, Sun. 3–9.*

SPORTS AND THE OUTDOORS

BIRD-WATCHING

Meadow Park. Bird-watchers come from all over to see eagles nesting in the sandstone cliffs at the south end of Meadow Park. Located along the banks of the St. Vrain River, this lovely park also has a white-water park for kayakers, a swimming hole, camping, and a zip line. ✉ *601 Park Dr.* ☎ *303/823–6622.*

HIKING AND MOUNTAIN BIKING

Hall Ranch. Nearly 14 miles of trails at Hall Ranch are open to hikers, mountain bikers, and equestrians (but not dogs). The **Bitterbrush Trail/ Nelson Loop** follows the Bitterbrush Trail for 3¾ miles, climbing 914 feet through meadows, pine trees, and rock outcroppings. It connects to the 2¼-mile Nelson Loop, which leads to the original Nelson Ranch House. The slight 300-foot elevation gain of the Nelson Loop brings you up onto a plateau that provides great views of the mountains to the north. Allow five to six hours to hike the trail, less for biking it. Mountain bikers who want to avoid the rock garden can approach the Nelson Loop from the other side via the **Antelope Trail**, which climbs a mile from the trailhead off Apple Valley Road. ✉ *Lyons* ✣ *¾ mile west of Lyons on Hwy. 7* 🌐 *www.co.boulder.co.us/openspace.*

Rabbit Mountain. Rabbit Mountain has several easy to moderate trails that afford views of the High Rockies and the plains. Pick up the interpretive pamphlet at the trailhead that explains the history of the area, including the dramatic metamorphosis of Rabbit Mountain from a lush, tropical swamp inhabited by dinosaurs to the present-day, mile-high desert that's home to raptors, prairie dogs, coyotes, and the occasional rattlesnake. The 2-mile round-trip **Little Thompson Overlook Trail** forks off to the left before you come to the gravel road and climbs a mere 500 feet to the point where you can see Longs Peak, the plains to the east, and Boulder Valley to the south. The 3½-mile **Eagle Wind Trail** loop has short spurs to viewpoints. From the parking area, head out on the trail to the gravel road and then right onto the single-track loop. ✉ *8 miles outside of Lyons to the east* ✣ *Follow CO–66 E out of Lyons for 4 miles, turn left on N. 75th St. and left on Rabbit Mountain Rd.* 🌐 *www.bouldercounty.org/os/parks.*

WHERE TO EAT

$$$ AMERICAN

🍴 **Lyons Fork.** Locals call it "the Fork," an upscale-for-Lyons spot that is known for its beer-friendly menu, outstanding margaritas, and delicious cooking—not to mention some of the best truffle fries in the West. The dining room is bright and cheery, with colorful walls and wooden booths, a long wood bar, and a red ceiling. If the weather permits, sit on the cozy back patio, though don't expect snappy service. Sit back, relax, and take in the view. [$] *Average main: $21* ✉ *450*

Main St. ☎ *303/823–5014* 🌐 *www.lyonsfork.com* 💳 *No credit cards* 🕒 *No lunch weekdays.*

$ AMERICAN 🍴 **Oskar Blues Grill & Brew.** The first American craft brewery to can its beer, Oskar Blues is a Lyons hot spot for beer (especially after a bike ride) as well as music and pub grub. Try Dale's Pale Ale, which packs a hoppy punch, or any of the other robust beers brewed on-site in small (20-barrel) batches. The burgers are consistently awesome, and come in interesting varieties, including two named in honor of music legends—B.B. King and Satchmo. Blues instruments and covers of blues CDs decorate the restaurant. In the basement, a "juke joint" frequently hosts live music, and there's a bluegrass jam every Tuesday night. [$] *Average main: $12* ✉ *303 Main St.* ☎ *303/823–6685* 🌐 *www.oskarblues.com.*

ESTES PARK

40 miles northwest of Boulder via U.S. 36 (28th St. in Boulder).

The vast scenery on the U.S. 36 approach to Estes Park gives little hint of the grandeur to come, but if ever there was a classic picture-postcard Rockies view, Estes Park has it. The town sits at an altitude of more than 7,500 feet, at the foot of a stunning backdrop of 14,259-foot Longs Peak, the majestic Stanley Hotel, and surrounding mountains. The town is family-oriented and very kitschy, with lots of stores selling Western-theme trinkets, sweets, and regional toys for the kids. Many of the small businesses and hotels lining the roads are mom-and-pop outfits that have been passed down through several generations. Estes Park is also the most popular gateway to Rocky Mountain National Park (aka RMNP, home of the world-famous Trail Ridge Road), which is a few miles down the road.

GETTING HERE AND AROUND

To get to Estes Park from Boulder, take U.S. 36 north through Lyons and the town of Pinewood Springs (about 38 miles). You also can reach Estes Park via the Peak to Peak Scenic and Historic Byway. To reach the byway from Boulder, take Highway 119 west to Nederland and turn right (north) onto Highway 72, or follow Sunshine Canyon Drive/Gold Hill Road into Ward, and pick up Highway 72 there.

Estes Park's main downtown area is walkable, which is good news on summer weekends, when traffic can be heavy (and parking can be challenging). Keep an eye out for parking signs throughout town, as the public lots are your best chance for a close-in spot.

The National Park Service operates a free bus service in and around Estes Park and between Estes Park and Rocky Mountain National Park. Buses operate daily from early June to Labor Day, then on weekends until the end of September.

ESSENTIALS

Transportation Contact **National Park Service Shuttle Buses.** ✉ *Estes Park* 🌐 *www.nps.gov/romo/planyourvisit/shuttle_bus_route.htm.*

Visitor Information **Estes Park Visitor Center.** ✉ *500 Big Thompson Ave.* ☎ *970/577–9900, 800/443–7837* 🌐 *www.visitestespark.com.*

EXPLORING

Estes Park Museum. The Native Americans of centuries past needed their getaways, too, and archaeological evidence displayed at the Estes Park Museum makes a potent case for them using this area as a summer resort. The museum has an assortment of pioneer artifacts, displays on the founding of Rocky Mountain National Park, and changing exhibits. It also publishes a self-guided walking tour of historic sites, which are mostly clustered along Elkhorn Avenue downtown. ⊠ *200 4th St.* ☎ *970/586–6256* ⊕ *www.estes.org/museum* ⊠ *Free* ⊗ *May–Oct., Mon.–Sat. 10–5, Sun. 1–5; Nov.–Apr., Fri. and Sat. 10–5, Sun. 1–5.*

MacGregor Ranch Museum. This working ranch, homesteaded in 1873, is on the National Register of Historic Places and provides a well-preserved record of typical ranch life. Take a 30-minute guided tour of the 1896 ranch house, then explore the outbuildings and machinery on your own as you take in views of the Twin Owls and Longs Peak (towering more than 14,000 feet). ⊠ *180 MacGregor Lane* ✛ *1½ miles north of town on U.S. 34. Turn right on MacGregor La., a dirt road* ☎ *970/586–3749* ⊕ *www.macgregorranch.org* ⊠ *$5* ⊗ *June–Aug., Tues.–Sat. 10–4.*

SPORTS AND THE OUTDOORS

FISHING

The Big Thompson River, which runs east of Estes Park along U.S. 34, is a good place to cast for rainbow and brown trout. See ⊕ *www. wildlife.state.co.us/fishing* for more information on fishing licenses, which are mandatory.

Estes Angler. This popular fishing guide arranges four-, six-, and eight-hour fly-fishing trips—as well as full-day horseback excursions—into the park's quieter regions, year-round, with a maximum of three people per guide. The best times for fishing are generally from April to mid-November. Equipment is also available for rent. ⊠ *338 W. Riverside Dr.* ☎ *970/586–2110, 800/586–2110* ⊕ *www.estesangler.com* ⊠ *From $125* ⊗ *Daily 8–6.*

Kirks Fly Shop. This Estes Park outfitter offers various guided fly-fishing trips, as well as backpacking, horseback, and llama pack trips. The store also carries fishing and backpacking gear. ⊠ *230 E. Elkhorn Ave.* ☎ *970/577–0790, 877/669–1859* ⊕ *www.kirksflyshop.com* ⊠ *From $50* ⊗ *Daily 7–7.*

HORSEBACK RIDING

Sombrero Ranches. From its several stables in the Estes Park region, including two in Rocky Mountain National Park, Sombrero Ranches offers guided trail rides (from one to 10 hours long), plus breakfast rides and steak dinner rides. Sombrero also offers "drop camps" to deliver your backcountry gear to your campsite. ⊠ *1895 Big Thompson Ave.* ☎ *970/586–4577* ⊕ *www.sombrero.com* ⊠ *From $40.*

7

RAFTING AND KAYAKING

White-water rafting trips fill up fast in high season, so it's a good idea to book with an outfitter a couple of days (if not weeks) in advance. Early-season trips in May catch the biggest runoff and the wilder rides, while late-season excursions (in August) will be tamer.

OUTFITTERS

Rapid Transit Rafting. This outfitter leads full-day rafting trips on the Colorado River and half-day trips on the Cache la Poudre River. ⊠ *161 Virginia Dr.* ☎ *970/577–7238, 800/367–8523* ⊕ *www.rapidtransitrafting. com* 🍽 *$60 for half day, $95 for full day* ☉ *Closed Sept.–mid-May.*

WHERE TO EAT

$ ✕ **Bighorn Restaurant.** An Estes Park staple since 1972, this family-run
AMERICAN   outfit is where the locals go for breakfast. Try a double-cheese omelet,
FAMILY   *huevos rancheros*, or grits before heading into the park in the morning. The owners are happy to pack a lunch for you—just place your order along with breakfast, and it will be ready when you leave. This homey spot also serves lunch and dinner, with specialties such as house-smoked pulled pork, housemade meatballs, and rib eye cut on-site. Expect a wait in the summer. $ *Average main: $12* ⊠ *401 W. Elkhorn Ave.* ☎ *970/586–2792* ⊕ *www.estesparkbighorn.com.*

$$ ✕ **Ed's Cantina & Grill.** The fajitas and well-stocked bar make this lively
MEXICAN   Mexican restaurant popular with locals and visitors alike. The decor
FAMILY   is bright, with light woods and large windows. When the sun is shining, ask for patio seating by the river. If you're hungry, try one of the enchilada platters (choose from bison, chicken mole, or vegetarian) or *carne asada*. The fish and bison tacos are other popular options. $ *Average main: $13* ⊠ *390 E. Elkhorn Ave.* ☎ *970/586–2919* ⊕ *www. edscantina.com.*

$ ✕ **Estes Park Brewery.** If you want to sample some local brews, check out
AMERICAN   the Estes Park Brewery, which has been crafting beer since 1993. Not sure what you will like? Head downstairs to the tasting area to sample a variety of brews on tap. The Stinger Wild Honey Wheat is the most popular, while the Bear Lake Blueberry Wheat has a hint of blueberries and is served with fruit in the glass. The food is no-frills (beer chili is the specialty), and the menu includes things like pizza, burgers, sandwiches, and house-made bratwurst. After eating, you can amuse yourself at the pool table or video games. $ *Average main: $11* ⊠ *470 Prospect Village Dr.* ☎ *970/586–5421* ⊕ *www.epbrewery.com.*

$ ✕ **Poppy's Pizza & Grill.** This casual riverside eatery serves creative sig-
PIZZA   nature pizzas. Try the spinach, artichoke, and feta pie made with sun-
FAMILY   dried tomato pesto. You can also create your own pie from five sauces and nearly 40 toppings. Other options include sandwiches, wraps, salads, and burgers. Poppy's has patio seating at the river and an extensive selection of beer. $ *Average main: $10* ⊠ *342 E. Elkhorn Ave.* ☎ *970/586–8282* ⊕ *www.poppyspizzaandgrill.com* ☉ *Closed Jan.* ⌨ *Reservations not accepted.*

WHERE TO STAY

Lodging options are clustered in several areas around Estes Park. Numerous cabins dot the banks of the Fall River along Fall River Road and the Big Thompson River along Highway 66. You can also choose from lodges south of town, or numerous motels that line the sides of Big Thompson Avenue (Highway 34) out the eastern edge of town. And, of course, the historic Stanley Hotel holds court on the prominent hill overlooking Estes Park. Wherever you stay, book well in advance for the summer months as hotels fill early in peak season.

STANLEY AND HIS SHINING HOTEL

On its road to becoming a resort town, Estes Park attracted the attention of entrepreneur F.O. Stanley, inventor of the Stanley Steamer automobile and several influential photographic processes. In 1905, after being told he would soon die of tuberculosis, he started construction on the regal **Stanley Hotel.** The hotel soon became one of the most glamorous resorts in the Rockies. It was the inspiration for Stephen King's horror novel *The Shining.* (While Stanley Kubrick's 1980 classic movie was not filmed on-site, the 1997 miniseries was—and King has said he prefers the latter.)

$$$$ HOTEL **Boulder Brook.** Watch elk stroll past your spacious luxury suite at this smart, secluded spot on the river amid towering pines, just 2 miles from Rocky Mountain National Park. **Pros:** scenic location; quiet area; attractive grounds. **Cons:** not within walking distance of attractions; no nearby dining. [$] *Rooms from: $250* ✉ *1900 Fall River Rd.* ☎ *970/586–0910, 800/238–0910* 🌐 *www.boulderbrook.com* 🛏 *20 suites* 🍴 *No meals.*

$$ RESORT FAMILY **Glacier Lodge.** Families are the specialty at this secluded, 22-acre guest resort on the banks of the Big Thompson River. **Pros:** great place for families; attractive grounds on the river; on free bus route. **Cons:** not within walking distance of attractions; along rather busy road. [$] *Rooms from: $160* ✉ *2166 Hwy. 66* ☎ *800/523–3920* 🌐 *www.glacierlodge.com* 🕒 *Closed Nov.–Apr.* 🛏 *22 single-family cabins, 4 cabins for 12–30, 2 sleeping rooms* 🍴 *No meals.*

$$ HOTEL **The Historic Mary's Lake Lodge.** The sound of a baby grand piano greets you in the lobby of this 1913 chalet-style lodge, which sits at the base of Rams Horn Mountain and overlooks peaceful Mary's Lake, a few miles south of town. **Pros:** historic charm; beautiful views. **Cons:** not within walking distance of attractions or other dining; large, older hotel. [$] *Rooms from: $149* ✉ *2625 Mary's Lake Rd.* ☎ *970/586–5958, 877/442–6279* 🌐 *www.maryslakelodge.com* 🛏 *13 rooms, 3 suites* 🍴 *No meals.*

$$ HOTEL Fodor's Choice ★ **The Maxwell Inn.** For a clean and comfortable place to rest your head within walking distance of downtown, check in to the Maxwell Inn, a friendly motel run by a husband-and-wife team. **Pros:** walking distance to downtown; relatively affordable for Estes Park; clean and comfortable. **Cons:** rooms are small; fairly basic accommodations. [$] *Rooms from: $139* ✉ *553 W. Elkhorn Ave.* ☎ *970/586–2833* 🌐 *www.themaxwellinn.com* 🕒 *Closed Jan. and Feb.* 🛏 *17 rooms* 🍴 *Breakfast.*

$$ HOTEL 🏨 **Riverview Pines.** Cast a line for stocked brown and rainbow trout, watch widlife visit the river's edge, or just sit and read on the expansive lawn at this peaceful property, the best value along beautiful Fall River Road between Estes and Rocky Mountain National Park. **Pros:** friendly and helpful owner-managers; quiet and scenic location on river; low rates for the area. **Cons:** very basic rooms without much decoration; on a busy road. [$] *Rooms from: $135* ✉ *1150 W. Elkhorn Ave.* ☎ *970/586–3627* 🌐 *www.riverviewpines.com* 🛏 *12 rooms, 8 cabins* 🍴 *No meals.*

$$$$ HOTEL Fodor's Choice ★ 🏨 **Stanley Hotel.** Perched regally on a hill, with a commanding view of town, the Stanley is one of Colorado's great old hotels, featuring Georgian colonial–style architecture and a storied, haunted history that includes being the inspiration for Stephen King's novel *The Shining*. **Pros:** historic hotel; many rooms have been updated; good restaurant. **Cons:** some rooms are small and tight; building is old; no air-conditioning. [$] *Rooms from: $279* ✉ *333 Wonderview Ave.* ☎ *970/577–4000, 800/976–1377* 🌐 *www.stanleyhotel.com* 🛏 *150 rooms, 10 suites, 18 condos* 🍴 *No meals.*

$$$ B&B/INN 🏨 **Taharaa Mountain Lodge.** Every room at this luxury B&B has access to its own balcony and views of the High Rockies and Estes Valley. **Pros:** beautiful mountain views; friendly hosts. **Cons:** not within walking distance of attractions nor on bus route; no young children allowed; two-day minimum stay (three-day minimum for summer and holidays). [$] *Rooms from: $209* ✉ *3110 S. St. Vrain Ave.* ✣ *4 miles south of downtown Estes Park* ☎ *970/577–0098, 800/597–0098* 🌐 *www.taharaa.com* 🛏 *9 rooms, 9 suites* 🍴 *Breakfast.*

$$ RESORT FAMILY 🏨 **YMCA of the Rockies – Estes Park Center.** Established in 1907—eight years before Rocky Mountain National Park—this 860-acre family-friendly property abuts the park and has an abundance of attractive, clean lodging options among its nine lodges and 217 cabins. **Pros:** good value for large groups and longer stays; lots of family-oriented activities and amenities; stunning scenery. **Cons:** very large, busy, and crowded property; fills fast; location requires vehicle to visit town or the national park. [$] *Rooms from: $129* ✉ *2515 Tunnel Rd.* ☎ *970/586–3341, 888/613–9622 family reservations, 800/777–9622 group reservations* 🌐 *www.ymcarockies.org* 🛏 *553 rooms, 217 cabins* 🍴 *Some meals.*

NIGHTLIFE AND PERFORMING ARTS

PERFORMING ARTS

Cultural Arts Council of Estes Park. This organization produces a self-guided art walk brochure, revised quarterly, that you can use to explore galleries and artists' studios around town. Pick one up at the council's offices or at one of the galleries along the way. During Plein Air Rockies each August, artists come to town to paint outdoors in the inspirational mountain setting. Watch the artists in action or see their completed work in the council's gallery. The council also hosts free concerts in Performance Park on Wednesday and Thursday evenings. ✉ *423 W. Elkhorn Ave.* ☎ *970/586–9203* 🌐 *www.estesarts.com.*

Rocky Ridge Music Center. Relax with some chamber music while taking in views of the mountains at the much-respected Rocky Ridge Music Center. Faculty members hold their own classical chamber music concerts June to September. ⊠ *465 Longs Peak Rd.* ✛ *South of Estes Park off Hwy. 7 at turnoff to Longs Peak Campground (mile marker 9)* ☎ *970/586–4031* ⊕ *www.rockyridge.org* ⌑ *$22.*

NIGHTLIFE

Lonigans Saloon, Nightclub & Grill. If you're in the mood for a fun Irish pub with "altitude," head over to Lonigans for drinks, bar food, and pool. Wednesday is open-mike night, and Friday and Saturday have Karaoke. ⊠ *110 W. Elkhorn Ave.* ☎ *970/586–4346* ⊕ *www.lonigans.com.*

Nagl's World Famous Wheel Bar. The venerable Wheel Bar (family owned since 1945) is one of the more historic watering holes in town and gets hopping at night. ⊠ *132 E. Elkhorn Ave.* ☎ *970/586–9381* ⊕ *www. thewheelbar.com.*

SHOPPING

CRAFTS AND ART GALLERIES

Earthwood Collections. This fine art and handcrafts shop sells a wide assortment of art, including ceramics, frames, jewelry, oil paintings, and more. ⊠ *141 E. Elkhorn Ave.* ☎ *970/577–8100* ⊕ *www. earthwoodcollections.com.*

Images of Rocky Mountain National Park. This shop showcases photographer Erik Stensland's stunning images of the park—a must-see collection of local photography. ⊠ *203 Park La.* ☎ *970/586–4352* ⊕ *www. imagesofrmnp.com.*

Patterson Glassworks of Estes Park. Watch glassblowing in action and browse a wide variety of glass creations. ⊠ *323 W. Elkhorn Ave.* ☎ *970/586–8619* ⊕ *www.glassworksofestespark.com.*

Wild Spirits Gallery. Shop for open and limited-edition prints, photographs, and paintings of the West and Rocky Mountain National Park. Custom framing and shipping are also available. ⊠ *148 W. Elkhorn Ave.* ☎ *970/586–4392* ⊕ *www.wildspiritsgallery.com.*

GIFTS

Rocky Mountain Chocolate Factory. Indulge in fudge, truffles, and fantastic caramel apples at this paradise of sweets. ⊠ *517 Big Thompson Ave.* ☎ *970/586–6601* ⊕ *www.rmcf.com.*

Wynbrier Home. This charming shop overflows with sophisticated jewelry, china, linens, home decor, gifts, and European antiques. ⊠ *240 E. Elkhorn Ave.* ☎ *970/586–3294* ⊕ *www.wynbrierhome.com.*

OUTDOOR GEAR

Outdoor World. At Outdoor World you can pick up maps, hiking shoes, rain gear, water bottles, or anything else you need for outdoor explorations. ⊠ *156 E. Elkhorn Ave.* ☎ *970/586–2114.*

7

Base Camp: Estes Park or Grand Lake?

CLOSE UP

More often than not, people choose to stay in **Estes Park** instead of Grand Lake because it's closer to the cities of the Front Range—but the traffic, particularly on summer weekends, reflects that. Expect parking in downtown Estes Park to be difficult and count on delays while driving through town. Estes Park also offers more options for lodging and meals than Grand Lake. A hotel room averages $159 per night, and a burger will run you about $8. The Safeway in Stanley Village at the intersection of U.S. 34 (Big Thompson Avenue) and U.S. 36 (St. Vrain Avenue) is the best place to pick up insect repellent, sunscreen, water, and snacks (including deli sandwiches) for hiking.

Grand Lake is a smaller resort than Estes Park. Getting around in a car is easier, and parking is rarely a problem. It's also a bit closer—only 2 miles—from Grand Lake village to the RMNP entrance, and some naturalists might argue that the Grand Lake side of the park is wilder because it's the road less traveled. The outdoor activities here are more diverse than in Estes Park; the list includes water sports on Grand Lake, mountain biking, and snowmobiling. Grand Lake village is also close to skiing and ice-fishing, and hiking in the Indian Peaks Wilderness and the Arapaho National Recreation Area. A hotel room is slightly less expensive than in Estes Park. The Mountain Food Market at 400 Grand Avenue is a handy spot to stock up on supplies before entering the park.

WESTERN PARAPHERNALIA

Rustic Mountain Charm. This expansive boutique sells gifts, local foodstuffs, and home accessories with the lodge look, including furniture, quilts, baskets, and throws. ⊠ *135 E. Elkhorn Ave.* ☎ *970/586–4344* ⊕ *www.rusticmountaincharm.com.*

The Twisted Pine Fur and Leather Company. If you're in the market for a new leather jacket or Native American items, you're in luck: the Twisted Pine Fur and Leather Company specializes in men's and women's clothing, and also carries weavings, pelts, bows and arrows, pipes, housewares, rugs, and jewelry. ⊠ *450 Moraine Ave.* ☎ *970/586–4539, 800/896–8086* ⊕ *www.thetwistedpine.com.*

GRAND COUNTY

Grand County combines high country and rolling ranch lands. Vistas of the Rockies to the east and south and of the Gore Range to the west frame these grasslands, which the early French explorers named Middle Park. By the time the Moffat Railroad came to Grand County in 1905, ranchers were already living on the flat, open meadows.

Although Grand County is ranching country, the word "range" today evokes more the excellent golf courses than the plains where cowboys herd cattle. The town of Granby has two golf courses, and Grand County hosts several annual tournaments. Golfers aren't the only sportspeople in town: summer brings droves of anglers and bicyclists, and large-game hunters replace them in the late fall. The area west of Granby along U.S. 40 is marked by a number of small towns with resorts and guest ranches.

GRAND LAKE

1½ miles west of Rocky Mountain National Park via U.S. 34.

The tiny town of Grand Lake, known to locals as Grand Lake Village, is doubly blessed by its surroundings. It's the western gateway to Rocky Mountain National Park and also sits on the shores of its namesake, the state's largest natural lake and the highest-altitude yacht anchorage in America. With views of snowy peaks and verdant mountains from just about any vantage point, Grand Lake is adored by Coloradans for sailing, canoeing, waterskiing, and fishing. In winter it's *the* snowmobiling and ice-fishing destination. Even with its wooden boardwalks, Old West–style storefronts, and assortment of souvenir shops and motels, Grand Lake seems less spoiled than many other resort towns and exudes friendliness.

GETTING HERE AND AROUND

Grand Lake is about 60 miles from Boulder or 96 miles from Denver, as the crow flies, but to get here by car you have to circle around the mountains and travel more than 100 miles from Boulder and 171 miles from Denver. You've got two options: Take the highway the whole way (U.S. 36, CO Highway 93, I–70, U.S. 40, and U.S. 34) or take the scenic route (U.S 36 north to Estes Park, then U.S. 34 across Rocky Mountain National Park). The section of U.S. 34 that passes through Rocky Mountain National Park, known as Trail Ridge Road, is the highest paved road in America, and you can stop for a photo op at the Continental Divide sign. Trail Ridge Road closes every winter, typically between mid-October and late May.

You can explore most of the town on foot, including the historic boardwalk on Grand Avenue, with more than 70 shops and restaurants. You won't be constantly rubbing elbows with others: Grand Lake doesn't get the hordes of tourists that can descend on Estes Park, meaning traffic and parking aren't a problem.

ESSENTIALS

Visitor Information Grand Lake Chamber of Commerce and Visitor Center. ⊠ *West Portal Rd. and U.S. 34, at the western entrance of Rocky Mountain National Park* ☎ *970/627–3402, 800/531–1019* ⊕ *www.grandlakechamber.com.*

EXPLORING

Grand Lake. According to Ute legend, the fine mists that shroud Grand Lake at dawn are the risen spirits of women and children whose raft capsized as they were fleeing a marauding party of Cheyennes and Arapahos. Grand Lake is the largest and deepest natural lake in Colorado. It feeds into two much larger man-made reservoirs, Lake Granby and Shadow Mountain Lake, and these three water bodies as well as Monarch Lake and Willow Creek and Meadow Creek reservoirs are called the "Great Lakes of Colorado." ⊠ *Grand Lake.*

**EN
ROUTE**

Colorado River Headwaters Scenic & Historic Byway. Whether you're staying in Grand Lake or merely stopping on your way to another destination, the 80-mile (one-way) Colorado River Headwaters Scenic & Historic Byway between Grand Lake and State Bridge is worth a side trip. The route takes you along the Colorado River, past hot springs, ranches, and reservoirs, through wide spaces with views of mountains, along deep canyons, and through a seemingly incongruous sage-covered desert. Follow U.S. 34 west out of Grand Lake toward Granby (about 15 miles) and take a right onto U.S. 40. Drive west on U.S. 40 to Kremmling (about 26 miles), which is a good place to fill up on gas and to get a cup of coffee or a snack before heading on. There are no facilities until the town of State Bridge. From Kremmling you continue on through an even more remote and beautiful route. Note that this route is not suitable for large RVs or buses as it is an improved dirt road rather than paved. From U.S. 40 (Park Avenue) in Kremmling, turn left onto 6th Street/Highway 9, and drive about 2¼ miles until you see Trough Road (County Road 1) on your right. This gravel road snakes along the precipices of Gore Canyon, and has several turnouts where you can get a good look at the roaring Colorado River and train tracks below. Stop by the viewing platform at the Gore Canyon Whitewater Park at Pumphouse to see paddlers and boarders playing in the waves. Follow the byway for about 26 miles to State Bridge. From there, you can loop back to Kremmling and then Grand Lake via Highways 131 and 134 and U.S. 40. ⊠ *Grand Lake* ☎ *303/757–9786.*

SPORTS AND THE OUTDOORS

BICYCLING

Willow Creek Pass. This route covers about 25 miles (one-way) from Granby and climbs 1,748 feet to the summit of one of the gentler passes on the Continental Divide, rewarding with stunning views of the Never Summer Range. The ride takes you through quiet aspen and pine forests where you'll encounter little traffic—but perhaps some moose and deer, which are often spotted just off the road. ⊠ *The route starts on U.S. 40 in Granby and then follows Hwy. 125 north for 23 miles.*

BIRD-WATCHING

The islands in Shadow Mountain Reservoir and Lake Granby are wild-life refuges that attract osprey and many other migrating birds. The best way to get close to them is by canoe or foot trail. Be sure to take binoculars, because you're not permitted to land on the islands.

East Shore Trail. Good bird-spotting opportunities await along the East Shore and Knight Ridge trails, which follow the shores of Shadow Mountain Reservoir and Lake Granby for 13 miles. Shadow Mountain Lake lies within the Arapaho National Recreation Area, and is maintained through the Sulphur Ranger District in Granby. ⊠ *Grand Lake* ✛ *Access trails either from Grand Lake between Grand Lake and Shadow Mountain Reservoir, or from Green Ridge Campground at the south end of Shadow Mountain Reservoir* ☎ *970/887–4100 Sulphur Ranger District.*

BOATING AND FISHING

OUTFITTERS **Beacon Landing Marina.** On the north shore of Lake Granby, Beacon Landing Marina rents 20-, 24-, and 25-foot pontoon boats and fishing equipment, and also winter equipment, including sleds, ice augers, and ice rods. ⊠ *1026 County Rd. 64* ✛ *Drive south 5 miles on U.S. 34 to County Rd. 64, turn left and go 1 mile* ☎ *970/627–3671* ⊕ *www. beaconlanding.us.*

Trail Ridge Marina. The Trail Ridge Marina is on the western shore of Shadow Mountain Lake, which is connected to Grand Lake by a channel. The marina rents pontoon, pleasure, and fishing boats, as well as kayaks and stand-up paddleboards. ⊠ *12634 U.S. 34* ✛ *2 miles south of Grand Lake on U.S. 34* ☎ *970/627–3586* ⊕ *www.trailridgemarina. com* ☺ *Closed Oct.–Apr.*

HIKING

A hike here can be a destination in itself: generally speaking, the trails on this side of the Continental Divide are longer than those on the Western Slope, meaning you'll trek farther and higher than you might expect to reach your destination. Many trails take you 5 miles one-way before you reach a lake or peak. If you hike in the backcountry, be prepared for adverse weather. For those who'd rather not venture quite so far, there are many shorter hikes in and around Grand Lake, all of which offer gorgeous scenery and wonderful relaxation, as the trails here tend to have fewer hikers than those near Estes Park.

7

Adams Falls. This short hike is a must-do that rewards with a gorgeous 55-foot waterfall. You can access it from the East Inlet Trailhead at the West Portal of Grand Lake. There are no dogs allowed. ⊠ *East Inlet Trailhead* ✛ *From downtown Grand Lake, drive west on W. Portal Rd. for 2½ miles.*

FAMILY **Indian Peaks Wilderness.** At the southeast end of Lake Granby, the Monarch Lake Trailhead is a popular access point for hiking to Indian Peaks Wilderness, located within the Arapaho National Recreation Area. The area around Monarch Lake is popular with families for the selection of trails and the views of the Indian Peaks and the Continental Divide. Trails range in distance from 1½ to 10¾ miles one-way. The easy **Monarch Lake Loop** is just over 3¾ miles and a mere 110 feet in elevation gain. You can get a day pass ($5) from the self-serve pay station. ⊠ *Grand Lake* ✛ *Take U.S. 34 south to County Rd. 6. Follow the lakeshore road about 10 miles* ☎ *970/887–4100* 🎟 *$5 per vehicle.*

HORSEBACK RIDING

Sombrero Ranches. The Grand Lake stable of Sombrero Ranches leads two-hour guided horseback rides along the Tonahutu Creek Trail in Rocky Mountain National Park. Sombrero can also arrange "drop camps" to deliver your backcountry gear to your campsite. ⊠ *304 W. Portal Rd.* ☎ *970/627–3514* ⊕ *www.sombrero.com* 🎟 *From $55* ☺ *Closed Sept.–May.*

NORDIC SKIING AND SNOWSHOEING

Grand Lake Metropolitan Recreation District. When snow glitters under the clear blue sky, it's time to strap on skis or snowshoes and hit the trails in Rocky Mountain National Park, the Arapaho National Recreation

Area, and Indian Peaks Wilderness. You also can stay in town: the Grand Lake Metropolitan Recreation District has nearly 22 miles (35 km) of cross-country ski trails with views of the Never Summer Range and the Continental Divide. Come summer, 15 miles of hiking and biking trails open. ✉ *1415 County Rd. 48* ☎ *970/627–8872* 🌐 *www.grandlakerecreation.com.*

Never Summer Mountain Products. Rent skis and snowshoes in the winter, or buy backpacks, tents, and other camping equipment for summer sports. Rocky Mountain National Park requires backpackers to use bear canisters (for overnight food storage), which Never Summer rents for $5 for 24 hours. ✉ *919 Grand Ave.* ☎ *970/627–3642* 🌐 *www.neversummermtn.com.*

SNOWMOBILING

Grand Lake is called the Snowmobiling Capital of Colorado, with more than 300 miles of trails (130 miles groomed), many winding through pristine forest. There are several rental and guide companies in the area. If you're visiting during the winter holidays, it's wise to make reservations about three weeks ahead. Bring a map as the trails are not always well marked.

Grand Adventures. Take a two- or four-hour guided snowmobile tour, or rent a machine and head out on your own. ✉ *304 W. Portal Rd.* ☎ *970/726–9247* 🌐 *www.grandadventures.com* 🎟 *From $55* 🕓 *Closed late spring–late fall.*

Lone Eagle Snowmobile Rental. You can rent snowmobiles here from $100 for two hours. ✉ *712-720 Grand Ave.* ☎ *970/627–3310, 800/282–3311* 🌐 *www.loneeaglelodge.com/wp/snowmobile-rental.*

On The Trail Rentals. This handy outfit a few miles northwest of town rents snowmobiles and also offers guided tours into Arapaho National Forest. During the summer, you can rent mountain bikes, ATVs, and side-by-sides here. ✉ *1447 County Rd. 491* ☎ *970/627–0171, 888/627–2429* 🌐 *www.onthetrailrentals.com* 🎟 *From $110* 🕓 *Snowmobile rental late Nov.–Mar.; ATV rental late May–Nov.*

WHERE TO EAT

$ DELI

🍴 **Cy's Deli.** The aroma of homemade bread and soup hint at the loving care this sandwich shop infuses into its food. This is a great place to grab a quick breakfast burrito or sandwich to take out on the trail. If you'd rather dine in-house, grab a table inside the cheerful blue deli, or relax on the sunny patio. [$] *Average main: $9* ✉ *717 Grand Ave.* ☎ *970/627–3354* 🌐 *www.cysdeli.com* 🕓 *Closed Nov.–mid-May.*

$ CAFÉ Fodor's Choice ★

🍴 **Fat Cat Cafe.** Located on the boardwalk, this cozy family-run café specializes in delicious breakfast and lunch at reasonable prices. The friendly owners serve up hearty helpings, as well as advice on local sightseeing. The $14.50 ($7.95 for kids) weekend breakfast buffet is downright amazing, with nearly 50 items—including biscuits and gravy, *huevos rancheros* casserole with house-made green chile sauce, and a wide selection of scones, pastries, and pies that are baked in-house. If you have to wait for a table (which you might on a summer Sunday), Fat Cat offers coffee and cinnamon rolls to tide you over. [$] *Average main: $10* ✉ *916 Grand Ave.* ☎ *970/627–0900* 🕓 *Closed Tues. No dinner.*

$ SOUTHERN Fodor'sChoice ★ 🍴 **Sagebrush BBQ & Grill.** Falling-off-the-bone, melt-in-your-mouth barbecue pork, chicken, and beef draw local and out-of-town attention to this homey café. You can munch on peanuts (and toss the shells on the floor) while dining at tables with cowhide-patterned tablecloths set against a backdrop of license plates from across the country. Comforting sides such as baked beans, corn bread, coleslaw, and potatoes top off the large plates. The breakfast menu includes omelets, pancakes, eggs Benedict, and biscuits, as well as chicken-fried steak and *huevos rancheros* platters for heartier appetites. Dinner reservations are recommended on summer weekends. [$] *Average main: $12* ✉ *1101 Grand Ave.* ☎ *970/627–1404* 🌐 *www.sagebrushbbq.com.*

WHERE TO STAY

$$ HOTEL Fodor'sChoice ★ 🏨 **Colorado Cabin Adventures.** The 1940s-era cabins at Colorado Cabin Adventures are rustic and cozy, with wood floors and trim, area rugs, stone fireplaces, slate tile bathrooms, soft Denali blankets, flat-screen televisions, full kitchens, and outdoor grills. **Pros:** lovely riverfront location; spacious grounds; comfortable, clean accommodations. **Cons:** outside town; no restaurants nearby. [$] *Rooms from: $139* ✉ *12082 U.S. Highway 34* ☎ *970/509–0810* 🌐 *www.coloradocabinadventures.com* 🛏 *13 cabins* 🍽 *No meals.*

$$ HOTEL 🏨 **Grand Lake Lodge.** Built in 1920 and on the National Register of Historic Places, this lodge is perched on the hillside overlooking Grand Lake and has 70 cabins nestled in the pines. **Pros:** stunning views of Grand Lake; historic charm; near Rocky Mountain National Park. **Cons:** service can be lacking; some rooms are small. [$] *Rooms from: $140* ✉ *15500 U.S. Highway 34* ✣ *Drive up Trail Ridge Rd. toward Rocky Mountain National Park and turn right on Tonahutu Ridge Rd.* ☎ *970/627–3967, 855/585–0004* 🌐 *www.grandlakelodge.com* ⏲ *Closed Oct.–mid-May* 🛏 *70 cabins* 🍽 *No meals.*

$ HOTEL Fodor'sChoice ★ 🏨 **Historic Rapids Lodge & Restaurant.** This handsome lodgepole-pine structure, which dates to 1915, is tucked on the banks of the Tonahutu River, and gives guests a dose of history amid a natural setting. **Pros:** in-house restaurant; condos are great for longer stays; quiet area of town. **Cons:** unpaved parking area; lodge rooms are above restaurant; all lodge rooms are on second floor and there's no elevator. [$] *Rooms from: $95* ✉ *210 Rapids La.* ☎ *970/627–3707* 🌐 *www.rapidslodge.com* ⏲ *Closed Apr. and Nov.* 🛏 *6 rooms, 9 suites, 4 cabins, 12 condos* 🍽 *No meals.*

$ HOTEL FAMILY 🏨 **Mountain Lakes Lodge.** Families and dog-lovers enjoy these comfortable, charming, whimsically decorated log cabins, which have such unique touches as cow-spotted walls, canoe-paddle headboards, and wooden ducks swimming on the ceiling. **Pros:** dog-friendly; close to fishing; good value. **Cons:** outside of town (and services); two-night minimum; no daily housekeeping. [$] *Rooms from: $99* ✉ *10480 U.S. 34* ☎ *970/627–8448* 🌐 *www.grandlakelodging.net* ⏲ *Closed for 10 days in Apr.* 🛏 *10 units, 2 houses* 🍽 *No meals.*

$$$ HOTEL 🏨 **Western Riviera Lakeside Lodging and Events.** This friendly property offers a wide variety of centrally located accommodations, including lakeside motel rooms, cabins, and condos, as well as a second block of cabins clustered around a courtyard a few blocks up the road.

7

Pros: helpful and friendly staff; lake views; clean rooms. **Cons:** rooms and bathrooms can be a little cramped; lobby is a bit small; no elevator. $ *Rooms from: $175* ⊠ *419 Garfield Ave.* ☎ *970/627–3580* ⊕ *www.westernriv.com* ⇆ *12 rooms, 2 suites, 1 apartment, 22 cabins, 3 condos* ⊙ *No meals.*

> ### GRAND LAKE LODGING ALTERNATIVES
>
> **Grand Mountain Rentals.** This family-owned property management business offers vacation rentals—some pet-friendly—in Grand Lake and the surrounding area for stays from three to 30 days. ⊠ *1028 Grand Ave.* ☎ *970/627–1131, 877/982-2155* ⊕ *www.grandmountainrentals.com* ⇆ *40 units* ⊙ *No meals.*

NIGHTLIFE AND PERFORMING ARTS

PERFORMING ARTS

Rocky Mountain Repertory Theatre. The professional Rocky Mountain Repertory Theatre stages performances of popular Broadway shows and musicals in a log cabin–style theater. ⊠ *404 Vine St.* ☎ *970/627–3421* ⊕ *www.rockymountainrep. com* ⬚ *From $35* ⊙ *Closed Oct.–May.*

NIGHTLIFE

Lariat Saloon. A local hot spot, this rustic bar has pinball, pool, and video games, plus live music on summer weekends. It's also the only spot in town for late-night eats. Look for the buffalo and dreadlock-adorned fox amid the eclectic Western decor. ⊠ *1121 Grand Ave.* ☎ *970/627–9965.*

SHOPPING

Grand Lake Art Gallery. This gallery sells photographs, original oil paintings, wood carvings, weavings, pottery, and stained glass by nearly 200 Colorado artists. ⊠ *1117 Grand Ave.* ☎ *970/627–3104* ⊕ *www. grandlakeartgallery.com.*

Humphrey's Cabin Fever. The ever-popular Humphrey's Cabin Fever, housed in a 135-year-old log building, sells an eclectic mix of upscale cabin collectibles, rustic home furnishings, clothes, bedding, and ceramics—and lots of moose-themed stuff. ⊠ *1100 Grand Ave.* ☎ *970/627–8939.*

Never Summer Mountain Products. For outdoor gear and clothing, head for Never Summer Mountain Products. ⊠ *919 Grand Ave.* ☎ *970/627–3642* ⊕ *www.neversummermtn.com.*

GRANBY

20 miles south of Grand Lake via U.S. 34.

The small, no-nonsense town of Granby (elevation 7,935 feet) serves the working ranches in Grand County, and you'll see plenty of cowboys, especially if you go to one of the weekly rodeos in summer. What the town lacks in attractions it makes up for with its views of Middle Park and the surrounding mountains of the Front and Gore ranges, and with its proximity to outdoor activities, particularly its top-class golf courses just south of town.

GETTING HERE AND AROUND

Granby is 20 minutes from Rocky Mountain National Park and 15 minutes from the ski resorts Winter Park and Mary Jane and the mountain-biking trails of the Fraser Valley.

To get here from Grand Lake, take U.S. 34 south for 20 miles. From Boulder, you'll drive about 18 miles south on CO–93, 28 miles west on I–70, then take U.S. 40 north about 46 miles. From Denver, take I–70 west (about 30 miles) to U.S. 40, then drive north about 45 miles. The town is pretty small, and you can easily find a parking spot and walk from one end to the other.

EXPLORING

Flying Heels Arena. Watch cowboys demonstrate their rodeo skills at the Flying Heels Arena, held a couple of weekends in early summer. The rodeo finale and fireworks show is on the Saturday nearest July 4. ⊠ *63032 U.S. 40, 1½ miles east of Granby* ☎ *970/887–2311* ⊕ *www.granbyrodeo.com* ⊟ *$10.*

SPORTS AND THE OUTDOORS

BIRD-WATCHING

Windy Gap Watchable Wildlife Area. On the path alongside the reservoir at Windy Gap Watchable Wildlife Area, you're likely to spot geese, pelicans, swans, eagles, killdeer, osprey, and more. The park has information kiosks, spotting scopes, viewing areas, covered picnic tables, and a nature trail that's wheelchair accessible. ⊠ *Granby* ⊹ *5 miles west of Granby on U.S. 40 where it meets Rte. 125* ☎ *970/725–6200* ⊕ *www.northernwater.org/waterprojects/howwindygapworks.aspx* ⊙ *May–Sept., daily dawn–dusk.*

FISHING

Serious fly-fishers head to the rivers and streams of Grand County. Angling on the **Fraser River** begins downstream from Tabernash, and is not appropriate for families or dogs. At **Willow Creek** you'll bag plenty of rainbow trout and brookies. The **Colorado River** between Shadow Mountain Dam and Lake Granby and downstream from Hot Sulphur Springs is also popular with anglers. See ⊕ *www.wildlife.state.co.us/fishing* for more information on fishing licenses.

GOLF

Golf Granby Ranch. Tucked back in a valley at the end of a gravel road, this Jack Nicklaus–designed course delivers beautiful views of meadows and mountains and is always in top-notch condition. It weaves through native grasses and wetlands along the meandering Poudre River. A new clubhouse debuts in summer 2016, including a restaurant and events pavilion. A cart is required on the back 9. ⊠ *2579 County Rd. 894* ⊹ *Turn off U.S. 40 onto Village Rd. Immediately after the Silver Creek Inn, turn left on Ten Mile Dr. Stay to the right on North Ranch Rd. and follow it to the clubhouse.* ☎ *970/887–2709, 888/850–4615* ⊕ *www.granbyranch.com* ⊟ *$90* ⅄ *18 holes, 6601 yards, par 70* ⬙ *Reservations essential.*

Grand Elk Golf Club. Designed by PGA great Craig Stadler, this challenging mountain course is reminiscent of traditional heathland greens in Britain yet brings its own blend of Colorado style, with expansive views of sagebrush-covered hills, aspen groves, and the Continental Divide.

The semi-private club is an excellent value compared to other Colorado mountain courses. Green fees include a cart, although it is a very walkable course. ✉ *1300 Tenmile Dr.* ☎ *970/887–9122* 🌐 *www.grandelk.com* 🎟 *$85 weekdays, $95 weekends* ⛳ *18 holes, 7144 yards, par 71* 🕒 *Closed mid-Oct.–mid-May* ✍ *Reservations essential.*

MOUNTAIN BIKING

Indian Peaks Wilderness Area is not open to mountain biking, but there are moderate and difficult trails in the **Arapaho National Forest** (☎ *970/887–4100* 🌐 *www.fs.usda.gov/arp*). In addition, Grand County has several hundred miles of easy to expert-level bike trails, many of which are former railroad rights-of-way and logging roads.

Doe Creek Trail. This roughly 3¼-mile one-way trail is a good workout of uphill climbs (and descents) with plenty of forest scenery. ✉ *Granby* ✥ *From Granby, take U.S. 34 to County Rd. 6 (Arapaho Bay Rd.) and follow it for about 3 miles. The trailhead is on your right* 🌐 *www.fs.usda.gov/recarea/arp/recreation/biking/recarea/?recid=28534&actid=50.*

SKIING AND SNOWBOARDING

FAMILY **Ski Granby Ranch.** Two miles south of Granby, this small ski area is a great place to teach the family to ski or snowboard. Terrain includes some good tree skiing, as well as beginner, intermediate, and expert runs, which all end at the same place so it's easy to keep track of your group. There's also a terrain park, as well as two Nordic-trail networks for cross-country skiing and snowshoeing. **Facilities:** 38 trails; 406 acres; 1,000-foot vertical drop; 6 lifts. ✉ *1000 Village Rd.* ☎ *888/850–4615* 🌐 *www.granbyranch.com* 🎟 *Lift ticket $61* 🕒 *Closed mid-Apr.–mid-Dec.*

WHERE TO STAY

$$$$ RESORT FAMILY 🏨 **C Lazy U Guest Ranch.** Secluded in a broad, verdant valley, this deluxe dude ranch offers a smorgasbord of activites as well as plush, Western-style accommodations with wood-paneled walls, beautiful furnishings, and bathrooms with copper sinks and custom vanities. **Pros:** kid- and family-friendly; helpful staff; deluxe in every respect. **Cons:** distant from other area attractions; no pets; very expensive. [$] *Rooms from: $3,000* ✉ *3640 Colorado Highway 125* ✥ *3½ miles north on Hwy. 125 from U.S. 40 junction* ☎ *970/887–3344* 🌐 *www.clazyu.com* 🛏 *43 rooms, 1 private house* 🍴 *All-inclusive.*

HOT SULPHUR SPRINGS

10 miles west of Granby via U.S. 40.

The county seat, Hot Sulphur Springs (population 639), is a faded resort town whose hot springs were once the destination for trains packed with people, including plenty of Hollywood types in the 1950s.

GETTING HERE AND AROUND

From Boulder, take U.S. 36 about 43 miles north to Estes Park. Take U.S. 34 west to Granby (53½ miles), then take U.S. 40 west for another 9 miles. From Fort Collins, take U.S. 287 south to Loveland (about 10 miles), then head west on U.S. 34 into Estes Park and then across Rocky Mountain National Park and into Granby (about 54 miles). Turn onto U.S. 40 and drive about 9 miles west.

You'll need a car to explore this area, as attractions, dining, and lodgings are spread out.

EXPLORING

Hot Sulphur Springs Resort & Spa. Soak or pamper yourself with a massage, wrap, or salt glow at the Hot Sulphur Springs Resort & Spa. Twenty open-air pools are sprinkled up the hillside, with temperatures ranging from 98°F to 112°F. The seasonal swimming pool is just right for recreation, at a comparatively frigid 80°F, and the resort also has four private, indoor pools (two reserved for spa treatments). Bring sandals if you have them, especially during snowy months when rock salt is used on icy walkways. ✉ *5609 County Rd. 20* ✣ *From U.S. 40, head north onto Aspen St., go left onto Grand Ave. and follow signs to the resort* ☎ *970/725–3306* 🌐 *www.hotsulphursprings.com* 🎟 *$18.50* 🕒 *Daily 8 am–10 pm.*

Pioneer Village Museum. The old Hot Sulphur Schoolhouse—built in 1924—houses the Pioneer Village Museum. Artifacts depict Grand County history dating back 8,500 years, including tools, clothing, a railroad snowplow, and the old Winter Park Ski Train caboose. The original county courthouse and jail are also on the site. ✉ *110 E. Byers Ave.* ☎ *970/725–3939* 🌐 *www.grandcountymuseum.com* 🎟 *$5* 🕒 *Tues.–Sat. 10–5.*

WHERE TO STAY

$ HOTEL 🏨 **Hot Sulphur Springs Resort & Spa.** The basic, no-nonsense rooms here have comfortable lodgepole beds and showers en suite; rates include unlimited use of the pools during your stay. **Pros:** quick access to hot pools and spa; close enough that a visit can be tacked onto an outdoor activity. **Cons:** trains passing through at night are noisy; no breakfast and most restaurants are at least 15 minutes away; very basic accommodations. [$] *Rooms from: $108* ✉ *5609 County Rd. 20* ☎ *970/725–3306* 🌐 *www.hotsulphursprings.com* 🛏 *17 rooms, 1 cabin, 1 apartment* 🍴 *No meals.*

$$$$ RESORT FAMILY 🏨 **Latigo Ranch.** Considerably more down-to-earth than other Colorado guest ranches, Latigo has a caring staff that helps create an authentic ranch experience. **Pros:** stunning scenery; quiet and secluded area; babysitting available for young children. **Cons:** no nearby restaurants or other attractions; 3-bedroom cabins have only one bathroom. [$] *Rooms from: $2,995* ✉ *County Rd. 1911* ☎ *970/724–9008, 800/227–9655* 🌐 *www.latigotrails.com* 🕒 *Closed Apr., May, Oct., and Dec.* 🛏 *10 cabins* 🍴 *All-inclusive.*

FORT COLLINS

65 miles north of Denver; 45 miles north of Boulder

The city sits on the cusp of the high plains of eastern Colorado, but is sheltered on the west by the lower foothills of the Rockies, giving residents plenty of nearby hiking and mountain biking opportunities. By plugging a couple of gaps in the foothills with dams, the city created Horsetooth Reservoir, which you can't see from town. To view the high mountains, you'll need to head up into Lory State Park or Horsetooth

Mountain Park, just west of town. A walk through Old Town Square and the neighborhoods to its south and west demonstrates Fort Collins's focus on historic preservation and the arts—music is everywhere, especially during summer.

The city was established in 1868 to protect traders from the natives, while the former negotiated the treacherous Overland Trail. After the flood of 1864 swept away Camp Collins—a cavalry post near today's town of LaPorte—Colonel Will Collins established a new camp on 6,000 acres where Fort Collins stands today. The town grew on two industries: education (Colorado State University was founded here in 1879) and agriculture (rich crops of alfalfa and sugar beets). Today there are plenty of shops and art galleries worth visiting in this relaxed university city. With more than 10 microbreweries—the most microbreweries per capita in the state—crafting ales, lagers, and stouts, as well as a Budweiser brewery, it's a fitting location for the two-day Colorado Brewers' Festival every June.

GETTING HERE AND AROUND

From Boulder, take U.S. 36 east to Interlocken Loop/Storage Tek Drive, follow for about ½ mile, then get onto Northwest Parkway for about 8½ miles. Take I–25 North for about 41 miles and get off at the Prospect Road exit. Head west on East Prospect Road for about 4 miles.

In October of 2012, Allegiant Air discontinued its service to Fort Collins/Loveland Airport (FNL), about 15 miles south of town, leaving the region without commercial flights. There's a local taxi service, and the city's bus system, Transfort, operates more than a dozen routes throughout the city, which run primarily Monday to Saturday.

Downtown is walkable, but you can also rent wheels from the city's Bike Library. There are three locations: the Hub in the Downtown Transit Center, CSU Surplus on the CSU campus, and at the Best Western University Inn.

Bike Library. At Bike Library, you can rent a bicycle to cruise around town. The $10 fee is waived if you return the bike by 1 pm the same day. Even though there are three locations, reservations are available only at The Hub and cost an extra $10, which is worthwhile on busy summer weekends. ⊠ *The Hub, 250 North Mason* ☎ *970/419–1050* ⊕ *www.fcbikelibrary.org* ☽ *Closed mid-Dec.–Mar.*

WHEN TO GO

Fort Collins's outdoor recreation and cultural pursuits attract visitors year-round, but it is definitely a college town, so expect a decidedly different atmosphere depending on whether CSU is in session.

FESTIVALS **Bohemian Nights at NewWestFest.** Fort Collins's largest community festival, this music-centered event is a proud showing of the bustling Colorado music community, which has produced the Fray, Tennis, 3OH!3, OneRepublic, Nathaniel Rateliff, and others in recent years. More than 70 bands play on five stages during the free three-day event. Bohemian Nights also hosts Thursday night concerts downtown during the summer. ⊠ *Old Town Square* ☎ *970/407–7867* ⊕ *www. bohemiannights.org.*

Colorado Brewers' Festival. During the last full weekend of June, more than 20,000 people flock to downtown Fort Collins to sample beers from more than 50 Colorado brewers at this event, which is the largest outdoor brewing festival in Colorado. You can roam the festival grounds for free, or pay $25 (in advance, or $30 same day) to sample beer. Enjoy a rotating line-up of live music by Colorado artists while you sip. ⊠ *Downtown Fort Collins – main entrance at Laporte Ave. and Mason St.* ☎ *970/484–6500* ⊕ *www.downtownfortcollins.com/events/ colorado-brewers-festival.*

ESSENTIALS

Transportation Contacts Fort Collins-Loveland Municipal Airport (FNL). ⊠ *4900 Earhart Rd., Loveland* ✈ *About 3 miles west of I–25, off S.W. Frontage Rd.* ☎ *970/962–2850* ⊕ *www.fortloveair.com.* **Fort Collins Yellow Cab.** ⊠ *Fort Collins* ☎ *970/224–2222* ⊕ *www.fortcollinstaxi.com.* **Transfort.** ⊠ *Fort Collins* ⊕ *www.ridetransfort.com.*

Visitor Information Visit Fort Collins. ⊠ *19 Old Town Sq., Suite 137* ☎ *970/232–3840, 800/274–3678* ⊕ *www.visitftcollins.com.*

EXPLORING

TOP ATTRACTIONS

Avery House. The stately sandstone Avery House was built in 1879 by Franklin Avery, who set the tone for Old Town's broad streets when he surveyed the city in 1873. You can tour the inside on weekends. The Avery House is just one of 36 sites on the Poudre Landmark Foundation's historic walking-tour map, which includes several self-guided options. ⊠ *328 W. Mountain Ave.* ☎ *970/221–0533* ⊕ *www. poudrelandmarks.com* ⊙ *Weekends 1–4.*

FAMILY **Fort Collins Museum of Discovery.** This museum entertains and informs visitors of all ages with interactive science, history, music, and natural history exhibits. The OtterBox Digital Dome Theater screens a mix of planetarium space shows and captivating educational films on its 35-foot dome screen. ⊠ *408 Mason Ct.* ☎ *970/221–6738* ⊕ *www. fcmod.org* ⊠ *$9.50* ⊙ *Tues.–Sun. 10–5, Thurs. 10–8.*

New Belgium Brewing Company. Bikes crowd the racks outside this pedal-friendly brewery, where visitors can sample the famous **Fat Tire** brand and take a free 90-minute tour. The New Belgium Brewing Company is the fourth-largest brewer of craft beer in the United States. A visit to the "mothership" (aka headquarters) allows you to taste some beers available only on-site. Tours are popular and first-come, first-served, so reserve online if you can. The brewery is north of Old Town, near Heritage Center Park. ⊠ *500 Linden St.* ☎ *970/221–0524* ⊕ *www. newbelgium.com* ⊠ *Free* ⊙ *Tours Tues.–Sat. 10–6 (7 in the summer).*

Old Town Square. In the National Historic District, Old Town Square is a bustling pedestrian zone with sculptures, fountains, and historic buildings, which house shops, galleries, jewelers, boutiques, bars, and, of course, breweries. Restaurants and cafés here have plenty of shaded outdoor seating for relaxing and watching the passing parade of people. A complete renovation of the square in 2015 injected new

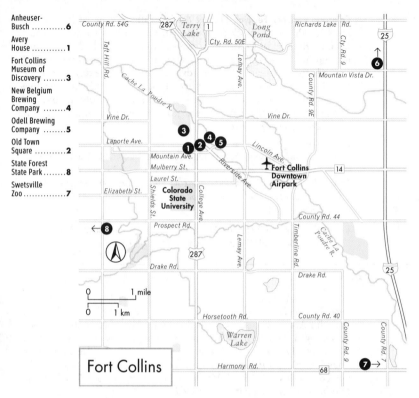

Fort Collins

life into this popular area. Musicians perform here Thursday and
Friday evenings during the summer. ✉ *Mountain and College Aves.*
☎ *970/484–6500* ⊕ *www.downtownfortcollins.com.*

WORTH NOTING

Anheuser-Busch. Learn about the large-scale Budweiser brewing process at Anheuser-Busch during one of the free tours, which start every
45 minutes and last about an hour and 15 minutes. You can also go
behind the scenes on a two-hour Brewmaster Tour ($35 per person,
reservations required). ✉ *2351 Busch Dr.* ☎ *970/490–4691* ⊕ *www.
budweisertours.com* ☉ *Oct.–Feb., Mon.–Sat. 11–6, Sun. 11–4; Mar.–
Sept., Mon–Sat. 10–6, Sun. 11–4.*

Odell Brewing Co. Take in the brewing process on a tour at Odell Brewing Company—one of the first craft breweries to open in Colorado.
Sample favorites like 90 Shilling Ale, Easy Street Wheat, and 5 Barrel Pale Ale in the taproom that was renovated in 2015 and features
long wood tables, as well as a massive outdoor patio. In winter, try
the seasonal Isolation Ale. ✉ *800 E. Lincoln Ave.* ☎ *970/498–9070,
888/887–2797* ⊕ *www.odellbrewing.com* ✉ *Free* ☉ *Tap Room: Sun.–
Tues. 11–6, Wed.–Sat. 11–7; Tours: 1–4.*

FAMILY **Swetsville Zoo.** This "zoo" is really an outdoor folk-art gallery. It is the unique creation of a former dairy farmer who has created more than 160 dinosaurs, birds, insects, and other fantastic creatures from scrap metal, car parts, and old farm equipment since 1985. ✉ *4801 E. Harmony Rd., ¼ mile east of I–25* ☎ *970/484–9509* ☉ *Daily dawn–dusk.*

OFF THE BEATEN PATH **State Forest State Park.** Rugged peaks, thick forests, and burbling streams make up this 71,000-acre park nestled in the Medicine Bow Mountains with views of the Never Summer Range. Fish for trout, boat in azure alpine lakes, ride horseback, hike or mountain bike, explore four-wheel-drive roads, or ski, snowmobile or snowshoe along miles of trails. Camping, cabins, and backcountry yurts are available year-round. ✉ *56750 Hwy. 14, Walden* ✛ *From Ft. Collins, drive 75 miles west on Rte. 14 to County Rd. 41. From Granby, take U.S. 125 north to Walden (about 53 miles), then Hwy. 14 south for about 32 miles to County Rd. 41* ☎ *970/723–8366* ⊕ *www.cpw.state.co.us/placestogo/parks/stateforest* ⊠ *$7 a day per vehicle.*

> ### NORTHERN FRONT RANGE BREWERIES
>
> The Front Range boasts several brewing firsts. In 1959 Coors, located in Golden, introduced the first beer in an aluminum can. Boulder Beer is Colorado's first microbrewery, founded in 1979. The Great American Beer Festival, which started in 1981 in Boulder (now held in Denver), was the nation's first beer festival. For a list of the operators that offer tours of local breweries as well as the individual breweries, visit ⊕ *www.colorado.com/colorado-breweries.*

SPORTS AND THE OUTDOORS

BICYCLING

Both paved-trail cycling and single-track mountain biking are within easy access of town.

For short, single-track rides, Pineridge and Maxwell trails do not disappoint, and they connect to other trails for longer adventures. Head west on Drake Road to where it bends right and becomes South Overland Trail; turn left on County Road 42C and drive almost 1 mile to the posted fence opening.

Horsetooth Mountain Park. Serious gearheads crank at Horsetooth Mountain Park on the southwest side of Horsetooth Reservoir. Several single-track and Jeep trails provide challenges. Park at the upper lot and head out on the **South Ridge Trail** to link to other trails. ✉ *6550 W. County Rd. 38E* ✛ *Drive west on Harmony Rd., which becomes County Rd. 38E. Follow for about 5 miles to park entrance.* ⊕ *www.co.larimer.co.us/parks/htmp.htm* ⊠ *$6 per vehicle.*

Poudre Trail. This paved multiple-use trail winds more than 10 miles through downtown, with several easy access points, including at the north end of Mason St. and off Linden, ¼ mile south of New Belgium. Download a map from the website. ✉ *Fort Collins* ⊕ *www.fcgov.com/parks.*

OUTFITTER

Recycled Cycles. Rent city bikes, mountain bikes, road bikes, kid trailers, and tandems here for $25–$40 per day. The company has multiple locations. ⊠ *4031-A S. Mason St.* ☎ *970/223–1969* ⊕ *www.recycledcycles.com.*

FISHING

The North Platte, Laramie, and Cache la Poudre rivers are renowned for excellent fishing. See ⊕ *www.wildlife.state.co.us/fishing* for more information on fishing licenses.

St. Peter's Fly Shop. The knowledgeable folks at this full-service fly shop in Old Town arrange half-day to full-day guided or instructional wade and float trips in northern Colorado and southern Wyoming that can include permits for waters not open to the public. The store also sells gear, and staff members gladly provide information on conditions to independent fishermen. ⊠ *202 Remington St.* ☎ *970/498–8968* ⊕ *www.stpetes.com* 🍴 *From $225 for a half day.*

GOLF

Mariana Butte Golf Course. This undulating public course in Loveland follows the banks of the Big Thompson River and delights with stunning scenery, including expansive views of mountain peaks. Designed by Dick Phelps, the course delivers plenty of challenges, skirting rock outcroppings and ponds. ⊠ *701 Clubhouse Dr., Loveland* ✛ *Go west on 1st St., take a right onto Rossum Dr. and another quick right onto Clubhouse Dr.* ☎ *970/667–8308 pro shop, 970/669–5800 tee times* 🍴 *$22 for 9 holes, $43 for 18 holes* ⅄ *18 holes, 6583 yards, par 72.*

HIKING

Horsetooth Mountain Park. Twenty-nine miles of trails in Horsetooth Mountain Park offer easy to difficult hikes, with views of the mountains to the west and the plains to the east. An easy 2¼-mile round-trip walk to **Horsetooth Falls** is a good way to explore the foothills for a couple of hours. From the upper parking area, head up the Horsetooth Falls Trail and keep right at the junction with the Soderberg Trail. Go left at the next junction to get to the falls. Arrive early, as the parking lot fills by 10 am on weekends. ⊠ *Fort Collins* ✛ *Drive west on Harmony Rd., which becomes County Rd. 38E. Follow for about 5 miles to park entrance* ☎ *970/679–4570* ⊕ *www.larimer.org/parks/htmp.htm* 🍴 *$6 per vehicle.*

Lory State Park. About 15 minutes west of downtown, Lory State Park is home to a vibrant diversity of wildlife, songbirds, and springtime wildflowers. Arrive before 10 or 11 am to avoid weekend crowds. ⊠ *708 Lodgepole Dr., Bellvue* ✛ *Drive north on Overland Trail and turn left on Bingham Hill Rd. Turn left at County Rd. 23 north, go 1¼ miles to County Rd. 25G and turn right. It's 1½ miles to park entrance* ☎ *970/493–1623* ⊕ *parks.state.co.us/Parks/lory* 🍴 *$7 per vehicle.*

Arthur's Rock Trail. For gorgeous views of the Front Range and the city from 7,000-foot Arthur's Rock, take Arthur's Rock Trail in Lory State Park. The trail climbs fast up switchbacks through sparse woods before leveling off in meadow, a welcome breather before the final steep approach to the summit. Allow about two hours to hike the trail (nearly 3½ miles round-trip and about 1,100 feet gain in elevation). ✉ *Lory State Park.*

RAFTING AND KAYAKING

The Cache la Poudre River is famous for its rapids, and river trips fill fast. It's wise to book with an outfitter at least two weeks in advance.

A-1 Wildwater Rafting. This long-standing outfitter will take you rafting on the nearby Poudre and other rivers (Clear Creek, North Platte, and the Upper Colorado). With advance notice, they can accommodate large groups. ✉ *2801 N. Shields St.* ☎ *970/224–3379* 🌐 *www.a1wildwater.com* 🎟 *From $55.*

Rocky Mountain Adventures. This outfitter offers white-water raft trips, guided fly-fishing, kayaking instruction, and gear rental. ✉ *1117 N. U.S. Hwy. 287* ☎ *970/493–4005, 800/888–6808* 🌐 *www.shoprma.com.*

WHERE TO EAT

$$ ITALIAN FAMILY

🍴 **Canino's.** Since 1976, Canino's has served hearty Italian specialties in an historic four-square house with original stained-glass windows. Tables are set in cozy wood-trim rooms with leafy burgundy carpets. The casual setting is the perfect backdrop for the menu of classic dishes, with appetizers like fried calamari, bruschetta, and steamed mussels. Entrées include traditional pasta dishes, plus favorites like chicken Marsala, veal parmigiana, and pizza, as well as plenty of seafood and vegetarian options. For dessert, indulge in the cheesecake (a Canino family recipe), or other house-made delights like cannoli, tiramisu, or gelato. The flower-rimmed patio is a nice spot to linger on summer nights. [$] *Average main: $18* ✉ *613 S. College Ave.* ☎ *970/493–7205* 🌐 *www.caninositalianrestaurant.com.*

$ PIZZA FAMILY

🍴 **Cozzola's Pizza.** At Cozzola's Pizza, you can base your pizza on thin New York–style crust, thick herb, or whole-wheat poppy-seed crust, and then select a sauce—sweet basil-tomato, fresh garlic, pesto, or spinach ricotta—and choose from the seemingly endless list of toppings that includes everything from artichoke hearts to feta cheese to smoked bacon. This roomy, family-friendly restaurant is done in rough-hewn wood and is bright and airy. At lunchtime, you can also get slices made to order with your choices of toppings. [$] *Average main: $12* ✉ *241 Linden St.* ☎ *970/482–3557* 🌐 *www.cozzolaspizza.com* ⏲ *No lunch Mon.*

$$$ CREOLE Fodor's Choice ★

🍴 **Jax Fish House & Oyster Bar.** A seafood hot spot, Jax has a hip vibe and delicious culinary creations. Dig into a plate of oysters or peel 'n' eat shrimp to start with, and then move on to seasonal combinations like potato-crusted salmon, buttermilk-fried duck confit, or the staple oyster po'boy. The restaurant also conjures up marvelous cocktails, like a cucumber-lemon press with cucumber-infused vodka, lemonade, and soda. Butcher paper–covered tables, exposed brick walls, and unique light fixtures contribute to a festive atmosphere. [$] *Average main: $25* ✉ *123 N. College Ave.* ☎ *970/682–2275* 🌐 *www.jaxfishhouse.com/fort-collins* ⏲ *No lunch.*

$$ ✕ **Rio Grande Mexican Restaurant.** Like its other Front Range brethren,
MEXICAN   the Fort Collins branch of this eight-location chain always satisfies,
with old favorites such as tacos, quesadillas, burritos, and flame-broiled shrimp fajitas, not to mention the infamous margaritas. This spacious restaurant in the heart of Old Town has exposed brick walls, hand-painted tables, and old storefront windows. When the weather is warm, it's worth the wait for a table on the inviting, enclosed patio with a giant Mexican fountain. $ *Average main: $13* ✉ *143 W. Mountain Ave.* ☎ *970/224–5428* ⊕ *www.riograndemexican.com.*

$ ✕ **Silver Grill Cafe.** This charming, historic café has soda-fountain
AMERICAN   stools, some boxy booths, and dozens of tables. Operating in its cur-
FAMILY   rent location since 1933, it spills into four dining rooms, and serves
legendary cinnamon rolls, along with a wide breakfast selection of omelets, Benedicts, biscuits and gravy, hotcakes, burritos, and grilled trout with eggs. Lunch features delicious sandwiches, soups, salads, burgers, chicken-fried steak, and other comfort foods. The café's coffee is custom roasted. Try the Café Royal, a house special that spruces up cappuccino with brown sugar, vanilla, and a lemon slice. Doors open at 6:30 for breakfast, and lunch is served until 2 pm. $ *Average main: $9* ✉ *218 Walnut St.* ☎ *970/484–4656* ⊕ *www.silvergrill. com* ☾ *No dinner.*

$ ✕ **Starry Night Espresso Café.** Espresso drinkers sip their sustenance
CAFÉ   while sitting on leather chairs or at tables under a night-blue ceiling.
Beyond breakfast, the café serves delicious quiche, salads, and sandwiches at lunch and dinnertime. For dessert, dig into decadent pastries and homemade cakes. Coffee and Crafts nights take place on the first Thursday of the month, with jewelry for sale, and live music livens things up on Friday evening. $ *Average main: $7* ✉ *112 S. College Ave.* ☎ *970/493–3039* ⊕ *www.cafestarrynight.com.*

WHERE TO STAY

$$ 🏨 **Armstrong Hotel.** For historic character in the heart of town, the Arm-
HOTEL   strong Hotel is in a 1923 building that's on the National Register of
Historic Places. **Pros:** helpful staff; downtown location; low rates for a classy, historic lodging. **Cons:** can be noisy; some rooms have limited storage space. $ *Rooms from: $149* ✉ *259 S. College Ave.* ☎ *970/484–3883, 866/384–3883* ⊕ *www.thearmstronghotel.com* ⇄ *35 rooms, 10 suites* ⦿ *No meals.*

$$$$ 🏨 **Colorado Cattle Company & Guest Ranch.** Live out your cowboy dreams
RESORT   at this real-deal working ranch, where guests stay in charming rustic
log cabins or bunkhouse rooms. **Pros:** authentic ranch experience; hot tub, pool, and sauna to soothe tired muscles; shuttle service from Denver International Airport. **Cons:** no kids allowed (minimum age is 18); a fair bit of work for a vacation; three-night minumum. $ *Rooms from: $2,199 for six nights* ✉ *70008 Weld County Rd. 132, New Raymer* ☎ *970/437–5345* ⊕ *www.coloradocattlecompany. com* ☾ *Closed mid-Oct.–Apr.* ⇄ *15 cabin and bunkhouse rooms* ⦿ *All-inclusive.*

$$ HOTEL **Edwards House.** Completely renovated in 2014, this quiet, intimate Victorian inn is impeccably furnished and just three blocks from downtown. **Pros:** on a busy but quiet street near downtown; helpful and professional staff; pleasant grounds. **Cons:** small inn; fills up quickly. [$] *Rooms from: $150* ✉ *402 W. Mountain Ave.* ☎ *970/493–9191, 800/281–9190* 🌐 *www.edwardshouse.com* 🛏 *7 rooms, 1 suite* 🍴 *Breakfast.*

$ HOTEL **La Quinta Inn Fort Collins.** For an affordable room near the highway and just 5 minutes from downtown, this chain hotel is a decent choice—bright, well maintained, and a better buy than many of its competitors. **Pros:** good value; pets welcome; near interstate for easy access. **Cons:** rather distant from dining and attractions; along busy and noisy thoroughfare. [$] *Rooms from: $120* ✉ *3709 E. Mulberry St.* ☎ *970/493–7800* 🌐 *www.lq.com* 🛏 *134 rooms, 1 suite* 🍴 *Breakfast.*

NIGHTLIFE

BARS AND CLUBS

Lucky Joe's Sidewalk Saloon. College students and young adults line the bar at Lucky Joe's Sidewalk Saloon for live music by local bands Wednesday through Saturday nights. Sunday is open-mike night. ✉ *25 Old Town Sq.* ☎ *970/493–2213* 🌐 *www.luckyjoes.com.*

Mishawaka Amphitheater. This intimate outdoor venue on the banks of the Poudre River, about 25 miles outside Fort Collins, corrals an eclectic mix of bands. Most shows are in the evening, but some are during the afternoon. Plan on reserving a shuttle from Fort Collins in advance, as parking is discouraged due to limited space along the highway. (See the Mishawaka website for details.) ✉ *13714 Poudre Canyon Hwy., Bellvue* ✥ *25 miles northwest of Fort Collins on Rte. 14* ☎ *970/482–4420* 🌐 *www.themishawaka.com.*

BREWPUBS AND MICROBREWERIES

CooperSmith's Pub & Brewery. After touring CooperSmith's brewery (by appointment only), you can enjoy a meal in the pub, which has gleaming wood floors and exposed brick walls. Or you can chow down on pizza while shooting pool across the alley at CooperSmith's Poolside. Quaff a Punjabi Pale Ale (an IPA) or one of another dozen beers on tap. ✉ *5 Old Town Sq.* ☎ *970/498–0483* 🌐 *www.coopersmithspub.com.*

SHOPPING

Alpine Arts. The family-owned Alpine Arts is the place to go for T-shirts, hats, and other souvenirs, as well as beautiful handcrafted pottery, carved wooden boxes, jewelry, and other gifts—most made by Colorado artists. ✉ *112 N. College Ave.* ☎ *970/493–1941.*

Clothes Pony and Dandelion Toys. The shopkeepers at Clothes Pony and Dandelion Toys enjoy playing with the toys as much as their young customers do. The shop carries books, CDs, imported toys, and classics like marbles, dolls, and stuffed animals, as well as adorable clothing. ✉ *111 N. College Ave.* ☎ *970/224–2866* 🌐 *www.clothespony.com.*

Nature's Own. At Nature's Own, you can browse an extensive collection of rocks, fossils, educational games, gifts, and beautiful onyx bowls. ⊠ *201 Linden St.* ☎ *970/484–9701* ⊕ *www.naturesown.com.*

Old Town Square. The historic buildings in Old Town Square and adjacent Linden Street house galleries, bookshops, cafés, brewpubs, and shops. Various Old Town art galleries host the **First Friday Gallery Walk** on the first Friday of each month—no matter the weather—with appetizers and music from 6 to 9 pm. ⊠ *College and Mountain Aves. and Jefferson St.*

Trimble Court Artisans. This co-op with more than 50 members sells paintings, jewelry, weavings, and pottery made by Colorado artists. ⊠ *118 Trimble Ct.* ☎ *970/221–0051* ⊕ *www.trimblecourt.com.*

ROCKY MOUNTAIN
NATIONAL PARK

WELCOME TO
ROCKY MOUNTAIN NATIONAL PARK

TOP REASONS TO GO

★ **Awesome ascents:**
Seasoned climbers can trek to the summit of 14,259-foot Longs Peak or attack the rounded granite domes of Lumpy Ridge. Novices can summit Twin Sisters Peaks or Mount Ida, both reaching more than 11,000 feet.

★ **Continental Divide:**
Straddle this great divide, which cuts through the western part of the park, separating water's flow to either the Pacific or Atlantic Ocean.

★ **Gorgeous scenery:**
Peer out over more than 100 lakes, gaze up at majestic mountain peaks, and soak in the splendor of lush wetlands, pine-scented woods, forests of spruce and fir, and alpine tundra in the park's four distinct ecosystems.

★ **More than 355 miles of trails:** Hike on dozens of marked trails, from easy lakeside strolls to strenuous mountain climbs.

★ **Wildlife viewing:**
Spot elk and bighorn sheep, along with moose, otters, and more than 280 species of birds.

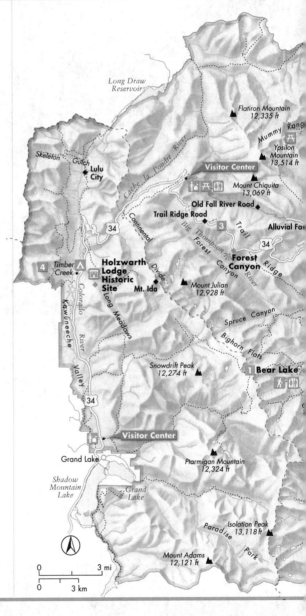

1 **Bear Lake.** One of the most photographed (and crowded) places in the park, Bear Lake is the hub for many trailheads and a major stop on the park's shuttle service.

2 **Longs Peak.** The highest peak in the park and the toughest to climb, this Fourteener pops up in many park vistas. A round-trip trek to the top takes 10 to 15 hours, so most visitors forego summit fever and opt for a (still spectacular) partial journey.

3 **Trail Ridge Road.** The alpine tundra of the park is the highlight here, as the road—the highest continuous highway in the United States—climbs to more than 12,000 feet (almost 700 feet above timberline).

4 **Timber Creek Campground.** The park's far-western area is much less crowded than most other sections, though it has its share of amenities and attractions, including evening programs, 98 camping sites, and a visitor center.

5 **Wild Basin Area.** Far from the crowds, the park's southeast quadrant consists of lovely expanses of subalpine forest punctuated by streams and lakes.

COLORADO

GETTING ORIENTED

Rocky Mountain National Park's 416-square-mile wilderness of meadows, mountains, and mirrorlike lakes lies about 70 miles from Denver. The park is roughly an eighth of the size of Yellowstone, yet it receives almost as many visitors—3 million a year.

8

KEY	
👫	Ranger Station
🔺	Campground
🛱	Picnic Area
🍴	Restaurant
🏨	Lodge
🚶	Trailhead
🚻	Restrooms
🔆	Scenic Viewpoint
-----	Walking/Hiking Trails
......	Bicycle Path

Map labels: Bighorn Mountain 11,463 ft, Black Canyon, Lumpy Ridge, Visitor Center, 34, Estes Park, Beaver Meadows, 36, 36, Moraine Park, Visitor Center and Park Headquarters, 66, 7, Sprague Lake, Glacier Basin, Bear Lake Rd., Twin Sisters Peaks, Boulder Brook, Longs Peak, Longs Peak 14,255 ft, Meeker Park, North St. Vrain Creek, 7, Wild Basin Area, Allenspark

Updated
by Lindsey
Galloway

Anyone who delights in alpine lakes, dense forests, and abundant wildlife—not to mention dizzying heights—should consider Rocky Mountain National Park. Here, a single hour's drive leads from a 7,800-foot elevation at park headquarters to the 12,183-foot apex of the twisting and turning Trail Ridge Road. More than 355 miles of hiking trails take you to the park's many treasures: meadows flush with wildflowers, cool dense forests of lodgepole pine and Engelmann spruce, and the noticeable presence of wildlife, including elk and bighorn sheep.

ROCKY MOUNTAIN PLANNER

WHEN TO GO

More than 80% of the park's annual 3 million visitors come in summer and fall. For thinner high-season crowds, come in early June or September. But there is a good reason to put up with summer crowds: only from Memorial Day to mid-October will you get the chance to make the unforgettable drive over Trail Ridge Road (note that the road may still be closed during those months if the weather turns bad).

Spring is capricious—75°F one day and a blizzard the next (March sees the most snow). June can range from hot and sunny to cool and rainy. July typically ushers in high summer, which can last through September. Up on Trail Ridge Road, it can be 15°F–20°F cooler than at the park's lower elevations. Wildlife viewing and fishing is best in any season but winter. In early fall, the trees blaze with brilliant foliage. Winter, when backcountry snow can be 4 feet deep, is the time for cross-country skiing, snowshoeing, and ice fishing.

AVG. HIGH/LOW TEMPS.

Jan.	Feb.	Mar.	Apr.	May	June
39/16	41/17	45/21	53/27	62/34	73/41

July	Aug.	Sept.	Oct.	Nov.	Dec.
78/46	76/45	70/38	60/30	46/23	40/18

FESTIVALS AND EVENTS

JUNE
FAMILY
Fiber Affair & Wool Market. Watch shearing, spinning, and sheepdog herding contests, plus angora goats, sheep, llamas, and alpacas being judged for their wool. Shop for knitting and weaving supplies as well as finished woolen items, such as hats, coats, and mittens. ⊠ *Estes Park Events Complex, 1125 Rooftop Way, Estes Park* ☎ *970/586–6104* ⊕ *www. visitestespark.com/events-calendar/special-events/wool-market.*

FAMILY **Jazz Fest & Art Walk.** Pack a picnic and bring the kids for a weekend afternoon of free jazz performances and an art walk at the outdoor theater in downtown Estes Park. ✉ *Performance Park Amphitheater, 417 W. Elkhorn Ave., Estes Park* ☎ *970/586–6104* ⊕ *www.visitestespark.com/ events-calendar/special-events/jazz-fest-and-art-walk.*

JULY **Estes Park Music Festival.** In July and August, the Colorado Music Festival Chamber Orchestra teams with the Estes Park Music Festival for a series of concerts at the historic Stanley Hotel Concert Hall ($31 for adults; children are free). Come winter, concerts featuring a variety of performances are held at 2 pm on Sunday afternoon from November through April ($7). ✉ *Stanley Hotel, 333 E. Wonderview Ave., Estes Park* ☎ *970/586–9519, 800/443–7837* ⊕ *www.estesparkmusicfestival.org.*

FAMILY **Rooftop Rodeo.** Consistently ranked one of the top small rodeos in the country (and a tradition since 1908), this six-day event features a parade and nightly rodeo events, such as barrel racing and saddle bronc riding. ✉ *Estes Park Fairgrounds, 1209 Manford Ave, Estes Park* ☎ *970/586– 6104* ⊕ *www.rooftoprodeo.com.*

SEPTEMBER– NOVEMBER FAMILY Fodor's Choice ★ **Elk Fest.** In early October, the calls of bull elk fill the forest as the animals make their way down the mountains for mating season. Estes Park celebrates with elk bugle contests, Native American music and performances, and elk educational seminars. For $5, tour buses take visitors to the best elk-viewing spots. ✉ *Bond Park, E. Elkhorn Ave. and MacGregor Ave., Estes Park* ⊕ *www.visitestespark.com/events-calendar/ special-events/elk-fest.*

Fall Back Beer Fest. In late October or early November, you can get a taste of the booming Colorado craft-beer craze and sample one of the 100 different beers created by 30 Colorado breweries at the Fall Back Beer Fest. DIYers can attend the Learn to Homebrew day, which includes equipment demonstrations and hops samples. ✉ *Estes Parks Event Complex, 1125 Rooftop Way, Estes Park* ⊕ *www.fallbackbeerfest. com* 🖃 *From $30.*

Longs Peak Scottish-Irish Highland Festival. A traditional tattoo (drum- and bugle-filled parade) kicks off this four-day fair of ancient Scottish athletic competitions, including full-armor jousting and throwing contests involving hammers and 20-foot-long, 140-pound wooden poles (called cabers). The festival also features Celtic music, Irish dancing, and events for dogs of the British Isles (such as terrier racing and sheepdog demonstrations). ✉ *Estes Park Fairgrounds, 1209 Manford Ave., Estes Park* ☎ *970/586–6308, 800/903–7837* ⊕ *www.scotfest.com.*

JANUARY FAMILY **Estes Park Winter Festival.** You'll find plenty of cures for cabin fever during this festival, including chili cook-offs, toboggan races, and ice skating. Be sure to check out the annual Winter Trails Day, which gives families the chance to try out snowshoeing equipment and learn proper techniques from instructors. ✉ *Estes Park Events Complex, 1125 Rooftop Way, Estes Park* ⊕ *www.visitestespark.com/events-calendar/ special-events/winter-festival.*

8

PLANNING YOUR TIME

ROCKY MOUNTAIN IN ONE DAY

Starting out in Estes Park, begin your day at the **Bighorn Restaurant,** a classic breakfast spot and a local favorite. While you're enjoying your short stack with apple-cinnamon-raisin topping, you can put in an order for a packed lunch (it's a good idea to bring your food with you, as dining options in the park consist of a single, seasonal snack bar at the top of Trail Ridge Road).

Drive west on U.S. 34 into the park, and stop at the **Beaver Meadows Visitor Center** to watch the orientation film and pick up a park map. Also inquire about road conditions on Trail Ridge Road, which you should plan to drive either in the morning or afternoon, depending on the weather. If possible, save the drive for the afternoon, and use the morning to get out on the trails, before the chance of an afternoon lightning storm.

For a beautiful and invigorating hike, head to Bear Lake and follow the route that takes you to **Nymph Lake** (an easy 0.5-mile hike), then onto **Dream Lake** (an additional 0.6 miles with a steeper ascent), and finally to **Emerald Lake** (an additional 0.7 miles of moderate terrain). You can stop at several places along the way. The trek down is much easier, and quicker, than the climb up. ■TIP➜ If you prefer a shorter, simpler (yet still scenic) walk, consider the Bear Lake Nature Trail, a 0.6-mile loop that is wheelchair- and stroller-accessible.

You'll need the better part of your afternoon to drive the scenic **Trail Ridge Road.** Start by heading west toward Grand Lake, stop at the lookout at the Alluvial Fan, and consider taking Old Fall River Road the rest of the way across the park. This single-lane dirt road delivers unbeatable views of waterfalls and mountain vistas. You'll take it westbound from Horseshoe Park (the cutoff is near the Endovalley Campground), then rejoin Trail Ridge Road at its summit, near the Alpine Visitor Center. If you're traveling on to Grand Lake or other points west, stay on Trail Ridge Road. If you're heading back to Estes Park, turn around and take Trail Ridge Road back (for a different set of awesome scenery). End your day with a ranger-led talk or evening campfire program.

GETTING HERE AND AROUND

AIR TRAVEL

The closest commercial airport is **Denver International Airport** (DEN). Its **Ground Transportation Information Center** (☎ *800/247–2336 or 303/342–4059 ⊕ www.flydenver.com*) assists visitors with car rentals, door-to-door shuttles, and limousine services. From the airport, the eastern entrance of the park is 80 miles (about two hours). **Estes Park Shuttle** (☎ *970/586–5151 ⊕ www.estesparkshuttle.com*; reservations essential) serves Estes Park and Rocky Mountain from both Denver International Airport and Longmont/Boulder.

CAR TRAVEL

Estes Park and Grand Lake are the Rocky Mountain's gateway communities; from these you can enter the park via U.S. 34 or 36 (Estes Park) or U.S. 34 (Grand Lake). U.S. 36 runs from Denver through Boulder, Lyons, and Estes Park to the park; the portion between Boulder and

Estes Park is heavily traveled—especially on summer weekends. Though less direct, Colorado Routes 119, 72, and 7 have much less traffic (and better scenery). If you're driving directly to Rocky Mountain from the airport, take the E–470 tollway from Peña Boulevard to I–25.

The **Colorado Department of Transportation** (for road conditions ☎ 303/639–1111 ⊕ www.cotrip.org) plows roads efficiently, but winter snowstorms can slow traffic and create wet or icy conditions. In summer, the roads into both Grand Lake and Estes Park can see heavy traffic, especially on weekends.

CAR TRAVEL WITHIN THE PARK
The main thoroughfare in the park is Trail Ridge Road (U.S. 34); in winter, it's closed from the first storm in the fall (typically in October) through the spring (depending on snowpack, this could be at any time between April and June). During that time, it's plowed only up to Many Parks Curve on the east side and the Colorado River trailhead on the west side. (For current road information: ☎ 970/586–1222 ⊕ www.coloradodot.info.)

The spectacular Old Fall River Road runs one-way between the Endovalley Picnic Area on the eastern edge of the park and the Alpine Visitor Center at the summit of Trail Ridge Road, on the western side. It is typically open from July to September, depending on snowfall. It's a steep, narrow road (no wider than 14 feet), and trailers and vehicles longer than 25 feet are prohibited, but a trip on this 90-year-old thoroughfare is well worth the effort. For information on road closures, contact the park: ☎ 970/586–1206 ⊕ www.nps.gov/romo.

SHUTTLES
Rocky Mountain has limited parking, but offers three free shuttle buses, which operate daily from 7 to 7, late May to early October. All three shuttles can be accessed from a large Park & Ride located within the park, 7 miles from the Beaver Meadows entrance. Visitors who don't want to drive into the park at all can hop on The Hiker Shuttle at the Estes Park Visitor Center. The hourly shuttle makes stops at the Beaver Meadows Visitor Center and the Park & Ride, where visitors can switch to one of the other two shuttles, which head to various trailheads. The Moraine Park Route shuttle runs every 30 minutes and stops at the Moraine Park Visitor Center and then continues on to the Fern Lake Trailhead. The Bear Lake Route shuttle runs every 15 minutes from the Park & Ride to the Bear Lake Trailhead.

TRAIN TRAVEL

Amtrak trains stop in downtown Denver, Winter Park/Fraser (80 miles away), and Granby (66 miles). ☎ 800/872–7245 ⊕ www.amtrak.com.

PARK ESSENTIALS

PARK FEES AND PERMITS

Entrance fees are $20 per automobile for a weekly pass, or $10 if you enter on bicycle, motorcycle, or foot. An annual pass costs $40.

Backcountry camping requires a permit that's $26 per party from May through October, and free the rest of the year. Visit ⊕ www.nps.gov/romo/planyourvisit/backcntry_guide.htm before you go for a planning guide to backcountry camping. You can get your permit online, by phone (☎ 970/586–1242), or in person. In person, you can get a day-of-trip permit year-round at one of the park's two backcountry offices, located next to the Beaver Meadows Visitor Center and in the Kawuneeche Visitor Center.

PARK HOURS

The park is open 24/7 year-round; some roads close in winter. It is in the mountain time zone.

CELL-PHONE RECEPTION

Cell phones work in some sections of the park, and free Wi-Fi can be accessed in and around the Beaver Meadows Visitor Center and the Kawuneeche Visitor Center.

EDUCATIONAL OFFERINGS

ART PROGRAM

Artist-in-Residence. Professional writers, sculptors, composers, and visual and performing artists can stay in a rustic cabin for two weeks in summer while working on their art. During their stay, they must make two presentations and donate a piece of original work to the park that relates to their stay. Applications must be received by November for requests for the following summer. ⊠ *Rocky Mountain National Park* ☎ *970/586–1206.*

CLASSES AND SEMINARS

FAMILY **Rocky Mountain Conservancy.** Each year, the Rocky Mountain Conservancy sponsors more than 200 hands-on field institute adventures for adults and children on such topics as natural history, fishing, geology, bird-watching, wildflower identification, wildlife biology, photography, and sketching. Classes range from lectures of a few hours to overnight and multiday camping trips. Most are fairly rigorous, incorporating hiking and other outdoor activities. All are taught by expert instructors. ⊠ *1895 Fall River Rd., Estes Park* ☎ *970/586–3262* ⊕ *rmconservancy. org* ⊡ *$10–$360 per class* ⊙ *Jan.–Oct.*

RANGER PROGRAMS

FAMILY **Junior Ranger Program.** Stop by the Junior Ranger Headquarters off Trail Ridge Road for ranger-led talks during the summer months. You can also pick up a Junior Ranger activity book (in English or Spanish) here or at any visitor center in the park. Program content has been developed for children ages 6 to 12; the material focuses on environmental education, identifying birds and wildlife, and outdoor safety skills. Once a child has completed all of the activities in the book, a ranger will look over his or her work and award a Junior Ranger badge. ⊠ *Rocky Mountain National Park* ☎ *970/586–1206* ⊕ *www.nps.gov/ romo/forkids* ⊡ *Free.*

FAMILY **Ranger Programs.** Join in on free hikes, talks, and activities conducted by those who know the park best. Topics may include wildlife, geology, vegetation, or park history. Don't miss special programs like "Skins and Things," a popular hands-on learning experience, and "Exploring with a Camera", which offers photography tips. In the evening, rangers lead twilight hikes, stargazing sessions, and storytelling around the campfire. Look for the extensive program schedule in the park's newspaper available at the main entrances. ⊠ *Rocky Mountain National Park* ☎ *970/586–1206* ⊡ *Free.*

RESTAURANTS

Restaurants in north central Colorado run the gamut from simple diners with tasty, homey basics to elegant establishments with extensive wine lists. Some restaurants take reservations, but many—particularly mid-range spots—seat on a first-come, first-served basis. In the park itself, there are no real dining establishments, though you can get snacks and light fare at the Trail Ridge Store, adjacent to the Alpine Visitor Center at the top of the Trail Ridge Road. The park also has a handful of scenic picnic areas, all with tables and pit or flush toilets.

HOTELS

Bed-and-breakfasts and small inns in north central Colorado vary from old-fashioned fluffy cottages to sleek, modern buildings with understated lodge themes. If you want some pampering, there are guest ranches and spas.

In Estes Park, Grand Lake, and other nearby towns, the elevation keeps the climate cool, and you'll scarcely need (and you'll have a tough time finding) air-conditioned lodging. For a historic spot, try the Stanley Hotel in Estes Park, which dates to 1909 and features 160 guestrooms. The park has no hotels or lodges. *Hotel reviews have been shortened. For full information, visit Fodors.com.*

WHAT IT COSTS				
	$	$$	$$$	$$$$
Restaurants	under $13	$13–$18	$19–$25	over $25
Hotels	under $121	$121–$170	$171–$230	over $230

Restaurant prices are the average cost of a main course at dinner or, if dinner is not served, at lunch. Hotel prices are the lowest cost of a standard double room in high season, excluding taxes and service charges.

TOURS

FAMILY **Green Jeep Tours.** From the back of an open-air, neon-green Jeep on these tours, you can enjoy the majestic scenery while your experienced guide points out wildlife along the way. Green Jeep Tours also offers a two-hour tour in September and October that focuses on finding elk. Admission includes the cost of the seven-day pass into the park. ⊠ *157 Moraine Ave., Estes Park* ☏ *970/577–0034* ⊕ *www.greenjeeptour.com* ⊡ *From $40.*

Rocky Mountain Rush. This company's most popular tour, the "Top of the World," takes visitors in an open-top vehicle all the way to Old Fall River Road and back down Trail Ridge. A waterfall tour and sunset valley tour offer great wildlife spottings at lower elevations. ⊠ *212 E. Elkhorn Ave., Estes Park* ☏ *970/586–8687* ⊕ *www.rockymountainrush.com* ⊡ *From $65.*

Fodor's Choice ★ **Yellow Wood Guiding.** Guided photo safaris, offered year-round, ensure visitors leave the Rocky Mountain National Park with more than just memories. Customized for either beginners or experts, the tours offer the use of professional digital cameras for visitors who don't have their own and plenty of tips on how to take animal and landscape photos.

8

Yellow Wood Guiding also offers hiking, snowshoe, and wildlife tours seasonally. ✉ *212 E. Elkhorn Ave., Estes Park* ☎ *970/586–8687* ⊕ *www.ywguiding.com* 🎫 *From $95.*

VISITOR INFORMATION

Park Contact Information Rocky Mountain National Park. ✉ *1000 U.S. 36, Estes Park* ☎ *970/586–1206* ⊕ *www.nps.gov/romo.*

VISITOR CENTERS

Alpine Visitor Center. At the top of Trail Ridge Road, this visitor center is open only when that road is navigable. The center also houses the park's only gift shop and snack bar. ✉ *Fall River Pass, at junction of Trail Ridge and Old Fall River Rds., 22 miles from Beaver Meadows entrance* ☎ *970/586–1206* ☉ *Late May–mid-June and Labor Day–Columbus Day, daily 10:30–4:30; mid-June–Labor Day, daily 9–5.*

Beaver Meadows Visitor Center. Housing the park headquarters, this visitor center was designed by students of the Frank Lloyd Wright School of Architecture at Taliesin West using the park's popular rustic style, which integrates buildings into their natural surroundings. Completed in 1966, it was named a National Historic Landmark in 2001. The surrounding utility buildings are noteworthy examples of the rustic-style buildings that the Civilian Conservation Corps constructed during the Depression. The center has a terrific 20-minute orientation film and a large relief map of the park. ✉ *U.S. 36, 3 miles west of Estes Park and 1 mile east of Beaver Meadows Entrance Station* ☎ *970/586–1206* ☉ *Daily 8–4:30.*

FAMILY **Fall River Visitor Center.** The Discovery Room, which houses everything from old ranger outfits to elk antlers, coyote pelts, and bighorn sheep skulls for hands-on exploration, is a favorite with kids at this visitor center. ✉ *U.S. 34, at the Fall River Entrance Station* ☎ *970/586–1206* ☉ *Daily 9–5.*

FAMILY **Kawuneeche Visitor Center.** The only visitor center on the park's far west side, Kawuneeche has exhibits on the plant and animal life of the area, as well as a large three-dimensional map of the park and an orientation film. ✉ *U.S. 34, 1 mile north of Grand Lake and ½ mile south of Grand Lake Entrance Station* ☎ *970/586–1206* ☉ *Daily 8–4:30.*

EXPLORING

SCENIC DRIVES

Bear Lake Road. This 23-mile round-trip drive offers superlative views of Longs Peak (14,259-foot summit) and the glaciers surrounding Bear Lake, winding past shimmering waterfalls shrouded with rainbows. You can either drive the road yourself (open year-round) or hop on one of the park's free shuttle buses. ✉ *Runs from the Beaver Meadow Entrance Station to Bear Lake.*

Old Fall River Road. Nearly 100 years old and never more than 14 feet wide, this road stretches for 11 miles, from the park's east side to the Fall River Pass (11,796 feet above sea level) on the west. The drive

CLOSE UP

Plants and Wildlife in Rocky Mountain

Volcanic uplifts and the savage clawing of receding glaciers created Rocky Mountain's majestic landscape. You'll find four distinct ecosystems here—a riparian (wetland) environment with 150 lakes and 450 miles of streams; verdant montane valleys teeming with proud ponderosa pines and lush grasses; higher and colder subalpine mountains with wind-whipped trees (krummholz) that grow at right angles; and harsh, unforgiving alpine tundra with dollhouse-size versions of familiar plants and wildflowers. Alpine tundra is seldom found outside the Arctic, yet it makes up one-third of the park's terrain. Few plants can survive at this elevation of 11,000–11,500 feet, but many beautiful wildflowers—including alpine forget-me-nots—bloom here briefly in late June or early July.

The park has so much wildlife that you can often enjoy prime viewing from the seat of your car. Fall, when many animals begin moving down from higher elevations, is an excellent time to spot some of the park's animal residents. This is also when you'll hear the male elk bugle mating calls (popular spots to see and hear bugling elk are Kawuneeche Valley, Horseshoe Park, Moraine Park, and Upper Beaver Meadows).

May through mid-October is the best time to see the bighorn sheep that congregate in the Horseshoe Park/ Sheep Lakes area, just past the Fall River entrance. If you want to glimpse a moose, try Kawuneeche Valley. Other animals in the park include mule deer, squirrels, chipmunks, pikas, beavers, and marmots. Common birds include broad-tailed and rufous hummingbirds, peregrine falcons, woodpeckers, mountain bluebirds, and Clark's nutcracker, as well as the white-tailed ptarmigan, which live year-round on the alpine tundra.

Mountain lions, black bears, and bobcats also inhabit the park but are rarely seen by visitors. Altogether, the park is home to roughly 60 species of mammals and 280 bird species.

provides spectacular views and a few white-knuckle moments, as the road is steep, serpentine, and lacking in guardrails. Start at West Horseshoe Park, which has the park's largest concentrations of sheep and elk, and head up the gravel road, passing Chasm Falls (there are a few places to park for a quick hike). ⊠ *Runs north of and roughly parallel to Trail Ridge Road, starting near Endovalley Campground (on east) and ending at Fall River Pass/Alpine Visitor Center (on west)* ☉ *July–Oct.*

Fodor's Choice **Trail Ridge Road.** This is the park's star attraction and the world's high-
★ est continuous paved highway, topping out at 12,183 feet. The 48-mile road connects the park's gateways of Estes Park and Grand Lake. The views around each bend—of moraines and glaciers, and craggy hills framing emerald meadows carpeted with columbine and Indian paintbrush—are truly awesome. As it passes through three ecosystems—montane, subalpine, and arctic tundra—the road climbs 4,300 feet in elevation. As you drive the road, take your time at the numerous turnouts to gaze over the verdant valleys, brushed with yellowing aspen in fall, that slope between the glacier-etched granite peaks.

Rainbow Curve affords views of nine separate mountain peaks, each more than 10,000 feet high, and of the **Alluvial Fan**, a 42-acre swath of rocks and boulders (some the size of cars) left behind after an earthen dam broke in 1982. You can complete a one-way trip across the park on Trail Ridge Road in two hours, but it's best to give yourself three or four hours to allow for leisurely breaks at the overlooks. Note that the middle part of the road closes with the first big snow (typically by mid-October) and most often reopens around Memorial Day, though you can still drive up about 10 miles from the west and 8 miles from the east. ⊠ *Trail Ridge Rd. (U.S. 34), runs between Estes Park and Grand Lake* ☉ *June–mid-Oct.*

HISTORIC SITES

Rocky Mountain has more than 1,000 archaeological sites and 150 buildings of historic significance; 47 of the buildings are listed in the National Register of Historic Places, which is reserved for structures that tie in strongly to the park's history in terms of architecture, archaeology, engineering, or culture. Most buildings at Rocky Mountain are done in the rustic style, a design preferred by the National Park Service's first director, Stephen Mather, that works to incorporate nature into these man-made structures.

FAMILY **Holzwarth Historic Site.** A scenic ½-mile interpretive trail leads you over the Colorado River to the original dude ranch that the Holzwarth family, some of the park's original homesteaders, ran between the 1920s and 1950s. Allow about an hour to view the buildings—including a dozen small guest cabins—and chat with a ranger. Though the site is open year-round, the inside of the buildings can be seen only in summer. It's a great place for families to learn about homesteading. ⊠ *Off U.S. 34, about 8 miles north of Kawuneeche Visitor Center, Estes Park.*

Lulu City. The remains of a few cabins are all that's left of this one-time silver-mining town, established around 1880. Reach it by hiking the 3.6-mile Colorado River Trail. Look for wagon ruts from the old Stewart Toll Road and mine tailings in nearby Shipler Park (this is also a good place to spot moose). The Colorado River is a mere stream at this point, flowing south from its headwaters at nearby La Poudre Pass. ⊠ *Off Trail Ridge Rd., 9½ miles north of Grand Lake Entrance Station.*

SCENIC STOPS

Bear Lake. Thanks to its picturesque location, easy accessibility, and the good hiking trails nearby, this small alpine lake below Flattop Mountain and Hallett Peak is one of the most popular destinations in the park. Free park shuttle buses can take you there May through October. ⊠ *Bear Lake Rd., 7 miles southwest of Moraine Park Visitor Center, off U.S. 36.*

Forest Canyon Overlook. Park at a dedicated lot to disembark on a wildflower-rich, 0.2-mile trail. Easy to access for all skill levels, this glacial valley overlook offers views of ice-blue pools (the Gorge Lakes) framed by ragged peaks. ⊠ *Trail Ridge Rd., 6 miles east of Alpine Visitor Center.*

Wild Basin Area. This section in the southeast region of the park consists of lovely expanses of subalpine forest punctuated by streams and lakes. The area's high peaks, along the Continental Divide, are not as easily accessible as those in the vicinity of Bear Lake; hiking to the base of the divide and back makes for a long day. Nonetheless, a visit here is worth the drive south from Estes Park, and because the Wild Basin trailhead is set apart from the park hub, crowding isn't a problem. ⊠ *Off Rte. 7, 13 miles south of Estes Park.*

> **ELK BUGLING**
>
> In September and October, there are traffic jams in the park as people drive up to listen to the elk bugling. Rangers and park volunteers keep track of where the elk are and direct visitors to the mating spots. The bugling is high-pitched, and if it's light enough, you can see the elk put his head in the air.

SPORTS AND THE OUTDOORS

BIRD-WATCHING

Spring and summer, early in the morning, are the best times for bird-watching in the park. **Lumpy Ridge** is a nesting ground for several kinds of birds of prey. Migratory songbirds from South America have summer breeding grounds near the **Endovalley Picnic Area.** The **alpine tundra** is habitat for white-tailed ptarmigan. The **Alluvial Fan** is the place for viewing broad-tailed hummingbirds, hairy woodpeckers, ouzels, and the occasional raptor.

FISHING

Rocky Mountain is a wonderful place to fish, especially for trout—German brown, brook, rainbow, cutthroat, and greenback cutthroat—but check at a visitor center about regulations and information on specific closures, catch-and-release areas, and limits on size and possession. No fishing is allowed at Bear Lake. To avoid the crowds, rangers recommend angling in the more-remote backcountry. To fish in the park, anyone 16 and older must have a valid Colorado fishing license, which you can obtain at local sporting-goods stores. See ⊕ *www.wildlife.state. co.us/fishing* for details.

TOURS AND OUTFITTERS

Estes Angler. This popular fishing guide arranges four-, six-, and eight-hour fly-fishing trips—as well as full-day horseback excursions—into the park's quieter regions, year-round, with a maximum of three people per guide. The best times for fishing are generally from April to mid-November. Equipment is also available for rent. ⊠ *338 W. Riverside Dr., Estes Park* ☎ *970/586–2110, 800/586–2110* ⊕ *www.estesangler. com* ⊠ *From $125* ☉ *Daily 8–6.*

Kirks Fly Shop. This Estes Park outfitter offers various guided fly-fishing trips, as well as backpacking, horseback, and llama pack trips. The store also carries fishing and backpacking gear. ✉ *230 E. Elkhorn Ave., Estes Park* ☎ *970/577–0790, 877/669–1859* ⊕ *www.kirksflyshop.com* 🖬 *From $50* ⊗ *Daily 7–7.*

Scot's Sporting Goods. This shop rents and sells fishing gear, and provides four-, six-, and eight-hour instruction trips daily from May through mid-October. Clinics, geared toward first-timers, focus on casting, reading the water, identifying insects for flies, and properly presenting natural and artificial flies to the fish. Half-day excursions into the park are available for three or more people. A range of camping and hiking equipment is also for sale. ✉ *870 Moraine Ave., Estes Park* ☎ *970/586–2877 May–Sept., 970/443–4932 Oct.–Apr.* ⊕ *www. scotssportinggoods.com* 🖬 *From $210* ⊗ *June–Aug., daily 8–8; May and Sept.–mid-Oct., daily 9–5.*

HIKING

Fodor's Choice
★

Rocky Mountain National Park contains more than 355 miles of hiking trails, so you could theoretically wander the park for weeks. Most visitors explore just a small portion of these trails—those that are closest to the roads and visitor centers—which means that some of the park's most accessible and scenic paths can resemble a backcountry highway on busy summer days. The high-alpine terrain around Bear Lake is the park's most popular hiking area, and although it's well worth exploring, you'll get a more frontierlike experience by hiking one of the trails in the less-explored sections of the park, such as the far northern end or in the Wild Basin area to the south.

Keep in mind that trails at higher elevations may have some snow on them, even in late summer. And because of afternoon thunderstorms on most summer days, an early morning start is highly recommended: the last place you want to be when a storm approaches is on a peak or anywhere above the tree line. All trail mileages are round-trip unless stated otherwise.

EASY

Bear Lake Trail. The virtually flat nature trail around Bear Lake is an easy, 0.6-mile loop that's wheelchair and stroller accessible. Sharing the route with you will likely be plenty of other hikers as well as songbirds and chipmunks. *Easy.* ✉ *Trailhead at Bear Lake, Bear Lake Rd.*

FAMILY **Copeland Falls.** The 0.3-mile hike to these Wild Basin Area falls is a good option for families, as the terrain is relatively flat (there's only a 15-foot elevation gain). *Easy.* ✉ *Trailhead at Wild Basin Ranger Station.*

East Inlet Trail. An easy hike of 0.3 miles from East Inlet trailhead, just outside the park in Grand Lake, will get you to **Adams Falls** in about 15 minutes. The area around the falls is often packed with visitors, so if you have time, continue east to enjoy more solitude, see wildlife, and catch views of **Mount Craig** from near the East Meadow campground. Note, however, that the trail beyond the falls has an elevation gain of between 1,500 and 1,900 feet, making it a more challenging hike. *Easy.*

Trailhead at East Inlet, end of W. Portal Road (CO 278) in Grand Lake, Grand Lake.

Fodor'sChoice ★ **Glacier Gorge Trail.** The 2.8-mile hike to **Mills Lake** can be crowded, but the reward is one of the park's prettiest lakes, set against the breathtaking backdrop of Longs Peak, Pagoda Mountain, and the Keyboard of the Winds. There's a modest elevation gain of 750 feet. On the way, about 1 mile in, you pass **Alberta Falls,** a popular destination in and of itself. The hike travels along Glacier Creek, under the shade of a subalpine forest. Give yourself at least four hours for hiking and lingering. *Easy.* *Trailhead off Bear Lake Rd., about 1 mile southeast of Bear Lake.*

Sprague Lake. With virtually no elevation gain, this 0.5-mile, pine-lined looped path near a popular backcountry campground is wheelchair accessible and provides views of Hallet Peak and Flattop Mountain. *Easy.* *Trailhead at Sprague Lake, Bear Lake Rd., 4½ miles southwest of Moraine Park Visitor Center.*

> **FREE PARK SHUTTLE BUSES**
>
> Free hiker shuttle buses connect the Estes Park Visitor Center, the Beaver Meadows Visitor Center, and a large Park & Ride facility. From the Park & Ride facility, two additional shuttle routes run through Moraine Park or Bear Lake, with stops at Cub Lake, Fern Lake, Glacier Gorge Junction, and Bear Lake trailheads. Buses run daily between late May and early October, from 7 to 7. The hiker shuttle runs hourly during off times, and every half hour during peak times. The Bear Lake shuttle runs every 15 minutes and the Moraine Park shuttle runs every 30 minutes.

MODERATE

Fodor'sChoice ★ **Bear Lake to Emerald Lake.** This scenic, calorie-burning hike begins with a moderately level, 0.5-mile journey to **Nymph Lake.** From here, the trail gets steeper, with a 425-foot elevation gain, as it winds around for 0.6 miles to **Dream Lake.** The last stretch is the most arduous part of the hike, an almost all-uphill 0.7-mile trek to lovely **Emerald Lake,** where you can perch on a boulder and enjoy the view. All told, the hike is 3.6 miles, with an elevation gain of 605 feet. Allow two hours or more, depending on stops. *Moderate.* *Trailhead at Bear Lake, off Bear Lake Rd., 8 miles southwest of the Moraine Park Visitor Center.*

Cub Lake. This 4.6-mile, three-hour (round-trip) hike takes you through meadows and stands of aspen trees and up 540 feet in elevation to a lake with water lilies. *Moderate.* *Trailhead at Cub Lake, about 1¾ miles from Moraine Park Campground.*

Colorado River Trail. This walk to the ghost town of Lulu City on the west side of the park is excellent for looking for the bighorn sheep, elk, and moose that reside in the area. Part of the former stagecoach route that went from Granby to Walden, the 3.7-mile trail parallels the infant Colorado River to the meadow where Lulu City once stood. The elevation gain is 350 feet. *Moderate.* *Trailhead at Colorado River, off Trail Ridge Rd., 1¾ miles north of the Timber Creek Campground.*

8

Bear Lake Region

Fern Lake Trail. Heading to Odessa Lake from the north involves a steep hike, but on most days you'll encounter fewer other hikers than if you had begun the trip at Bear Lake. Along the way, you'll come to the Arch Rocks; the Pool, an eroded formation in the Big Thompson River; two waterfalls; and Fern Lake (3.8 miles from your starting point). Less than a mile farther, Odessa Lake itself lies at the foot of Tourmaline Gorge, below the craggy summits of Gabletop Mountain, Little Matterhorn, Knobtop Mountain, and Notchtop Mountain. For a full day of spectacular scenery, continue past Odessa to Bear Lake (9 miles total), where you can pick up the shuttle back to the Fern Lake Trailhead. *Moderate.* ⊠ *Trailhead off Fern Lake Rd., about 2½ miles south of Moraine Park Visitor Center.*

DIFFICULT

Chasm Lake Trail. Nestled in the shadow of Longs Peak and Mount Meeker, Chasm Lake offers one of Colorado's most impressive backdrops, which also means you can expect to encounter plenty of other hikers on the way. The 4.2-mile Chasm Lake Trail, reached via the Longs Peak Trail, has a 2,360-foot elevation gain. Just before the lake, you'll need to climb a small rock ledge, which can be a bit of a challenge for the less sure-footed; follow the cairns for the most straightforward route. Once atop the ledge, you'll catch your first memorable view of

CLOSE UP

Longs Peak: The Northernmost Fourteener

At 14,259 feet above sea level, **Longs Peak** has long fascinated explorers to the region. Explorer and author Isabella L. Bird wrote of it, "It is one of the noblest of mountains, but in one's imagination it grows to be much more than a mountain. It becomes invested with a personality."

It was named after Major Stephen H. Long, who led an expedition in 1820 up the Platte River to the base of the Rockies. Long never ascended the mountain—in fact, he didn't even get within 40 miles of it—but a few decades later, in 1868, the one-armed Civil War veteran John Wesley Powell climbed to its summit.

Longs Peak is the northernmost of the Fourteeners—the 54 mountains in Colorado that reach above the 14,000-foot mark—and one of more than 114 named mountains in the park that are higher than 10,000 feet. The peak, in the park's southeast quadrant, has a distinctive flat-topped, rectangular summit that is visible from many spots on the park's east side and on Trail Ridge Road.

The ambitious climb to Longs summit is only recommended for those who are strong climbers and well acclimated to the altitude. If you're up for it, be sure to begin before dawn so that you're down from the summit when the typical afternoon thunderstorm hits.

the lake. *Difficult.* ✉ *Trailhead at Longs Peak Ranger Station, off Rte. 7, 10 miles from the Beaver Meadows Visitor Center.*

Deer Mountain Trail. This 6-mile round-trip trek to the top of 10,083-foot Deer Mountain is a great way for hikers who don't mind a bit of a climb to enjoy the views from the summit of a more manageable peak. You'll gain more than 1,000 feet in elevation as you follow the switchbacking trail through ponderosa pine, aspen, and fir trees. The reward at the top is a panoramic view of the park's eastern mountains. *Difficult.* ✉ *Trailhead at Deer Ridge Junction, about 4 miles west of Moraine Park Visitor Center, U.S. 34 at U.S. 36.*

Longs Peak Trail. Climbing this 14,259-foot mountain (one of 53 "Four-teeners" in Colorado) is an ambitious goal for almost anyone—but only those who are very fit and acclimated to the altitude should attempt it. The 16-mile round-trip climb requires a predawn start (3 am is ideal), so that you're off the summit before the typical summer afternoon thunderstorm hits. Also, the last 2 miles or so of the trail are very exposed—you have to traverse narrow ledges with vertigo-inducing drop-offs. That said, summiting Longs can be one of the most reward-ing experiences you'll ever have. The Keyhole route is the most popular means of ascent, and the number of people going up it on a summer day can be astounding, given the rigors of the climb. Though just as scenic, the Loft route, between Longs and Mount Meeker from Chasm Lake, is less crowded but not as clearly marked and therefore more difficult to navigate. *Difficult.* ✉ *Trailhead at Longs Peak Ranger Station, off Rte. 7, 10 miles from Beaver Meadows Visitor Center.*

8

Best Campgrounds in Rocky Mountain

CLOSE UP

The park's five campgrounds accommodate campers looking to stay in a tent, trailer, or RV (only three campgrounds accept reservations—up to six months in advance at ⊕ www.recreation.gov or ⊕ www.reserveamerica.com; the others fill up on a first-come, first-served basis).

Aspenglen Campground. This quiet, eastside spot near the north entrance is set in open pine woodland along Fall River. There are a few excellent walk-in sites for those who want to pitch a tent away from the crowds but still be close to the car. Reservations are recommended in summer. ✉ *Drive past Fall River Visitor Center on U.S. 34 and turn left at the campground road.*

Glacier Basin Campground. This spot offers expansive views of the Continental Divide, easy access to the free summer shuttles to Bear Lake and Estes Park, and ranger-led evening programs in the summer. Reservations are essential. ✉ *Drive 5 miles south on Bear Lake Rd. from U.S. 36.* ☎ *877/444-6777.*

Longs Peak Campground. Open May to November, this campgound is only a short walk from the Longs Peak trailhead, making it a favorite among hikers looking to get an early start there. The tent-only sites, which are first-come, first-served, are limited to eight people; firewood, lighting fluid, and charcoal are sold in summer. ✉ *9 miles south of Estes Park on Rte. 7.*

Moraine Park Campground. The only campground in Rocky Mountain open year-round, this spot connects to many hiking trails and has easy access to the free summer shuttles. Rangers lead evening programs in the summer. You'll hear elk bugling if you camp here in September or October. Reservations are essential from mid-May to late September. ✉ *Drive south on Bear Lake Rd. from U.S. 36, 1 mile to campground entrance.*

Timber Creek Campground. Anglers love this spot on the Colorado River, 10 miles from Grand Lake village and the only east-side campground. In the evening you can sit in on ranger-led campfire programs. The 98 campsites are first-come, first-served. ✉ *1 Trail Ridge Rd., 2 miles west of Alpine Visitor Center.*

Backcountry Camping, Rocky Mountain National Park. Experienced hikers can camp at one of the park's many designated backcountry sites with advance reservations or a day-of-trip permit (which comes with a $26 fee in May through October). Contact the Backcountry Permits office before starting out to get a sense of current conditions. ✉ *Beaver Meadows Visitor Center, Kawuneeche Visitor Center* ☎ *970/586-1242.*

ROCK CLIMBING

Expert rock climbers as well as novices can try hundreds of classic and big wall climbs here (there's also ample opportunity for bouldering and mountaineering). The burgeoning sport of ice climbing also thrives in the park. The Diamond, Lumpy Ridge, and Petit Grepon are the places for serious rock climbing, while well-known ice-climbing spots include Hidden Falls, Loch Vale, and Emerald and Black lakes.

TOURS AND OUTFITTERS

FAMILY **Colorado Mountain School.** Guiding climbers since 1877, Colorado
Fodor's Choice Mountain School is an invaluable resource for climbers in the Rocky
★ Mountain area (they're also the park's only official provider of technical climbing services). They can teach you rock climbing, mountaineering, ice climbing, avalanche survival, and many other skills. Take introductory half-day and one- to five-day courses on climbing and rappelling technique, or sign up for guided introductory trips, full-day climbs, and longer expeditions. Make reservations a month in advance for summer climbs. ⊠ *341 Moraine Ave., Estes Park* ☎ *800/836–4008, 303/447–2804* ⊕ *coloradomountainschool.com* ▣ *From $90.*

WINTER SPORTS

Each winter, the popularity of snowshoeing in the park increases. It's a wonderful way to experience Rocky Mountain's majestic winter side, when the jagged peaks are softened with a blanket of snow and the summer hordes are nonexistent. You can snowshoe any of the summer hiking trails that are accessible by road; many of them also become well-traveled cross-country-ski trails. Two trails to try are Tonahutu Creek Trail (near Kawuneeche Visitor Center) and the Colorado River Trail to Lulu City (start at the Timber Creek Campground).

Backcountry skiing within the park ranges from gentle cross-country outings to full-on, experts-only adventures down steep chutes and open bowls. Ask a ranger about conditions, and gear up as if you were spending the night. If you plan on venturing off trail, take a shovel, probe pole, and avalanche transceiver. Only on the west side of the park are you permitted to snowmobile, and you must register at Kawuneeche Visitor Center before traveling the unplowed section of Trail Ridge Road up to Milner Pass. Check the park newspaper for ranger-guided tours.

TOURS AND OUTFITTERS

Estes Park Mountain Shop. You can rent or buy snowshoes and skis here, as well as fishing, hiking, and climbing equipment. The store is open year-round and gives four-, six-, and eight-hour guided snowshoeing, fly-fishing, and climbing trips to areas in and around Rocky Mountain National Park. ⊠ *2050 Big Thompson Ave., Estes Park* ☎ *970/586–6548, 866/303–6548* ⊕ *www.estesparkmountainshop. com* ▣ *From $54.*

Never Summer Mountain Products. This well-stocked shop sells and rents all sorts of outdoor equipment, including cross-country skis, hiking gear, kayaks, and camping supplies. ⊠ *919 Grand Ave., Grand Lake* ☎ *970/627–3642* ⊕ *www.neversummermtn.com.*

8

WHAT'S NEARBY

NEARBY TOWNS

Estes Park, 5 miles east of Rocky Mountain, is the park's most popular gateway. The town sits at an altitude of more than 7,500 feet, with 14,259-foot Longs Peak and a legion of surrounding mountains as its stunning backdrop. Many of the small hotels lining the roads are mom-and-pop outfits that have been passed down through several generations.

Estes Park's quieter cousin, **Grand Lake,** 1½ miles outside the park's west entrance, gets busy in summer, but has a low-key, quintessentially Western graciousness. In winter, it's *the* snowmobiling and ice-fishing destination for Front Range Coloradans. At the park's southwestern entrance are the Arapaho and Roosevelt National Forests, Arapaho National Recreational Area, and the small town of **Granby,** the place to go for big-game hunting and mountain biking. There are also skiing and other mountain activities (both summer and winter varieties) at nearby SolVista Basin and the Winter Park/Mary Jane ski areas.

WHERE TO EAT

IN THE PARK

$ AMERICAN 🍴 **Cafe at Trail Ridge.** The park's only source for food, this small café offers snacks, sandwiches, hot dogs, and soups. A coffee bar also serves fair-trade coffee, espresso drinks, and tea, plus water, juice, and salads. The café is in the same building as the Trail Ridge Store, adjacent to the Alpine Visitor Center, and is open seasonally, whenever Trail Ridge Road is open. [$] *Average main: $7* ✉ *Trail Ridge Rd., at Alpine Visitor Center* ☎ *970/586–3097* 🌐 *www.trailridgegiftstore.com* 🕒 *Closed mid-Oct.–mid-May. No dinner.*

PICNIC AREAS

Endovalley. With 32 tables and 30 fire grates, this is the largest picnic area in the park. Here, you'll find aspen groves, nice views of Fall River Pass—and lovely Fan Lake a short hike away. ✉ *Off U.S. 34, at beginning of Old Fall River Rd., about 4½ miles from Fall River Visitor Center.*

Hollowell Park. In a meadow near Mill Creek, this lovely spot for a picnic has 10 tables and is open year-round. It's also close to the Hollowell Park and Mill Creek Basin Trailheads. ✉ *Off Bear Lake Rd., about 2½ miles from Moraine Park Visitor Center.*

FAMILY **Sprague Lake.** With 27 tables and 16 pedestal grills, there's plenty of room for the whole gang at this alfresco dining spot. It's open year-round, with flush toilets in the summer and vault toilets the rest of the year. ✉ *About ½ mile from intersection of Bear Lake Rd. and U.S. 36, 4 miles from Bear Lake.*

NORTHWEST COLORADO AND STEAMBOAT SPRINGS

Updated by
Kyle Wagner

Varied terrain attracts bold outdoors enthusiasts, and genteel towns are tucked among the craggy cliffs for those seeking quieter pursuits. Whatever your choice, the northwest region's more remote location and mountain-dominated landscape give it a largely undiscovered feel, and many of the activities lack the crowds and frenzy attached to those in more heavily populated areas.

Adventures in these far-western and northern regions of the state might range from a bone-jarring mountain-bike ride on Kokopelli's Trail—a 142-mile route through remote desert sandstone and shale canyon from Grand Junction to Moab—to a heart-pounding raft trip down the Green River, where Major John Wesley Powell made his epic exploration of this continent's last uncharted wilderness in 1869. Colorado National Monument and Dinosaur National Monument have endless opportunities for hiking. For the less adventurous, a visit to the wine country makes for a relaxing afternoon, or try your hand at excavating prehistoric bones from a dinosaur quarry. Rich in more recent history as well, the area is home to the Museum of Western Colorado and Escalante Canyon, named after Spanish missionary explorer Francisco Silvestre Velez de Escalante, who with Father Francisco Atanasio Dominguez led an expedition through the area in 1776.

Farther east, flanked by mountains with some of the softest snow in the world, even the cowboys don skis. Steamboat Springs is Colorado at its most authentic, where hay bales and cattle crowd pastures, McMansions are regarded with disdain, high-schoolers compete in local rodeos, deer hang from front porches during hunting season, and high fashion means clean jeans. Steamboat Ski Resort has none of the pretensions of the glitzier Colorado resorts.

Even the less visited corners of the region have plenty of cultural opportunities for those willing to seek them out. Dotting the area are art galleries, antiques shops, and many small eateries with alfresco seating. People are friendly and share plenty of tourist tips just for the asking. As for quirky festivals, you might have a hard time choosing between the Olathe Sweet Corn Festival, Country Jam, or the Mike the Headless Chicken Festival. The laid-back lifestyle here is the perfect example to follow—chill out and explore the region at your own pace.

TOP REASONS TO GO

Colorado National Monument:
Gaze out over Grand Junction
toward the Book Cliffs along the
23-mile Rim Rock Drive or hike one
of the many trails through sandstone canyons.

Dinosaur National Monument:
Wander among thousands of
fossilized skeletons that remain
embedded in the rugged hillsides
or take a raft trip down the Green
or Yampa rivers.

**Grand Junction and Palisade wine
tasting:** More than two dozen local

wineries have garnered attention
for their grapes grown in the unique
high-altitude soil.

**Steamboat Springs horseback
riding:** Choose from an authentic
dude ranch experience, a pack trip
into the wilderness, or a gentle
alpine trail ride.

Strawberry Park Hot Springs:
Though it takes some work to get
here, it's well worth the effort to
soak away what ails you in the
rustic, rock-lined setting.

ORIENTATION AND PLANNING

GETTING ORIENTED

A little planning goes a long way when visiting this region. Grand Junction, the largest city between Denver and Salt Lake City, makes an ideal hub for exploring. Many of the sights, except for Steamboat Springs, are less than two hours from Grand Junction. You can make the loop from Delta to Cedaredge and Grand Mesa to Palisade easily in a day. If you want to break up the trip, stop in Cedaredge. The loop in the opposite direction—includ-ing Meeker, Craig, Dinosaur National Monument, and Rangely—is longer, but there's decent lodging along the way, with the exception of Dinosaur National Monument, where there's only one nearby motel and camping.

If you're headed to Steamboat Springs from Denver in winter, exercise caution on Highway 40. It sees less traffic than I-70, but it can be treacherous in the Berthoud Pass stretch during snowstorms.

Grand Junction and Around. This narrow city is a quiet, gracious locale that easily balances raucous outdoor adventures and a thriving cultural scene. The Colorado National Monument and Book Cliffs dominate the landscape, but Palisade, with its peaches and wines, and Fruita, a thriving mountain-biking mecca, command ever-increasing attention.

Steamboat Springs. Unlike some of the other ski towns, Steamboat has always been a "real" town. With its touch of the Old West and plenty of cowboys still hanging around, visitors are usually torn—hot springs, horseback riding, or skiing?

Northwest Corner. The world's largest flat-topped mountain, the Grand Mesa, has a 55-mile Scenic Byway that feels a little like Land of the Lost. Meanwhile, Dinosaur National Monument offers thousands of fossils and hiking trails. Stop in nearby Craig or Rangely to refuel yourself and your vehicle.

PLANNING

WHEN TO GO

The region has four distinct seasons. The heaviest concentration of tourists is in summer, when school is out and families hit the road for a little together time. Temperatures in summer frequently reach into the high 80s and 90s, although the mercury has been known to top triple digits on occasion. You might have a hard time finding a hotel room during late May and late June thanks to the National Junior College World Series (baseball) and Country Jam music festival, both in Grand Junction. Hotels fill quickly in fall, which brings an explosion of colors. Days are warm, but nights are crisp and cool. There's still time to enjoy activities like fishing, hiking, and backpacking before the snow flies. Grand Mesa is a winter favorite among locals looking for a quick fix for cabin fever. Powder hounds can't wait to strap on their newly waxed skis and hit the slopes at Steamboat and Powderhorn ski resorts.

PLANNING YOUR TIME

The remoteness of northwest Colorado makes it appealing for those looking to escape the big crowds of more heavily visited areas of the state, but it also requires more careful planning. Steamboat Springs is a good place to start and usually requires 2–3 days to explore, particularly if hiking, biking, skiing, horseback riding, or other adventure activities are on the itinerary, with optional day trips to Craig. From there, it's a commitment to spend time at Dinosaur National Monument, but one that is well worth the effort if dinosaurs or white-water rafting are on your must-do list.

Dropping down to Grand Junction is possible from Dinosaur through Rangely—which gives you the chance to do a little fishing—or you can skip the fossil tour and go through Meeker, secure in the knowledge that you'll still get your dino fix around this part of the Western Slope. Plan on several days to explore Grand Junction, with wine tasting in Palisade and the extensive outdoors options on the Grand Mesa nearby.

GETTING HERE AND AROUND

AIR TRAVEL

Grand Junction Regional Airport (GJT) is served by Allegiant Air, American, Delta Airlines, United, and US Airways.

Yampa Valley Regional Airport (HDN) is in Hayden, 22 miles from Steamboat Springs. Alaska, American, Delta, and United fly nonstop from various gateways during ski season.

Taxis and shuttle services are available in Grand Junction and Steamboat Springs.

Airport Contacts Grand Junction Regional Airport (GJT). ✉ *2828 Walker Field Dr., Grand Junction* ☎ *970/244–9100* ⊕ *www.gjairport.com.* **Yampa Valley Regional Airport (HDN).** ✉ *Hayden* ☎ *970/276–5000* ⊕ *www.co.routt.co.us.*

CAR TRAVEL

In northwestern Colorado I–70 (U.S. 6) is the major thoroughfare, accessing Grand Junction and Grand Mesa (via Route 65, which runs to Delta). Meeker is reached via Route 13, and Rangely and Dinosaur via Route 64. U.S. 40 east from Utah is the best way to reach Dinosaur National Monument and Craig.

From Denver, Steamboat Springs is about a three-hour drive northwest via I–70 and U.S. 40. The route traverses some high-mountain passes, so it's a good idea to check road conditions before you travel.

Grand Junction has gas stations that are open 24 hours. Most gas stations in the smaller towns are open until 10 pm in summer, and even some automated credit-card pumps shut down at that hour.

Most roads are paved and in fairly good condition. Summer is peak road-construction season, so expect some delays. Be prepared for winter driving conditions at all times. Enterprise car rental is in downtown Grand Junction, with free pickup. Alamo, Avis, Budget, Enterprise, Hertz, and National Car Rental are in the Grand Junction Airport terminal. Depending on where you're traveling, you might want a four-wheel drive. Avis has car rentals in Steamboat Springs.

Car Travel Contacts AAA Colorado. ☎ 970/245–2236 ⊕ www.aaa.com. **Colorado State Patrol.** ☎ 970/249–4392 ⊕ www.csp.state.co.us. **Road Report.** ☎ 511, 877/315–7623 in Colorado but outside Denver ⊕ www.cotrip.org.

TRAIN TRAVEL

Amtrak provides daily service to the East and West coasts through downtown Grand Junction.

PARKS AND RECREATION AREAS

The blushing red-rock cliffs of the **Colorado National Monument** are easily accessible by winding roads that open to miles of hiking trails. **Dinosaur National Monument** holds a stunning cache of fossils as well as spectacular scenery aboveground for family-friendly hiking.

9

Browns Park Wildlife Refuge. A bird-watcher's destination with species from ducks to bald eagles, the remote Browns Park Wildlife Refuge northwest of Maybell can be navigated by car or horseback, or on foot. ⊕ www.fws.gov/brownspark.

Flat Tops Wilderness. This alpine mesa has good stream and lake fishing and excellent deer and elk hunting. It's southwest of Steamboat Springs. ⊕ www.fs.fed.us/r2/whiteriver.

Grand Mesa National Forest. This forest shimmers with peaceful alpine lakes and great fishing and hiking in summer, along with trails for snowmobiling in winter. ⊕ www.fs.usda.gov/gmug.

Medicine Bow/Routt National Forests. Steamboat Springs is surrounded by the Medicine Bow/Routt National Forests, which stretch across northern Colorado and into southern Wyoming, embracing more than half a dozen mountain ranges, including the Gore, Flat Tops, Park, Medicine Bow, Sierra Madre, and Laramie. ⊕ www.fs.usda.gov/mbr.

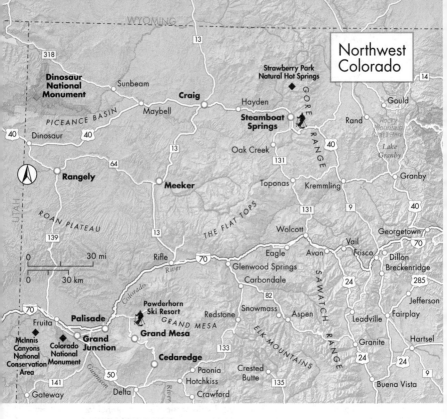

RESTAURANTS

The usual chain restaurants ring Grand Junction, but they're joined by eclectic gourmet pizza joints and authentic Mexican restaurants. Look for made-from-scratch delicacies at mom-and-pop bakeries—especially worth seeking out during summer fruit harvests. In season, Palisade peaches, Olathe sweet corn, and Cedaredge apples find their way onto menus, and they're sometimes paired with a multitude of local wines. For something traditional, it's hard to beat a great hand-battered chicken-fried steak smothered in creamy gravy—which is available in just about any town in the area.

The town of Steamboat Springs, in the heart of cattle country, has far more carnivorous delights—including elk, deer, and bison—than you're likely to find in the trendier resorts of Aspen, Telluride, and Vail. The Steamboat ski resort, separated geographically from town, is more eclectic, with small sushi bars and Mediterranean cafés hidden among the boutiques.

HOTELS

In Grand Junction, Horizon Drive has the largest concentration of hotels and motels, conveniently near the airport and within walking distance of a handful of restaurants. For the budget conscious, there are many no-frills motels as well as hotel branches of the well-known chains. History buffs might enjoy a stay at a dude ranch, one of the many rustic cabin rentals, or the famed Meeker Hotel, once frequented by Teddy Roosevelt. For those looking for the comforts of home, the area has a nice selection of bed-and-breakfasts; be sure to ask for off-season lodging rates, which could save you a bundle.

Steamboat Springs is unique in the state because it has high-end dude ranches and ranch resorts, which are less abundant in resort areas like Aspen, Summit County, and Vail. *Hotel reviews have been shortened. For full information, visit Fodors.com.*

WHAT IT COSTS				
	$	**$$**	**$$$**	**$$$$**
Restaurants	under $13	$13–$18	$19–$25	over $25
Hotels	under $121	$121–$170	$171–$230	over $230

Restaurant prices are the average price of a main course at dinner or, if dinner is not served, at lunch, excluding 6.5%–8.4% tax. Hotel prices are the lowest cost of a standard double room in high season, excluding service charges and 9.4%–10.65% tax.

GRAND JUNCTION AND AROUND

With its mild climate and healthy economy, Grand Junction and the surrounding area make northwestern Colorado an inviting destination. A thriving retirement community and mountain-biking headquarters, the Grand Valley also counts superior soil and top-notch ranching among its assets. The contrast between the sandstone of the Book Cliffs and the canyons of the Colorado National Monument with the greenery of the lush orchards below, particularly in nearby Palisade, makes for a pleasant road trip.

9

GRAND JUNCTION

255 miles west of Denver via I–70.

Grand Junction is where the mountains and desert meet at the confluence of the mighty Colorado and Gunnison rivers—a grand junction indeed. No matter which direction you look, there's an adventure waiting to happen. The city, with a population of more than 59,000, is nestled between the picturesque Grand Mesa to the south and the towering Book Cliffs to the north. It's a great base camp for a vacation—whether you're into art galleries, boutiques, hiking, horseback riding, rafting, mountain biking, or winery tours.

The Art on the Corner exhibit showcases leading regional sculptors, whose latest works are installed on the Main Street Mall. Passersby may find their faces reflected in an enormous chrome buffalo (titled *Chrome on the Range II*) or, a few streets down, encounter an enormous cactus made entirely of rusted (but still prickly) chainsaw chains.

GETTING HERE AND AROUND

A Touch With Class has regular limo service into Grand Junction and outlying communities. Sunshine Taxi serves Grand Junction. Amtrak runs the *California Zephyr* round-trip from San Francisco to Chicago, which stops in Grand Junction, Glenwood Springs, Winter Park, and Denver. Grand Valley Transit operates 11 public bus routes that are geared to commuters between Grand Junction, Palisade, Clifton, Orchard Mesa, and Fruita.

FESTIVALS

Country Jam and Loudwire Music Festival. Country Jam is held every June and draws the biggest names in country music, followed by Loudwire Music Festival, also in June. ⊠ *Jam Ranch, 1065 Hwy. 6 and 50, Mack* ☎ *800/780–0526* ⊕ *countryjam.com, loudwire.com.*

ESSENTIALS

Transportation Contacts A Touch With Class. ☎ 970/245–5466 ⊕ *www.colorado-limo.com.* **Amtrak.** ☎ *800/872–7245* ⊕ *www.amtrak.com.* **Grand Valley Transit.** ☎ *970/256–7433* ⊕ *www.gvt.mesacounty.us.* **Sunshine Taxi.** ⊠ *1321 Ute Ave.* ☎ *970/245–8294.*

Visitor Information Grand Junction Visitor & Convention Bureau. ⊠ *740 Horizon Dr.* ☎ *800/962–2547, 970/244–1480* ⊕ *www.visitgrandjunction.com.*

TOURS

FAMILY **Dino Digs.** Ever wonder what it's like to be on a dinosaur expedition? Here's your chance. The Museum of Western Colorado sponsors one-to five-day Dino Digs all over northwestern Colorado, and folks find fresh fossils all the time. The area includes some rich Late Jurassic soil, Morrison Formation sites, and other well-preserved zones that make for impressive discoveries. You never know what might be unearthed. ⊠ *Grand Junction* ☎ *888/488–3466* ⊕ *www.dinodigs.org* 🖃 *From $65.*

Dinosaur Journey. Dinosaur Journey leads one- to five-day paleontological treks that include work in a dinosaur quarry. ⊠ *550 Jurassic Ct., Fruita* ☎ *970/858–7282* ⊕ *www.dinosaurjourney.org* 🖃 *From $8.50.*

EXPLORING

The Art Center. This center rotates a fine permanent collection of Native American tapestries and Western contemporary art, including the only complete series of lithographs by noted printmaker Paul Pletka. The fantastically carved doors—done by a WPA artist in the 1930s—alone are worth the visit. Take time to view the elegant historic homes along North 7th Street afterward. Admission is free on Tuesdays and always for children under 12. ⊠ *1803 N. 7th St.* ☎ *970/243–7337* ⊕ *www. gjartcenter.org* 🖃 *$3* ☉ *Mon.–Sat. 9–4.*

Museum of Western Colorado/Museum of the West. This museum relates the history of the area since the 1880s, with a time line, a firearms display, and a Southwest pottery collection. The area's rich mining heritage is perfectly captured in the uranium mine that educates with interactive sound and exhibit stations. The museum also runs the Cross Orchards Living History Farm and the Dinosaur Journey Museum, and oversees paleontological excavations. ⊠ *462 Ute Ave.* ☎ *970/242–0971* ⊕ *www. museumofwesternco.com* 🖃 *$7* ☉ *May–Sept., Mon.–Sat. 9–5; Oct.–Apr., Mon.–Sat. 10–4.*

**OFF THE
BEATEN
PATH**

Little Book Cliffs Wild Horse Range. One of just three ranges in the United States set aside for wild horses, this range encompasses 36,113 acres of rugged canyons and plateaus in the Book Cliffs. Eighty to 120 wild horses roam the sagebrush-covered hills. Most years new foals can be spotted with their mothers in spring and early summer on the hillsides just off the main trails. Local favorites for riding include the Coal Canyon Trail and Main Canyon Trail, where the herd often goes in winter. Vehicles are permitted on designated trails. ✉ *2815 H Rd., about 8 miles northeast of Grand Junction* ☎ *970/244–3000, 800/417–9647* ⊕ *www. co.blm.gov* ✉ *Free* ⊙ *Daily dawn–dusk.*

SPORTS AND THE OUTDOORS

GOLF

The Golf Club at Redlands Mesa. The 18-hole, Jim Engh-designed championship course sits in a natural desert setting at an elevation of 4,600 feet in the shadows of the Colorado National Monument, just minutes from downtown. Sunset across the monument is spectacular, and the game is a challenge of red-rock walls and sloping stone formations. ✉ *2325 W. Ridges Blvd.* ☎ *970/263–9270, 866/863–9270* ⊕ *www.redlandsmesa. com* ✉ *$50 weekdays, $60 weekends* ⚑ *Monument Course: 18 holes, 7007 yards, par 72; Redlands Course: 18 holes, 6486 yards, par 72; Canyon Course: 18 holes, 5281 yards, par 72; Desert Course: 18 holes, 4890 yards, par 72* ⚐ *Reservations essential.*

MOUNTAIN BIKING

Several routes through Grand Junction are well suited to bicycle use. The city also has designated bike lanes in some areas. You can bike along the Colorado Riverfront Trails, a network that winds along the Colorado River, stretching from the Redlands Parkway to Palisade.

Colorado Plateau Mountain Bike Trail Association. Those interested in bike tours should contact the Colorado Plateau Mountain Bike Trail Association. ✉ *Grand Junction* ☎ *970/244–8877* ⊕ *www.copmoba.org.*

Kokopelli's Trail. This trail links Grand Junction with the famed Slickrock Trail outside Moab, Utah. The 142-mile stretch winds through high desert and the Colorado River Valley before climbing the La Sal Mountains. ✉ *Loma.*

OUTFITTERS **Brown Cycles.** This company rents road, mountain, and hybrid bikes that start around $45 a day. It also sells and fixes bikes, and offers a full line of tandems for families, with expanded kid options for rent and sale, as well. Aficionados should allow some extra time to check out the interesting bike museum, with models from as early as the 1860s. ✉ *549 Main St.* ☎ *970/245–7939* ⊕ *www.browncycles.com.*

Over the Edge Sports. Over the Edge Sports offers mountain-biking lessons and half- or full-day customized bike tours. ✉ *202 E. Aspen Ave., Fruita* ☎ *970/858–7220* ⊕ *www.otesports.com.*

Ruby Canyon Cycles. This outfitter rents high-end, 29-inch, full-suspension mountain bikes for $60 the first day and $50 on subsequent days. The cycle shop also sponsors weekly evening rides around the area. ✉ *301 Main St.* ☎ *970/241–0141* ⊕ *www.rubycanyoncycles.com.*

9

WHERE TO EAT

$ MEXICAN FAMILY 🍴 **Dos Hombres.** Casual and colorful, Dos Hombres serves the usual variety of combination platters and Mexican specialties, and loads up the plates for low prices. The fajitas and enchiladas are particularly well made, with quality meats and a noticeable lack of grease, and they have an unusually large menu of interesting salads (check out the Cancun version, with pineapple and fried tortilla strips). Service is snappy and friendly, and the staff is accommodating to kids. The margaritas and cervezas are inexpensive, too—they're half-price during the weekday three-hour happy hour and all day Tuesday. [$] *Average main: $11* ✉ *421 Brach Dr.* ☎ *970/242–8861* 🌐 *www.go2dos.com.*

$$ ITALIAN 🍴 **Il Bistro Italiano.** With a chef hailing from the birthplace of Parmigiano-Reggiano, this restaurant's authenticity is assured, down to that perfectly delivered final shredded topping. Diners are greeted by a case of pasta made fresh daily and assisted by a staff that knows the origins of each home-style dish. Entrées include shrimp, prosciutto, and avocado tossed with spinach pasta; wood-fired pizzas; and meat dishes finished with innovative sauces such as capers, orange juice, and tomatoes in a vodka cream sauce. The standout, though, is the Rosetta, a dish of house-made noodles wrapped around rosemary ham and provolone in a spicy tomato sauce. [$] *Average main: $17* ✉ *400 Main St.* ☎ *970/243–8622* 🌐 *www.ilbistroitaliano.com* 🕒 *No lunch weekends* ✍ *Reservations essential.*

$ PIZZA FAMILY 🍴 **Pablo's Pizza.** Drawing inspiration from Pablo Picasso's artwork, the pizzas at this funky joint make for a diverse palette of flavors and fun. Specialties include creations such as Popeye's Passion (featuring spinach and "olive oyl") or Dracula's Nemesis (studded with roasted garlic). For kids, they even serve (we're not making this up) a peanut-butter-and-jelly pizza. With brick walls covered only by eclectic local paintings, Pablo's can get loud when busy. They pour local wines by the glass and Palisade Brewery beer and root beer by the bottle. [$] *Average main: $8* ✉ *319 Main St.* ☎ *970/255–8879* 🌐 *www.pablospizza.com* ✍ *Reservations not accepted.*

$$$$ AMERICAN 🍴 **The Winery.** This is *the* place for that big night out and other special occasions. It's awash in stained glass, wood beams, exposed brick, and hanging plants, with dark nooks and crannies and ends of aging barrels as art, all of which combine for an intimate atmosphere. The menu isn't terribly adventuresome, but the kitchen does turn out fresh-fish specials and top-notch steak, chicken, prime rib, and shrimp in simple, flavorful sauces. The real draw is for wine fans who want to try a more obscure bottle from the extensive, domestic-heavy roster. [$] *Average main: $28* ✉ *642 Main St.* ☎ *970/242–4100* 🌐 *www.winery-restaurant.com* 🕒 *No lunch* ✍ *Reservations essential.*

WHERE TO STAY

$$ HOTEL FAMILY 🏨 **DoubleTree Hotel.** At this sprawling full-service property, service begins with a warm cookie at check-in, and the attention to detail continues from there; many of the large rooms have vast mountain views, along with a long list of amenities. **Pros:** outdoor heated pool and hot tub; kid-friendly; friendly staff. **Cons:** restaurant and room service food is so-so. [$] *Rooms from: $123* ✉ *743 Horizon*

Dr. ☎ *970/241–8888, 800/222–8733* ⊕ *www.doubletree.com* ➪ *259 rooms, 14 suites* ◉ *No meals.*

$$ 🔲 **Fairfield Inn & Suites Grand Junction.** Well situated in the middle of the
HOTEL downtown shopping district, this Marriott-owned property is ideal for
business travelers, with spacious rooms that sport small sitting areas
and large desks. **Pros:** downtown locale; cavernous rooms. **Cons:** chain-
hotel atmosphere; service is hit or miss. $ *Rooms from: $140* ✉ *225
Main St.* ☎ *970/242–2525* ⊕ *www.marriott.com* ➪ *60 rooms, 10 suites*
◉ *Breakfast.*

$ 🔲 **Grand Vista Hotel.** Plush high-back chairs invite visitors to relax in the
HOTEL spacious lobby of this hotel that lives up to its name. **Pros:** you can't
FAMILY beat the views; they will store your bike for you; the price is right. **Cons:**
the breakfast buffet is mediocre; service is patchy. $ *Rooms from: $78*
✉ *2790 Crossroads Blvd.* ☎ *970/241–8411, 800/800–7796* ⊕ *www.
grandvistahotel.com* ➪ *158 rooms* ◉ *No meals.*

$ 🔲 **Los Altos Bed & Breakfast.** This luxurious, panoramic hilltop is a
B&B/INN peaceful, centralized home base for exploring the area. **Pros:** close to
downtown but quiet; stunning views; private baths. **Cons:** thin walls
mean that sometimes you can hear your neighbors. $ *Rooms from:
$119* ✉ *375 Hillview Dr.* ☎ *970/256–0964, 888/774–0982* ⊕ *www.
losaltosgrandjunction.com* ➪ *5 rooms, 2 suites* ◉ *Breakfast.*

$$ 🔲 **Two Rivers Winery & Chateau.** Open a bottle of wine inside the vineyard
B&B/INN where it was created at this rustic French-styled inn set among acres of
vines. **Pros:** idyllic locale for weddings or other special occasions; tasty
wines always at hand; expansive Continental breakfast. **Cons:** winery
and functions make this noisier than the usual B&B; rooms are chilly
in winter. $ *Rooms from: $145* ✉ *2087 Broadway* ☎ *970/255–1471,
866/312–9463* ⊕ *www.tworiverswinery.com* ➪ *10 rooms* ◉ *Breakfast.*

NIGHTLIFE AND PERFORMING ARTS

PERFORMING ARTS

Avalon Theatre. The Avalon Theatre is one of the largest performing
arts complexes in western Colorado, offering traveling lectures, dance,
theater, and other cultural performances. The popular monthly "Dinner
and a Movie" Tuesday nights bring classic and popular old blockbusters to the big screen, with receipts from a meal in town garnering free
admission. A $9 million renovation, completed in late 2014, restored
and upgraded the 1923 facility, adding seating, reception areas, and a
rooftop terrace, while making audio/visual improvements and allowing
the theater to expand its cultural offerings. ✉ *645 Main St.* ☎ *970/263–
5700* ⊕ *www.tworiversconvention.com.*

Grand Junction Symphony. The highly regarded, 95-piece Grand Junction
Symphony performs in venues throughout the city, including Stocker
Stadium and area vineyards. ✉ *Grand Junction* ☎ *970/243–6787*
⊕ *www.gjsymphony.org.*

NIGHTLIFE

Bistro 743 Lounge. This lounge inside the DoubleTree Hotel serves beverages, appetizers, and light snacks. On weekends, entertainers perform
in the bar, and occasionally outside on the beer-garden stage. ✉ *743
Horizon Dr.* ☎ *970/241–8888* ⊕ *doubletreegrandjunction.com.*

Blue Moon. This local bar, which serves decent wings, sandwiches, and other typical pub grub, is a popular spot for patrons to nurse their favorite brew while catching up with colleagues and friends. ⊠ *120 N. 7th St.* ☎ *970/242–4506* ⊕ *www.bluemoongj.com* ☉ *Closed Sun.*

Rockslide Brewery. This brewery has won awards for its ales, porters, and stouts. The menu of burgers and other sandwiches, steaks, and pastas has something for just about everyone. The patio is open in summer. ⊠ *401 Main St.* ☎ *970/245–2111* ⊕ *www.rockslidebrewpub.com.*

SHOPPING

Champion Boots & Saddlery. The best place in the area for Tony Lama boots and Minnetonka moccasins is Champion Boots & Saddlery, in business since 1936. ⊠ *545 Main St.* ☎ *970/242–2465.*

FAMILY **Enstrom Candies.** The sweetest deal in town, Enstrom Candies is known for its scrumptious candy and renowned toffee. ⊠ *701 Colorado Ave.* ☎ *970/683–1000* ⊕ *enstrom.com.*

Girlfriends. The Main Street boutique Girlfriends sells a line of comfy clothes, pottery, benches, candles, and one-of-a-kind gifts. ⊠ *316 Main St.* ☎ *970/242–3234.*

Heirlooms for Hospice. The cute but upscale boutique Heirlooms for Hospice has great secondhand designer clothing and shabby-chic furniture. ⊠ *635 Main St.* ☎ *970/254–8556, 866/310–8900* ⊕ *www. heirloomsforhospice.com.*

Working Artists Studio and Gallery. This studio and gallery carries prints, pottery, stained glass, and unique gifts. ⊠ *520 Main St.* ☎ *970/256–9952.*

PALISADE

12 miles east of Grand Junction via I–70.

Palisade is Colorado's version of Napa Valley, with the highest concentration of wineries in the state. It's an easy day trip from Grand Junction; meander through the vineyards and stop for lunch in the tiny, slow-paced town framed by stately Victorian homes and sweetened by homespun festivals. The orchards also are a big draw; the long, frost-free growing season intensifies the fruit sugars, resulting in intensely flavorful peaches, cherries, apricots, and nectarines. At harvest time the area sees a steady flow of visitors stopping by the orchards themselves, many of which have on-site sales, as well as the roadside stands that pop up seasonally to sell preserves, salsas, pies, and other fruit-based products.

GETTING HERE AND AROUND

A car is the best way to get to and around Palisade. Public transportation options are limited.

WHEN TO GO

A variety of produce is available through the summer months, but the peaches and other fruits famous in the Palisade area are at the height of their season from late June to early October.

FESTIVALS **Grande River Vineyards.** In summer Grande River Vineyards hosts a concert series featuring classical, country, blues, and rock music. The natural landscape contributes to the good acoustics, not to mention the spectacular sunsets. Concertgoers lounge in lawn chairs, enjoying picnics and dancing barefoot on the grass, and sometimes the concerts are held in the cellars. ✉ *787 Elberta Ave.* ☎ *970/464–5867* 🌐 *www.granderiverwines.com* 🎟 *From $15.*

Palisade Peach Festival. Palisade celebrates the harvest for four days every August during the Palisade Peach Festival, most of which is held at Riverbend Park. ✉ *Palisade* ☎ *970/464–7458* 🌐 *www.palisadepeachfest.com* 🎟 *$7.*

ESSENTIALS

Visitor Information **Palisade Chamber of Commerce.** ✉ *319 Main St.* ☎ *970/464–7458* 🌐 *www.palisadecoc.com.*

EXPLORING

American Spirit Shuttle. This company operates scheduled tours in passenger vans seating up to 11 on Saturday that visit at least four wineries and last approximately four hours. Wine lovers get to sample a variety of Colorado wines in the tasting rooms, with the added benefit of having someone else do the driving. Cost is $225 for groups up to six people and $35 per person up to 10. ✉ *204 4th St., Clifton* ☎ *970/523–7662* 🌐 *www.americanspiritshuttle.net* 🎟 *From $35* 🕒 *May–Oct., Sat. noon–4.*

QUICK BITES

Palisade Café. Changing artwork decorates the light and airy Palisade Café, which offers a nice selection of breakfast (only on weekends), lunch, and dinner choices, including soups, salads, burgers, French dips, Reuben sandwiches, and vegetarian dishes. ✉ ***113 W. 3rd St.*** ☎ ***970/464–0657*** 🌐 ***www.palisadecafe.com*** 🕒 ***No dinner Sun.–Wed. Closed Tues. in winter*** ✍ ***Reservations not accepted.***

Fodor's Choice ★ **Winery Tours.** One of Colorado's best-kept secrets is its winery tours. It's a great way to see how your favorite wine goes from vineyard to glass. You can learn about the grape-growing process and what varieties of grapes grow best in western Colorado's mild climate. Depending on the time of year, you may also see the grape harvesting and crushing process. For a self-guided tour, visit Grand Junction's website for maps and directions to the wineries. If you're taking the self-guided route, call to reserve tours that take you beyond the tasting room and into the winemaking process. Of course, the best part of the tour is sampling the wines. ✉ *Palisade* 🌐 *www.visitgrandjunction.com.*

WHERE TO EAT AND STAY

$ CAFÉ FAMILY Fodor's Choice ★

🍴 **Slice O' Life Bakery.** Aromatic goodies are baked with whole grains and fresh local fruits at this down-home–style bakery known around the region for its melt-in-your-mouth pastries, sweet rolls, "jamocha" brownies, and fresh-fruit cobblers. Owners Tim and Mary Lincoln have made their fruitcakes craveable commodities, studding them with fresh Palisade peaches and mailing them around the country (in fact, they do lots of great things with peaches, including pie). Cold sandwiches and fresh-baked bread are also available. [$] *Average main: $4* ✉ *105 W. 3rd St.* ☎ *970/464–0577* 💳 *No credit cards* 🕒 *Closed Sun. and Mon. No dinner* ✍ *Reservations not accepted.*

9

$$
B&B/INN
🖼 **Wine Country Inn.** The richly colored fabrics and spacious design of the rooms in a well-established vineyard give an upscale feel to what's an appealingly casual and welcoming farmhouse-style lodging. **Pros:** convenient location off the interstate; vineyard property evokes surrounding locale; convenient to rest of wine properties. **Cons:** nearby truck traffic can be noisy; service spotty, especially when the place is full. 💲 *Rooms from: $169* ✉ *777 Grande River Dr.* ☎ *888/855–8330, 970/464–5777* ⊕ *www.coloradowinecountryinn.com* ⊟ *No credit cards* ⇆ *80 rooms, 6 suites* ◯| *Breakfast.*

SHOPPING

Alida's Fruits. This market sells a wide range of fresh and dried fruits, including cherries, pears, apricots, and peaches, as well as chocolate-dipped fruits, nuts, and locally produced jams, jellies, and syrups. During the growing season, the market sells fresh produce as well. There's a second location in Grand Junction. ✉ *3402 C 1/2 Rd.* ☎ *970/434–8769* ⊕ *www.alidasfruits.com.*

Talbott Farms Mountain Gold Market. This market puts out nearly two dozen kinds of peaches, as well as apples and pears and the juices of all three. The huge, fourth generation–run operation sells local products and will take you on a tour of the place if you ask. ✉ *3782 F 1/4 Rd.* ☎ *970/464–5943* ⊕ *www.talbottfarms.com* ◷ *Mid-July–Dec., Mon.– Sat. 9–5:30.*

COLORADO NATIONAL MONUMENT

23 miles west of Grand Junction via Rte. 340.

Colorado's version of red rock is nowhere more spectacularly on display than at Colorado National Monument. Created between 65 and 225 million years ago, the monument was designated in 1911 and has been popular with photographers, hikers, and those eager to drive its paved road, Rim Rock Drive, ever since.

GETTING HERE AND AROUND
From I–70 westbound, take Exit 31 (Horizon Drive) and follow signs through Grand Junction; eastbound take Exit 19 (Fruita) and drive south 3 miles on Highway 340 to the west entrance.

FESTIVALS
Fruita Fat Tire Festival. The town's Fat Tire Festival brings mountain bikers from all over together to take on the area's trails every April. ☎ *970/858–7228* ⊕ *fruitafattirefestival.com.*

Mike the Headless Chicken Days. Fruita celebrates Mike the Headless Chicken Days every May with the Chicken Dance and the Run Like A Headless Chicken 5K Race. ✉ *Fruita* ☎ *970/858–0360* ⊕ *www. miketheheadlesschicken.org.*

TOURS
American Spirit Shuttle. American Spirit Shuttle offers scheduled and customized tours of Colorado National Monument. ✉ *204 4th St., Clifton* ☎ *970/523–7662* ⊕ *www.americanspiritshuttle.net* 🎫 *From $35.*

EXPLORING

Fodor's Choice ★ **Colorado National Monument.** Sheer red-rock cliffs open to 23 miles of steep canyons and thin monoliths that sprout as high as 450 feet from the floor of Colorado National Monument. This vast tract of rugged, ragged terrain was declared a national monument in 1911 at the urging of an eccentric visionary named John Otto. Now it's popular for rock climbing, horseback riding, cross-country skiing, biking, and camping. Cold Shivers Point is just one of the many dramatic overlooks along **Rim Rock Drive,** a 23-mile scenic route with breathtaking views. The town of Fruita, at the base of Colorado National Monument, is a haven for mountain bikers and hikers. It makes a great center for exploring the area's canyons—whether from the seat of a bike or the middle of a raft, heading for a leisurely float trip. ⊠ *Fruita* ☎ *970/858–3617* ⊕ *www. nps.gov/colm* ⌨ *$10 per wk per vehicle. Visitors entering on bicycle, motorcycle, or foot pay $5 for weekly pass.*

FAMILY **Dinosaur Journey.** Roaring robotic stegosaurs and meat-shredding animatronic allosaurs prowl Dinosaur Journey, a fun, informative attraction just off I–70 a few minutes from the western entrance to Colorado National Monument. Unlike many museums, this one encourages kids to touch everything—friendly paleontologists may even allow kids to hold a chunk of fossilized dino dung. In addition to the amazing lifelike replicas, there are more than 20 interactive displays. Children can stand in an earthquake simulator; dig up "fossils" in a mock quarry (the pit is made of crushed walnut shells); or make dino prints in dirt, along with reptile and bird tracks for comparison. The museum also sponsors daily digs nearby, where many of the fossils were found. Local volunteers are at work cleaning and preparing fossils for study. ⊠ *550 Jurassic Ct., Fruita* ☎ *970/858–7282* ⊕ *www.museumofwesternco.com/ visit/dinosaur-journey* ⌨ *$9* ☉ *May–Sept., daily 9–5; Oct.–Apr., Mon.– Sat. 10–4, Sun. noon–4.*

Fodor's Choice ★ **McInnis Canyons National Conservation Area.** Ten miles west of Grand Junction, stretching from Fruita to just across the Utah border, the McInnis Canyons National Conservation Area (formerly Colorado Canyons National Conservation Area) is rife with natural arches, along with numerous rock canyons, caves, coves, and spires. **Rattlesnake Canyon** has nine arches, making it the second-largest concentration of natural arches in the country. The canyon can be reached in summer from the upper end of Rim Rock Drive with four-wheel-drive vehicles or via a 7-mile hike by the intrepid.

Though much of the territory complements the red-dirt canyons of Colorado National Monument, McInnis Canyons is more accessible to horseback riding, mountain biking, all-terrain vehicle and motorcycle trails, and for trips with dogs (most of these activities aren't allowed at the monument). Designated in 2000 by act of Congress, the conservation area was created from a desire of nearby communities to preserve the area's unique scenery while allowing multiple-use recreation. Be prepared for biting gnats from late May to late July. Contact the Bureau of Land Management for a map before venturing out. ⊠ *2815 H Rd., Grand Junction* ☎ *970/244–3000* ⊕ *www.blm.gov/co/st/en/nca/mcnca. html* ⌨ *Free.*

CLOSE UP

The Legacy of Mike the Headless Chicken

Mike the Headless Chicken was a freak bound for fame. It all started with a run-in with a Fruita farmer who had bad aim, or so the tale goes. The year was 1945. Mike, a young Wyandotte rooster, was minding his own business in the barnyard when farmer Lloyd Olsen snatched him from the chicken coop. It seems that Clara, the farmer's wife, wanted chicken for dinner that night. Mike was put on death row. Well, faster than you can say pinfeathers, farmer Olsen stretched Mike's neck across the chopping block and whacked off his head. Apparently undaunted by the ordeal, Mike promptly got up, dusted off his feathers and went about his daily business pecking for food, fluffing his feathers, and crowing, except Mike's crow was now reduced to a gurgle.

Scientists surmised that Mike's brain stem was largely untouched, leaving his reflex actions intact. A blood clot prevented him from bleeding to death. The headless chicken dubbed "Miracle Mike" toured the freak-show circuit, where the morbidly curious could sneak a peek at his nogginless nub for a quarter. Mike's incredible story of survival (he lived for 18 months without a head!) soon hit the pages of two national magazines, *Time* and *Life*. The headless wonder, who was fed with an eyedropper, eventually met his demise in an Arizona motel room, where he choked to death. His legacy lives on in Fruita, where the tiny town throws a gigantic party every May to celebrate Mike's life. Even in death, Mike is still making headlines.

SPORTS AND THE OUTDOORS

HIKING

Colorado National Monument Hiking Trails. A good way to explore Colorado National Monument is by trail. There are more than 40 miles of short and backcountry trails, with more than a dozen well-marked hikes ranging from a ¼ mile to 14 miles. ⊠ *Fruita* ☎ *970/858–3617* ⊕ *www.nps.gov/colm.*

Otto's Trail. An easy 30-minute stroll with sweeping canyon views, Otto's Trail greets hikers with breezes scented by sagebrush and juniper, which stand out from the dull red rock and sand. The trail leads to stunning sheer drop-offs and endless views. At the end of the half-mile trail at Otto's Overlook you can hear the wind in the feathers of birds as they soar out of the canyon. ⊠ *Fruita* ✛ *Trailhead: Rim Rock Dr., 1 mile from western gate visitor center.*

Serpents Trail. This trail has been called the "Crookedest Road in the World" because of its more than 50 switchbacks. The fairly steep but rewarding trail, which ascends several hundred feet, takes about two hours to complete, depending on your ability (and the heat). ✛ *Trailhead: Serpents Trail parking lot, ¼ mile from east gate.*

HORSEBACK RIDING

Rimrock Adventures. This company runs horseback rides near Colorado National Monument as well as through Little Book Cliffs Wild Horse Preserve. Rimrock Adventures also runs a variety of rafting excursions and easygoing float trips. ✉ *927 Hwy. 340, Fruita* ☎ *970/858–9555, 888/712–9555* ⊕ *www.rradventures.com.*

RAFTING

Adventure Bound River Expeditions. This company runs trips on the Colorado, Green, and Yampa rivers—the latter through the canyons of Dinosaur National Monument. ✉ *2392 H Rd., Grand Junction* ☎ *970/245–5428, 800/423–4668* ⊕ *www.adventureboundusa.com.*

ROCK CLIMBING

The stunning stark sandstone and shale formations of Colorado National Monument are a rock climber's paradise. Independence Monument is a favorite climb.

Desert Crags & Cracks. Experienced desert-rock guide Kris Hjelle owns and operates Desert Crags & Cracks, specializing in guiding and instruction on the desert rocks of western Colorado and eastern Utah. ☎ *970/245–8513* ⊕ *www.desertcrags.com.*

WHERE TO EAT AND STAY

$
MEXICAN
FAMILY
✕ **Fiesta Guadalajara Restaurant.** Authentic and family-friendly, this Mexican restaurant serves up good food in huge portions. Try the chiles rellenos, super nachos, and especially the chili Colorado: fork-tender beef simmered in a savory red-pepper sauce. The appetizer combo plate is a meal in itself, and to feed an army, order Fiesta Fajitas. There's a second location in Grand Junction. $ *Average main: $12* ✉ *103 Hwy. 6 and 50, Fruita* ☎ *970/858–1228* ⚠ *Reservations not accepted.*

$
HOTEL
FAMILY
Comfort Inn. Some rooms in this Southwestern-style budget motel have views of the Colorado National Monument. **Pros:** kid-friendly; great views; close to the monument. **Cons:** rooms and furniture showing age; chain-hotel feel. $ *Rooms from: $85* ✉ *400 Jurassic Ave., Fruita* ☎ *970/858–1333* ⊕ *www.choicehotels.com* ⇆ *53 rooms, 13 suites* ✦ *Breakfast.*

GRAND MESA

47 miles southeast of Grand Junction via I–70 and Hwy. 65.

Small, quiet towns along the 63-mile Grand Mesa Scenic and Historic Byway (Highway 65) provide just enough support for the plethora of outdoor opportunities available in the diverse range of ecosystems on the world's largest flat-topped mountain.

GETTING HERE AND AROUND

A car is needed to explore Grand Mesa. In northwestern Colorado I–70 (U.S. 6) is the major thoroughfare, accessing Grand Junction and Grand Mesa (via Route 65, which runs to Delta).

ESSENTIALS

Transportation Contacts Grand Junction Regional Airport (GJT). ✉ *2828 Walker Field Dr., Grand Junction* ☎ *970/244–9100* ⊕ *www.gjairport.com.*

Visitor Information Parachute/Battlement Mesa Chamber of Commerce. ☎ *970/285–7934.*

EXPLORING

Grand Mesa National Forest. The world's largest flattop mountain towers nearly 11,000 feet above the surrounding terrain and sprawls an astounding 53 square miles. Grand Mesa National Forest attracts the outdoor enthusiast who craves the simple life: fresh air, biting fish, spectacular sunsets, a roaring campfire under the stars, and a little elbow room to take it all in. The landscape is filled with more than 300 sparkling lakes—a fisherman's paradise in summer. The mesa, as it's referred to by locals, offers excellent hiking and camping (try Island Lake Campground) opportunities. There are also a handful of lodges that rent modern cabins. You can downhill ski at Powderhorn Resort, cross-country ski, snowshoe, snowmobile, or ice fish. ✉ *2250 Hwy. 50, Delta* ☎ *970/874–6600* 🌐 *www.fs.usda.gov/gmug.*

SPORTS AND THE OUTDOORS

DOWNHILL SKIING

Powderhorn Mountain Resort. The slopes at this resort intriguingly follow the fall line of the mesa, carving out natural bowls. Those bowls on the western side are steeper than they first appear. Lift tickets are reasonable, the skiing is surprisingly good, and the addition of a half-pipe and an improved terrain park have gone a long way toward modernizing the resort. Powderhorn averages 250 inches of snowfall per year. **Facilities:** 63 trails; 1,600 acres; 1,650-foot vertical drop; 4 lifts. ✉ *Rte. 65, 48338 Powderhorn Rd., Mesa* ☎ *970/268–5700* 🌐 *www.powderhorn.com* 🎫 *Lift ticket $59* 🕒 *Dec.–Apr., daily 9–4.*

HIKING

FAMILY **Grand Mesa Discovery Trail.** This trail is a great beginning hike for kids and adults attempting to acclimate themselves to the altitude—and the slow-paced attitude—of the mesa. Pick up a brochure at the visitor center for information on the landscape. The gently sloping 20-minute trail offers a taste of what to expect on longer hikes. ✉ *Trailhead: Grand Mesa visitor center, near intersection of Hwy. 65 and Trickel Park Rd.*

WHERE TO STAY

$ HOTEL 🏨 **Alexander Lake Lodge.** The mirror-calm Alexander Lake reflects towering pine trees that also overlook the majority of this resort's cozy cabins, which are designed for tranquility. **Pros:** fishing and snowmobiling right on the property; quiet and peaceful. **Cons:** rather remote; must bring your own food for most meals. [$] *Rooms from: $95* ✉ *21221 Baron Lake Dr., Cedaredge* ✢ *17 miles north of Cedaredge, 2 miles from Grand Mesa visitor center on Forest Rd. 121* ☎ *970/856–2539, 800/850–7221* 🌐 *www.alexanderlakelodge.com* 🛏 *4 rooms, 7 cabins* 🍴 *No meals.*

EN ROUTE **Grand Mesa Scenic Byway.** This byway is 63 miles long and winds its way along Highway 65 through meadows sprinkled with wildflowers, shimmering aspen groves, aromatic pine forests, and endless lakes. Scenic overlooks (Land-O-Lakes is a standout), rest areas, and picnic areas are clearly marked. There are two visitor centers on the byway, which has endpoints at I–70 near Palisade and in Cedaredge. ☎ *970/856–3100* 🌐 *www.grandmesabyway.com.*

CEDAREDGE

15 miles south of Grand Mesa via Hwy. 65.

Cedaredge is called the gateway to the Grand Mesa, the world's largest flat-topped mountain. An elevation of 6,100 feet makes for a mild climate that is perfect for ranching, as well as for growing apples, peaches, and cherries. It's also rich in galleries, gift shops, antiques stores, and wineries.

GETTING HERE AND AROUND

Driving is the best way to get around the area; the small town is best explored on foot.

ESSENTIALS

Visitor Information Cedaredge Chamber of Commerce. ⊠ *245 W. Main St.* ☎ *970/856–6961* ⊕ *www.cedaredgechamber.com.*

EXPLORING

Pioneer Town. The town site was originally the headquarters of a cattle spread, the Bar-I Ranch. Pioneer Town, a cluster of 23 authentic buildings that re-create turn-of-the-20th-century life, includes a country chapel, the Lizard Head Saloon, original silos from the Bar-I Ranch, and a working blacksmith shop. ⊠ *336 S. Grand Mesa Dr.* ☎ *970/856–7554* ⊕ *www.pioneertown.org* 🖾 *$5* ☉ *Memorial Day weekend–late Sept., Mon.–Sat. 10–4, Sun. 1–4.*

SHOPPING

Fodor'sChoice ★ **Apple Shed.** Once an apple-packing shed, the Apple Shed has been restored and remodeled into a series of unusual gift shops and arts and crafts galleries, as well as a tasting room that offers locally produced wines and ciders. The attached Loading Dock Deli ($) serves fresh peach milk shakes in season and top-notch sandwiches, sure to fuel your drive up the next pass. ⊠ *250 S. Grand Mesa Dr.* ☎ *970/856–7007* ⊕ *www.theappleshed.net.*

STEAMBOAT SPRINGS

42 miles east of Craig via U.S. 40; 160 miles west of Denver via I–70, Rte. 9, and U.S. 40.

Steamboat got its name from French trappers who, after hearing the bubbling and churning hot springs, mistakenly thought a steamboat was chugging up the Yampa River. Here Stetson hats are sold for shade and not for souvenirs, and the Victorian-era buildings, most of them fronting the main drag of Lincoln Avenue, were built to be functional, not ornamental.

Steamboat Springs is aptly nicknamed Ski Town, U.S.A., because it has sent more athletes to the Winter Olympics than any other ski town in the nation. When sizing up the mountain, keep in mind that the part that's visible from below is only the tip of the iceberg—much more terrain lies concealed in back. Steamboat is famed for its eider-down-soft snow; in fact, the term "champagne powder" was coined (and amusingly enough registered as a trademark) here to describe the

9

area's unique feathery drifts, the result of Steamboat's fortuitous position between the arid desert to the west and the moisture-magnet of the Continental Divide to the east, where storm fronts duke it out.

The mountain village, with its maze of upscale condos, boutiques, and nightclubs, is certainly attractive, but spread out and a little lacking in character. To its credit, though, this increasingly trendy destination has retained much of its down-home friendliness.

GETTING HERE AND AROUND

Yampa Valley Regional Airport (HDN) is in Hayden, 22 miles from Steamboat Springs. Alaska, American, Delta, and United fly non-stop from various gateways during ski season. Go Alpine and Storm Mountain Express provide door-to-door service to Steamboat Springs from Yampa Valley Regional Airport. A one-way trip with either costs $36.

Steamboat Springs Transit (SST) provides free shuttle service between the ski area and downtown Steamboat year-round. Most of the major properties also provide shuttles between the two areas for their guests.

From Denver, Steamboat Springs is about a three-hour drive northwest via I–70 and U.S. 40. The route traverses some high-mountain passes, so it's a good idea to check road conditions before you travel.

WHEN TO GO

A popular year-round destination, Steamboat becomes most dramatic in mid-September, when the leaves turn brilliant gold in the forests along the highways and the air cools considerably. By the first week of November, the ski season has begun, and it doesn't end until mid-April.

FESTIVALS

FAMILY   **Hot Air Balloon Rodeo and Annual Art in the Park.** Every year since 1980, mid-July in Steamboat has meant hot-air balloons and fine art, a combination that draws folks from miles around to watch more than 40 balloons float out over the valley from Bald Eagle Lake each morning. The rest of the weekend is devoted to the display and sale of hundreds of works of art from all over the world at West Lincoln Park. ⊠ *2305 Mt. Werner Circle* ☎ *970/879–0880* ⊕ *www. steamboat-chamber.com.*

Strings in the Mountains Music Festival. The focus is on chamber music and chamber-orchestra music presented by more than 150 musicians, including Grammy winners and other internationally renowned talents, throughout summer, primarily in the tent on the weekends. But Strings also offers big names in jazz, country, big band, bluegrass, and world music (Pink Martini, Lyle Lovett, and Dirty Dozen Brass Band, to name a few), as well as free concerts during its "Music on the Green" lunchtime series at Yampa River Botanic Park on Thursday in summer. ⊠ *Steamboat Springs Music Festival Tent at the corner of Mt. Werner and Pine Grove Rds.* ☎ *970/879–5056* ⊕ *www. stringsmusicfestival.com.*

ESSENTIALS

Transportation Contacts Go Alpine Taxi. ⊠ *Steamboat Springs* ☎ *800/343–7433* ⊕ *www.alpinetaxi.com.* **Steamboat Springs Transit.** ☎ *970/879–3717* ⊕ *steamboatsprings.net/transit.* **Storm Mountain Express.** ⊠ *Steamboat Springs* ☎ *877/844–8787* ⊕ *www.stormmountainexpress.com.* **Sunshine Taxi.** ⊠ *Grand Junction* ☎ *970/245–8294.* **Yampa Valley Regional Airport (HDN).** ⊠ *11005 County Rd. 51A, Hayden* ☎ *970/276–3669* ⊕ *yampavalleyregionalairport.com.*

Visitor Information Steamboat Ski & Resort Corporation. ⊠ *2305 Mount Werner Circle* ☎ *970/879–6111* ⊕ *www.steamboat.com.* **Steamboat Springs Chamber Resort Association.** ⊠ *125 Anglers Dr.* ☎ *970/879–0880* ⊕ *www. steamboat-chamber.com.* **Steamboat Springs Snow Report.** ☎ *970/879–7300* ⊕ *www.steamboat.com/the-mountain/snow-and-weather-report.*

TOURS

Sweet Pea Tours. Steamboat's Sweet Pea Tours visits nearby hot springs. The ride takes about 25 minutes each way, and rates are higher in winter and on weekends. ⊠ *Steamboat Springs* ☎ *970/879–5820* ⊕ *www. sweetpeatours.com* ⊠ *From $40.*

EXPLORING

Medicine Bow/Routt National Forests. In summer Steamboat serves as the gateway to the magnificent Medicine Bow/Routt National Forests, with a wealth of activities from hiking to mountain biking to fishing. Among the nearby attractions are the 283-foot **Fish Creek Falls** and the splendidly rugged **Mount Zirkel Wilderness Area.** To the north, two sparkling man-made lakes, **Steamboat** and **Pearl**, each in its own state park, are a draw for those into fishing and sailing. In winter the area is just as popular. Snowshoers and backcountry skiers are permitted to use the west side of Rabbit Ears Pass, whereas snowmobilers are confined to the east side. ⊠ *Hahns Peak-Bears Ears Ranger District Office* ☎ *970/870–2187* ⊕ *www.fs.usda.gov/mbr.*

FAMILY **Old Town Hot Springs.** There are more than 150 mineral springs of varying temperatures in the Steamboat Springs area, including this one, in the middle of town. Old Town Hot Springs gets its waters from the all-natural Heart Spring. The modern facility has a lap pool, relaxation pool, climbing wall, and health club. Two waterslides are open noon to 6 pm in summer and 4 to 8 pm in winter; they require an additional fee. A new feature, an inflatable playground called The Wibit, is open Friday to Sunday from noon to 6 pm between June and September, and also requires an additional fee. ⊠ *136 Lincoln Ave.* ☎ *970/879–1828* ⊕ *www.steamboathotsprings.org* ⊠ *$17.50* ☉ *Weekdays 5:30 am–10 pm, Sat. 7 am–9 pm, Sun. 8 am–9 pm.*

Fodor's Choice ★ **Strawberry Park Hot Springs.** About 7 miles west of town, the Strawberry Park Hot Springs is a bit remote and rustic, although only the winter drive on the gravel portion on the road is challenging. The way the pool is set up to offer semi-privacy makes for an intimate setting and relaxation. It's family-oriented during the day, but after dark clothing is optional, and no one under 18 is admitted. Feel free to bring food to eat in the picnic areas. A variety of massages, including aquatic-style, are offered next to the pools. Admission is cash or check only. ⊠ *Strawberry Park Rd., 44200 County Rd. #36* ☎ *970/879–0342* ⊕ *www.strawberryhotsprings.com* ⊠ *$12* ☉ *Sun.–Thurs. 10 am–10:30 pm; Fri. and Sat. 10 am–midnight.*

Tread of Pioneers Museum. In a restored Queen Anne–style house, the Tread of Pioneers Museum is an excellent spot to bone up on local history. It includes ski memorabilia dating to the turn of the 20th century, when Carl Howelsen opened Howelsen Hill, still the country's preeminent ski-jumping facility. ⊠ *800 Oak St.* ☎ *970/879–2214* ⊕ *www.treadofpioneers.org* ⊠ *$5* ☉ *Tues.–Sat. 11–5.*

DOWNHILL SKIING AND SNOWBOARDING

Howelsen Hill Ski Area. The tiny Howelsen Hill Ski Area, in the heart of Steamboat Springs, is the oldest ski area still open in Colorado. Howelsen, with 4 lifts, 15 trails, 1 terrain park, and a 440-foot vertical drop, is home to the Steamboat Springs Winter Sports Club, which has more than 800 members. The ski area not only has an awesome terrain park, but has night skiing as well. It's the largest ski-jumping complex in America and a major Olympic training ground. **Facilities:** 15 trails; 50 acres; 440-foot vertical drop; 4 lifts. ⊠ *845 Howelsen Pkwy.* ☎ *970/879–8499* ⊕ *www.steamboatsprings.net/ski* ⊠ *Lift ticket $25* ☉ *Nov.–Mar., Tues. and Fri. 1–6, Wed. and Thurs. 1–8, weekends 10–4.*

Fodor'sChoice ★ **Steamboat Springs Ski Area.** The Steamboat Springs Ski Area is perhaps best known for its tree skiing and "cruising" terrain—the latter term referring to wide, groomed runs perfect for intermediate-level skiers. The abundance of cruising terrain has made Steamboat immensely popular with those who ski once or twice a year and who aren't looking to tax their abilities. On a predominantly western exposure—most ski areas sit on north-facing exposures—the resort benefits from intense sun, which contributes to the mellow atmosphere. In addition, one of the most extensive lift systems in the region allows skiers to get in lots of runs without having to spend much time waiting in line. The Storm Peak and Sundown high-speed quads, for example, each send you about 2,000 vertical feet in less than seven minutes. Do the math: a day of more than 60,000 vertical feet is entirely within the realm of possibility.

All this is not to suggest, however, that Steamboat is a piece of cake for more experienced skiers. Pioneer Ridge encompasses advanced and intermediate terrain. Steamboat is renowned as a breeding ground for top mogul skiers, and for good reason. There are numerous mogul runs, but most are not particularly steep. The few with a vertical challenge, such as Chute One, are not especially long. If you're looking for challenging skiing at Steamboat, take on the trees. The ski area has done an admirable job of clearing many gladed areas of such nuisances as saplings, underbrush, and fallen timber, making Steamboat tree skiing much less hazardous than at other areas. The trees are also where advanced skiers—as well as, in some places, confident intermediates—can find the best of Steamboat's much-ballyhooed powder.

Statistically, Steamboat doesn't report significantly more snowfall than other Colorado resorts, but somehow snow piles up here better than at the others. Ask well-traveled Colorado skiers, and they'll confirm that when it comes to consistently good, deep snow, Steamboat is hard to beat. Also, when conditions permit, the ski area opens up for night skiing. **Facilities:** 165 trails; 2,965 acres; 3,668-foot vertical drop; 18 lifts. ⊠ *2305 Mount Werner Circle* ☎ *970/879–6111* ⊕ *www.steamboat. com* ⊠ *Lift ticket $119* ⊙ *Late Nov.–mid-Apr., daily 8:30–3:30.*

LESSONS AND PROGRAMS

Half-day group lessons begin at $169; all-day lessons are $199. Clinics in moguls, powder, snowboarding, and "hyper-carving"—made possible by the design of shaped skis—are available.

Snow-cat skiing—where a vehicle delivers you to hard-to-reach slopes—has been called the poor man's version of helicopter skiing, although at $400 to $450 a day that's probably a misnomer. It's true that snow cat users don't have to worry about landing, and can get to places that would be inaccessible by helicopter.

Billy Kidd Center for Performance Skiing. Intensive one- and three-day training camps in racing and advanced skiing are available through the Billy Kidd Center for Performance Skiing. ⊠ *Steamboat Springs* ☎ *800/299–5017, 970/879–6111* ⊠ *From $200.*

FAMILY **Kids' Vacation Center.** Programs for children from 6 months to 15 years of age are given through the Kids' Vacation Center. Day care is also available. ⊠ *Steamboat Springs* ☎ *970/879–0740.*

Steamboat Powder Cats. Buffalo Pass, northeast of Steamboat, is one of the snowiest spots in Colorado, and that's why it's the base for Steamboat Powder Cats. There's a maximum of 12 skiers per group, so the open-meadow skiing is never crowded. ⊠ *1724 Mt. Werner Circle* ☎ *970/879–5188* ⊕ *www.steamboatpowdercats.com* ⊠ *From $475.*

Steamboat Ski and Resort Corporation. General information about the Steamboat Springs ski areas is available through the Steamboat Ski and Resort Corporation. ⊠ *Steamboat Springs* ☎ *970/879–6111, 877/237–2628 reservations* ⊕ *www.steamboat.com.*

RENTALS

Steamboat Central Reservations. Equipment packages are available at the gondola base as well as at ski shops in town. Packages (skis, boots, and poles) average about $45 a day, less for multiday rentals. Call Steamboat Central Reservations for rental information. ⊠ *Steamboat Springs* ☎ *970/879–0740* ⊕ *www.steamboat.com.*

9

NORDIC SKIING

BACKCOUNTRY SKIING

The most popular area for backcountry skiing around Steamboat Springs is Rabbit Ears Pass, southeast of town. It's the last pass you cross if you're driving from Denver to Steamboat. Much of the appeal is its easy access to high-country trails from U.S. 40. There are plenty of routes you can take.

Hahns Peak Ranger Office. A popular backcountry spot is Seedhouse Road, about 26 miles north of Steamboat, near the town of Clark. A marked network of trails across the rolling hills has good views of distant peaks. For maps and information on snow conditions, contact the Hahns Peak Ranger Office. ⊠ *400 Seedhouse Rd.* ☎ *970/870–2299.*

Ski Haus. Touring and telemarking rentals are available at ski shops in the Steamboat area. One of the best is the Ski Haus. ⊠ *1457 Pine Grove Rd.* ☎ *970/879–0385* ⊕ *www.skihaussteamboat.com.*

Steamboat Ski Touring Center. Arrangements for backcountry tours can be made through Steamboat Ski Touring Center. Trail passes cost $20. ⊠ *Steamboat Springs* ✛ *Left on Steamboat Blvd. from Mt. Werner Rd.; second right at Steamboat Ski Touring Center sign* ☎ *970/879–8180* ⊕ *www.steamboatnordiccenter.com.*

TRACK SKIING

Steamboat Ski Touring Center. Laid out on and along the Sheraton Steamboat Golf Club, Steamboat Ski Touring Center has a relatively gentle 18½-mile trail network. A good option for a relaxed afternoon of skiing is to pick up some vittles at the Picnic Basket in the main building and enjoy a picnic along Fish Creek Trail, a 3-mile-long loop that winds through pine and aspen groves. Rental packages (skis, boots, and poles) are available. ⊠ *1230 Steamboat Blvd.* ☎ *970/879–8180* ⊕ *www.steamboatnordiccenter.com* ⊡ *Trail fee $20.*

Vista Verde Guest Ranch. This guest ranch has a well-groomed network of tracks (about 9 miles), as well as access to the adjacent national forest. ⊠ *58000 Cowboy Way, Clark* ☎ *970/879–3858* ⊕ *www.vistaverde.com.*

OTHER SPORTS AND THE OUTDOORS

Steamboat Central Reservations. Dogsledding, hot-air ballooning, and snowmobiling can be arranged by calling the activities department at Steamboat Central Reservations. ⊠ *1475 Pine Grove Rd.* ☎ *970/879–0740.*

GOLF

Haymaker Golf Course. Three miles south of Steamboat Springs, this public-access 18-hole Keith Foster course has a pro shop and café. The challenging, rolling course has hills, streams, and native grasses, as well as exceptional views. The course is noted for being well maintained, with large greens and a 10,000-square-foot putting green. ⊠ *34855 U.S. 40* ☎ *970/870–1846* ⊕ *www.haymakergolf.com* ⊡ *$119* ⊼. *Silver course: 18 holes, 7308 yards, par 72; Blue course: 18 holes, 5059 yards, par 72; Gold course: 18 holes, 6728 yards, par 72; White course: 18 holes, 6151 yards, par 72* ⌖ *Reservations essential.*

Rollingstone Ranch Golf Club at the Sheraton Steamboat Resort. Expect to see plenty of wildlife on this 18-hole championship course, which was designed by the legendary Robert Trent Jones Jr. The extensive practice facilities include a driving range, a bunker, and a putting green. The Fish Creek Grille ($) serves lunch and a well-rounded happy hour and appetizer menu after 3 pm and until 6. ⊠ *1230 Steamboat Blvd.* ☎ *970/879–1391* ⊕ *www.rollingstoneranchgolf.com* ⊡ *$159* ⊼. *Black* *course: 18 holes, 6902 yards, par 72; Green course: 18 holes, 5205 yards, par 72 ⌕ Reservations essential.*

HORSEBACK RIDING

Because of the ranches surrounding the Yampa and Elk rivers, Steamboat is full of real cowboys as well as visitors trying to act the part. Horseback riding is popular here for good reason: seeing the area on horseback is not only easier on the legs, but it also allows riders to get deeper into the backcountry—which is crisscrossed by a web of deer and elk trails—and sometimes closer to wildlife than is possible on foot.

Del's Triangle 3 Ranch. This facility can organize rides from hour-long tours to journeys lasting several days. It's about 20 miles north of Steamboat via Highway 129. ⌖ *55675 County Rd. 62, Clark* ☎ *970/879–3495* ⊕ *www.steamboathorses.com.*

Howelsen Rodeo Grounds. Every Friday and Saturday evening in summer, rodeos are held at the Howelsen Rodeo Grounds. ⌖ *5th St. and Howelsen Pkwy.* ☎ *970/879–1818* ⊕ *steamboatprorodeo.com* ⌑ *$18.*

Sombrero Ranch. This ranch is right in Steamboat Springs and has one-hour guided tours that are perfect for novices. ⌖ *835 River Rd.* ☎ *970/879–2306* ⊕ *www.sombrero.com/steamboatsprings.*

MOUNTAIN BIKING

Steamboat Springs' rolling mountains, endless aspen glades, mellow valleys, and miles and miles of Jeep trails and single-track make for great mountain biking. In summer, when Front Range trails are baking in the harsh summer sun and cluttered with mountain bikers, horse riders, and hikers, you can pedal some of the cool backcountry trails in Steamboat without passing a single cyclist.

Gore Pass Loop. The 27½-mile Gore Pass Loop takes you through aspen and pine forests, with gradual hill climbs and long, sweet descents. ⌖ *Hwy. 134 and Forest Rd. 185* ⊹ *Trailhead: Follow Hwy. 134 to Gore Pass Park.*

Orange Peel Bicycle Service. This bike shop offers a sweet line of demos that cost about double the regular rental rates, which start at $28 for a half day. It's a good deal if you're in the market for a new bike. ⌖ *1136 Yampa St.* ☎ *970/879–2957* ⊕ *www.orangepeelbikes.com.*

RAFTING

Bucking Rainbow Outfitters. This outfitter runs rafting excursions to the Yampa, Elk, Colorado, North Platte, and Eagle rivers. Half-day to two-day trips are available for all levels. ⌖ *730 Lincoln Ave.* ☎ *970/879–8747* ⊕ *www.buckingrainbow.com* ⌑ *From $50.*

WHERE TO EAT

$$$$
MODERN
AMERICAN
Fodor'sChoice
★

✕ **Cafe Diva.** A pretty, egg yolk–yellow but unfussy dining room is an ideal backdrop for fresh, locally sourced modern American dishes from a menu that lists a fair number of vegan and gluten-free options that put some effort into their creation, such as a tower of quinoa falafels with fried green tomatoes. Meat eaters will be happy here, too, though: Elk and pork belly tenderloins are lightly sauced (Cabernet veal demi-glace, say) and treated to savory sides. The well-varied wine list starts off with a dozen by-the-glass options you won't see elsewhere, and the savvy staff is excited to share their picks as well as entice guests to try something new. It's easy to choose only from the small-plate selections and make a meal of it, but don't forget about things like salted caramel ice-cream sandwiches or cherry-pie empanadas waiting at the end. [$] *Average main: $35* ✉ *1855 Ski Time Square Dr.* ☎ *970/871–0508* 🌐 *www.cafediva.com* ⏲ *No lunch* ✍ *Reservations essential* 💳 *No credit cards.*

$$ AMERICAN 🍴 **Carl's Tavern.** Named after Karl Hovelsen, the Norwegian ski jumper who brought the sport to Colorado in the early 1900s and who also lent his name to Steamboat's Howelsen Hill, this modern tavern serves updated takes on comfort food, with an emphasis on locally sourced ingredients and as many items produced in-house as possible. Local favorites include chicken-fried steak, three-cheese mac, and lemon icebox pie, but it's also tough to pass up the pot roast made from Angus beef or the banana-chocolate bread pudding. Sunday brunch is packed, so be prepared to wait. [$] *Average main: $16* ✉ *700 Yampa Ave.* ☎ *970/761–2060* 🌐 *www.carlstavern.com* 💳 *No credit cards* ⏲ *No lunch Mon.* ✍ *Reservations essential.*

$ AMERICAN FAMILY 🍴 **Creekside Café & Grill.** This café's hearty breakfasts and lunches, which are crafted to get folks through a day of skiing or biking, are served in a casual atmosphere that's family—and group—friendly. The most popular item on the menu, and for good reason, is the roster of a dozen eggs Benedict choices, including "the Arnold," with smoked bacon, ham, and chorizo. On nice days, ask to sit on the patio next to pretty Soda Creek. In season the place is usually jam-packed. Everything on the great kids' menu is $5. [$] *Average main: $12* ✉ *131 11th St.* ☎ *970/879–4925* 🌐 *www.creekside-cafe.com* ⏲ *No dinner* ✍ *Reservations essential.*

$$ ITALIAN FAMILY 🍴 **Cugino's Pizzeria & Italian Restaurant.** The South Philly sensibility of this pizzeria lends authenticity to its filling strombolis, stuffed pizzas that may have originated just outside Philadelphia. The casual dining room offers a lot of breathing room, with the wooden tables that allow plenty of space for big groups to maneuver, a spacious patio deck, and a small bar area with a TV and an attached deck. Food comes in big portions, the patios are great for people-watching and views of the Yampa River, and the staff here will take good care of you. Try the crispy New York–style pizza and the authentic-tasting spaghetti. [$] *Average main: $14* ✉ *41 8th St.* ☎ *970/879–5805* 🌐 *www.cuginosrestaurant.com.*

$$$$ FRENCH Fodor's Choice ★ 🍴 **Harwigs.** Steamboat's most intimate restaurant is in a building that once housed Harwig's Saddlery and Western Wear. There are two dining rooms, one that is more formal, the other casual. The classic French cuisine, with subtle Asian influences, is well crafted, and the menu changes monthly. Especially fine are the innovative duck and seafood dishes, and the rotating foie gras appetizers. Still, the menu takes a backseat to the admirable wine list: owner Jamie Jenny is a collector whose wine cellar contains more than 10,000 bottles, and you can order more than 40 wines by the glass. [$] *Average main: $34* ✉ *911 Lincoln Ave.* ☎ *970/879–1919* 🌐 *www.lapogee.com* ⏲ *No lunch* ✍ *Reservations essential.*

$ AMERICAN FAMILY 🍴 **Johnny B. Good's Diner.** Between the appealing kids' menu and the memorabilia that suggests Elvis has not left the building, Johnny's is all about fun and family. Breakfast (until 2 pm), lunch, and dinner are served daily, and they are all budget minded and large portioned. The menu is mostly what you'd expect—comfort food like meat loaf and mashed potatoes, burgers, milkshakes, and biscuits and gravy—but they also do an above-average rib eye and some tasty Mexican, as well as a popular list of hot "dawgs." [$] *Average main: $10* ✉ *738 Lincoln Ave.* ☎ *970/870–8400* 🌐 *www.johnnybgoodsdiner.com* ✍ *Reservations not accepted.*

$$$ MEXICAN FAMILY 🍴 **La Montaña.** This Southwestern and Tex-Mex establishment is among Steamboat's most popular restaurants, and with good reason. The kitchen incorporates indigenous specialties into the traditional menu. Among the standouts are sunflower seed–crusted tuna with a margarita beurre blanc, enchiladas layered with Monterey Jack and goat cheese and roasted peppers, and buffalo loin crusted with pecan nuts and bourbon cream sauce. Excellent (read; strong) margaritas, and the light, cinnamon-spicy Mexican twist on bananas Foster is a worthy finale. [$] *Average main: $20* ✉ *2500 Village Dr., at Après Ski Way* ☎ *970/879–5800* 🌐 *www.lamontanasteamboat.com* 🕒 *No lunch* ✍ *Reservations essential.*

$$$$ MODERN AMERICAN Fodor's Choice ★ 🍴 **Laundry Kitchen & Cocktails.** Small plates are the way to go in this convivial, casual setting, which was indeed the Steamboat Laundry from 1910 to 1977 but now serves tasty modern American tidbits such as fried shoestring potatoes sprinkled with duck fat powder and house-smoked trout with goat cheese in a jar (the "jar" offering routinely changes). House-cured meats and hand-crafted cocktails are also specialties. The dining room is rustic and cozy—exposed brick and original wood—and the service is spot-on. If you show up without reservations, the spacious bar is just as good, with its high-top tables and the roomy bar itself; the impeccable service spills over into this area, too. [$] *Average main: $28* ✉ *127 11th St.* ☎ *970/870–0681* 🌐 *www.thelaundryrestaurant.com* 🕒 *No lunch* ✍ *Reservations essential.*

$$$ ITALIAN 🍴 **Riggio's.** In a dramatic industrial space, this Italian eatery evokes the Old Country with tapestries, murals, and landscape photos. The menu includes tasty pizzas (with toppings such as goat cheese and clams) and pasta dishes (the lobster and basil gnocchi with potatoes and artichokes is superb). Standards such as manicotti, chicken cacciatore, and saltimbocca are also well prepared, but one of the best dishes is the Capo, with sea scallops and prawns in tomato cream sauce over penne. Try the house salad with Gorgonzola vinaigrette. [$] *Average main: $22* ✉ *1106 Lincoln Ave.* ☎ *970/879–9010* 🕒 *No lunch* ✍ *Reservations essential.*

WHERE TO STAY

$$ B&B/INN 🏨 **Alpine Rose Bed and Breakfast.** Views of Strawberry Park and an easy walk into town make the Alpine Rose a wonderful alternative to pricey hotels, especially during ski season. **Pros:** close to town; relatively close to ski area (five-minute drive); reasonably priced. **Cons:** not right next to ski area; two-night minimum can be an issue. [$] *Rooms from: $125* ✉ *724 Grand St.* ☎ *970/879–1528* 🌐 *www.alpinerosesteamboat.com* 🛏 *4 rooms, 1 suite* 🍽 *Breakfast.*

LODGING ALTERNATIVES

Mountain Resorts. This vacation rental company manages condominiums at more than two dozen locations. ✉ *2145 Resort Dr., Suite 100* ☎ *888/686–8075* 🌐 *www.mtn-resorts.com* 🍴 *No meals.*

Steamboat Resorts. Steamboat Resorts rents plenty of properties near the slopes. ☎ *800/276–6719* 🌐 *www.steamboatresorts.com* 🍴 *No meals.*

Wyndham Vacation Rentals. Torian Plum, one of the properties managed by Wyndham Vacation Rentals has elegant one- to six-bedroom units in a ski-in ski-out location, some with hot tubs. ✉ *1855 Ski Time Sq.* ☎ *970/879–8811* 🌐 *www.wyndhamvacationrentals.com* 🛏 *64 condos* 🍴 *No meals.*

$$$$ RESORT FAMILY 🏨 **Home Ranch.** You won't be roughing it at this all-inclusive retreat, a high-end property set among towering stands of aspen north of Steamboat near Clark. **Pros:** luxury experience; excellent food; family-friendly. **Cons:** pricey; seven-day stay can be prohibitive in summer; less authentic. [$] *Rooms from: $710* ✉ *54880 County Rd. 129, Clark* ☎ *970/879–1780* 🌐 *www.homeranch.com* 🕒 *Closed mid-April–May and early Oct.–late Dec.* 🛏 *6 rooms, 8 cabins* 🍴 *All meals.*

$$ HOTEL FAMILY 🏨 **Hotel Bristol.** A delightful small hotel nestled in a 1948 building, the Bristol not only has location working for it, but also old-fashioned personalized service. **Pros:** families and groups can stay comfortably for a little bit extra; convenient location; ski lockers. **Cons:** rooms may seem uncomfortably small, bathrooms even more so. [$] *Rooms from: $139* ✉ *917 Lincoln Ave.* ☎ *970/879–3083* 🌐 *www.steamboathotelbristol.com* 🛏 *22 rooms, 2 suites* 🍴 *No meals.*

$$ B&B/INN 🏨 **Inn at Steamboat.** Rustic knotty pine, leather furniture, comfortable linens, and panoramic views of the Yampa Valley make this inn a good choice for visitors looking to stay somewhere that feels like a mountain lodge at lower-than-ski-resort prices. **Pros:** magnificent views, even from the heated pool and particularly in fall; reasonable rates. **Cons:** not ski-in ski-out. [$] *Rooms from: $149* ✉ *3070 Columbine Dr.* ☎ *970/879–2600* 🌐 *www.innatsteamboat.com* 🛏 *28 rooms, 6 suites* 🍴 *Breakfast.*

$$$ HOTEL FAMILY 🏨 **Ptarmigan Inn.** Situated on the slopes, this laid-back lodging couldn't have a more convenient location. **Pros:** great location; ski-in ski-out; mountain views. **Cons:** feels a bit like a chain hotel. [$] *Rooms from: $189* ✉ *2304 Après Ski Way* ☎ *970/879–1730* 🌐 *www.theptarmigan.com* 🛏 *77 rooms* 🍴 *No meals.*

$ HOTEL FAMILY 🏨 **Rabbit Ears Motel.** The playful, pink-neon bunny sign outside this motel has been a local landmark since 1952, making it an unofficial gateway to Steamboat Springs. **Pros:** great location; family- and pet-friendly. **Cons:** kitschy; nothing fancy; it can be noisy along the main drag. [$] *Rooms from: $79* ✉ *201 Lincoln Ave.* ☎ *970/879–1150* 🌐 *www.rabbitearsmotel.com* 🛏 *65 rooms* 🍴 *Breakfast.*

$$$$ HOTEL FAMILY Fodor's Choice ★ [hotel] **Sheraton Steamboat Resort & Villas.** This bustling high-rise is one of Steamboat's few ski-in ski-out properties. **Pros:** convenient location, with the slopes, five restaurants, and town right there; large size means lots of amenities. **Cons:** lobby areas can be chaotic; prices now on par with major ski areas. [$] *Rooms from: $379* ✉ *2200 Village End Ct.* ☎ *970/879–2220* 🌐 *www.sheratonsteamboatresort.com* 🛏 *188 rooms, 52 suites, 20 condos, 21 villas* 🍴 *Breakfast.*

$$ B&B/INN FAMILY [hotel] **Steamboat Mountain Lodge.** River or mountain views await you at this budget-minded spot, which counts a river-rock fireplace surrounded by cozy couches and a Jacuzzi on the deck among its charms. **Pros:** great views; spacious rooms; bargain prices. **Cons:** very simple decor; breakfast is nothing special. [$] *Rooms from: $137* ✉ *3155 S. Lincoln St.* ☎ *970/871–9121* 🌐 *www.steamboatmountainlodge.com* 🛏 *38 rooms* 🍴 *Breakfast.*

$$$$ B&B/INN Fodor's Choice ★ [hotel] **Vista Verde Guest Ranch.** On a working ranch, the luxurious Vista Verde provides city slickers with an authentic Western experience. **Pros:** authentic experience; variable stays; family-friendly. **Cons:** pricey; remote. [$] *Rooms from: $431* ✉ *31100 County Rd. 64, Clark* ☎ *970/879–3858* 🌐 *www.vistaverde.com* ⏲ *Closed mid-Mar.–early June and Oct.–mid-Dec.* 🛏 *3 rooms, 9 cabins* 🍴 *All meals.*

NIGHTLIFE

Mahogany Ridge Brewery & Grill. Mahogany Ridge Brewery & Grill serves superior pub grub and pours an assortment of its own ales, lagers, porters, and stouts. Live music is a nice bonus on weekends. ✉ *435 Lincoln Ave.* ☎ *970/879–3773* 🌐 *www.mahoganyridgesteamboat.com.*

Old Town Pub. This pub serves juicy burgers accompanied by music from some great bands. A limited bar menu and homemade pizza is served until 1 am. ✉ *600 Lincoln Ave.* ☎ *970/879–2101* 🌐 *www.theoldtownpub.com.*

SHOPPING

At the base of the ski area are three expansive shopping centers—Ski Time Square, Torian Plum Plaza, and Gondola Square.

Old Town Square. Downtown Steamboat's Old Town Square is a collection of upscale boutiques and retailers. There are also plenty of places to sit and people-watch or get a good cup of coffee. ✉ *7th St. and Lincoln Ave.*

BOOKSTORES

Off the Beaten Path. Off the Beaten Path is a throwback to the Beat Generation, with poetry readings, lectures, and concerts. It has an excellent selection of New Age works, in addition to the usual best sellers and travel guides. The on-site coffee shop is the best in town, with fresh baked goods and sandwiches. Hours vary so call ahead to confirm. ✉ *68 9th St.* ☎ *970/879–6830* 🌐 *www.steamboatbooks.com.*

BOUTIQUES AND GALLERIES

Silver Lining. This shop displays beautifully designed jewelry from around the world, such as Peruvian opal necklaces, as well as locally crafted Western pieces using turquoise and silver. They carry an extensive and well-organized selection of beads and found objects for making your own, which you can do on a small scale at one end of the tiny store. They also offer jewelry repair and pearl knotting. ⊠ *Torian Plum Plaza, 1855 Ski Time Sq. Dr.* ☎ *970/879–7474* ⊕ *www.silverlininginsteamboat.com.*

White Hart Gallery. This gallery is a magnificent clutter of Western-theme paintings and furniture, as well as objets d'art. ⊠ *843 Lincoln Ave.* ☎ *970/879–1015.*

Wild Horse Gallery. Native American images, local landscapes, and wildlife adorn the walls of the Wild Horse Gallery. This shop across from the Steamboat Art Museum is the place to buy artwork, jewelry, and blown glass. ⊠ *802 Lincoln Ave.* ☎ *970/879–5515* ⊕ *www. wildhorsegallery.com.*

SPORTING GOODS

Ski Haus. If you need to be outfitted for the slopes, look no further than Ski Haus, which has a full line of winter gear and also offers rentals. ⊠ *1457 Pine Grove Rd.* ☎ *970/879–0385* ⊕ *www. skihaussteamboat.com.*

Straightline Sports. This sporting-goods store is a good bet for downhill necessities. ⊠ *744 Lincoln Ave.* ☎ *970/879–7568* ⊕ *www. straightlinesports.com.*

WESTERN WEAR

F.M. Light and Sons. Owned by the same family for four generations, F.M. Light and Sons caters to the cowpoke in all of us. If you're lucky you'll find a bargain on the Western wear here. ⊠ *830 Lincoln Ave.* ☎ *800/530–8908* ⊕ *www.fmlight.com.*

Romick's Into the West. A former member of the U.S. Ski Team and a veteran of the rodeo circuit, Jace Romick crafts splendid textured lodgepole furniture. His cavernous store also includes antiques (including ornate potbellied stoves), cowhide mirrors, and handicrafts such as Native American–drum tables and fanciful candleholders fashioned from branding irons. ⊠ *402 Lincoln Ave.* ☎ *970/879–8377.*

Soda Creek Western Outfitters. This outfitter is about 30 miles west of Steamboat and worth the drive if authentic Western attire, including boots and hats, is on your shopping list. They also sell all manner of cowboy collectibles; home-decor items; gear; kitschy stuff for your dog, horse, and truck; and locally crafted jewelry. ⊠ *224 Arthur Ave., Oak Creek* ☎ *970/736–2811* ⊕ *www.soda-creek.com.*

NORTHWEST CORNER

Between the Flat Tops Scenic Byway and Dinosaur National Monument, the northwest corner of the state, which feels remote and desolate in parts, overflows with history. Dinosaur fans will delight in exploring the monument, and folks looking for evidence of early Indian habitation will delight in the petroglyphs and pictographs. The towns are small and sleepy, but their inhabitants, many devoted to fishing, hunting, and other area outdoor pursuits, could not be more welcoming.

MEEKER

43 miles north of Rifle via Rte. 13.

Once an outpost of the U.S. Army, Meeker is still a place where anyone in camouflage is in fashion. Famous for its annual sheepdog championships—a sheepdog statue keeps watch over the sleepy town—it remains a favorite spot for hunting, fishing, and snowmobiling. Interesting historical buildings include the Meeker Hotel on Main Street, where Teddy Roosevelt stayed.

GETTING HERE AND AROUND

Meeker is fairly isolated, and nearly equidistant between Grand Junction and Steamboat Springs. There is no public transportation in town, and a car is needed.

ESSENTIALS

Visitor Information Meeker Chamber of Commerce. ⊠ *878 Market St.* ☎ *970/878-5510* ⊕ *www.meekerchamber.com.*

EXPLORING

White River Museum. This museum is housed in a long building that served as a barracks for U.S. Army officers. Inside are exhibits such as a collection of guns dating to the Civil War and the plow used by Nathan Meeker to dig up the Ute's pony racetrack. ⊠ *565 Park Ave.* ☎ *970/878-9982* ⊕ *www.meekercolorado.com/museum.htm* 🖅 *Free* ⊙ *Mid-Apr.–Nov., weekdays 9–5, weekends 10–5; Dec.–mid-Apr., daily 10–4.*

SPORTS AND THE OUTDOORS

FISHING

JML Outfitters. The White River valley is home to some of the best fishing holes in Colorado, including Meeker Town Park, Sleepy Cat Access, and Trappers Lake. Some of the best fishing is on private land, so you need to ask permission, and you might have to pay. Your best bet—if you don't want to go it alone—is to hire a guide familiar with the area, such as JML Outfitters, which has been in the outfitting business for three generations, offering photography and wildlife-viewing trips, kids' camps, and trail rides. Rates vary by excursion. ⊠ *300 County Rd. 75* ☎ *970/878-4749* ⊕ *www.jmloutfitters.com* 🖅 *From $125.*

SNOWMOBILING

Welder Outfitting Services. One of Meeker's best-kept secrets is the fantastic snowmobiling through pristine powder in the backcountry, which some say rivals Yellowstone—without the crowds. Trail maps for self-guided rides are available through the Chamber of Commerce or the U.S. Forest Service, or from Welder Outfitting Services, a hunting and fishing service that also organizes snowmobile trips in the White River National Forest and Flat Tops Wilderness. Rates vary by excursion. ⊠ *Meeker* ☎ *970/878-9869* ⊕ *www.welderoutfitters.com* 🖅 *From $55.*

9

WHERE TO STAY

$ HOTEL **Meeker Hotel and Cafe.** The lobby is lined with framed broadsheet biographies of famous figures—such as Teddy Roosevelt—who stayed in this landmark, which is on the National Register of Historic Places. **Pros:** delightful decor; delicious food in the café; accommodating staff. **Cons:** the café can get crowded and noisy; the walls are paper-thin. [$] *Rooms from: $80* ✉ *560 Main St.* ☎ *970/878–5255* 🌐 *www.themeekerhotel.com* 🛏 *9 rooms, 5 suites* 🍴 *No meals.*

SHOPPING

Fawn Creek Gallery. Featuring original watercolor paintings and limited-edition prints by Colorado artist John T. Myers, Fawn Creek Gallery also sells Fremont and Ute rock-art replicas and duck carvings made from 100-year-old cedar fence posts. ✉ *315 6th St.* ☎ *970/878–0955* 🌐 *www.fawncreekgallery.com.*

Wendll's Wondrous Things. An old-fashioned mercantile building with original display cases, tin ceilings, and wood floors, Wendll's Wondrous Things (open at 6 am) sells an eclectic mix of clothing, housewares, body-care products, greeting cards, Brighton jewelry, and Native American turquoise and sterling silver from Arizona. The attached coffee shop, Cuppa Joe, makes a welcoming stop. ✉ *594 Main St.* ☎ *970/878–3688.*

CRAIG

48 miles north of Meeker via Rte. 13; 42 miles west of Steamboat Springs via U.S. 40.

Craig is home to some of the best fishing in the area. Guided trips to the hottest fishing spots are available, as are horseback pack trips into the wilderness. Depending on the season, you might spot bighorn sheep, antelope, or nesting waterfowl, including the Great Basin Canada goose.

GETTING HERE AND AROUND

U.S. 40 west from Denver or east from Utah is the best way to reach Craig. All Around Taxi provides service in town.

ESSENTIALS

Transportation Contacts **All Around Taxi.** ✉ *Craig* ☎ *970/824–1177.*

Visitor Information **Craig Chamber of Commerce.** ✉ *360 E. Victory Way* ☎ *970/824–5689* 🌐 *www.craig-chamber.com.*

EXPLORING

Marcia Car. One of Craig's most prized historical possessions, the Marcia Car in City Park was the private Pullman car of Colorado magnate David Moffat, who at one time was full or partial owner of more than 100 gold and silver mines. Moffat was also instrumental in bringing railroad transportation to northwest Colorado. He used his private car to inspect construction work on the Moffat Railroad line. Named after his only child, the car has been restored and makes for an interesting tour. ✉ *360 E. Victory Way* ☎ *970/824–5689* 🎟 *Free* 🕒 *Tours weekdays 8–5.*

Museum of Northwest Colorado. This museum elegantly displays an eclectic collection of everything from arrowheads to a fire truck. The upstairs of this restored county courthouse holds the largest privately owned collection of working cowboy artifacts in the world. Bill Mackin, one of the leading traders in cowboy collectibles, has spent a lifetime gathering guns, bits, saddles, bootjacks, holsters, and spurs of all descriptions. ⊠ *590 Yampa Ave.* ☎ *970/824–6360* ⊕ *www.museumnwco.org* ✉ *Free, donations accepted* ☉ *Weekdays 9–5, Sat. 10–4.*

SPORTS AND THE OUTDOORS
FISHING
Sportsman's Center at the Craig Chamber of Commerce. The Yampa and Green rivers, Trappers Lake, Lake Avery, and Elkhead Reservoir are known for pike and trout. Contact the Sportsman's Center at the Craig Chamber of Commerce for information. ⊠ *360 E. Victory Way* ☎ *970/864–4405* ⊕ *www.craig-chamber.com/hunting.html.*

WHERE TO EAT AND STAY
$ ✕ **Gino's Neighborhood Pizzeria & Grill.** The staff is friendly and the pizzas
ITALIAN are excellent, thin-crust, and "Philly-style," which means they also offer
FAMILY that town's famous stromboli with the same thin, crispy crust. If you'd rather have pasta, the homemade lasagna is a rare treat. An exposition kitchen means lots of give-and-take between the dining room and the family that runs the place, and they still have the large, foliage-lined patio with its backyard feel. $ *Average main: $12* ⊠ *572 Breeze St.* ☎ *970/824–6323* ⊗ *Reservations not accepted.*

$ ⊡ **Clarion Inn & Suites.** The amenities at Craig's largest hotel include a rec-
HOTEL reational center with a pool, whirlpool, and exercise and game rooms, all inside a lush atrium. **Pros:** on-site restaurant; spacious rooms. **Cons:** area around hotel can be noisy at night. $ *Rooms from: $74* ⊠ *300 Rte. 13 S* ☎ *970/824–4000* ⊕ *www.choicehotels.com* ⇔ *152 rooms, 19 suites* ⦿❘ *Breakfast.*

DINOSAUR NATIONAL MONUMENT

90 miles west of Craig via U.S. 40.

Overlapping the border between Colorado and Utah, Dinosaur National Monument offers river runners and dinosaur enthusiasts a remote and magnificent attraction that more than rewards the effort to get here. Colorful canyons and endless opportunities to examine fossils and bones make the monument a unique destination, and the Yampa and Green rivers provide cooling relief from what is much of the year a hot and dry desert landscape.

GETTING HERE AND AROUND
U.S. 40 west from Denver or east from Utah is the best way to reach Dinosaur National Monument. You also can take Highway 139 and Route 64 from Grand Junction. The town of Dinosaur, with a few somewhat dilapidated concrete dinosaur statues watching over their namesake town, merits only a brief stop on the way to the real thing: the bones at Dinosaur National Monument.

EXPLORING

FAMILY
Fodor's Choice ★

Dinosaur National Monument. Straddling the Colorado–Utah border, Dinosaur National Monument is a must for any dinosaur enthusiast. A two-story hill teeming with fossils—many still in the complete skeletal shapes of the dinosaurs—greets visitors at one of the few places in the world where you can touch a dinosaur bone still embedded in the earth. The Colorado side of the park offers some of the best hiking in the West, along the Harpers Corner and Echo Park Drive routes and the ominous-sounding Canyon of Lodore (where the Green River rapids buffet rafts). The drive is only accessible in summer—even then, four-wheel drive is preferable—and some of the most breathtaking overlooks are well off the beaten path. ✉ *4545 E. Hwy. 40, Dinosaur* ☎ *435/781–7700* 🌐 *www.nps.gov/dino* 🎟 *$10 per vehicle; $5 per individual.*

Dinosaur Quarry. After its predecessor was closed for five years because of structural damage, the much-anticipated Dinosaur Quarry Exhibit Hall opened in 2011, showcasing an estimated 1,500 dinosaur bones that date to the late Jurassic Period still embedded in the clay. Open daily, the Exhibit Hall is ranger-guided only in the winter; check the website or call ahead for shuttle hours and access availability. Fossils are visible only from the Utah side of the monument, not the Colorado side. A half mile away is a massive 7,595-square-foot visitor center. ✉ *Visitor center: 7 miles north of Jensen, Utah, on Rte. 139, Dinosaur* ☎ *970/374–3000 Canyon Visitor Center in Colorado, 435/781–7700 Quarry Visitor Center in Utah* 🌐 *nps.gov/dino* 🎟 *$10 per vehicle; $5 per individual* ⏲ *Daily, hrs vary.*

SPORTS AND THE OUTDOORS

HIKING

FAMILY
Desert Voices Nature Trail. This nature trail is near the Dinosaur Quarry. The 1½-mile loop is moderate in difficulty and has a series of trail signs produced for kids by kids. ✉ *Split Mountain area, across from boat ramp, Dinosaur* 🌐 *nps.gov/dino.*

RAFTING

Adventure Bound River Expeditions. One of the best ways to experience the rugged beauty of the park is on a white-water raft trip. Adventure Bound River Expeditions runs two- to five-day excursions on the Colorado, Yampa, and Green rivers. ✉ *2392 H Rd., Grand Junction* ☎ *800/423–4668, 970/245–5428* 🌐 *www.adventureboundusa.com.*

WHERE TO EAT

$
AMERICAN
FAMILY

🍴 **BedRock Depot.** Co-owners and longtime residents Leona Hemmerich and Bill Mitchem understand both the cravings of the area's visitors and the spectacular vistas they come to see. New batches of homemade ice cream show up almost every day at their roadside shop, where the walls are a gallery for their photography and artwork. The shop sells fresh sandwiches—including a terrific roast beef on house-baked rolls—and specialty coffees (with names like "Mochasaurus") and bottled root beer, cream soda, and ginger ale. The Depot's immaculate restroom makes for one of the most pleasant pit stops on the long drive ahead. [$] *Average main: $6* ✉ *214 Brontosaurus W. Blvd., Dinosaur* ☎ *970/374–2336* 🌐 *www.bedrockdepot.com* ⏲ *No lunch Sun. Call for hrs Nov.–Mar.* ✍ *Reservations not accepted.*

$$ AMERICAN 🍴 **Massadona Tavern & Steak House.** A restaurant and bar, Massadona is small, homey, and rustic, with a smattering of Western decor items and a mixture of tables and booths. It's also a casual, inviting, and relaxing place to stop after a day of digging around in dinosaur dirt, even if it's kind of in the middle of nowhere (20 minutes east of Dinosaur and a half-hour drive from the monument). The inexpensive steaks go down well with a cocktail (also reasonably priced). They also do excellent breaded shrimp, good burgers (try the bacon cheeseburger), fish-and-chips, and classic Reubens. [$] *Average main: $14* ✉ *22927 Hwy. 40, Dinosaur* ☎ *970/374–2324* ⏲ *Closed Mon. No lunch weekdays* ✍ *Reservations not accepted.*

RANGELY

20 miles southeast of Dinosaur National Monument; 96 miles northwest of Grand Junction via Rte. 139 and 1–70.

The center of one of the last areas in the state to be explored by European settlers, Rangely was dubbed an "isolated empire" by early pioneers. You can search out the petroglyphs left by Native American civilizations or just stroll the farmers' market in Town Square. If you enjoy back-road mountain biking, the Raven Rims have an abundance of trails. You may even spot elk, mules, deer, coyotes, and other wildlife as you spin your wheels through the multihued sandstone rims and mesas north of town. Kenney Reservoir 5 miles north of town offers fishing and swimming, and a trip on the Cathedral Bluffs trail gives new definition to "isolated empire."

GETTING HERE AND AROUND

U.S. 40 west from Denver or east from Utah and then Route 64 south is the best way to get to Rangely. You can also take Highway 139 from Grand Junction. There are no transportation services in town.

ESSENTIALS

Visitor Information **Rangely Chamber of Commerce.** ✉ *209 E. Main St.* ☎ *970/675–5290* 🌐 *www.rangelychamber.com.*

EXPLORING

Canyon Pintado National Historic District. One of Rangely's most compelling sights is the superb Fremont petroglyphs—carved between AD 600 and 1300—in Douglas Creek canyon, south of town along Route 139. This stretch is known as the Canyon Pintado National Historic District, and the examples of rock art are among the best-preserved in the West; half the fun is clambering up the rocks to find them. A brochure listing the sights is available at the Rangely Chamber of Commerce. ✉ *Rangely* ☎ *970/675–5290* 🌐 *www.blm.gov/co* 🎟 *Free.*

SPORTS AND THE OUTDOORS

FISHING

Kenney Reservoir. Just below Taylor Draw Dam, Kenney Reservoir draws anglers in search of black crappie, channel catfish, and rainbow trout. The best fishing is right below the dam. If you hook one of Colorado's endangered pikeminnow, you'll have to throw it back. You can also go camping, boating, waterskiing, wildlife-watching, and picnicking. Locals come to the reservoir to watch the sun's last rays color the bluffs behind the lake. ⊠ *Rangely* ⊕ *www.rangely.com/ fishing.htm.*

MOUNTAIN BIKING

Town of Rangely. The best mountain-biking trails north of town are in the Raven Rims, named in honor of the abundant population of the large, noisy birds that live in the area. Contact the Town of Rangely for trail information. ⊠ *209 E. Main St.* ☎ *970/675–8476* ⊕ *www.rangely.com.*

WHERE TO EAT AND STAY

$$ ✕ **Giovanni's Italian Grill.** Between the thick, hearty pizzas, big-as-your-
ITALIAN head strombolis, and overflowing plates of pasta, it's hard to walk out
FAMILY of this friendly, casual eatery without feeling stuffed. The sauces are homemade, and the red sauce in particular is flavorful and authentic. The reasonably priced kids' menu, with nothing over $4, helps families feel welcome, and so does the staff, which is sometimes made up of the owners' family members. $ *Average main: $14* ⊠ *855 E. Main St.* ☎ *970/675–2670* ⊕ *www.letseat.at/GiovannisItalianGrill* ⊗ *Closed Sun.* ⚠ *Reservations essential.*

$ 🏨 **Blue Mountain Inn & Suites.** Rooms are simple but spacious at this reli-
HOTEL able hotel, which is next to a grocery store. **Pros:** inviting heated indoor pool and hot tub; pleasant lobby with soft, cozy chairs; centrally located. **Cons:** has a chain feel; rooms are sparsely decorated. $ *Rooms from: $105* ⊠ *37 Park St.* ☎ *970/675–8888* ⊕ *www.bluemountaininnrangely. com* ⇱ *47 rooms, 3 suites* ⦿| *Breakfast.*

SHOPPING

Sweetbriar. A wood-burning stove graces the front of charming Sweet-briar, a little store that sells a variety of gifts and home decor. ⊠ *781 W. Hwy. 64* ☎ *970/675–5353* ⊕ *sweetbriaronline.com.*

SOUTHWEST COLORADO

with the San Juan Mountains and
Black Canyon of the Gunnison

Updated by
Kellee Katagi

The reddish rocks found in much of the state, particularly in the southwest, give Colorado its name. The region's terrain varies widely—from yawning black canyons and desolate moonscapes to pastel deserts and mesas, glistening sapphire lakes, and wide expanses of those stunning red rocks. It's so rugged in the southwest that a four-wheel-drive vehicle or a pair of sturdy hiker's legs is necessary to explore much of the wild and beautiful backcountry.

The region's history and people are as colorful as the landscape. Southwestern Colorado, as well as the "Four Corners" neighbors of northwestern New Mexico, northeastern Arizona, and southeastern Utah, was home to the Ancestral Puebloans formerly known as Anasazi, meaning "ancient ones." These people, ancestors of today's Puebloan peoples (including the Zuni and Hopi tribes) constructed impressive cliff dwellings in what are now Mesa Verde National Park, Ute Mountain Tribal Park, and other nearby sites. This wild and woolly region, dotted with rowdy mining camps and boomtowns, also witnessed the antics of such notorious outlaws as Butch Cassidy, who embarked on his storied career by robbing the San Miguel Valley Bank in Telluride in 1889, and Robert "Bob" Ford, who hid out in Creede after shooting Jesse James in 1882.

Southwest Colorado has such diversity that, depending on where you go, you can have radically different vacations. You can spiral from the towering peaks of the San Juan range to the plunging Black Canyon of the Gunnison, taking in alpine scenery along the way, as well as the eerie remains of old mining camps, before winding through striking desert landscapes and Old West railroad towns. Even if you're not here to ski or golf in the resorts of Crested Butte, Durango, or Telluride, you'll still find plenty to experience in this part of the state.

ORIENTATION AND PLANNING

GETTING ORIENTED

Southwest Colorado is the land beyond the interstates. Old mining roads, legacies of the late 19th and early 20th centuries, when gold and silver mining was ascendant, lead through drop-dead-gorgeous mountain valleys and rugged high country. Much of this part of the state is designated as a wilderness area, which means that no roads may be built and no wheeled or motorized vehicles are permitted. Even some state highways are unpaved, and a federal highway known as U.S. 550 corkscrews over Red Mountain Pass, best known for its cliff-hugging turns and lack of guardrails. While backcountry roads demand four-wheel-drive vehicles in summer and snowmobiles in winter, regular roads are no problem for passenger cars.

TOP REASONS TO GO

Downhill skiing and snowboarding in Telluride: There's never much of a wait to take a lift up to the sweeping, groomed trails and challenging tree and mogul runs at this world-famous ski area, tucked among the highest concentration of 14,000-foot peaks in North America.

Driving the Million Dollar Highway: The scenery is unparalleled on this narrow, hairpin-turning road that winds over Red Mountain Pass between Ouray and Silverton.

Exploring Mesa Verde: Discover what life was like for ancient peoples in this region as you climb ladders to access the incredible cliff dwellings of Mesa Verde National Park.

Hiking the Colorado Trail: Bike, hike, or photograph along the nearly 500 miles of volunteer-maintained trails traversing eight major mountain ranges, seven national forests, and six wilderness areas from Durango to Denver.

Mountain biking in Crested Butte: The town is one of the birthplaces of fat-tire biking, and it's completely surrounded by up-close mountain scenery.

Crested Butte and Gunnison. Explore this mountain paradise on single-track in summer and Nordic track in winter. The Taylor and Gunnison rivers round out the adventure possibilities, with white-water rafting, kayaking, and great fly-fishing.

Black Canyon of the Gunnison National Park. The western town of Montrose makes a great base for exploring the majestic canyon, which plunges 2,000 feet down sheer vertical cliffs to the roaring Gunnison River.

Lake City and Creede. Route 149 meanders south from the Black Canyon of the Gunnison through a scattering of cozy, laid-back communities with deep mining roots.

Telluride and the San Juan Mountains. Old mining camps including Silverton, Ouray, and Telluride now welcome adventurers seeking other riches—wilderness trekking, rugged four-wheeling, mountain biking, skiing, and horseback riding.

Durango and Mesa Country. Durango is an ideal springboard for exploring nearby Mesa Country and its star attraction, Mesa Verde National Park. This college town is known for its eclectic eateries and historic hotels, as well as its many hiking and mountain-biking options.

PLANNING

WHEN TO GO

Like the rest of the state, southwestern Colorado is intensely seasonal. Snow typically begins falling in the high country in late September or early October, and by Halloween seasonal closures turn some unpaved alpine roads into routes for snowmobiles. The San Juan Mountains see average annual snowfalls approaching 400 inches in the highest spots. Winter lingers well into the season that is called spring on the calendar—the greatest snowfalls generally occur in March and April.

Skiing winds down in mid-April, as the snow in the higher elevations begins to melt. Some resort towns shut down almost completely from mid-April until late May, when cresting streams provide thrilling, if chilling, white-water rafting and kayaking. Hiking and biking trails become accessible, and wildflowers begin their short, intense season of show. Summer is glorious in the mountains, with brilliant sunshine and cobalt-blue skies. But it also brings brief and often intense showers on many an afternoon, sometimes accompanied by dramatic thunder and lightning. Summer tourism winds down after Labor Day, although fluttering, golden aspens increasingly draw leaf-peepers to the region in September and early October. After that, some resort towns take another hiatus for a few weeks. The mountains are popular year-round, but spring and fall are the best times to visit the hot, dry climate of the Mesa Country around the Four Corners.

PLANNING YOUR TIME

For the full southwestern Colorado experience, you'll need at least a week or 10 days. After all, there are no speedy interstates here—just winding two-lane highways over steep mountain passes.

If you're coming from Denver, start your visit with a couple of days in the mountain-biking, fishing, and skiing havens of Crested Butte and Gunnison. If time allows, take a day trip to the towns of Lake City and Creede for a taste of history and off-the-beaten-path beauty. Either way, for the next leg of your trip, travel west from Gunnison on U.S. 50 past the sprawling Curecanti National Recreation Area to the Black Canyon of the Gunnison. Be sure to carve out at least half a day here (more if you love hiking) to take in the panoramic views.

From there, you'll head southwest to Telluride for a couple of relaxing days, enjoying the region's best cuisine, toniest hotels, and most rewarding scenery. Next, continue southwest (via highways 145, 184, and 160) for a few days in Mesa Country. Plan to base yourself in Durango, with daytime excursions to Mesa Verde National Park (a must-see), Purgatory Resort, and the vast wilderness areas surrounding the town. Finally, head back north on U.S. 550, stopping for lunch in Silverton before the slow but ultrascenic trek over Red Mountain Pass, also known as the Million Dollar Highway (depending on whom you ask, the highway got its name from the views or from the precious metals under the mountain). Spend the night in Ouray—dubbed "The Switzerland of America" for its dramatic, jagged peaks—and take a soak in one of the town's hot springs before making your way back to Denver.

GETTING HERE AND AROUND

AIR TRAVEL

The Gunnison–Crested Butte Regional Airport (GUC) serves the nearby resort area. GUC is served by American, United, and United Express.

The closest regional airport to the Black Canyon of the Gunnison National Park is Montrose Regional Airport (MTJ). It's served by Allegiant, American, Delta, and United.

The Durango–La Plata County Airport (DRO) is your closest option for Silverton, Durango, Pagosa Springs, Mesa Verde National Park, and the Four Corners region. It's served by American Eagle, United, and US Airways. ■ TIP→ **Depending on your final destination in the Four Corners** region and airline schedules, you might want to consider flying to Albuquerque instead of Denver. The Albuquerque International Sunport (ABQ) is host to many of the major airlines and is closer than Denver.

TRANSFERS Several companies run transportation options between the airports and the resort towns of Telluride and Crested Butte. Shuttle fares vary; it's about $100 per person round-trip between Montrose Regional Airport and Telluride, and $67 per person round-trip between Gunnison–Crested Butte Regional Airport and Crested Butte. To get to Crested Butte from Gunnison or Montrose, try Alpine Express. Telluride Express offers service to Telluride from Durango, Montrose, Cortez, Gunnison, and Grand Junction.

In addition, the towns of Crested Butte and Durango operate shuttles to and from the ski areas.

Airport Contacts Albuquerque International Sunport (ABQ). ⊠ *2200 Sunport Blvd. SE, Albuquerque* ☎ *505/244–7700* ⊕ *www.cabq.gov/airport.* **Durango–La Plata County Airport (DRO).** ⊠ *1000 Airport Rd., Durango* ☎ *970/382–6050* ⊕ *www.flydurango.com.* **Gunnison–Crested Butte Regional Airport (GUC).** ⊠ *711 Rio Grande Ave., Gunnison* ☎ *970/641–2304* ⊕ *www. gunnisoncounty.org/airport.* **Montrose Regional Airport (MTJ).** ⊠ *2100 Airport Rd., Montrose* ☎ *970/249–3203* ⊕ *www.montroseairport.com.*

Airport Transfers Alpine Express. ⊠ *Gunnison Airport Terminal, 711 Rio Grande Ave., Gunnison* ☎ *970/641–5074, 800/822–4844* ⊕ *www. alpineexpressshuttle.com.* **Buck Horn Limousine.** ⊠ *Durango* ☎ *970/769–0933* ⊕ *www.buckhornlimousine.com.* **Telluride Express.** ⊠ *Telluride* ☎ *970/728– 6000, 888/212–8294* ⊕ *www.tellurideexpress.com.*

CAR TRAVEL

Alamo, Avis, Budget, Hertz, and National have car-rental counters at the Montrose Regional Airport. Alamo, Avis, Enterprise, Hertz, and National all have counters at Durango–La Plata County Airport. Gunnison–Crested Butte Regional Airport has Avis, Budget, and Hertz.

The main roads in the region are Highway 135 between Crested Butte and Gunnison; U.S. 50 linking Gunnison, Montrose, and Delta; Route 149 between Gunnison, Lake City, and Creede; U.S. 550 from Montrose to Ridgway, Ouray, Silverton, and Durango; Highway 62 and Route 145 linking Ridgway with Telluride, Dolores, and Cortez; and U.S. 160, which passes from Cortez to Durango to Pagosa Springs via Mesa Verde National Park. None of these roads officially close for winter, but be prepared at any time during snowy months for portions of the roads to be closed or down to one lane for avalanche control or to clear ice or snowdrifts.

TAXI TRAVEL

In the resort towns, you'll probably never need to call for a cab. You're most likely to use one to get to or from the airport.

PARKS AND RECREATION AREAS

Southwest Colorado includes a wealth of national and state parks and recreation areas. Three of the 13 rivers designated as "gold medal" waters by the Colorado Wildlife Commission—the Animas, Gunnison, and Rio Grande—are here. Blue Mesa and McPhee reservoirs, the state's largest bodies of water, are destinations for boaters, water-skiers, windsurfers, and anglers (including the ice-fishing kind). Up in rustic Almont, a small community near the Gunnison headwaters, they love—and live—fly-fishing. Anglers also love Ridgway State Park, with access to rainbow trout and other prize fish. ■ TIP➡ **Anyone older than 16 needs a Colorado fishing license, which you can obtain at local sporting-goods stores.**

The precipitous Black Canyon of the Gunnison National Park is a mysterious and powerful attraction. Some of the most intact remains of the ancient, little-known Ancestral Puebloan culture are inside Mesa Verde National Park and Canyons of the Ancients National Monument.

The San Juan Mountains stretch through 12,000 square miles of southwest Colorado, encompassing three national forests and seven wilderness areas. The enormous San Juan National Forest is a virtual paradise for all kinds of adventuring. Directly north, the Uncompahgre National Forest encompasses nearly a million acres of alpine wilderness and the picturesque peaks of Mount Sneffels and Lizard Head. To the east, the Rio Grande National Forest stretches from the magisterial Sangre de Cristo Mountains across the San Luis Valley.

RESTAURANTS

With dining options ranging from creative international cuisine in the resort towns of Telluride, Crested Butte, and Durango to no-frills American fare in down-home communities like Montrose and Creede, no one has any excuse to visit a chain restaurant here. The leading chefs are tapping into the region's local bounty, so you can find innovative recipes for ranch-raised game, lamb, and trout. Many serve only locally raised, grass-fed meats. Olathe sweet corn is a delicacy enjoyed across the state (and found in grocery stores and roadside stands as well as restaurants). Seasonal produce is highlighted on the best menus.

HOTELS

No matter what you're looking for in vacation lodging—luxurious slope-side condominium, landmark inn in a historic town, riverside cabin, guest ranch, country inn, budget motel, or chock-full-of-RVs campground—southwest Colorado has it in abundance. Rates vary season to season, particularly in the resort towns. Some properties close in fall once the aspens have shed their golden leaves, open in winter when the lifts begin running, close in spring after the snow melts, and open again in mid-May. *Hotel reviews have been shortened. For full information, visit Fodors.com.*

WHAT IT COSTS			
$	$$	$$$	$$$$
Restaurants	under $13	$13–$18	$19–$25	over $25
Hotels	under $121	$121–$170	$171–$230	over $230

Restaurant prices are the average cost of a main course at dinner or, if dinner is not served, at lunch, excluding 5.9%–8.1% tax. Hotel prices are the lowest cost of a standard double room in high season, excluding service charges and 7.6%–9.9% tax.

VISITOR INFORMATION
Contact **Southwest Colorado Travel Region.** ☎ ⊕ *www.swcolotravel.org.*

CRESTED BUTTE AND GUNNISON

This area is dominated and shaped by the Gunnison River, which gathers water from the Taylor and East rivers at Almont, meets the Uncompahgre River near Delta, and finally hooks up with the Colorado River near Grand Junction. West of Gunnison, the river cuts the Black Canyon of the Gunnison, a forbidding, 48-mile-long abyss often deeper than it is wide. The Elk Mountains stretch from the northern edge of the Black Canyon through Crested Butte. Almont, off Highway 135 between Crested Butte and Gunnison, is a still-rustic fly-fishing hideaway.

CRESTED BUTTE

28 miles north of Gunnison via Hwy. 135; 92 miles northeast of Montrose via U.S. 50 and Hwy. 135.

Like Aspen, the town of Crested Butte was once a small mining village (albeit for coal, not silver). The Victorian gingerbread-trim houses remain, many of them now painted in whimsical shades of hot pink, magenta, and chartreuse. Unlike Aspen, however, Crested Butte has retained much of its small-town charm despite its development as a ski area.

A lovelier setting could not be imagined. The town sits at the top of a long, broad valley that stretches 17 miles south toward Gunnison. Mount Crested Butte, which looms over the town, is the most visible landmark. It's surrounded by the Gunnison National Forest and the Elk Mountain Range.

It's as an extreme-skiing mecca that Crested Butte earned its reputation with some of the best skiers in the land. Over the years, Crested Butte has steadily increased its extreme-skiing terrain to 550 ungroomed acres. Although this area, known as the Extreme Limits, should only be attempted by experts, there are plenty of cruise-worthy trails for skiers of all levels. The groomed trails are rarely crowded, which allows for plenty of long, fast, sweeping turns.

10

GETTING HERE AND AROUND

Crested Butte is just over the mountain from Aspen, but there are no paved roads—just unpaved routes over the challenging Pearl, Taylor, and Schofield passes and hiking trails through White River National Forest. If you're coming from the north or west, the most direct route is over Kebler Pass. The drive is one of the state's prettiest, passing through one of the state's largest stands of aspens. If you're coming from the east, the beautiful Cottonwood Pass will deposit you on Highway 135, just south of town. Both graded gravel roads are closed in winter, making it necessary to take a circuitous route on U.S. 24 and U.S. 50 through Poncha Springs and Gunnison, and then up Highway 135 to Crested Butte.

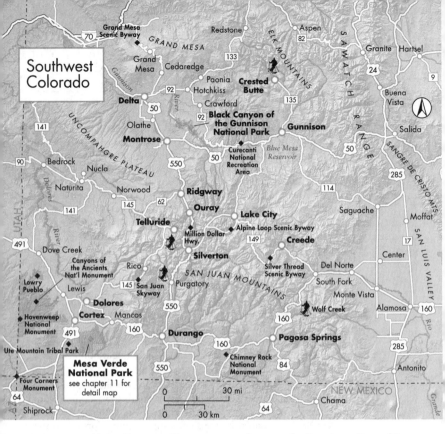

Southwest Colorado

Alpine Express will transport you between the Gunnison–Crested Butte Regional Airport and the resort for $67 round-trip. Mountain Express is a reliable free shuttle bus that travels the 3 miles between the town and the resort throughout the year.

WHEN TO GO

Ski season—mid-December to mid-April—is definitely the busiest time in Crested Butte. The weeks between Memorial Day and Labor Day are hopping, as well. Things slow down dramatically in the in-between times, with some businesses closing completely.

ESSENTIALS

Transportation Contacts Alpine Express. ☎ 970/641–5074, 800/822–4844 ⊕ www.alpineexpressshuttle.com. **Mountain Express.** ✉ 803 Butte Ave. ☎ 970/349–5616 ⊕ www.mtnexp.org.

Visitor Information Crested Butte–Mt. Crested Butte Chamber of Commerce. ✉ 601 Elk Ave. ☎ 970/349–6438, 855/681–0941 ⊕ www. cbchamber.com. **Crested Butte Snow Report.** ✉ Crested Butte ☎ 970/349–2323 ⊕ www.skicb.com. **Crested Butte Vacations.** ✉ 12 Snowmass Rd. ☎ 877/547–5143 ⊕ www.skicb.com.

EXPLORING

Crested Butte Mountain Heritage Museum. Housed in an 1893 hardware store, this museum showcases the essentials for life in an 1880s mining town, such as clothing, furniture, and household items. There's an intricate diorama of the town in the 1920s, complete with a moving train, plus exhibits on skiing, sledding, biking, and Flauschink, a quirky local ceremony that welcomes the return of spring. ⊠ *331 Elk Ave.* ☎ *970/349–1880* ⊕ *crestedbuttemuseum.com* ⊠ *$4* ⊙ *Memorial Day–late Oct., daily 10–8; late Nov.–mid-Apr., daily 10–6.*

FAMILY **Mt. Crested Butte Adventure Park.** Make a day of it at Mt. Crested Butte Adventure Park, where for one ticket price, you can access unlimited lift-served hiking and biking, mini-golf, bungee trampolines, a climbing wall, an inflated-bag jump, and a hands-on kids' mining exhibit. A la carte pricing and guided hiking are also available. The lift-served hiking and biking are summer-only, but the rest of the Adventure Park is open year-round. ⊠ *12 Snowmass Rd., Mt. Crested Butte* ☎ *800/600–2083* ⊕ *www.skicb.com* ⊠ *$41, kids $33.*

DOWNHILL SKIING AND SNOWBOARDING

Crested Butte Mountain Resort. The skiing here has a split personality, which is plain to see when you check out the skiers who descend on the place year after year. Its mellow half is the network of trails on the front side of the mountain, characterized by long intermediate runs. Families flock to Crested Butte for these trails, as well as the children's ski-school facilities and the laid-back and friendly vibe.

The wilder side of Crested Butte's personality is the **Extreme Limits,** more than 500 acres of backcountry-like terrain (all double black diamond), with steep bowls, gnarly chutes, and tight tree skiing. It's some of the toughest in-bounds skiing in North America. Sign up for one of the guided programs for expert instruction (and insider info on the best powder stashes on the mountain).

The best expert skiing on the front side of the mountain is off the Silver Queen high-speed quad, which shoots you up 2,078 vertical feet in one quick ride. For beginners there's a wonderful expanse of easy terrain from the Red Lady Express lift. **Facilities:** 121 trails; 1,547 acres; 2,755-foot vertical drop; 13 lifts. ⊠ *12 Snowmass Rd.* ☎ *855/969–3022* ⊕ *www.skicb.com* ⊠ *Lift ticket from $108* ⊙ *Late Nov.–early Apr., daily 9–4.*

LESSONS AND PROGRAMS

Crested Butte Ski and Ride School. A full-day adult group lesson costs $134 (lift ticket not included) and is available for all levels. For kids ages 3 through 16, Camp CB offers single all-day lessons starting at $164, which includes lunch. Private lessons are also available. ⊠ *12 Snowmass Rd.* ☎ *800/444–9236.*

RENTALS

Crested Butte Sports. Full rental packages (including skis, boots, and poles), as well as telemark, snowshoe, and snowboard equipment, are available at this outfitter. Rates start at $24 per day. There's also a retail store and full repair shop. ⊠ *35 Emmons Loop Rd.* ☎ *970/349–7516, 800/970–9704* ⊕ *www.crestedbuttesports.com.*

NORDIC SKIING
BACKCOUNTRY SKIING

Crested Butte Nordic Center. Crested Butte abounds with backcountry possibilities. You can rent cross-country skis or snowshoes, then head out on one of the Forest Service roads that radiate from town—particularly Washington Gulch, Slate River Road, and Gothic Road. You can also head into the backcountry on a guided tour. You can hike up the slopes for above-treeline trips, but this requires strong legs and lungs, the right equipment, and lots of experience. This is the high country—the town itself is around 9,000 feet, and things go up from there—and weather and snow conditions can change with little or no warning.

> ### ICE BAR
>
> **The Ice Bar at Uley's Cabin.**
> Mount Crested Butte's cool Ice Bar relies on temperatures in the freezing range. Made partly of ice, the bar is constructed each December near Twister Lift, midway up the mountain, next to Uley's Cabin. On busier days, Uley's dining spills outside, serving upscale barbecue fare like elk sausage and bison chili. On any winter day, the wine list is lengthy and the signature cocktails are delightful at this chilly, but very hot, après-ski and lunch spot. ⊠ *At base of Twister Lift.*

The Crested Butte Nordic Center offers half- and full-day packages that include transportation, guides, and equipment. If you're traveling with a group you can rent one of two ski huts in the old town site of Gothic. The center also hosts the Annual Alley Loop Nordic Marathon, held in early February. This is an American Birkebeiner qualifying race, but local amateurs and visitors can join the experts in their cross-country race through the town's snow-covered streets and alleys, past snow-corniced homes, and down the scenic trails along the edge of town. ⊠ *620 2nd St.* ☏ *970/349–1707* ⊕ *www.cbnordic.org* ⊠ *Tours from $65.*

RENTALS **The Alpineer.** This iconic Crested Butte shop rents top-notch backcountry and telemark equipment, as well as classic Nordic and skate skis. The staff offers expert advice on routes and snow conditions. ⊠ *419 6th St.* ☏ *970/349–5210* ⊕ *www.alpineer.com.*

TRACK SKIING

FAMILY **Crested Butte Nordic Center.** The community-owned Crested Butte Nordic Center maintains an extensive network of cross-country ski and snowshoe trails. There are 34 miles of trails radiating out to the northwest, south, and east of Crested Butte. The trails cover flat and moderately rolling terrain across meadows and through aspen groves near the valley floor. A one-day adult trail pass costs $18. The views of some of the distant peaks are stunning. The Moonlight Dinner—on full-moon nights from December to March—includes a trek to a cozy yurt for a five-course dinner prepared by local chefs; the $70 per-person cost includes a trail pass and ski rentals. You can also buy hot drinks and pastries every Sunday from 10 to 2 at the Magic Meadows Yurt. ■ TIP➔ **Kids 17 and younger get free ski passes and rentals all season long.** ⊠ *620 2nd St.* ☏ *970/349–1707* ⊕ *www.cbnordic.org.*

OTHER SPORTS AND THE OUTDOORS
FISHING

Almont. Located where the East and Taylor rivers join to form the Gunnison River, this tiny angler-oriented hamlet is one of Colorado's top fly-fishing centers. It's also one of the most crowded. Local fishing outfitters rent equipment, teach fly-fishing, and lead guided wading or float trips to both public and private waters. ⊠ *Almont.*

TOURS AND **Almont Anglers.** This outfitter and guide has a solid fly and tackle shop OUTFITTERS with an enormous selection. There are clinics for beginners as well as guided wading and float-fishing excursions on the East, Taylor, and Gunnison rivers. ⊠ *10209 Hwy. 135, Almont* ☎ *970/641–7404* ⊕ *www. almontanglers.com* ✉ *Lessons from $75; trips from $240.*

Dragonfly Anglers. Crested Butte's oldest year-round guide service and fly-fishing outfitter, Dragonfly Anglers offers guided half-day, full-day, and multiday trips to choice fly-fishing spots, including the famed Gunnison Gorge. The shop sells a wide variety of rods and has a solid selection of reels, flies, and outdoor gear, including Patagonia items. ⊠ *307 Elk Ave.* ☎ *970/349–1228, 800/491–3079* ⊕ *www.dragonflyanglers.com* ✉ *From $275.*

Willowfly Anglers at Three Rivers Resort. A branch of Three Rivers Resort and Outfitting, Willowfly Anglers offers half- and full-day trips for all skill levels and has a full-service fly shop. Trip prices include all necessary equipment. ⊠ *130 County Rd. 742, Almont* ☎ *970/641–1303, 888/761–3474* ⊕ *www.willowflyanglers.com* ✉ *Trips start at $245.*

FOUR-WHEELING

Alpine Express. Take an open-top four-wheel-drive tour on the Forest Service roads that crisscross the Elk Mountain range, heading past meadows of wildflowers and pristine mountain streams. Half-day Jeep tours are $55 for adults. ⊠ *Crested Butte* ☎ *970/641–5074, 800/822–4844* ⊕ *www.alpineexpressshuttle.com.*

GOLF

Fodor's Choice **The Club at Crested Butte.** Golf legend Robert Trent Jones Jr. designed this
★ ravishing 18-hole course surrounded by gorgeous mountain peaks. The first nine holes follow a traditional format, but the back nine offer a Highlands-style surprise with a Scottish-links design. Water hazards are present on 14 of the 18 holes, so be sure to bring extra balls. The semi-private course belongs to the country club, but it's open to the public daily after 12 pm. The dress code bars denim and mandates stand-up collars for all. ⊠ *385 Country Club Dr.* ☎ *970/349–8601* ⊕ *www.theclubatcrestedbutte. com* ✉ *$85 for 9 holes, $149 for 18 holes* ⌗ *18 holes, 7208 yards, par 72* ⚑ *Reservations essential* ☞ *Rates include golf cart and practice balls.*

HIKING

FAMILY **Judd Falls.** Nestled among three designated wilderness areas (Maroon Bells–Snowmass to the north, Raggeds to the west, and Collegiate Peaks to the east), Crested Butte is close to an extensive system of trails. One of the easiest—and most kid-friendly—hiking trails is the 2-miles round-trip to Judd Falls, located within the Gunnison National Forest near the former mining town of Gothic. The path slices through groves of aspen and, in summer, a crop of more than

70 local wildflower varieties. At the end, look over Judd Falls from a bench named after Garwood Judd, "the man who stayed" in the old mining town. In the wilderness areas you can find splendid trails far off the beaten path. ☒ *Gunnison National Forest, off Gothic Rd.* ☎ *970/874–6600* ⊕ *www.fs.usda.gov/gmug.*

HORSEBACK RIDING

Fantasy Ranch. One of the best ways to see the Crested Butte area is from atop a horse. Fantasy Ranch gives guided horseback tours into the Elk Mountains, Maroon Bells, and Gunnison National Forest. Trips range from 90-minute trail rides to full-day wilderness adventures. Riders must be at least seven years old, but younger children can do 15-minute pony rides. The company also offers multiday pack trips in the fall. ☒ *935 Gothic Rd., Mt. Crested Butte* ☎ *970/349–5425, 888/688–3488* ⊕ *www.fantasyranchoutfitters.com* ☷ *From $65.*

ICE-SKATING

FAMILY **Crested Butte Nordic Center.** If you're eager to practice a figure eight, the Crested Butte Nordic Center operates an outdoor skating rink. Skating is free and open to the public when the rink isn't reserved for hockey. The lodge rents skates for $7–$9. ☒ *620 2nd St.* ☎ *970/349–1707* ⊕ *www.cbnordic.org* ☷ *Free* ☉ *Closed Mar.–Nov.*

KAYAKING AND RAFTING

Three Rivers Resort & Outfitting. The rivers around Crested Butte are at their best from May through early August. Three Rivers offers rafting trips and kayaking lessons on the Taylor and Gunnison rivers. ☒ *130 County Rd. 742, Almont* ☎ *970/641–1303, 888/761–3474* ⊕ *www.3riversresort.com* ☷ *Raft trips start at $45.*

MOUNTAIN BIKING

Crested Butte is the mountain-biking center of Colorado. This is a place where there are more bikes than cars, and probably more bikes than residents. Many locals own two: a cruiser (or "townie") for hacking around and a mountain bike for *serious* hacking around. Nearby Pearl Pass is known as the route that got the fat-tire craze started.

Strand Hill. Starting southeast of town along Brush Creek Road, Strand Hill Trail is about 6 miles out and back. It includes a 900-foot climb on a double-track road followed by a twisting, roller-coaster-like single-track descent that will leave you feeling exhilarated. ☒ *Brush Creek Rd.* ⊕ *www.travelcrestedbutte.com.*

Upper Loop. Great for beginners, the Upper Loop is a popular 1½-mile ride that will help orient you to the area. The views up the Slate River valley to the peaks of Paradise Divide are wonderful. **Tony's Trail** consists of a short, moderate climb leading to an intersection with the Upper Upper Loop Trail. Here you can take in the view of the town below and the mountains above, then enjoy a fun descent back down or venture further in either direction on the Upper Upper Loop. ☒ *Crested Butte* ⊕ *www.travelcrestedbutte.com.*

TOURS AND
OUTFITTERS
Big Al's Bicycle Heaven. This full-service downtown bike shop, a favorite with locals, sells and rents all manner of two-wheelers, from knockaround "townies" to state-of-the-art mountain bikes. The shop also carries road and cross-country bikes and a full line of clothing, helmets,

and other necessities. Best of all, the staff is willing to share the inside scoop on the best local trails. ⊠ *207 Elk Ave.* ☎ *970/349–0515* ⊕ *www. bigalsbicycleheaven.com.*

Irwin Guides. Guided rides on the area's legendary single-track trails are available for riders of all skill levels. Experienced riders can take overnight tours with meals, lodging, and transportation included. ⊠ *330 Belleview Ave.* ☎ *970/349–5430* ⊕ *www.irwinguides.com* ✉ *Guided rides from $100 per person, per day; overnight trips from $275 per person, per day.*

RENTALS **Crested Butte Sports.** Come here to rent Cannondale mountain bikes, plus helmets and other gear. It also has a full repair shop. ⊠ *35 Emmons Loop Rd.* ☎ *970/349–7516, 800/970–9704* ⊕ *www.crestedbuttesports.com.*

ZIPLINING

Crested Butte Mountain Resort Zipline Tour. Friendly guides and superior views make this two-hour, five-line tour worth your time. The tour runs in both winter and summer at the base of the mountain, where you can watch the skiers or bikers below as you zip from tree to tree. ⊠ *Mountaineer Square, 12 Snowmass Rd., Mt. Crested Butte* ⊕ *www. skicb.com* ✉ *A two-hour tour costs $62.*

WHERE TO EAT

$$$ × **Django's.** End your ski (or biking) day with delectable small plates
MODERN   from this sophisticated eatery at the base of an otherwise laid-back
AMERICAN   mountain resort. The modern, elegant decor—breezy, floor-to-ceiling tapestries and Alice-in-Wonderland booths—suits the creative, gourmet menu. Try the super-popular crispy Brussels sprouts and the lacquered duck breast with tart cherry sauce, and ask your server for a pairing from the lengthy list of wines, served in bottles or quartinos. $ *Average main: $25* ⊠ *Mountaineer Square, 620 Gothic Rd., Mt. Crested Butte* ☎ *970/349–7574* ⊕ *www.djangosrestaurantcrestedbutte.com* ⊗ *Closed Mon. and mid-Apr.–mid-June and Oct.–late Nov.*

$$ × **Ginger Cafe.** The small, sunny dining room and welcoming street-side
ASIAN   deck provide a cheerful backdrop for the superb East–West fusion and Pan-Asian food, with a good selection of vegetarian and gluten-free options, as well as several dishes featuring deliciously tender Colorado lamb. There is also a full bar with an inventive cocktail menu, including ginger-infused martinis and mango-ginger mojitos. $ *Average main: $16* ⊠ *425 Elk Ave.* ☎ *970/349–7291* ⊕ *www.thegingercafe.com* ⊗ *Closed Mid-Apr.–Mid-May.*

$ × **Montanya Distillers Tasting Room.** Stop here for artisan cocktails and
TAPAS   tasty tapas before dinner and it just might end up being your dinner spot. The rum is divine—there's a light and a dark, both skillfully distilled on-site in copper stills from Portugal using fresh local-spring water (come by between noon and five for a distillery tour). Try the rum straight or in an inventive cocktail, such as the local favorite Maharaja, which blends chai spices with ginger and lime. $ *Average main: $10* ⊠ *212 Elk Ave.* ☎ *970/799–3206* ⊕ *www.montanyarum.com.*

$ × **Secret Stash.** The secret is out about this tasty, trendy pizza place,
PIZZA   which has moved from a tucked-away location to a building three times the size, right on the town's main strip. It still serves amazing pizza in

a mind-bending array of formulations—from the "Notorious F.I.G." (prosciutto, dried figs, and truffle oil) to the "Mac Daddy" (with Thousand Island, shaved rib eye, pickles, and a sesame seed crust). There's a full bar with an impressive list of specialty drinks, and a daily Poorboy special—a slice of cheese pizza, a shot of tequila, and a beer—for $6. Sit inside beneath sweeping tapestries in a Japanese-style booth or opt for a table on the lively deck. The wait can be long, so order an appetizer. [$] *Average main: $10* ✉ *303 Elk Ave.* ☎ *970/349–6245* 🌐 *www.stashpizza.com* 💳 *No credit cards.*

$$$ AMERICAN 🍴 **Slogar.** In a lovingly renovated Victorian tavern awash in handmade lace and stained glass, this restaurant is just plain cozy. A fixed-price menu spotlights skillet-fried chicken or 12-ounce New York strip steak paired with sides such as flaky biscuits fresh from the oven, creamy mashed potatoes swimming in chicken gravy, homemade tomato chutney, and sweet-and-sour coleslaw from a Pennsylvania Dutch recipe. Served family style, dinner is $22 for chicken or $38 for steak. Reservations are recommended. [$] *Average main: $22* ✉ *517 2nd St., at Whiterock Ave.* ☎ *970/349–5765* ⏲ *Closed mid-Oct.–Nov. and mid-Apr.–mid-May. No lunch.*

$$$$ FRENCH Fodor's Choice ★ 🍴 **Soupçon.** "Soup's on" (get it?) occupies two intimate rooms in a historic cabin tucked away in an alley and dishes up Nouveau American cuisine with a strong French accent. Organic herbs grown on the premises accent local produce, and everything, including soups, stocks, and sauces, is made from scratch. The menu changes every few weeks, but always includes locally influenced entrées such as stuffed quail and Colorado lamb. Pair your meal with a glass of wine from the comprehensive wine cellar. Call ahead for your seating time: 6 or 8:30. [$] *Average main: $40* ✉ *127A Elk Ave.* ☎ *970/349–5448* 🌐 *www.soupcon-cb.com* ⏲ *Closed Nov. and mid-Apr.–mid-May. No lunch* ✍ *Reservations essential.*

$$$ MODERN AMERICAN 🍴 **Supper at the Sunflower.** By day, Sunflower is a small but cheery breakfast and lunch spot. The reins change hands in the evening at this co-op kitchen, becoming a lively, gourmet farm-to-table dining room. New menus are printed nightly, creatively crafted to accommodate the fresh, organic meats and produce available that day from local farm suppliers. Choose from a short list of entrées such as Colorado trout or smoked flank steak, or share several of the delectable apps, salads, and veggies. An excellent and ever-changing wine list complements the menu brilliantly. The owners are very personable: Don't be surprised if one of them sits down at your table to chat. [$] *Average main: $23* ✉ *214 Elk Ave.* ☎ *970/417–7767* ⏲ *Closed Sun. and Mon. No lunch* ✍ *Reservations essential.*

$ MEXICAN 🍴 **Teocalli Tamale.** Known as "Teo's," this Mexican restaurant is housed in a small, historic building and is a local favorite venue for tasty, inexpensive takeout (or a claustrophobic eat-in experience). You can get a generous portion of tamales, burritos, or tacos (try the mahimahi or spicy shredded beef)—topped with delicious homemade salsas—for about $10. The place also serves margaritas and bottled beers. Lines can be long, so allow plenty of time. [$] *Average main: $11* ✉ *311 Elk Ave.* ☎ *970/349–2005* 🌐 *www.teocallitamale.com.*

WHERE TO STAY

$$ B&B/INN **Cristiana Guesthaus.** With a huge stone fireplace in a wood-beamed lobby, this alpine-style ski lodge provides a cozy, unpretentious haven. **Pros:** comfortable lodge; knowledgeable hosts; great value. **Cons:** TV only in common area; no air-conditioning; pets not allowed in July or August. [$] *Rooms from: $130* ✉ *621 Maroon Ave.* ☎ *800/824–7899* 🌐 *www.cristianaguesthaus.com* ⏲ *Closed early Apr.–mid-Apr.* 🛏 *21 rooms* 🍴 *Breakfast.*

$$$$ HOTEL **Elevation Hotel & Spa.** Top-notch service, mountain-modern luxury, and ample amenities make this upscale ski-in ski-out hotel worth the splurge. **Pros:** complimentary wine hour; complimentary ski valet and storage; turndown service. **Cons:** parking is $20 per day; pool is small. [$] *Rooms from: $259* ✉ *500 Gothic Rd., Mt. Crested Butte* ☎ *970/251–3000, 877/569–2754* 🌐 *www.elevationresort.com* 🛏 *211 rooms, 51 suites* 🍴 *No meals.*

$$ B&B/INN **Elk Mountain Lodge.** Step into the lobby of the Elk Mountain Lodge and encounter a slower pace of life and extraordinary attention to detail. **Pros:** good breakfast; intimate feel; provides locked ski storage on-site and on-mountain. **Cons:** 3 miles from ski area; there's no elevator and stairs are a bit steep. [$] *Rooms from: $169* ✉ *129 Gothic Ave.* ☎ *970/349–7533, 800/374–6521* 🌐 *www.elkmountainlodge.com* ⏲ *Closed mid-Apr.–late Apr.* 🛏 *19 rooms* 🍴 *Breakfast.*

$$ B&B/INN **Old Town Inn.** Friendly, knowledgeable staff and an excellent in-town location make this a great base for adventures in town or the mountains. **Pros:** good deluxe Continental breakfast; outdoor hot tub; convenient location. **Cons:** no pool; no elevator to second story. [$] *Rooms from: $139* ✉ *708 6th St.* ☎ *970/349–6184, 888/349–6184* 🌐 *www.oldtowninn.net* 🛏 *32 rooms, 1 suite* 🍴 *Breakfast.*

$$ B&B/INN Fodor's Choice ★ **Pioneer Guest Cabins.** On a creekside meadow about 8 miles from Crested Butte, this pleasant getaway for outdoors lovers was once the base area of the original ski area. **Pros:** secluded setting; close to trails and fishing. **Cons:** bedrooms are small; no restaurant; minimum stay required. [$] *Rooms from: $151* ✉ *2094 County Rd. 740* ☎ *970/349–5517* 🌐 *www.pioneerguestcabins.com* 🛏 *8 cabins* 🍴 *No meals.*

NIGHTLIFE

Kochevar's Saloon and Gaming Hall. An 1899 cabin built from hand-hewn logs, Kochevar's is a classic saloon where locals play pool. ✉ *127 Elk Ave.* ☎ *970/349–7117.*

Wooden Nickel. This popular place is packed for happy hour each day from 4 to 6. Stay for dinner, as the steaks are terrific. ✉ *222 Elk Ave.* ☎ *970/349–6350* 🌐 *www.woodennickelcb.com* ⏲ *Closed mid-Apr.–early May.*

SHOPPING

SPAS

Elevation Spa. With an elevation of 9,385 feet, Mount Crested Butte can drain the life out of your skin. Rejuvenate with the Elevation Spa's signature massage, using hydrating lotion and grapeseed oil. In all of its treatments, Elevation employs either high-end skin-care products such as Eminence or simple, natural ingredients—brown sugar to exfoliate and honey to hydrate, for example. The 11,000-square-foot, earth-toned spa is simply decorated, but provides all the amenities you need to unwind: robes, sandals, steam rooms, and three relaxation rooms—men's, women's, and coed—plus a large, well-equipped fitness center overlooking the slopes. ⊠ *500 Gothic Rd., Mt. Crested Butte* ☎ *970/251–3500* ⊕ *www.elevationspa.com* ☞ *$105 50-min massage, $410 3-hr signature package. Hair salon, hot tubs (indoor and outdoor), indoor pool, saunas, steam rooms. Gym with: cardiovascular machines, free weights, weight-training equipment. Services: body wraps and scrubs, facials, massage.*

GUNNISON

64 miles east of Montrose via U.S. 50; 28 miles south of Crested Butte via Hwy. 135.

At the confluence of the Gunnison River and Tomichi Creek, Gunnison is an old mining and ranching community and college town. It's been adopted by nature lovers because of the excellent outdoor activities, including hiking, climbing, fishing, and hunting. In fact, long before any settlers arrived, the Ute Indians used the area as summer hunting grounds. Gunnison provides economical lodging and easy access to Crested Butte and Blue Mesa Reservoir. Locals (for good reason) call it "Sunny Gunny," despite its claim to fame of having recorded some of the coldest temperatures ever reported in the continental United States.

GETTING HERE AND AROUND

Getting in and out of Gunnison is a breeze. U.S. 50 travels right through town, heading east to I–25 in Pueblo and northwest to I–70 in Grand Junction. U.S. 50 goes by the name Tomichi Avenue as it travels 18 blocks through town. Western State Colorado University and the Pioneer Museum are on the east side of town, and the rodeo grounds and airport are to the south.

WHEN TO GO
ESSENTIALS

Visitor Information **Gunnison County Chamber of Commerce.** ⊠ *500 E. Tomichi Ave.* ☎ *970/641–1501* ⊕ *www.gunnisonchamber.com.*

EXPLORING

Curecanti National Recreation Area. This sprawling recreation area, named in honor of a Ute Indian sub-chief, stretches for 40 miles along U.S. 50, between Gunnison and Montrose. It encompasses three reservoirs along the Gunnison River: Blue Mesa, Colorado's largest lake at almost 20 miles long, and Morrow Point and Crystal, fjord-like reservoirs in the upper Black Canyon of the Gunnison. All three are excellent spots for fishing, boating, and paddling, although only Blue Mesa offers boat ramps. You'll find great fly-fishing east of the Blue Mesa Reservoir, on the Gunnison River. Camping and hiking are also available. The Elk Creek Visitor Center on U.S. 50 is open year-round for trip planning, boat-tour reservations, and pass/permit sales; call for hours. Entrance to the recreation area is free, unless you use the east entrance, which is inside Black Canyon of the Gunnison National Park ($15 entrance fee). ⊠ *102 Elk Creek* ☎ *970/641–2337* ⊕ *www.nps.gov/cure* ⌖ *Free.*

FAMILY **Gunnison Pioneer Museum.** Anyone interested in the region's history shouldn't miss the Pioneer Museum. The complex spreads across 6 acres, and includes an extensive collection of vehicles from Model Ts to 1960s sedans. There are also two old schoolhouses; an impressive display of arrowheads; mining exhibits; a red barn with wagons and displays of ranch life; and a great train, complete with coal tender, caboose, and boxcar. ⊠ *803 E. Tomichi Ave.* ☎ *970/641–4530* ⊕ *www.gunnisonpioneermuseum.com* ⊡ *$10* ⊗ *Late May–Sept., daily 9–5.*

SPORTS AND THE OUTDOORS

FISHING

Gunnison Sports Outfitters. Take a guided fishing trip on the Blue Mesa Reservoir, which teems with brown trout, rainbow trout, and kokanee salmon. Full-day trips are $325 per person; kids 12 and younger pay nothing. ⊠ *201 W. Tomichi Ave.* ☎ *970/641–1845* ⊕ *www. gunnisonsportsoutfitters.com.*

High Mountain Drifters. Choose from half- and full-day fly-fishing tours on the East and Gunnison rivers, as well as trophy lake-trout fishing on the Blue Mesa Reservoir. Both walk-wade trips and float trips are available. ⊠ *201 W. Tomichi Ave.* ☎ *970/471–5829* ⊕ *www.highmtndrifters.com* ⊡ *Trips start at $275 per person.*

WATER SPORTS

At 20 miles long, with 96 miles of shoreline, Blue Mesa Reservoir ranks as Colorado's largest body of water. Located within Curecanti National Recreation Area, the reservoir was created in the mid-1960s when the Gunnison River was dammed as part of the Colorado River Storage Project. This cold-water reservoir has become a mecca for water-sports enthusiasts. Anglers are drawn by the 3 million stocked kokanee salmon, as well as rainbow, lake, brown, and brook trout.

Five boat ramps and two marinas operate through the summer with varying hours and amenities. Boat permits are required and are available at the Elk Creek Visitor Center. A two-day boat permit is $4, and a two-week permit is $10. Annual boat permits run $30.

Elk Creek Marina. About 16 miles west of Gunnison, this marina on Blue Mesa Reservoir offers a range of services: boat and slip rentals, mechanical and towing services, gas, ice, bait, and supplies. You can also book guided fishing trips here. A small restaurant, Pappy's, is located above the dock, where you can enjoy a light meal while watching anglers try their luck. ⊠ *24830 U.S. 50* ☎ *970/641–0707* ⊕ *www.thebluemesa. com* ⊗ *Closed Oct.–Apr.*

WHERE TO EAT

$ ✕ **The Bean.** This brightly hued coffee shop is a great place to grab
CAFÉ and go (or stay and hang out). The walls are decorated with frequently changing art exhibits, and for light reading there are plenty of newspapers and magazines (and of course free Wi-Fi). There's an impressive selection of espresso drinks, juices, and smoothies (try the strawberry-ginger) plus crepes, burritos, and savory sandwiches, many of which are made with organic ingredients. Get here

10

early, as it closes at 6 pm in the winter and 7 pm in the summer. [$] *Average main: $5* ✉ *120 N. Main St.* ☎ *970/641–2408* 🌐 *www.thebeancoffeehouseandeatery.com.*

$$$ MODERN AMERICAN 🍴 **Blue Mesa Grill.** The seafood is surprisingly fresh, and the weekend brunches are fabulous at this upscale-for-the-area restaurant, 2 miles east of downtown Gunnison. There is a small but tasty selection of sushi rolls, and turf options include the usual steaks, chicken, and pork, as well as braised buffalo short ribs. A large portion of the menu items are designated gluten-free. For a more casual atmosphere, sit at the bar or on the patio, or enjoy a more luxe ambience in the dining room. [$] *Average main: $19* ✉ *41883 U.S. 50 E* ☎ *970/641–1131* 🌐 *www.theinntv.com* ⏲ *No lunch Mon.–Sat. No dinner Sun. Closed Nov.*

$$$ ITALIAN 🍴 **Garlic Mike's.** The menu at this unpretentious Italian spot is surprisingly rich and complex. Good bets include the garlic fries, thin-crust pizza, minestrone soup, the house-favorite steak carbonara, and perhaps the best prime rib in the valley. The heated outdoor patio overlooking the Gunnison River is a divine place to relax in summer, especially on Friday nights when you can enjoy live music. Be prepared for a leisurely dinner, as the service can be slow. Or call ahead and ask about guided, summertime dinner float trips. [$] *Average main: $21* ✉ *2674 Hwy. 135* ☎ *970/641–2493* 🌐 *www.garlicmikes.com* ⏲ *No lunch.*

$$ STEAKHOUSE 🍴 **Ol' Miner Steakhouse.** Join the locals here for steak—choose T-bone, strip, rib eye, or prime rib cooked the way you like it—in a rustic, down-home setting, complete with elk and deer mounts, tin ceilings, and scarred wood furniture. Rocky Mountain oysters (bull testicles) are available for culinary risk-takers. There's also seafood offerings, an unlimited soup-and-salad bar for $8, a respectable array of sandwiches, a full bar, and traditional breakfasts. [$] *Average main: $18* ✉ *139 N. Main St.* ☎ *970/641–5153* 🌐 *www.olminersteakhouse.com.*

WHERE TO STAY

$$ HOTEL 🏨 **The Inn at Tomichi Village.** The rooms at this completely remodeled hotel feature modern-rustic decor, comfortable beds (including a variety of pillow styles to suit various tastes), and amenities such as refrigerators and microwaves. **Pros:** ample amenities; refurbished property; great restaurant. **Cons:** motel-style entrances; bathrooms are a bit dated. [$] *Rooms from: $129* ✉ *41833 U.S. 50 E* ☎ *970/641–1131* 🌐 *www.theinntv.com* 🛏 *50 rooms, 1 suite* 🍽 *Breakfast.*

$ RESORT FAMILY 🏨 **Rockey River Resort.** A tetherball on the turf, a riverside fire pit, and welcoming front porches: these are just a few of the touches that make this old homestead a uniquely pleasant place to stay. **Pros:** close to fishing; a lot of activities available on the property; pet-friendly. **Cons:** 6 miles from Gunnison; TV only in common areas. [$] *Rooms from: $110* ✉ *4359 County Rd. 10* ☎ *970/641–0174* 🌐 *www.gunnisoncabins.com* ⏲ *Closed mid-Nov.–Apr.* 🛏 *14 cabins* 🍽 *No meals.*

BLACK CANYON OF THE GUNNISON NATIONAL PARK

South Rim: 15 miles east of Montrose, via U.S. 50 and Rte. 347. North Rim: 11 miles south of Crawford, via Rte. 92 and North Rim Rd.

The Black Canyon of the Gunnison River is one of Colorado's, and indeed the West's, most awe-inspiring places. A vivid testament to the powers of erosion, the canyon is roughly 2,000 feet deep. At its narrowest point, it spans 1,000 feet at the rim and only 40 feet at the bottom. The steep angles of the cliffs make it difficult for sunlight to fully break through during much of the day, and ever-present shadows blanket the canyon walls, leaving some places in almost perpetual darkness. No wonder it's called the "Black Canyon."

The primary gateway to Black Canyon is **Montrose**, 15 miles west of the park. The legendary Ute chief, Ouray, and his wife, Chipeta, lived near here in the late 1800s. Today, Montrose straddles the important agricultural and mining regions along the Uncompahgre River, and is the area's main shopping hub.

GETTING ORIENTED

Black Canyon of the Gunnison is a park of extremes—great depths, narrow widths, tall cliffs, and steep descents. It is not a large park, but it offers incredible scenery and unforgettable experiences, whether you're hiking, fishing, camping, or just taking it all in from the overlooks.

East Portal. The only way you can get down to the river via automobile in Black Canyon is on the steep East Portal Road.

North Rim. The area's remoteness and difficult location mean the North Rim is never crowded; the road is unpaved and closes in the winter. There's also a small ranger station here, but the rangers are often in the field.

South Rim. This is the main area of the park. The park's only visitor center is here, along with a campground and a few picnic areas.

WHEN TO GO

Summer is the busiest season, with July experiencing the greatest crowds. However, a spring or fall visit gives you two advantages: fewer people and cooler temperatures. In summer, especially in years with little rainfall, daytime temperatures can reach into the 90s. A winter visit to the park brings even more solitude, as all but one section of campsites are shut down and only about 2 miles of South Rim Road, the park main road, are plowed.

November through March is when the snow hits, with an average of about 3 to 8 inches of it monthly. April through May and September and October are the rainiest, with about an inch of precipitation each month. June is generally the driest month. Temperatures at the bottom of the canyon are about 8 degrees warmer than at the rim.

PLANNING YOUR TIME

BLACK CANYON OF THE GUNNISON IN ONE DAY Pack a lunch and head to the canyon's South Rim, beginning with a stop at the **South Rim Visitor Center.** Before getting back into the car, take in your first view of Black Canyon from **Gunnison Point,** adjacent to the visitor center. Then set out on a driving tour of the 7-mile **South Rim**

10

Road, allowing the rest of the morning to stop at the various viewpoints that overlook the canyon. Don't miss **Chasm View** and **Painted Wall View,** and be sure to stretch your legs along the short (0.4-mile round-trip) **Cedar Point Trail.** If your timing is good, you'll reach **High Point,** the end of the road, around lunchtime.

After lunch, head out on **Warner Point Nature Trail** for an hour-long hike (1.5 miles round-trip). Then retrace your drive along South Rim Road back to the visitor center.

GETTING HERE AND AROUND

AIR TRAVEL   The Black Canyon of the Gunnison lies between the cities of Gunnison and Montrose, both of which have small regional airports.

CAR TRAVEL   The park has three roads. South Rim Road, reached by Route 347, is the primary thoroughfare and winds along the canyon's South Rim. From about late November to early April, the road is not plowed past the visitor center at Gunnison Point. North Rim Road, reached by Route 92, is usually open from May through Thanksgiving; in winter, the road is unplowed. On the park's south side, the serpentine East Portal Road descends abruptly to the Gunnison River below. The road is usually open from the beginning of May through the end of November. Because of the grade, vehicles or vehicle-trailer combinations longer than 22 feet are not permitted. The park has no public transportation.

PARK ESSENTIALS

PARK FEES AND PERMITS   Entrance fees are $15 per week per vehicle. Visitors entering on bicycle, motorcycle, or on foot pay $7 for a weekly pass. To access the inner canyon, you must pick up a wilderness permit (no fee).

PARK HOURS   The park is open 24/7 year-round. It's in the mountain time zone.

CELL-PHONE RECEPTION   Cell-phone reception in the park is unreliable and sporadic. There are public telephones at South Rim Visitor Center and South Rim Campground.

VISITOR INFORMATION

Black Canyon of the Gunnison National Park. ⊠ *102 Elk Creek, Gunnison* ☎ *970/641–2337* ⊕ *www.nps.gov/blca.*

VISITOR CENTERS   **North Rim Ranger Station.** This small facility on the park's North Rim is open only in summer. Rangers can provide information and assistance and can issue permits for wilderness use and rock climbing. If rangers are out in the field, which they often are, guests can find directions for obtaining permits posted in the station. ⊠ *North Rim Rd., 11 miles from Rte. 92 turnoff, Black Canyon of the Gunnison National Park* ☎ *970/641–2337* ⊗ *Late May–Labor Day.*

South Rim Visitor Center. The park's only visitor center offers interactive exhibits and introductory films detailing the park's geology and wildlife. Inquire at the center about free guided tours and informational ranger programs. ⊠ *Black Canyon of the Gunnison National Park* ✛ *1½ mile from the entrance station on South Rim Rd.* ☎ *970/249–1914* ⊗ *Late May–early Sept., daily 8–6; early Sept.–late May, daily 8:30–4.*

EXPLORING

SCENIC DRIVES

The scenic South and North Rim roads offer deep and distant views into the canyon. Both also offer several lookout points and short hiking trails along the rim. The trails that go down into the canyon are steep and strenuous, and essentially unmarked, and so are reserved for experienced (and very fit) hikers.

East Portal Road. The only way to access the Gunnison River from the park by car is via this paved route, which drops approximately 2,000 feet down to the water in only 5 miles, giving it an extremely steep grade. Vehicles longer than 22 feet are not allowed on the road. If you're towing a trailer, you can unhitch it near the entrance to South Rim campground. The bottom of the road is actually in the adjacent Curecanti National Recreation Area. A tour of East Portal Road, with a brief stop at the bottom, takes about 45 minutes.

North Rim Road. Black Canyon's North Rim is much less frequented, but no less spectacular—the walls here are near vertical—than the South Rim. To reach the 15½-mile-long North Rim Road, take the signed turnoff from Route 92 about 3 miles south of Crawford. The road is paved for about the first 4 miles; the rest is gravel. After 11 miles, turn left at the intersection (the North Rim Campground is to the right). There are six overlooks along the road as it snakes along the rim's edge. Kneeling Camel, at the road's east end, provides the broadest view of the canyon. Set aside about two hours for a tour of the North Rim.

South Rim Road. This paved 7-mile stretch from Tomichi Point to High Point is the park's main road. The drive follows the canyon's level South Rim; 12 overlooks are accessible from the road, most via short gravel trails. Several short hikes along the rim also begin roadside. Allow between two and three hours round-trip.

SCENIC STOPS

The vast depths that draw thousands of visitors each year to Black Canyon have also historically prevented any extensive human habitation from taking root, so cultural attractions are largely absent here. But what the park lacks in historic sites it more than makes up for in scenery.

10

Chasm and Painted Wall Views. At the heart-in-your-throat Chasm viewpoint, the canyon walls plummet 1,820 feet to the river, but are only 1,100 feet apart at the top. As you peer down into the depths, keep in mind that this section is where the Gunnison River descends at its steepest rate, dropping 240 feet within the span of a mile. A few hundred yards farther is the best place from which to see Painted Wall, Colorado's tallest cliff. Pinkish swaths of pegmatite (a crystalline, granite-like rock) give the wall its colorful, marbled appearance. ⊠ *Black Canyon of the Gunnison National Park* ⊕ *Approximately 3½ miles from the Visitor Center on South Rim Rd.*

Narrows View. Look upriver from this North Rim viewing spot and you'll be able to see into the canyon's narrowest section, just a slot really, with only 40 feet between the walls at the bottom. The canyon is also taller (1,725 feet) here than it is wide at the rim (1,150 feet). ⊠ *North Rim Rd., first overlook past the ranger station, Black Canyon of the Gunnison National Park.*

Warner Point. This viewpoint, at the end of the Warner Point Nature Trail, delivers awesome views of the canyon's deepest point (2,722 feet), plus the nearby San Juan and West Elk mountain ranges. ⊠ *End of Warner Point Nature Trail, westernmost end of South Rim Rd., Black Canyon of the Gunnison National Park.*

SPORTS AND THE OUTDOORS

Recreational activities in Black Canyon run the gamut from short and easy nature trails to world-class (and experts-only) rock climbing and kayaking. The cold waters of the Gunnison River are well known to trout anglers.

BIRD-WATCHING

The sheer cliffs of Black Canyon, though not suited for human habitation, provide a great habitat for birds. Peregrine falcons, white-throated swifts, and other cliff-dwelling birds revel in the dizzying heights, while at river level you'll find American dippers foraging for food in the rushing waters. Canyon wrens, which nest in the cliffs, are more often heard than seen, but their hauntingly beautiful songs are unforgettable. Dusky grouse are common in the sagebrush areas above the canyon, and red-tailed and Cooper's hawks and turkey vultures frequent the canyon rims. Best times for birding: spring and early summer.

BOATING AND KAYAKING

Fodor's Choice ★ With Class V rapids, the Gunnison River is one of the premier kayak challenges in North America. The spectacular 14-mile stretch of the river that passes through the park is so narrow in some sections that the rim seems to be closing up above your head. Once you're downstream from the rapids (and out of the park), the canyon opens up into what is called the Gunnison Gorge. The rapids ease considerably, and the trip becomes more of a quiet float on Class I to Class IV water.

Kayaking the river through the park requires a wilderness use permit (and lots of expertise), and rafting is not allowed. Access to the Gunnison Gorge is only by foot or horseback. However, several outfitters offer guided raft and kayak trips in the Gunnison Gorge and other sections of the Gunnison River.

TOURS **Morrow Point Boat Tours.** Starting in neighboring Curecanti National Recreation Area, these guided tours run twice daily (except Tuesday) in the summer, at 10 am and 12:30 pm. Morrow Point Boat Tours take passengers on a 90-minute tour via pontoon boat, and require a 1-mile walk to the boat dock. Reservations are required. ⊠ *Pine Creek Trail and Boat Dock, U.S. 50, milepost 130, 25 miles west of Gunnison, Gunnison* ☎ *970/641–2337* ⌨ *$16.*

FISHING

The three dams built upriver from the park in Curecanti National Recreation Area have created prime trout fishing in the waters below. Certain restrictions apply: Only artificial flies and lures are permitted, and a Colorado fishing license is required for people age 16 and older. Rainbow trout are catch-and-release only, and there are size and possession limits on brown trout (check at the visitor center). Most anglers access the river from the bottom of East Portal Road; an undeveloped trail goes along the riverbank for about ¾ mile.

CLOSE UP

Best Campgrounds in Black Canyon

There are three campgrounds in Black Canyon National Park. The small North Rim Campground is first-come, first served, and is closed in the winter. Vehicles longer than 35 feet are discouraged from this campground. South Rim Campground is considerably larger, and has a loop that's open year-round. Reservations are accepted in South Rim Loops A and B. Power hookups only exist in Loop B. The East Portal campground is at the bottom of the steep East Portal Road and is open whenever the road is open. It offers 15 first-come, first-served tent sites in a pretty setting. Water has to be trucked up to the campgrounds, so use it in moderation; it's shut off in mid- to late September. Generators are not allowed at South Rim and are highly discouraged on the North Rim.

South Rim Campground. Stay on the canyon rim at this main campground right inside the park entrance. Loops A and C have tent sites only. The RV hookups are in Loop B, and those sites are priced higher than those in other parts of the campground. It's possible to camp here year-round (Loop A stays open all winter), but the loops are not plowed, so you'll have to hike in with your tent. ⊠ *S. Rim Rd., 1 mile from the visitor center.*

North Rim Campground. This small campground, nestled amid pine trees, offers the basics along the quiet North Rim. ⊠ *N. Rim Rd., 11¼ miles from Rte. 92.*

East Portal Campground. Its location next to the Gunnison River makes it perfect for fishing. ⊠ *E. Portal Rd., 5 miles from the main entrance.*

HIKING

All trails can be hot in summer and most don't receive much shade, so bring water, a hat, and plenty of sunscreen. Dogs are permitted, on leash, on Rim Rock, Cedar Point Nature, and Chasm View Nature trails, and at any of the overlooks. Hiking into the inner canyon, while doable, is not for the faint of heart—or step. Six named routes lead down to the river, but they are not maintained or marked. In fact, the park staff won't even call them trails; they refer to them as "controlled slides." These supersteep, rocky routes vary in one-way distance from 1 to 2.75 miles, and the descent can be anywhere from 1,800 to 2,722 feet. Your reward, of course, is a rare look at the bottom of the canyon and the fast-flowing Gunnison. ■TIP→ **Don't attempt an inner-canyon hike without plenty of water (the park's recommendation is one gallon per person, per day).** For descriptions of the routes and the necessary permit to hike them, stop at the visitor center at the South Rim or North Rim ranger station. Dogs are not permitted in the inner canyon.

EASY
FAMILY
Cedar Point Trail. This 0.4-mile round-trip interpretive trail leads out from South Rim Road to two overlooks. It's an easy stroll, and signs along the way detail the surrounding plants. *Easy.* ⊠ *Trailhead off South Rim Rd., Black Canyon of the Gunnison National Park ⊹ 4¼ miles from South Rim Visitor Center.*

10

Deadhorse Trail. Despite its name, the 5-mile Deadhorse Trail is actually a pleasant hike, starting on an old service road from the Kneeling Camel View on the North Rim Road. The trail's farthest point provides the park's easternmost viewpoint. From this overlook, the canyon is much more open, with pinnacles and spires rising along its sides. *Easy.* ⊠ *Black Canyon of the Gunnison National Park* ✛ *Trailhead at the southernmost end of North Rim Rd.*

MODERATE **Chasm View Nature Trail.** The park's shortest trail (0.3 mile round-trip) starts at North Rim Campground and offers an impressive 50-yard walk right along the canyon rim as well as an eye-popping view of Painted Wall and Serpent Point. This is also an excellent place to spot raptors, swifts, and other birds. *Moderate.* ⊠ *, Trailhead at North Rim Campground, Black Canyon of the Gunnison National Park* ✛ *11¼ miles from Rte. 92.*

North Vista Trail. The round-trip hike to Exclamation Point is 3 miles; a more difficult foray to the top of 8,563-foot Green Mountain (a mesa, really) is 7 miles. The trail leads you along the North Rim; keep an eye out for especially gnarled pinyon pines—the North Rim is the site of some of the oldest groves of pinyons in North America, between 400 and 700 years old. *Moderate.* ⊠ *Trailhead at North Rim ranger station, off North Rim Rd., Black Canyon of the Gunnison National Park* ✛ *11 miles from Rte. 92 turnoff.*

Fodor'sChoice **Warner Point Nature Trail.** The 1.5-mile round-trip hike starts from High
★ Point. It provides fabulous vistas of the San Juan and West Elk Mountains and Uncompahgre Valley. Warner Point, at trail's end, has the steepest drop-off from rim to river: a dizzying 2,722 feet. *Moderate.* ⊠ *Black Canyon of the Gunnison National Park* ✛ *Trailhead at the end of South Rim Rd.*

DIFFICULT **Oak Flat Loop Trail.** This 2-mile loop is the most demanding of the South Rim hikes, as it brings you about 400 feet below the canyon rim. In places, the trail is narrow and crosses some steep slopes, but you won't have to navigate any steep drop-offs. Oak Flat is the shadiest of all the South Rim trails; small groves of aspen and thick stands of Douglas fir along the loop offer some respite from the sun. *Difficult.* ⊠ *Black Canyon of the Gunnison National Park* ✛ *Trailhead just west of the South Rim Visitor Center.*

HORSEBACK RIDING

TOURS AND **Elk Ridge Ranch and Trail Rides.** You can take 90-minute and two-hour
OUTFITTERS rides at this ranch. Elk Ridge also offers a half-day ride to the rim of the Black Canyon. ⊠ *10203 Bostwick Park Rd., Montrose* ☎ *970/240–6007* ☉ *May–Sept., daily.*

ROCK CLIMBING

Fodor'sChoice For expert rock climbers, the sheer cliffs of the Black Canyon represent
★ one of Colorado's premier big-wall challenges. Some routes can take several days to complete, with climbers sleeping on narrow ledges, or "portaledges." Though there's no official guide to climbing in the park, reports from individual climbers are kept on file at the South Rim Visitor Center. Nesting birds of prey may lead to wall closure at certain times of year.

Rock climbing in the park is for experts only, but you can do some bouldering at the Marmot Rocks area, about 100 feet south of South Rim Road between Painted Wall and Cedar Point overlooks (park at Painted Wall). Four boulder groupings offer a variety of routes rated from easy to very difficult; a pamphlet with a diagrammed map of the area is available at the South Rim Visitor Center.

TOURS AND OUTFITTERS

Irwin Guides. Intermediate and expert climbers can take full-day rock-climbing guided tours on routes from 6 to 15 pitches in length. ⊠ *330 Belleview Ave., Crested Butte* ☎ *970/349–5430* ⊕ *www.irwinguides. com* ✉ *From $195 per person, per day.*

Skyward Mountaineering. Intermediate and advanced climbers can take lessons and guided tours on the Black Canyon's fabled climbs with this internationally certified guide and outfitter. ⊠ *2392 Ridgeway Ct., Grand Junction* ☎ *541/639–9913* ⊕ *www.skywardmountaineering.com* ✉ *From $500 per day* ⊗ *Closed Dec.–Feb.*

WINTER SPORTS

From late November to early April, South Rim Road is not plowed past the visitor center, offering park guests a unique opportunity to cross-country ski or snowshoe on the road. The Park Service also grooms a cross-country ski trail and marks a snowshoe trail through the woods, both starting at the visitor center. It's possible to ski or snowshoe on the unplowed North Rim Road, too, but it's about 4 miles from where the road closes, through sagebrush flats, to the canyon rim.

MONTROSE

15 miles west of Black Canyon of the Gunnison; 64 miles west of Gunnison; 22 miles south of Delta, all via U.S. 50.

The self-described "Home of the Black Canyon" sits amid glorious surroundings, but it's otherwise a typical Western town with a small historic center, where you'll find a smattering of trendy shops and restaurants, and a collection of truck stops, strip malls, and big-box stores along its outskirts. Montrose also has a small airport that's a major gateway for skiers heading to Telluride and Crested Butte. Montrose is perfectly placed for exploring the Black Canyon of the Gunnison National Park and Curecanti National Recreation Area to the east, the San Juan Mountains to the south, Grand Mesa to the north, and the spectacular Uncompahgre National Forest to the southwest.

10

GETTING HERE AND AROUND

U.S. 550 enters Montrose from the south; it's known as Townsend Avenue as it passes through town. At Main Street, U.S. 550 merges with U.S. 50, which continues north to Delta and east to Black Canyon of the Gunnison National Park and the town of Gunnison.

ESSENTIALS

Visitor Information Montrose Visitor Center. ⊠ *107 S. Cascade Ave.* ☎ *970/497–8558* ⊕ *www.visitmontrose.com.*

EXPLORING

FAMILY **Museum of the Mountain West.** Run by a retired archaeologist, the museum depicts life in Colorado from the late 1800s to the 1940s. It features roughly 500,000 artifacts and 23 buildings, including a schoolhouse, church, carriage works, and several homesteads and a few teepee replicas. ✉ *68169 E. Miami Rd.* ✣ *2 miles east of Montrose, off U.S. 50* ☎ *970/240–3400* 🌐 *www.museumofthemountainwest.org* 🎟 *$10* 🕒 *Mon.–Sat., 8–4:30.*

SPORTS AND THE OUTDOORS

BOATING

Lake Fork Marina. Located on the western end of Blue Mesa Reservoir off U.S. 92, the Lake Fork Marina rents all types of boats. If you have your own, there's a ramp at the marina and slips for rent. ✉ *Off U.S. 92, near Lake Fork Campground, Gunnison* ☎ *970/641–3048* 🌐 *www.thebluemesa.com.*

HIKING

Grand Mesa, Uncompahgre, and Gunnison National Forests. With some of the most spectacular scenery in the Colorado Rockies, this trio of national forests has a total of more than 3 million acres. The area contains many historic mining sites, 3,600 miles of streams, 3,500 miles of trails, and 300-plus lakes. ✉ *2250 U.S. 50, Delta* ☎ *970/874–6600* 🌐 *www.fs.usda.gov/gmug.*

WHERE TO EAT AND STAY

$$ SOUTHWESTERN 🍴 **Camp Robber.** This simply decorated restaurant serves some of Montrose's most creative cuisine. Start with the famous green-chili chicken and potato soup, and follow with entrées such as spicy shrimp *chimayo* (New Mexican chili pepper) or the house specialty: pork medallions covered with pistachios. At lunch, salads with housemade dressings, hearty sandwiches, and blue-corn enchiladas fuel hungry hikers. The Sunday brunch will leave you happily stuffed, and locals flock here for the delicious homemade desserts. When the weather permits, you can sit on the shaded patio. ■ TIP→ **The green and red chili is mild, so ask them to spice it up if you prefer your chili sauce with a kick.** [$] *Average main: $15* ✉ *1515 Ogden Rd.* ☎ *970/240–1590* 🌐 *www.camprobber.com* 🕒 *No dinner Sun.*

$ PIZZA 🍴 **Colorado Boy Pizzeria & Brewery.** The dough is homemade and the beer is home-brewed at this trendy downtown pizzeria with high ceilings, brick walls, and contemporary decor. Colorado Boy also makes and bottles its own hot garlic oil, which is featured on several of its pizzas. Ingredients are often sourced locally, which also makes for delicious salads. Sit at the pizza bar in the back and enjoy an English-style ale while you watch the chefs craft your tasty pie. You can also visit the original Colorado Boy Pub & Brewery in downtown Ridgway. [$] *Average main: $10* ✉ *320 E. Main St.* ☎ *970/240–2790* 🌐 *www.coloradoboy.com* 🕒 *Closed Mon.*

$ HOTEL 🏨 **Country Lodge.** A log cabin–style building and rooms ringing a pretty garden and pool make this hotel feel remote even though it's on Montrose's main drag. **Pros:** great value; intimate feel; nice pool and hot tub. **Cons:** small bathrooms and TVs; on main highway, so it can sometimes be noisy. [$] *Rooms from: $85* ✉ *1624 E. Main St.* ☎ *970/249–4567* 🌐 *www.countrylodgecolorado.com* ⇆ *22 rooms, 1 cabin* 🍴 *Breakfast.*

$ HOTEL 🏨 **Red Arrow Inn & Suites.** This low-key establishment is a great value, with very reasonable prices for one of the nicest lodgings in the area, mainly because of the large, pretty rooms filled with handsome wood furnishings. **Pros:** spacious and comfortable rooms; good breakfast; pleasant pool. **Cons:** motel-style entrances; next to busy street. [$] *Rooms from: $89* ✉ *1702 E. Main St.* ☎ *970/249–9641* 🌐 *www.redarrowinn.com* ⇆ *57 rooms, 2 suites* 🍴 *Breakfast.*

DELTA

40 miles south of Grand Junction via U.S. 50; 22 miles north of Montrose via U.S. 50.

Delta is a no-frills town that makes a good jumping-off point for visiting Black Canyon of the Gunnison National Park and the nearby farming and ranching communities of Crawford, Hotchkiss, and Paonia—the last is known for its many vineyards and orchards. The main in-town attractions are colorful murals painted throughout downtown by local artists.

GETTING HERE AND AROUND

From Delta, Highway 65 heads north to Cedaredge, which is the starting point for the Grand Mesa Scenic and Historic Byway. Highway 92 heads east to Hotchkiss and south through the tiny town of Crawford, where you can access Black Canyon of the Gunnison National Park. From Hotchkiss, a 9-mile jaunt on Highway 133 leads to Paonia.

WHEN TO GO

The abundance of ripening fruits and vegetables paired with a delightful array of local wines make summer the best time to visit this remote area.

ESSENTIALS

Visitor Information **Cedaredge Area Chamber of Commerce.** ✉ *245 W. Main St., Cedaredge* ☎ *970/856–6961* 🌐 *www.cedaredgechamber.com.* **Crawford Area Chamber of Commerce.** ✉ *Crawford* ☎ *970/921–4000* 🌐 *www.crawfordcountry.org.* **Delta County Tourism.** ✉ *Delta* ☎ *970/874–9532* 🌐 *www.deltacountycolorado.com.* **Hotchkiss Community Chamber of Commerce.** ✉ *Hotchkiss* ☎ *970/872–3226* 🌐 *www.hotchkisschamber.com.* **Paonia Chamber of Commerce.** ✉ *130 Grand Ave., Paonia* ☎ *970/527–3886* 🌐 *www.paoniachamber.com.*

EXPLORING

Creamery Arts Center. In a renovated milk-processing plant, the two-story Creamery Arts Center showcases the work of more than 50 regional artists. Exhibits include paintings, photographs, sculptures, jewelry, crafts, and more. In a nod to the building's former use, you can buy ice cream on-site. ■ TIP→ **Find an excuse to visit both unisex bathrooms, which were exquisitely designed by two local artists.** ✉ *165 W. Bridge St., Hotchkiss* ☎ *970/872–4848* 🌐 *www.creameryartscenter.org* ⌚ *May–Dec., Mon.–Sat. 11–6; Jan.–Apr., Mon.–Sat. 11–5.*

10

Delicious Orchards Organic Farm Market. This lovely orchard markets its own organic apples, apricots, cherries, nectarines, peaches, pears, and plums throughout the summer. You can also shop for local wines and other products, or stop by the tasting room for homemade Big B's organic juices or hard cider on tap (plus lunch items at the deli). ⊠ *39126 Hwy. 133, Hotchkiss* ☎ *970/527–1110* ⊕ *www.bigbs.com* ☾ *Mid-May–Nov., daily 9–6.*

Delta County Historical Society Museum. One of the more interesting artifacts at the Delta County Museum is a collection of guns used in a failed bank robbery in 1893. Other attractions include dinosaur bones, pioneer-era housewares, an impressive collection of antique bells, and a family-history research archive. ■TIP➔ **Admission is free for ages 18 and younger.** ⊠ *251 Meeker St., Delta* ☎ *970/874–8721* 🖾 *$2* ☾ *May–Sept., Tues.–Fri. 10–4; Oct.–Apr., Tues. and Wed. 10–4.*

Fort Uncompahgre. Learn about the area's rich history with a visit to Fort Uncompahgre, which has a self-guided tour that takes you through the 1826 fur-trading post. In summer months, you might catch demonstrations of weaving, spinning, and other 19th-century activities. ⊠ *Confluence Park, 230 Gunnison River Dr., Delta* ☎ *970/874–8349* 🖾 *$4.50* ☾ *Apr.–Sept., Mon.–Sat. 9–4, Sun. noon–4.*

Orchard Valley Farms & Market. Family fun takes an organic approach at this friendly farm. Take a stroll through the gardens and orchards and pick your own fruits and vegetables or choose from a nice selection at the farm market. The on-site Black Bridge Winery offers free tastings of its Chardonnay, Riesling, Merlot, Pinot Noir, and other wines. ⊠ *15836 Black Bridge Rd., Paonia* ☎ *970/527–6838* ⊕ *www. orchardvalleyfarms.com* ☾ *Late May–Oct., daily 10–6.*

FAMILY **Tru-Vu Drive-in Theater.** A blast from the past, the Tru-Vu Drive-in Theater is one of the country's 335 remaining drive-in movie theaters. ■TIP➔ **Kids ages 11 and younger get in free.** ⊠ *1001 Hwy. 92, Delta* ☎ *970/874–9556* 🖾 *$8 per person* ☾ *May–Sept.* ☞ *Cash only.*

OFF THE
BEATEN
PATH

Dominguez-Escalante National Conservation Area. Explore hiking trails and view Native American rock art in this 210,000-acre conservation area. You can also visit 19th-century homesteads, one of which was built by Captain H.A. Smith. His stone cabin, built into the side of a boulder, has a hollowed-out slab for a bed and a smaller niche carved out of the stone wall to hold a bedside pistol. And don't miss 1,300-foot-deep Escalante Canyon, which harbors the Escalante Potholes, a popular swimming and wading spot. ⊠ *Escalante Canyon Rd., Delta* ✛ *12 miles west of Delta on U.S. 50* ☎ *970/244–3000* ⊕ *www.blm.gov/co/st/en/ nca/denca.html* 🖾 *Free.*

WINERIES

Located in eastern Delta County, the West Elks American Viticultural Area contains some of the highest-altitude vineyards in the Northern Hemisphere and produces an array of Central European varietals, including Merlot and Chardonnay. ■TIP➔ **Check out www.coloradowine. com for a wine trail map, then hit a few of the highlights while enjoying the fresh mountain air and scenery.**

Alfred Eames Cellars. Located at the Puesta del Sol Vineyards, 3 miles south of Paonia, this casual winery offers a nice selection of top-notch reds. ✉ *11931 4050 Rd., Paonia* ☎ *970/527–3269* 🌐 *www.alfredeamescellars.com* 🕒 *Call ahead for an appt.*

Black Bridge Winery. This winery, part of Orchard Valley Farms, has made great strides with its nice selection of Cabernet, Merlot, Pinot Noir, Syrah, and Chardonnay wines. Try them for free in the Tasting Room. ✉ *15836 Black Bridge Rd., Paonia* ☎ *970/527–6838* 🌐 *www.blackbridgewinery.com/bbhome.cfm* 🕒 *Late May–Oct., daily 10–6.*

Peak Spirits Farm Distillery. Spice things up a bit with the spirited selections at this organic distillery. Peak uses organic fruits to create CapRock spirits, including gin, vodka, brandys, grappas, and bitters. Free tours and tastings are available if you call ahead. ✉ *26567 North Rd., Hotchkiss* ☎ *970/361–4249* 🌐 *www.peakspirits.com* 🕒 *Call for hrs.*

Stone Cottage Cellars. This North Fork Valley Winery specializes in Chardonnay, Merlot, Syrah, Pinot Noir, Pinot Gris, and Gewürztraminer varietals. Stop by for a free vineyard tour and wine tasting. ✉ *41716 Reds Rd., Paonia* ☎ *970/527–3444* 🌐 *www.stonecottagecellars.com* 🕒 *Late May–Oct., daily 11–6.*

WHERE TO EAT AND STAY

$$ ITALIAN 🍴 **Flying Fork Cafe & Bakery.** This charming café serves tasty Italian fare in a comfortable dining room and, in the summer, a shady outdoor garden. An assortment of artisan breads and pastries is sold in the small bakery at the front of the building, with a growing selection of gluten-free items. Local ingredients are used whenever possible to create dishes like braised Colorado lamb shank or farfalle in a sauce of smoked chicken, pear, and Gorgonzola. The homemade fettuccine noodles are delicious, and the individual pizzas, made with whole-wheat flour and fresh basil and mozzarella, are good for smaller appetites. [$] *Average main: $18* ✉ *101 3rd St., Paonia* ☎ *970/527–3203* 🌐 *www.flyingforkcafe.com* 🕒 *Closed Mon.*

$ HOTEL 🏨 **Days Inn Delta.** Within walking distance of Delta's downtown, this motel has comfortable rooms, a full-service restaurant and lounge, heated seasonal pool, indoor hot tub, and fitness room. **Pros:** reasonably good restaurant; full hot breakfast. **Cons:** chain-hotel feel. [$] *Rooms from: $99* ✉ *903 Main St., Delta* ☎ *970/874–9781, 800/626–1994* 🌐 *www.daysinn.com* 🛏 *41 rooms* 🍽 *Breakfast.*

$$ B&B/INN 🏨 **Fresh & Wyld Farmhouse Inn and Gardens.** This well-kept, classic farmhouse has three suites on the main floor and four smaller rooms on the second floor, three of which have shared bathrooms. **Pros:** comfortable rooms; delicious food; farmhouse setting. **Cons:** the rooms upstairs are basic and have shared bathrooms; no TVs. [$] *Rooms from: $125* ✉ *1978 Harding Rd., Paonia* ☎ *970/527–4374* 🌐 *www.freshandwyld.com* 🛏 *5 rooms, 2 suites* 🍽 *Breakfast.*

$$$$ RESORT FAMILY 🏨 **Smith Fork Ranch.** Rustic charm and warm hospitality are the keys to success at this historic ranch, where rooms and log cabins combine modern amenities with Western art and handcrafted furniture. **Pros:** fabulous staff; luxurious accommodations; variety of ranch activities. **Cons:** very expensive; no refund for cancellations 90 days prior to

arrival date. [$] *Rooms from: $1,200* ✉ *45362 Needle Rock Rd., Crawford* ☎ *970/921–3454* 🌐 *www.smithforkranch.com* ⏲ *Closed Nov.–late May* 🛏 *5 rooms, 4 cabins* 🍴 *All-inclusive.*

OFF THE BEATEN PATH

Grand Mesa National Scenic and Historic Byway. For spectacular views of wildflower meadows, evergreen mesa forests, and high-mountain lakes, take a drive through Grand Mesa, Uncompahgre, and Gunnison National Forests on the 63-mile-long Grand Mesa Scenic and Historic Byway. Dubbed the "Playground in the Sky," this National Scenic Byway travels along the rim of the world's largest flat-top mountain, offering breathtaking views of Grand Valley more than a mile below. Plan on at least an hour and a half. It follows Highway 65 from Cedaredge at the southern end to I–70 on the northern end (a spur road takes you to the see-forever Lands End Overlook). ✉ *Cedaredge* 🌐 *www.grandmesabyway.com.*

LAKE CITY AND CREEDE

Lake City and Creede are in one of the most beautiful areas of Colorado. Both have colorful histories and excellent access to the many hiking and mountain-biking trails in the Gunnison National Forest and the Rio Grande National Forest. If you're driving through here, especially on the Silver Thread Scenic Byway or the Alpine Loop Scenic Byway, allow plenty of time, because you'll want to keep stopping to take pictures of the surrounding mountains.

LAKE CITY

45 miles from Ouray via Alpine Loop Scenic Byway (summer only); 55 miles southwest of Gunnison via U.S. 50 and Rte. 149; 52 miles northwest of Creede via Rte. 149.

Lake City—with its collection of lacy gingerbread-trim houses and other Victorian buildings—has one of the largest National Historic Districts in Colorado (more than 200 structures). Lake City is a quaint little town and a point of departure for superb hiking, fishing, and four-wheel driving in the Gunnison National Forest. A geological phenomenon known as the Slumgullion Earthflow occurred some 700 years ago, when a mountainside sloughed off into the valley, blocking the Lake Fork of the Gunnison River and creating Lake San Cristobal, the state's second-largest natural lake. There's a scenic overlook along Highway 149, just south of town, with a sign explaining how this happened.

GETTING HERE AND AROUND

Highway 149 turns into Gunnison Avenue as it passes through the seven blocks of Lake City. The majority of the town's shops and historic homes are one block west on Silver Street.

ESSENTIALS

Visitor Information Lake City/Hinsdale County Chamber of Commerce. ✉ *800 Gunnison Ave.* ☎ *970/944–2527* 🌐 *www.lakecity.com.*

EXPLORING

Alpine Loop Scenic Byway. The inspiring 63-mile Alpine Loop Scenic Byway joins Lake City with Ouray and Silverton. The road, typically open late May or early June through October, has unpaved sections that require a high-clearance, four-wheel-drive vehicle. Dizzily spiraling from 12,800-foot-high passes to gaping valleys, past seven ghost towns, the trip is well worth the effort. ⊠ *Lake City*.

Silver Thread Scenic Byway. Lake City used to be at the northern tip of the Silver Thread Scenic Byway, which in the past few years has been extended north to its intersection with U.S. 50 at Blue Mesa Reservoir, for a total of 117 miles. From Lake City, the byway (also called Highway 149) travels south 75 miles to Southfork, climbing over Slumgullion and Spring Creek passes. The route then overlooks the headwaters of the Rio Grande before dropping into the lush Rio Grande Valley. Along the way, you'll see plenty of old gold- and silver-mining camps and spectacular North Clear Creek Falls.

SPORTS AND THE OUTDOORS

FISHING

Numerous high-alpine lakes and mountain streams make the area around Lake City an angler's heaven. Lake San Cristobal is known around the region for its rainbow and mackinaw trout, while the Lake Fork of the Gunnison attracts anglers for rainbow and brown trout.

The Sportsman Outdoors. This full-service outfitter offers half- and full-day guided fly-fishing trips, as well as lessons for both novice and advanced anglers. The Sportsman also runs hiking, 4-wheel-drive, snowshoeing, and backcountry skiing trips. At the shop, you can buy and rent all manner of outdoor gear. ⊠ *238 S. Gunnison* ☎ *970/944–2526* ⊕ *www.lakecitysportsman.com* ⊠ *Lessons from $85; fly-fishing tours from $215.*

CREEDE

105 miles south of Gunnison via U.S. 50 and Rte. 149; 52 miles southeast of Lake City via Rte. 149.

Creede, a flash-in-the-pan silver town, was known in its heyday as Colorado's rowdiest mining camp. When silver was discovered here in 1889, hotels, saloons, banks, and brothels opened virtually overnight, often in tents and other makeshift structures. By 1892, Creede had become a collection of wood-framed buildings, at least 30 of which were saloons and dance halls. That year, Creede was immortalized in a poem written by the local newspaper editor Cy Warman: "It's day all day in daytime," he wrote, "and there is no night in Creede."

As delightful as the town's history may be, its location is even more glorious. Mineral County is almost entirely public land, including the nearby Weminuche Wilderness to the south and west and the Wheeler Geological Area to the east, where the unusual rock formations resemble playful abstract sculptures or M.C. Escher creations. The Colorado Trail and the Continental Divide Trail, two of the country's most significant long-distance recreational paths, pass through Mineral County.

10

GETTING HERE AND AROUND

Highway 149 connects with Main Street before it turns and heads out of Creede. The town encompasses about 15 blocks.

ESSENTIALS

Visitor Information **Creede & Mineral County Chamber of Commerce.** ✉ *904 S. Main St.* ☎ *800/327-2102* 🌐 *www.creede.com.*

EXPLORING

Creede Historic Museum. Occupying the original Denver & Rio Grande Railroad Depot, the museum paints a vivid portrait of the town's rough-and-tumble early days. It also includes World War I and World War II exhibits. ✉ *17 Main St.* ☎ *719/658-2004* 🌐 *www.creedehistoricalsociety.com* 🎟 *$2* 🕓 *Memorial Day–mid-Sept., daily 10–4.*

Underground Mining Museum. This museum is housed in rooms that modern miners blasted out of solid rock to commemorate the lives of 1880s-era miners. Exhibits tracing the history of mining reveal the difference between a *winze* (reinforced shaft leading straight down) and a *windlass* (hand-operated hoist). In summer, there are guided tours at 10 and 3 daily, but before 2:15 pm you can also take a self-guided audio tour. ✉ *503 Forest Service Rd. No. 9* ☎ *719/658-0811* 🌐 *www.undergroundminingmuseum.com* 🎟 *$7 self-guided tour, $15 guided tour* 🕓 *May–Sept., daily 10–4; Oct.–Apr., weekdays 10–3.*

WHERE TO EAT AND STAY

$$ B&B/INN FAMILY 🏨 **Antler's Rio Grande Lodge.** Dating back to the late 1800s, this cozy lodge has rooms in the main building as well as rustic, secluded cabins with their own kitchens. **Pros:** views of river; solid restaurant. **Cons:** off the beaten path; restaurant is a bit spendy. [$] *Rooms from: $145* ✉ *26222 Hwy. 149* ☎ *719/658-2423* 🌐 *www.antlerslodge.com* 🕓 *Closed Oct.–Apr.* 🛏 *9 rooms, 15 cabins* 🍴 *No meals.*

$$ B&B/INN 🏨 **Creede Firemens Inn.** In a historic building that once provided accommodation for firefighters, you'll now find comfortable but simple rooms with brick accent walls and private baths. **Pros:** private baths. **Cons:** no pets; basic rooms; no elevator. [$] *Rooms from: $135* ✉ *123 N. Main St.* ☎ *719/332-8806* 🌐 *www.theoldfirehouse.com* 🕓 *Closed Oct.–Apr.* 🛏 *3 rooms, 1 suite* 🍴 *Breakfast.*

$ B&B/INN 🏨 **Creede Hotel.** A relic of silver-mining days, this charming 1890s structure with a street-front balcony has been fully restored. **Pros:** in-town location; full breakfast. **Cons:** town can be noisy at night; closed in winter. [$] *Rooms from: $105* ✉ *120 N. Main St.* ☎ *719/658-2608* 🌐 *www.creedehotel.com* 🕓 *Closed Oct.–Mar.* 🛏 *4 rooms* 🍴 *Breakfast.*

TELLURIDE AND THE SAN JUAN MOUNTAINS

The San Juan Mountains cover more than 12,000 square miles of southwestern Colorado. This striking mountain range ranks as one of the most rugged in the country, and is defined by the hundreds of peaks rising to an elevation of 13,000 feet or more. This high mountain country is the perfect playground for laid-back camping and hiking, and extreme sports like ice climbing and heli-skiing.

TELLURIDE

66 miles south of Montrose via U.S. 550 and Hwy. 62; 111 miles north of Durango via U.S. 160 and Rtes. 184 and 145.

Tucked away between the azure sky and the gunmetal mountains is Telluride, the colorful mining town–turned–ski resort famous for its celebrity visitors (Oprah Winfrey, Tom Cruise, and Oliver Stone spend time here).

Telluride's first mines were established in the 1870s, and by the early 1890s the town was booming. The allure of the place was such that Butch Cassidy robbed his first bank here in 1889. These days the savage but beautiful San Juan range attracts mountain people of a different sort—skiers, snowboarders, mountain bikers, and four-wheelers—who attack any incline, up or down, with abandon.

GETTING HERE AND AROUND

Although Telluride and the ski resort town of Mountain Village are two distinct areas, you can travel between them via a 2½-mile, over-the-mountain gondola ride, arguably one of the most beautiful commutes in Colorado. The gondola makes a car unnecessary, as both the village and the town are pedestrian-friendly.

The free Galloping Goose shuttle loops around Telluride every 10 minutes in winter, 20 minutes in summer, and less often in the off-season. The Dial-a-Ride shuttle, also free, serves the Mountain Village area during high season. Telluride Express, a private taxi company, serves Telluride Regional Airport and the rest of the surrounding area, including other regional airports.

At about 15 blocks long and 6 blocks wide, Telluride is easy to cover on foot. And interesting, too—it's made up of one pastel Victorian residence or frontier trading post after another. It's hard to believe that the lovingly restored shops and restaurants once housed gaming parlors and saloons known for the quality of their "waitressing." That party-hearty spirit lives on, evidenced by numerous annual summer celebrations.

WHEN TO GO

Telluride has two short off-seasons, when most restaurants and many lodgings take a breather. The town closes up from late October until ski season gets going in late November. Many people also flee town during "mud season," leaving after the ski area shuts down in mid-April and returning in mid- to late May. But with the growing popularity of Mountainfilm, a film festival held over Memorial Day weekend, more places are staying open. Off-season rates offer you a chance to enjoy the town's charm for less. However, when the summer festivals are in full swing, prices skyrocket and rooms book up fast. The biggies are the Telluride Bluegrass Festival in June, the Telluride Jazz Festival in early August, the Telluride Film Festival over Labor Day weekend, and the Telluride Blues and Brews Festival in mid-September. Whenever you decide to go, you should check for upcoming events at least three months in advance.

FESTIVALS **Telluride Bluegrass Festival.** The Telluride Bluegrass Festival in June has gone far beyond its bluegrass roots and is now one of the country's premier acoustic folk–rock gatherings. ⊠ *Telluride* ☎ *800/624–2422* ⊕ *www.bluegrass.com/telluride.*

Fodor's Choice ★ **Telluride Film Festival.** Held each year over Labor Day, the Telluride Film Festival is up there with Sundance as one of the world's leading showcases for foreign and domestic films. ⊠ *Telluride* ☎ *510/665–9494* ⊕ *www.telluridefilmfestival.org.*

ESSENTIALS

Transportation Contacts Dial-a-Ride. ⊠ *Telluride Ski Resort* ☎ *970/728–8888.* **Galloping Goose.** ⊠ *Telluride* ☎ *970/728–5700* ⊕ *www.telluride-co.gov.* **Telluride Express.** ☎ *970/728–6000, 888/212–8294* ⊕ *www.tellurideexpress.com.*

Visitor Information Telluride Visitor Information Center. ⊠ *700 W. Colorado Ave.* ☎ *970/728–3041, 888/605–2578* ⊕ *www.visittelluride.com.* **Telluride Ski Resort.** ⊠ *565 Mountain Village Blvd.* ☎ *970/728–6900, 800/778–8581* ⊕ *www.tellurideskiresort.com.* **Telluride Snow Report.** ☎ *970/728–7425* ⊕ *www.tellurideskiresort.com.*

EXPLORING

Historical Tours of Telluride. Operated by local thespian Ashley Boling, Historical Tours of Telluride provides humorous walking tours through the downtown streets and buildings, adding anecdotes about infamous figures such as Butch Cassidy and Jack Dempsey. Tours last about 90 minutes. ⊠ *Telluride* ☎ *970/728–6639* 🎫 *$20* ☞ *By reservation only; no credit cards.*

Telluride Historical Museum. Housed in the 1896 Miner's Hospital, the Telluride Historical Museum hosts exhibits on the town's past, including work in the nearby mines, techniques used by local doctors, and an 860-year-old Native American blanket. It is one of only five Smithsonian-affiliated museums in Colorado. ⊠ *201 W. Gregory Ave.* ☎ *970/728–3344* ⊕ *www.telluridemuseum.org* 🎫 *$5* ☉ *Late May–mid-Oct., Mon.–Sat. 11–5, Sun. 1–5; mid-Oct.–mid-May Tues.–Sat. 11–5.*

EN ROUTE
San Juan Skyway. One of the country's most stupendously scenic drives, the 236-mile San Juan Skyway weaves through an impressive series of Fourteeners (peaks reaching more than 14,000 feet). From Telluride, it heads north on Route 145 to Placerville, where it turns east on Highway 62. On U.S. 550 it continues south to historic Ouray and over Red Mountain Pass to Silverton and then on to Durango, Mancos, and Cortez via U.S. 160. From Cortez, Route 145 heads north, passing through Rico and over lovely Lizard Head Pass before heading back into Telluride. In late September and early October, this route has some of the state's most spectacular aspen viewing. ⊠ *Telluride.*

DOWNHILL SKIING AND SNOWBOARDING

Fodor's Choice ★ **Telluride Ski Resort.** Dubbed "the most beautiful place you'll ever ski," Telluride Ski Resort once was known as an experts-only ski area. Indeed, the north-facing trails are impressively steep and long, and the moguls can be massive. Chairlift 9 services primarily expert terrain, including the famed Spiral Stairs and the Plunge, while Gold Hill, Bald Mountain, Black Iron Bowl, and Palmyra Peak provide challenging chutes and other double-diamond runs, as well as hiking options for expert skiers.

Telluride Bluegrass Festival

Bluegrass may have evolved from country's "Appalachian mountain music," but Telluride's Bluegrass Festival has added a distinctive Rocky Mountain note to the mix.

Since its inception in 1973, the festival has featured traditional bluegrass bands from across the nation, but when contemporary Colorado bands started adding the quintessential bluegrass instruments—mandolin, fiddle, guitar, upright bass, and banjo—to their lineups, their version of the "high lonesome sound" garnered national attention. It forced bluegrass to undergo several transformations, sometimes right before the Telluride audience's eyes, as the crowd's enthusiasm prompted more and more on-stage experimentation.

As the festival gained in popularity, it brought more bluegrass artists to Colorado, and crossover between bluegrass and other musical styles became more common. The festival earned the moniker "Woodstock of the West." Colorado bands such as String Cheese Incident, Leftover Salmon, and Yonder Mountain String Band performed regularly at the event, appealing to a younger audience and encouraging more experimentation.

Now the Telluride Bluegrass Festival draws such popular acts as Emmylou Harris, Alison Krauss, Bonnie Raitt, and Counting Crows—not exactly bluegrass purists. It has also boosted the popularity of other bluegrass gatherings around the state, including a sister festival held each July at Planet Bluegrass Ranch in Lyons, Colorado, a town of about 1,600 that has become a bluegrass artists' colony.

But then there is the other side—literally—of the ski area, the gently sloping valley called the Gorrono Basin, with long groomed runs excellent for intermediates and beginners. On the ridge that wraps around the ski area's core is the aptly named See Forever, a long cruiser that starts at 12,570 feet and delivers views over the San Juan Mountains and into Utah's La Sal mountain range. The best areas for beginners are the Meadows, off Lift 1, and Galloping Goose, a long winding trail off Lifts 12 or 10. Near Gorrono Basin, off Lift 4 (the ski area's main artery), is another section that includes supersteep, double-diamond tree runs on one side and glorious cruisers on the other.

Midmountain, Lift 5 accesses a wealth of intermediate runs. From there, slide through a Western-style gate and you come to Prospect Bowl, a 733-acre area with a network of runs cut around islands of trees. Prospect Express (Lift 12) appeases not only experts–who can navigate double-diamond chutes, cliff bands, and open glades–but also beginners and intermediates, who can ski some of the highest green and blue terrain in North America.

Telluride also has three terrain parks for skiers and snowboarders of all levels. **Facilities:** 127 trails; 2,000 acres; 4,425-foot vertical drop; 16 lifts. ✉ *565 Mountain Village Blvd.* ☎ *800/778–8581* ⊕ *www.tellurideskiresort.com* ▣ *Lift ticket $114.*

LESSONS AND PROGRAMS

Telluride Ski & Snowboard School. At this well-regarded school, adult half-day group clinics are $80, and full-day classes are $160. Lessons are available for alpine and telemark skiers as well as snowboarders. Children's programs are $185 per day and include a lift ticket, lesson, and lunch. The school also offers Women's Week programs, which include three or five days of skills-building classes with female instructors; cost is $550 to $875, not including lift tickets. Bumps and steeps camps are available as well. ⊠ *565 Mountain Village Blvd.* ☎ *970/728–7540* ⊕ *www.tellurideskiresort.com.*

RENTALS

Bootdoctors. Despite its name, Bootdoctors services go way beyond boots, renting all manner of skis, boots, and snowboards, along with backcountry gear and snowshoes. It also offers ski tuning, boot fitting, and repairs. It has two sister locations: one in Mountain Village and another on the city's main street that also serves as a year-round bike shop. ⊠ *236 S. Oak St.* ☎ *970/728–4587* ⊕ *www.bootdoctors.com.*

Telluride Sports. All manner of ski and snowboard rentals are available from the ubiquitous Telluride Sports, with several locations in Telluride and Mountain Village. The shop will deliver everything to your hotel for no extra charge. ⊠ *150 W. Colorado Ave.* ☎ *970/728–4477* ⊕ *www. telluridesports.com.*

NORDIC SKIING

TRACK SKIING

Telluride Nordic Center. Operated by the Telluride Nordic Association, the center offers ski and snowshoe tours and cross-country ski lessons. It also rents ski equipment, ice skates, and sleds for adults and children. ⊠ *500 W. Colorado Ave.* ☎ *970/728–1144* ⊕ *www.telluridetrails.org* ⌨ *Tours start at $95 per person for two people; group lessons start at $65 per person.*

TopAten Snowshoe and Nordic Area. There are 6 miles of rolling trails groomed for cross-country skiing and snowshoeing, as well as a warming teepee, a picnic deck, and restroom facilities. To access TopAten, you'll need to buy a "foot passenger" lift ticket for $25. ⊠ *Telluride Ski Resort* ✛ *Located near the unloading area for Chair 10* ☎ *970/728–7517* ⊕ *www.tellurideskiresort.com.*

OTHER SPORTS AND THE OUTDOORS

FISHING

For an afternoon in some of the finest fishing spots around, with abundant rainbow, cutthroat, brown, and brook trout, head for the beautiful San Miguel and Dolores rivers.

Telluride Outside. This service runs clinics and guided fly-fishing trips from its store, the Telluride Angler. You can also buy fishing gear and licenses here. ⊠ *Telluride Angler, 121 W. Colorado Ave.* ☎ *970/728–3895, 800/831–6230* ⊕ *www.tellurideoutside.com* ⌨ *Clinics from $100, tours from $295.*

GLIDER RIDES

Glide Telluride. Offering a rare and beautiful bird's-eye view of the town, the ski area, and the San Juans, Glider Bob operates out of the Telluride Regional Airport. Rides are conducted daily, weather permitting. ✉ *Telluride Regional Airport, 1500 Last Dollar Rd.* ☎ *970/708–0862* ⊕ *www.glidetelluride.com* ☞ *$130 for 30 minutes, $180 for 1 hour.*

GOLF

Telluride Golf Club. The soul-stirring, 360-degree mountain views at Telluride Golf Club may just elevate your game. Ease into play on the front nine, which includes downhill holes and a few par 3s. On the back nine, the holes lengthen, stretch uphill, and bend around doglegs for an invigorating challenge. The club is designated an Audubon Cooperative Sanctuary for its wildlife-habitat protection and water and biodiversity conservation efforts. Green fees include cart rental. ✉ *The Peaks Resort & Spa, 136 Country Club Dr., Mountain Village* ☎ *970/728–2606* ⊕ *www.tellurideskiresort.com* ☞ *$195* ⚑ *18 holes, 6574 yards, par 70.*

HIKING

The peaks of the rugged San Juan Mountains around Telluride require some scrambling, occasionally bordering on real climbing, to get to the top. A local favorite is Wilson Peak, which is one of the easier Fourteeners to climb if you take the Navajo Lake Approach. July and August are the most popular months on this 9½-mile round-trip hike.

Bear Creek Falls. An immensely popular trail leads to Bear Creek Falls, 2½ miles from the trailhead. The route is also used by mountain bikers. ✉ *Telluride ✛ Trailhead at end of S. Pine St.*

Bridal Veil Falls. A 1¾-mile road (it's advisable to travel in a 4WD) from the old Pandora Mill leads to spectacular Bridal Veil Falls, which, at 365 feet, tumbles lavishly from the top of the box canyon. A beautifully restored powerhouse sits beside the falls. ✉ *Telluride ✛ Trailhead near Pandora Mill, at the east end of Colorado Ave.*

Jud Wiebe Trail. This 3-mile loop is an excellent hike that is generally passable from spring until late fall. The first segment of the trail is fairly steep, so this is not the best choice for novices. It links with the Sneffels Highline Trail, a 13-mile loop that leads through wildflower-covered meadows. ✉ *Telluride ✛ Trailhead at north end of Aspen St.*

HORSEBACK RIDING

Telluride Horseback Adventures. Roudy Roudebush is a cowboy straight out of central casting (he starred in a television commercial and in Disney's 2004 film *America's Heart and Soul*). His company, Telluride Horseback Adventures, offers ultrascenic trail rides departing from his ranch in Norwood, 33 miles northwest of Telluride. You can also book sleigh rides in the winter. ✉ *4019 County Rd. 43ZS* ☎ *970/728–9611* ⊕ *www.ridewithroudy.com.*

MOUNTAIN BIKING

San Juan Hut System. Having a fully equipped hut waiting at the end of a tough day of riding makes the San Juan Hut System a backcountry biker's dream come true. The company, which started out as a hut-to-hut service for backcountry skiers, operates a 190-mile route from Telluride to Moab, Utah, suitable for novice and intermediate riders. Trips

10

run from June to October and last five or seven days, covering alpine meadows, desert slick rock, canyon country, and the Porcupine Rim Trail. Along the way, the six one-room huts are supplied with bunks, sleeping bags, heating and cooking stoves, food, and water. ✉ *770 N. Cora St., Ridgway* ☎ *970/626–3033* 🌐 *www.sanjuanhuts.com* 🎫 *Prices start at $695 per person.*

WHERE TO EAT

$$$$ MODERN AMERICAN Fodor's Choice ★ 🍴 **Allred's.** Unless you're planning some serious hiking, the only way to reach this sky-high eatery is via the gondola that connects Telluride with the Mountain Village. The view is understandably awesome, as are the meals. In the airy, stone-walled dining room, you'll find a locally inspired menu with offerings such as cider-brined Colorado Berkshire pork chops and veal scaloppine with a lemon-beurre fondue and Cabernet reduction, as well as a seasonal vegan entrée. Even if your wallet isn't ready for a full-dinner splurge, you owe it to your eyes to soak in the views over a drink and truffle fries in the bar. [$] *Average main: $36* ✉ *Top of St. Sophia gondola station* ☎ *970/728–7474* 🌐 *www.allredsrestaurant.com* 🕒 *No lunch.*

$ CAFÉ 🍴 **Baked in Telluride.** This Telluride institution has expanded enormously over the years, as you can tell from the racks of fresh-baked breads, rolls, bagels, and other pastries that are on display. The kitchen turns out heavenly sandwiches, pizzas, and pastas (try the Alfredo), as well as huge, inexpensive salads. Order your meal to go or grab a seat at one of the communal-style tables, where you can enjoy displays from a local art school. The front porch is especially busy as locals meet, greet, and enjoy the views. [$] *Average main: $8* ✉ *127 S. Fir St.* ☎ *970/728–4775.*

$$ PIZZA 🍴 **Brown Dog Pizza.** This local hangout serves a mean pizza in a pub-style atmosphere. Choose from three pizza styles—Detroit square (an international award winner), medium crust, and ultrathin crust—and load it up with specialty toppings such as artichoke hearts, broccoli, pickles, jalepeño peppers, and sun-dried tomatoes. However, the most popular choices are also the meatiest. The barbecued chicken with bacon is a favorite, as is the Boone's Meaty, loaded with pepperoni, sausage, meatballs, bacon, and Canadian bacon. Slices are served until midnight. There's also a good selection of pastas, burgers, and subs, as well as a decent gluten-free menu. Brown Dog is one of the few places in town that will feed your family for less than the cost of a lift ticket. [$] *Average main: $13* ✉ *110 E. Colorado Ave.* ☎ *970/728–8046* 🌐 *www.browndogpizza.com.*

$$ CAFÉ 🍴 **The Butcher & The Baker.** Fresh farm-to-table fare lures guests to The Butcher & The Baker, a bustling and recently expanded café on the town's main strip. White walls with blue wainscoting and decorative touches like metal-milk-bucket light fixtures give the eatery a modern-farmhouse feel. The breakfast, lunch, and dinner menus follow suit: hearty hashes and scrumptious egg dishes for breakfast; fresh sandwiches, salads (including daily salads by the scoop in the deli case), and soups for lunch; steak and fish entrées in the evening. An outdoor patio and an espresso bar make this a popular gathering place for locals. [$] *Average main: $17* ✉ *201 E. Colorado Ave.* ☎ *970/728–2899* 🌐 *www.butcherandbakercafe.com* 🕒 *No dinner Sun.*

$$$$
CONTEMPORARY

✕ Cosmopolitan. The trendy Cosmopolitan lures guests with half-price happy-hour sushi rolls and keeps them there for some of Telluride's finest dining. Fresh sustainable seafood is flown in regularly, which is obvious in dishes such as the seafood-loaded fish stew and the barbecued Verlasso salmon. "Turf" options include ultratender Colorado braised lamb and Wagyu rib eye. Locals rave about the bread, and an exhaustive wine list means there's a proper pairing no matter which dish you choose. Finish with the New Orleans–style beignets with a cappuccino for dessert, cheekily listed as "coffee and donuts" on the menu. $ *Average main: $36 ⊠ Hotel Columbia, 300 W. San Juan Ave. ☎ 970/728–1292 ⊕ www. cosmotelluride.com ⊗ No lunch. Closed Apr. and May.*

$$$$
CONTEMPORARY
Fodor's Choice
★

✕ La Marmotte. La Marmotte may be housed in one of Telluride's oldest buildings, but it provides one of its freshest dining experiences. A French influence is obvious in favorites such as coq au vin with bacon mashed potatoes, but local inspiration is here, too (try the braised Colorado lamb shank with salsa verde). Start your meal with the seared sea scallops or the house favorite—roasted red beet salad—and finish with the chocolate and sour cherry mousse terrine. The candlelight-and-white-tablecloth aura and simple, contemporary decor is, like the cuisine, sophisticated without being snooty, and the outdoor seating is divine on summer evenings. $ *Average main: $35 ⊠ 150 W. San Juan Ave. ☎ 970/728–6232 ⊕ www.lamarmotte.com ⊗ Closed Wed. in summer. No lunch, except for summer Fri. ⌕ Reservations essential.*

$$$$
STEAKHOUSE

✕ New Sheridan Chop House. This upscale steakhouse is arguably Telluride's best—and spendiest. Here you can choose your meat (sirloin, filet mignon, and succulent bison rib eye are among the choices), then your topping (think caramelized onions, blue cheese, or glazed wild mushrooms), then your sauce (anything from béarnaise to chimichurri). Other options include elk loin and Colorado striped bass. The extensive wine list includes many by the glass. Dark wood, mirrors aged with gold patina, and white tablecloths complement the red-hued tapestries and brightly colored murals. $ *Average main: $36 ⊠ New Sheridan Hotel, 231 W. Colorado Ave. ☎ 970/728–9100 ⊕ www.newsheridan. com ⊗ Closed mid-Apr.–mid-May and mid-Oct.–mid-Nov.*

$$
SOUTHERN

✕ Oak. In the Camel's Garden Hotel, this place serves messy, mouthwatering ribs and Carolina-style pulled-pork sandwiches. You'll find the famous sides—fried okra, red beans and rice, and sweet potato fries— and rich desserts, plus the Southern-style beverages. There are a dozen or so beers (including Schlitz), 30 bourbons, and homemade sweet tea. Some lighter options have joined the menu, which is good news to anyone concerned with cholesterol. There's outdoor seating, with a huge patio that's hopping every afternoon throughout the year. $ *Average main: $15 ⊠ Camel's Garden Hotel, 250 San Juan Ave. ☎ 970/728– 3985 ⊕ www.oakstelluride.com ⌕ Reservations not accepted.*

$$$$
THAI

✕ Siam. The atmosphere is low-key, but the food is exquisite at Siam, a simultaneously authentic and creative Thai restaurant one block off main street. Seafood selections abound on the enormous menu, which also includes plenty of chicken, beef, and pork, all prepared by native Thai chefs. The innovative hand rolls are delicious (don't miss the local favorite: zesty asparagus with the addictive house "Thailandaise"

10

sauce). A large portion of the menu items are gluten-free, and you can designate your preferred level of spiciness in most dishes. Siam also has a sister restaurant on the mountain: Siam's Talay Grille. ⓢ *Average main: $28* ✉ *200 S. Davis* ☎ *970/728–6886* ⊕ *www.siamtelluride. com* ☉ *No lunch*.

$$$$
EUROPEAN

✕ **221 South Oak.** Housed in a beautifully restored Victorian, this classy bistro with two lovely patios entices you to linger with its cozy ambience and scrumptuous meals. Sunday brunch, in summer only, draws locals and visitors alike with a fabulous menu that includes several varieties of frittatas, French toast, and homemade sausage. The dinner menu changes frequently but always includes dishes made with locally sourced fish (like Rocky Mountain trout or Colorado striped bass) and meat (elk, lamb, and bison); plus, there's a hearty vegetarian menu. ■ TIP➜ **Stop in on a Wednesday for Mussels & Martinis night.** While you're there, sign up for the popular wine-and-app-pairing class. ⓢ *Average main: $33* ✉ *221 S. Oak St.* ☎ *970/728–9507* ⊕ *www.221southoak. com* ☉ *Closed early Apr.–May, and mid-Oct.–mid-Dec. No lunch*.

WHERE TO STAY

$$$$
HOTEL

🏨 **Camel's Garden.** An ultramodern lodge that's all sharp lines and sleek surfaces is just steps from the gondola and features huge rooms and suites. **Pros:** convenient to lifts; ski valet service; creekside location. **Cons:** modern look makes it feel a bit sterile; no amenities for kids. ⓢ *Rooms from: $250* ✉ *250 W. San Juan Ave.* ☎ *970/728–9300, 888/772–2635* ⊕ *www.camelsgarden.com* ⇌ *30 rooms, 6 condos* ⦿| *Breakfast*.

$$$$
HOTEL

🏨 **Hotel Columbia Telluride.** Conveniently located right at the base of the gondola, this hotel has a crisp and contemporary vibe. **Pros:** spacious rooms; steps from gondola; stunning views. **Cons:** expensive; some rooms can be noisy. ⓢ *Rooms from: $250* ✉ *301 W. San Juan Ave.* ☎ *970/728–0660, 800/201–9505* ⊕ *www.columbiatelluride.com* ⇌ *14 rooms, 7 suites* ⦿| *Breakfast*.

$$$$
HOTEL

🏨 **The Hotel Telluride.** With luxurious rooms, tasteful Western-style decor, and dramatic views from private patios or balconies, The Hotel Telluride is an ideal place to immerse yourself in mountain culture. **Pros:** free shuttle to the gondola; pets are welcome; great views. **Cons:** $20 parking fee; a few blocks from downtown; restaurant not open for lunch. ⓢ *Rooms from: $249* ✉ *199 N. Cornet St.* ☎ *970/369–1188* ⊕ *www. thehoteltelluride.com* ⇌ *55 rooms, 4 suites* ⦿| *No meals*.

$$
HOTEL

🏨 **Inn at Lost Creek.** A grand stone-and-wood structure, this luxury ski-in ski-out hotel in the Mountain Village resembles an alpine lodge with contemporary furnishings. **Pros:** ski-in ski-out convenience; upscale but friendly atmosphere; excellent service. **Cons:** minimum stay during holidays; $20 nightly fee for parking. ⓢ *Rooms from: $129* ✉ *119 Lost Creek La., Mountain Village* ☎ *970/728–5678, 888/601–5678* ⊕ *www. innatlostcreek.com* ⇌ *4 studios, 25 suites, 3 condos* ⦿| *Breakfast*.

$$$$
HOTEL
Fodor'sChoice
★

🏨 **Lumière.** "Lumière" means "light" in French, and this luxury lodge lives up to its name—suites open onto beautiful views, and the airy decor brings the outside in with a warm color palette of orange, cream, and brown. **Pros:** very large bathrooms; sumptuous rooms; friendly and attentive staff. **Cons:** incredibly pricey; minimum stay during holidays;

layout can be confusing. $ *Rooms from: $400* ✉ *118 Lost Creek La.* ☎ *970/369–0400* ⊕ *www. lumieretelluride.com* ⇥ *11 rooms, 18 residences* ᵀᴼ⎮ *Breakfast.*

$$$$ ⊞ **Madeline Hotel and Residences.**
HOTEL Attentive service and minimalist, contemporary decor give this Mountain Village hotel a well-deserved air of luxury. **Pros:** feels very posh; ample amenities. **Cons:** $25 parking fee; labyrinthine design is hard to navigate. $ *Rooms from: $359* ✉ *568 Mountain Village Blvd.* ☎ *970/369–0880* ⊕ *www. madelinetelluride.com* ⇥ *84 rooms, 46 suites* ᵀᴼ⎮ *No meals.*

$$$ ⊞ **New Sheridan Hotel.** Contemporary furnishings and historic black-and-white photos adorn this

> **TELLURIDE LODGING ALTERNATIVES**
>
> **Telluride Rentals.** This agency books many of the town's and mountain's most luxurious properties, including private homes and condos. ✉ *209 E. Colorado Ave.* ☎ *800/970–7541, 970/728–5262* ⊕ *www.telluride-rentals.com.*
>
> **Telluride Resort Reservations.** This central reservations system handles most of the properties at Telluride Mountain Village and several more in town. ✉ *Telluride* ☎ *970/728–7350, 800/778–8581* ⊕ *www.tellurideskiresort.com.*

beautifully restored century-old landmark on Telluride's main drag. **Pros:** accommodating staff; secure ski storage with boot warmers; luxurious feel. **Cons:** fitness center not on-site; noise from the bar can drift upstairs at night; no fridge or microwave. $ *Rooms from: $203* ✉ *231 W. Colorado Ave.* ☎ *970/728–4351, 800/200–1891* ⊕ *www. newsheridan.com* ⊘ *Closed mid-Apr.–mid-May and mid-Oct.–mid-Nov.* ⇥ *24 rooms, 2 suites* ᵀᴼ⎮ *No meals.*

NIGHTLIFE AND PERFORMING ARTS

PERFORMING ARTS

Sheridan Opera House. Miners built the opera house in 1913 as a venue primarily for vaudeville acts. Today the landmark opera house presents a variety of shows year-round, including live theater, concerts, and comedy acts. Over the years it has hosted performances by such popular artists as Jackson Browne, Jimmy Buffett, and Jewel. The nonprofit Sheridan Arts Foundation operates the opera house. ✉ *110 N. Oak St.* ☎ *970/728–6363* ⊕ *www.sheridanoperahouse.com.*

Telluride Theatre. This semiprofessional group performs a variety of shows year-round in various venues. Productions include popular musicals, Shakespeare-in-the-park performances, and original, experimental shows. ✉ *Administrative office, 220 W. Colorado Ave.* ☎ *970/708–3934* ⊕ *www.telluridetheatre.org.*

NIGHTLIFE

Fly Me to the Moon Saloon. Telluride's favorite spot to catch a band, this saloon has live music—jazz, blues, funk, ska, rock, you name it—several nights each week. The bands are a mix of local and national touring acts; past artists have included Jack Johnson and Sheryl Crow. On band breaks, you can enjoy free pool and shuffleboard. ✉ *136 E. Colorado Ave.* ☎ *970/728–4100* ⊕ *www.flymetothemoonsaloon.com* ⊘ *Closed Mon.*

10

Last Dollar Saloon. A favorite après-ski and after-hours destination, the Last Dollar (locals know it as "The Buck") has scads of beers, great margaritas, and a modern jukebox filled with old favorites. It's housed in an authentic Victorian building with original brick walls and high tin ceilings. ⊠ *100 E. Colorado Ave.* ☎ *970/728–4800* ⊕ *www.lastdollarsaloon.com.*

New Sheridan Bar. The century-old bar at the New Sheridan Hotel is a favorite hangout for skiers returning from the slopes and, in summer, for everybody else. There's occasionally live music. ⊠ *New Sheridan Hotel, 231 W. Colorado Ave.* ☎ *970/728–9100* ⊕ *www.newsheridan.com.*

There. Tucked off the main strip, this tiny bar serves scrumptious small plates and killer cocktails (we suggest the brussels sprouts and the grapefruit martini) in a speak-easy atmosphere accented by a funky design (for the full experience, find an excuse to visit the restroom). It's packed from 5 until midnight, so call ahead to reserve a table. ■ TIP→ After you recover from Saturday night, stop back in for a tasty Sunday brunch. ⊠ *627 W. Pacific Ave.* ☎ *970/728–1213* ⊕ *www.therebars. com* ☉ *Closed mid-Oct.–early Dec. and mid-Apr.–mid-May.*

SHOPPING

BOOKS

Between the Covers Bookstore. This locally owned bookstore is perfect for browsing through the latest releases while sipping a foam-capped cappuccino from the coffee bar at the back of the shop. You'll also find a good selection of field guides and books on local history. ⊠ *224 W. Colorado Ave.* ☎ *970/728–4504* ⊕ *www.between-the-covers.com.*

BOUTIQUES

Telluride Trappings & Toggery. Check The Toggery—the town's longest-standing retail store—for stylish Telluride and Colorado souvenir tees and sweatshirts. You'll also find a large selection of men's and women's clothing and shoes, as well as some jewelry, household items, and children's clothing. ⊠ *109 E. Colorado Ave.* ☎ *970/728–3338* ⊕ *www. thetelluridetoggery.com.*

SPAS

The Peaks Spa. Plan for a full-day retreat at The Peaks, which at 42,000 feet is Colorado's largest spa. Its sheer size guarantees there is plenty to keep you occupied: a half-Olympic-size pool, indoor/outdoor pool with a two-story waterslide, full fitness center, a generous lineup of exercise classes, steam rooms, large Roman soaking tubs, saunas, an oxygen bar, and large, modern relaxation lounges, for a start. With 32 treatment rooms stretched down a long corridor, The Peaks can feel a bit clinical, but your gem-stone massage with organic herbal oils and semi-precious stones or your herbal Thai poultice treatment will rub that worry away. ⊠ *136 Country Club Dr.* ☎ *800/772–5482, 970/728–2590* ⊕ *www.thepeaksresort.com/ spa* ☞ *$140 60-min massage, $385 3½-hr package. Hair salon, hot tubs (indoor and outdoor), oxygen inhalation, pools (indoor and outdoor), nail salon, saunas, steam rooms. Gym: cardiovascular machines, free weights, weight-training machines, squash court. Services: Aromatherapy, body scrubs and wraps, facials, massage. Classes and programs: Body com-position analysis, conditioning and stretching, movement classes, Nordic walks, personal training, Pilates, Spinning, yoga.*

RIDGWAY

40 miles from Telluride via Hwy. 62 and Rte. 145; 26 miles south of Montrose via U.S. 550.

The 19th-century railroad town of Ridgway has been the setting for some classic Westerns, including *True Grit* (the original John Wayne version) and *How the West Was Won*. Though you'd never know it from the rustic town center, the area is also home to many swank ranches, including one belonging to fashion designer Ralph Lauren.

GETTING HERE AND AROUND

U.S. 550 runs along the eastern side of town, heading north to Montrose and south to Ouray. Highway 62 heads right through the middle of town on its way to Telluride. The rest of the main part of town encompasses all of seven blocks, making side travel a breeze.

SPORTS AND THE OUTDOORS

BACKCOUNTRY SKIING

San Juan Hut System. Among the better backcountry skiing routes is the San Juan Hut System. The route starts about 15 miles south of Ridgway in Ouray and leads toward Telluride along the Sneffels Range. The five huts in the system are about 7 miles apart, and are well equipped with bunks, wood-burning stoves, propane lights, and cooking stoves and utensils. Previous backcountry experience is highly recommended, and staff members can steer guests to terrain that best fits their backcountry knowledge and skill levels. Reservations are recommended at least two weeks in advance. ⊠ *770 N. Cora. St.* ☎ *970/626–3033.*

FISHING

Ridgway State Park. At this peaceful state park, 4 miles north of Ridgway, the 5-mile-long reservoir is stocked with plenty of rainbow trout, as well as the larger and tougher brown trout. Anglers also pull up kokanee salmon and yellow perch. There's a boat ramp, swimming beach, picnic areas, playgrounds, and a campground. ⊠ *28555 U.S. 550* ☎ *970/626–5822* ⊕ *www.cpw.state.co.us* ⊠ *$7 per vehicle.*

GOLF

Divide Ranch and Club. This semiprivate 18-hole, Byron Coker–designed course twists through a maze of high-mesa forest, complete with mountain views and wildlife. It's long and often demanding, but at 8,000 feet your drives might go a little farther and higher than they do at sea level. Course and driving range are open from May to October, and prices include cart fees. ⊠ *151 Divide Ranch Cir.* ☎ *970/626–5284* ⊕ *www. divideranchandclub.com* ⊠ *$55 weekdays, $65 weekends* ⅄ *18 holes, 7039 yards, par 72.*

WHERE TO EAT AND STAY

$$
AMERICAN
✕ **True Grit Cafè.** This local hangout is a shrine to the original 1968 film that starred John Wayne—one of the restaurant's walls actually appears in the movie. The huge stone fireplace, second-floor outdoor balcony, and cozy interior would make even the Duke feel at home. The Grit serves cowboy-type fare—homemade chili, burgers (locals rave about them), and delicious chicken-fried steak—along with Tex-Mex offerings like burritos and tacos. You can also now get breakfast on summer

10

weekends. $ *Average main: $13* ⊠ *123 N. Lena Ave.* ☎ *970/626–5739* ⊕ *www.truegritcafe.com.*

$$ **Chipeta Solar Springs Resort.** Enjoy the stunning views from the decks
HOTEL   of the dramatic Southwestern-style adobe rooms and suites, which have
rough-hewn log beds and hand-painted Mexican tiles. **Pros:** saltwa-
ter swimming and soaking pools; on-site restaurant; ideal for outdoor
activities. **Cons:** fills up on weekends; limited parking. $ *Rooms from:*
$159 ⊠ *304 S. Lena St.* ☎ *970/626–3737, 800/633–5868* ⊕ *www.*
chipeta.com ☽ *Restaurant is closed for dinner Mon. and Tues.* ⇨ *17*
rooms, 8 condos ⍟ *No meals.*

OURAY

10 miles south of Ridgway; 23 miles north of Silverton via U.S. 550.

The town of Ouray (pronounced *you-ray*) is nestled in a narrow, steep-
walled canyon in the shadow of the San Juan Mountains. It was named
for the great Southern Ute chief Ouray, labeled a visionary by the U.S.
Army and branded a traitor by his people because he attempted to
assimilate the Utes into white society. The former mining town is only
a few blocks wide, but is filled with lavish old hotels, commercial build-
ings, and residences. More than 25 classic edifices are included in the
walking-tour brochure issued by the Ouray County Historical Society
and available at the town visitor center. Among the points of interest
are the grandiose Wright's Opera House and the Western Hotel. The
town's ultimate glory lies in its surroundings, and it has become an
increasingly popular destination for climbers (both the mountain and
ice varieties), mountain-bike fanatics, and hikers.

GETTING HERE AND AROUND

U.S. 550 runs straight through town and turns into Main Street for the
six blocks from 3rd Avenue to 9th Avenue. The Ouray Visitors Center
and the Hot Springs Park are on the north end of town, and the historic
landmark hotel, the Beaumont, is smack in the middle of town between
5th and 6th avenues. The Uncompahgre River runs parallel to Main
Street just a couple blocks west of town, and Box Cañon Park is just
southwest of Main Street, at the confluence of Canyon Creek and the
Uncompahgre River.

ESSENTIALS

Visitor Information Ouray Visitors Center. ⊠ *1230 Main St.* ☎ *970/325–*
4746, 800/228–1876 ⊕ *www.ouraycolorado.com.*

EXPLORING

TOP ATTRACTIONS

Box Cañon Falls. One particularly gorgeous jaunt is to Box Cañon Falls,
where the turbulent waters of Clear Creek thunder 285 feet down a
narrow gorge. A steel suspension bridge and well-marked trails afford
breathtaking views. Birders flock to the park to see the rare black
swift and other species, and a visitor center has interpretive displays.
⊠ *Ouray* ✛ *West end of 3rd Ave. off U.S. 550* ☎ *970/325–7080* 🖅 *$4*
☽ *May–Oct., daily 8–8.*

Historic Wiesbaden Hot Springs Spa & Lodgings. At the source of several of Ouray's famed springs, this European-style spa and inn features rock-hewn vapor caves with a steamy soaking pool. In addition, there's a small outdoor pool, fed by continuously flowing hot-spring water. Massages, herbal wraps, and other treatments are offered at the spa. This is a strictly no-smoking facility, and no children under 6 are allowed in the caves. ⊠ *625 5th St.* ☎*970/325–4347* ⊕ *www. wiesbadenhotsprings.com* 🖃 *$15 for 3 hrs* ☉ *Daily 8 am–9:45 pm in summer; call for winter hrs.*

Fodor'sChoice
★ **Million Dollar Highway.** Ouray is also the northern end of the Million Dollar Highway, the awesome stretch of U.S. 550 that climbs over Red Mountain Pass (arguably the most spectacular part of the 236-mile San Juan Skyway). As it ascends steeply from Ouray, the road clings to the cliffs hanging over the Uncompahgre River. Guardrails are few, hairpin turns are many, and behemoth RVs seem to take more than their share of road. This priceless road is kept open all winter by heroic plow crews. The road on the Ouray side of the Pass is more dramatic (and intimidating) than the Silverton side. ⊠ *Ouray.*

WORTH NOTING

Bachelor-Syracuse Mine Tour. On this hour-long tour, visitors trek 1,500 feet into one of the region's great silver mines. Tour guides are actual miners and they explain various mining techniques and point out remaining silver veins and other mineral deposits. Tours depart every hour, and light jackets are wise year-round, as it's chilly in the mine. Gold-panning lessons in the adjacent stream are included in the tour price. ■TIP→ **Come early for a tasty, inexpensive breakfast and receive a $2 discount on your tour.** ⊠ *1222 County Rd. 14* ☎*970/325–0220* ⊕ *www.bachelorsyracusemine.com* 🖃 *$15* ☉ *Daily in summer; call for hrs.*

Ouray County Museum. This small, but surprisingly stocked museum highlights the history of mining, ranching, and railroading in the San Juan Mountains. The basement features a life-size model mine shaft, as well as an impressive collection of locally found gems and minerals. Other exhibits include Native American artifacts and depictions of domestic and commercial life in the late 1800s. The building itself is a former 1887 hospital. ⊠ *420 6th Ave.* ☎*970/325–4576* ⊕ *www. ouraycountyhistoricalsociety.org* 🖃 *$6* ☉ *Call for hrs.*

FAMILY **Ouray Hot Springs Pool & Fitness Center.** After a day of hiking, biking, or skiing, hit one of the area's hot springs. The massive Ouray Hot Springs Pool is brimming with a million gallons of naturally heated water kept between 88°F and 105°F (80°F in the lap lanes). Kids love the two large, twisting slides and the inflatable obstacle course. ⊠ *1220 Main St.* ☎*970/325–7073* ⊕ *www.ourayhotsprings.com* 🖃 *$12* ☉ *Weekdays noon–9, weekends 11–9 in winter; daily 10–10 in summer.*

SPORTS AND THE OUTDOORS

FOUR-WHEELING

Off-roaders delight in the more than 500 miles of four-wheel-drive roads around Ouray. Popular routes include the Alpine Loop Scenic Byway to the Silverton and Lake City areas, and Imogene Pass to Telluride.

Switzerland of America Jeep Rentals & Tours. If you have the skill and confidence but not the four-wheel-drive vehicle, you can rent one from Switzerland of America. The company also operates guided tours in open-air six-passenger trucks, and can conduct custom tours upon request. ✉ *226 7th Ave.* ☎ *970/325–4484, 866/990–5337* ⊕ *www. soajeep.com* 💲 *From $60.*

Yankee Boy Basin. About the first 7 miles of the road to Yankee Boy Basin are accessible by regular cars, but it takes a four-wheel drive to reach the heart of this awesome alpine landscape. After leaving Ouray, the route climbs west into a vast basin ringed with soaring summits and carpeted with lavish displays of wildflowers. At 17 miles round-trip, this is one of the region's premier day-trip destinations. ✉ *County Rd. 361.*

HIKING

Ouray Perimeter Trail. For a glimpse of many of Ouray's most famous features—including Cascade Falls, Baby Bathtubs, the Potato Patch (where miners once grew potatoes), the Ouray Ice Park, Box Cañon Falls, and Ouray's old water tunnel—take this 5-mile trek around the town's outskirts. The trail starts at the Ouray Visitors Center, which is at about 7,800 feet. It climbs steeply at the beginning, but mostly undulates through the forests surrounding Ouray. The trail currently ends at South Pinecrest Street, but it's a beautiful walk back to your starting point past the Victorian homes on Oak Street. ■ TIP→ **You can also pick a smaller section of the trail like Baby Bathtubs or Lower Cascade Falls for a short, family-friendly hike.** ✉ *Ouray Visitors Center, 1230 Main St.* ☎ *970/325–4746* ⊕ *www.ouraycolorado.com.*

Uncompahgre River Trail. This 2-mile loop follows the riverbank of the Uncompahgre River, just north of Ouray. The terrain is relatively flat, and the trail meanders past stands of trees, a wildflower-filled meadow, and interpretive signs about the river ecosystem from its trailhead to the city's north boundary. Trail entry points are located near the Ouray Visitors Center, the north corridor hotel locations, and along Oak Street. ✉ *Ouray Visitors Center, 1230 Main St.* ☎ *970/325–4746* ⊕ *www. ouraycolorado.com.*

ICE CLIMBING

Ouray Ice Park. Ouray is known in ice-climbing circles for its abundance of frozen waterfalls. The Ouray Ice Festival, held each January, helped to cement the town's reputation as America's ice-climbing mecca. The Ouray Ice Park is the world's first facility dedicated to the sport. In the Uncompahgre Gorge, just south of town, the Ice Park has 11 climbing areas with more than 200 routes. ✉ *280 County Rd. 361* ☎ *970/325– 4288* ⊕ *www.ourayicepark.com.*

Ouray Mountain Sports. This outfitter sells and rents all sorts of out-door-sports equipment, including ice-climbing gear. The staff will also sharpen your ice screws, generally within a day or two, using the only Grivel sharpening machine in North America. ✉ *732 Main St.* ☎ *970/325–4284* ⊕ *www.ouraysports.com.*

NORDIC SKIING

Ironton Park. Managed by the Ouray Trail Group, Ironton Park is a marked trail system for Nordic skiers and snowshoers. About 8 miles south of town, it has several interconnecting loops that let you spend a day on the trails. Local merchants stock trail maps. ⊠ *8 miles south of Ouray, Hwy. 550* ⊕ *www.ouraytrails.org.*

WHERE TO EAT

$$ ✕ **Cavallo's Restaurant.** From street level, wind down a spiral staircase to
CAJUN the little slice of Bourbon Street that is Cavallo's, a New Orleans–style eatery that provides a nice departure from Ouray's typical steak and burger establishments. Cavallo's delivers perhaps the town's best breakfast (served until closing time), with creative Cajun omelettes and Benedicts, as well as "daily inspirations" such as strawberry-basil–cream cheese French toast. The lunch menu offers soups, salads, and sandwiches, while the heavenly dinners (served Friday through Sunday) range from seafood étouffée to black-pepper and sage–crusted duck breast. Peruse Cavallo's signature cocktails list to find a nice complement for your entrée. Ⓢ *Average main: $15* ⊠ *630 Main St.* ☎ *970/325– 2042* ⊕ *www.cavallosrestaurant.com* ◐ *No dinner Mon.–Thurs.*

$ ✕ **Maggie's Kitchen.** Your enormous burger might be served on a plastic
BURGER lid or a piece of cardboard, but it will still probably taste better than
FAMILY any other burger in town. This anti-frills, order-at-the-counter burger-and-sandwich joint also serves homemade onion rings that are worth any artery-clogging they might foster. Before you leave, grab a Sharpie and add your signature to the wall or bench or ceiling, or anywhere you can find a spot. Ⓢ *Average main: $9* ⊠ *705 Main St.* ☎ *970/325–0259* ▭ *No credit cards.*

$$ ✕ **Ouray Brewery.** This brewpub boasts the town's only rooftop deck—
AMERICAN now twice the size it used to be—and it has great views of the surrounding canyon as well as the goings-on below on Main Street. There are actually three levels; the first features a small bar with swings in place of stools. On the second floor, there is loft seating where you can watch the brewing in action. The beers—four standards plus a few seasonal offerings—cover the gamut, from Carson's Chocolate Stout to blonde San Juan IPA. A local favorite is the Camp Bird Blonde, a German-style ale. The food is typical pub fare, with a sprinkling of more upscale entrées like grilled salmon. Ⓢ *Average main: $13* ⊠ *607 Main St.* ☎ *970/325–7388* ⊕ *www.ouraybrewery.com.*

$$$ ✕ **The Outlaw.** Live ragtime piano music welcomes you most nights to
STEAKHOUSE this saloon-style eatery, specializing in steak, seafood, and pasta. Portions are generous and loaded with extras (each entrée comes with rice or potato, vegetables, soup or salad, and bread). Prime rib is the house favorite, and the homemade salad dressings are fabulous. Before you leave, direct your eyes past the wagon-wheel chandeliers to just above the bar where you'll see John Wayne's hat hanging on the wall (he left it here in 1968). Ⓢ *Average main: $24* ⊠ *610 Main St.* ☎ *970/325–4366* ⊕ *www.outlawrestaurant.com.*

10

WHERE TO STAY

$$$
HOTEL
Fodor's Choice
★

Beaumont Hotel and Spa. No detail has been overlooked at this beautifully restored 1886 hotel, a gold-rush-era landmark that has hosted such VIPs as Theodore Roosevelt and Oprah Winfrey. **Pros:** sound-paneled rooms mean a quiet stay; good value. **Cons:** hot tubs cost extra; no children under 16. $ *Rooms from: $189* ✉ *505 Main St.* ☎ *970/325–7000, 888/447–3255* ⊕ *www.beaumonthotel.com* ⇄ *3 rooms, 10 suites* ❍ *Breakfast.*

$$
B&B/INN

Black Bear Manor Bed & Breakfast. Tucked away on a quiet side street, this tidy B&B has terrific views of the surrounding San Juan Mountains from its outdoor decks. **Pros:** welcoming hosts; plenty of privacy; generous amenities. **Cons:** no children under 16. $ *Rooms from: $149* ✉ *118 6th Ave.* ☎ *970/325–4219, 800/845–7512* ⊕ *www.blackbearmanor. com* ⇄ *9 rooms* ❍ *Breakfast.*

$
HOTEL

Box Canyon Lodge & Hot Springs. If bathing with the masses at the local hot springs is not your cup of tea, opt for a semiprivate plunge at this friendly lodge. **Pros:** proximity to hot springs; welcoming staff; off-the-beaten-path feel. **Cons:** looks dated; no-frills rooms; no pets. $ *Rooms from: $115* ✉ *45 3rd Ave.* ☎ *970/325–4981, 800/327–5080* ⊕ *www. boxcanyonouray.com* ⇄ *33 rooms, 6 suites* ❍ *Breakfast.*

$$
B&B/INN

China Clipper Inn. Although it was built in the mid-1990s, this stately inn fits in perfectly with its Victorian neighbors. **Pros:** beautiful property; small and romantic. **Cons:** minimum stay on some holidays and weekends; can be noisy between rooms. $ *Rooms from: $145* ✉ *525 2nd St.* ☎ *970/325–0565, 800/315–0565* ⊕ *ouraylodging-inns.com* ⇄ *10 rooms, 3 suites* ❍ *Breakfast.*

SILVERTON

23 miles south of Ouray; 47 miles north of Durango via U.S. 550.

Glorious peaks surround Silverton, an old mining community. The town reputedly got its name when a miner exclaimed, "We ain't got much gold but we got silver by the ton!" Silverton is the county seat, as well as the only remaining town, in San Juan County. The last mine here went bust in 1991 (which is recent as such things go), leaving Silverton to boom only in summer, when the Durango & Silverton Narrow Gauge Railroad deposits three trainloads of tourists a day. But the Silverton Mountain ski area has also helped the town to shake off its long slumber, and more businesses are finding it worthwhile to stay open year-round.

The downtown area has been designated a National Historic Landmark District. Be sure to pick up the walking-tour brochure that describes—among other things—the most impressive buildings lining Greene Street: Miners' Union Hall, Teller House, the Town Hall, the San Juan County Courthouse (home of the county historical museum), and the Grand Imperial Hotel. These structures have historical significance, but more history was probably made in the raucous red-light district along Blair Street.

GETTING HERE AND AROUND

U.S. 550 North and U.S. 550 South meet at a junction in front of the Silverton Chamber of Commerce and Visitor Center. At the intersection, Greene Street—with the main stores, restaurants, hotels, and the only paved street in town—heads northeast from 6th Street to 15th Street before splitting into County Road 110 heading to the Silverton Mountain Ski Area to the north and County Road 2 heading to the Old Hundred Gold Mine and the Mayflower Gold Mill to the east.

ESSENTIALS

Visitor Information Silverton Chamber of Commerce and Visitor Center. ⊠ *414 Greene St.* ☎ *970/387–5654, 800/752–4494* ⊕ *www.silvertoncolorado.com.*

EXPLORING

Christ of the Mines Shrine. If you look north toward Anvil Mountain, you'll see the Christ of the Mines Shrine, the centerpiece of which is a 12-ton statue of Jesus carved of Italian marble. The shrine was erected in 1959, and has been credited with a handful of miracles over the subsequent years. A moderately strenuous 1-mile hike leads to the shrine, which has memorable views of the surrounding San Juan Mountains. ⊠ *Silverton* ✛ *Trailhead at end of 10th St.*

Mayflower Gold Mill. Northeast of Silverton, the Mayflower Gold Mill (also known as the Shenandoah-Dives Mill) is a beautifully restored landmark with tours that explain how precious gold, silver, and other metals were extracted and processed. ⊠ *135 County Rd. 2* ☎ *970/387–0294* ⊕ *www.sanjuancountyhistoricalsociety.org* ✎ *$8* ⊙ *mid-June–Sept. daily 10–5 (last self-guided tour starts at 4:30).*

Old Hundred Gold Mine. A tram takes you 1,500 feet into the Old Hundred Gold Mine for a tour of one of the area's oldest mining facilities. Old Hundred operated for about a century, from the first strike in 1872 until the last haul in the early 1970s. Temperatures remain at a steady 47°F, so be sure to bring a sweater or a jacket. Guided tours leave every hour on the hour (arrive 15 minutes early to secure your spot). Your ticket price also covers panning for silver and copper in the sluice boxes outside the mine. ⊠ *721 County Rd. 4A* ✛ *5 miles north of Silverton* ☎ *970/387–5444, 800/872–3009* ⊕ *www.minetour.com* ✎ *$19* ⊙ *Mid-May–Sept., daily 10–4.*

Fodor's Choice ★ **San Juan County Historical Society Mining Heritage Center.** This large, well-kept museum houses an assortment of mining memorabilia, minerals, and local artifacts, including walk-in mining-shaft replicas. The museum also includes the old San Jaun County Jail, built in 1902. Here you can get a glimpse of turn-of-the-20th-century life in the region. ⊠ *1559 Greene St.* ☎ *970/387–5838* ⊕ *www.sanjuancountyhistoricalsociety.org* ✎ *$7* ⊙ *Memorial Day–mid-Oct., daily 10–5.*

SPORTS AND THE OUTDOORS

DOWNHILL SKIING AND SNOWBOARDING

Kendall Mountain Recreation Area. Run by the town, Kendall Mountain Recreation Area is a single-lift ski center open Friday through Sunday during ski season, weather permitting. It's not a challenging slope, so it's perfect for beginners. You can also skate, sled, and cross-country ski here. Rentals are available. ⊠ *1 Kendall Mountain Pl.* ☎ *970/387–5522* ⊕ *www.skikendall.com* ✎ *$20.*

10

Silverton Mountain. About 6 miles north of town, Silverton Mountain is one of the country's simplest yet most innovative ski areas. Open to expert skiers and boarders only, Silverton Mountain operates one double lift that accesses more than 1,800 acres of never-groomed backcountry steeps. It's the highest ski area in North America, as well as the steepest. The mountain sets a limit of roughly 80 people per day, and most of the time you feel like you have the mountain to yourself. There's no fancy lodge, either—in fact, there's no running water, but you can buy bottled water, along with simple lunches, at the base area. You can rent equipment, including a mandatory avalanche beacon, and other gear. Guided and unguided excursions are available. The ski area also now offers helicopter skiing seven days a week by reservation, which expands the skiable territory to more than 20,000 acres. **Facilities:** 69 trails; 1,819 acres; 3,000-foot vertical drop; 1 lift. ⊠ *Off Hwy. 110* ☎ *970/387–5706* ⊕ *www.silvertonmountain. com* ⊡ *Lift ticket from $49* ☉ *Dec.–Apr., Thurs.–Sun. 9–4 (dates can vary, so check website before you go).*

FOUR-WHEELING

Silverton provides easy access to such popular four-wheel-drive routes as Ophir Pass to the Telluride side of the San Juans, Stony Pass to the Rio Grande Valley, and Engineer and Cinnamon passes, components of the Alpine Loop. With an all-terrain vehicle you can see some of Colorado's most famous ghost towns, remnants of mining communities, and jaw-dropping scenery. The four-wheeling season is May to mid-October, weather permitting. In winter these unplowed trails are transformed into fabulous snowmobile routes.

Silver Summit RV Park and Jeep Rentals. You can rent a four-wheel-drive vehicle starting at $150 per day. ⊠ *640 Mineral St.* ☎ *970/387–0240, 970/210–3683 in winter* ⊕ *www.silversummitrvpark.com.*

ICE-SKATING

FAMILY **Silverton Town Rink.** At the Kendall Mountain Recreation Area, the Silverton Town Rink lets you skate for free, weather permitting. Rentals are available. ⊠ *Kendall Mountain Recreation Area, 1 Kendall Mountain Pl.* ☎ *970/387–5522.*

NORDIC SKIING

The local snowmobile club grooms nearly 170 miles of cross-country skiing and snowshoeing trails around Silverton, so the route is flat, easy, and safe. Molas Pass, 6 miles south of Silverton on U.S. 550, has a variety of Nordic routes, from easy half-milers in broad valleys to longer, more demanding ascents.

St. Paul Lodge & Hut. This place is an incredible find for anyone enchanted by remote high country. Above 11,000 feet and about a 40-minute ski-in from the summit of Red Mountain Pass (between Ouray and Silverton), the St. Paul Lodge (a converted mining camp) & Hut provide access to above–tree line exploring via telemark or cross-country skis, snowboard, or snowshoes. The Hut is also available in the summer, when you can reach the property via four-wheel-drive vehicle (or by hiking in). The hut has two bedrooms and sleeps 6, and the lodge offers dormitory-style accommodations; both buildings have shared baths. Reservations are essential. ■ TIP→ **The hut has running water only in summer; the lodge has it year-round.** ✉ *Silverton* ✥ *Top of Red Mountain Pass* ☎ *970/799–0785* 🌐 *www.skistpaul.com* 🏨 *$150, includes three meals.*

WHERE TO EAT AND STAY

$$ AMERICAN 🍴 **Handlebars.** As much a museum as an eatery, the restaurant is crammed with mining artifacts, odd antiques, and stuffed animals—including a full-grown elk. Don't pass up the huge platter of baby back ribs basted with the restaurant's own barbecue sauce (bottles of it are also for sale). The hearty menu also includes steaks, hamburgers, chicken, pasta, prime rib, and chicken-fried steak, all with homemade sides and sauces. [$] *Average main: $16* ✉ *117 W. 13th St.* ☎ *970/387–5395* 🌐 *www.handlebarssilverton.com* ⏲ *Closed Nov.–Apr.*

$$$$ B&B/INN Fodor's Choice ★ 🏨 **The Wyman Hotel and Inn.** On the National Register of Historic Places, this wonderful red-sandstone building dates from 1902. **Pros:** quiet; centrally located; updated amenities. **Cons:** stairs are steep; smaller rooms can feel cramped. [$] *Rooms from: $240* ✉ *1371 Greene St.* ☎ *970/387–5372, 800/609–7845* 🌐 *www.thewyman.com* ⏲ *Closed Nov. and Apr.* 🛏 *13 rooms, 4 suites* 🍽 *Breakfast.*

DURANGO AND MESA COUNTRY

Discover the southern reaches of the San Juan Mountains and Mesa Verde National Park in the high country of southwestern Colorado, known as Mesa Country. You can ride the rails on the Durango & Silverton Narrow Gauge Railroad, raft the Animas River, explore 2,000 miles of hiking and biking trails, and ski at the Durango Mountain Resort.

DURANGO

47 miles south of Silverton via U.S. 550; 45 miles east of Cortez via U.S. 160; 60 miles west of Pagosa Springs via U.S. 160.

Wisecracking Will Rogers had this to say about Durango: "It's out of the way and glad of it." His statement is a bit unfair, considering that as a railroad town Durango has always been a cultural crossroads and melting pot (as well as a place to raise hell). Resting at 6,500 feet along the winding Animas River, with the San Juan Mountains as backdrop, the town was founded in 1879 by General William Palmer, president of the all-powerful Denver & Rio Grande Railroad, at a time when nearby Animas City haughtily refused to donate land for a depot. Within a decade, Durango had completely absorbed its rival. The booming town quickly became the region's main metropolis and a gateway to the Southwest.

A walking tour of the historic downtown offers ample proof of Durango's prosperity during the late 19th century, although the northern end of Main Avenue has the usual assortment of cheap motels and fast-food outlets.

About 27 miles north of town, the down-home ski resort of Purgatory welcomes a clientele that includes cowboys, families, and college students. The mountain is named for the nearby Purgatory Creek, a tributary of the River of Lost Souls.

GETTING HERE AND AROUND

Durango Transit operates regular trolleys and bus service throughout town. Purgatory at Durango Mountain Resort runs a $10 skier shuttle between the town and the mountain during the winter. Buck Horn Limousine is your best bet for airport transfers.

ESSENTIALS

Transportation Contacts Buck Horn Limousine. ☎ 970/769-0933 ⊕ www.buckhornlimousine.com. **Durango Transit.** ☎ 970/259-5438 ⊕ www.durangotransit.com. **Purgatory Resort Skier Shuttle.** ⊠ Purgatory ☎ 970/426-7282 ⊕ www.skipurg.com.

Visitor Information Durango Welcome Center. ⊠ 802 Main Ave. ☎ 970/247-3500, 888/631-7011 ⊕ www.durango.org.

EXPLORING

FAMILY

Fodor's Choice

★

Durango & Silverton Narrow Gauge Railroad. The most entertaining way to relive the halcyon days of the Old West is to take a ride on the Durango & Silverton Narrow Gauge Railroad, a nine-hour round-trip journey along the 45-mile railway to Silverton. You'll travel in comfort in lovingly restored coaches or in the open-air cars called gondolas as you listen to the train's shrill whistle as it chugs along. On the way, you get a good look at the Animas Valley, which in some parts is broad and green and in others narrow and rimmed with rock. A shorter excursion—to Cascade Canyon, 26 miles away—in heated coaches is available in winter. The train departs from the Durango Depot, constructed in 1882 and beautifully restored. Next door is the Durango & Silverton Narrow Gauge Railroad Museum. ⊠ 479 Main Ave. ☎ 970/247-2733, 877/872-4607 ⊕ www.durangotrain.com 🎫 $91–$199 ☉ Train: early May–late Oct. daily.

Main Avenue National Historic District. The intersection of 13th Avenue and Main Avenue marks the northern edge of Durango's Main Avenue National Historic District. Old-fashioned streetlamps line the streets, casting a warm glow on the elegant buildings filled with upscale galleries, restaurants, and shops. Dating from 1887, the Strater Hotel is a reminder of the time when this town was a stop for many people headed west. The town visitor center's website provides information for self-guided walking tours. ⊠ Main Ave., between 13th St. and 12th St. ⊕ www.durango.org.

Purgatory at Durango Mountain Resort. A trip to the ski area in summer will earn you huge points with your kids. They'll enjoy the alpine slide, a family-friendly ropes course, a short zip line, bungee trampolines, Water Runners (giant balls that let you walk and roll on water), lift-served hiking and biking, and, of course, the obligatory climbing wall and mini-golf course. ⊠ 1 Skier Pl., Purgatory ☎ 970/385-2168 ⊕ www.skipurg.com 🎫 $79 for 10 activities, $50 for 5, or choose à la carte pricing.

FAMILY **Trimble Spa and Natural Hot Springs.** Come here to soak your aching bones after a day of hiking or skiing. The complex includes an Olympic-size swimming pool and two natural mineral pools ranging from 98°F to 110°F; all are open year-round. The pools are outdoors, next to a large, partly shaded lawn with picnic tables. Massage and spa treatments are also available. ⊠ *6475 County Rd. 205 ✛ About 5 miles north of Durango* ☎ *970/247–0111, 970/247–0212 spa* ⊕ *www. trimblehotsprings.com* ⊠ *$18* ⊗ *Memorial Day–Labor Day, Wed.– Mon. 9–8:45, Tues. 9–7:45; Labor Day–mid-Oct. and mid-Apr.–Memorial Day, Wed.–Mon. 10–8:45, Tues. 10–7:45; mid-Oct.–mid-Apr., Thurs.–Mon. 11–8:45, Tues. 11–7:45.*

DOWNHILL SKIING AND SNOWBOARDING

Fodor's Choice ★ **Purgatory Resort.** This unpretentious ski resort 27 miles north of Durango has plenty of intermediate runs and gladed tree skiing, but what's unique about it is its stepped terrain: lots of humps and dips and steep pitches followed by virtual flats. A great powder day on the mountain's back side will convince anyone that Purgatory isn't just "Pleasant Ridge," as it's sometimes known in the bigger resorts of Crested Butte and Telluride. The truth is that Purgatory is just plain fun, and return visitors like it that way. It's not all old-school, however: A new high-speed quad now conveys skiers to the top of the mountain in five minutes and accesses three new advanced trails. The ski area is perfect for families and those who are open to other diversions, such as dog sledding, horse-drawn sleigh rides, snowshoeing, cross-country skiing, and snowmobiling. **Facilities:** 88 trails; 1,360 acres; 2,029-foot vertical drop; 10 lifts. ⊠ *1 Skier Pl., Purgatory* ☎ *970/247–9000, 800/525–0892* ⊕ *www.skipurg.com* ⊠ *Lift ticket $81* ⊗ *Late Nov.–early Apr., daily 9–4.*

LESSONS AND PROGRAMS

Adult & Teen Ski and Ride School. On the second level of the Village Center, the Adult & Teen Ski and Ride School runs full-day and half-day group lessons during the season. It also offers a "First-Timer" package, including a lesson, equipment rental, and lift ticket. The school also provides private lessons, as well as specialty clinics for telemark and bump skiers of all levels. ⊠ *Village Center, Purgatory* ☎ *970/385–2149* ⊕ *www.skipurg.com* ⊠ *From $TK.*

Kids Ski and Ride School. Getting kids onto the slopes is a cinch at the Kids Ski and Ride School, which offers programs for skiers and snowboarders ages 4 to 12. Choose from a full-day package—which includes lunch, a lesson, equipment rental, and a lift ticket—or a half-day package. ⊠ *Village Center, Purgatory* ☎ *970/385–2149* ⊠ *Half-day packages $TK, full-day $TK.*

San Juan Untracked. Out-of-bounds types can explore 35,000 acres of untamed wilderness with the San Juan Untracked. A day of guided snowcat skiing or riding includes safety gear and a hearty lunch. The company guarantees five runs and averages eight to 12. ⊠ *Village Center, Purgatory* ☎ *800/208–1780* ⊕ *www.sanjuanuntracked.com* ⊠ *$385.*

10

RENTALS

Expert Edge Ski & Board Shop. This is the go-to shop at the base village for demos, retail, and repair. It features top-of-the-line men's and women's skis, snowboards, boots, bindings, poles, and more from top brands, including K2, Rossignol, Burton, and Venture. Expert Edge also does custom boot fitting, ski tuning, and equipment repair. ⊠ *Village Center, Purgatory* ☎ *970/385–2181* ⊕ *www.skipurg.com* ☉ *Mid-Nov.–mid-Apr., daily 8–5.*

Purgatory Rentals. This base-area shop has skis, boots, and poles, plus snowboards, helmets, and other equipment for kids and adults. You should make advance reservations on their website if you'll be renting during the busy holiday periods. ⊠ *1 Skier Pl., Purgatory* ☎ *970/385–2182* ⊕ *www.skipurg.com* ☉ *Mid-Nov.–mid-Apr., daily 8–5.*

OTHER SPORTS AND THE OUTDOORS

San Juan Public Lands Center. Stop at this office for information from the San Juan Mountains Association on hiking, fishing, and camping, as well as cross-country skiing, snowshoeing, and snowmobiling in the San Juan Public Lands. The 2½ million acres of land includes three designated wilderness areas and other federal lands in southwestern Colorado. The center also includes a bookstore where you can purchase field guides, clothing, and other items. ⊠ *15 Burnett Ct.* ☎ *970/247–4874* ⊕ *www.sjma.org* ☉ *Weekdays 8–4:30.*

BICYCLING

Animas River Trail. Thanks to recent upgrades linking the northern and southern sections of the trail, this 7-mile paved path parallels the river from Animas City Park south to Dallabetta Park in one smooth stroke. It's the main artery, linking up with several of the town's other trail systems. ⊠ *Durango.*

Durango Mountain Bike Tours. Take a guided ride tailored to your skill level and interests with Durango Mountain Bike Tours. Rides range from a two-hour "Town & Trails" tour for beginners, complete with riding instruction, to full-day excursions on the area's most challenging singletrack. If you don't have a bike, you can rent one here. ⊠ *Durango* ☎ *970/749–5328* ⊕ *www.durangobiketours.com* ⧆ *From $90.*

Hermosa Creek Trail. This single-track trail travels roughly 19 miles from Purgatory Resort to lower Hermosa parking area. It's an intermediate-to-difficult ride with a couple of steep spots and switchbacks along with mellow rolls through open meadows and towering aspen and pine forests. The trail hugs the steep riverbank at a few places and there are a few creek crossings, so you shouldn't try it too early in the season, while the snow is still melting (the water can be waist-high in the spring and early summer). To minimize the fight against gravity, you can leave your car at the lower trailhead and catch a shuttle to the top—even so, there will still be plenty of climbing. ⊠ *Durango* ⊹ *Trailhead: 2 miles from Purgatory's upper parking lot.*

TOURS AND **San Juan Hut Systems.** Having a fully equipped hut waiting at the end of
EXPEDITIONS a tough day of riding makes the San Juan Hut System a backcountry biker's dream come true. The company, which started out as a hut-to-hut service for backcountry skiers, operates a 215-mile route from Durango

to Moab, Utah, suitable for intermediate and advanced riders. Trips run from June to October and last five or seven days, covering alpine meadows, desert slick rock, canyon country, and the famous Whole Enchilada Trail. Along the way, the six one-room huts are supplied with bunks, sleeping bags, heating and cooking stoves, food, and water. ☎ 970/626–3033 ⊕ www.sanjuanhuts.com ✉ Prices start at $695 per person.

GOLF

Dalton Ranch Golf Club. Inspiring views of the Animas River Valley and surrounding San Juans beckon golfers to this semiprivate 18-hole championship course, about 6 miles north of Durango. Carts cost $15 per person for 18 holes, and nonmembers are required to use a cart. Swing, the clubhouse's full-service restaurant and bar, is a popular hangout for golfers and locals who like watching the resident elk herd take its afternoon stroll. The golf season is early April to late October, weather permitting. ✉ 589 County Rd. 252, off U.S. 550 ☎ 970/247–8774 ⊕ www.daltonranch.com ✉ $120; $16 for golf cart ⚐ 18 holes, 6934 yards, par 72 ⚑ Reservations essential.

Hillcrest Golf Club. Since 1969, a relaxed atmosphere, affordable rates, and gorgeous views have attracted golfers to this 18-hole public course, perched on a mesa near the campus of Fort Lewis College. Carts are $16 per person for 18 holes, but the tee-to-green distance is relatively short, so most patrons opt to walk. The course is open from February to December, weather permitting. ✉ 2300 Rim Dr. ☎ 970/247–1499 ⊕ www.golfhillcrest.com ✉ $39 ⚐ 18 holes, 6912 yards, par 71 ⚑ Reservations essential.

HIKING

Hiking trails are everywhere in and around Durango. Many trailheads at the edges of town lead to backcountry settings, and the San Juan Forest has plenty of mind-boggling walks and trails for those with the urge to explore.

Across from the Fort Lewis College Recreation Complex is a kid-friendly hike called **Lion's Den Trail.** It connects with the **Chapman Hill Trail** for a nice moderate hike, climbing switchbacks that take you away from town and hook up with the **Rim Trail.**

Animas View Overlook Trail. If you're looking for a great view without the effort, try the ¾-mile Animas View Overlook Trail. It takes you past signs explaining local geology, flora, and fauna before bringing you to a precipice with an unparalleled view of the valley and the surrounding Needle Mountains. It's the only wheelchair-accessible trail in the area. From town, it's a 45-minute drive up Junction Creek Road. ✉ Durango ⊹ Trailhead at Forest Rd. 171, Milepost 8.

Fodor'sChoice ★ **Colorado Trail.** This epic trail starts a few miles northwest of Durango and covers about 500 miles on its way to Denver. You're not obliged to go that far, of course. Just a few miles in and out will give you a taste of the grandeur of this trail, which winds through mountain ranges and high passes and some of the most amazing mountain scenery around. ✉ Trailhead off County Rd. 204 ⊹ From town, take 25th St. west; it turns into Junction St. and continues on to the lower parking lot ⊕ www.coloradotrail.org.

10

RAFTING

Durango Rivertrippers. This outfitter runs two- and four-hour trips down the Animas River. You can up your adrenaline output by swapping the raft for an inflatable kayak on any of the Animas River trips. Or ask about zip line and rafting packages, or Jeep tours or rentals. ✉ *724 Main Ave.* ☎ *970/259–0289* 🌐 *www.durangorivertrippers.com.*

ROCK-CLIMBING

East Animas. You'll find some of the best crack and face climbing at East Animas, just a few miles east of town. Don't miss the "Watch Crystal" route, a favorite with the locals. The parking area is on the east side of the road. ✉ *Off County Rd. 250, 2 miles east of U.S. 550.*

San Juan National Forest. There are plenty of opportunities for climbing in the Columbine Ranger District of the San Juan National Forest, just outside of Durango. Some of the more popular spots are Julia's Spire, Golf Wall, and Fume Wall. ✉ *U.S. Forestry office, 15 Burnett Ct.* ☎ *970/247–4874* 🌐 *www.fs.usda.gov/sanjuan.*

X-Rock. Just north of town, X-Rock offers a little bit of everything—slag, crack climbs, bouldering—for novice and intermediate climbers. It's also a great place to learn (or just brush up on) basic climbing skills. One look at the distinctive natural cracks that cross its face will tell you how it got its name. ✉ *Off U.S. 550, just north of 32nd St.*

TOURS AND EXPEDITIONS

San Juan Mountain Guides. For classes and guided trips to some of the area's most beautiful and challenging crags and peaks, talk to San Juan Mountain Guides. Seasonal courses run year-round and cover the basics (beginning climbing techniques, belaying, and rappeling) as well as specifics such as alpine canyoneering, rock rescue, and desert crack climbing. Trips run from one to five days. ✉ *1111 Camino del Rio, Suite 105* ☎ *800/642–5389* 🌐 *www.mtnguide.net* 🎫 *Tours and classes from $160.*

SNOWMOBILING

Snowmobile Adventures. With access to more than 75 miles of trails traversing mountain passes, old stagecoach roads, and mining sites, Snowmobile Adventures leads one- to four-hour tours from the base area of Purgatory Resort. Rides are available daily during ski season between 9 and 5. ✉ *Village Center, Purgatory* ☎ *970/385–2141* 🌐 *www.skipurg.com.*

WHERE TO EAT

$$ AMERICAN

🍴 **Carver Brewing Company.** The "Brews Brothers," Bill and Jim Carver, have about 12 beers on tap at any given time at this Durango favorite. Popular brews include the Raspberry Wheat Ale, Jackrabbit Pale Ale, and Colorado Trail Nut Brown Ale. If you're hungry, try one of the signature bread bowls filled with chili, soup, or chicken stew. There's a spacious, shaded patio out back where you can relax at a table or in a hammock chair. From breakfast to late evening, the place is always hopping. [$] *Average main: $13* ✉ *1022 Main Ave.* ☎ *970/259–2545* 🌐 *www.carverbrewing.com.*

$$ CONTEMPORARY

🍴 **Chimayo.** The former chef for Michael Andretti's racing team runs this trendy bistro, in which every dish is cooked in one of two stone-fired ovens. The house specialty is artisan pizza (try the four-mushroom variety and add the house fennel sausage), and most dishes have a Southwestern touch (a favorite is the stuffed poblano chili pepper with a pepita crust).

Check both the board and the menu for creative cocktails such as blueberry-Bacardi mojitos and jalapeño margaritas. Housed in a century-old building, Chimayo blends historic elements like restored tin ceilings and the original hardwood floor with classy, contemporary decor. [$] *Average main: $18* ✉ *862 Main Ave.* ☎ *970/259–2749* 🌐 *www.chimayodurango.com* ☞ *Reservations accepted only for parties of six or more.*

$$$ MEDITERRANEAN 🍴 **Cyprus Cafe.** In warm weather you can sit on the patio to enjoy fresh mountain air, and the rest of the year you'll have to cozy up to your fellow diners in the 10-table Cyprus Cafe, housed in a quaint Victorian just off Main Avenue. Mediterranean food receives the upscale treatment, with selections such as grape-leaf-wrapped salmon baked with goat cheese and olive-caper tapenade, and braised lamb shank with dijon cream and beluga lentils. Afterward, head next door to the trendy Eno wine, coffee, and tapas bar (same owner) for Portuguese coffee or a wine flight. [$] *Average main: $19* ✉ *725 E. 2nd Ave.* ☎ *970/385–6884* 🌐 *www.cypruscafe.com* 🕓 *Closed Sun. and Oct.–Apr.*

$$$ ASIAN FUSION 🍴 **East by Southwest.** Asian food gets a bit of a Latin treatment in this snazzy but inviting space. The menu has a strong Japanese bent, with sushi and sashimi, tempura, and other traditional dishes elegantly presented and layered with complementary flavors. Also among the favorites are entrées cooked on the "ishiyaki" grilling stone, including lobster and American Wagyu beef. The sake, beer, and wine list is well varied, and the tea and tonic selections are fun, too. [$] *Average main: $23* ✉ *160 E. College Dr.* ☎ *970/247–5533* 🌐 *www.eastbysouthwest.com* 🕓 *No lunch Sun.*

$$ MODERN AMERICAN 🍴 **Ken & Sue's.** Plates are big and the selection is creative at Ken & Sue's, one of Durango's favorite restaurants. Locals are wild for the contemporary American cuisine with an Asian flair, served in an intimate space. Try the pistachio-crusted grouper with vanilla-rum butter, or Aunt Lydia's meatloaf with red-wine gravy and mashed potatoes. If the weather allows, ask for a table on the large, pretty patio in the back. [$] *Average main: $18* ✉ *636 Main Ave.* ☎ *970/385–1810* 🌐 *www.kenandsues.com* 🕓 *No lunch weekends.*

$ PIZZA 🍴 **The Olde Schoolhouse Cafe & Saloon.** The sign is new, but the building that houses this funky pizza tavern near the ski area lives up to its name as the "Olde" Schoolhouse. Here the pizza and calzones are made with homemade dough and fresh ingredients, and plenty of local brews are on tap. The great food, plus a dart board, pool table, and old shuffleboard make this a favorite local hangout. Before you leave, be sure to add your autographed $1 bill to the hundreds already lining the walls. Dinner ends around 9:45, but the bar keeps hopping till 1:30 am, seven days a week. [$] *Average main: $11* ✉ *46778 U.S. 550* ☎ *970/259–2257* 🕓 *No lunch weekdays.*

$ AMERICAN 🍴 **Olde Tymers Cafe.** If you're looking for the locals, look no further than Olde Tymers Cafe—known in these parts as OTC—a bustling café and bar in a beautiful old building on Main Avenue with an inviting patio in the back. The hamburger is a huge specimen on a fat, fresh bun, and the salads and sandwiches are piled high. There's a different special every night—including $6 burgers on Monday—and a respectable roster of beers on tap, including local Durango brews. [$] *Average main: $10* ✉ *1000 Main Ave.* ☎ *970/259–2990* 🌐 *www.otcdgo.com.*

$$$$ ✕ **Ore House.** Durango is a meat-and-potatoes kind of town, and the
STEAKHOUSE rustic Ore House is Durango's idea of a steak house. The aroma of
beef smacks you in the face as you walk past, but there are also
chicken, pork, and wild-caught seafood dishes available. This local
favorite serves enormous slabs of aged Angus that are hand cut daily.
For a special occasion try the chateaubriand for two ($73). $ *Average main: $37* ✉ *147 E. College Dr.* ☎ *970/247–5707* ⊕ *www.
orehouserestaurant.com.*

$$$$ ✕ **The Red Snapper.** If you're in the mood for fresh fish head to Durango's
SEAFOOD best seafood spot. There are the seafood "musts"—lobster tail, Alas-
kan king crab legs, and the like—as well as some interesting twists,
such as lobster potpie and tequila shrimp. The "landfood" dishes hold
their own, too (try the one-pound prime rib or, for smaller appetites
and budgets, the drunken Hawaiian chicken). The salad bar is enormous and a good value at $12. It features a few main-course options
and comes with potatoes, wild rice, or soup. Reservations are recommended. $ *Average main: $26* ✉ *144 E. 9th St.* ☎ *970/259–3417*
⊕ *www.durangoredsnapper.com* ☉ *No lunch weekends.*

$$$$ ✕ **Sow's Ear.** This airy eatery in Silverpick Lodge is known for providing
STEAKHOUSE "the best steaks on the mountain," which it does with aplomb. Opt
for the house specialty filet au poivre, or try a wild-game entrée, such
as elk tenderloin. There are also several delicious seafood options, and
those with smaller appetites will appreciate the assortment of equally
imaginative "small plates." Request a seat by the window, as the quality
of the views rivals the cuisine. ■TIP➔ **Sow's Ear is closed many Saturdays in summer for weddings.** $ *Average main: $30* ✉ *48475 U.S. 550*
☎ *970/247–3527* ⊕ *www.sowseardurango.com* ☉ *No lunch.*

WHERE TO STAY

$$ ⌂ **Apple Orchard Inn.** This quiet B&B sits on 5 acres in the lush Ani-
B&B/INN mas Valley with an apple orchard, flower gardens, and trout ponds
on the grounds. **Pros:** inspiring views; peaceful and quiet setting; cot-
tages are intimate and romantic. **Cons:** no dinner on-site; several miles
from town; rooms in the house are all upstairs (no elevator). $ *Rooms
from: $160* ✉ *7758 County Rd. 203* ⊹ *About 8 miles from downtown
Durango* ☎ *970/247–0751, 800/426–0751* ⊕ *www.appleorchardinn.
com* ➦ *4 rooms, 6 cottages* ⦿ *Breakfast.*

$ ⌂ **Durango Quality Inn.** This is one of the better budget properties along
HOTEL Durango's strip: it's reliable, comfortable, and has sizable rooms, as
well as a hot breakfast. **Pros:** spacious rooms; reasonable rates. **Cons:**
on busy street; away from historic downtown area. $ *Rooms from:
$100* ✉ *2930 N. Main Ave.* ☎ *970/259–5373, 888/770–6800* ⊕ *www.
qualityinn.com* ➦ *48 rooms* ⦿ *Breakfast.*

$$ ⌂ **General Palmer Hotel.** Named after William Jackson Palmer, owner
HOTEL of the Denver & Rio Grande Railroad, the General Palmer Hotel is a
faithfully restored historic property with a clean, bright look as well as
period furniture and Victorian touches that reinforce an old-timey feel.
Pros: nicely restored lodging; rooms are quiet; free off-street parking.
Cons: no restaurant or bar; elevator is claustrophobic; pricey in season.
$ *Rooms from: $170* ✉ *567 Main Ave.* ☎ *970/247–4747, 800/523–
3358* ⊕ *www.generalpalmer.com* ➦ *34 rooms, 5 suites* ⦿ *Breakfast.*

$$$$ 🏨 **Purgatory Lodge.** This mountain-luxe slope-side hotel provides an
HOTEL upscale retreat at a down-home resort, featuring roomy two- to four-
FAMILY bedroom suites decorated with contemporary furnishings. **Pros:** slope-
side location; good restaurants; ample amenities. **Cons:** can be pricey;
far from town. 💲 *Rooms from: $315* ✉ *Purgatory Resort, 24 Sheol
St.* ☎ *970/385–2100, 800/525–0892* ⊕ *www.skipurg.com* 🛏 *37 suites*
🍽 *No meals.*

$$$ 🏨 **Rochester Hotel.** The renovated Rochester Hotel is funky yet chic,
B&B/INN with marquee-lighted movie posters from Hollywood Westerns filmed
nearby lining the airy hallways. **Pros:** free guest parking; large rooms;
free use of cruiser bikes in town. **Cons:** can be noisy; no counter space
in bathrooms. 💲 *Rooms from: $179* ✉ *726 E. 2nd Ave.* ☎ *970/385–
1920, 800/664–1920* ⊕ *www.rochesterhotel.com* 🛏 *19 rooms, 8 suites*
🍽 *Breakfast.*

$$$ 🏨 **Strater Hotel.** Still the hottest spot in town, this Western grande dame
HOTEL opened for business in 1887 and has been visited by Butch Cassidy,
Fodor'sChoice Louis L'Amour (he wrote many of the *Sacketts* novels here), Francis
★ Ford Coppola, John Kennedy, or Marilyn Monroe (the latter two stayed
here at separate times). **Pros:** right in the thick of things; genuine Old
West feel. **Cons:** breakfast not included in all rates; when the bar gets
going, rooms above it get no peace. 💲 *Rooms from: $190* ✉ *699 Main
Ave.* ☎ *970/247–4431, 800/247–4431* ⊕ *www.strater.com* 🛏 *93 rooms*
🍽 *No meals.*

NIGHTLIFE AND PERFORMING ARTS

PERFORMING ARTS

Durango Arts Center. You can see stage productions as well as visual
arts exhibits, concerts, and films at the Durango Arts Center. Its resident performing groups include Durango Dot Comedy, the Durango
Performing Arts Company, the San Juan Symphony, and the Durango
Independent Film Festival. The free gallery and gallery shops are open
10–5 Tuesday through Saturday. ✉ *802 E. 2nd Ave.* ☎ *970/259–2606*
⊕ *www.durangoarts.org.*

Durango Melodrama and Vaudeville. This group stages rip-roaring productions in the classic Victorian music-hall style, all summer long, in the historic Henry Strater Theatre. ✉ *699 Main Ave.* ☎ *970/375–7160* ⊕ *www.
durangomelodrama.com* ⊗ *Closed Mon. and late Sept.–early June.*

BARS AND CLUBS

Diamond Belle Saloon. Awash in flocked wallpaper and lace, the Diamond
Belle Saloon is dominated by a gilt-and-mahogany bar. With its prime
location—on the ground floor of the historic Strater Hotel—and a staff
of ragtime piano players and waitresses dressed as saloon girls, the Diamond Belle can really pack them in. Be sure to try the Brazilian mint
martini; if you're hungry, try the much-hailed Diamond burger. ✉ *699
Main Ave.* ☎ *970/247–4431* ⊕ *www.diamondbelle.com.*

Lady Falconburgh's Alehouse and Kitchen. A popular spot with locals and
tourists alike, the subterranean Lady Falconburgh's Alehouse and
Kitchen has 38 beers on tap at any given time; the lineup is constantly
rotating. The pub's restaurant serves burgers, sandwiches, and ribs.
✉ *640 Main Ave.* ☎ *970/382–9664.*

10

Fodor's Choice
★

Ska Brewing Company. Beer fans shouldn't miss Ska Brewing, a home-grown brewery that boasts an airy "tasting room" with 12 taps. The decor is bowling-alley inspired, including tables crafted with wood from former lanes at a Denver bowling alley. Ska is known for its many fine craft brews, such as True Blonde Ale, Mexican Logger, and Modus Operandi, as well as creative seasonal stouts. If the weather allows, you can sip your beer of choice on the park-like patio or second-story deck, beneath enormous, metal brew tanks. Pair your beer with a sandwich or artisan pizza from The Container restaurant, made from two repurposed shipping containers that are attached to the brewery. ■TIP→ **Stop by on a Thursday night for live music.** ✉ *255 Girard St.* ☎ *970/247–5792* ⊕ *www.skabrewing.com.*

CASINOS

Sky Ute Casino & Resort. The Southern Ute tribe operates this 45,000-square-foot facility, with hundreds of slot machines and tables for blackjack, poker, roulette, and craps. ✉ *14324 Hwy. 172 N, Ignacio* ✛ *About 23 miles southeast of Durango* ☎ *970/563–7777, 888/842–4180* ⊕ *www.skyutecasino.com.*

DINNER SHOWS

FAMILY **Bar D Chuckwagon Suppers.** This old-style-cowboy venue, about 10 miles from Durango, serves steaks, barbecued beef and chicken, and biscuits under the stars every summer evening. After supper, the Bar D Wranglers entertain the crowd with guitar music, singing, and corny comedy. Reservations are required. ✉ *8080 County Rd. 250* ☎ *970/247–5753, 888/800–5753* ⊕ *www.bardchuckwagon.com* 🎫 *From $26* ⊙ *Closed Labor Day–Memorial Day.*

SHOPPING
BOOKS

Maria's Bookshop. This well-stocked general-interest shop specializes in regional literature, guidebooks, and other nonfiction, and carries a good selection of kids' books and toys. You'll also find works from local and regional authors. ✉ *960 Main Ave.* ☎ *970/247–1438* ⊕ *www.mariasbookshop.com.*

BOUTIQUES

Appaloosa Trading Co. Your best source for all things leather, Appaloosa Trading Co. stocks everything from jackets and purses to boots and canteens. The dog collars, fitted with silver coins, are an especially nice find. ■TIP→ **You can also visit Appaloosa's factory store north of town at 850 County Road 203.** ✉ *640 Main Ave.* ☎ *970/385–1722* ⊕ *www.appaloosadurango.com.*

FOOD

Honeyville. About 10 miles north of Durango, Honeyville sells honey, jams, jellies (try the wild chokecherry), syrups, sauces, and other goodies. You can watch the bees go about their work in glass hives and, on weekdays, view honey being processed and bottled. ✉ *33633 U.S. 550* ☎ *800/676–7690* ⊕ *www.honeyvillecolorado.com.*

GIFTS

Toh-Atin Gallery. Recognized as one of the region's best Native American galleries, Toh-Atin specializes in Navajo rugs and weavings. There's also a wide range of paintings and prints, pottery, baskets, and jewelry made by the artisans of many Southwestern tribes. ⊠ *145 W. 9th St.* ☎ *970/247–8277, 800/525–0384* ⊕ *www.toh-atin.com.*

SPORTING GOODS

Mountain Bike Specialists. Although everybody in town seems to be an expert, the staff at this shop can help direct you to the trail of your dreams and outfit you for the excursion. It also does expert repairs. ⊠ *949 Main Ave.* ☎ *970/247–4066* ⊕ *www.mountainbikespecialists. com* ⊗ *Mon.–Sat. 9–6.*

TOYS

FAMILY **Durango Toy Depot.** A wide range of prices and merchandise—from classics such as Parcheesi and Chinese checkers to unique building sets and a fantastic marble collection—make this toy shop worth a look. But be warned if you bring the kids: Fuzziwig's Candy Factory is next door. ⊠ *658 Main Ave.* ☎ *970/403–8697* ⊕ *www. durangotoydepot.com.*

PAGOSA SPRINGS

60 miles east of Durango via U.S. 160; 165 miles south of Gunnison via Hwy. 114, U.S. 285, and U.S. 160.

Although not a large town, Pagosa Springs has become a major center for outdoor sports. Hiking, biking, and cross-country skiing opportunities abound here, and there's excellent downhill skiing and snowboarding at the nearby Wolf Creek ski area.

GETTING HERE AND AROUND

Highway 160 turns into Pagosa Street when it enters the town limits and serves as the main drag, with the majority of restaurants, shops, and hotels. The other main thoroughfare, Lewis Avenue, runs parallel to Pagosa Street from 1st Street to 5th Street.

ESSENTIALS

Visitor Information Pagosa Springs Visitor Center. ⊠ *105 Hot Springs Blvd.* ☎ *970/264–2360, 800/252–2204* ⊕ *www.visitpagosasprings.com.* **Wolf Creek Snow Report.** ☎ *800/754–9653* ⊕ *www.wolfcreekski.com/wolf-creek-snow-report.php.*

EXPLORING

Chimney Rock National Monument. About 16 miles west of Pagosa Springs, State Highway 151 heads south to Chimney Rock National Monument. Twin spires of rock loom over the ruins of more than 100 homes and ceremonial buildings built about 1,000 years ago on a high mesa. Open in the summer, the area offers 2½-hour guided walking tours. The trail is short, but steep and exposed, so bring plenty of water. You can also take a self-guided tour of the Great Kiva Trail. ⊠ *Off Hwy. 151* ☎ *970/883–5359* ⊕ *www.chimneyrockco.org* 🎫 *$12* ⊗ *May–Sept., daily 9–4:30.*

10

FAMILY
Fodor's Choice
★

The Springs Resort. In a beautiful setting overlooking the San Juan River, the Springs Resort draws from the Guinness World Record–verified deepest geothermal hot spring to heat its 23 outdoor pools, ranging in temperature from 89°F to 114°F. The multitiered layout includes several waterfalls; a large, cooler-water swimming pool; two jetted tubs; a goldfish pond; and plenty of lounge chairs and shaded tables for taking breaks from the steamy pools. There is also a full-service spa on-site. ✉ *165 Hot Springs Blvd.* ☎ *866/338–7404, 970/264–4168* ⊕ *www.pagosahotsprings.com* ✉ *$26* ⊙ *June–Aug., daily 7 am–midnight; Sept.–May, daily 7 am–11 pm.*

DOWNHILL SKIING AND SNOWBOARDING

Wolf Creek Ski Area. With more than 430 average inches of snow annually, Wolf Creek Ski Area is Colorado's best-kept secret. The trails accommodate all ability levels offering a variety of terrain, from beginner to wide-open bowls and steep glades, with commanding views of remote valleys and towering peaks. Because there are no slopeside accommodations, Wolf Creek has a reputation as a laid-back place for those with an aversion to the long lift lines and the other hassles of faster-paced, better-known ski areas. The quant mountain towns of Pagosa Springs, which is home to the healing waters of the Pagosa Hot Springs, and South Fork offer comfortable and affordable accommodations.

At 2 miles, the longest run at Wolf Creek is Navajo Trail. Beginners can start on the Raven chairlift to Upper Bunny Hop or Kelly Boyce Trail; both hook up with the Lower Bunny Hop back down the hill.

The best area for advanced skiers stretches back to the Waterfall area, serviced by the Alberta lift. The more intrepid will want to climb the Knife Ridge Staircase to the more-demanding Knife Ridge Chutes and out to the Horseshoe Bowl. **Facilities:** 77 trails; 1,600 acres; 1,604-foot vertical drop; 9 lifts. ✉ *U.S. Hwy. 160* ☎ *970/264–5639* ⊕ *www.wolfcreekski.com* ✉ *Lift ticket $65* ⊙ *Early Nov.–mid-Apr., daily 8:30–4.*

LESSONS AND PROGRAMS

Wolf Creek Ski School. Group lessons are a good bet here—they're $52 for two hours and $77 for four hours. Beginner packages start at $65, and private one-hour lessons are $85. Children older than 4 can join the Wolf Pups program, which includes lift tickets and lunch. Kids ages 9 to 12 can join the Hot Shots program, which takes both skiers and boarders. ✉ *Wolf Creek Ski Area, U.S. 160* ☎ *970/264–5639* ⊕ *www.wolfcreekski.com.*

OTHER SPORTS AND THE OUTDOORS
GOLF

Pagosa Springs Golf Club. The 27 championship holes here can be played in three combinations, essentially creating three different 18-hole courses. A bonus at this public course is the gorgeous mountain scenery. The regular season runs from June to mid-September. Cart rental is included in the green fee, and reservations are recommended. ✉ *1 Pine Club Pl.* ☎ *970/731–4755* ⊕ *www.golfpagosa.com* ✉ *$35 for 9 holes, $86 for 18 holes* ⌣ *Meadows-Pinon Course: 18 holes, 6412* *yards, par 72; Pinon-Ponderosa Course: 18 holes, 6134 yards, par 72; Meadows-Ponderosa Course: 18 holes, 6026 yards, par 72.* ⏲ *Closed mid-Sept.–May.*

HIKING

Continental Divide Trail. Serious hikers in the Pagosa Springs area head to the Continental Divide Trail, which has a major access point near Wolf Creek Pass. The trail can be a fairly easy out-and-back day hike or the starting point for a longer backcountry trip. ✉ *Pagosa Springs* ✥ *Trailhead at end of short gravel road that starts on east side of Wolf Creek Pass* 🌐 *www.continentaldividetrail.org.*

FAMILY **Piedra Falls Trail.** This popular trail delivers an easy 1¼-mile (round-trip) hike through conifer and aspen forest to the falls, which tumble in two big steps down a narrow wedge cut through volcanic rocks. ✉ *Pagosa Springs* ✥ *Trailhead at end of East Toner Road (Forest Rd. 637)* ☎ *800/252–2204* 🌐 *www.visitpagosasprings.com.*

WHERE TO EAT AND STAY

$ SOUTHWESTERN 🍴 **Kip's Grill.** Locals pack out this small restaurant, famous for its Baja-style tacos. Favorites include the grilled ono and the Dos Dynamite Diablos: two Hatch green chilis stuffed with mozzarella cheese and top sirloin. Kip's also serves Southwestern-style burgers and sandwiches. ■ TIP→ **In summer, request a spot on the deck overlooking main street.** [$] *Average main: $10* ✉ *121 Pagosa St.* ☎ *970/264–3663* 🌐 *www.kipsgrill.com.*

$$$ HOTEL Fodor's Choice ★ 🏨 **The Springs Resort and Spa.** Wrap yourself in a big white spa robe and head directly for the 23 soaking pools that are terraced on several levels overlooking the San Juan River; as a hotel guest you'll have 24-hour access. **Pros:** access to hot springs; tranquil setting. **Cons:** service can be indifferent; no breakfast. [$] *Rooms from: $199* ✉ *165 Hot Springs Blvd.* ☎ *970/264–4168, 866/338–7404* 🌐 *www.pagosahotsprings.com* 🛏 *46 rooms, 33 suites* 🍽 *No meals.*

CORTEZ

45 miles west of Durango via U.S. 160; 78 miles southwest of Telluride via Hwy. 145.

The northern escarpment of Mesa Verde to the southeast and the volcanic blisters of La Plata Mountains to the east dominate the views around sprawling Cortez. With its Days Inns, Dairy Queens, and Best Westerns, the town has a layout that seems to have been determined by neon-sign and aluminum-siding salesmen of the 1950s. Hidden among these eyesores, however, are fine galleries, shops showcasing Native American art, and a host of secondhand shops that can yield surprising finds.

The gently rising hump to the southwest of town is Sleeping Ute Mountain, which resembles the reclining silhouette of a Native American, complete with headdress. This site is sacred to the Ute Mountain tribe, as it represents a great warrior god who, after being mortally wounded in a titanic battle with evil gods, lapsed into eternal sleep, his flowing blood turning into the life-giving Dolores and Animas rivers.

GETTING HERE AND AROUND

Cortez sits at the junction of Highway 160 and Highway 491, making it a busy town for people heading north to Dolores and Telluride, south into New Mexico and Arizona, and east to Durango. Highway 491 turns into Broadway heading north, and Highway 160 splits off due east, turning into Main Street as it passes through the center of town on its way to Durango.

ESSENTIALS

Visitor Information Colorado Welcome Center. ⊠ *928 E. Main St.* ☎ *970/565-4048.* **Cortez Area Chamber of Commerce.** ⊠ *31 W. Main St.* ☎ *970/565-3414* ⊕ *www.cortezchamber.com.* **Mesa Verde Country.** ⊠ *928 E. Main St.* ☎ *800/253-1616, 970/565-8227* ⊕ *www.mesaverdecountry.com.*

EXPLORING

Cortez Cultural Center. The cultural center has exhibits on regional artists and Ancestral Puebloan culture, as well as events and fairs. Summer evening programs include Native American dances and storytelling. ⊠ *25 N. Market St.* ☎ *970/565-1151* ⊕ *www.cortezculturalcenter.org* 🎫 *Free* ☉ *Memorial Day–Labor Day, daily 10 to 10; Sept. and May, daily 10–6; Oct.–Apr., daily 10–5.*

Crow Canyon Archaeological Center. Professionals, students, and any would-be Indiana Joneses come here to learn about ancient relics. Among the more popular offerings of the center's educational programs are weeklong "Archaeology Adventures," which allow visitors to work alongside professional archaeologists as they search for pottery, stone tools, and other artifacts at excavation sites throughout the area, then clean and catalog their finds in the lab. The program includes a special guided tour of Mesa Verde National Park. ⊠ *23390 County Rd. K* ☎ *970/565-8975, 800/422-8975* ⊕ *www.crowcanyon.org.*

Ute Mountain Tribal Park. The only way to see this spectacular 125,000-acre park, located inside the Ute reservation, is by taking a guided tour. Expert tribal guides lead strenuous daylong hikes into this dazzling repository of Ancestral Puebloan ruins, including beautifully preserved cliff dwellings, pictographs, and petroglyphs. There are also less-demanding half-day tours, as well as private and custom tour options. Tours start at the park's visitor center, off Highway 160. ⊠ *Hwy. 160/491* ☎ *970/565-3751, 800/847-5485* ⊕ *www.utemountaintribalpark.info* 🎫 *From $29.*

| OFF THE BEATEN PATH | **Four Corners Monument.** The Navajo Nation manages this interesting landmark about 65 miles southeast of Bluff and 6 miles north of Teec Nos Pos, Arizona. Primarily a photo op, you'll also find Navajo and Ute artisans selling authentic jewelry and crafts, as well as traditional foods. It's the only place in the United States where four states meet at one single point. Bring plenty of water. You'll need cash for the entry fee. No cards or checks are accepted, and the nearest ATM is in Teec Nos Pos. ⊠ *Four Corners Monument Rd., off U.S. 160, Teec Nos Pos* ⊕ *www.navajonationparks.org* 🎫 *$5* ☉ *May–mid-Sept., daily 8–8; mid-Sept.–Apr., 8–6.* |

OFF THE BEATEN PATH

Mud Creek Hogan. This endearing bit of classic American kitsch has about a dozen enormous arrows (made from telephone poles) stuck into the ground as if shot from gigantic bows. There are also a few faux teepees and a big plastic horse. The main attraction here is the trading post, which sells an assortment of Native American arts and crafts. Out back, there's a frontier town, complete with saloon, hotel, bank, jail, and livery station. Don't breathe too hard, or you'll blow the town over: the paper-thin buildings are only facades. ✉ *38651 U.S. 160, Mancos* ☎ *970/533–7117* 🎟 *Free.*

WHERE TO EAT AND STAY

$$ ITALIAN

🍴 **Nero's.** The menu at this unpretentious Italian eatery is fairly basic, with classic pasta dishes as well as steak, veal, and seafood, but the food is terrific. It has a full bar and a respectable wine list. The atmosphere is casual and the decor is clean and simple. The dining area is small, so reservations are a good idea in the busy summer months. [$] *Average main: $14* ✉ *303 W. Main St.* ☎ *970/565–7366* 🌐 *www.neroscortez.com* 🕒 *No lunch. Closed Tues.*

$ HOTEL

🏨 **American Holiday Mesa Verde Inn.** This is arguably the nicest motel on the strip, mostly because its air-conditioned rooms are spacious and pleasantly decorated. **Pros:** reasonably priced; near the national park; outdoor pool. **Cons:** can get noisy; nothing fancy. [$] *Rooms from: $65* ✉ *640 S. Broadway* ☎ *970/565–3773* 🌐 *www.mesaverdeinncolorado.com* 🛏 *84 rooms* 🍽 *No meals.*

NIGHTLIFE

Ute Mountain Casino. At the base of Sleeping Ute Mountain, the state's first tribal casino rings with the sound of more than 800 slot machines. Ute Mountain Casino also draws crowds for bingo, blackjack, roulette, and craps. The resort is 11 miles south of Cortez on U.S. 160. ✉ *3 Weeminuche Dr., Towaoc* ☎ *970/565–8800, 800/258–8007* 🌐 *www.utemountaincasino.com.*

SHOPPING

CRAFTS AND ART GALLERIES

Notah Dineh Trading Company and Museum. This store specializing in Navajo rugs has the largest collection in the area. There are also handmade baskets, beadwork, pottery, and jewelry. If you stop in the free museum you can see relics of the Old West. ✉ *345 W. Main St.* ☎ *800/444–2024* 🌐 *www.notahdineh.com.*

Ute Mountain Indian Trading Company. Stop by this Native American–owned factory store to watch the traditional and painstaking processes of molding, trimming, cleaning, painting, and glazing pottery. In the showroom you can buy pieces straight from the source, as well as Native American jewelry, rugs, and other crafts from local artists. ✉ *27601 E. Hwy. 160* ☎ *970/565–0195.*

DOLORES

11 miles northeast of Cortez via Rte. 145.

On the bank of the Dolores River, just downstream from the McPhee Reservoir, the tiny town of Dolores is midway between Durango and Telluride on State Highway 145. The river runs along the south edge of town, while beautiful cliffs flank the northern edge. Delores attracts visitors with its spectacular scenery, fabulous fly-fishing, water sports, mountain hiking, and other outdoor adventures.

EXPLORING

FAMILY **Anasazi Heritage Center.** Operated by the Federal Bureau of Land Management, this museum houses artifacts culled from more than 1,500 excavations in the region. The center has permanent exhibits showcasing the archaeology, history, and culture of the Ancestral Puebloans and other indigenous peoples. There are also two 12th-century pueblos, named after the Spanish friars Dominguez and Escalante, within walking distance. A full-scale replica of an ancient pit-house dwelling illustrates how the people lived around AD 850. It also houses the visitor center and jumping-off point for the **Canyons of the Ancients National Monument.** ⊠ *27501 State Hwy. 184* ✛ *3 miles west of Dolores* ☎ *970/882–5600* ⊕ *www.blm.gov/co/st/en/fo/ahc.html* ⊠ *$3* ⊙ *Mar.–Oct., daily 9–5; Nov.–Feb., daily 10–4.*

Canyons of the Ancients National Monument. Spread across 176,000 acres of arid mesa and canyon country, the Canyons of the Ancients National Monument holds more than 20,000 archaeological sites, the greatest concentration anywhere in the United States. Some sites, like apartment-style cliff dwellings and hewn-rock towers, are impossible to miss. Others are as subtle as evidence of agricultural fields, springs, and water systems. They are powerful evidence of the complex civilization of the Ancestral Puebloan people. **Lowry Pueblo,** in the northern part of the monument, is a 40-room pueblo with eight kivas (round chambers used for sacred rituals). Its Great Kiva is one of the largest known in the Southwest.

Exploring the monument area can be a challenge: roads are few, hiking trails are sparse, and visitor services are all but nonexistent. The Anasazi Heritage Center, 3 miles west of Dolores on Highway 184, serves as the visitor center. A brochure, which details the self-guided tour, is available at the entrance to the site. ⊠ *27501 State Hwy. 184* ✛ *3 miles west of Dolores* ☎ *970/882–5600* ⊕ *www.blm.gov/co/st/en/nm/canm.html* ⊠ *Free.*

Hovenweep National Monument. Straddling the Colorado–Utah border, this monument is known for distinctive square, oval, round, and D-shape towers that were engineering marvels when they were built around AD 1200. The buildings are spread throughout a series of ancient villages, once home to 2,500 people. The visitor center is on the Utah side of the monument. ■TIP➔ **Per rangers, don't attempt to use your GPS to find Hovenweep. Most devices will take you either over rough dirt roads or to more remote parts of the monument.** ✛ *From Dolores,* *take Hwy. 184 west to U.S. 491, then head west onto County Rd. CC for 9 miles* ☎ *970/562–4282* 🌐 *www.nps.gov/hove* 🎟 *Free.*

McPhee Reservoir. In 1985, crews completed construction of an irrigation dam across the Dolores River, forming the McPhee Reservoir, the second largest in the state. It draws anglers looking to bag a variety of warm- and cold-water fish along its 50 miles of shoreline, which is surrounded by spectacular specimens of juniper and sage as well as large stands of pinyon pine. There are two boat ramps; the McPhee Boat Ramp also has a new marina and convenience store. The area also has camping, hiking, and a relatively easy mountain-bike trail, and the mesa offers panoramic views of the surrounding San Juan National Forest. ✉ *Forest Service Rd. 271, off State Hwy. 184* ✣ *About 9 miles northwest of Dolores* 🎟 *Free.*

Rio Grande Southern Railroad Museum. Housed in a replica of the town's 1880s-era train station, this museum displays Galloping Goose No. 5, one of only seven specially designed engines built in the 1930s. The "Geese" were motored vehicles built from touring-car bodies that could operate for much less than steam-powered engines. ✉ *5th St. at Railroad Ave.* ☎ *970/882–7082* 🌐 *www.gallopinggoose5.com* 🎟 *Free* 🕓 *Mid-May–mid-Oct., Mon.–Sat., 9–5; mid-Oct.–early May, Tues.–Thurs., 10–2.*

SPORTS AND THE OUTDOORS

RAFTING

Beginning in the mountains outside the town of Dolores, the Dolores River travels more than 150 miles before joining the Colorado River near Moab, Utah. This is one of those rivers that tend to flow madly in spring and diminish considerably by midsummer, meaning that most rafting trips run between May and June. Sandstone canyons, Ancestral Puebloan ruins, and the spring bloom of wildflowers and cacti are trip highlights. The current's strength depends mostly on how much water is released from McPhee Reservoir, but for the most part a Dolores River trip is a float interrupted by rapids that, depending on the flow level, can rate a Class IV.

Dvorak Expeditions. This outfitter offers rafting trips on the Dolores River that cover Class II to Class IV rapids and last up to 10 days. Or you can book a "Build-Your-Own-Adventure" trip that pairs rafting with other adventurous options, including ziplining, mountain biking, horseback riding, and rock climbing. ✉ *17921 U.S. 285, Nathrop* ☎ *719/539–6851, 800/824–3795* 🌐 *www.dvorakexpeditions.com* 🎟 *From $122.*

WHERE TO EAT

$ AMERICAN

🍴 **Dolores River Brewery.** This brewpub playfully advertises itself as "Dolores's Oldest Operating Brewery." (It's also the only one in town.) Order an ale or a stout to wash down good pub grub (don't miss the amazing wood-fired pizzas). Bonus: if you've hit it just right, you'll also get to hear live music from a local band. [$] *Average main: $10* ✉ *100 S. 4th St.* ☎ *970/882–4677* 🌐 *www.doloresriverbrewery.com* 🕓 *Closed Mon. No lunch.*

MESA VERDE
NATIONAL PARK

WELCOME TO
MESA VERDE NATIONAL PARK

TOP REASONS TO GO

★ **Ancient artifacts:** Mesa Verde is a time capsule for the Ancestral Puebloan culture, which flourished between 700 and 1,400 years ago; more than 4,000 archaeological sites and 3 million objects have been unearthed here.

★ **Bright nights:** Mesa Verde's lack of light and air pollution, along with its high elevation make for spectacular views of the heavens.

★ **Active adventures:** Get your heart pumping outdoors with hiking, biking, and exploring on trails of varying difficulties.

★ **Cliff dwellings:** Built atop the pinyon-covered mesa tops and hidden in the park's valleys is a wondrous collection of 600 ancient dwellings, some carved directly into the sandstone cliff faces.

★ **Geological marvels:** View the unique geology that drew the Ancient Puebloan people to the area: protected desert canyons, massive alcoves in the cliff walls, thick bands of sandstone, continuous seep springs, and soils that could be used for both agriculture and architecture.

1 **Morefield Campground.** Near the park entrance, this large campground (the only one in Mesa Verde) includes a village area with a gas station and store. The best-known sites are farther in, but this one is close to some of the best hiking trails in the park.

2 **Visitor and Research Center.** Turn left at the entrance for the park's visitor center. Buy tickets for the popular ranger-led tours here and learn everything you need to know to plan a great trip.

← TO CORTEZ

11

COLORADO

160

2

k Entrance
Station

Visitor Center

TO
MANCOS

Mancos Valley
Overlook

1

Morefield Campground

Prater Ridge
Trail

Tunnel

EAST RIM

PRATER CANYON

MOREFIELD CANYON

WATERS CANYON

WHITES CANYON

BIG MESA

MANCOS CANYON

EAST RIM

2 mi

2 km

3 Far View. Almost an hour's drive (but just 18 miles) from Mesa Verde's entrance, Far View is the park's epicenter, with several restaurants and the park's only overnight lodge. The fork in the road here takes you west toward the sites at Wetherill Mesa or south toward Chapin Mesa.

4 Chapin Mesa. Home to the park's most famous cliff dwellings and archaeological sites, the Chapin Mesa area includes the famous 150-room Cliff House dwelling and other man-made and natural wonders. It's also home to the Chapin Mesa Archeological Museum, where you can take a free tour of nearby Spruce Tree House.

5 Wetherill Mesa. It's less visited than Chapin Mesa, but just as rewarding for visitors. See Long House, Two Raven House, Kodak House, and the Badger House Community.

GETTING ORIENTED

Perhaps no other area offers as much evidence into the Ancestral Puebloan culture as Mesa Verde National Park. Several thousand archaeological sites have been found, and research is ongoing to discover more. The carved-out homes and assorted artifacts, many of which are displayed at the park's Chapin Mesa Archeological Museum, belonged to ancestors of today's Hopi, Zuni, and Pueblo tribes, among others. Due to the sensitive nature of these sites, hiking in the park is restricted to designated trails, and certain cliff dwellings may be accessed only on ranger-led tours during the peak summer season.

KEY	
👫	Ranger Station
🛆	Campground
🎪	Picnic Area
🍴	Restaurant
🏨	Lodge
🚶	Trailhead
🚻	Restrooms
⋟	Scenic Viewpoint
····	Walking/Hiking Trails
⋯⋯	Bicycle Path

Updated by
Aimee Heckel

Unlike the other national parks, Mesa Verde earned its status from its ancient cultural history rather than its geological treasures. President Theodore Roosevelt established it in 1906 as the first national park to "preserve the works of man," in this case that of the Ancestral Puebloans, also known as the Anasazi. They lived in the region from roughly 550 to 1300; they left behind more than 4,000 archaeological sites spread out over 80 square miles. Their ancient dwellings, set high into the sandstone cliffs, are the heart of the park.

Mesa Verde (which in Spanish means, literally, "Green Table," but translates more accurately to something like "green flat-topped plateau") is much more than an archaeologist's dreamland, however. It's one of those windswept places where man's footprints and nature's paintbrush—some would say chisel—meet. Rising dramatically from the San Juan Basin, the jutting cliffs are cut by a series of complex canyons and covered in several shades of green, from pines in the higher elevations down to sage and other mountain brush on the desert floor. From the tops of the smaller mesas, you can look across to the cliff dwellings in the opposite rock faces. Dwarfed by the towering cliffs, the sand-color dwellings look almost like a natural occurrence in the midst of the desert's harsh beauty.

MESA VERDE PLANNER

WHEN TO GO

The best times to visit the park are late May, early June, and most of September, when the weather is fine but the summer crowds have thinned. Mid-June through August is Mesa Verde's most crowded time. In July and August, lines at the museum and visitor center may last half an hour. Afternoon thunderstorms are common in July and August.

The park gets as much as 100 inches of snow in winter. Snow may fall as late as May and as early as October, but there's rarely enough to hamper travel. In winter, the Wetherill Mesa Road is closed, but you can still get a glimpse of some of the Wetherill Mesa sandstone dwellings, sheltered from the snow in their cliff coves, from the Chapin Mesa area.

AVG. HIGH/LOW TEMPS.

Jan.	Feb.	Mar.	Apr.	May	June
40/18	44/19	50/26	52/34	71/44	83/52
July	Aug.	Sept.	Oct.	Nov.	Dec.
88/58	85/56	76/48	66/39	51/28	42/21

FESTIVALS AND EVENTS

MAY OR JUNE **Mountain Ute Bear Dance.** This traditional dance, the local version of a Sadie Hawkins (in which the women choose their dance partners—and the selected men can't refuse), is held in May or June on the Towaoc Ute reservation south of Cortez. The event celebrates spring and the legacy of a mythical bear who taught the Ute people her secrets. It's part of a multiday festival that includes music, races, and softball games, and culminates with an hour-long dance that's over when only one couple remains. ⊠ *124 Mike Wash Rd., Towaoc* ☎ *970/565–3751* ⊕ *www.utemountainutetribe.com.*

JULY **Durango Fiesta Days.** A parade, rodeo, barbecue, street dance, cook-offs, live music, and more come to the Durango Fairgrounds in July. ⊠ *La Plata County Fairgrounds, 2500 Main Ave., Durango* ☎ *970/749–4960* ⊕ *www.durangofiestadays.com.*

OCTOBER
FAMILY **Durango Cowboy Poetry Gathering.** A parade and dance accompany art exhibitions, poetry readings, music, and storytelling in this four-day event run by the Durango Cowboy Poetry Gathering, a non-profit set up to preserve the traditions of the American West. It's held the first weekend in October. ⊠ *Durango* ☎ *970/749–2995* ⊕ *www.durangocowboypoetrygathering.org.*

PLANNING YOUR TIME

MESA VERDE IN ONE DAY

For a full experience, take at least one ranger-led tour of a major cliff dwelling site, as well as a few self-guided walks. Arrive early and stop first at the Visitor and Research Center, where you can purchase tickets for Cliff Palace and Balcony House tours on Chapin Mesa. If it's going to be a hot day, you might want to take an early-morning or late-afternoon bus tour. Drive to the **Chapin Mesa Museum** to watch a 25-minute film introducing you to the area and its history. Just behind the museum is the trailhead for the 0.5-mile-long **Spruce Tree House Trail**, which leads to the best-preserved cliff dwelling in the park. Then drive to **Balcony House** for an hour-long, ranger-led tour.

Have lunch at the Spruce Tree House cafeteria or the Cliff Palace picnic area. Afterward take the ranger-led tour of **Cliff Palace** (one hour). Use the rest of the day to explore the overlooks and trails off the 6-mile loop of **Mesa Top Loop Road.** Or head back to the museum and take **Petroglyph Point Trail** to see a great example of Ancestral Puebloan rock carvings. A leisurely walk along the Mesa Top's **Soda Canyon Overlook Trail** (off Cliff Palace Loop Road) gives you a beautiful bird's-eye view of the canyon below. On the drive back toward the park entrance, be sure to check out the view from **Park Point.**

GETTING HERE AND AROUND

AIR TRAVEL

The cities of Durango (36 miles east of the park entrance) and Cortez (11 miles to the west) have airports.

CAR TRAVEL

The park has just one entrance, off U.S. 160, between Cortez and Durango in what's known as the Four Corners area (which spans the intersection of Colorado, New Mexico, Arizona, and Utah). Most of the roads at Mesa Verde involve steep grades and hairpin turns, particularly on Wetherill Mesa. Vehicles over 8,000 pounds or 25 feet are prohibited on this road. Trailers and towed vehicles are prohibited past Morefield Campground. Check the condition of your vehicle's brakes before driving the road to Wetherill Mesa. For the latest road information, tune to 1610 AM, or call ☎ 970/529–4461. Off-road vehicles are prohibited in the park. At less-visited Wetherill Mesa, you must leave your car behind and hike to the Long House, Kodak House, and Badger House Community.

PARK ESSENTIALS

PARK FEES AND PERMITS

Admission is $15 per vehicle for a seven-day permit. An annual pass is $30. Ranger-led tours of Cliff Palace, Long House, and Balcony House are $3 per person. You can also take ranger-guided bus tours from the Far View Lodge, which last between 3½ and 4 hours and cost $41–$48 ($26–$35 for kids; under 5 free). Backcountry hiking and fishing are not permitted at Mesa Verde.

PARK HOURS

Mesa Verde's facilities each operate on their own schedule, but most are open daily, from Memorial Day through Labor Day, between about 8 am and sunset. The rest of the year, they open at 9. In winter, the Spruce Tree House is open only to offer a few scheduled tours each day. Wetherill Mesa (and all the sites it services) is open only from Memorial Day through Labor Day. Far View Visitor Center, Far View Terrace, and Far View Lodge are open between April and October. Morefield Campground and the sites nearby are open from mid-May through mid-October. Specific hours are subject to change, so check with the visitor center upon arrival.

CELL-PHONE RECEPTION AND INTERNET

You can get patchy cell service in the park. Best service is typically at the Morefield Campground area, which is the closest to the neighboring towns of Cortez and Mancos. Public telephones can be found at all the major visitor areas (Morefield, Far View, and Spruce Tree). You can get free Wi-Fi throughout the Far View Lodge and at the Morefield Campground store.

EDUCATIONAL OFFERINGS

RANGER PROGRAMS

FAMILY **Evening Ranger Campfire Program.** Every night in summer at the Morefield Campground Amphitheater, park rangers present a different 45- to 60-minute program on topics such as stargazing, history, wildlife, and archaeology. Several evenings a week, you can also find free, hour-long ranger talks in the Far View Lodge library. ⊠ *Morefield Campground Amphitheater, 4 miles south of park entrance* ☎ *970/529–4465* ✉ *Free* ☉ *Memorial Day–Labor Day, daily at 9 pm. Lodge program time and days vary.*

Far View Sites Walk. This one-hour, self-guided walk winds through the mesa top sites in the Far View area. ⊠ *Far View House, 1 mile south of Far View Visitor Center* ☎ *970/529–4465* ⊕ *www.nps.gov/meve* ✉ *Free* ☉ *8 am–sunset during open seasons.*

FAMILY **Junior Ranger Program.** Children ages 4 through 12 can earn a certificate and badge for successfully completing at least three activities in the park's Junior Ranger booklet (available at the park or online). ⊠ *Mesa Verde Visitor and Research Center or Chapin Mesa Archeological Museum* ☎ *970/529–4465* ⊕ *www.nps.gov/meve/forkids/beajuniorranger.htm.*

Ranger-Led Tours. The cliff dwellings known as Balcony House, Cliff Palace, and Long House can be explored only on ranger-led tours; the first two last about an hour, the third is 90 minutes. Buy tickets at the Visitor and Research Center. These are active tours and may not be suitable for some children; each requires climbing ladders without handrails and squeezing through tight spaces. Be sure to bring water and sunscreen. ⊠ *Mesa Verde National Park* ☎ *970/529–4465* ⊕ *www.nps.gov/meve/planyourvisit/visitcliffdwelling.htm* ⊠ *$4 per site.*

RESTAURANTS

Dining options in Mesa Verde are limited inside the park, but comparatively plentiful and varied if you're staying in Cortez or Durango. In surrounding communities, Southwestern restaurants and steak houses are common options.

HOTELS

All 150 rooms of the park's Far View Lodge, open April through October, fill up quickly—so reservations are recommended, especially if you plan to visit on a weekend in summer. Options in the surrounding area include chain hotels, cabins, and bed-and-breakfast inns. Durango in particular has a number of hotels in fine old buildings reminiscent of the Old West. *Hotel reviews have been shortened. For full information, visit Fodors.com.*

WHAT IT COSTS				
	$	$$	$$$	$$$$
Restaurants	under $13	$13–$18	$19–$25	over $25
Hotels	under $121	$121–$170	$171–$230	over $230

Restaurant prices are the average cost of a main course at dinner or, if dinner is not served, at lunch. Hotel reviews are the lowest cost of a standard double room in high season, excluding taxes and service charges.

TOURS

BUS TOURS

FAMILY **ARAMARK Tours.** If you want a well-rounded visit to Mesa Verde's most popular sites, consider a group tour. The park concessionaire provides all-day and half-day guided tours of the Chapin Mesa and Far View sites, departing in buses from either Morefield Campground or Far View Lodge. Tours are led by Aramark guides or park rangers, who share information about the park's history, geology, and excavation processes. Cold water is provided, but you'll need to bring your own snacks. Buy tickets at Far View Lodge, Far View Terrace, the Morefield Campground, or online. Tours sell out, so reserve in advance. ⊠ *1 Navajo Hill, Box 277* ☎ *970/529–4422, 800/449–2288* ⊕ *www.visitmesaverde.com* ⊠ *From $41* ⊙ *Mid-Apr.–mid-Oct., daily, departs at 8 am and 1:30 pm.*

VISITOR INFORMATION

PARK CONTACT INFORMATION

Mesa Verde National Park. ✉ *Mesa Verde National Park* ☎ *970/529–4465* ⊕ *www.nps.gov/meve.*

VISITOR CENTERS

Chapin Mesa Archeological Museum. This is an excellent first stop for an introduction to Ancestral Puebloan culture, as well as the area's development into a national park. Exhibits showcase original textiles and other artifacts, and a theater plays an informative film every 30 minutes. Rangers are available to answer your questions, and there's also a sign-in sheet for hiking trails. The museum sits at the south end of the park entrance road and overlooks Spruce Tree House. Nearby, you'll find park headquarters, a gift shop, a post office, snack bar, and bathrooms. ✉ *Park entrance road, 5 miles south of Far View Visitor Center, 20 miles from park entrance* ☎ *970/529–4465* ⊕ *www.nps. gov/meve/planyourvisit/museum.htm* 🎟 *Free* ☉ *Open year-round. Hrs vary by season.*

Mesa Verde Visitor and Research Center. Mesa Verde's visitor center is the place to go to sign up for tours and get the information you need to plan a successful trip. This is the only place in the park to buy tickets for the Cliff Palace, Balcony House, and Long House ranger-led tours. The sleek, energy-efficient research center is filled with more than 3 million artifacts and archives. The center features indoor and outdoor exhibits, a gift shop, picnic tables, and a museum. A selection of books, maps, and videos on the history of the park are available, and rangers are on hand to answer questions and explain the history of the Ancestral Puebloans. ✉ *Park entrance on the left* ☎ *970/529–4465* ⊕ *www.nps.gov/meve/ planyourvisit/meve_vc.htm* ☉ *Open year-round. Hrs vary by season.*

EXPLORING

SCENIC DRIVES

Mesa Top Loop Road. This 6-mile drive skirts the scenic rim of Chapin Mesa and takes you to several overlooks and short, paved trails. You'll get great views of Sun Temple and Square Tower, as well as Cliff Palace, Sunset House, and several other cliff dwellings visible from the Sun Point Overlook. ✉ *Mesa Verde National Park.*

Park Entrance Road. The main park road, also known as SH 10, leads you from the entrance off U.S. 160 to the Far View complex, 15 miles from the park entrance. As a break from the switchbacks, you can stop at a couple of pretty overlooks along the way, but hold out for Park Point, which, at the mesa's highest elevation (8,572 feet), gives you unobstructed, 360-degree views. Note that trailers and towed vehicles are not permitted beyond Morefield Campground. ✉ *Mesa Verde National Park.*

Wetherill Mesa Road. This 12-mile mountain road, stretching from the Far View Visitor Center to the Wetherill Mesa, has sharp curves and steep grades (and is restricted to vehicles less than 25 feet long and 8,000

CLOSE UP

Plants and Wildlife in Mesa Verde

Mesa Verde is home to 640 species of plants, including a number of native plants found nowhere else. Its lower elevations feature many varieties of shrubs, including rabbitbrush and sagebrush. Higher up, you'll find mountain mahogany, yucca, pinyon, juniper, and Douglas fir. During warmer months, brightly colored blossoms, like the yellow perky Sue, blue lupines, and bright-red Indian paintbrushes, are scattered throughout the park.

The park is also home to a variety of migratory and resident animals, including 74 species of mammals. Drive slowly along the park's roads; mule deer are everywhere. You may spot wild turkeys, and black bear encounters are not unheard of on the hiking trails. Bobcats, coyotes, and mountain lions are also around, but they are seen less frequently. About 200 species of birds, including threatened Mexican spotted owls,

red-tailed hawks, golden eagles, and noisy ravens, also live here. On the ground, you should keep your eyes and ears open for lizards and snakes, including the poisonous—but shy— prairie rattlesnake. As a general rule, animals are most active in the early morning and at dusk.

Many areas of the park have had extensive fire damage over the years. In fact, wildfires here have been so destructive they are given names, just like hurricanes. For example, the Bircher Fire in 2000 consumed nearly 20,000 acres of brush and forest, much of it covering the eastern half of the park. It will take several centuries for the woodland there to look as verdant as the area atop Chapin Mesa, which escaped the fire. But in the meantime, you'll have a chance to glimpse nature's powerful rejuvenating processes in action; the landscape in the fire-ravaged sections of the park is already filling in with vegetation.

pounds). Roadside pull-outs offer unobstructed views of the Four Corners region. At the end of the road, you can access Step House, Long House, and Badger House. ⊠ *Mesa Verde National Park* ☉ *Memorial Day–Labor Day, weather permitting.*

HISTORIC SITES

Badger House Community. A self-guided walk along paved and gravel trails takes you through a group of four mesa-top dwellings. The community, which covers nearly 7 acres, dates back to the year 650, the Basketmaker Period, and includes a primitive, semisubterranean pit house and what's left of a multistoried stone pueblo. Allow about 45 minutes to see the sites. The trail is 2.4 miles round-trip. The park plans to offer bike rentals, too. ⊠ *Wetherill Mesa Rd., 12 miles from Far View Visitor Center* ⊕ *www.nps.gov/meve/historyculture/mt_badger_house. htm* 🎟 *Free.*

Balcony House. The stonework of this 40-room cliff dwelling, which housed about 40 or 50 people, is impressive, but you're likely to be even more awed by the skill it must have taken to reach this place. Perched in a sandstone cove 600 feet above the floor of Soda Canyon,

Balcony House seems almost suspended in space. Even with the aid of modern passageways and a partially paved trail, today's visitors must climb a 32-foot ladder and crawl through a 12-foot-long tunnel to enter. Surrounding the house is a courtyard with a parapet wall and the intact balcony for which the house is named. A favorite with kids, the dwelling is accessible only on a ranger-led tour. Purchase tickets at the Visitor and Research Center, Morefield Ranger Station, or the Colorado Welcome Center in Cortez. ⊠ *Cliff Palace/Balcony House Rd., 10 miles south of Far View Visitor Center, Cliff Palace Loop* 🖭 *$4.*

Fodor'sChoice
★ **Cliff Palace.** This was the first major Mesa Verde dwelling seen by cowboys Charlie Mason and Richard Wetherill in 1888. It is also the largest, containing about 150 rooms and 23 kivas on three levels. Getting there involves a steep downhill hike and three ladders. Purchase tickets at the Visitor and Research Center, Morefield Ranger Station, and at the Colorado Welcome Center in Cortez. From Memorial Day through Labor Day, rangers in historical costumes lead a 90-minute Twilight Tour of the site. These tours run daily just before twilight; tickets are available only at the Visitor and Research Center. Also check out 90-minute, small-group photography tours at sunset. ⊠ *Cliff Palace Overlook, about 2½ miles south of Chapin Mesa Archeological Museum* 🖭 *Basic tour $4; twilight tour $12; photography tour $20.*

FAMILY **Far View Sites Complex.** This was probably one of the most densely populated areas in Mesa Verde, comprising as many as 50 villages in a ½-square-mile area at the top of Chapin Mesa. Most of the sites here were built between 900 and 1300. Begin the self-guided tour at the interpretive panels in the parking lot, then proceed down a ½-mile, level trail. ⊠ *Park entrance road, near the Chapin Mesa area* ⊕ *www.nps.gov/meve* 🖭 *Free.*

Long House. This Wetherill Mesa cliff dwelling is the second largest in Mesa Verde. It is believed that about 150 people lived in Long House, so named because of the size of its cliff alcove. The spring at the back of the cave is still active today. The in-depth, ranger-led tour begins a short distance from the parking lot and takes about 90 minutes. Even though you will hike less than a mile, be prepared to climb two 15-foot ladders. Buy your ticket at the Visitor and Research Center, Morefield Ranger Station, or at the Colorado Welcome Center in Cortez. ⊠ *On Wetherill Mesa, 29 miles past the Visitor Center, near mile marker 15* ⊕ *www.nps.gov/meve* 🖭 *Tours $4.*

Pit Houses and Early Pueblo Villages. Three dwellings, built on top of each other from 700 to 950, at first look like a mass of jumbled walls, but an informational panel helps identify the dwellings—and the stories behind them are fascinating. The 325-foot trail from the walking area is paved, wheelchair accessible, and near a restroom. ⊠ *Mesa Top Loop Rd., about 2½ miles south of Chapin Mesa Archeological Museum* ☒ *Free.*

FAMILY **Spruce Tree House.** This 138-room complex is the best-preserved site in the park, and the rooms and ceremonial chambers are more accessible to visitors than those in other sites. Here you can actually enter a kiva, via a short ladder that goes underground, just as the original inhabitants did. It's a great place for kids to explore, but because of its location in the heart of the Chapin Mesa area, Spruce Tree House can resemble a crowded playground during busy periods. Tours are self-guided from spring to fall (allow 45 minutes to an hour), but a park ranger is on-site to answer questions. Sign up for ranger-guided tours in the winter. The trail leading to Spruce Tree House starts behind the museum and leads you 100 feet down into the canyon. You may find yourself breathing hard by the time you make it back up to the parking lot. ⊠ *At the Chapin Mesa Archeological Museum, 5 miles south of Far View Visitor Center* ☒ *Free.*

Step House. So named because of a crumbling prehistoric stairway leading up from the dwelling, Step House is reached via a paved (but steep) trail that's ¾ mile long. The house is unique in that it shows clear evidence of two separate occupations: the first around 626, the second a full 600 years later. The self-guided tour takes about 45 minutes. ⊠ *Wetherill Mesa Rd., 12 miles from Far View Visitor Center* ⊕ *www. nps.gov/meve/historyculture/cd_step_house.htm* ☒ *Free.*

Sun Temple. Although researchers assume it was probably a ceremonial structure, they're unsure of the exact purpose of this complex, which has no doors or windows in most of its chambers. Because the building was not quite half-finished when it was left in 1276, some researchers surmise it might have been constructed to stave off whatever disaster caused its builders—and the other inhabitants of Mesa Verde—to leave. ⊠ *Mesa Top Loop Rd., about 2 miles south of Chapin Mesa Archeological Museum* ⊕ *www.nps.gov/meve/historyculture/mt_sun_temple. htm* ☒ *Free.*

SCENIC STOPS

Cedar Tree Tower. A self-guided tour takes you to, but not through, a tower and kiva built between 1100 and 1300 and connected by a tunnel. The tower-and-kiva combinations in the park are thought to have been either religious structures or signal towers. ⊠ *Near the four-way intersection on Chapin Mesa; park entrance road, 1½ miles north of Chapin Mesa Archeological Museum* ☒ *Free.*

Kodak House Overlook. Get an impressive view into the 60-room Kodak House and its several small kivas from here. The house, closed to the public, was named for a Swedish researcher who absentmindedly left his Kodak camera behind here in 1891. ⊠ *Wetherill Mesa Rd.* ⊕ *www. nps.gov/meve.*

Soda Canyon Overlook. Get your best view of Balcony House here. You can also read interpretive panels about the site and the surrounding canyon geology. ⊠ *Cliff Palace Loop Rd., about 1 mile north of Balcony House parking area.*

SPORTS AND THE OUTDOORS

At Mesa Verde, outdoor activities are restricted, due to the fragile nature of the archaeological treasures here. Hiking (allowed on marked trails only) is the best option, especially as a way to view some of the Ancestral Puebloan dwellings.

BIRD-WATCHING

Turkey vultures soar between April and October, and large flocks of ravens hang around all summer. Among the park's other large birds are red-tailed hawks, great horned owls, and a few golden eagles. The Steller's jay (the male looks like a blue jay with a dark hat on) frequently pierces the pinyon-juniper forest with its cries, and hummingbirds dart from flower to flower in the summer and fall. Any visit to cliff dwellings late in the day will include frolicking white-throated swifts, which make their home in rock crevices overhead.

Pick up a copy of the park's "Checklist of the Birds" brochure or visit the National Park Service's website (⊕ *www.nps.gov/meve/ planyourvisit/birdwatching.htm*) for a detailed listing of the feathered inhabitants here.

HIKING

A handful of trails lead beyond Mesa Verde's most visited sites and offer more solitude than the often-crowded cliff dwellings. The best canyon vistas can be reached if you're willing to huff and puff your way through elevation changes and switchbacks. Carry more water than you think you'll need, wear sunscreen, and bring rain gear—cloudbursts can come seemingly out of nowhere. Certain trails are open seasonally, so check with a ranger before heading out. No backcountry hiking is permitted in Mesa Verde, and pets are prohibited.

EASY

FAMILY **Farming Terrace Trail.** This 30-minute, ½-mile loop begins and ends on the spur road to Cedar Tree Tower, about 1 mile north of the Chapin Mesa area. It meanders through a series of check dams, which the Ancestral Puebloans built to create farming terraces. *Easy.* ⊠ *Park entrance road, 4 miles south of Far View Visitor Center* ⊕ *www.nps. gov/meve/planyourvisit/hiking.htm.*

Knife Edge Trail. Perfect for a sunset stroll, this easy 2-mile (round-trip) walk around the north rim of the park leads to an overlook of the Montezuma Valley. If you stop at all the flora identification points that the trail guide pamphlet suggests, the hike should take about 1½ to 2 hours. The patches of asphalt you're likely to spot along the way are leftovers from old Knife Edge Road, built in 1914 as the main entryway into the park. *Easy. ⊠ Morefield Campground, 4 miles from park entrance ⊕ www.nps.gov/meve/planyourvisit/hiking.htm.*

FAMILY **Soda Canyon Overlook Trail.** One of the easiest and most rewarding hikes in the park, this little trail travels 1½ miles round-trip through the forest on almost completely level ground. The overlook is an excellent point from which to photograph the Chapin Mesa–area cliff dwellings. *Easy. ⊠ Cliff Palace Loop Rd., about 1 mile north of Balcony House parking area ⊕ www.nps.gov/meve/planyourvisit/ hiking.htm.*

MODERATE

Fodor'sChoice **Petroglyph Point Trail.** Scramble along a narrow canyon wall to reach
★ the largest and best-known petroglyphs in Mesa Verde. Older literature occasionally refers to the destination of this 2.4-mile loop hike as "Pictograph Point," but that's a misnomer. Pictographs are painted onto the rock, and petroglyphs are carved into it. If you pose for a photo just right, you can just manage to block out the gigantic "don't touch" sign next to the rock art. A map—available at any ranger station—points out three dozen points of interest along the trail. The trail is open only when Spruce Tree House is open; check with a ranger to verify times. *Moderate. ⊠ Spruce Tree House, next to Chapin Mesa Archeological Museum ⊕ www.nps.gov/meve/ planyourvisit/hiking.htm.*

Spruce Canyon Trail. While Petroglyph Point Trail takes you along the side of the canyon, this trail ventures down into its depths. It's only 2.4 miles long, but you descend about 600 feet in elevation. Remember to save your strength; what goes down must come up again. Access to the trail is limited to times when Spruce Tree House is open; check with a ranger beforehand. *Moderate. ⊠ Spruce Tree House, next to Chapin Mesa Archeological Museum ⊕ www.nps.gov/meve/planyourvisit/hiking.htm ☞ Registration required.*

DIFFICULT

Prater Ridge Trail. This 7.8-mile round-trip loop, which starts and finishes at Morefield Campground, is the longest hike you can take inside the park. It provides fine views of Morefield Canyon to the south and the San Juan Mountains to the north. About halfway through the hike, you'll see a cut-off trail that you can take, which shortens the trip to 5 miles. *Difficult. ⊠ West end of Morefield Campground, 4 miles from park entrance ⊕ www.nps.gov/meve/planyourvisit/hiking.htm.*

STARGAZING

There are no large cities in the Four Corners area, so there is little artificial light to detract from the stars in the night sky. Far View Lodge and Morefield Campground are great for sky watching.

SHOPPING

Chapin Mesa Archeological Museum Shop. Books and videos are the primary offering here, with more than 400 titles on Ancestral Puebloan and southwestern topics. You can also find a selection of touristy T-shirts and hats. ✉ *Spruce Tree Terrace, near Chapin Mesa Archeological Museum, 5 miles from Far View Visitor Center* ☎ *970/529–4445.*

Far View Terrace Shop. In the same building as the Far View Terrace Cafe, this is the largest gift shop in the park, with gifts, souvenirs, Native American art, toys, and T-shirts galore. ✉ *Mesa Top Loop Rd., 15 miles south of park entrance* ☎ *970/529–4421, 800/449–2288* ⏲ *Daily 7 am–8 pm.*

WHAT'S NEARBY

NEARBY TOWNS

A onetime market center for cattle and crops, **Cortez,** 11 miles west of the park, is now the largest gateway town to Mesa Verde and a base for tourists visiting the Four Corners region. You can still see a rodeo here at least once a year. **Dolores,** steeped in a rich railroad history, is on the Dolores River, 19 miles north of Mesa Verde. Near both the San Juan National Forest and McPhee Reservoir, Dolores is a favorite of outdoor enthusiasts. East of Mesa Verde by 36 miles, **Durango,** the region's main hub, comes complete with a variety of restaurants and hotels, shopping, and outdoor equipment shops. Durango became a town in 1881 when the Denver and Rio Grande Railroad pushed its tracks across the neighboring San Juan Mountains.

WHERE TO EAT

IN THE PARK

$ AMERICAN

🍴 **Far View Terrace Cafe.** This full-service cafeteria offers great views, but it's nothing fancy. Grab a simple coffee here or head across the dining room to Mesa Mocha for a latte. Order an omelet cooked to order, or if you're in a hurry to hit the park trails, you can grab a to-go lunch. Dinner options include a Navajo taco piled high with all the fixings. [$] *Average main: $8* ✉ *Across from Far View Visitor Center* ☎ *970/529–4444* 🌐 *www.visitmesaverde.com/dining/far-view-terrace-cafe.aspx* ⏲ *Closed late Oct.–early May.*

$ CAFÉ FAMILY

🍴 **Knife Edge Cafe.** Located in the Morefield Campground, this simple restaurant in a covered outdoor terrace with picnic tables serves a hearty all-you-can-eat pancake breakfast with sausage every morning. Coffee and beverages are also available. It also offers lunch and dinner. [$] *Average main: $6* ✉ *4 miles south of park entrance* ☎ *970/565–2133* 🌐 *www.nps.gove/meve/planyourvisit/restaurants.htm* ⏲ *Closed mid-Sept.–early May.*

CLOSE UP

Best Campgrounds in Mesa Verde

Morefield Campground is the only option within the park, and it's an excellent one. Reservations are accepted; it's open late May through early September. In nearby Mancos, just across the highway from the park entrance, there's a campground with full amenities (but no electrical hookups), while the San Juan National Forest offers backcountry camping.

Morefield Campground. With 267 campsites, including 15 full-hookup RV sites, access to trailheads, and plenty of amenities, the only campground in the park is an appealing mini-city for campers. It's a 40-minute drive to reach the park's most popular sites. Reservations are accepted. 4 miles south of park entrance, ☎ *970/564–4300, 800/449–2288* 🌐 *www.visitmesaverde.com.*

$$$ AMERICAN Fodor's Choice ★ 🍴 **Metate Room.** The park's rugged terrain contrasts with this relaxing space just off the lobby of the Far View Lodge. The well-regarded dining room is upscale, but the atmosphere remains casual. A wall of windows affords wonderful Mesa Verde vistas. The menu is based on regional heritage foods, including corn, beans, and squash (all staples for the Ancestral Puebloans). Many entrées are unique, such as cinnamon-chile pork tenderloin or regional quail with prickly-pear red-pepper jam. Every table gets mesa bread and black bean hummus for starters. There's an array of local wines (try Cortez's own Guy Drew) and cocktails with kitschy names, like the "Long House Lemonade." Gluten-free and vegan options are available. [$] *Average main: $25* ✉ *Far View Lodge, 1 Navajo Road, across from Far View Visitor Center, 15 miles southwest of park entrance* ☎ *970/529–4421* 🌐 *www.visitmesaverde.com/dining/metate-room.aspx* 🕒 *Closed late Oct.–mid Apr. No lunch.*

$ AMERICAN 🍴 **Spruce Tree Terrace Cafe.** This small cafeteria has a limited selection of hot food, coffee, salads, and sandwiches. The patio is pleasant, and it's conveniently located across the street from the museum. The Spruce Tree Terrace is also the only food concession in the park that's open year-round. Try the popular Navajo tacos. [$] *Average main: $8* ✉ *Near Chapin Mesa Archeological Museum, 5 miles south of the Far View Visitor Center* ☎ *970/529–4521* 🌐 *www.visitmesaverde.com/dining/spruce-tree-terrace-cafe.aspx* 🕒 *No dinner.*

PICNIC AREAS

FAMILY **Chapin Mesa Picnic Area.** This is the nicest and largest picnic area in the park. It has about 40 tables under shade trees and a great view into Spruce Canyon, as well as flushing toilets. ✉ *Near Chapin Mesa Archeological Museum, 5 miles south of Far View Visitor Center* 🌐 *www.nps.gov/meve* 🎫 *Free.*

FAMILY **Wetherill Mesa Picnic Area.** Ten tables placed under lush shade trees, along with nearby drinking water and restrooms, make this a pleasant spot for lunch. ✉ *12 miles southwest of Far View Visitor Center* 🎫 *Free.*

WHERE TO STAY

IN THE PARK

$$
HOTEL
Fodor's Choice
★

Far View Lodge. Talk about a view—all rooms have a private balcony, from which you can admire views of the neighboring states of Arizona, Utah, and New Mexico up to 100 miles in the distance. **Pros:** close to the key sites; views are spectacular. **Cons:** simple rooms and amenities, with no TV; walls are thin and less than soundproof; limited cell phone service. $ *Rooms from: $135* ⊠ *Across from Far View Visitor Center, 1 Navajo Road, 15 miles southwest of park entrance* ☎ *602/331–5210, 800/449–2288* ⊕ *www.visitmesaverde.com* ☯ *Closed Nov.–Mar.* ➹ *150 rooms* ❚◯❙ *No meals.*

SOUTH CENTRAL COLORADO

with Colorado Springs, Royal Gorge
& Great Sand Dunes

Updated by
Whitney Bryen

Stretching from majestic mountains into rugged, high desert plains, south central Colorado has plenty of 14,000-foot peaks, astounding natural hot springs, striking red-rock out-croppings, rivers that roll with white-water rapids in spring, and even the incongruous sight of towering sand dunes dwarfed by a mountain range at their back. It's worth a few days for white-water rafting, hiking in the backcountry, and exploring historic gold-mining towns. Colorado Springs is one of the fastest growing cities in the West, but other parts of the area have a barely discovered feel.

Framed by Pikes Peak, Colorado Springs is the region's population center and a hub for the military and the high-tech industry. The city has been a destination for out-of-towners since its founding in 1870, due to the alleged healing power of the local spring water and clean air. The gold rush fueled the city's boom through the early 20th century, as the military boom did following World War II. With more than 650,000 residents in the metro area, Colorado Springs offers a mix of history and modernity, as well as incredible access to the trails and red-rock scenery in this section of the Rockies.

Surrounding Colorado Springs is a ring of smaller cities and alluring natural attractions. To the west, between alpine and desert scenery, are the Florissant Fossil Beds, the Royal Gorge, and Cripple Creek, which offers gambling in casinos housed in historic buildings. You can go rafting near Cañon City, while Pueblo has a dash of public art and history museums.

Outdoorsy types love the entire area: camping and hiking are especially superb in the San Isabel and Pike national forests. Climbers head to the Collegiate Peaks around Buena Vista and Salida (west of Colorado Springs) and the Cañon City area for a variety of ascents from moderate to difficult. Farther south, you can take the Highway of Legends Scenic Byway, which travels through the San Isabel National Forest and over high mountain passes. You can even take a day trip on the Rio Grande Scenic Railroad or the Cumbres & Toltec Scenic Railroad, which travels through regions not reachable by car.

TOP REASONS TO GO

Hike a Fourteener: Coloradans collect hikes to the summit of Four-teeners—mountains that top 14,000 feet above sea level—like trophies.

Play on the Sand Dunes: At Great Sand Dunes, one of nature's most spectacular sandboxes, you'll feel like a kid again as you hike up a 750-foot dune then roll down (or sandboard) the other side.

Raft on the Arkansas: The Arkansas River is one of the most popular rivers for rafting and kayaking—from gentle floats to Class V rapids—in the United States.

Ride Up Pikes Peak: Katharine Bates wrote "America the Beautiful" after riding to the top of Pikes Peak. Today you can drive or ride the cog railway to the top for the same see-forever views.

Visit the U.S. Air Force Academy: Here you can learn more about the academy that trains future Air Force leaders and visit the stunning, nondenominational Cadet Chapel.

ORIENTATION AND PLANNING

GETTING ORIENTED

This region, which encompasses the south central section of Colorado, stretches from a collection of the state's 14,000-foot-high mountains in the heart of the Rockies eastward to Kansas, and from Colorado Springs south to the New Mexico state line. Pikes Peak, one of the most famous of Colorado's Fourteeners, forms the backdrop for Colorado Springs. Farther west, the Arkansas River towns of Buena Vista and Salida are within view of the Fourteeners of the Collegiate Peaks. Farther south, the Rio Grande runs through the flat San Luis Valley, which is lined by the Sangre de Cristo range. Cuchara Valley, just north of New Mexico, is framed by the Spanish Peaks.

Colorado Springs. About 70 miles south of Denver, Colorado Springs is a comfortable base camp for travelers headed for high altitude and high adventure. Colorado's second-largest city has natural attractions like Pikes Peak and Garden of the Gods, and man-made additions like the Broadmoor luxury hotel and the U.S. Air Force Academy.

Side Trips from Colorado Springs. You could gamble or visit a gold mine and learn more about the gold rush in Cripple Creek. If you prefer outdoor adventures, take a walk among petrified tree trunks in Florissant Fossil Beds or go river rafting through the Royal Gorge near Cañon City.

The Collegiate Peaks. Buena Vista and Salida provide easy access to the largest collection of 14,000-foot-or-higher peaks in Colorado, perfect for hiking, boating, river rafting, horseback riding, and mountain biking in wilderness areas.

Southeast Colorado. If you're looking for a mountain drive with spectacular and diverse scenery, take the Highway of Legends Scenic Byway. Tiny towns along the way are in Cuchara Valley; Pueblo and Trinidad are larger hubs.

The San Luis Valley. You can play like a child rolling around the dunes at the Great Sand Dunes National Park and Preserve. Leave time for a drive through the tiny nearby towns or a ride on one of the two scenic railroads.

PLANNING

WHEN TO GO

Colorado Springs is a good year-round choice because winters are relatively mild. Late spring or early summer is best if you want adrenaline-rush rafting, because the snowmelt is feeding the rivers. Summer is tourist season everywhere in south central Colorado. Early fall is another good time to visit, especially when the aspen leaves are turning gold. Some of the lodging properties in the smaller towns are closed in winter, although there are always some open for the cross-country skiers who enjoy staying in the small high-mountain towns.

PLANNING YOUR TIME

If you have a short amount of time in the region, base yourself in Colorado Springs, or in neighboring Manitou Springs. On the first day, take the Pikes Peak Cog Railway to the top of the mountain and explore the shops in Manitou Springs. The following day, explore the "natural" sites, such as Cave of the Winds, Seven Falls, and Garden of the Gods. Visit the Broadmoor for a look at its palatial architecture, perhaps stopping for lunch or ending the day there in the Golden Bee. If the kids are along, try one of the outdoor settings above, then visit the Cheyenne Mountain Zoo and the Ghost Town Museum. End the day at the Flying W Chuckwagon Suppers & Western Stage Show. End your stint by hiking in Red Rock Canyon park or visiting Cripple Creek if you enjoy gaming. If you prefer kid-oriented choices, head to the Royal Gorge and Buckskin Joe Frontier Town, both in Cañon City.

GETTING HERE AND AROUND

AIR TRAVEL

Colorado Springs Airport (COS) is the major airport in the region, with more than a dozen nonstop destinations. Most south central residents south of Colorado Springs drive to this city to fly out.

Alternatively, you can choose to fly to Denver International Airport (DEN), which has a lot more nonstop flights from other major cities to Colorado. It's a 70-mile drive from Denver to the Springs, but during rush hour it might take a solid two hours, whether you're in your own car or in one of the Denver–Colorado Springs shuttles. It's fastest to take the E–470 toll road. Another option is Pueblo Memorial Airport (PUB), which has direct flights to Denver on United, Delta, and American Airlines.

Airport Contacts Colorado Springs Airport (COS). ☎ 719/550–1900 ⊕ www.flycos.com. **Denver International Airport (DEN).** ☎ 303/342–2000, 800/247–2336 ⊕ www.flydenver.com. **Pueblo Memorial Airport (PUB).** ☎ 719/553–2760 ⊕ flypueblo.com.

CAR TRAVEL

In Colorado Springs (whose airport has the typical lineup of car-rental agencies), the main north–south roads are I–25, Academy Boulevard, Nevada Avenue, and Powers Boulevard, and each will get you where you want to go in good time; east–west routes along Woodmen Road (far north), Austin Bluffs Parkway (north central), and Platte Boulevard (south central) can get backed up.

Running north–south from Wyoming to New Mexico, I–25 bisects Colorado and is the major artery into the area.

TRAIN TRAVEL

Amtrak's *Southwest Chief* stops daily in Trinidad and La Junta.

PARKS AND RECREATION AREAS

South central Colorado is chock-full of parks and recreational areas. Almost every chamber of commerce will have a list of trails in the near vicinity, so when you're asking for general information about the city, ask for a list of trails, too. ■ TIP→ **Many cities are still recovering from the 2013 flood that caused significant damage across the state so call the local parks department or forest service for closures before venturing out.** The Arkansas River flows through this region, so every spring and summer people come here to raft through a mix of challenging white-water rapids interspersed with smoothly flowing sections. Pike, bass, and trout are plentiful in this region: popular fishing spots include Spinney Mountain Reservoir (between Florissant and Buena Vista), the Arkansas and South Platte rivers, and Trinidad Lake. Great Sand Dunes National Park and Preserve in the San Luis Valley is perfect for walking up (and sliding down) the dunes, hiking on mountain trails, kite flying, and wildlife viewing. Monarch, west of Salida, is the nearest ski area.

Arkansas Headwaters Recreation Area. This area is unique because it follows a linear 152-mile stretch of the Arkansas River, from the mountains near Leadville to Lake Pueblo. The Arkansas River is popular for rafting and kayaking, and fishermen love it for its brown trout. (Anglers near Salida reported good luck with 'hoppers, not to mention the caddis hatch every Mother's Day.) There are six campgrounds along the river. ⊠ *Arkansas Headwaters Recreation Area, 307 W. Sackett Ave., Salida* ☎ *719/539–7289* ⊕ *www.parks.state.co.us/ parks/arkansasheadwaters.*

Collegiate Peaks Wilderness. This wilderness region northwest of Buena Vista includes 14 mountains above 14,000 feet and is known for superb hiking, mountain biking, and climbing and a few ghost towns. ⊠ *Leadville Ranger District, San Isabel National Forest, 810 Front St., Leadville* ☎ *719/486–0749.*

Pike National Forest. This massive forest encompasses millions of acres of public land that stretch along the Front Range and go deep into the Rockies. Pikes Peak is the best-known 14,000-footer in Pike—and one of the most famous in the state. Forest entry is always free. ⊠ *Forest Service Office, 2840 Kachina Dr., Pueblo* ☎ *719/553–1400* ⊕ *www. fs.usda.gov/psicc.*

Ring of the Peak. This collection of trails, four-wheel-drive roads, and a few paved roads circles Pikes Peak. Altitudes range between 6,400 and 11,400 feet. Check the website for trail access. ⊕ *www. ringthepeak.com.*

RESTAURANTS

Many restaurants serve regional trout and game, as well as locally grown fruits and vegetables. In summer, look for cantaloupe from the town of Rocky Ford, the self-proclaimed "Melon Capital of the World." Colorado Springs offers unique Colorado cuisine that zings taste buds without zapping budgets.

HOTELS

The lodging star is the Broadmoor resort in Colorado Springs, built from the booty of the late 19th-century gold-rush days, but there are also predictable boxy-bed motel rooms awaiting travelers at the junctions of major highways throughout the region. Interspersed are quaint mom-and-pop motels, as well as bed-and-breakfasts and rustic lodges in tourist districts. *Hotel reviews have been shortened. For full information, visit Fodors.com.*

WHAT IT COSTS				
	$	**$$**	**$$$**	**$$$$**
Restaurants	under $13	$13–$18	$19–$25	over $25
Hotels	under $121	$121–$170	$171–$230	over $230

Restaurant prices are for a main course at dinner, excluding 7.4% tax. Hotel prices are for two people in a standard double room in high season, excluding service charges and 9.4%–11.7% tax.

COLORADO SPRINGS

The contented residents of the Colorado Springs area believe they live in an ideal location, and it's hard to argue with them. To the west the Rockies form a majestic backdrop. To the east the plains stretch for miles. Taken together, the setting ensures a mild, sunny climate year-round, and makes skiing and golfing on the same day feasible with no more than a two- or three-hour drive. You don't have to choose between adventures here: you can climb the Collegiate Peaks one day and go white-water rafting on the Arkansas River the next.

The state's second-largest city, it has a strong cultural scene, between the outstanding Colorado Springs Fine Arts Center, the Colorado Springs Philharmonic, and the variety of plays and musicals offered at several independent theaters.

The region abounds in natural and man-made wonders, from the red sandstone monoliths of the Garden of the Gods to the space-age architecture of the U.S. Air Force Academy's Cadet Chapel. The most indelible landmark is unquestionably Pikes Peak (14,115 feet); after seeing the view from the peak, Katharine Lee Bates penned "America the Beautiful." Pikes Peak is a constant reminder that this contemporary city is still close to nature. Purple in the early morning, snow-packed after winter storms, capped with clouds on windy days, the mountain is a landmark for directions and, when needed, a focus of contemplation.

GETTING HERE AND AROUND

It's easiest to explore this region in a private car because the attractions are spread out. If you're staying in the heart of town and don't intend to head out to Pikes Peak, the Air Force Academy, or other attractions farther away, you could use the Mountain Metropolitan Transit bus system or grab a taxi.

ESSENTIALS

Transportation Contacts Colorado Springs Shuttle. ☎ *719/687–3456* ⊕ *www.coloradoshuttle.com.* **Mountain Metropolitan Transit.** ☎ *719/385–7433* ⊕ *www.mmtransit.com.* **Yellow Cab.** ☎ *719/634–5000* ⊕ *www.yccos.com.*

Visitor Information Colorado Springs Convention and Visitors Bureau. ⊠ *515 S. Cascade Ave.* ☎ *719/635–7506, 800/888–4748* ⊕ *www.visitcos. com.* **Colorado Springs Parks, Recreation and Cultural Services Department.** ☎ *719/385–5940* ⊕ *coloradosprings.gov.* **Manitou Springs Chamber of Commerce.** ⊠ *354 Manitou Ave.* ☎ *719/685–5089, 800/642–2567* ⊕ *www. manitousprings.org.* **Tri-Lakes Chamber of Commerce (Palmer Lake).** ⊠ *166 2nd St., Monument* ☎ *719/481–3282* ⊕ *www.trilakeschamber.com.*

EXPLORING

Pikes Peak is a must-do and pairs nicely with an afternoon of poking around in the shops of Manitou Springs. The red rocks of Garden of the Gods and Cheyenne Cañon Park are the other natural showstoppers—mix and match them with exploring the surrounding neighborhoods and tourist attractions. And don't forget the U.S. Air Force Academy, just north of town.

PIKES PEAK AND MANITOU SPRINGS

Access points for scaling the mighty Pikes Peak are in the Manitou Springs area, a quaint National Historic Landmark District that exudes an informal charm. Stop at the chamber for a free map of the 8 mineral-springs drinking fountains and historic sites. On your self-guided tour, stop by 7 Minute Spring or Twin Springs during the day, or for an after-dinner spritz (it tastes and acts just like Alka-Seltzer).

TIMING

It takes a full day to visit Pikes Peak, explore Manitou Springs, and visit some of the attractions along U.S. 24, if you want to enjoy each without doing a marathon sprint. Whether you head up Pikes Peak in a car and stop for lunch at the top or take the train (which includes a stop at the summit), plan at least four hours. Visiting the variety of shops, which sell souvenirs to antiques, along historic Manitou Springs's main street, is a good way to stretch your legs after the journey to the peak. Heading underground into Cave of the Winds or visiting the Cliff Dwellings Museum will easily fill up the rest of the day.

TOP ATTRACTIONS

FAMILY **Cave of the Winds.** Discovered by two boys in 1880, the cave has been exploited as a tourist sensation ever since. The only way to enter the site is by purchasing a tour, but once inside the cave you'll forget the hype and commercialism of the gimmicky entrance. The cave contains examples of every major sort of limestone formation, from icicle-shaped stalactites and stump-like stalagmites to delicate cave flowers, fragile anthodite crystals, flowstone (or frozen waterfalls), and cave popcorn. Enthusiastic guides host easy 45-minute walking tours, adventurous cave expeditions, and lantern tours that last 1½ hours. Games like laser tag and rides like the Terror-dactyl, which swings riders off a 200-foot cliff, offer more fun outside of the cave. ⊠ *100 Cave of the Winds Rd., off U.S. 24* ☎ *719/685–5444* ⊕ *www.caveofthewinds.com* ⊠ *$15–$45* ⊙ *Memorial Day to Labor Day, daily 9–9; early Sept.–late May, daily 10–5.*

FAMILY **Pikes Peak.** If you want to see the view from the top of Pikes Peak, which
Fodor's Choice Katharine Bates described in "America the Beautiful," head up this
★ 14,115-foot-high mountain on a train, in a car, or in a pair of hiking boots if you've got the stamina. Stop for a donut at the Summit House café and trading post at the very top of the mountain or for souvenirs at gift shops located at miles 6 and 13 along the highway. Whichever route you choose to take up the prominent peak, you'll understand why the pioneers heading West via wagon train used to say: "Pikes Peak or Bust." ⊠ *U.S. 24 ✛ 5 miles west of Manitou Springs* ☎ *719/684–9383* ⊕ *pikespeak.us.com* ⊠ *$12 per person, $40 per vehicle May–Nov.; $10 per person, $35 per vehicle Dec.–Apr.* ⊙ *Summit House June–Aug., daily 8–8; Nov.–Apr., daily 9–3:30.*

Pikes Peak Highway. You can drive the 19-mile Pikes Peak Highway, which rises nearly 7,000 feet in its precipitous, dizzying climb; stop at the top for lunch and to enjoy the view; then be at the base again in approximately three hours. This is the same route that leading race-car drivers follow every year in the famed Pikes Peak Hill Climb, at speeds that have reached 123 miles per hour. ⊠ *Colorado Springs* 🎫 *$12 per person; $40 per vehicle.*

12

Barr Trail. The 11¾-mile hike up Barr Trail gains 7,900 feet in elevation before you reach the summit. Halfway up the steep trail is Barr Camp, where many hikers spend the night. ⊠ *Colorado Springs* ⊕ *www.barrtrail.net.*

Pikes Peak Cog Railway. The world's highest cog train departs from Manitou Springs and follows a frolicking stream up a steep canyon, through stands of quaking aspen and towering lodgepole pines, before reaching the timberline, where you can see far into the plains until arriving at the summit. Advance reservations are recommended in summer and on weekends, as this three-hour trip sells out regularly. ⊠ *515 Ruxton Ave.* 🕾 *719/685–5401* ⊕ *www.cograilway.com* 🎫 *$37* ⊙ *Daily; call for schedule* ⚠ *Reservations essential.*

WORTH NOTING

Manitou Cliff Dwellings. Some Ancestral Puebloan cliff dwellings that date from the 1100s to the 1400s have been moved from other sites in southern Colorado to this museum. Two rooms of artifacts in the museum offer information on the history of the dwellings. Smartphone codes provide a free audio tour through the space and a local woman occasionally brings rescue wolves to the museum, bringing the history to life. ⊠ *10 Cliff Rd., off U.S. 24* 🕾 *719/685–5242, 800/354–9971* ⊕ *www.cliffdwellingsmuseum.com* 🎫 *$9.50* ⊙ *May–Sept., daily 9–6; Oct., Nov., Mar., and Apr., daily 9–5; Dec.–Feb., daily 10–4.*

Manitou Springs Mineral Springs. The town grew around the springs, so there are eight mineral springs open to the public in or near downtown. Competitions to design the fountains that bring the spring water to the public ensured that each fountain design is unique. It's a bring-your-own-cup affair; the water (frequently tested) is potable and free. The chamber of commerce publishes a free guide to the springs and the Mineral Springs Foundation offers tours. ⊠ *Colorado Springs* 🕾 *719/685–5089* ⊕ *www.visitcos.com/manitou-mineral-springs* 🎫 *Free.*

Miramont Castle Museum. Commissioned in 1895 as the private home of French priest Jean-Baptiste Francolon, this museum in Manitou Springs is still decorated, in part, as if a family lived here. More than 30 rooms in this 14,000-square-foot space offer a wide variety of displays and furnishings primarily from the Victorian era. Have lunch or high tea in the Queens Parlour Tea Room. ⊠ *9 Capitol Hill Ave., Manitou Springs* 🕾 *719/685–1011* ⊕ *www.miramontcastle.org* 🎫 *$9* ⊙ *June–Aug., daily 9–5; Sept.–May, Tues.–Sat. 10–4, Sun. noon–4.*

THE BROADMOOR AND CHEYENNE CAÑON

Up in the Cheyenne Cañon section of town there are some terrific natural sites. Along the way you can view some of the city's exclusive neighborhoods and stop for lunch at the Broadmoor.

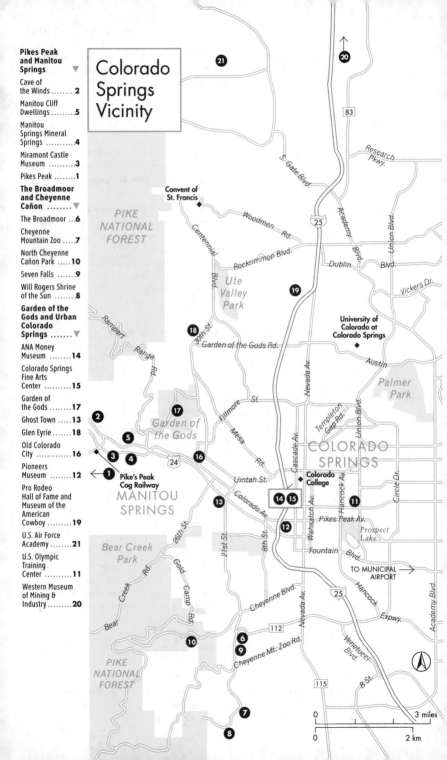

Colorado Springs Vicinity

12

TIMING

This is a good drive if there are kids in your group, because you can include stops at the Cheyenne Mountain Zoo and the Will Rogers Shrine of the Sun. Young ones can also blow off any extra energy racing up and down the paths at Seven Falls. Depending upon where you decide to stop, this could take a half to a full day.

TOP ATTRACTIONS

Fodor'sChoice
★
The Broadmoor. This pink-stucco Italianate complex, built in 1918, is truly one of the world's finest luxury resorts. Even if you don't stay here, stop by for lunch on one of the many restaurant patios in summer and to take a paddleboat ride on Lake Cheyenne, which anchors several of the resort's buildings. The Sunday brunch here is legendary (reservations are almost mandatory), and don't miss Play, the hotel's new gaming bar with six luxurious lanes of bowling, shuffleboard, and plenty of other diversions. ⊠ *1 Lake Circle* ☎ *719/634–7711, 800/634-7711* ⊕ *www. broadmoor.com.*

FAMILY **Cheyenne Mountain Zoo.** America's highest zoo, at 6,700 feet, has more than 950 animals housed amid mossy boulders and ponderosa pines. You can hand-feed the giraffe herd in the zoo's African Rift Valley and check out the animals living in Primate World, Rocky Mountain Wild, or the Asian Highlands. ⊠ *4250 Cheyenne Mountain Zoo Rd.* ☎ *719/633–9925* ⊕ *www.cmzoo.org* ☒ *$17.25, includes admission to Will Rogers Shrine* ⊙ *Daily 9–5.*

FAMILY **North Cheyenne Cañon Park.** This is Colorado Springs at its best. The 1,600 acres of this city park, which is open year-round, manifest nature and natural history without a hint of commercialism—or charge. The canyon's moderate hikes include the Lower Columbine and Mount Cutler trails, each less than a 3-mile round-trip. Both afford a view of the city and a sense of accomplishment. ⊠ *2120 S. Cheyenne Cañon Rd.* ☎ *719/385–6086* ⊕ *parks.coloradosprings.gov* ☒ *Free* ⊙ *daily 6 am–11 pm.*

Starsmore Discovery Center. At the mouth of the canyon off Cheyenne Boulevard, this center is chock-full of nature exhibits. ⊠ *2120 S. Cheyenne Cañon Rd.* ☎ *719/385–6086* ⊕ *parks.coloradosprings.gov/ starsmore* ⊙ *May–Sept., daily 9–5. Call for seasonal hrs.*

Seven Falls. After flooding badly damaged the stunning red-rock canyon in 2013, the falls, which plummet into a tiny emerald pool, reopened in the summer of 2015 with new life. Visitors can no longer drive the canyon road to the falls but parking is free at the Broadmoor Hotel where a shuttle will take passengers to and from the site. A series of zip lines ranging from 300 to more than 1,722 feet long send adventurers sailing nearly 500 feet above the canyon floor, and rope bridges that hang about 300 feet high provide a similar bird's-eye view at a slower pace. The new Restaurant 1859 has a patio overlooking the falls where patrons will find buttermilk biscuits and Virginia country ham, local trout prepared eight different ways, and a mixed game grill. ⊠ *1 Lake Ave.* ⊹ *Free parking at the Broadmoor where a shuttle takes passengers* ☎ *855/923–7272* ⊕ *www.sevenfalls.com* ☒ *$14* ⊙ *Call for seasonal hrs.*

WORTH NOTING

FAMILY **Will Rogers Shrine of the Sun.** This five-story tower was dedicated in 1937, after the tragic plane crash that claimed Rogers's life. Its interior is painted with all manner of Western murals in which Colorado Springs benefactor Spencer Penrose figures prominently, and is plastered with photos and homespun sayings of Rogers, America's favorite cowboy. In the chapel are 15th- and 16th-century European artworks. ⊠ *4250 Cheyenne Mountain Zoo Rd.* ☎ *719/578–5367* ⊕ *www.cmzoo.org/ index.php/about-the-zoo/history/will-rogers-shrine/* ⊠ *$17.25, includes admission to Cheyenne Mountain Zoo* ⊙ *Daily 9–5.*

GARDEN OF THE GODS AND URBAN COLORADO SPRINGS

Depending on which museums you decide to visit, a tour of Garden of the Gods and urban Colorado Springs could take from two-thirds of a day to a full day to take everything in, from learning how the pioneers struggled to survive and thrive to strolling through the stunning red-rock cliffs and visiting the effortlessly educational and entertaining Trading Post at Garden of the Gods.

TOP ATTRACTIONS

Colorado Springs Fine Arts Center. This regional museum has a fine permanent collection of modern art and excellent rotating exhibits. Some highlight the cultural contributions of regional artists; others focus on famous artists such as the glassmaker Dale Chihuly and American modernist Georgia O'Keeffe. Enjoy the view of Pikes Peak and the mountains from the patio in the summer. ⊠ *30 W. Dale St.* ☎ *719/634–5581* ⊕ *www.csfineartscenter.org* ⊠ *$12* ⊙ *Tues.–Sun. 10–5.*

Fodor's Choice ★ **Garden of the Gods.** These magnificent, eroded red-sandstone formations—from gnarled jutting spires to sensuously abstract monoliths—were sculpted more than 300 million years ago. Follow the road as it loops past such oddities as the Three Graces, the Siamese Twins, and the Kissing Camels or get an up-close look at the rocks with a guided climbing expedition booked at the visitor center. High Point, near the south entrance, provides camera hounds with the ultimate photo op: a formation known as Balanced Rock and jagged formations that frame Pikes Peak. The visitor center has maps of the trails and several geological, historical, and interactive, hands-on displays, as well as a café. It's a short, paved hike into the park from the parking lot. ⊠ *Visitor and Nature Center, 1805 N. 30th St., at Gateway Rd.* ☎ *719/634–6666* ⊕ *www.gardenofgods.com* ⊠ *Free* ⊙ *May–Oct., daily 5 am–11 pm; Nov.–Apr., daily 5 am–9 pm.*

Pioneers Museum. Once the Old El Paso County Courthouse, this repository has artifacts relating to the entire Pikes Peak area. The historic courtroom is absolutely elegant, and so perfectly appointed that it looks as if a judge will walk in any minute to start a trial. It's most notable for the special exhibits the museum puts together or receives on loan from institutions like the Smithsonian. ⊠ *215 S. Tejon St.* ☎ *719/385–5990* ⊕ *www.cspm.org* ⊠ *Free* ⊙ *Tues.–Sat. 10–5.*

Fodor's Choice ★ **U.S. Air Force Academy.** The academy, which set up camp in 1954, is one of the most popular attractions in Colorado. Highlights include the futuristic design, 18,000 beautiful acres of land, and antique and

12

historic aircraft displays. At the visitor center you'll find photo exhibits, a model of a cadet's room, a gift shop, a snack bar, and a 21-minute film designed to make you want to enlist on the spot. Other stops on the tour include a B-52 display, sports facilities, a parade ground, and the chapel. Some days you can catch the impressive cadet lunch formation that begins at 11:45. The Air Force chapel, which can accommodate simultaneous Catholic, Jewish, and Protestant services, is easily recognized by its unconventional design, which features 17 spires that resemble airplane wings. Don't miss the smaller chapels, including the downstairs Buddhist room. Visitors can enter only through the North Gate. ⊠ *N. Gate Blvd., off I–25, Exit 156* ☎ *719/333–2025* ⊕ *www. usafa.af.mil/information/visitors* 🖾 *Free* ☉ *Daily 9–5.*

FAMILY **U.S. Olympic Training Center.** America's hopefuls come to train and be tested at this flagship training center for the U.S. Olympic Committee and Olympic Training Center programs—the U.S. swimming and shooting teams are headquartered here. And, depending on which teams are in residence at the time, you might catch a glimpse of some future Wheaties-box material. Guided tours are hosted every half hour in the summer and every hour in the off season and begin with a video, followed by a 30-minute walk around the facilities. You can also find red, white, and blue souvenirs at the Team USA gift shop. ⊠ *1750 E. Boulder St.* ☎ *719/866–4618* ⊕ *www.teamusa.org* 🖾 *Free* ☉ *June–Aug., Mon.– Sat. 9–4:30; Sept.–May, Mon.–Sat. 9–4.*

WORTH NOTING

FAMILY **ANA Money Museum.** The American Numismatic Association's fascinating Money Museum has a collection of old gold coins, mistakes made at the U.S. Mint, and currency from around the world. Tours are available Tuesday to Friday. ⊠ *818 N. Cascade Ave.* ☎ *800/367–9723, 719/482– 9834* ⊕ *www.money.org* 🖾 *$5* ☉ *Tues.–Sat. 10:30–5.*

FAMILY **Ghost Town.** You can play a real player piano and a nickelodeon at this Western town with a sheriff's office, general store, saloon, and smithy. There's also gold panning in the summer. ⊠ *400 S. 21st St.* ☎ *719/634– 0696* ⊕ *www.ghosttownmuseum.com* 🖾 *$7.50* ☉ *June–Aug., Mon.– Sat. 9–6, Sun. 10–6; Sept.–May, Mon.–Sat. 10–5, Sun. 10–6.*

Glen Eyrie. General William Jackson Palmer, the founder of Colorado Springs, was greatly influenced by European architecture and lifestyle, and lived in this grandiose estate from its beginnings in the 1870s until his death in 1909. Original fireplaces with stone, metal, and tile details are one of the highlights of this mansion-turned-castle. Many of its rocks were hewn with the moss still clinging, to give them an aged look. The center is maintained by a fundamentalist Christian ministry called the Navigators, which runs programs and seminars. An afternoon English tea is offered daily. ⊠ *3820 30th St.* ☎ *719/634–0808* ⊕ *www.gleneyrie. org* 🖾 *$8* ☉ *Tours: June–Aug., daily at 1; Sept.–May, Thurs.–Mon. at 1.*

Old Colorado City. Once a separate, rowdier town where miners caroused, today the stretch of Colorado Avenue between 24th Street and 28th Street, west of downtown, is a kitchy National Historic Landmark District whose restored buildings house galleries and boutiques as well as shops with inexpensive souvenirs and restaurants. ⊠ *Colorado Ave., between 24th and 28th Sts.* ⊕ *www.shopoldcoloradocity.com.*

FAMILY **Pro Rodeo Hall of Fame and Museum of the American Cowboy.** Even a ten-derfoot would get a kick out of this museum, which includes changing displays of Western art; permanent photo exhibits that capture the excitement of bronco-bustin' and the lonely life of the cowpoke; and gorgeous saddles and belt buckles. ⊠ *101 Pro Rodeo Dr., off I–25* ☎ *719/528–4764* ⊕ *www.prorodeohalloffame.com* ⊡ *$8* ⊘ *May–Aug., daily 9–5; Sept.–Apr., Wed.–Sun. 9–5.*

Western Museum of Mining & Industry. The region's rich history of mining is represented through comprehensive exhibits of equipment and techniques and hands-on demonstrations, including gold panning. The 27-acre mountain site has several outdoor exhibits, and is a great spot for a picnic. ⊠ *225 N. Gate Blvd., off I–25* ☎ *719/488–0880, 800/752–6558* ⊕ *www.wmmi.org* ⊡ *$8* ⊘ *Mon.–Sat. 9–4.*

SPORTS AND THE OUTDOORS

ADVENTURE TOURS

Adventures Out West. This outfitter offers Jeep tours of Colorado Springs and Manitou Springs covering local sites like Garden of the Gods, Pike National Forest, and North Cheyenne Cañon Park. It can also arrange other activities, such as ballooning, horseback riding, zip-lining, and rafting. ⊠ *1680 S. 21st St.* ☎ *719/578–0935, 800/755–0935* ⊕ *www. adventuresoutwest.com.*

Echo Canyon River Expeditions. Rafting on the Arkansas and Colorado rivers is offered by this established company. A Raft and Rail trip includes a morning ride on the Royal Gorge Railroad and rafting on the Arkansas River in the afternoon. The company will also customize trips pairing rafting with zip-lining, ATV tours, and more. ⊠ *45000 U.S. 50, Cañon City* ☎ *800/755–3246* ⊕ *www.raftecho.com.*

GOLF

Fodor'sChoice ★ **The Broadmoor Golf Club.** The three courses here offer distinctly diverse challenges, in part because they travel over a variety of terrain on the resort's 3,000 acres in the Rocky Mountain foothills. Donald Ross designed the original resort course in 1918, but today the East Course is a mix including nine of the original holes and nine more designed by Robert Trent Jones Sr. in 1952. The West Course is also a combination of holes designed by the golf-course architects, but it's at a higher elevation (6,800 feet above sea level), and has more-vicious doglegs, rolling fairways, tree-lined holes, and multilevel greens. The Mountain Course has some wide forgiving fairways and large greens, but major elevation changes add special challenges while providing outstanding mountain views. ⊠ *The Broadmoor, 1 Lake Circle* ☎ *719/577–5790* ⊕ *www. broadmoor.com* ⊡ *East Course, $150 for 9 holes, $275 for 18 holes; Mountain Course, $125 for 9 holes, $220 for 18 holes; West Course, $125 for 9 holes, $220 for 18 holes* ⌦ *East Course: 18 holes, 6651 yards, par 72; Mountain Course: 18 holes, 6325 yards, par 72; West Course: 18 holes, 6173 yards, par 72* ⊘ *Mountain Course closed Nov.–Apr.; West Course closed mid-Nov.–Mar.* ⛴ *Reservations essential.*

12

HIKING

Pikes Peak Greenway Trail. This trail combines with the New Santa Fe Regional Trail for 35 miles of multisurface hiking and biking trails running from Palmer Lake to the town of Fountain. At this writing, a 7-mile section that goes through the Air Force Academy was not accessible to the public due to a recent upgrade in the facility's security clearance, though locals say the clearance could be downgraded, reopening the trail. Past the academy, the trail then flows over gently rolling hills and finally follows a straight line and level course over an abandoned railroad track for the last 6½ miles into Palmer. With many uncertainties, your safest bet is to start at America the Beautiful Park in the heart of downtown and ride north to the Airforce Academy for a scenic tour of the city that guarantees at least 10 miles of open trail. You can also take the route west from the park for a 6-mile ride into Manitou Springs. ■ TIP→ **City and county officials are working hard to repair and reopen the full trail but it's wise to call before planning your trip.** ⊠ *126 Cimino Dr.* ☎ *719/325–6404* ⊕ *www.elpasocountyparks.com.*

HORSEBACK RIDING

Academy Riding Stables. Trail rides, most notably through the Garden of the Gods, are offered here. ⊠ *4 El Paso Blvd.* ☎ *719/633–5667, 888/700–0410* ⊕ *www.arsriding.com.*

MOUNTAIN BIKING

Challenge Unlimited. For more than 25 years this outfitter has been leading bike tours throughout Colorado, including the daily 20-mile bike tour down Pikes Peak from May through mid-October. The tours include helmets and bikes, and breakfast and lunch. Other trips combine biking and zip-lining. ⊠ *204 S. 24th St.* ☎ *800/798–5954* ⊕ *www. bikithikit.com.*

Pikes Peak Mountain Bike Tours. The guides with this company will take you to the top of Pikes Peak, then let you ride all the way down on one of their lightweight mountain bikes. An alternative tour is the 20-mile tour on Upper Gold Camp Road, which is a self-paced downhill ride along an old railroad tract converted to a hiking–bicycling trail that cuts through the mountains. Another option allows you to saddle up and pedal down, a partnership with the Stables at the Broadmoor. ⊠ *306 S. 25th St.* ☎ *888/593–3062* ⊕ *www.bikepikespeak.com.*

WHERE TO EAT

$$
CAFÉ

✕ **Adam's Mountain Café.** Join the locals sitting at mismatched tables, viewing drawings by regional artists, and mingling at the community table. The food has an organic bent, with many vegetarian options. Smashing breakfasts include orange-almond French toast and huevos rancheros; dinners such as Senegalese vegetables or rustic Italian lasagna are hits as well. ⑤ *Average main: $15* ⊠ *26 Manitou Ave.* ☎ *719/685–1430* ⊕ *www.adamsmountain.com* ⊘ *No dinner Sun. and Mon.*

$$$
MODERN
AMERICAN

✕ **Blue Star.** Perch on a high stool in the bar while enjoying tapas like PEI mussels or fried shishito pepper, or head to the simple and elegant dining room for a leisurely dinner with seasonal dishes designed around local meats, like Alamosa bass and Boulder chicken. Influences drift around the globe, from Asia to the Mediterranean. It's a place frequented by everyone from blue-haired ladies to college students, so it's best to make a reservation. $ *Average main: $25* ⊠ *1645 S. Tejon St.* ☎ *719/632–1086* ⊕ *www.thebluestar.net.*

$$$$
MODERN
EUROPEAN

✕ **Briarhurst Manor.** One of the most exquisitely romantic restaurants in Colorado, Briarhurst Manor has several dining rooms, each with its own look and mood. The rich decor includes cherrywood wainscoting, balustrades, and furnishings, Van Briggle wood-and-ceramic fireplaces, tapestries, chinoiserie, and stained glass. Dine in the Garden Room, which has massive bow windows and original wallpaper from the 1880s, or in the book-lined Library. In the Drawing Room, with its ornate chandelier and fireplace, the tables are nicely spaced for conversation. The menu regularly features lamb, poultry, fish, and wild game dishes, which change as the chef adds a seasonal flair. $ *Average main: $32* ⊠ *404 Manitou Ave.* ☎ *719/685–1864* ⊕ *www.briarhurst. com* ☾ *Closed Mon. No lunch.*

$$$$
MODERN
AMERICAN

✕ **Carlos' Bistro.** Although this chic spot with copper-and-black decor is a ways from downtown, it's a local favorite thanks to its great food and casual ambience. Here you'll find patrons—some wearing jeans, others in suits—dining in the dim light on what appear to be pieces of art framed by triangular white plates. Start with fresh oysters or a lump blue crab cake, then move on to seared filet mignon with a black-peppercorn brandy sauce or covered in lump blue crab meat, topped with béarnaise sauce. If you're not full, try the New Orleans chocolate bread pudding, or the white-chocolate bread pudding with macadamia nuts. $ *Average main: $34* ⊠ *1025 S. 21st St.* ☎ *719/471–2905* ⊕ *www.carlosbistrocos. com* ☾ *Closed Mar. and Sun.–Tues. Sept.–Apr. No lunch.*

$$
ECLECTIC

✕ **Nosh 121.** Small plates are the focus at this popular restaurant. People often share the more than 25 "noshers," ranging from the char sui Ramen bowl to rainbow trout. The koi murals represent the restaurant's flow of energy and good service. Happy hour specials are offered on weekdays. $ *Average main: $14* ⊠ *121 S. Tejon St.* ☎ *719/635–6674* ⊕ *www.nosh121.com* ☾ *No lunch Sat.*

$$
ITALIAN

✕ **Paravicini's Italian Bistro.** Named for the proprietor's grandmother, Paravicini lives up to its Italian name which translates to "for the neighborhood." Locals of all ages gather in the colorful and well-lit space that provides a balance of fun and romance while sipping glasses of wine and sharing the family-style salad, fresh bread, and heaping piles of noodles. Pasta reigns on this traditional Italian menu with a surf-and-turf dish that displays a 10-ounce New York Strip and shrimp atop a mound of tomato-basil cream–soaked linguine and classics like spaghetti and meatballs. $ *Average main: $18* ⊠ *2802 W. Colorado Ave.* ☎ *719/471–8200* ⊕ *paravicinis.com* ☐ *No credit cards.*

$$$$
MODERN
AMERICAN

✕ **Penrose Room at the Broadmoor.** Whatever number of courses you choose from the prix-fixe menu, you're guaranteed a memorable culinary experience. Executive chef Greg Vassos varies the dishes seasonally, offering fine dining without the constraints of French, American, or any other single cuisine. Appetizers such as foie gras torchon with burnt pineapple, and entrées such as veal tenderloin with sherry au jus and duo of rabbit in a reduction, are plated to look like edible works of art. Indulge yourself with the seven-course chef's tasting menu with wine pairings ($215). Request a table in the small glassed-in area, and you can watch the sun set behind Cheyenne Mountain, or ask about sitting at the 16-seat chef's table. $ *Average main: $84* ✉ *The Broadmoor South, 1 Lake Circle* ☎ *719/577–5733* 🌐 *www.broadmoor.com* 🕑 *Closed Sun. and Mon.* ✍ *Reservations essential* 👔 *Jacket required.*

$ AMERICAN FAMILY 🍴 **Poor Richards.** This is a six-in-one store loved by locals of all ages. On one side there's a pizza parlor, where you stand in line to order hand-tossed pies, salads, and sandwiches. Step through a doorway and you're in a toy store. Step through another and you'll find yourself in Rico's Cafe and Wine Bar, where the ambience is more upscale and the menu veers toward organic. Order a sandwich, a salad, or try a cheese plate. Step though another doorway and you've entered a used-book store. You can also enter each store from outside. $ *Average main: $9* ✉ *320–324½ N. Tejon St.* ☎ *719/578–5549* 🌐 *www.poorrichardsdowntown.com.*

$$ ITALIAN 🍴 **Ristorante Del Lago at the Broadmoor.** With stunning views of Cheyenne Lake and the main hotel, this "restaurant of the lake" opened in 2015 as part of the newly renovated Broadmoor West. The open kitchen and cozy lounge are inviting and relaxed. Smaller portions allow guests to try a variety of authentic Italian dishes from antipasti and wood-fired pizzas to lasagne and house-made sausage. Ask your server or the house sommelier which of the restaurant's 150 selections of wine to pair with each course. $ *Average main: $18* ✉ *1 Lake Ave.* ☎ *719/577–5774, 866/381–8432* 🌐 *www.broadmoor.com/ristorante-del-lago* 🕑 *No dinner Tues. and Wed. No lunch.*

$$$$ MODERN AMERICAN Fodor's Choice ★ 🍴 **Summit at the Broadmoor.** The ambience at this "American brasserie" is a successful blend of big-city elegance and Western casualness. The 14-foot wine tower revolving slowly behind the bar is impossible to miss. The menu includes year-round favorites like escargots and pan-roasted swordfish and a seasonal section that revolves around fresh ingredients. Thirty wines are served by the glass, and half the fun of dining here is the conversation with the sommelier or the knowledgeable waitstaff about pairing the wine to the food. $ *Average main: $30* ✉ *The Broadmoor, 1 Lake Ave.* ☎ *719/577–5775* 🌐 *www.broadmoor.com* 🕑 *Closed Mon. No lunch.*

WHERE TO STAY

$$ HOTEL 🏨 **Antlers Hilton Colorado Springs.** The marble-and-granite lobby strikes an immediate note of class at this downtown hotel, whose location provides easy access to restaurants and shops. **Pros:** good service; convenient location. **Cons:** little ambience; few amenities. $ *Rooms from: $159* ✉ *4 S. Cascade Ave.* ☎ *719/955–5600, 866/299–4602* 🌐 *www.antlers.com* 🛏 *292 rooms, 7 suites* 🍽 *Breakfast.*

$$$$ HOTEL Fodor's Choice ★ 🏨 **The Broadmoor.** The Broadmoor continues to redefine itself with settings where guests can unwind and be pampered. **Pros:** you'll feel thoroughly pampered; choosing where to eat may be difficult, because there are so many good options. **Cons:** very expensive. $ *Rooms from: $400* ✉ *1 Lake Circle* ☎ *719/634–7711, 800/634–7711* 🌐 *www.broadmoor.com* 🛏 *619 rooms, 114 suites, 44 cottages* 🍽 *No meals.*

$$$$ RESORT **Cheyenne Mountain Resort.** At this 217-acre resort on the slopes of Cheyenne Mountain, superb swimming facilities (including an Olympic-size pool), a variety of tennis courts, and a Pete Dye championship golf course tempt you to remain on-property, despite the easy access to the high country. **Pros:** resort ambience; outstanding views; lobby and fitness center renovated in 2015. **Cons:** you must walk outside to get to the main lodge; can get crowded for conferences. [$] *Rooms from: $229* ✉ *3225 Broadmoor Valley Rd.* ☎ *719/538–4000, 800/588–0250* 🌐 *www.cheyennemountain.com* 🛏 *304 rooms, 12 suites* 🍴 *No meals.*

$$$ HOTEL **Cliff House.** This Victorian-era jewel was built in 1874 as a stagecoach stop between Colorado Springs and Leadville. **Pros:** convenient location; old-fashioned charm. **Cons:** might be a little too old-fashioned for some. [$] *Rooms from: $200* ✉ *306 Cañon Ave., Manitou Springs* ☎ *719/685–3000, 888/212–7000* 🌐 *www.thecliffhouse.com* 🛏 *35 rooms, 17 suites* 🍴 *Breakfast.*

$$$$ RESORT **Garden of the Gods Club and Resort.** The views are spectacular from this longtime private club overlooking the red rocks in the Garden of the Gods. **Pros:** great views; access to great golf on the Kissing Camels course. **Cons:** a car is needed to get downtown; expensive. [$] *Rooms from: $310* ✉ *3320 Mesa Rd.* ☎ *719/632–5541, 800/923–8838* 🌐 *www.gardenofthegodsclub.com* 🛏 *69 rooms, 12 suites* 🍴 *No meals.*

$$ B&B/INN Fodor's Choice ★ **Holden House.** Innkeepers Sallie and Welling Clark realized their dream when they restored this 1902 home and transformed it into a B&B. **Pros:** good choice for travelers who want something homey; excellent breakfasts. **Cons:** old-fashioned ambience may not suit all tastes; not suitable for young children. [$] *Rooms from: $150* ✉ *1102 W. Pikes Peak Ave.* ☎ *719/471–3980, 888/565–3980* 🌐 *www.holdenhouse.com* 🛏 *6 rooms* 🍴 *Breakfast.*

NIGHTLIFE AND PERFORMING ARTS

PERFORMING ARTS

Pikes Peak Center. This downtown venue presents a wide range of musical events as well as touring theater and dance companies. ✉ *190 S. Cascade Ave.* ☎ *719/520–7469* 🌐 *www.pikespeakcenter.com.*

NIGHTLIFE

BARS AND CLUBS

Cowboys. This is a favorite hangout for country music lovers and two-steppers. ✉ *25 N. Tejon St.* ☎ *719/596–1212* 🌐 *www.cowboyscs.com.*

Golden Bee. Remnants of a 19th-century English pub were discovered in a warehouse in New York City in the 1950s and moved to the Broadmoor site where the original mahogany bar, wood carvings, mirrors, and tin ceilings still define the Golden Bee's charm. The old-fashioned bar features a piano player leading sing-alongs. Watch out for the bees—as part of a long-standing tradition, they flick bee stickers into the audience during the show. ✉ *International Center at the Broadmoor, 1 Lake Circle* ☎ *719/634–7711* 🌐 *www.broadmoordining.com.*

Ritz. Located downtown, the Ritz fills up at cocktail hour and has a bistro-style menu for dining. The real action is Thursday–Saturday, when there's a DJ or live music. Locals recommend arriving before 7 pm if you plan to eat. ⊠ *15 S. Tejon St.* ☎ *719/635–8484* ⊕ *www.ritzgrill.com.*

BREWPUBS

Fodor's Choice ★ **Ivywild School.** Student art still lingers on the bathroom walls of this historic elementary school turned hipster haunt. On one end of the 1916 school, Bristol Brewing Company schools patrons with its Laughing Lab Scottish Ale and Beehive Honey Wheat microbrews while creative libations are shaken and stirred down the hall at The Principal's Office. Trendy locals flock to the historic site with large patios and lots of charm for the tastiest cafeteria grub around served up by The Meat Locker and Old School Bakery lining the art-covered hallway between the two bars. Despite the weekend crowds, you'll find yourself quickly lost in the surroundings wondering if you're going to get detention for drinking on school grounds. ⊠ *1604 S. Cascade Ave.* ☎ *719/368–6100* ⊕ *ivywildschool.com.*

Judge Baldwin's. In the Antlers Hilton Colorado Springs, a stunning wood bar and trim gives the restaurant and bar a rich pub feel. Customers come back for the custom cocktails—like the Mile High Martini with gin, lime and grapefruit juice, and simple syrup or the Metro Tea, a twist on the Long Island iced tea—and a selection of Colorado craft beers are always on tap. Lunch and dinner are also served here daily. ⊠ *Antlers Hilton, 4 S. Cascade Ave.* ☎ *719/473–5600.*

Phantom Canyon Brewing Co. In a century-old brick building, this noted brewpub has shuffle board and billiards in an upstairs hall. There's great pub grub, plus sinful desserts like goat cheese cheesecake, prickly pear chocolate cake, and hops-infused panna cotta. ⊠ *2 E. Pikes Peak Ave.* ☎ *719/635–2800* ⊕ *www.phantomcanyon.com.*

COMEDY AND SHOWS

Iron Springs Chateau. This club across from Pikes Peak Cog Railway offers comic melodramas along with dinner year-round. ⊠ *444 Ruxton Ave.* ☎ *719/685–5104* ⊕ *www.ironspringschateau.com.*

Loonees Comedy Corner. This club showcases live stand-up comedy Thursday to Saturday evening. Some of the performers are nationally known. ⊠ *1305 N. Academy Blvd.* ☎ *719/591–0707* ⊕ *www.loonees.com.*

SHOPPING

Colorado Springs has a mix of upscale shopping in boutiques and major chain stores. Many boutiques and galleries cluster in Old Colorado City and the posh Broadmoor One Lake Avenue Shopping Arcade.

Manitou Springs, a small town between Garden of the Gods and Pikes Peak, has a historic district, and the chamber of commerce has free maps. There's a large artists' population; walk along Manitou Avenue and Ruxton Avenue, where you'll find a mix of galleries, quaint shops, and stores selling souvenirs.

ANTIQUES AND COLLECTIBLES

Ruxton's Trading Post. Look here for cowboy-and-Indian antiques and collectibles, Native American art, and nostalgia items from old TV programs and movies. ⊠ *22 Ruxton Ave., Manitou Springs* ☎ *719/685–9024* ⊕ *www.oldwestantiques.com.*

CRAFT AND ART GALLERIES

Commonwheel Artists Co-Op. This longtime co-op gallery is packed with art in various mediums, jewelry, paintings, sculpture and fiber, clay, and glass art. ⊠ *102 Cañon Ave., Manitou Springs* ☎ *719/685–1008* ⊕ *www.commonwheel.com.*

Sculpture by Michael Garman. This gallery in Old Colorado City carries the contemporary sculptures of renowned artist Michael Garman, including Western-themed pieces and a firefighter series. ⊠ *2418 W. Colorado Ave.* ☎ *719/471–9391* ⊕ *www.michaelgarman.com.*

FOOD

Patsy's Candies. Renowned for its saltwater taffy and chocolate, Patsy's Candies offers tours weekdays mid-May to mid-September. ⊠ *1540 S. 21st St.* ☎ *719/633–7215* ⊕ *www.patsyscandies.com.*

SHOPPING CENTER

Promenade Shops at Briargate. Among the tenants at this upscale shopping center are clothiers Chico's and White House Black Market, plus other retailers such as Pottery Barn and Williams-Sonoma. ⊠ *1885 Briargate Pkwy.* ☎ *719/265–6264* ⊕ *www.thepromenadeshopsatbriargate.com.*

SIDE TRIPS FROM COLORADO SPRINGS

Easy day trips from Colorado Springs can lead you to the gambling or mining heritage in Cripple Creek. Florissant Fossil Beds attracts geology buffs. If you like heights, head to Cañon City and walk over the Royal Gorge Bridge, or take a lunchtime ride on the train that runs on a track through the most dramatic part of the canyon.

CRIPPLE CREEK

46 miles west of Colorado Springs via U.S. 24 and Hwy. 67.

One of Colorado's three legalized gambling towns, Cripple Creek once had the most lucrative mines in the state—and 10,000 boozing, brawling, bawdy citizens. Today the charming main street is lined with casinos housed in quaint Victorian buildings. Outside the central area, old mining structures and the stupendous curtain of the Collegiate Peaks are marred by slag heaps and parking lots. Take a side trip to nearby Victor, walk down streets where hundreds of miners once took streetcars to the mines, and learn about their lives.

GETTING HERE AND AROUND

The town is tiny, though a bit hilly off the main drag, so it's easy to walk around and explore. Drive here in a private car, or hitch a ride on one of the Ramblin' Express casino shuttles from Colorado Springs to Cripple Creek. Ramblin' Express also runs between Cripple Creek and nearby Victor.

ESSENTIALS

Transportation Contacts Ramblin' Express. ☎ 719/590–8687 ⊕ www.ramblinexpress.com.

Visitor Information Pikes Peak Heritage Center. ✉ 9283 S. Hwy. 67 ☎ 877/858–4653, 719/689–3315 ⊕ www.visitcripplecreek.com.

EXPLORING

Miners gathered around card games in most of the nearly 100 saloons in Cripple Creek, which opened during the wild years after Bob Womack discovered gold in 1890. Today there's a lineup of casinos set into storefronts and buildings with exteriors meticulously maintained to retain the aura they had a century ago. But inside the casinos and gambling parlors here today there's no question that these are gambling halls, chock-full of slot machines, video and live poker tables, and blackjack tables. Today there are even a few casinos in modern buildings, too. In 2009 the maximum bet limit was raised from $5 to $100. You can play craps and roulette at many of the casinos, some of which stay open 24 hours a day.

Most of the casinos on East Bennett Avenue house predictable (albeit inexpensive) restaurants. Beef is the common denominator across all the menus. Some casinos also have hotel rooms.

Bronco Billy's. This longtime, locally-owned casino embodies the atmosphere of Cripple Creek's main drag with its Western theme and friendly staff. Known for its customer service, Bronco Billy's is a favorite among locals and tourists. Stay overnight in the affordable and cozy rooms upstairs and dine on-site at The Steakhouse where quality cuts reign, Baja Billy's Mexican restaurant and cantina, or diner-style breakfast, lunch, and dinner dishes at Home Cafe. ✉ 151 E. Bennett Ave. ☎ 719/689–0353, 866/689–0353 ⊕ www.broncobillyscasino.com.

FAMILY **Cripple Creek and Victor Narrow Gauge Railroad.** A favorite with kids, the Cripple Creek and Victor Narrow Gauge Railroad weaves over reconstructed trestles and past abandoned mines to the Anaconda ghost town, then returns to Cripple Creek during the 4-mile, 45-minute ride. In the boom days of the 1870s through the silver crash of 1893, more than 50 ore-laden trains made this run daily. For years Victor has been a sad town, virtually a ghost of its former self. Walking the streets—past abandoned or partially restored buildings—has been an eerie experience. But there's a partial renewal of the town, because Victor is again home to a gold mine, the Cripple Creek and Victor Mining Company. Trains depart every 40 minutes. ✉ 520 E. Carr St., at Bennett Ave. ☎ 719/689–2640 ⊕ www.cripplecreekrailroad.com ☑ $14 ☉ Late May–early Oct., daily 10–5.

Cripple Creek District Museum. The museum set in five historic buildings—including a vintage railway depot—contains a vast collection of artifacts, photos, and exhibits that provide a glimpse into mining life at the turn of the 20th century. ✉ 500 Bennett Ave. ☎ 719/689–2634 ⊕ cripplecreekmuseum.com ☑ $5 ☉ Mid-May–mid-Oct., daily 10–5; late Oct.–early May, weekends 10–4.

Mollie Kathleen Gold Mine Tour. Descending 1,000 feet, the Mollie Kathleen Gold Mine Tour tours a mine that operated continuously from 1892 to 1961. The tours are fascinating, sometimes led by a former miner, and definitely not for the claustrophobic. Tours depart about every 30 minutes. On-site, the Hard Rock Diner serves burgers and light fare. ✉ *9388 Hwy. 67, northeast of town* ☎ *719/689–2466* ⊕ *www. goldminetours.com* ✆ *$20* ⊙ *Late May–mid-Sept., daily 8:45–5; late Apr.–mid-May and late Sept.–Oct., daily 9:45–5.*

FAMILY **Victor Lowell Thomas Museum.** This two-story house museum makes the already worthwhile trip to Victor even better. Kids can learn how to pan for gold while adults get a glimpse at mountain mining life in the late 1800s and early 1900s. World traveler, author, journalist, and broadcaster Lowell Thomas left some of his estate to the museum, which is also on display inside the museum. ✉ *298 Victor Ave., Victor* ☎ *719/689–5509* ⊕ *www.victorcolorado.com/museum.htm* ✆ *$6* ⊙ *Late May–early Sept., daily 9:30–5:30; limited hrs mid-Sept.–late Dec.*

FLORISSANT FOSSIL BEDS

35 miles west of Colorado Springs via U.S. 24.

GETTING HERE AND AROUND

From Cripple Creek, take Teller County Road 1, which goes right through the monument. It's about 17 miles from town.

EXPLORING

Florissant Fossil Beds National Monument. Once a temperate rain forest, Florissant Fossil Beds National Monument was perfectly preserved by volcanic ash and mud flow 34 million years ago. This little-known site is a haven for paleontologists. The visitor center offers a daily guided walk and ranger talks in the amphitheater in summer, or you can follow 14 miles of well-marked hiking trails and lose yourself in the remnants of 56 million-year-old petrified redwoods from the Eocene epoch. ✉ *15807 Teller County Rd. 1, Florissant* ☎ *719/748–3253* ⊕ *www.nps.gov/flfo* ✆ *$3* ⊙ *Late May–early Sept., daily 8–6; mid-Sept.–mid-May, daily 9–5.*

PALMER LAKE

25 miles north of Colorado Springs via I–25 and Hwy. 105.

Artsy, and very sleepy, Palmer Lake is a magnet for hikers who set out for the evergreen-clad peaks at several in-town trailheads. There are more good restaurants and working artists than one would expect from a population of about 2,400. The town developed around the railroad tracks that were laid here in 1871—the lake itself was used as a refueling point for steam engines. ■ TIP➡ **The lake is a few miles off the highway, so you need a car to get here.**

EXPLORING

FAMILY **Colorado Renaissance Festival.** Larkspur is home to just a few hundred residents, but it knows how to throw a heck of a party—and a medieval one at that. The Colorado Renaissance Festival annually throws open its gates to throngs of families, chain mail–clad fantasy enthusiasts, tattooed bikers, and fun lovers of every other kind. Within the wooded 350-acre "kingdom" there are performers who deliver everything from juggling stunts and fire-eating to hypnotism and comedy. The big event happens three times a day, when knights square off in the arena for a theatrical joust. There are also more than 200 artisans selling their wares, games, rides, and myriad food and drink booths. It's a great way to while away a summer day, though it can be a bit much to handle in the hottest weather. ✉ *650 W. Perry Park Ave., off Larkspur Rd.* ✣ *Larkspur is 9 miles north of Palmer Lake via Hwy. 18* ☎ *303/688–6010* 🌐 *www.coloradorenaissance.com* 🎟 *$21* 🕓 *Mid-June–early Aug., weekends 10–6:30.*

Tri-Lakes Center for the Arts. In a landmark Kaiser-Frazer building on the north fringe of town, the Tri-Lakes Center for the Arts hangs rotating exhibits in its auditorium-gallery that also serves as a venue for music and theater. Classes and workshops are offered, and several resident artists work from studios on-site. ✉ *304 Hwy. 105* ☎ *719/481–0475* 🌐 *www.trilakesarts.org* 🎟 *Free* 🕓 *Tues.–Fri. noon–4, Sat. 10–3.*

QUICK BITES

Rock House Ice Cream. This is a popular stop for hikers on their way home. Choose from among more than 24 different types, including raspberry truffle, coconut-almond fudge, and—seasonally—pumpkin, for your cone, sundae, or milkshake. ✉ *24 Hwy. 105* ☎ *719/488–6917* 🌐 *www.rockhouseicecream.com.*

SPORTS AND THE OUTDOORS

HIKING

Palmer Lake Reservoirs Trail. One of the most popular hiking trails between Denver and Colorado Springs, the Palmer Lake Reservoirs Trail begins near Glen Park. After a fairly steep incline, the 3-mile trail levels out and follows the shoreline of Upper and Lower Palmer Lake reservoirs between forested mountains. Bikes and leashed dogs are permitted. **TIP→ Work has been underway since 2013 to repair extensive flood damge to the trail so call about possible closures before your trip.** ✉ *Palmer Lake* ✣ *Trailhead starts at bottom of Old Palmer Rd.* ☎ *719/633–6884.*

WHERE TO EAT

$$ ITALIAN 🍴 **Bella Panini.** This popular restaurant has a heavy Italian focus. But the chefs here aren't afraid to mix things up, whipping out such creative concoctions as crawfish-and-jalapeño pizza. The owner also hosts cooking classes and food and wine pairings. [$] *Average main: $13* ✉ *4 Hwy. 105* ☎ *719/481–3244* 🌐 *www.bellapanini.com* 💳 *No credit cards* 🕓 *Closed Sun. and Mon.*

CAÑON CITY AND ROYAL GORGE

45 miles southwest of Colorado Springs via Hwy. 115 and U.S. 50.

Cañon City is an undeniably quirky town. From its easy access to the nearby Royal Gorge, a dramatic slash in the earth, to its aggressive strip-mall veneer (softened, fortunately, by some handsome old buildings), you'd think Cañon City existed solely for tourism. Nothing could be further from the truth: Cañon City is in Fremont County, called "Colorado's Prison Capital" by some. In Cañon City and nearby Florence there are more than a dozen prisons, including Supermax. While this may seem like a perverse source of income to court, the prisons have pumped millions of dollars into the local economy.

GETTING HERE AND AROUND

The route from Colorado Springs to Cañon City (on Highway 115 and U.S. 50) goes through Red Rock Canyon, with lovely views. You'll need a car to get to Cañon City, where there are limited transportation options.

ESSENTIALS

Visitor Information Cañon City Chamber of Commerce. ⊠ *403 Royal Gorge Blvd., Cañon City* ☎ *719/275–2331, 800/876–7922* ⊕ *www.canoncitycolorado.com.*

EXPLORING

Museum of Colorado Prisons. Introduce yourself and your kids to what life is like behind bars at the Museum of Colorado Prisons, which formerly housed the Women's State Correctional Facility and where many of the exhibits are housed in cells. The museum exhaustively documents prison life in Colorado through old photos and newspaper accounts, as well as with inmates' confiscated weapons and contraband. The gas chamber sits in the courtyard. Many parents bring their children to this museum, but it might be disturbing for young kids. ⊠ *201 N. 1st St., Cañon City* ☎ *719/269–3015* ⊕ *www.prisonmuseum.org* ⊠ *$7* ⊙ *Late May–Sept., daily 10–6; Oct.–mid-May, Wed.–Sun. 10–5.*

FAMILY

Fodor'sChoice

★

Royal Gorge. Cañon City is the gateway to the Royal Gorge, whose canyon walls tower up to 1,200 feet high and were carved by the Arkansas River more than 3 million years ago. The famed Royal Gorge War between the Denver & Rio Grande and Santa Fe railroads occurred here in 1877. The battle was over the right-of-way through the canyon, which could only accommodate one rail line. Rival crews would lay tracks during the day and dynamite each other's work at night. The dispute was finally settled in court—the Denver & Rio Grande won. Today there's a commercially run site, the Royal Gorge Bridge and Park, along one part of the gorge. A wildfire swept through this region in 2013, but quick-acting locals revived the touristic hub, which launched a new children's area in 2015. Rafting remains a strong and prosperous draw to the region. ⊠ *U.S. 50, Cañon City* ✛ *12 miles west of Cañon City* ⊕ *royalgorgebridge.com.*

Royal Gorge Bridge and Park. The Royal Gorge Bridge and Park has the highest **suspension bridge** in North America. Never intended for traffic, it was constructed in 1929 as a tourist attraction. The 1,053-foot-high bridge sways on gusty afternoons and the river can be seen clearly

12

between gaps in the boards, adding to the thrill of a crossing. You can cross the suspension bridge and also ride the astonishing **aerial tram** (2,400 feet long and more than 1,000 feet above the canyon floor). Remnants of a wildfire that ravaged the area in 2013 can be seen in the charred incline rail line, which remains on display but not functional on the canyon wall. As part of the renovations following the fire, the park opened a Children's Playland in 2015 with a playground, carousel, maze, and splash pad. A ride on the **Royal Rush Skycoaster** ensures an adrenaline rush—you'll swing from a free-fall tower and momentarily hang over the gorge. Also on hand are a theater that presents a 17-minute multimedia show, outdoor musical entertainment in summer, and the usual assortment of food and gift shops. Visiting this attraction can prove to be expensive for a family. ✉ *4218 Fremont County Rd. 3A, Cañon City* ☎ *719/275–7507, 888/333–5597* ⊕ *www. royalgorgebridge.com* ⌸ *$23* ⊙ *Call ahead for hrs.*

FAMILY **Royal Gorge Route Railroad.** A ride on the Royal Gorge Route Railroad takes you under the bridge and through one of the most dramatic parts of the canyon. From the Santa Fe depot in Cañon City, the train leaves several times a day for the two-hour ride. The lunch and dinner rides are pleasant, and the food is good, although not exactly "gourmet" as advertised, and a murder mystery ride adds additional entertainment from the end of May through October. For an extra fee you can ride in the cab with the engineer. ✉ *330 Royal Gorge Blvd., Cañon City* ☎ *888/724–5748* ⊕ *www.royalgorgeroute.com* ⌸ *$39–$119* ⊙ *Early Mar.–early Jan.*

OFF THE BEATEN PATH
Winery at Holy Cross Abbey. The Benedictine monks once cloistered at Holy Cross Abbey came to Cañon City for spiritual repose. But for the faithful who frequent the winery on the eastern edge of the property, redemption is more easily found in a nice bottle of Revelation, a Bordeaux-style blend. Tours of the winery's production facility are by advance reservation in spring and summer. The Tasting Room, in a historic building, is open year-round. For a truly divine experience, reserve a wine and cheese tasting ($25 per person) on the terrace that includes a private hostess, sampling of all wines and an artisanal cheese, bread, fruit, and chocolate plate. ✉ *3011 E. U.S. 50, Cañon City* ☎ *719/276–5191, 877/422–9463* ⊕ *www.abbeywinery.com* ⊙ *Apr.–Dec., Mon.–Sat. 10–6, Sun. noon–5; Jan.–Mar., Mon.–Sat. 10–5, Sun. noon–5.*

SPORTS AND THE OUTDOORS

HIKING

Arkansas River Walk. For a pleasant stroll, try the Arkansas River Walk. The 7-mile trail is virtually flat, and the elevation is only 5,320 feet. It follows the Arkansas River for 3 miles through woods, wetlands, and the riparian river environment. ✉ *Cañon City* ✛ *Trailhead: Heading south on 9th St., turn east immediately past the bridge.*

Red Canyon Park. Cañon City–owned Red Canyon Park, 12 miles north of town, offers splendid easy to moderate hiking among the rose-color sandstone spires. The easy-to-find park features towering red-rock formations, fossils, and the world's most complete *Stegosaurus* skeleton. ✉ *Red Canyon Rd. and Field Ave., Cañon City.*

RAFTING

TOURS AND OUTFITTERS

Colorado River Outfitters Association. With dozens of outfitters working from Salida, Buena Vista, and Cañon City, south-central Colorado is one of the top places in the country to go rafting. The Colorado River Outfitters Association is an organization of more than 50 licensed outfitters who run rafting trips on Colorado's 13 river systems. ✉ *Cañon City* ☎ *720/260–4135* 🌐 *www.croa.org.*

WHERE TO EAT AND STAY

$ PIZZA FAMILY

🍴 **Pizza Madness.** There is no shortage of fun or food in the family-friendly Pizza Madness. Arcade games and weekend magicians (you read that right—magicians) keep kids and adults entertained while you wait for your hand-tossed pie. This is where you'll find the Cañon City locals on a Saturday afternoon—sitting against mural-covered walls munching on slices, salads, and sandwiches. Pick your own ingredients or try one of the specialties like the Colorado with chicken, green chilies, black olives, and bacon. [$] *Average main: $9* ✉ *509 Main St., Cañon City* ☎ *719/276–3088* 🌐 *www.mypizzamadness.com.*

$ HOTEL

🏨 **Quality Inn and Suites.** Some of the famous people who have stayed here (back when it was the Canon Inn)—John Belushi, Jane Fonda, John Wayne, and Goldie Hawn among them—now have their names emblazoned on the door of a room. **Pros:** close to Royal Gorge; pet-friendly; full breakfast included. **Cons:** dated and in need of a makeover; rooms above diner noisy in the mornings; spotty TV and Wi-Fi reception. [$] *Rooms from: $100* ✉ *3075 E. U.S. 50, Cañon City* ☎ *719/275–8676, 800/525–7727* 🌐 *www.qualityinncanoncity.com* 🛏 *150 rooms* 🍽 *Breakfast.*

THE COLLEGIATE PEAKS

Buena Vista and Salida are comfortable base towns for vacationers who love hiking and mountain biking the trails that zigzag up and down the 14,000-footers called the Collegiate Peaks. These towns are also favorites for folks who want to stay in rustic cabins or small mom-and-pop motels, perhaps take a rafting trip on the Arkansas River, and come home with a wallet still intact.

BUENA VISTA

94 miles west of Colorado Springs on U.S. 24.

Skyscraping mountains, the most impressive being the Collegiate Peaks, ring Buena Vista (pronounced *byoo*-na *vis*-ta by locals). The 14,000-foot, often snowcapped peaks were first summited by alumni from Yale, Princeton, Harvard, and Columbia, who named them for their respective alma maters. A small mining town–turned–casual resort community, Buena Vista's main street is lined with Wild West–style historic buildings. On U.S. 24, which bisects the town, there are inexpensive roadside motels. The town is also a hub for the white-water rafting industry that plies its trade on the popular Arkansas River, and a great central location for hiking, fishing, rafting, and horseback riding.

GETTING HERE AND AROUND

You'll need your own car to explore this region. Everything outdoors from hiking and mountain biking to rafting on the Arkansas is an easy drive from Buena Vista.

ESSENTIALS

Visitor Information Buena Vista Chamber of Commerce. ⊠ *343 U.S. 24*
☎ *719/395–6612* ⊕ *www.buenavistacolorado.org.*

EXPLORING

Buena Vista Heritage Museum. Before leaving downtown, meander through the Buena Vista Heritage Museum in the 1882 brick courthouse. A falling-down stagecoach cabin near the back of the property and pretty carriage outside give a hint of what's inside. Each room is devoted to a different aspect of regional history from the 1860s to the 1900s: one to mining equipment, another to fashions, and another to household utensils. There are working models of the three railroads that serviced the area in its heyday, a schoolroom, and historical photos in the archives. A rafting and kayaking exhibit will have you itching to experience the thrill of the area's water sports for yourself. ⊠ *506 E. Main St.* ☎ *719/395–8458* ⊕ *www.buenavistaheritage.org* 🖭 *$5* ☉ *June–Sept., Mon.–Sat. 10–5, Sun. noon–5.*

Fodor'sChoice
★

Collegiate Peaks Wilderness Area. Taking its own name from the many peaks named after famous universities, the 168,000-acre Collegiate Peaks Wilderness Area includes more 14,000-foot-high mountains than any other wilderness area in the Lower 48 states. Forty miles of the Continental Divide snake through the area as well. The most compelling reason to visit Buena Vista is for the almost unequaled variety of hikes, climbs, biking trails, and fishing streams here. (Keep an eye out for hot springs, too.) Two ranger offices, one in Leadville and one in Salida, handle inquiries about this region. ⊠ *Leadville Ranger District, 810 Front St., Leadville* ☎ *719/486–0749* ⊕ *www.fs.fed.us/r2/whiteriver/ recreation/wilderness/collegiatepeaks/index.shtml* ⊠ *Salida Ranger District, 5575 Cleora Rd., Salida* ☎ *719/539–3591* ⊕ *www.fs.usda.gov/ detail/psicc/about-forest/offices/?cid=fsm9_032697.*

Mount Princeton Hot Springs Resort. To relax sore muscles after your outdoor adventure, visit Mount Princeton Hot Springs Resort, 8 miles from Buena Vista. The resort has four pools open year-round and a fifth in the summer plus several "hot spots in the creek"—the water temperature ranges between 97°F and 108°F. The restaurant features mostly fish and steak entrées with creative seasonal specials and has a large stone fireplace and a dramatic view of the Chalk Cliffs. If you're too relaxed to drive home, stay in one of the resort's 49 hotel rooms or 30 cabins beginning at $160 per night during the summer. ⊠ *15870 County Rd. 162, Nathrop* ✛ *4½ miles west of U.S. 285* ☎ *719/395–2447* ⊕ *www. mtprinceton.com* 🖭 *$18 Mon.–Thurs.; $22 Fri.–Sun.*

SPORTS AND THE OUTDOORS

HIKING

The Trailhead. This outdoor specialty shop shares a space with Spoon-It-Up café in the heart of downtown Buena Vista. Stop in for trail maps, guidebooks, hiking and climbing gear, and clothing before grabbing a soup and salad or some frozen yogurt. Local and foreign outdoor enthusiasts congregate in this Main Street hub throughout the year. ✉ *402 E. Main St.* ☎ *719/395–8001* 🌐 *www.thetrailheadco.com.*

RAFTING

Arkansas River. Adrenaline-charging rapids range from Class II to Class V on Colorado's Arkansas River, one of the most commercially rafted and challenging rivers in the world. Among the most fabled stretches of the Arkansas are the Narrows, the Numbers, and Browns Canyon, but extreme paddlers tend to jump on trips through the Royal Gorge, which the river has carved out over eons. Plan your trip for the early summer snowmelt for the biggest thrills. ✉ *Buena Vista.*

TOURS AND OUTFITTERS

Fodor's Choice ★ **River Runners.** This long-respected outfitter offers rafting trips on the Arkansas River, including the Royal Gorge stretch, which is classed expert, but there are other choices on the river for families who want a gentler experience. ✉ *24070 County Rd. 301* ☎ *800/723–8987* 🌐 *www.whitewater.net.*

WHERE TO EAT AND STAY

$$ AMERICAN Fodor's Choice ★ 🍴 **Eddyline Restaurant & Brewery.** The steel community table at this casual brewpub gives the dining area and tiny bar a sophisticated vibe. The pub is by South Main River Park, so after dining on wood-fired pizzas, steaks, or seafood, washed down with ales brewed on-site, you can tackle the nearby miles of hiking and biking trails. If you want a peek at the brewery's operations, you can head to Eddyline's taproom where all of the company's beers including the River Runners Pale Ale are brewed just off of Highway 24 and Linderman Avenue. [$] *Average main: $13* ✉ *926 S. Main St.* ☎ *719/966–6000* 🌐 *www.eddylinepub.com.*

$$$ B&B/INN 🏨 **Ghost Town Guest House.** Although it looks like one of the old buildings in this authentic ghost town, this guesthouse is actually a modern structure built by a couple who decided to get away from urban living. **Pros:** unusual setting; friendly hosts. **Cons:** 30-minute drive to civilization (Buena Vista), part of which is on a dirt road; some rooms up many stairs. [$] *Rooms from: $185* ✉ *25850 County Rd. 162, Nathrop* ☎ *719/395–2120* 🌐 *www.ghosttownguesthouse.com* 💳 *No credit cards* 🛏 *3 rooms* 🍽 *Some meals.*

$$ B&B/INN 🏨 **Liars' Lodge.** On the banks of the Arkansas River, this fishing lodge–inspired B&B surrounded by 23 acres of woodland is just a mile north of downtown. **Pros:** gorgeous setting; river views (and sounds). **Cons:** not the best choice if you have young kids. [$] *Rooms from: $138* ✉ *30000 County Rd. 371* ☎ *719/395–3444, 888/542–7756* 🌐 *www.liarslodge.com* 🛏 *5 rooms, 1 house* 🍽 *Breakfast.*

NIGHTLIFE

Deerhammer Distilling Company. Be sure to sit at the bar in this Main Street joint and chat up the local bartenders that serve up opinions on town politics and advice on where to eat as well as delicious cocktails. The Green Grind includes a cucumber-and-mint garnish over a solid pour of the shop's Whitewater white whiskey, apple, and sugar. Single malt whiskey, brandy, and gin are also made on-site. Live bands liven up Main Street on weekends and throughout the summer bringing in tourists and plenty of local flavor. ✉ *321 E. Main St.* ☎ *719/395–9464* 🌐 *www.deerhammer.com.*

OFF THE BEATEN PATH

St. Elmo. If you want to see an authentic ghost town, head 15 miles west on County Road 162. Once the supply center for the Mary Murphy Mine and dozens of smaller mines, St. Elmo is the best-preserved ghost town in Colorado. It doesn't take long to walk along the main street and peer into some of the rickety old buildings. There is a B&B, as well as a general store that's open in the summer. Don't forget to feed the chipmunks! ⊠ *Western end of County Rd.162.*

SALIDA

25 miles south of Buena Vista via U.S. 285 and Hwy. 291; 102 miles southwest of Colorado Springs via Hwy. 115 and U.S. 50.

Imposing peaks, including 14,000-plus-foot Mount Shavano, dominate the town of Salida, which is on the Arkansas River. Salida draws some of the musicians who appear at the Aspen Music Festival—classical pianists, brass ensembles, and the like—for its Salida–Aspen Concerts in July and August. The town's other big event is the annual **Kayak and Rafting White-Water Rodeo** in June, on a section of river that cuts right through downtown. It's been taking place since 1949.

GETTING HERE AND AROUND

You need a private car to explore this area. There's a compact, walkable downtown area, but you'll need to drive to most lodgings, rivers, attractions, and the trailheads in the mountains.

ESSENTIALS

Visitor Information Salida Colorado Chamber of Commerce. ⊠ *406 W. U.S. 50* ☎ *719/539–2068, 877/772–5432* ⊕ *www.salidachamber.org.*

SPORTS AND THE OUTDOORS

BIKING

Absolute Bikes. This downtown shop rents cruisers starting at $15 per day and mountain bikes starting at $40 per day, and provides repair service, maps, and good advice. ⊠ *330 W. Sackett Ave.* ☎ *719/539–9295* ⊕ *www.absolutebikes.com.*

DOWNHILL SKIING

Monarch Mountain. A small ski resort that tops out on the Continental Divide, Monarch Mountain is a family-friendly place with moderate pricing—one-day lift tickets cost $69. The resort also offers snowcat skiing on steep runs off the Divide, plus the 130 acres of extreme terrain in Mirkwood Basin. **Facilities:** 53 trails; 800 acres; 1,162-foot vertical drop; 5 lifts. ⊠ *22720 U.S. 50* ✛ *18 miles west of Salida* ☎ *719/530–5000, 888/996–7669* ⊕ *www.skimonarch.com* ⊠ *Lift ticket $69* ☉ *Mid-Nov.–mid-Apr., daily 9–4.*

FISHING

The Arkansas River, as it spills out of the central Colorado Rockies on its course through the south central part of the state, reputedly supports a brown-trout population exceeding 5,000 fish per mile. Some of the river's canyons are deep, and some of the best fishing locations are difficult to access, making a guide or outfitter a near necessity. See ⊕ *www.wildlife.state.co.us/fishing* for more information.

OUTFITTERS **ArkAnglers.** A good fly shop with an experienced staff, ArkAnglers offers guided float and wade trips, fly-fishing lessons, and equipment rentals. ✉ *7500 W. U.S. 50* ☎ *719/539–4223* 🌐 *www.arkanglers.com.*

Independent Whitewater. This family-owned company has been running the Arkansas River since the 1980s. Groups are small, and the take-out is at a private area after running Seidel's Suckhole and Twin Falls on regular half-day trips. ✉ *10830 County Rd. 165* ☎ *800/428–1479, 719/539–7737* 🌐 *www.raftsalida.com.*

HORSEBACK RIDING

Mt. Princeton Hot Springs Stables. Here you can book trail rides along the dramatic Chalk Creek Cliffs; the cost is $35 per hour or day rides starting at $155 (including lunch). ✉ *14582 County Rd. 162* ☎ *866/877–3630, 719/395–3630* 🌐 *www.coloradotrailrides.com.*

JEEP TOURS

High Country Jeep Tours. These four-wheel-drive trips venture to old mines, ghost towns, and mountain vistas. ✉ *410 U.S. Hwy. 24, Buena Vista* ☎ *719/395–6111, 866/458–6877* 🌐 *www.highcountryjeeptours.com.*

RAFTING

The Salida area is a magnet for rafting aficionados, and there are dozens of outfitters. Salida jockeys with Buena Vista for the title of "Colorado's White-Water Capital." *For outfitters, see the Buena Vista section.*

SNOWMOBILING

Monarch Snowmobile Tours. This snowmobile outfitter takes customers on winter excursions around Monarch Park. Family-friendly introductory tours start at $40 per person and six-hour tours that include lunch go up to $230. ✉ *22763 U.S. 50, Garfield* ✣ *18 miles west of Salida* ☎ *719/539–2572, 800/539–2573* 🌐 *www.snowmobilemonarch.com.*

WHERE TO EAT

$ PIZZA 🍴 **Amicas Pizza and Microbrewery.** The wood-fired pizzas and craft brews at this downtown grub hub come highly recommended by locals. Families stop in for a giant pie that can easily feed a family of four while white-water rafters, hikers, and bikers unwind at the next table with one of the brewery's well-known chili beers. Artful pizzas like the Michelangelo with pesto sauce, sausage, goat cheese, and green chilies give the popular dishes a unique twist but the Salsiccia pie boasts classic pepperoni, sausage, and tomato for the restaurant's most popular pick. Local and organic ingredients are also offered in salads, calzones, and paninis, as well as plenty of vegetarian and gluten-free options. Peer into the working brewery with glass walls that is centrally located and visible from most tables in this lively space. TIP→ **Pies are also available to go.** [$] *Average main: $11* ✉ *136 E. 2nd St.* ☎ *719/539–5219* 🌐 *amicassalida.com* 💳 *No credit cards.*

$$ MODERN AMERICAN Fodor's Choice ★ 🍴 **The Fritz.** A relative newcomer in the building that formerly housed the well-respected (but now defunct) Butcher's Table, this hip small-plates restaurant is as trendy as Salida dining gets. The intimate bar and expansive patio are some of the region's best spaces for socializing. Lunch here is all about sandwiches and quick bites. Dinner is more relaxed with creative tapas alongside a few more substantial entrées. Don't miss the grilled asparagus with hollandaise and

the potent margaritas. $ *Average main: $15* ✉ *113 E. Sackett St.* ☎ *719/539–0364* ⊕ *www.thefritzsalida.com.*

$$$
ECLECTIC
✗ **Shallots.** This inviting café in the historic district presents an eclectic menu of American and Southwest dishes, with the pork "street" tacos highly recommended. The island half smoked chicken with orange-honey Jamaican jerk sauce and a smoked pork belly with Hawaiian barbecue shine on the revamped menu. A fresh look including a wood bar mounted on a half brick wall maintains the locally-owned restaurant's mountain café feel. Sunday brunch is very popular. For those seeking a morning pick-me-up, try the huevos, chorizo, and corn muffin covered in red sauce. $ *Average main: $22* ✉ *137 E. 1st St.* ☎ *719/539–4759* ⊗ *No dinner Sun.*

12

WHERE TO STAY

$
B&B/INN
⊡ **Tudor Rose.** With beautiful furnishings and an idyllic setting, this rustic mountain lodge sits on a 37-acre spread of pine forest and mountain ridges. **Pros:** owners will stable horses in their barn. **Cons:** not for guests with young children; no pool. $ *Rooms from: $105* ✉ *6720 County Rd. 104* ☎ *719/539–2002, 800/379–0889* ⊕ *www.thetudorrose.com* ➷ *4 rooms, 2 suites, 5 chalets* |◯| *Breakfast.*

$
HOTEL
⊡ **Woodland Motel.** Since 1975, Steve and Viva Borbas have run this impeccable mom-and-pop motel on the outskirts of downtown Salida. **Pros:** reliable; inexpensive rooms. **Cons:** a 12-minute walk to downtown. $ *Rooms from: $80* ✉ *903 W. 1st St.* ☎ *719/539–4980, 800/488–0456* ⊕ *www.woodlandmotel.com* ➷ *16 rooms, 2 condos* |◯| *No meals.*

PERFORMING ARTS

Salida Steam Plant Events Center. In a former power plant overlooking the Arkansas River, Salida Steam Plant Events Center has a theater that has put on several productions each summer, ranging from drama to comedy to music to cabaret. ✉ *Sackett St. and G St.* ☎ *719/530–0933* ⊕ *www.salidasteamplant.com.*

SHOPPING

All Booked Up. In this downtown space, browse Native American art and jewelry, mixed media artwork, and more. ✉ *134 E. 1st St.* ☎ *719/539–2344.*

Culture Clash. This is a good source for original artwork, glass, and intricately handcrafted jewelry. ✉ *101 N. F St.* ☎ *719/539–3118.*

Gallery 150. Check out this gallery's jewelry and wearable art, plus blown glass, furniture, sculpture, pottery, and fiber art. ✉ *150 W. 1st St.* ☎ *719/539–2971* ⊕ *www.gallery150.com.*

Maverick Potter. Brice Turnbill's wonderful blown-glass creations are at the Maverick Potter gallery, where the artist rents space. The gallery also displays work from owner Mark Rittmann, a brewer-turned-potter who has shown pieces all over the country. ✉ *119 F St.* ☎ *719/539–5112* ⊕ *www.maverickpotter.com.*

Rock Doc at Prospectors Village. Midway between Salida and Buena Vista, the Rock Doc is an enormous shop with gold-panning equipment, metal detectors, and rock art. ✉ *17897 U.S. 285, Nathrop* ☎ *719/539–2019* ⊕ *www.therockdoc.net.*

Salida ArtWalk. First Street and F Street are home to many antiques shops and art galleries, including specialists in contemporary art, photography, and jewelry. The annual Salida ArtWalk takes place in late June. Ask the chamber of commerce for the *Art in Salida* or *Antique Dealers* brochures for information about the ArtWalk. ⊠ *Salida.*

Spirit Mountain, Antler & Design. This shop has stunning handcrafted tables inlaid with turquoise and other handmade furniture. ⊠ *223 E. 1st St.* ☎ *719/539–1500.*

SOUTHEAST COLORADO

Pueblo is the biggest city along I–25 between Colorado Springs and the New Mexico border. South of Pueblo, Trinidad is close to the state border, and there are a few small towns sprinkled around the region. West of I–25 there's easy access to the mountains along picturesque routes such as the Highway of Legends, a scenic byway that runs through the Cuchara Valley.

PUEBLO

40 miles east of Cañon City via U.S. 50; 42 miles south of Colorado Springs via I–25.

In 1842 El Pueblo trading post, on the bank of the Arkansas River, was a gathering place for trappers and traders. Today the trading post is an archaeological dig set in a pavilion next to the new El Pueblo History Museum. The thriving city of Pueblo surrounds the museum, and the Arkansas River runs through the city in a concrete channel, tamed by the Pueblo Dam.

To get a sense of the city and its offerings, start at the museum, stroll through the Union Avenue Historic District, and then take a ride on one of the tour boats leaving from the Historic Arkansas Riverwalk, an urban waterfront area that restored the Arkansas River channel to its original location. More than 682 acres of parkland, in addition to hiking and bicycling trails, help to define Pueblo as a sports and recreation center.

GETTING HERE AND AROUND
A car is the best way to explore this sprawling city.

ESSENTIALS
Visitor Information Pueblo Chamber of Commerce. ⊠ *302 N. Santa Fe Ave.* ☎ *719/542–1704, 800/233–3446* ⊕ *www.pueblochamber.org.*

EXPLORING
TOP ATTRACTIONS
FAMILY **El Pueblo History Museum.** A nicely designed repository for the city's history, El Pueblo History Museum extends its scope to chronicle life on the plains since the prehistoric era. It tells of Pueblo's role as a cultural and geographic crossroads, beginning when it was a trading post in the 1840s. Hands-on features—a giant teepee where guests can go inside and play historic drum replicas; a dress-up chest full of pioneer clothing and hats; and a covered wagon that is just the right height for small

hands to discover the trinkets on board—make this museum fun for the whole family. Remnants of the original trading post are now an archaeological dig enclosed in a pavilion next to the museum. ✉ *301 N. Union Ave.* ☎ *719/583–0453* ⊕ *www.historycolorado.org* ▤ *$5* ⊘ *Mon.–Sat. 10–4, Sun. noon–4.*

Union Avenue Historic District. The century-old stores and warehouses of Union Avenue Historic District make for a commercial district filled with a mix of stores ranging from kitschy to good. Among the landmarks are the glorious 1889 sandstone-and-brick Union Avenue Depot and Mesa Junction. Pitkin Avenue, lined with fabulous gabled and turreted mansions, attests to the town's more prosperous times. Walking-tour brochures are available at the chamber of commerce. ✉ *Pueblo.*

WORTH NOTING

FAMILY **Buell Children's Museum.** Ranked among the best in the country, the Buell Children's Museum provides fun, interactive experiences for kids of all ages. The 12,000-square-foot facility has innovative exhibits on art, science, and history. It's in the same complex as the Sangre de Cristo Arts Center. ✉ *210 N. Santa Fe Ave.* ☎ *719/295–7200* ⊕ *www.sdc-arts.org/ museum/current_exhibits* ▤ *$8* ⊘ *Tues.–Fri. 11–5, weekends noon–5.*

FAMILY **City Park.** The fine City Park has fishing lakes, playgrounds, a carousel, a mini train ride, and tennis courts and a swimming pool. ✉ *Pueblo Blvd. and Goodnight Ave.*

Pueblo Zoo. In City Park, this biopark is home to black-footed penguins, ringtail lemurs, and pythons—housed separately of course. Favorites here include African painted dogs, lions, river otters, and the annual holiday feature ElectriCritters, an evening light display that involves more than 250,000 lights, which runs from late November through the end of the year. ✉ *3455 Nuckolls Ave.* ☎ *719/561–1452* ⊕ *www.pueblozoo.org* ▤ *$10* ⊘ *May–Sept., daily 9–5; Oct.–Apr., Mon.–Sat. 9–4, Sun. noon–4.*

Historic Arkansas Riverwalk of Pueblo. Stroll on the paths or take to the water on a boat tour or in a paddleboat to explore this 32-acre urban waterfront park. Boat rides are available at the riverwalk center at 101 South Union Avenue. ✉ *Pueblo* ☎ *719/595–1589 boat reservations* ⊕ *www.puebloharp.com.*

Pueblo-Weisbrod Aircraft Museum. At the city's airport, the Pueblo-Weisbrod Aircraft Museum traces the development of American military aviation with nearly 30 aircraft in mint condition, ranging from a Lockheed F-80 fighter plane to a MiG-15. Curator Shawn Kirst is restoring a Boeing B-29 Super Fortress of atomic-bomb fame on-site. Admission also includes entry to the International B-24 Memorial Museum, which is also on this site. ✉ *Pueblo Memorial Airport, 31001 Magnuson Ave.* ☎ *719/948–9219* ⊕ *www.pwam.org* ▤ *$9* ⊘ *Mon.–Sat. 10–4, Sun. 1–4.*

Rosemount Museum. Exquisite maple, oak, and mahogany woodwork gleams throughout this splendid 37-room mansion, with ivory glaze and gold-leaf trim. Italian marble fireplaces, Tiffany-glass fixtures, and frescoed ceilings complete the opulent look. The top floor—originally servants' quarters—features the odd Andrew McClelland Collection: objects of curiosity this eccentric philanthropist garnered on his worldwide travels, including an Egyptian mummy. ✉ *419 W. 14th St.* ☎ *719/545–5290* ⊕ *www.rosemount.org* 🎫 *$6* ⊙ *Feb.–Dec., Tues.–Sat. 10–3:30; tours every half hr.*

**OFF THE
BEATEN
PATH**

Bishop Castle. This elaborate creation, which resembles a medieval castle replete with turrets, buttresses, and ornamental iron, is the prodigious (some might say monomaniacal) one-man undertaking of Jim Bishop, a self-taught architect who began work in 1969. Once considered a blight on pastoral Highway 165, the castle is now a popular attraction. Not yet complete, it is three stories high with a nearly 165-foot tower. Those who endeavor to climb into the structure must sign the guest book–cum–liability waiver. Bishop finances this enormous endeavor through donations and a gift shop. ✉ *12705 Hwy. 165* ☎ *719/485–3040* ⊕ *www.bishopcastle.org* 🎫 *Free* ⊙ *Daily, sunrise–sunset.*

SPORTS AND THE OUTDOORS

BIKING

Pueblo Bike Trail System. An extensive network of bike trails loops around the city, following the Arkansas River for part of the way before heading out to the reservoir. There are paved portions of the trail that are popular in-line skating routes, too. You can get trail maps at the chamber of commerce. ✉ *Pueblo.*

BOATING, KAYAKING, AND FISHING

Edge Ski, Paddle and Pack. Along the Arkansas River near the Pueblo Levee you'll notice a kayak course. The Edge Ski, Paddle and Pack rents kayaks and gives lessons. ✉ *107 N. Union Ave.* ☎ *719/583–2021* ⊕ *www.edgeskiandpaddle.com.*

Lake Pueblo State Park. There's excellent camping and fishing at Lake Pueblo State Park, as well as many other outdoor activities. ✉ *Hwy. 96* ✛ *8 miles west of downtown* ☎ *719/561–9320* ⊕ *www.parks.state. co.us/parks/LakePueblo.*

South Shore Marina. At this marina in Lake Pueblo State Park, you can rent 10-passenger pontoon boats for $210 per half-day. ✉ *Lake Pueblo State Park, Hwy. 96* ✛ *8 miles west of downtown* ☎ *719/564–1043* ⊕ *www.thesouthshoremarina.com.*

GOLF

Walking Stick Golf Course. This challenging links-style course is named after the native cholla, the cacti in the rugged terrain and arroyos that surround the rolling green fairways. ✉ *4301 Walking Stick Blvd.* ☎ *719/553–1181* ⊕ *www.pueblocitygolf.com* 🎫 *$44* 🏌 *18 holes, 7147 yards, par 72.*

HIKING

Nature & Raptor Center of Pueblo. You can bike, hike, and canoe along the 35 miles in the river trail system that follows the Arkansas River into City Park or out to Lake Pueblo State Park. For more information, call the Nature & Raptor Center of Pueblo. A small interpretive center describes the flora and fauna unique to the area, and it also cares for injured birds of prey. Volunteers bring the tamer birds out of their cage for occasional show-and-tell when visitors are around. ✉ *5200 Nature Center Rd., off Hwy. 45* ☎ *719/549–2414* ⊕ *www.natureandraptor.org.*

San Isabel National Forest. You can hike in relative solitude on many trails threading the San Isabel National Forest, 45 minutes southwest of Pueblo. The forest service station in Pueblo is open 7:30 am–4:30 pm weekdays. Check in with them for backpacking permits. ✉ *2840 Kachina Dr.* ☎ *719/553–1670* ⊕ *www.fs.usda.gov/psicc.*

WHERE TO EAT

$$$ ✕ **dc's on b street.** There are two dining areas in this restaurant, housed
AMERICAN in the historic redbrick Coors building across from the Union Depot. At lunch you can order sandwiches, salads, and other light fare in a room with simple tables, brick walls, and a tin ceiling. For dinner in the more elegant dining room, try the moist crab cakes followed by pork or steak beautifully dripping with well-matched, decadent sauces. $ *Average main: $24* ✉ *115 B St.* ☎ *719/584–3410.*

$ ✕ **Gray's Coors Tavern.** Locals constantly debate where to find the city's
AMERICAN best "slopper"—an open-faced burger smothered in cheese, red or green chili, and onions—but there is no question you will find an authentic Pueblo experience at this dive bar where the dish was first served. Bikers and families converge on the large outdoor patio during the summers to devour the messy burger. Add a pile of fries to the top for the true slopper taste, and make sure to pair it all with an ice-cold Coors in honor of the building that was once a distribution center for the state's largest brewery. $ *Average main: $9* ✉ *515 W. 4th St.* ☎ *719/544–0455* ▭ *No credit cards.*

$$ ✕ **Shamrock Brewing Company.** This consistently jam-packed hot spot is
IRISH a bar and grill with a good kitchen. With dishes like corned beef and cabbage and Jameson meat loaf, it's the place for authentic Irish pub grub. And of course they brew their own beer—six or seven varieties are usually on tap including the Irish Red Ale and PAPA, the Pueblo American Pale Ale. It's especially popular with the after-work crowd. $ *Average main: $14* ✉ *108 W. 3rd St.* ☎ *719/542–9974* ⊕ *www. shamrockbrewing.com.*

WHERE TO STAY

$ ☷ **Courtyard Marriott Pueblo.** A reliably good choice in downtown Pueblo,
HOTEL the Marriott offers excellent value and service. **Pros:** close to downtown destinations; concierge floor. **Cons:** not much nearby for tourists; because it's a convention hotel, your neighbors may be early risers. $ *Rooms from: $99* ✉ *110 City Center Dr.* ☎ *719/542–3200, 866/706–7815* ⊕ *www.marriott.com* ⇆ *160 rooms, 6 suites* ⦿*No meals.*

$$ ☷ **Rusted Poppy Inn.** The playful gardens and large porch with plenty
B&B/INN of seating beckon visitors to this 1900 brick home situated among a
Fodor's Choice treasure trove of well-preserved houses in this historic neighborhood.
★ **Pros:** clean with lots of charm; knowledgable local staff. **Cons:** not best for young children; 12 blocks from downtown and riverwalk. $ *Rooms from: $130* ✉ *130 W. Orman Ave.* ☎ *719/544–1350* ⊕ *www. therustedpoppyinn.com* ⇆ *5 rooms* ⦿ *Breakfast* ▭ *No credit cards.*

NIGHTLIFE AND PERFORMING ARTS

PERFORMING ARTS

Broadway Theatre League. This downtown theater company brings three touring Broadway blockbusters to the restored Memorial Hall every year. ⊠ *Memorial Hall, 1 City Hall Place* ☎ *719/295–7222* ⊕ *www. broadwaytheatreleaguepueblo.com.*

Pueblo Symphony. The city's symphony performs all types of music, from pops to classical. Concerts are held at the Hoag Recital Hall on the Colorado State University–Pueblo campus. ⊠ *Hoag Recital Hall, 2200 Bonforte Blvd.* ☎ *719/545–7967* ⊕ *www.pueblosymphony.com.*

Sangre de Cristo Arts Center. Rotating exhibits at this impressive performance and gallery center celebrate regional arts and crafts. The center also houses the superb Western art collection donated by Francis King and a theater with a performing-arts series that ranges from plays to ballets. ⊠ *210 N. Santa Fe Ave.* ☎ *719/295–7200* ⊕ *www.sdc-arts.org.*

NIGHTLIFE

Gus' Place. A legendary Pueblo dive bar, this quintessential locals' hangout has been going strong since the 1930s. ⊠ *1201 Elm St.* ☎ *719/542–0755.*

EN ROUTE **Rocky Ford.** Leaving the Rockies far behind, U.S. 50 takes you toward the eastern plains, where rolling prairies give way to hardier desert blooms and the land is stubbled with sage and stunted pinyon pines. One fertile spot—50 miles along the highway—is the town of Rocky Ford, dubbed the "Melon Capital of the World" for its famously succulent cantaloupes. ⊠ *Rocky Ford.*

LA JUNTA

60 miles east of Pueblo via U.S. 50.

For an easy day trip from Pueblo into Colorado's past, head east to La Junta. The Koshare Indian Museum is in town, and Bent's Old Fort National Historic Site and the dinosaur tracks and ancient rock art of the canyonlands are nearby.

GETTING HERE AND AROUND

Amtrak stops in La Junta but a private car is best to explore this remote area.

ESSENTIALS

Visitor Information La Junta Chamber of Commerce. ⊠ *110 Santa Fe Ave.* ☎ *719/384–7411* ⊕ *www.lajuntachamber.com.*

EXPLORING

Bent's Old Fort National Historic Site. About 8 miles east of La Junta, Bent's Old Fort National Historic Site painstakingly re-creates what life was like in this adobe fort. Founded in 1833 by trader William Bent, the fort was situated along the commercially vital Santa Fe Trail, providing both protection and a meeting place for the soldiers, trappers, and traders of the era. The museum's interior reveals daily life at a trading post, providing looks at a smithy and carpenter's workshop and featuring educational films and guided tours. Guided tours are offered daily during the summer. ⊠ *35110 Hwy. 194* ☎ *719/383–5010* ⊕ *www.nps. gov/beol* ⊠ *$3* ⊙ *June–Aug., daily 8–5:30; Sept.–May, daily 9–4.*

Koshare Indian Museum. With Navajo silver, Zuni pottery, and Shoshone buckskin clothing, the Koshare Indian Museum contains extensive holdings of Native American artifacts and crafts. It also displays pieces from Anglo artists, such as Remington, known for their depictions of Native Americans. The Koshare Indian Dancers—actually local youth—perform regularly. ✉ *115 W. 18th St.* ☎ *719/384–4411* 🌐 *www.kosharehistory.org* 🎟 *$5* 🕒 *May–Sept., daily noon–5; Oct.–Apr., Wed. and Fri.–Mon. noon–5.*

QUICK BITES

Boss Hogg's. For a quick bite, try this Western-themed watering hole and barbecue-steak joint with a quirky personality. Boss Hogg's is a local institution. ✉ *808 E. 3rd St.* ☎ *719/384-7879.*

SPORTS AND THE OUTDOORS

Comanche National Grassland. This vast 444,000-acre tract has a pair of canyon loops where there's a fair amount of rock art. Some of the largest documented sets of fossilized dinosaur tracks in the United States are in **Picket Wire Canyonlands**, a part of the grassland. There are tables for when you want an impromptu picnic. ✉ *Ranger Office, 1420 E. 3rd St.* ✥ *From La Junta, drive south on Hwy. 109 for 13 miles, west on County Rd. 802 for 8 miles, and south on County Rd. 25 for 6 miles. Turn left at Picket Wire Corrals onto Forest Service Rd. 2185 and follow signs to Withers Canyon Trailhead* ☎ *719/384–2181* 🌐 *www.fs.usda.gov/detail/psicc.*

WESTCLIFFE

55 miles west of Pueblo via Hwy. 96 and 47 miles southwest of Cañon City via scenic Hwys. 50 and 69.

In a joint effort with neighboring Silver Cliff, this remote town at the base of the Sangre de Cristo Mountains became the state's first International Dark Sky Community in 2015. Nestled in the quiet Custer County, mountains shade the town from light pollution to the east preserving the dark nights that provide a perfect backdrop for stargazing year-round. Once a mining town, Westcliffe's 568 residents now thrive mostly on agriculture and ranching but spring and summer festivals attract tourists from around the world. In July, the town's bluegrass festival and jazz camp bring a lively soundtrack to the scenic setting, and the Ride the Rockies bike race ended in Westcliffe in 2015 putting it "on the map" as a cycling destination. Abutting the slightly denser Silver Cliff to the east, Westcliffe's mile-long Main Street is host to charming shops, lodging, dining, and friendly locals.

WHERE TO EAT AND STAY

$ ITALIAN

🍴 **Westcliffe Wine Mine.** At this favorite for locals, the food complements the wine, not the other way around. And with house wines starting at $4 a glass (nothing's over $10) you can indulge your taste buds trying several selections recommended by new friends easily met in the intimate space. Tapas, paninis, and pastas taste better on the outdoor patio in the summer with a view of snowcapped peaks. [$] *Average main: $11* ✉ *109 N. 3rd St., Westcliffe* ☎ *719/783–2490* 🌐 *www.westcliffewinemine.com.*

$ 🖼 **Lamp Post Lodge.** This impeccably clean B&B has large rooms, plenty
B&B/INN of natural light, and incredible mountain views from west-facing rooms
on the second floor. **Pros:** stargazing for miles; well maintained; mountain views. **Cons:** remote location; no pedestrian sidewalk to nearby
Main Street. $ *Rooms from: $120* ✉ *59450 Hwy. 69, Westcliffe*
☎ *719/783–2876* ⊕ *www.lamppostlodge.com* ⤳ *7 rooms* ⦿ *Breakfast.*

TRINIDAD

*85 miles south of Pueblo and 13 miles north of New Mexico border
via I–25.*

If you're traveling on I–25 and want to stop for a night in a historic
town with character instead of a motel on the outskirts of a bigger city,
check out Trinidad. Walk around Corazon de Trinidad, the downtown
area where some of the streets still have the original bricks—instead of
pavement—and visit a few of the town's superb museums, a remarkably
large number for a town of about 8,500 residents.

Trinidad was founded in 1862 as a rest-and-repair station along the
Santa Fe Trail. Starting in 1878 with the construction of the railroad
and the development of the coal industry, the town grew and expanded,
especially from 1880 to 1910. But the advent of natural gas, coupled
with the Depression, ushered in a gradual decline in population. Since
the 1990s there's been a modest increase in the population and a major
interest in the upkeep of the city's rich cultural heritage. Although new-
comers are moving in and Trinidad is coming to life again, with restaurants, cafés, and galleries, the streets in the heart of town are still paved
with brick, keeping a sense of the town's history alive.

GETTING HERE AND AROUND

Amtrak stops here. You'll need a private car or you can take the Trinidad Trolley around the downtown area.

TOURS

From June to August you can take the free Trinidad Trolley, and the
driver will give you an informal history of Trinidad between the stops
and at all the museums.

ESSENTIALS

Visitor Information Trinidad & Las Animas Chamber of Commerce. ✉ *136
W. Main St.* ☎ *719/846–9285* ⊕ *www.historictrinidad.com.*

EXPLORING

A.R. Mitchell Memorial Museum and Gallery. This museum celebrates the life
and work of the famous Western illustrator, whose distinctive oils, charcoal drawings, and watercolors graced the pages of ranch romances.
Original works that were featured in pulp magazines are on display at
the museum, which is in a historic building with the original tin ceiling.
Western paintings by Arthur Roy Mitchell, Harvey Dunn, and Harold
Von Schmidt are also on display. Cowboy prints and collectibles are sold
in the museum's gift shop. ✉ *150 E. Main St.* ☎ *719/846–4224* ⊕ *www.
armitchellmuseum.com* 🎫 *$5* ⦿ *Wed.–Sun. 11–5.*

Corazon de Trinidad (*Heart of Trinidad*). Downtown Trinidad, called the Corazon de Trinidad, is a National Historic Landmark District, with the original brick-paved streets, several Victorian mansions, graceful churches, and the bright-red domes and turrets of Temple Aaron, Colorado's oldest continuously used Reform synagogue. ✉ *Trinidad.*

Louden-Henritze Archaeology Museum. On the other side of the Purgatoire River, this museum at Trinidad State Junior College takes viewers back millions of years to examine the true origins of the region, including early geological formations, plant and marine-animal fossils, and prehistoric artifacts. ✉ *Trinidad State Junior College, 600 Prospect St.* ☎ *719/846–5508* 🌐 *www.trinidadstate.edu/museum* 🎟 *Free* 🕒 *Jan.–Nov., Mon.–Thurs. 10–3.*

FAMILY **Old Firehouse No. 1 Children's Museum.** Set in the delightful Old Firehouse Number 1, the museum displays fire-fighting memorabilia, such as a 1947 American LaFrance fire truck (children love clanging the bell) and the city's original fire alarm system. Upstairs is a fine re-creation of an early 1900s schoolroom. This is a favorite with the kids, but call ahead to make sure they're open—or to schedule a tour—as the hours can be sporadic. ✉ *314 N. Commercial St.* ☎ *719/846–7721* 🌐 *www.santafetrailscenicandhistoricbyway.org/fhsmus.html* 🎟 *Free* 🕒 *Call for hrs.*

Trinidad History Museum. This complex with three separate museums and a garden is a place to learn about the town's history. The first museum is **Baca House**, the 1870s residence of Felipe Baca, a prominent Hispanic farmer and businessman. Displays convey a mix of Anglo (clothes, furniture) and Hispanic (santos, textiles) influences. Next door, the 1882 **Bloom Mansion** was built by Frank Bloom, who made his money through ranching and banking. He filled his ornate Second Empire–style Victorian with fine furnishings and fabrics brought from the East Coast and abroad. The adjacent **Santa Fe Trail Museum**—the only free-entrance building—is dedicated to the effect of the trail and railroad on the community. Inside are exhibits covering Trinidad's heyday as a commercial and cultural center. Finish up with a stop in the **Heritage Gardens,** which are open year-round and filled with native plants and century-old grapevines similar to those tended by the pioneers. ✉ *312 E. Main St.* ☎ *719/846–7217* 🌐 *www.trinidadhistorymuseum.org* 🎟 *$5 per house* 🕒 *May–Sept., Mon.–Sat. 10–4. Gardens: daily 10–4.*

SPORTS AND THE OUTDOORS

Trinidad Lake State Park. There's hiking, fishing, horseback riding, and camping at this park in the Purgatoire River Valley. ✉ *Hwy. 12* ✣ *3 miles west of Trinidad* ☎ *719/846–6951* 🌐 *parks.state.co.us/parks/trinidadlake.*

WHERE TO EAT AND STAY

$ CAFÉ 🍴 **The Café.** Set in a downtown historic building with red umbrellas marking the front patio, this eatery serves imaginative and delicious sandwiches. Try the Baca House, hot roast beef with pepper jack cheese and crema fresca served on a ciabatta roll. This spot is usually crowded at breakfast and lunch, but you order at the counter, so things move quickly. Drop in for a muffin or cinammon rolls and a cup of strong coffee or chai tea if you don't want a full meal. [$] *Average main: $9* ✉ *135 E. Main St.* ☎ *719/846–7119* 🕒 *Closed Sun. No dinner.*

$ ITALIAN 🍴 **Nana and Nano's Pasta House.** The aroma of garlic and tomato sauce saturates this tiny, unpretentious eatery. Pastas, including standards like ravioli with homemade sauce and rigatoni with luscious meatballs, are consistently excellent. If you don't have time for a sit-down lunch, stop at the deli counter for sandwiches or takeouts of imported cheeses and olives. [$] *Average main: $10* ✉ *418 E. Main St.* ☎ *719/846–2696* 🕓 *Closed Sun.–Tues.*

$ B&B/INN 🏨 **Tarabino Inn.** This Italianate–Victorian B&B sits in the middle of the Corazon de Trinidad National Historic District. **Pros:** inn is filled with work by local artists; within walking distance of museums. **Cons:** feels like staying in someone's private home. [$] *Rooms from: $84* ✉ *310 E. 2nd St.* ☎ *719/846–2115, 866/846–8808* 🌐 *www.tarabinoinn.com* 🛏 *3 suites, 2 rooms without bath* 🍽 *Breakfast.*

CUCHARA VALLEY

55 miles northwest of Trinidad and 64 miles southwest of Pueblo to the town of La Veta via I–25, U.S. 160, and Hwy. 12.

If you want a true mountain rural setting, head to the Cuchara Valley. From here or La Veta you can go camping or hiking in the San Isabel National Forest, go horseback riding on trails through the woods, or go fishing in streams.

GETTING HERE AND AROUND

The Cuchara Valley is along the Highway of Legends. You need a private car to get here and move around this region.

ESSENTIALS

Visitor Information La Veta–Cuchara Chamber of Commerce. ☎ *719/742-3676* 🌐 *www.lavetacucharachamber.com.*

EXPLORING

Cokedale. This entire town is a National Historic Landmark District, and it's the most significant example of a turn-of-the-20th-century coal–coke camp in Colorado. As you drive through the area, note the telltale streaks of black in the sandstone and granite bluffs fronting the Purgatoire River and its tributaries, the unsightly slag heaps, and the spooky abandoned mining camps dotting the hillsides. ✉ *Hwy. 12, Cokedale* ✣ *9 miles west of Trinidad.*

Highway of Legends. From Trinidad, the scenic Highway of Legends curls north through the Cuchara Valley. As it starts its climb, you'll pass a series of company towns built to house coal miners. The Highway of Legends, also known as Highway 12, takes you through some of the wildest and most beautiful scenery in southern Colorado. You can start the drive in Trinidad or La Veta. 🌐 *www.trinidadco.com/main/highway-of-legends.*

La Veta. The Highway of Legends passes through the tiny, laid-back resort town of La Veta before intersecting with U.S. 160 and turning east toward Walsenburg, another settlement built on coal and the largest town between Pueblo and Trinidad. ✉ *La Veta.*

San Isabel National Forest. As you approach Cuchara Pass, several switchbacks snake through rolling grasslands and dance in and out of spruce stands whose clearings afford views of Monument Lake. You can camp, fish, and hike throughout this tranquil part of the San Isabel National Forest, which in spring and summer is emblazoned with a color wheel of wildflowers. Four corkscrewing miles later you'll reach a dirt road that leads to Bear Lake and Blue Lake. The resort town of Cuchara is about 4 miles from the Highway 12 turnoff to the lakes. Nestled in a spoon valley (*cuchara* means "spoon"), the area became popular as a turn-of-the-20th-century camping getaway for Texans and Oklahomans because of its cool temperatures and stunning scenery. 🌐 *www.fs.usda.gov/psicc.*

Spanish Peaks. In the Cuchara Valley you'll see fantastic rock formations with equally fanciful names, such as Profile Rock, Devil's Staircase, and Giant's Spoon. With a little imagination you can devise your own legends about the names' origins. There are more than 400 of these upthrusts, which radiate like the spokes of a wheel from the valley's dominating landmark, the Spanish Peaks. In Spanish they are known as *Dos Hermanos,* or "Two Brothers." In Ute, their name *Huajatolla* means "breasts of the world." The haunting formations are considered to be a unique geologic phenomenon for their sheer abundance and variety of rock types.

SPORTS AND THE OUTDOORS

HIKING

San Isabel National Forest. In this vast wilderness, you can explore myriad hiking trails, not to mention campgrounds, fishing streams, and mountain-biking terrain. In winter it's a cross-country skiing destination. ✉ *Ranger Office, 2840 Kachina Dr., Pueblo* ☎ *719/553–1400* 🌐 *www.fs.usda.gov/psicc.*

WHERE TO EAT AND STAY

$$$ CONTEMPORARY Fodor's Choice ★

🍴 **Alys' Restaurant.** Dinner at Alys' is a simple treat: for $25 apiece, you'll be fed an "international eclectic" protein (perhaps chicken paprikash or lamb shanks braised in Pinot Noir); fresh vegetables; potato, rice, or pasta; soup or salad; and soft drinks, tea, or coffee. (Vegetarian dinners are $20.) Wine is extra, and you'll appreciate the attentive care taken with the thoughtful wine list—you might even have the opportunity to ask chef Alys Romer what she recommends. Lunch is à la carte. [$] *Average main: $25* ✉ *604 S. Oak St., La Veta* ☎ *719/742–3742* 🌐 *www.alysrestaurant.com* 💳 *No credit cards* 🕒 *Closed Mon.–Wed.* ✍ *Reservations essential.*

$ B&B/INN

🏨 **Inn at the Spanish Peaks Bed & Breakfast.** This Southwestern-style B&B is set in an adobe-style home with open beams and high ceilings. **Pros:** mountain views; friendly owners; good breakfasts. **Cons:** you are really in the outback of Colorado; no air-conditioning. [$] *Rooms from: $100* ✉ *310 E. Francisco St., La Veta* ☎ *719/742–5313* 🌐 *www.innatthespanishpeaks.com* 🛏 *3 suites* 🍽 *Breakfast.*

THE SAN LUIS VALLEY

The San Luis Valley is considered to be the world's largest alpine valley, sprawling on a broad, flat, dry plain between the San Juan and La Garita mountains to the west and the Sangre de Cristo range to the east. But equally important is that the valley, like the Southwest, remains culturally rooted in the early Hispanic tradition rather than the northern European one that early prospectors and settlers brought to central and northern Colorado.

Despite an average elevation of more than 7,500 feet, the San Luis Valley's sheltering peaks help to create a relatively mild climate. The area is one of the state's major agricultural producers, with huge annual crops of potatoes, carrots, canola, barley, and lettuce. In many ways it's self-sufficient; in the 1950s local business owners threatened to secede to prove that the state couldn't get along without the valley and its valuable products. Half a century later, however, the reality is that the region is economically disadvantaged and contains two of the state's poorer counties. The large and sparsely populated valley contains some real oddities, including an alligator farm, a UFO-viewing tower, and the New Age town of Crestone, with its many spiritual centers.

This area was settled first by the Ute, then by the Spanish, who left their indelible imprint in the town names and architecture. The oldest town (San Luis), the oldest military post (Fort Garland), and the oldest church (Our Lady of Guadalupe in Conejos) in the state are in this valley.

GREAT SAND DUNES NATIONAL PARK AND PRESERVE

Created by winds that sweep the San Luis Valley floor, the enormous sand dunes that form the heart of Great Sand Dunes National Park and Preserve are an improbable, unforgettable sight. The dunes, as curvaceous as Rubens's nudes, stretch for more than 30 square miles. Because they're made of sand, the dunes' very existence seems tenuous, as if they might blow away before your eyes, yet they're solid enough to withstand 440,000 years of Mother Nature—and the modern stress of hikers and saucer-riding thrill-seekers.

GETTING ORIENTED

The Great Sand Dunes Park and Preserve encompasses 150,000 acres (about 234 square miles) of land and mountains surrounding the dunes. Looking at the dunes from the west, your eye sweeps over the grassland and sand sheet, a vast expanse of smaller dunes and flatter sections of sand and knee-high brush. The Sangre de Cristo Mountains rear up in the east behind the dunes, forming a dramatic backdrop and creating a stunning juxtaposition of color and form.

Sand dunes. The 30-square-mile field of sand has no designated trails. The highest dune in the park—and, in fact, in North America—is 750-foot-high Star Dune.

Sangre de Cristo Mountains. Named the "Blood of Christ" Mountains by Spanish explorers because of their ruddy color—especially at sunrise and sunset—the range contains 10 of Colorado's 58 Fourteeners (mountains taller than 14,000 feet).

WHEN TO GO

About 300,000 visitors come to the park each year, most on summer weekends; they tend to congregate around the main parking area and Medano Creek. To avoid the crowds, hike away from the main area up to the High Dune. Or come in the winter, when the park is a place for contemplation and repose—as well as skiing and sledding.

Fall and spring are the prettiest times to visit, with the surrounding mountains still capped with snow in May, and leaves on the aspen trees turning gold in September and early October. In summer, the surface temperature of the sand can climb to 150°F in the afternoon, so climbing the dunes is best in the morning or late afternoon. Since you're at a high altitude—about 8,200 feet at the visitor center—the air temperatures in the park itself remain in the 70s most of the summer.

GETTING HERE AND AROUND

Great Sand Dunes National Park and Preserve is about 240 miles from both Denver and Albuquerque, and roughly 180 miles from Colorado Springs and Santa Fe. The fastest route from Denver is I–25 south to U.S. 160, heading west to just past Blanca, to Highway 150 north, which goes right to the park's main entrance. For a more scenic route, take U.S. 285 over Kenosha, Red Hill, and Poncha Passes, turn onto Highway 17 just south of Villa Grove, then take County Lane 6 to the park (watch for signs just south of Hooper). From Albuquerque, go north on I–25 to Santa Fe, then north on U.S. 285 to Alamosa, then U.S. 160 east to Highway 150. From the west, Highway 17 and County Lane 6 take you to the park. The park entrance station is about 3 miles from the park boundary, and it's about a mile from there to the visitor center; the main parking lot is about a mile farther.

PARK ESSENTIALS

PARK FEES
AND PERMITS

Entrance fees are $3 per adult above age 16 and are valid for one week from date of purchase. Children are admitted free at all times. Pick up camping permits ($20 per night per site at Pinyon Flats Campground) and backpacking permits (free) at the visitor center.

PARK HOURS

The park is open 24/7. It is in the mountain time zone.

CELL-PHONE
RECEPTION

Cell-phone reception in the park is sporadic. Public telephones are at the visitor center, dunes parking lot, and at the Pinyon Flats campground—you need a calling card (these aren't coin-operated phones).

EDUCATIONAL OFFERINGS

FAMILY

Bison Tour. The Nature Conservancy, an international nonprofit conservation organization, owns a 103,000-acre ranch that includes a herd of roughly 2,000 bison in the 50,000-acre Medano Ranch section, in the southwest corner of the park. The conservancy offers a two-hour tour focused on the section of the park, where bison—along with coyotes, elk, deer, pronghorns, porcupines, and birds such as great horned owls and red-tailed hawks—roam in the grasslands and wetlands. Depending on the season, the tour will be led by wagon or a four-wheel-drive vehicle. Tours begin at the Nature Conservancy's Zapata Ranch Headquarters and reservations are required at least 24 hours in advance. ⊠ *Zapata Ranch Headquarters, 5305 Hwy. 150, Mosca* ☎ *888/592–7282, 719/378–2356* ⊕ *www.zranch. org* ☛ *Tours $50* ⊙ *daily 8–5; tours Wed., Fri., and Sat. 9 am and noon.*

RANGER
PROGRAMS
FAMILY

Interpretive Programs. Family-friendly nature walks designed to help visitors learn more about the Great Sand Dunes National Park are scheduled most days from late May through September, and sporadically in April and October. Call or drop in to ask about sunset walks, afternoon weekend tours and evening stargazing programs. ✉ *Programs begin at the visitor center, Great Sand Dunes National Park* ☎ *719/378–6399* ▧ *Free.*

FAMILY

Junior Ranger Programs. In summer, children ages 3 through 12 can join age-appropriate activities to learn about plants, animals, and the park's ecology, and they can become Junior Rangers by working successfully through an activity booklet available at the visitor center. If they complete the self-led program, they'll receive a patch or a badge. ✉ *Visitor Center, 11999 Hwy. 150, Great Sand Dunes National Park* ☎ *719/378–6399.*

VISITOR INFORMATION

Park Contact Information Great Sand Dunes National Park and Preserve. ✉ *11999 Hwy. 150, Mosca* ☎ *719/378–6399* ⊕ *www.nps.gov/grsa.*

VISITOR
CENTER

Great Sand Dunes Visitor Center. View exhibits and artwork, browse in the bookstore, and watch a 20-minute film with an overview of the dunes. Rangers are on hand to answer questions. Facilities include restrooms and a vending machine stocked with soft drinks and snacks, but no other food. (The Great Sand Dunes Oasis, just outside the park boundary, has a café that is open generally late April through early October.) ✉ *Near the park entrance, Great Sand Dunes National Park* ☎ *719/378–6399* ⊕ *www.nps.gov/grsa/planyourvisit/visitor-center. htm* ☉ *Late May–early Sept., daily 8:30–6; early Sept.–late May, daily 9–4:30 (sometimes until 5 in late spring and early fall—call ahead).*

EXPLORING

SCENIC DRIVES

Medano Pass Primitive Road. This 22-mile road connects Great Sand Dunes with the Wet Mountain Valley and Highway 69 on the east side of the Sangre de Cristo Mountains via a climb to Medano Pass (about 10,000 feet above sea level) and affords stunning views, especially in late September when the aspen trees change color. It also provides access to campsites in the national preserve. It is a four-wheel-drive-only road that is best driven by someone who already has good driving skills on rough, unpaved roads. (Your four-wheel-drive vehicle must have high clearance and be engineered to go over rough roads, and you may need to drop your tires' air pressure.) The road has sections of deep, loose sand, and it crosses Medano Creek nine times. Before you go, stop at the visitor center for a map and ask about current road conditions. Drive time pavement to pavement is 2½ to 3 hours. ✉ *Great Sand Dunes National Park.*

SCENIC STOPS

There's one paved road in the park, and it goes to the park visitor center, the amphitheater, and about another mile to the Pinyon Flats Campground. Past the campground, you can take a regular car another mile on the Medano Pass Primitive Road to the Point of No Return. Beyond that only four-wheel high-clearance vehicles are allowed.

Dune Field. The more than 30 square miles of big dunes in the heart of the park is the main attraction, although the surrounding sand sheet does have some smaller dunes. You can start putting your feet in the sand 3 miles past the main park entrance. ⊠ *Great Sand Dunes National Park.*

High Dune. This isn't the park's highest dune, but it's high enough in the dune field to provide a view of all the dunes from its summit. It's on the first ridge of dunes you see from the main parking area. ⊠ *Great Sand Dunes National Park.*

SPORTS AND THE OUTDOORS

BIRD-WATCHING

The San Luis Valley is famous for its migratory birds, many of which make a stop in the park. Great Sand Dunes also has many permanent feathered residents. In the wetlands, you might see American white pelicans and the American avocet. On the forested sections of the mountains there are goshawks, northern harriers, gray jays, and Steller's jays. And in the alpine tundra there are golden eagles, hawks, horned larks, and white-tailed ptarmigan.

FISHING

Fly fishermen can angle for Rio Grande cutthroat trout in the upper reaches of Medano Creek, which is accessible by four-wheel-drive vehicle. It's catch-and-release only, and a Colorado license is required (☎ 800/244–5613). There's also fishing in Upper and Lower Sand Creek Lakes, but it's a very long hike (3 or 4 miles from the Music Pass trail, located on the far side of the park in the San Isabel National Forest).

HIKING

Visitors can walk just about anywhere on the sand dunes in the heart of the park. The best view of all the dunes is from the top of High Dune. There are no formal trails because the sand keeps shifting, but you don't really need them: You can easily spot the crowds near the main parking lot from any high point.

■TIP➔ **Before taking any of the trails in the preserve, rangers recommend stopping at the visitor center and picking up the handout that lists the trails, including their degree of difficulty.** The dunes can get very hot in summer, reaching up to 150°F in the afternoon. If you're hiking, carry plenty of water; if you're going into the backcountry to camp overnight, carry even more water and a water filtration system. A free permit is needed to backpack in the park. Also, watch for weather changes. If there's a thunderstorm and lightning, get off the dunes or trail immediately, and seek shelter. Before hiking, leave word with someone indicating where you're going to hike and when you expect to be back. Tell that contact to call 911 if you don't show up when expected.

> **BEST CAMPGROUNDS IN GREAT SAND DUNES**
>
> Great Sand Dunes has one campground that is open year-round. During weekends in the summer, it can fill up with RVs and tents by midafternoon. Black bears live in the preserve, so when camping there, keep your food, trash, and toiletries in the trunk of your car (or use bear-proof containers). There is one campground and RV park near the entrance to Great Sand Dunes and several others in the area.

EASY **Hike to High Dune.** Get a panoramic view of all the surrounding dunes
FAMILY from the top of High Dune. Since there's no formal path, the smartest
approach is to zigzag up the dune ridgelines. High Dune is 650 feet
high, and to get there and back takes about 1½ to 2 hours. It's just
over a mile each way, but it can feel like a lot longer if there's been no
rain for some time and the sand is soft. If you add on the walk to the
750-foot Star Dune, which is another 1 mile there and back, plan on
another two hours and a strenuous workout up and down the dunes.
Easy. ⊠ *Great Sand Dunes National Park* ✛ *Start from main dune field.*

MODERATE **Mosca Pass Trail.** This moderately challenging route follows the Mont-
FAMILY ville Trail laid out centuries ago by Native Americans, which became
Fodor'sChoice the Mosca Pass toll road used in the late 1800s and early 1900s. This
★ is a good afternoon hike, because the trail rises through the trees and
subalpine meadows, often following Mosca Creek. It is 3½ miles one
way, with a 1,500-foot gain in elevation. Hiking time is two to three
hours each way. *Moderate.* ⊠ *Great Sand Dunes National Park* ✛ *The
lower end of the trail begins at the Montville Trailhead, just north of
the visitor center.*

DIFFICULT **Music Pass Trail.** This steep trail offers superb views of the glacially carved
Upper Sand Creek Basin, ringed by several 13,000-foot peaks and the
Wet Mountain Valley to the east. The top of the pass can be covered
in snow through midsummer and reaches about 11,000 feet above sea
level, surrounded by even higher mountain peaks. It's 3½ miles and a
2,000-foot elevation gain one way from the lower parking lot on the
east side of the preserve, off Forest Service Road 119, and 1 mile from
the upper parking lot (reachable only by four-wheel-drive). Depending on how fit you are and how often you stop, it can take six hours
round-trip from the lower lot. *Difficult.* ⊠ *Great Sand Dunes National
Park* ✛ *Trail begins on eastern side of park, reached via Hwy. 69, 4½
miles south of Westcliffe. Turn off Hwy. 69 to the west at the sign for
Music Pass and South Colony Lakes Trails. At the "T" junction, turn
left onto South Colony Rd. At the end of the ranch fence on the right
you'll see another sign for Music Pass.*

ALAMOSA

*35 miles southwest of Great Sand Dunes via U.S. 160 and Rte. 150;
163 miles southwest of Colorado Springs.*

The San Luis Valley's major city is a casual, central base from which to
explore the region and visit the Great Sand Dunes.

EXPLORING

Adams State University. The campus here contains several superlative
examples of 1930s WPA-commissioned murals in its administrative
building. The college's **Luther Bean Museum and Art Gallery** displays European porcelain and furniture collections in a handsome, wood-paneled
19th-century drawing room, and exhibits of regional arts and crafts.
⊠ *Richardson Hall, Richardson and 3rd Sts.* ☏ *719/587–7151* ⊕ *www.
adams.edu.*

Alamosa National Wildlife Refuge. Less than an hour's drive southwest of Great Sand Dunes is a sanctuary for songbirds, waterbirds, and raptors (it's also home to many other types of birds, along with mule deer, beavers, and coyotes). The Rio Grande runs through the park comprising more than 12,000 acres of natural and man-made wetlands. You can take a 4-mile hike round-trip along the river or a 3½-mile wildlife drive on the park's western side or a drive along Bluff Road to an overlook on the park's eastern side. The refuge office is staffed by volunteers sporadically from March through November and closed in winter—it's wise to call first. ✉ *9383 El Rancho La., off U.S. 160* ☎ *719/589–4021* 🌐 *www.fws.gov/alamosa* 🎫 *Free* 🕑 *Daily sunrise–sunset.*

Monte Vista National Wildlife Refuge. Just west of the Alamosa wildlife refuge is its sister sanctuary, the Monte Vista National Wildlife Refuge, a 15,000-acre park that's a stopping point for up to 20,000 migrating cranes in the spring and fall. It hosts an annual Crane Festival, held one weekend in mid-March in the nearby town of Monte Vista and a children's Crane Festival in mid-October at the park with kid-friendly activities. You can see the sanctuary via a 2½-mile driving tour. ✉ *6120 Hwy. 15, south off U.S. 160/285, Monte Vista* ☎ *719/589–4021* 🌐 *www.fws.gov/refuge/monte_vista/* 🎫 *Free* 🕑 *Daily sunrise–sunset.*

WHERE TO EAT AND STAY

$ ASIAN 🍴 **East West Grill.** Noodles, salads, and teriyaki top the menu at this casual, almost fast-food-style place with dine-in or carry-out options. [$] *Average main: $8* ✉ *408 4th St.* ☎ *719/589–4600* 🌐 *www.east-westgrill.com.*

$ CAFÉ 🍴 **Milagros Coffeehouse.** The coffee is full-bodied at this combination coffeehouse, café, and used-book store, where all profits go to local charities. The breakfast bagels are especially tasty and organic; local food dominates the menu, which includes plenty of vegetarian and gluten-free options. [$] *Average main: $7* ✉ *529 Main St.* ☎ *719/589–9299.*

$ HOTEL 🏨 **Best Western Alamosa Inn.** This sprawling, well-maintained complex is your best bet for reasonably priced lodgings. **Pros:** reliable basic accommodations; easy to find. **Cons:** noisy street; nothing but fast food nearby. [$] *Rooms from: $108* ✉ *2005 Main St.* ☎ *719/589–2567, 800/459–5123* 🌐 *www.bestwestern.com/alamosainn* 🛏 *52 rooms, 1 suite* 🍽 *Breakfast.*

SAN LUIS AND FORT GARLAND LOOP

To get a real feel for this area, take an easy driving loop from Alamosa that includes San Luis and Fort Garland. In summer, take a few hours to ride one of the scenic railroads that take you into wilderness areas in this region.

EXPLORING

FAMILY **Cumbres & Toltec Scenic Railroad.** Take a day trip on the Cumbres & Toltec Scenic Railroad, an 1880s steam locomotive that chugs through portions of Colorado's and northern New Mexico's rugged mountains that you can't reach via roads. It's the country's longest and highest narrow-gauge railroad. The company offers two round-trip train routes—either Antonito to Osier or Chama, NM, to Osier—plus several bus-and-train combinations and one-way trips. Cumbres & Toltec offers themed rides, including a special Christmastime train ride called "The Cinder Bear." ⊠ *5234 U.S. 285, Antonito* ☎ *888/286–2737* ⊕ *www. cumbrestoltec.com* 🖅 *$95–$179* ⊘ *Late May–mid-Oct.*

Fort Garland. One of Colorado's first military posts, Fort Garland was established in 1858 to protect settlers. It lies in the shadow of the Sangre de Cristo Mountains. The mountains were named for the "Blood of Christ" because of their ruddy color, especially at dawn. The legendary Kit Carson commanded the outfit, and five of the original adobe structures are still standing. The **Fort Garland State Museum** features a re-creation of the commandant's quarters and period military displays. The museum is 16 miles north of San Luis via Highway 159 and 24 miles east of Alamosa via U.S. 160. ⊠ *U.S. 160 and Hwy. 159, Fort Garland* ☎ *719/379–3512* ⊕ *www.museumtrail.org/fortgarlandmuseum. asp* 🖅 *$5* ⊘ *Apr.–Oct., daily 9–5; call for winter hrs.*

FAMILY   **Rio Grande Scenic Railroad.** This railroad carries passengers on excursions between Alamosa and La Veta some weekdays. You can also take a weekend ride from Alamosa to the Fir Summit Amphitheater where a wind- and solar-powered performance stage at 9,400 feet attracts regional and national Western and folk artists. The Rio Grande also offers a round-trip "Train to Christmas Town" from Alamosa to La Veta several times in late November and December. ⊠ *610 State Ave., Alamosa* ☎ *877/726–7245, 719/587–0509* ⊕ *www.coloradotrain.com* 🖅 *$19–$169* ⊘ *Late May–mid-Oct.*

San Luis. Founded in 1851, San Luis is the oldest incorporated town in Colorado. Murals depicting famous stories and legends of the area adorn several buildings in the town. A latter-day masterpiece is the **Stations of the Cross Shrine,** created by renowned local sculptor Huberto Maestas. The shrine is formally known as La Mesa de la Piedad y de la Misericordia (Hill of Piety and Mercy), and its 15 stations illustrate the last hours of Christ's life. The trail leads up to a chapel called La Capilla de Todos Los Santos. ⊠ *San Luis.*

TRAVEL SMART
COLORADO

GETTING HERE AND AROUND

Denver is Colorado's hub; the state's two major interstates, I–25 and I–70, intersect here, and most of the state's population lives within a one- or two-hour drive of the city. The high plains expand to the east from Denver, and the western edge of the metro area ends at the foothills of the Rocky Mountains. A corridor of cities along I–25 parallels the foothills from Fort Collins to Pueblo, and the most lonely stretches of highway are in the eastern portion of the state on the plains. Although air, rail, and bus service connects Denver to many smaller cities and towns, a car is the most practical way to explore the state.

■ AIR TRAVEL

It takes about two hours to fly to Denver from Los Angeles or Dallas, and 2½ hours from Chicago. From New York and Boston the flight is about 4½ hours. If you'll be checking skis, arrive even earlier.

AIRPORTS

The major air gateway to the Colorado Rockies is Denver International Airport (DEN), usually referred to by its nickname, DIA. It's about 25 miles northeast of downtown Denver and 45 miles from Boulder. Flights to smaller, resort-town airports generally connect through it. Inclement weather, fairly common in winter, occasionally delays or cancels flights. In recent years, the airport has expanded its restaurant offerings to include higher-end spots like Elway's steak house and the Denver Chophouse, but also includes more casual fare. Currently, all airport hotels are located 7 miles west toward Denver, but an airport expansion slated to open in late-2015 will include a 14-story luxury hotel next to the airport's terminal.

Colorado Springs Airport (COS) has direct flights from many major cities and is slightly less subject to bad winter storms than Denver. The airport is sometimes still open when bad weather closes other airports (especially those in the ski towns). Some of the major airlines and their subsidiaries serve communities around the state: Grand Junction (GJT), Durango (DRO), Steamboat Springs (HDN), Gunnison–Crested Butte (GUC), Montrose (MTJ), Telluride (TEX), Aspen (ASE), and Vail (EGE). Some major airlines have scheduled service from points within the United States to Colorado Springs Airport (COS); the relatively mild weather in Colorado Springs means that its airport is sometimes still functional when bad weather farther north and west affects the state's other airports. Many ski towns increase their seasonal service, adding direct flights.

Airport Information Colorado Springs Airport (COS). ✉ *Colorado Springs* ☎ 719/550–1900 ⊕ *flycos.coloradosprings. gov.* **Denver International Airport (DEN).** ✉ *Denver* ☎ 800/247–2336 ⊕ *www.flydenver.com.*

GROUND TRANSPORTATION

If you are driving, the best route from Denver International Airport to Denver, the ski resorts, or the mountains is to drive west on I–70. You can bypass some traffic by using the E–470 tollway, which you can access west of the airport. It connects to I–25 both south and north of Denver. When flying into Colorado Springs, take I–25 north and south. Vail, Aspen, Telluride, and the surrounding towns are accessible on Highway 24 without going through Denver.

RTD, the city's public transit, has frequent bus service to Denver and Boulder; visit their booth in the main terminal for destinations, times, and tickets. There are taxis and various private airport shuttles to cities along the Front Range from the airport, and some offer door-to-door service. Many hotels and ski resorts have their own buses;

check with your lodging or ski resort to see if they offer service. The Ground Transportation Information Center is on the fifth level of the main terminal, and can direct travelers to companies' service counters.

FLIGHTS

Denver International Airport (DEN) has direct flights from most major U.S. cities, as well as quite a few smaller ones, especially in the West. A few international carriers serve Denver with nonstop flights from London, England; Frankfurt, Germany; Tokyo, Japan; Reykjavik, Iceland; as well as Canadian cities like Vancouver, Toronto, and Montréal. United Airlines, Southwest Airlines, and Frontier Airlines (based in Colorado) are Denver's largest carriers, with the most flights and the longest list of destinations. Colorado Springs is served by Allegiant Airlines as well as by most major domestic airlines. United Express and Great Lakes Airlines connect Denver with smaller cities and ski resorts within Colorado.

Airline Contacts Aero Mexico. ☎ *800/237–6639* ⊕ *www.aeromexico.com.* **Air Canada.** ☎ *888/247–2262* ⊕ *www.aircanada. com.* **Alaska Airlines.** ☎ *800/252-7522* ⊕ *www.alaskaair.com.* **Allegiant Airlines.** ☎ *702/505–8888* ⊕ *www.allegiantair.com.* **American Airlines.** ☎ *800/433–7300* ⊕ *www.aa.com.* **British Airways.** ☎ *800/247–9297* ⊕ *www.britishairways.com.* **Delta Airlines.** ☎ *800/221–1212* ⊕ *www.delta.com.* **Frontier.** ☎ *800/432–1359* ⊕ *www.frontierairlines.com.* **Great Lakes.** ☎ *800/554–5111* ⊕ *www.flygreatlakes.com.* **JetBlue.** ☎ *800/538–2583* ⊕ *www.jetblue.com.* **Lufthansa.** ☎ *800/645–3880* ⊕ *www.lufthansa.com.* **Southwest Airlines.** ☎ *800/435–9792* ⊕ *www.southwest. com.* **United Airlines.** ☎ *800/864–8331* ⊕ *www.united.com.* **US Airways.** ☎ *800/428–4322* ⊕ *www.usairways.com.*

▌ BUS TRAVEL

Traveling by bus within the Denver–Boulder region is fairly easy with RTD, because the coverage of the area is dense and most routes are not too circuitous. The free 16th Street MallRide and the light-rail routes within Denver make travel to and from downtown attractions easy.

Mountain Metropolitan Transit serves the Colorado Springs area. Colorado Mountain Express offers both shared-ride shuttles and private-car airport services from Denver International Airport (DEN) and Eagle County Regional Airport.

Bus Information Colorado Mountain Express. ☎ *800/525–6363, 970/754–7433* ⊕ *www.coloradomountainexpress.com.* **Mountain Metropolitan Transit.** ✉ *Colorado Springs* ☎ *719/385–7433* ⊕ *transit. coloradosprings.gov.* **RTD.** ☎ *303/299–6000* ⊕ *www.rtd-denver.com.*

▌ CAR TRAVEL

Car travel within the urban corridor north and south of Denver can be congested, particularly weekday mornings and afternoons. Weekends, too, can have quite a bit of traffic, particularly along I–70 between Denver and the high mountains. Heavy traffic is not limited to ski season or bad weather. It is nearly a matter of course now for eastbound I–70 to be heavily congested on Sunday afternoons. If you are returning to Denver International Airport for a Sunday afternoon or evening flight, allow more than enough time to reach the airport.

GASOLINE

At this writing, gasoline costs between $2.50 and $3 a gallon. Gas prices in larger communities are comparable to those elsewhere in the country, but can be considerably higher in rural towns and mountain resorts. Although gas stations are plentiful in many areas, you can drive more than 100 miles in remote areas without finding gas.

LICENSE PLATE TOLL

Denver's Eastern Beltway, the E–470, and the connecting Northwest Parkway are both toll roads. You are automatically a License Plate Toll customer on both roads if you're not an EXpressToll or GO-PASS customer with a transponder. No advance registration is required, and customers drive nonstop through the tolls. Cameras photograph the license plates and a bill is sent one month later to the registered owner of the vehicle for tolls incurred during that period.

PARKING

On-street metered parking as well as by-the-hour garages and lots are fairly plentiful in larger cities. Meters take coins and credit cards almost everywhere.

ROAD CONDITIONS

Colorado offers some of the most spectacular vistas and challenging driving in the world. Roads range from multilane blacktop to barely graveled backcountry trails; from twisting switchbacks considerately marked with guardrails to primitive campgrounds with a lane so narrow that you must back up to the edge of a steep cliff to make a turn. Scenic routes and lookout points are clearly marked, enabling you to slow down and pull over to take in the views.

One of the more unpleasant sights along the highway is roadkill—animals struck by vehicles. Deer, elk, and moose may try to get to the other side of a road just as you come along, so watch out for wildlife on the highways. Exercise caution both for the sake of the animal in danger and your car, which could be totaled in a collision.

Emergency Services AAA Colorado. ☎ 866/625–3601, 303/753–8800 ⊕ www.colorado.aaa.com. **Colorado State Patrol.** ☎ 303/239–4501, *277 from a cell phone ⊕ www.colorado.gov/pacific/csp.

License Plate Toll E-470. ☎ 303/537–3470, 888/946–3470 ⊕ www.expresstoll.com. **Northwest Parkway.** ☎ 303/533–1200 ⊕ www.northwestparkway.org.

Road Condition Information CO Trip. ☎ 303/639–1111 from outside Colorado, 511 from inside Colorado ⊕ www.cotrip.org.

For police or ambulance, dial 911.

FROM	TO	DRIVE TIME
Denver	Boulder	40–60 mins
Denver	Fort Collins	60 mins
Denver	Colorado Springs	60–75 mins
Denver	Estes Park	1½–2 hrs
Denver	Glenwood Springs	2½–3 hrs
Glenwood Springs	Aspen	1 hr
Glenwood Springs	Crested Butte	3 hrs
Denver	Grand Junction	4 hrs
Grand Junction	Telluride	2–3 hrs
Denver	Durango	6–7 hrs

RULES OF THE ROAD

You'll find highways and national parks crowded in summer, and almost deserted (and occasionally impassable) in winter. Follow the posted speed limit, drive defensively, and make sure your gas tank is full. The law requires that drivers and front-seat passengers wear seat belts.

Always strap children under age five or under 40 pounds into approved child-safety seats. You may turn right at a red light after stopping if there's no sign stating otherwise and no oncoming traffic. When in doubt, wait for the green.

If your vehicle breaks down, or you are involved in an accident, move your vehicle out of the traffic flow, if possible, and call for help: 911 for emergencies and *277 from a cell phone for the Colorado State Patrol.

The speed limit on U.S. interstates in Colorado is up to 75 mph in rural areas and between 55 mph and 65 mph in urban zones. Mountain stretches of I–70 have lower limits—between 55 mph and 70 mph.

WINTER DRIVING

Modern highways make mountain driving safe and generally trouble-free even in cold weather. Although winter driving can occasionally present real challenges, road maintenance is good and plowing is prompt. However, in mountain areas tire chains, studs, or snow tires are essential. If you're planning to drive into high elevations, be sure to check the weather forecast and call for road conditions beforehand. Even main highways can close.

It's a good idea to carry an emergency kit and a cellphone, but be aware that the mountains can disrupt service. If you do get stalled by deep snow, do not leave your car. Wait for help, running the engine only if needed, and remember that assistance is never far away. Winter weather isn't confined to winter months in the high country (it's been known to snow in July), so be prepared year-round.

CAR RENTAL

Rates in most major cities run about $70 to $95 a day and $490 to $660 a week for an economy car with air-conditioning, automatic transmission, and unlimited mileage. Rates can vary greatly from company to company, so it's worth comparing online. Keep in mind if you're venturing into the Rockies that you'll need a little oomph in your engine to get over the passes. If you plan to explore any back roads, an SUV is the best bet, because it will have higher clearance. Unless you plan to do much mountain exploring, a four-wheel drive is usually needed only in winter.

To rent a car in Colorado you must be at least 25 years old (or be willing to pay surcharges) and have a valid driver's license; most companies also require a major credit card. Some companies at certain locations set their minimum age at 21, and then add a daily surcharge. In Colorado, child-safety seats or booster seats are compulsory for children under five (with certain height and weight criteria).

You'll pay extra for child seats ($5–$13 a day), drivers under age 25 (at least $25 a day), and usually for additional drivers (about $10 per day). When returning your car to Denver International Airport, allow 15 minutes (30 minutes during busy weekends and around the holidays) to return the vehicle and to ride the shuttle bus to the terminal.

Major Rental Agencies

Alamo. ☎ *888/233-8749* ⊕ *www.alamo. com.* **Avis.** ☎ *800/633-3469* ⊕ *www.avis.com.* **Budget.** ☎ *800/218-7992* ⊕ *www.budget. com.* **Hertz.** ☎ *800/654-3131* ⊕ *www.hertz. com.* **National Car Rental.** ☎ *877/222-9058* ⊕ *www.nationalcar.com.*

∎ TRAIN TRAVEL

Amtrak connects several stations in Colorado to both coasts and major American cities. The *California Zephyr* and the *Southwest Chief* pass once per day with east- and west-bound trains that stop in Denver, Winter Park, Granby, Glenwood Springs, Grand Junction, and Trinidad. There are also several scenic narrow-gauge sightseeing railroads all over the state.

Information Amtrak. ☎ *800/872-7245* ⊕ *www.amtrak.com.* **Cumbres & Toltec Scenic Railroad.** ☎ *888/286-2737* ⊕ *www.cumbrestoltec.com.* **Durango & Silverton Narrow Gauge Railroad.** ☎ *888/872-4607* ⊕ *www.durangotrain.com.* **Georgetown Loop Railroad.** ☎ *888/456-6777* ⊕ *www.georgetownlooprr.com.* **Royal Gorge Route Railroad.** ☎ *888/724-5748* ⊕ *www.royalgorgeroute.com.* **Leadville, Co. & Southern Railroad Company.** ☎ *719/486-3936, 866/386-3936* ⊕ *www.leadville-train.com.* **Rio Grande Scenic Railroad.** ☎ *719/587-0520, 877/726-7245* ⊕ *www.riograndescenicrailroad.com.*

ESSENTIALS

▮ ACCOMMODATIONS

Accommodations in Colorado vary from the posh ski resorts in Vail, Aspen, and Telluride to basic chain hotels and independent motels. Dude and guest ranches often require a one-week stay, and the cost is all-inclusive. Bed-and-breakfasts can be found throughout the state. Hotel rates peak during the height of the ski season, which generally runs from late November through March or April; although rates are high all season, they top out during Christmas week and in February and March. In summer months, a popular time for hiking and rafting, hotel rates are often half the winter price.

⇨ *Properties are assigned price categories based on the cost of a standard double room during high season. Lodging taxes vary throughout the state.*

Most hotels and other lodgings require you to give your credit-card details before they will confirm your reservation. However you book, get confirmation in writing and have a copy of it handy when you check in.

Be sure you understand the hotel's cancellation policy. Some places allow you to cancel without any kind of penalty—even if you prepaid to secure a discounted rate—if you cancel at least 24 hours in advance. Others require you to cancel a week in advance or penalize you the cost of one night. Small inns and B&Bs are most likely to require you to cancel far in advance. Most hotels allow children under a certain age to stay in their parents' room at no extra charge, but others charge them as extra adults; find out the cutoff age for discounts.

Hotels in Denver and Colorado Springs cater heavily to business travelers, often with facilities like restaurants, cocktail lounges, swimming pools, fitness centers, and meeting rooms. Many properties offer considerably lower rates on weekends, particularly during the colder months. In resort towns, hotels are decidedly more deluxe; rural areas generally offer simple, sometimes rustic accommodations.

Ski towns throughout Colorado are home to dozens of resorts in all price ranges; the activities lacking at any individual property can usually be found in the town itself—in summer as well as winter. Off the slopes, there are both wonderful rustic and luxurious resorts, particularly in out-of-the-way spots near Rocky Mountain National Park and other alpine areas.

General Information Colorado Hotel and Lodging Association. ☎ *303/297–8335* ⊕ *www.coloradolodging.com.*

APARTMENT AND HOUSE RENTALS

Rental accommodations are quite popular in Colorado's ski resorts and mountain towns. Condominiums and luxurious vacation homes dominate the Vail Valley and other ski-oriented areas, but there are scads of cabins in smaller, summer-oriented towns in the Rockies and the Western Slope. Many towns and resort areas have rental agencies.

With a direct home exchange you stay in someone else's home while they stay in yours. Some outfits also deal with vacation homes, so you're not actually staying in someone's full-time residence, just their vacant weekend place.

Exchange Clubs Airbnb. ⊕ *www.airbnb. com.* **forGetaway.** ⊕ *www.forgetaway.com.* **Home Away.** ⊕ *www.homeaway.com.* **Home Exchange.** ☎ *800/877–8723, 310/798–3864* ⊕ *www.homeexchange.com.* **HomeLink International.** ☎ *800/638–3841* ⊕ *www.homelink. org.* **Intervac Home Exchange.** ☎ *866/884–7567* ⊕ *us.intervac-homeexchange.com.*

Local Rental Agencies Colorado Mountain Cabins & Vacation Home Rentals. ☎ 719/636–5147, 866/425–4974 ⊕ www.coloradomountaincabins.com. **Colorado Vacation Directory.** ☎ 303/499–9343, 888/222–4641 ⊕ www.coloradodirectory.com.

BED-AND-BREAKFASTS

Charm is the long suit of these establishments, which often occupy a restored older building with some historical or architectural significance. They're generally small, with fewer than 20 rooms. Breakfast is usually included in the rates. The owners often manage the B&B, and you'll likely meet them and get to know them a bit. Breakfasts are usually substantial, with hot beverages, cold fruit juices, and a hot entrée. Bed & Breakfast Innkeepers of Colorado prints a free annual directory of its members.

Reservation Services BedandBreakfast.com. ☎ 512/322–2710, 800/462–2632 ⊕ www.bedandbreakfast.com. **Bed & Breakfast Innkeepers of Colorado.** ☎ 800/265–7696 ⊕ www.innsofcolorado.org. **Bed & Breakfast Inns Online.** ☎ 800/215–7365 ⊕ www.bbonline.com. **BnBFinder.** ☎ 888/469–6663 ⊕ www.bnbfinder.com.

GUEST RANCHES

If the thought of sitting around a campfire after a hard day on the range is your idea of a vacation, consider playing dude on a guest ranch. Wilderness-rimmed working ranches accept guests and encourage them to pitch in with chores and other ranch activities; you might even be able to participate in a cattle roundup. Most dude ranches don't require previous experience with horses. Luxurious resorts on the fringes of small cities offer swimming pools, tennis courts, and a lively roster of horse-related activities such as breakfast rides, moonlight rides, and all-day trail rides. Rafting, fishing, tubing, and other activities are usually available at both types of ranches. In winter, cross-country skiing and snowshoeing keep you busy.

Lodgings can run the gamut from charmingly rustic cabins to the kind of deluxe quarters you expect at a first-class hotel. Meals may be sophisticated or plain but hearty. Be sure to check with the ranch for a list of items you might be expected to bring. If you plan to do much riding, a couple of pairs of sturdy pants, boots, a wide-brim hat to shield you from the sun, and outerwear that protects from rain and cold should be packed. Nearly all dude ranches in Colorado offer all-inclusive packages: meals, lodging, and generally all activities. Weeklong stays cost between $1,300 and $4,000 per adult, depending on the ranch's amenities and activities.

Information Colorado Dude & Guest Ranch Association. ☎ 866/942–3472 ⊕ www.coloradoranch.com.

❚ BUSINESS SERVICES AND FACILITIES

Several cities throughout Colorado have business services where you can print photographs, photocopy documents, send a fax, and check your email. The larger cities along the I–25 corridor have more selection and locations. A few are locally owned, but most are franchises of FedEx.

Contacts FedEx Office. ☎ 800/463–3339 ⊕ www.fedex.com/us/office.

❚ CHILDREN IN COLORADO

Colorado is tailor-made for family vacations, offering dude ranches, historic railroads, mining towns, rafting, and many outdoor activities.

Visitor centers and lodgings are often good at recommending places to spend time with children. The guides issued by the tourism office of Colorado have sections geared toward children. If you are renting a car, don't forget to arrange for a car seat when you reserve.

The free monthly magazine *Colorado Parent* (⊕ *www.coloradoparent.com*) is available online and in the lobbies of office buildings, hotels, and other businesses.

▌ COMMUNICATIONS

INTERNET

Internet access is available throughout Colorado. Most lodgings have wireless access for laptops, and many have computers available for guests. Many cafés, coffee shops, and restaurants have Wi-Fi, though some charge a fee for access. Many municipal public libraries will allow patrons to use the Internet, either free or for a small fee.

▌ EATING OUT

Dining in Colorado is generally casual. Dinner hours are typically from 6 pm to 10 pm, but many small-town and rural eateries close by 9 pm. Authentic ethnic food is hard to find outside the big cities and major resort towns.

MEALS AND MEALTIMES

⇨ *Unless otherwise noted, the restaurants listed in this guide are open daily for lunch and dinner.*

Although you can find all types of cuisine in Colorado's major cities and resort towns, don't forget to try native dishes like trout, elk, and buffalo (the latter two have less fat than beef and are just as tasty). Steak is a mainstay in the Rocky Mountains. Chile verde, also known as green chile, is a popular menu item at Mexican restaurants in Colorado. Many restaurants serve vegetarian items, and some are exclusively vegetarian. Organic fruits and vegetables are also readily available.

ITEM	AVERAGE COST
Cup of Coffee	$1–$2.50
Glass of Wine	$5–$8
Glass of Beer	$4–$6
Sandwich	$6–$8
One-Mile Taxi Ride in Denver	$4.75
Museum Admission	$8–$15

RESERVATIONS AND DRESS

Regardless of where you are, it's a good idea to make a reservation if you can. In some places it's expected. We only mention them specifically when reservations are essential (there's no other way you'll ever get a table) or when they are not accepted. For popular restaurants, book as far ahead as you can (often 30 days), and reconfirm as soon as you arrive. Large parties should always call ahead to check the reservations policy. We mention dress only when men are required to wear a jacket or a jacket and tie—which is almost never in the Rockies.

SMOKING AND MARIJUANA LAWS

Cigarette smoking is prohibited in Colorado's public places, including restaurants and bars.

Since December 2012, Colorado has allowed the legalized sale, possession, cultivation, and use of recreational marijuana for persons 21 years of age and older. It is important to note that the law varies between residents and visitors, and statutes are subject to change by the year. The industry is highly regulated and taxed by the state government, but certain municipalities statewide have their own local ordinances banning the sale of marijuana outside of prior medicinal laws that date back to 2000.

Retail marijuana must be purchased at authorized dispensaries, which are available in most major cities and towns, but not all outlets provide both recreational and medicinal marijuana. All use, be it smoked or consumed in edibles like drinks or candies, must take place in private residences or in the increasingly popular "420-friendly" hotels or other rentals. It is prohibited to smoke or consume marijuana in any public space. Consumption in motor vehicles or public transportation is also illegal. When in doubt, do your research before partaking. Be aware that transporting marijuana through airports or neighboring states remains a federal crime as of this writing.

WINES, BEER, AND SPIRITS

The legal drinking age in Colorado is 21. Colorado liquor laws do not allow anyone to bring their own alcohol to restaurants. You'll find renowned breweries throughout Colorado, including, of course, the nation's second-largest brewer: Miller-Coors. There are dozens of microbreweries in Denver, Colorado Springs, Boulder, and the resort towns—if you're a beer drinker, be sure to try some local brews. Although the region is not known for its wines, the wineries in the Grand Junction area and along the Front Range are earning increased acclaim.

■ ECOTOURISM

Although neither the Bureau of Land Management (BLM) nor the National Park Service has designated any parts of Colorado as endangered ecosystems, many areas are open only to hikers; vehicles, mountain bikes, and horses are banned. It's wise to respect these closures, as well as the old adage **leave only footprints, take only pictures.** It is considered poor form to pick wildflowers while hiking, and it is illegal to pick columbine, the state flower of Colorado. Recycling is taken seriously throughout Colorado, and you will find yourself unpopular if you litter—which is also illegal—or fail to recycle your cans and bottles.

All archaeological artifacts, including rock etchings and paintings, are protected by federal law and must be left untouched and undisturbed.

Contacts National Park Reservation Service. ☎ 877/444–6777 ⊕ www.recreation. gov. **U.S. Bureau of Land Management.** ☎ 303/239–3600 ⊕ www.blm.gov/co.

■ HEALTH

You may feel dizzy and weak and find yourself breathing heavily—signs that the thin mountain air isn't giving you your accustomed dose of oxygen. Take it easy, and rest often for a few days until you're

acclimatized. Throughout your stay, drink plenty of water and watch your alcohol consumption. If you experience severe headaches and nausea, see a doctor. It's easy—especially in a state where highways climb to 11,000 feet and higher—to go too high too fast. The remedy for altitude-related discomfort is to descend into heavier air.

■ PACKING

For the most part, informality reigns in the Centennial State; jeans, sport shirts, and T-shirts fit in almost everywhere. If you plan to golf, a collared shirt may be required for men. No matter what your vacation plans are, don't forget to pack sunscreen, lip balm with SPF, sunglasses, and a cap or hat. The sunshine is intense at Colorado's altitude, and there are plenty of souvenirs available that you'll prefer over a sunburn.

If you plan to spend much time outdoors, and certainly if you go in winter, choose clothing appropriate for cold and wet weather. Cotton clothing, including denim, can be uncomfortable when it gets wet or when the weather's cold. Better choices are clothing made of wool or any of a number of synthetics that provide warmth without bulk and maintain their insulating properties when wet. It's not a bad idea to save your shopping for when you arrive in Colorado, where you'll find a huge selection of suitable clothing and gear.

In summer you'll probably want to wear shorts during the day. Because early morning and night can be cool, particularly in the mountains, pack a sweater and a light jacket, and perhaps a wool cap and gloves. For walks and hikes, you'll need sturdy footwear. Boots should have thick soles and plenty of ankle support; if your shoes are new and you plan to do a lot of hiking, break them in at home. Bring a day pack for short hikes, along with a canteen or water bottle, and don't forget rain gear, a hat, sunscreen, and insect repellent.

In winter, prepare for subzero temperatures with good boots, warm socks and liners, long underwear, a well-insulated jacket, and a warm hat and mittens. Layers are the best preparation for fluctuating temperatures.

▌SAFETY

Although Colorado is considered to be generally safe, travelers should take ordinary precautions—unfortunate incidents can happen anywhere. At your hotel, lock your valuables either in the hotel's safe or in the safe in your room, if one is available. Be aware of your surroundings, and keep your wallet and passport in a buttoned pocket, or keep your handbag in front of you where you can see it. At night, avoid dimly lighted areas as well as those where there are few people. Consider a taxi ride to your hotel if it is a long walk or you are alone.

Regardless of the outdoor activity or your level of skill, safety must come first. When hiking or taking part in any other outdoor activity, it's best (and often more fun) to go in pairs or small groups. If you do hike, cycle, kayak, or backcountry ski alone, it is essential that you tell someone where you are going and when you plan to return, whether it's a park ranger or the host of your B&B. Let them know, of course, when you've returned safely.

Many trails are at high altitudes, where oxygen is scarce. They're also frequently desolate. Hikers and bikers should carry emergency supplies in their backpacks. Proper equipment includes a flashlight, a compass, waterproof matches, a first-aid kit, a knife, a space blanket, and a light plastic tarp for shelter. Backcountry skiers should add a repair kit, a blanket, an avalanche beacon, and a lightweight shovel to their lists. Always bring extra food and a canteen of water, as dehydration is a real danger at high altitudes. Never drink from streams or lakes, unless you boil the water first or purify it with tablets. Giardia, an intestinal parasite, may be present.

Although you may tan easily, the sun is intense even at mile-high elevations (which are relatively low for the state), and sunburn can develop in just a few hours of hiking or sightseeing. Coloradans slather on sunscreen as a matter of course. Be sure to pack plenty of it, and don't forget to put it on when skiing—there's nothing glamorous about a goggle tan. The state's dry climate and thin air can also dehydrate you quickly. Carry a couple of liters of water with you each day and sip frequently.

Flash floods can strike at any time and any place with little or no warning. The danger in mountainous terrain is heightened when distant rains are channeled into gullies and ravines, turning a quiet streamside campsite or wash into a rampaging torrent in seconds. Check weather reports before heading into the backcountry, and be prepared to head for higher ground if the weather turns severe.

One of the most wonderful parts of the Rockies is the abundant wildlife. And although a herd of grazing elk or a bighorn sheep high on a hillside is most certainly a picturesque moment, an encounter with a bear or mountain lion is not. To avoid such an unpleasant situation while hiking, make plenty of noise and keep dogs on leashes and small children between adults. While camping, be sure to store all food, utensils, and clothing with food odors far away from your tent, preferably high in a tree. If you do come across a bear or big cat, do not run. For bears, back away quietly; for mountain lions, make yourself look as big as possible. In either case, be prepared to fend off the animal with loud noises, rocks, sticks, etc. And, as the saying goes, do not feed the bears—or any wild animals—whether they're dangerous or not.

When in any park, give all animals their space. If you want to take a photograph, use a long lens rather than a long sneak to approach closely. Approaching an animal can cause stress and affect its ability to survive the sometimes brutal climate. In all cases, remember that animals have the right-of-way; this is their home, you are the visitor.

Contacts Transportation Security Administration. ☎ 866/289–9673 ⊕ www.tsa.gov.

▮ SPORTS AND THE OUTDOORS

The Colorado Rockies are one of America's greatest playgrounds. Information about Colorado's recreational areas and activities is provided in each regional section; the following is general information.

Outfitter Listings Colorado Outfitters Association. ☎ 970/824–2468 ⊕ www.coloradooutfitters.org.

GROUP TRIPS

Group sizes for organized trips vary considerably, depending on the organizer and the activity. Often, if you're planning a trip with a large group, trip organizers or outfitters will offer discounts of 10% or more and are willing to customize trips. For example, if you're with a group interested in photography or in wildlife, trip organizers have been known to get professional photographers or naturalists to join the group.

One way to travel with a group is to join an organization before going. Conservation-minded travelers might want to contact the Sierra Club, a nonprofit organization, which offers both vacation and work trips. Hiking trails tend to be maintained by volunteers (this is more often done by local hiking clubs). Park or forest rangers are the best resource for information about groups involved in this sort of work.

Individuals or groups wanting to test their mettle can learn wilderness skills through "outdoor schools."

Contacts American Hiking Society. ☎ 800/972–8608, 301/565–6704 ⊕ www.americanhiking.org. **Boulder Outdoor Survival School.** ✉ Boulder ☎ 800/335–7404 ⊕ www.boss-inc.com. **Sierra Club.** ✉ 1536 Wynkoop St., Ste 200, Denver ☎ 303/861–8819 ⊕ www.sierraclub.org/rocky-mountain-chapter.

▮ TAXES

Colorado's state sales tax is 2.9%, but after that it gets a little tricky, as there are additional city and county taxes that raise the total to as high as 10.4%, depending on the municipality. Lodging taxes also vary around the state, and can be as high as nearly 15% in Denver and less than 10% in other areas.

▮ TIME

All of Colorado is in the mountain time zone. Mountain time is two hours earlier than eastern time and one hour later than Pacific time, so Colorado is two hours behind New York and one hour ahead of California.

Information Timeanddate.com. ⊕ www.timeanddate.com/worldclock.

▮ TIPPING

It's customary to tip 15% to 20% at restaurants in cities; in resort towns, 20% is increasingly the norm. For coat checks and bellmen, $1 per coat or bag is the minimum. Taxi drivers expect 10% to 15%. In resort towns, ski technicians, sandwich makers, coffee baristas, and the like also appreciate tips.

▌ TOURS

Culinary Connectors. Culinary Connectors offers Denver-based culinary tours of the city's best restaurants, cafés, and craft-beer havens. Each tour is a private event that must be scheduled in advance. ☎ *303/495–5487* ⊕ *www.culinaryconnectors.com* ✉ *From $34.*

Field Guides. Field Guides takes birders on 10-day trips in search of Colorado's prairie chickens and grouse every April. ☎ *800/728–4953, 512/263–7295* ⊕ *www.fieldguides.com* ✉ *From $3,150 (requires $325 deposit).*

OARS. OARS offers multiday rafting trips on the Yampa and Green rivers and hiking vacations in Chaco Canyon, Mesa Verde National Park, Ute Mountain Tribal Park, and National Bridges Monument. ☎ *800/346–6277* ⊕ *www.oars.com/colorado* ✉ *From $79 for day trips.*

Victor Emanuel Nature Tours. Victor Emanuel Nature Tours offers several Colorado-based birding tours in the spring and summer. ☎ *512/328–5221, 800/328–8368* ⊕ *www.ventbird.com* ✉ *From $2,895.*

▌ TRIP INSURANCE

Comprehensive trip insurance is valuable if you're booking a very expensive or complicated trip (particularly to an isolated region) or if you're reserving far in advance. Comprehensive policies typically cover trip cancellation and interruptions, letting you cancel or cut your trip short because of illness, or, in some cases, acts of terrorism in your destination. Such policies might also cover evacuation and medical care. (For trips abroad you should have at least medical-only coverage.) Some also cover you for trip delays because of bad weather or mechanical problems as well as for lost or delayed luggage.

Another type of coverage to consider is financial default—that is, when your trip is disrupted because a tour operator, airline, or cruise line goes out of business. Generally you must buy this when you book your trip or shortly thereafter, and it's available to you only if your operator isn't on a list of excluded companies.

Always read the fine print of your policy to make sure that you're covered for the risks that most concern you. Compare several policies to be sure you're getting the best price and range of coverage available.

Comprehensive Insurers

Allianz Global Assistance. ☎ *866/884–3556* ⊕ *www.allianztravelinsurance.com.* **CSA Travel Protection.** ☎ *800/711–1197* ⊕ *www.csatravelprotection.com.* **Travel Guard.** ☎ *800/826–4919* ⊕ *www.travelguard.com.* **Travelex Insurance.** ☎ *800/228–9792* ⊕ *www.travelexinsurance.com.* **Travel Insured International.** ☎ *800/243–3174* ⊕ *www.travelinsured.com.*

Insurance Comparison Information

Insure My Trip. ☎ *800/487–4722* ⊕ *www.insuremytrip.com.* **Square Mouth.** ☎ *800/240–0369* ⊕ *www.squaremouth.com.*

▌ VISITOR INFORMATION

Almost every town, county, and resort area has its own tourist office.

Contact Colorado Tourism Office. ☎ *800/265–6723* ⊕ *www.colorado.com.*

INDEX

PHOTO CREDITS

NOTES

NOTES

NOTES

NOTES

NOTES

NOTES

NOTES

NOTES

NOTES

Fodor's COLORADO

Publisher: Amanda D'Acierno, *Senior Vice President*

Editorial: Arabella Bowen, *Editor in Chief*; Linda Cabasin, *Editorial Director*

Design: Tina Malaney, *Associate Art Director*; Chie Ushio, *Senior Designer;* Erica Cuoco, *Production Designer*

Photography: Jennifer Arnow, *Senior Photo Editor*; Mary Robnett, *Photo Researcher*

Production: Linda Schmidt, *Managing Editor*; Evangelos Vasilakis, *Associate Managing Editor*; Angela L. McLean, *Senior Production Manager*

Maps: Rebecca Baer, *Senior Map Editor*; Mark Stroud (Moon Street Cartography), David Lindroth, *Cartographers*

Sales: Jacqueline Lebow, *Sales Director*

Marketing & Publicity: Heather Dalton, *Marketing Director*; Katherine Punia, *Publicity Director*

Business & Operations: Susan Livingston, *Vice President, Strategic Business Planning*; Sue Daulton, *Vice President, Operations*

Fodors.com: Megan Bell, *Executive Director, Revenue & Business Development*; Yasmin Marinaro, *Senior Director, Marketing & Partnerships*

Copyright © 2016 by Fodor's Travel, a division of Penguin Random House LLC

Writers: Whitney Bryen, Kevin Fixler, Lindsey Galloway, Aimee Heckel, Kellee Katagi, Hudson Lindenberger, Avery Stonich, Kyle Wagner

Editor: Luke Epplin

Editorial Contributors: Alexis Kelly, Jacinta O'Halloran

Production Editor: Carolyn Roth

12th Edition

ISBN 978-1-101-87965-8

ISSN 0276-9018

SPECIAL SALES

This book is available at special discounts for bulk purchases for sales promotions or premiums. For more information, e-mail specialmarkets@penguinrandomhouse.com.

PRINTED IN THE UNITED STATES OF AMERICA

10 9 8 7 6 5 4 3 2 1

ABOUT OUR WRITERS

Whitney Bryen has been exploring Colorado since she moved to the state in 2010. She is the assistant editor and community reporter for *Colorado Hometown Weekly* and the east Boulder County reporter for the *Boulder Daily Camera* and *Longmont Times-Call*. Whitney is also a contributor to About.com's Colorado travel page and has written for Colorado Public Radio, the *Denver Post,* and the *Colorado Springs Independent,* among others. Whitney updated the South Central Colorado and Aspen and the Roaring Fork Valley chapters.

Kevin Fixler is a Colorado native and long-time Denver resident who enjoys running and hiking, and is also a local high school lacrosse coach. He holds a master's from UC Berkeley, and sports are near and dear to his heart. His work as a freelancer has appeared with a variety of publications, among them the *Guardian, The Atlantic, ESPN The Magazine,* and OZY.com. For this edition, Kevin updated the Travel Smart chapter.

Lindsey Galloway lives in Boulder, Colorado, and frequently overeats at the many restaurants on Pearl Street. Like any good Boulderite, she loves yoga and is particularly proud of her tree pose; however, the state of Colorado has threatened to revoke her license if she doesn't climb a Fourteener soon. She contributes regularly to BBC Travel and AOL Travel, and founded TravelPretty.com to document her perils in packing. Lindsey updated the Rocky Mountain National Park chapter for this edition.

Aimee Heckel is a Colorado native who has been working at Colorado newspapers for 15 years. She is currently features writer at the *Boulder Daily Camera,* as well as the Colorado Travel Expert for About.com, a regular travel writer for USA Today's 10Best.com, and a travel writer for ShopBlog. Her passion for storytelling has brought her around the world as a journalist, but still, one of her favorite places to explore is the miraculous mountains in her home state. For this edition, she updated the Mesa Verde, Summit County, and Vail Valley chapters.

Kellee Katagi has lived in eight U.S. states, but Colorado is by far her favorite—not least because of the glorious scenery and the adventures to be had in its southwest region. A former managing editor of *SKI Magazine,* Katagi is now a freelance writer/editor specializing in travel, sports, fitness, health, and food. When not at her desk, she enjoys playing in the Colorado mountains with her husband, her three grade-school-age budding explorers (Shaelyn, David, and A.J.), and their trusty raft dubbed *K-5 Shark*. Katagi updated the Southwest Colorado chapter.

Hudson Lindenberger is a longtime resident of Boulder, Colorado, who enjoys hiking, biking, and just about any other outdoor pursuit. He regularly contributes to *Men's Journal, 5280 Magazine,* and *Elevation Outdoors*. As a freelance writer, he spends most of his time searching out adventures. For this edition, Hudson updated the Experience Colorado chapter.

Avery Stonich is a Boulder-based writer who has traveled to more than 45 countries and still thinks Colorado is one of the greatest places on Earth. When not playing with prose, she likes to ski, hike, kiteboard, bike, camp, travel, and climb mountains. Her work has been published by *National Geographic Adventure, National Geographic Travel, Outside, Mountain Magazine, Elevation Outdoors, Women's Adventure, RootsRated, Bicycle Times,* and more. Visit her website at ⊕ *averystonich. com*. For this edition, Avery updated the Boulder and North Central Colorado chapter.

Kyle Wagner wrote about restaurants and food in Denver for 12 years, first for the alternative weekly *Westword* and then for the *Denver Post,* before being named travel editor for the *Post* in 2005, a position she held until 2014. The Denver resident, an avid mountain biker, river rafter, and skier, now writes freelance food and travel stories for regional and national magazines. For this edition, Kyle updated Denver, the Rockies Near Denver, and Northwest Colorado and Steamboat Springs.